D1475217

Barbarossa 1941

Barbarossa 1941

Reframing
Hitler's Invasion
of Stalin's Soviet
Empire

Frank Ellis

 University Press of Kansas

Published by the University Press of Kansas (Lawrence, Kansas 66045), which was organized by the Kansas Board of Regents and is operated and funded by Emporia State University, Fort Hays State University, Kansas State University, Pittsburg State University, the University of Kansas, and Wichita State University

Published by the University Press of Kansas (Lawrence, Kansas 66045), which was organized by the Kansas Board of Regents and is operated and funded by Emporia State University, Fort Hays State University, Kansas State University, Pittsburg State University, the University of Kansas, and Wichita State University

Library of Congress Cataloging-in-Publication Data

Ellis, Frank, 1953– author.
Barbarossa 1941 : reframing Hitler's invasion of Stalin's Soviet empire / Frank Ellis.
pages cm. — (Modern war studies)
Includes bibliographical references and index.
ISBN 978-0-7006-2145-3 (cloth : alk. paper)
ISBN 978-0-7006-2146-0 (ebook)
1. World War, 1939–1945—Campaigns—Eastern Front.
2. World War, 1939–1945—Campaigns—Soviet Union.
3. Soviet Union—History—German occupation, 1941–1944.
I. Title.
D764.E287 2015
940.54′217—dc23
2015026181

British Library Cataloguing-in-Publication Data is available.

Printed in the United States of America

10 9 8 7 6 5 4 3 2 1

The paper used in this publication is recycled and contains 30 percent postconsumer waste. It is acid free and meets the minimum requirements of the American National Standard for Permanence of Paper for Printed Library Materials z39.48–1992.

There were no reasonable explanations for the Soviet failures, nothing to assuage our humiliation. Poland had been surprised, then stabbed in the back by its eastern neighbor. France had been smaller, weaker than the assailant. But should prodigious Russia two years after the outbreak of war, with every advantage of numbers, time, military concentration, behave like a backward little country caught off guard? Had we been no bigger than France, we would have been crushed four times over in the first four months.

—Viktor Kravchenko, *I Chose Freedom*

A woman had come out onto the road. Vigorously waving as if she was in a cornfield sowing seed, she devoutly made the sign of the cross after the troops. Each company, each platoon, each soldier was blessed with the cross by this Russian woman in the custom of the ancients, according to the ways of our fathers, forefathers and the Heavenly Father, bidding the soldiers well on their long road, for their martial deeds, for the successful completion of the battle on the part of our eternal protectors.

—Viktor Astaf'ev, *The Damned and the Dead*

CONTENTS

A photo section appears following page 232.

Given the reinforced library shelves already groaning under the weight of tomes dedicated to *Unternehmen* (Operation) Barbarossa, the obvious and reasonable question is why another study is required. The answer to this question is essentially one of source material. A large part of this study is based on a number of Soviet documents that were placed in the public domain as part of the declassification process that started in 1991 and continues, intermittently, to this day. The primary documentation I relied on can be found in the relevant volumes of *Organy gosudarstvennoi bezopasnosti SSSR v Velikoi Otechestvennoi voine* covering the second half of 1941 and the first half of 1942—*Nachalo 22 iiunia–31 avgusta 1941 goda* (2000), *Nachalo 1 sentiabria–31 dekabria 1941 goda* (2000), and *Krushenie "Blitzkriga" 1 ianvaria–30 iiunia 1942 goda* (2003)—and the two volumes of documents specifically relating to the period before and just after 22 June 1941 contained in *1941 god* (1998).

Although this material has been available to scholars for more than a decade, I am not aware of any study of the central problems associated with Barbarossa—Soviet intelligence assessments, German-Soviet diplomacy, and NKVD (People's Commissariat of Internal Affairs) operations—based on a systematic and detailed analysis of the material published in the aforementioned volumes. In chapters 3, 4, and 5 I seek to remedy this deficiency. Chapter 4 makes it quite clear that the Soviet intelligence agencies were doing a thorough and professional job, which makes Stalin's failure to act in good time and in good order all the more perplexing. A detailed analysis of the documents raises other intelligence-related questions to which there are no clear answers. For example, is one to assume that the Soviet air force conducted no systematic reconnaissance flights at all over German-controlled territory in the period leading up to 22 June 1941?

German-Soviet diplomatic relations between 1939 and 1941 have been covered in detail by Gerhard Weinberg in *Germany and the Soviet Union, 1939–1941* (1954), although as the author acknowledges, "largely on the basis of German sources."[1] Soviet documents available since 1998 permit certain lacunae that existed throughout the Cold War and beyond to be filled. In this regard, it is noteworthy that the author of one of the most recent studies of the Non-Aggression Pact, published in 2014, does not exploit the detailed material in the two volumes of 1941 god.[2] Soviet documents published in 1941 god strongly suggest that both the German and the Soviet states were using trade agreements as a device not just to extract strategic and economic advantage but also to deceive each other. On balance, it seems to me that deception was the primary purpose. Thus, Weinberg's view that "during the period from 1939 to 1941 the dynamic element in German-Soviet relations is provided by Germany, while Soviet policy is essentially a reactive one which attempts to make the best of opportunities offered and avert the worst of the threatening dangers," requires some adjustment.[3]

German-Soviet diplomatic exchanges, along with other material, also hint that the Germans were aware of the mass murders of Poles at Katyn and other sites in 1940, carried out by the NKVD's murder squads. If so, the question arises whether knowledge of these murders played a part in the formulation of two of the most notorious orders that emerged from the offices of Hitler's planning staff: *Erlaß über die Ausübung der Kriegsgerichtsbarkeit im Gebiet „Barbarossa" und über besondere Maßnahmen der Truppe* (Decree Concerning the Implementation of Military Jurisdiction in the Barbarossa Zone and Concerning Special Measures for the Troops; hereafter, the Barbarossa Jurisdiction Decree), dated 13 May 1941, and *Richtlinien für die Behandlung politischer Kommissare* (Guidelines for the Treatment of Political Commissars; hereafter, the Commissar Order), dated 6 June 1941. It can be argued that even if German planners had foreknowledge of the Katyn murders, this in no way diminishes the criminal nature of the Barbarossa Jurisdiction Decree and the Commissar Order. And if that is the case, one would have expected the Nürnberg prosecutors to pursue the question of responsibility for the Katyn murders with the same determination and dedication with which they looked into the origins, drafting, and execution of the Barbarossa Jurisdiction Decree and the Commissar Order. Unfortunately, they did nothing of the sort. As Robert Conquest has noted, the Katyn murders were examined by the judges at Nürnberg "in a derisory fashion."[4] Indeed, the Soviet fiction that the Katyn murders were the work of National Socialist (NS) death squads was upheld and unchallenged.

The Katyn murders are important for an examination of the Commissar Order because Soviet thinking behind the decision to murder Polish prisoners of war has much in common with Nazi thinking behind the decision to kill commissars. This is just one of several indices demonstrating the closeness of the two totalitarian regimes. In my opinion, this ideological propinquity of the Commissar Order and the earlier Katyn Memorandum—the theme of chapter 2—undermines some of the conclusions of Felix Römer's *Der Kommissarbefehl: Wehrmacht und NS-Verbrechen an der Ostfront 1941/42* (2008). His impressive statistical analysis notwithstanding, he adopts what I can only describe as a system-immanent or text-immanent approach to the origins and execution of the Commissar Order, thus ignoring the very real objective and external influences on German planners that, as I argue, informed—and could not help but inform—their attitudes toward the ideological functionaries known as military commissars and the action to be taken against them and the Soviet state. This reluctance by some German historians to consider Soviet behavior and ideological influences on German planning for Barbarossa is nothing new. For example, of the nine research essays published in part II of *Unternehmen „Barbarossa": Der deutsche Überfall auf die Sowjetunion 1941, Berichte, Analysen, Dokumente* (1984), none provide any insights into the rapacious nature of Soviet foreign policy or the Soviet Union's murderous internal policies in the 1920s and 1930s.[5] This failure to document Soviet criminality creates a false picture that attributes all the horrors of the mid-twentieth century to the NS regime and implies that they can be understood only by examining the contents of a large black box with a red lid depicting a white circle circumscribing a satanic black *Hakenkreuz* (bent cross, i.e., Swastika).

Social, ideological, and military manifestations such as the rise of NS Germany cannot be studied in isolation. In a similar vein, to understand the forces and trends that led to the Bolshevik seizure of power in 1917, one would have to examine the history of tsarist Russia and key events such as the Emancipation Edict of 1861, the influence of *Das Kapital* (1867, 1885, 1894), the failure of movements such as *Khozhdenie v narod* (Going to the People, 1874) and the consequent rise of revolutionary terrorism in the 1870s, the development of Marxism-Leninism, the various events of 1905, and the disastrous outcome of Russian involvement in World War I, which prepared the way for the Leninist coup d'état. In *Marching into Darkness: The Wehrmacht and the Holocaust in Belarus* (2014), Waitman Beorn at least shows some awareness (unlike Römer) that German fear and hatred of Bolshevism were not without substance and could not be solely ascribed to specific features of NS ideology or Hitler's psychopathy: "Generals and enlisted men alike," he notes, "many of them shocked and horrified by the anarchic Weimar years and the associated Bolshevik terror, saw the Soviet Union as a very real threat to Germany's survival." Beorn also realizes the importance of "long and short term historical trends."[6]

These long- and short-term trends are indispensable for understanding not just the origins and evolution of the NS regime and the way it behaved but also the nature of the Soviet regime and its actions and thus why German planners felt compelled to pursue some of the policies they did. Before 22 June 1941 the Soviet regime enjoyed an unrivaled record for the use of terror (mass, arbitrary, and selective), genocide, judicial murder, annexation, forced labor, and deportation. Thanks to the introduction of a system of censorship unique in human history, the Soviet regime was able to hide a great deal of its murderous activity from the outside world. For example, the existence of Order № 00447, signed by Nikolai Ezhov on 30 July 1937 and providing for the execution of tens of thousands of so-called enemies of the people (vragi naroda) and automatic sentences of ten years' hard labor—in effect, death sentences—for thousands more came to light only after the end of the Cold War.[7] Only in the last months of the Soviet Union's existence did its officials finally acknowledge NKVD responsibility for the mass murders of Polish prisoners of war at Katyn and other sites in 1940 (considered by the Polish government to be genocide).[8] Up until this moment of truth, Soviet officials had issued one fanatical denial after another, insisting that the Katyn murders were the work of the German occupation forces and that any assertions to the contrary were simply anti-Soviet Cold War propaganda. Likewise, when confronted with the publication of the secret protocol annexed to the Non-Aggression Pact just after the end of World War II, Soviet commentators denounced it as a forgery. In fact, as Roger Moorhouse reminds us, Viacheslav Molotov, Stalin's foreign minister and the man who actually signed the document, stubbornly maintained to the day he died that no such secret protocol existed.[9]

Soviet censorship could not, however, hide everything. Western states, including Germany, knew a great deal about the Red Terror, the genocide in Ukraine (Holodomor), the purges, and the forced labor camps. Despite the best efforts of Soviet fellow travelers such as Walter Duranty, the New York Times correspondent in Moscow, to mislead Westerners, the scale of the genocide in Ukraine could not be hidden from those who wanted to know the truth. I propose to readers of this book that it is implausible (to put it mildly) to believe that knowledge of this monstrous crime and others committed by the Soviet state did not shape German attitudes toward that state, never mind the attitudes of fanatical Nazis. And it was here that objective, veracious, and verifiable evidence of Soviet criminality combined with Hitler's psychopathic hatred of Jews to form a fateful and utterly catastrophic union. It is undoubtedly true that the NS regime exploited the truth about the Soviet regime to justify the Holocaust, and knowledge of Soviet (NKVD) crimes, disseminated by the NS propaganda apparatus, made it easier for the Wehrmacht to become an accomplice to NS crimes.

If by propaganda one means organized lying and an attempt to change people's attitudes by the methods used in a Maoist reeducation camp, then propaganda alone could not have achieved Wehrmacht complicity, This point, it seems to me, is the flaw in Omer Bartov's interpretation of German behavior in The Eastern Front 1941–45, German Troops and the Barbarisation of Warfare (1985). In his view, the Germans' actions overwhelmingly arose from, and can be explained by, NS ideology and propaganda. Thus, according to Bartov: "When Hitler came to power, all the resources of the new Reich were mobilised in an attempt to produce a massive and incessant stream of propaganda aimed at brainwashing the public into a 'blind belief' in the Führer and a complete and uncritical acceptance of the tenets of National Socialism."[10] Bartov effectively describes the cult of Stalin that was initiated in the Soviet Union in 1929 and lasted until Stalin's death in 1953. Furthermore, the belief in Hitler was not compelled only by propaganda; it arose from internal and foreign policy successes that convinced large numbers of Germans that Hitler was a great leader who would bring Germany out of the wilderness of Weimar. Propaganda film masterpieces such as Leni Riefenstahl's Triumph des Willens (1935) helped create and project images of power, modernity, and success, as did the autobahns and the 1936 Berlin Olympic Games. Propaganda and success reinforced each other, whereas the cult of Stalin was based on extreme ideological coercion and terror. Boris Pasternak, the author of Doktor Zhivago (1957), has argued that one aim of the physical and psychological terror unleashed by Stalin in the 1930s was to obliterate the memory of the genocide in Ukraine and to compel people to accept the picture of Soviet society being generated and imposed by Soviet mass media (radio, press, and cinema) and the Soviet agitprop network.[11]

According to Bartov, German soldiers were not expected to understand National Socialism; they were merely expected to believe in it. But that claim is thoroughly erroneous, since it portrays German soldiers as unthinking robots. If the Wehrmacht had comprised automatons, it would not have been such a fearful and highly effective war machine. Moreover, belief that is coerced by the threat of violence is nothing but psychological terrorism, such as that used by the NKVD against German prisoners of war, by the Chinese in the Korean War, and against enemies of the people during Mao's Red Terror to purge their minds of politically incorrect thoughts. Belief that emerges from satisfying the psychological, cultural, political, historical, emotional, and intellectual requirements of would-be or potential believers leads to acceptance and conviction. Such conviction, when combined with first-class military training and a military tradition that stresses personal initiative (*Auftragstaktik*) in battle, enhances the chance of success and, as the Western Allies and the Red Army both discovered after the fall of North Africa and Stalingrad, produces soldiers who stand fast in the face of defeat.[12] NS slogans alone could not have produced such an outcome, either in victory or in looming defeat; rather, those slogans were characteristics of belief, not its catalysts. Some of the ideas exploited in NS ideology predate the rise of Hitler, as Bartov acknowledges. However, ideas and cultural norms that were peculiar to Wilhelmine Germany cannot, on their own, explain the rapid rise and appeal of National Socialism. Utterly decisive was the seizure of power by Lenin in Russia in 1917 and the consequences of the emergence of this totalitarian state, a new type of state for Germany (and others).

Lenin, for example, had no doubt that a new type of state was emerging from the revolution. As far as Lenin was concerned, this new type of state also meant that the war being waged by the Soviet regime and its proletariat was unique. Wars between slaves and slave owners have occurred throughout history, Lenin acknowledged, "but wars of state power against the bourgeoisie of its own country and against the united bourgeoisie of all countries: such a war as this has never occurred before."[13] Thus, the war of the proletariat against the hated bourgeoisie within and beyond the borders of the Soviet state was a war that would determine not just the survival of that state but whether the global revolution would succeed; it would be a war of unprecedented ruthlessness and bitter hatred. Victory would be all that mattered, and to that end, everything must be sacrificed. Such was Lenin's position.

Regarding NS ideological influence on German troops, Bartov addresses two questions: whether soldiers were affected by the barrage of propaganda directed at them, and whether events on the Eastern Front in World War II were "essentially different from numerous other brutal and barbarous military confrontations."[14] On one obvious criterion—scale—the war on the Eastern Front was unique. However, the war's ideological, quasi-religious aspects were not unique to the Eastern Front. There is no doubt that German soldiers were subjected to NS indoctrination and propaganda, but this was also the norm in the Red Army from its inception. This explains the role of military commissars and *politruks* (political instructors) and the large, ubiquitous, invasive network of volunteer and professional agitators that penetrated all levels of the Soviet state. The other World War II army to which Bartov's thesis is germane is the Imperial Japanese Army. Discipline was harsh and atrocities were common before and during the war, one of the worst being the rape and sacking of Nanking from December 1937 to January 1938 in the second Sino-Japanese War.[15] Japanese treatment of Allied prisoners of war was also abominable. While committed Nazis admired Hitler, and Soviet citizens were coerced into accepting Stalin as some kind of father-figure genius, Japanese soldiers worshipped their emperor and considered him a god. In all three states the leadership cult encouraged atrocities. Moreover, the ideological fanaticism that justifies unspeakable atrocities, including genocide, in the eyes of the perpetrator was certainly not unique to the Soviet Union and NS Germany. It was present in Mao's China and Cambodia, and it exists today in North Korea, where the grotesque leadership cult is a mixture of the black comedy in *Team America: World Police* (2004) and the paranoia-inspired violence of Stalin and Mao. The leaders of various fanatical Islamic groups and their disciples also believe, like Lenin, Hitler, Stalin, and Mao, that any abomination is justified in pursuit of their ideotheocratic ambitions.

Bartov seems reluctant to consider the question of Soviet behavior when examining the Wehrmacht's behavior in the Soviet Union. Concerning the Red Army, he notes that "it is often claimed that the Red Army was just as brutal as the Wehrmacht, a particularly convenient assumption for those who say that in Russia one had to behave like the Russians."[16] The claim of Red Army brutality is certainly not baseless, but the real problem was the existence of the NKVD (references to which are entirely absent from Bartov's study). The NKVD, with Red Army complicity, was responsible for the genocide in Ukraine; the NKVD executed enemies of the people in the tens of thousands; the NKVD was responsible for mass deportations and administration of the forced labor camps; and the NKVD murdered Polish prisoners of war.

Red Army and NKVD collusion in genocide and state-directed terror clearly anticipates the same sort of collusion between the Wehrmacht and the *Schutzstaffel* (SS) and *Sicherheitsdienst* (SD) in expediting the "final solution" in the occupied territories. Again, it may well be true that claims of Red Army (and NKVD) brutality are a "convenient assumption," but that changes nothing because, first, the assumption of Red Army (and NKVD) brutality is fully justified and verifiable, and second, one must consider the question of how any armed forces, not just the Wehrmacht, would behave when confronted with the brutality of the Red Army (and the NKVD). The mass death of Soviet prisoners of war in German camps—what I call the *Höllenqual* (see chapter 1)—was indisputably a dreadful crime, but the very high Soviet combat losses relative to those of the German invader were attributable more to the Red Army's battlefield incompetence. Ultimate responsibility for the number of Red Army soldiers killed, wounded, and captured rests with Stalin, who murdered his senior commanders. It also suited Stalin that Red Army soldiers, whose lives meant nothing to him, perished in German camps, since it could be used for propaganda purposes. Order № 270 (16 August 1941) removes all doubt about what the Great Benefactor and Father of the Soviet People really thought about his soldiers and their grieving mothers.

Bartov argues, not unconvincingly, that although other wars—the Thirty Years' War and Japan's war in China—"had a strong element of racial or religious fanaticism, they do not appear to have been conducted with the single-minded intention of exterminating whole peoples as was the 'war of ideologies' unleashed by Germany in the East."[17] The first objection to this claim is that it was the Soviet state that unleashed the "war of ideologies" with its commitment to incite revolution and class war. From its inception, the Soviet state regarded itself as being in a permanent state of war: war against internal enemies of all kinds, including whole populations,[18] and a cold war against Western states (Britain, United States, France, and Germany). This cold war, which started with the Allied intervention after 1918, ended when Germany invaded the Soviet Union in June 1941. The Soviet state's prosecution of this cold war was based on class fanaticism, and it envisaged the extermination of millions of class enemies. The ideology of class war and class hatred led directly to genocide in Ukraine during the 1930s, when some 6 million peasants were exterminated by a deliberate and utterly cruel policy of starvation. The entire weight of the Soviet agitprop apparatus was also turned against the so-called kulaks. The dehumanization and demonization of the kulaks foreshadows the same process against the Jews in NS Germany and in the eastern occupied territories. Kulaks were portrayed as greedy and unscrupulous usurers, bloodsuckers, and parasites who exploited others. Here, there is a striking parallel between the Soviet propagandistic exploitation of the economic motive to demonize the kulaks and the Jews' demonization as an exploitative and parasitic group in NS ideology. In fact, when one examines the various motives that have inspired other mass murders and genocides, the real or imagined superiority of one group in financial matters and the envy it arouses are consistent features.

Although Lenin was not the first demagogue to incite hatred of the rich, he once again blazed a distinctive ideological trail for Hitler. Lenin's writings on how to deal with the rich, with capitalists, or with any other class enemy demonstrate and adumbrate the psychopathic, irrational, and ineffably insane hatred with which Hitler would later target Jews. In an address written in January 1918 but not published until 20 January 1929, Lenin directed revolutionary mobs to dispossess and kill the rich. Using the same kind of language Hitler would use to dehumanize Jews—"parasites," "the dregs of humanity," "hopelessly rotten," "contagion," "plague," and "scum"[19]—Lenin let it be known that the main aim of registration and control was "the *cleansing* of the Russian lands from all kinds of harmful insects, from petty thieving fleas, from the rich bedbugs and so on and so on."[20] Of all the actions Lenin goads these mobs to take against the class enemy—including immediate incarceration, public humiliation (cleaning toilets), and arbitrary execution—two catch the historian's eye. The first is Lenin's insistence that the class enemy be subjected to registration and control so that none can escape the retribution of the proletariat. The second is Lenin's demand that those victims being dragged off to prison cells for "correction" (*ispravlenie*) must wear the same yellow cards given to prostitutes so that, in Lenin's words, "all the people, can keep them under observation as *harmful* people."[21] Registration and control—perhaps it would be more accurate to say registration *in order to control*—were the same bureaucratic methods later adopted by the Nazis to target and isolate Jews in Germany and then by the German occupation forces in the east (registration of Jews was essential for *Einsatzgruppen* operations). Furthermore, compelling so-called class enemies to wear distinctive forms of identification in public, with the express intention of humiliating them as a prelude to their being executed or being sent to forced-labor camps, was one of the most widely known and certainly one of the defining features of Hitler's persecution of Jews: Jews were made to wear armbands or badges identifying them as Jews in public—the same psychological terror tactic advocated by Lenin as early as 1918 (well before the NS regime adopted the same method), with the aim of socially isolating a specific group and concentrating public hatred on its members.

Although Lenin's war of ideological fanaticism bears some resemblance to the fanaticism engendered by the Thirty Years' War, that war's savagery ended when the war did. Ideological war, once started, cannot end until the enemy has been defeated; thus, the formal boundary between war and peace that belongs to the Western understanding of war was not accepted as binding by the Soviet state. Treaties of any kind were weapons of war and subterfuge, as far as the Soviet Union was concerned. Lenin's war of ideologies was total war that embraced all elements of the state and mandated totalitarian control.

The Western view is that wars have a beginning and an end and that what occurs in between is called peace. This view distorts the study of German war crimes unless, in the case of the war on the Eastern Front, it acknowledges that the total ideological war pioneered by Lenin was a new way of waging war that led to the crimes committed by the Soviet Union before June 1941. Since the Soviet Union was not involved in war with Germany before 22 June 1941, these Soviet crimes were regarded as an internal Soviet matter and did not constitute war crimes in any established Western understanding of that term. They could therefore be dismissed as irrelevant with regard to the genesis and consideration of NS war crimes, a position maintained to this day. This lack of interest in Soviet criminality as a factor in German war planning was clearly demonstrated during the Nürnberg trials, when the origins of the National Socialist German Workers' Party, its rise to power, and its various domestic policies were examined in detail. Since no such scrutiny of the origins of the Soviet state and the rise of Stalin and his policies took place (or was not permitted to occur), the inevitable conclusion was that the Soviet Union was an innocent victim of monstrous Nazi aggression on 22 June 1941, not that both states were vying for the totalitarian domination of Europe.

One obvious consequence of this failure to take into account the Soviet state's criminality was that the Barbarossa Jurisdiction Decree, the Commissar Order, and, above all, the Holocaust appear to be unique crimes, whereas Soviet criminality before 22 June 1941—the Red Terror, Holodomor, the Great Terror, mass deportations, Order № 00447, and Katyn—was tantamount to NS crimes. The fact that Germany more or less observed the requirements of the Hague and Geneva Conventions with regard to Western prisoners of war but not Soviet prisoners of war was not based solely on Nazi racial theories; it was based on the view that the Soviet state was fully committed to a war of ideology in which everything was permitted. Committed to a doctrine of war in which the Soviet state reserved the right to behave as it wished, Soviet ideologues had no grounds for complaining that Hitler attacked the Soviet Union without any formal declaration of war.

Both NS Germany and the Soviet state were committed to a war without rules and with no respect for the customs and laws of war. This posed hideously complicated (if not insuperable) legal, moral, and intellectual problems for the International Military Tribunal at Nürnberg. Max Hastings grasps part of the problem when he notes: "If the law had been enforced against all Germans who committed crimes against humanity in the countries occupied by Hitler, post-war executions on a Soviet scale would have been necessary."[22] According to this view, many Nazi murderers escaped justice—which they undoubtedly did—but Soviet crimes against humanity before, during, and after World War II were not condemned as such and have remained unpunished. The Soviet Union's responsibility for crimes as ghastly as anything perpetrated by the NS regime undoubtedly left an ugly stain on the postwar trials, but it does not totally invalidate them. Some form of retribution, however flawed and imperfect, was essential, and even though the Soviet Union was not in the dock with its totalitarian rival in 1946, the evidence of Soviet criminality is there for those who wish to see it.

Christian Hartmann exhibits a far greater awareness of the ideological as well as the external and objective factors influencing NS planning for Barbarossa in *Wehrmacht im Ostkrieg: Front und militärisches Hinterland* (2010). He examines the key moments on the Eastern Front—the invasion, the Commissar Order, the early battles, the beginnings of the Holocaust, the failure of the Blitzkrieg, the onset of partisan warfare, the nature of the rear areas, and the dreadful fate of Soviet prisoners of war—primarily through the files of five Wehrmacht divisions: 45th Infantry Division, 296th Infantry Division, 4th Panzer Division, 221st Security Division, and Kommandant/Kommandantur des Rückwärtigen Armeegebiets 580 (Commandant/Command of the Rear Area of Army Region 580, abbreviated Korück 580). Adding value to Hartmann's book is the fact that he harbors no illusions about the Soviet regime and makes a number of compelling comparisons between it and its NS rival. Further comparisons between the two totalitarian regimes can be found in Hartmann's *Operation Barbarossa: Nazi Germany's War in the East, 1941–1945* (2013).[23] The mere statement of these comparisons indicates that Hartmann is asserting not only that NS and Soviet totalitarianism can be compared and analyzed but also, and more importantly, that failing to do so provides an incomplete picture of what took place between 1939 and 1945.

Hartmann's many comparisons between NS Germany and the Soviet state recall the *Historikerstreit* (historians' dispute) that erupted in 1986 and led to the publication of a series of arguments and counterarguments in Germany.

The key element in this bitter dispute was whether the final solution—the Holocaust—was unique and therefore whether any comparisons with genocide and mass murder by the Soviet regime were morally, intellectually, and historically reasonable. The key proponents of the view that the crimes of the two regimes were comparable were Ernst Nolte, Michael Stürmer, and Andreas Hillgruber. Opposition to these historians was initiated largely by Jürgen Habermas.[24]

Unlike Römer, Hartmann is willing to consider the reasons why German planners and soldiers were so obsessed with the threat posed by military commissars. First, Hartmann acknowledges the highly influential role of commissars in the Red Army, their distinct administrative infrastructure, the fact that they "closely cooperated with the Special Section that the NKVD had established in each division," and their role in setting up blocking detachments. Second, he recognizes "that no group in the Red Army was ideologically indoctrinated to such a degree as the commissars" and that the "Soviet commissars and functionaries were no ordinary group of victims."[25] Indeed, they were not; together with the NKVD, they were representatives of a regime that had always been fully committed to the use of terror and the physical extermination of class enemies. Furthermore, this ideological and enforcement role was well known to German planners. The fact that commissars formed an ideological elite indoctrinated in the worldview of Marxism-Leninism-Stalinism and that they represented the Communist Party's interests clearly shows that the Red Army was always intended to be a new type of army—one that was committed to a specific ideological worldview and bound first and foremost by Soviet ideological tenets.

World War I also provides critical insights into the origins of NS (and Soviet) policies, since behavior that tends to be seen as unique to the totalitarian states of NS Germany and the Soviet Union was, in fact, common during World War I, especially on the Eastern Front. Ruthless countermeasures against partisans and armed civilians (francs tireurs)—including arbitrary shootings and the imposition of collective punishment—mass deportations, policies aimed at maintaining or facilitating racial unity, pitiless measures to ensure food security, appropriation of private property, scorched-earth policies, and a selective approach to the provisions of international law can all be demonstrated and are well documented. Yet these policies are not as firmly associated with World War I as they are with the World War II. One reason, perhaps, is that there were no major war crimes trials after the armistice.

The tsarist army, for example, employed mass deportation as an effective device to enhance its own security, to break resistance, and to weaken Germany's war economy. Anticipating the Soviet NKVD, it deported hundreds of thousands of ethnic Germans from the border zones and left them in the Volga region or between it and the Urals, where these people endured untold misery and suffering. Moreover, as the Russians were forced out by the German army, they engaged in a scorched-earth policy and deported some 3.3 million civilians along with them. Alexander Watson records the effect on German soldiers: "Advancing into the deliberately devastated landscape, encountering scattered, desperate and dispossessed inhabitants, German soldiers could be left in no doubt that they faced an evil empire."[26] Memories among Germans were long lasting. It is difficult to see how German officers and civilian functionaries who later assumed important positions in the Third Reich could not have been profoundly affected by what they saw in the east. That this experience shaped planning for Barbarossa strikes me as a given.

World War I and the major conflict that preceded it, the Franco-Prussian War, also provided plenty of precedents for ruthless and summary measures against those deemed to be operating outside the conventions of war, at least as understood by the Germans. *Francs tireurs* were seen as the main illegal enemy, and twenty-two years later, detestation of them was easily transferred to partisans, commissars, and other Soviet political functionaries during the planning for Barbarossa. In World War I the total number of civilians killed by the Germans in Belgium as suspected *francs tireurs* was 6,427,[27] comparable to the number of Red Army commissars—a far more ruthless enemy—killed in accordance with the Commissar Order. I am of the opinion (unlike Watson) that the killing of *francs tireurs* and the policy of so-called active deterrence point the way to events in World War II, especially with regard to the drafting of the Barbarossa Jurisdiction Decree and the Commissar Order. Nor was hatred of the *franc tireur* confined to the Germans. The reaction of the Habsburg officer corps to the threat posed by Serbian irregulars, the *Komitadjis*, was just as brutal: because they were deemed to be outside international law, there were no qualms about eliminating them. Obsessed by spy mania and convinced of the ubiquity of German fifth columnists, the tsarist army behaved every bit as ruthlessly in the east.

Facing starvation because of the British naval blockade—which, Watson convincingly argues, was a violation of international law—the Germans took various measures to guarantee food security in the east during World War I.

The Germans identified two areas as critical for meeting their agricultural needs: Lithuania and Courland, referred to as *Ober Ost*. The later Nazi plan drawn up by Herbert Backe, under Göring's supervision, for the agricultural exploitation of Soviet territory bears more than a passing resemblance to that drawn up for *Ober Ost*, although to be fair to Ludendorff and other German administrators in World War I, there were no plans to starve people to death. From Backe's plan, however, it is clear that the British starvation blockade aimed primarily against Germany in World War I played a major part in inspiring NS policies of mass exploitation of Soviet territories in World War II and a willingness to countenance mass starvation among the indigenous population if that was the price to be paid for meeting Germany's needs.

The data and the documentary evidence presented and examined in Watson's *Ring of Steel* show that, in terms of planning and execution, many of the policies pursued by NS Germany and the Soviet Union in World War II were not new, although they were implemented on a much greater scale than those carried out by Germany, Austria-Hungary, and tsarist Russia in the east during World War I. They were derived from obvious templates and precedents that Soviet and NS planners were able to modify. Moreover, in 1915 the feasibility of genocide, using war as a cover, had been clearly demonstrated with the killing of some 1.5 million Armenians by the Turkish regime. This genocide, the first in the twentieth century, is now known as the Armenian genocide or, among Armenians, as the Great Crime (*Medz yeghern*). The Soviet Union and later NS Germany perfected the techniques of genocide pioneered by the Turks in World War I, taking organized and systematic mass killing, and organized lying about such killing, to new levels, as evidenced by the Holodomor in Ukraine and the Holocaust in the German-occupied territories in the east.

A systematic and detailed analysis of the documentation pertaining to the NKVD reveals the critical role played by this feared organization. Very much like the SS in NS Germany, the NKVD operated as a state within a state. It assumed responsibility for imposing *revoliutsionnyi poriadok* (revolutionary order), uncovering spies, intercepting and filtrating *okruzhentsy* (soldiers from encircled units) and deserters, ensuring the security of the rail network and industrial plant, disrupting the operations of German airborne units, and executing and deporting Soviet citizens deemed likely to collaborate with the German invaders. In the first half of 1941 the main victims were Finns and Germans, but later in the war this policy was applied to other Soviet ethnic groups, including the Chechens, Tartars, and Kalmyks. After the mass deportation of Germans from the Volga region, Lavrentii Beria, head of the NKVD, boasted that the region had been *cleansed*. Beria's language matches that found in SS documents (e.g., *judenrein* or *judenfrei*) to characterize areas from which Jews had been deported or where they had been murdered en masse. Once again, this confirms the close affinity between the terror agencies of the NS state and the Soviet Union.

The systematic analysis of previously available material can yield new insights, but it is especially gratifying to come across new and valuable documents that enrich the subject. Such is the diary of Gefreiter Hans Caspar von Wiedebach-Nostitz, who served in the 20th Panzer Division. My translation of this diary is the first time it has been published in any language (see chapter 6). It starts just before the launch of Barbarossa on 17 June 1941 and ends on 17 February 1942, and although there are gaps, it is an almost daily account of the campaign, including the dangers and frustrations faced by German troops. The diary was made available to me by von Wiedebach-Nostitz's widow, and I would like to thank her and her family for allowing me the honor and privilege of studying the diary and other material.

The first phase of the German invasion figures prominently in the work of large numbers of Soviet-Russian authors (see chapter 7). On its face, an analysis of the portrayal of the invasion in novels may seem out of place in a study of Barbarossa. But given the way literature was intended to function in the Soviet state, the role allocated to writers, and the censorship apparatus, it is my opinion that published works are important historical documents and primary source material in their own right. Because of the unique ideological conditions and restrictions under which Soviet writers had to function, Soviet-Russian war novels provide a record of what themes mattered to the censors and their party controllers. They are not just novels in the normal sense of the word; they are documents that reveal how the Soviet state insisted that its view of the Great Fatherland War be presented. Soviet-Russian war novels are, therefore, literary, historical, and political-ideological documents in a way that Western war novels are not. The critical distinction is not that Western war novels cannot have political significance—clearly, they can—but that the Soviet state demanded political and ideological significance (and orthodoxy) from *its* writers. That is, Soviet writers were not permitted to operate independently of the state; they were required to serve the Soviet state and support its Marxist-Leninist *Weltanschauung*. Those who dissented, succumbing to *politicheskaia nepravil'nost'* (political incorrectness), suffered severe penalties: arrest, incarceration, expulsion from the Union of Writers, deportation, and execution.

It is important to note that the restrictions imposed on the writing of the history of World War II in the Soviet Union were not applicable to German postwar writing. This distinction is not fully recognized even now, when so much is known about the destructive impact of Soviet censorship on literature, history, and all forms of intellectual endeavor. Thus, Geoffrey Megargee takes a rather dim view of postwar German memoirs and insists that, "for reasons both innocent and insidious, their accounts constitute a mix of truth, half-truth, omission, and outright lies that has been difficult to untangle."[28] Even if these authors chose to bypass certain themes, memoirs written by, for example, Heinz Guderian and Erich von Manstein have much to commend them; Guderian's for his insights into the origins and development of the German panzer formations, and von Manstein's—possibly the most outstanding general on any side in World War II—for his tactical and strategic insights. In any case, Megargee's comments are far more applicable to Soviet memoirs, war literature, and official histories and statements. If von Manstein and others sought to mislead German readers about the war, they did so of their own volition, not because they were compelled to relate history in a certain way. Nor did they have to be concerned about being arrested and imprisoned for challenging the Bonn government's views on World War II. The main obstacle to getting a truthful account of the war on the Eastern Front has been not German memoirists but the massive Soviet censorship apparatus, which was abolished only in 1990. In fact, a quarter century after the collapse of the Soviet regime, there are renewed signs that the government of the Russian Federation is taking steps to block access to archives.

★ ★ ★

This study begins with Hitler's conundrum: attack Britain or the Soviet Union? All aspects of German planning for Barbarossa are covered. Here, the value of returning to source material that has long been in the public domain—in this case, the forty-two volumes of *Trial of the Major War Criminals before the International Military Tribunal Nuremberg*, the so-called Blue Series, and the fifteen volumes constituting the Green Series, dealing, *inter alia*, with the High Command case and the *Einsatzgruppen* case—is evident. These documents were downloaded from the Library of Congress website, and I am duty bound to express my gratitude to the librarians and archivists of that august institution for their diligence and dedication. Returning to this huge collection of documents with the benefit of modern research casts new light on German agricultural policy for the occupied territories. The penultimate chapter of this book is dedicated to a detailed analysis of Viktor Suvorov's book *Ledokol: Kto nachal vtoruiu mirovuiu voinu?* (Icebreaker: Who Started the Second World War? [1992]). Suvorov is a talented maverick whose views on the origins of World War II have to be taken seriously in order to rebut them.

Each chapter in this book is a discrete analysis. Taken together, they form a corpus of new material and close analysis of *Unternehmen* Barbarossa that I hope historians, especially those without access to Russian and German source material, will find valuable.

Transliteration conforms to that used by the Library of Congress, with some exceptions. Most notably, I use *Alexander* instead of *Aleksandr*. According to the Library of Congress, SMERSh is the correct transliteration, but I prefer SMERSH: it looks, appropriately, more sinister. Since *Belorussia* and *Belorussian* pertain to the period in question, I use them instead of the current *Belarus* and *Belarusian*. There are also variations on the name of the German city that hosted the International Military Tribunal. When quoting sources that use the anglicized transliterations *Nuremberg* or sometimes *Nuremburg*, I retain such usage. In all other instances I use the German spelling: *Nürnberg*. Since the German word *Panzer* is so well known among military-historical scholars, I treat it like an English word, lowercase and in roman type. Unless otherwise stated or indicated, all translations from all languages are mine. Likewise, all errors and interpretations contained in this book are mine.

Finally, so that my interpretation of *Unternehmen* Barbarossa is not misconstrued, I would like to point out that my view of the German campaign undoubtedly represents, in part, something of a challenge—even a disorienting and threatening one—to the scholarly consensus, especially that which has emerged since the end of the 1970s. This is often an inherent part of writing about history, and for this I make no apologies. However, I hope it is obvious that in highlighting and criticizing aspects of Soviet behavior before, during, and after the war and reexamining the way it has been interpreted, I am not providing an alibi for Hitler and his regime. I merely wish to explain and draw attention to some aspects of Barbarossa that, in my opinion, have not been properly examined. *Nihil obstat, imprimatur!*

★ ★ ★

The thirteen-part Russian television series *Shtrafbat* (The Penal Battalion), which was first shown in the autumn of 2004, begins with German wartime footage of Soviet soldiers being taken prisoner by German troops. The footage ends with the profoundly moving scene of a captured Red Army soldier. He is sitting and sobbing in his moment of abject misery and humiliation. I dedicate this book to that unknown Red Army soldier, in the fervent hope that he returned from hell.

Frank Ellis
Ampleforth, North Yorkshire, England, 2014

Barbarossa 1941

1 *Unternehmen* Barbarossa
Conception, Planning, and Execution

If, then, civilized nations do not put their prisoners
to death or devastate cities and countries, it is
because intelligence plays a larger part in their
methods of warfare and has taught them more
effective ways of using force than the crude
expression of instinct.

Carl von Clausewitz, On War

The vast area must, of course, be pacified as quickly
as possible. The best way for this to happen is that
any person who so much as looks askance is shot
dead.

Adolf Hitler, 16 July 1941

Planning for Barbarossa was set in motion by Adolf Hitler's Weisung (Directive) Nr. 21 and began in earnest in December 1940. Every significant agency
in the National Socialist (NS) state was involved. Experts in economics,
diplomacy, agriculture, meteorology, and metallurgy worked alongside
ethnologists, military planners, lawyers, and propagandists. Dreaming
of personal empires and estates, future administrators maneuvered for
appointments as Reichskommissare and Gauleiter. Meanwhile, in the nether
regions of this planning, the mass murderers of the SS and Einsatzgruppen
were preparing for the day when the vast areas behind the German front
line would be turned into an experimental killing laboratory where the
theories of Hitler, Alfred Rosenberg, and Heinrich Himmler would be
translated into genocidal reality by efficient technocrats and willing, obe-
dient, or indifferent executioners. Once these rear areas had been formed,
German civilian agencies became part of the occupation administration;

these agencies included the Todt Organization, the Reich Work Service, the National Socialist Vehicle Corps, the Reich Railway, the Reich Postal Service, the German Red Cross, the National Socialist People's Welfare Organization, and the National Socialist Women's Organization.[1] The aim of Barbarossa was the swift destruction of the Soviet state apparatus, which would pave the way for German occupation of the vast territories of the east, to Germany's long-term advantage. Poles, Russians, Ukrainians, and Belorussians would form a new class of helots, and the huge reservoir of Jewish populations would be exterminated. This chapter examines the considerations confronting the multifarious planners, the doctrinal and operational changes that had made the Wehrmacht so formidable by 1941, and some of the problems facing its Soviet opponent.

Introduction

They planned, they invaded, they conquered: the French were defeated, the British were ejected from the European continent, 1918 was avenged. So whither now Germany's victorious legions? Would the Germans undertake an all-out assault on southern England to complete the task in the west? Or could Britain be contained until Germany's remaining continental adversary, the Soviet Union, had been vanquished in another lightning campaign? These were the options facing Hitler and his generals as they enjoyed their moment of triumph and pondered the future in the summer of 1940.

The decision whether to launch an invasion of Britain (*Unternehmen Seelöwe*, or Operation Sea Lion) had all kinds of consequences for the outcome of Barbarossa. Defeating the British in the late summer of 1940 would have transformed the entire strategic situation in Europe and beyond: there would have been no air campaign against Germany, no resistance movements controlled and equipped from across the English Channel, no reason to allocate vast resources to a large U-boat fleet, no British troops in the Mediterranean, no need to raise Rommel's Afrika Korps, and no Anglo-American second front; in addition, with Britain out of the war, Germany might have developed an atomic bomb ahead of the United States. For the Soviet Union, the consequences of Britain's defeat would have been dire: no Lend-Lease; no access to British secrets derived from ULTRA; and the full weight of the German armed forces, now bolstered by the advanced industrial economies of western Europe, deployed against the Red Army. That the invasion of Britain would have entailed enormous risks is a given, but considering the astonishing advantages accruing to Germany in the event of success, the attempt now seems justified. The Germans' recent successes in Poland, the Low Countries, Scandinavia, and France further support this view.

In fact, the invasion of France—the Germans' main focus in the late spring and summer of 1940—ended with the rapid collapse of French arms and the exit of the British Expeditionary Forces (BEF) in disarray from the European continent. It is considered one of the most immaculate operations in military history. In nearly every aspect of this campaign, the German commanders and their technical support staffs introduced major innovations and, crucially, pioneered a new way of waging war that became known as *Blitzkrieg*. This fast-moving combined-arms doctrine was prefigured in the deployment of German mechanized forces in the *Anschluß* and the occupation of Czechoslovakia; it was fully implemented for the first time in the Polish campaign and was demonstrated again on a much larger scale in the summer of 1940.

The potential of airborne and glider forces had been appreciated before 1940, as demonstrated by the Italians and the Red Army, but it was left to the Germans to show what could be done with genuinely elite troops and bold leadership. British irregulars, such as T. E. Lawrence, had ably assisted the pursuit of British goals in the Middle East a generation earlier. Yet it fell to the Abwehr, combining the thorough training of the regular soldier with the ethos of the irregular, to come up with the Brandenburg zur besonderen Verwendung (zbV). These Brandenburg 800 units—the precursor of modern special forces—inspired the British to raise commando units and to form the Special Operations Executive (SOE). They also corroborated the views of British officers such as Colonels Mayne and Stirling that the Special Air Service (SAS) and similar units could wreak havoc behind the German lines in North Africa, as they did indeed in 1942 and 1943.

To defeat Britain, a proper plan was required to exploit German military excellence, but no such strategy existed. Hitler's hopes were pinned on the expectation that after Dunkirk, the British would be prepared to reach some kind of accommodation. Rebuffed by Winston Churchill, Hitler had to think seriously about the risks and opportunities of an invasion of Britain. Erich von Manstein's thoughts on the impasse immediately after Dunkirk, set out in his 1955 autobiography *Verlorene Siege* (Lost Victories), provide detailed insight into German military thinking at this juncture in the war. Paying full tribute to the leadership of Churchill and the tenacity of the British, he nevertheless argues that in pursuing its determined opposition to Hitler and the NS regime, Britain failed to recognize the much greater danger posed by the Soviet Union. This argument carries weight—hindsight is certainly not required to identify the Soviet threat—but it seems improbable that Churchill would have made a deal with Hitler. Hitler undoubtedly would have given all kinds of assurances that Britain and its empire would be left alone in return for guarantees that the British would not interfere in Europe. However, no agreement between Britain and Germany could have resulted in a long-term solution to the essential problem arising from a German-dominated Europe facing an offshore imperial rival.

The obvious advantage for Germany was that a deal with Britain would have removed the burden of a two-front war, allowing Germany to attack the Soviet Union and immeasurably enhancing its chances of success. Then the question confronting Hitler after the defeat of France would have arisen again: *Was nun?* (What now?) Having vanquished the Soviet state, would Hitler respect the agreement with Britain, or would he decide to solve the British problem by force? I cannot envisage any kind of agreement between Britain and Germany being maintained while Europe—from the French coast to Moscow and beyond—remained under Nazi occupation. That state of affairs would have been intolerable to both parties: Britain could never realistically accept Nazi domination of Europe, since it would represent a permanent threat to British interests—above all, national security. Hitler's new order would be jeopardized by the existence of an independent and militarily strong Britain with close links to the United States, given the threat to German hegemony implicit in the Anglo-US relationship. These tensions could be resolved only by war. In that case, it would not be in Britain's interests to conclude any kind of deal with Hitler, certainly not one that would help neutralize the Soviet Union. Churchill, like von Manstein, would have recognized that despite the Non-Aggression Pact, the Soviet Union posed a threat to Germany in the east. Therefore, from the British perspective, it made sense *not* to strike a deal with Hitler and thus maintain the possibility of a war on two fronts. Time worked in Britain's favor, not Germany's.

Commenting on the Anglo-German conflict in 1940, von Manstein writes, "It is the tragedy of this brief time span in which the long-term fate of Europe was decided that neither of the two sides had seriously sought to find a way to an understanding based on a reasonable foundation."[2] The basis of any understanding would have been, first and foremost, Britain's recognition of Germany as the undisputed hegemon of Europe, thus giving Germany a free hand not only to exterminate millions of Jews but also to implement its occupation policies in the eastern territories undisturbed by war. It may well be true, as von Manstein claims, that outside of a few National Socialist Party fanatics, ideas associated with the *Herrenvolk* (master race) were not taken seriously. Unfortunately, these fanatics were able to pursue their policies in the eastern territories. Writing after the end of the war, von Manstein would have been well aware of what happened in the rear areas, assuming he did not know during the war, which strikes me as scarcely credible. Had he, in 1940, bemoaned the lack of an understanding between Britain and Germany, this might be seen as an appeal to mutual Anglo-German interests and realpolitik (*vernünftig*, to use his word), but doing so after the war ignores the enormity of Nazi crimes in the east—crimes that were possible because of the outstanding success of German arms, of which von Manstein was one of the chief architects. From the perspective of the summer of 1940, Britain had every reason to refuse to strike a deal with Hitler; from a post-1945 perspective, Churchill's defiance shows a sure and inspired historical and moral understanding of what was at stake.

According to von Manstein's view, any invasion had to be launched immediately to ensure the best chance of success. Delays would mean the loss of good summer weather, complicating any landings undertaken in the autumn. Moreover, Germany had to defeat Britain as quickly as possible because of the ever-present threat posed by the Soviet Union. A long war may well have encouraged US entry sooner rather than later, whereas it would be too late for the United States to make any difference in the event of a German invasion.

Von Manstein also addresses the assertion that Hitler thought only in terms of war on the European continent and failed to grasp the importance of sea power and the need to attack British interests in the Mediterranean. In his view, loss of the Mediterranean would not have been a deadly blow to Britain, even allowing for the loss of Gibraltar and Malta and access to the Middle East. Von Manstein argues that trying to achieve a decisive solution in the Mediterranean would have had negative consequences for Germany. If Germany had made the Mediterranean the center—the *Schwerpunkt*—of its operations, Britain could have been defeated. But if Spain and Portugal refused to permit German troops access to Gibraltar and had to be subjugated by force, this would have required a permanent German presence, adversely affecting Germany's position relative to South America and the United States. A German presence in the Middle East would have exacerbated relations with the Soviet Union. Von Manstein also maintains that conquest of the Mediterranean would have required vast amounts of troops, and "the temptation for the Soviet Union to get involved in the war against Germany would have risen extraordinarily."[3] A major German commitment in the Mediterranean would have repeated the mistake made by Napoleon, tying down large forces. In any case, a campaign in the Mediterranean constituted a deviation from the main task: the invasion of Britain, the motherland, herself.

The main conclusion drawn by von Manstein is that an invasion of Britain, assuming it had a chance of success, was the right solution. After the Dunkirk evacuations, the British were in disarray, and this worked in the Germans' favor in the summer of 1940. The capture or destruction of the BEF would have had profound military and political consequences. First, the loss of so many men—as well as the equipment—would have seriously weakened not just the defense of Britain but also large-scale operations in North Africa. Second, it may have brought down the Churchill government and led to serious consideration of Hitler's overtures for a deal. Regardless of the specific outcomes, the loss of the BEF would have been a deadly blow to Britain. The failure to either capture or destroy the BEF—both entirely possible—was Hitler's, and it had far-reaching consequences for the outcome of World War II.

Von Manstein cites two factors as critical for any invasion of Britain. First, the invasion had to be launched as soon as possible to derive maximum advantage from Britain's weak defenses. Second, the effectiveness of the Royal Air Force (RAF) and Royal Navy had to be reduced "to a *sufficient level*" for the duration of the operation.[4] In other words, total destruction of the RAF was not required; rather, its impact and interference had to be reduced only enough to allow the invasion to occur. Deploying the Luftwaffe in the hopes of destroying the RAF before attempting a landing was, von Manstein argues, an error. The German air attack played to British strengths. The RAF was able to concentrate its entire fighter arm, backed up by a superior command and control system (including radar), on defeating the Luftwaffe. It was unencumbered by the need to attack German shipping or German troops on the bridgeheads or to provide support to British troops on the ground. Had the Luftwaffe attacks been part of an invasion with airborne troops, beach landings, and lodgment battles, the RAF would not have been able to concentrate solely on defeating the Luftwaffe. Its efforts would have been dissipated by the necessity of dealing with all the other facets of the invasion.

The Luftwaffe's attempt to defeat the RAF alone marked a significant departure from the all-arms concept of Blitzkrieg—a simultaneous assault in the air and on land. The Germans envisaged a seaborne landing after a successful air battle, a one-dimensional attack that lacked the concentrated violence of an all-arms assault, the defining feature of Blitzkrieg. Moreover, since the RAF bore the brunt of the Luftwaffe's attack, the British had time to improve their land defenses and recover their physical and psychological balance after the evacuation from Dunkirk. No such reorganization would have been possible had the British army been thrown into the battle immediately after Dunkirk. In von Manstein's view, even if the invasion had not succeeded, the losses could have been made good. The real damage would have been political, and it would have been considerable. Conversely, the failure to deal with Britain carried enormous long-term risks, since it facilitated the concentration of military, economic, and political forces, which ultimately destroyed the Third Reich.

Heinz Guderian and the Development of German Armored Warfare Doctrine

The so-called tanks were first deployed by the British on the western front in World War I, yet it was a German officer, Heinz Guderian, who went on to formulate and test a doctrine of armored warfare that had devastating consequences for the Poles in 1939, the Anglo-French armies in 1940, and the Red Army in 1941. The new armored warfare doctrine pioneered by Guderian and fully grasped by von Manstein and Hitler placed certain demands on commanders that were appreciated by the Germans but not properly understood or even accepted by the Anglo-French and Red armies. Its armored warfare doctrine may be the single most important element in Germany's success in the east.

The Treaty of Versailles proscribed the raising of armored units in the post–World War I German army. Yet this did not prevent enlightened officers such as Guderian and others from studying and developing the theoretical foundations that could lead, at some point in the future, to the formation of armored forces. In fact, in the decade after Versailles, this prohibition may have assisted in the development of German armored forces because officers like Guderian had to concentrate on the theoretical aspects of the armored weapon before any major practical measures could be implemented. Thus, by the time Hitler came to power in 1933, theoretical foundations had been laid based on a thorough study of the best available experience, the last two years of World War I, and the work of pioneers in the field, such as Major

General John Fuller, Basil Liddell-Hart, and Giffard Martel. Guderian also derived insight from Fritz Heigl's *Taschenbuch der Tanks* (The Tank Handbook) and the unpublished manuscript *Kampfwagenkrieg* (Combat Vehicles at War), by Austrian general Ritter von Eimannsberger. Despite the possibility that other states would pick up its ideas, Guderian pressed for the publication of von Eimannsberger's book. Opposition to his ideas in Germany compelled Guderian to submit his own views to a robust analysis and to synthesize the insights of Fuller and others to counter objections and gain support for his proposals.

Guderian's insights and arguments for the use of the panzers were set out in various articles published in the 1930s and then compiled in 1937 in *Achtung-Panzer! Die Entwicklung der Panzerwaffe, ihre Kampftaktik und ihre operativen Möglichkeiten* (Attention Tanks! The Development of the Tank Arm, Its Combat Tactics and Operational Potential). A second edition, unchanged apart from the title—*Die Panzerwaffe. Ihre Entwicklung und ihre operativen Möglichkeiten bis zum Beginn des grossdeutschen Freiheitskampfes* (The Panzer Arm. Its Development and Its Operational Potential to the Beginning of the Pan-German Struggle for Freedom)—was published in 1943. The most likely reason for the publication of a second edition was to signal Guderian's rehabilitation and return to active duty after his dismissal by Hitler in December 1941, prior to his appointment as general inspector of panzer troops on 28 February 1943. Moreover, the book's new title—especially the emphasis on the struggle for freedom—reflected an awareness that after the British victory at El Alamein, the Allied landings in North Africa, and the Soviet victory at Stalingrad, the initiative had passed to the Allies, and for Germany, the war had entered a new phase. Guderian's postwar autobiography, *Erinnerungen eines Soldaten* (A Soldier's Recollections [1950]), is also a valuable source of insights into the doctrines being pioneered in Germany.

Though acknowledging that the Germans could learn from the British, French, and Soviets, Guderian understood that not everything from all sources could be incorporated into his armored warfare model. Overwhelmingly, the British model was preferred, and the relevant manuals were translated to serve as the basis for training and refining German experiences. Although the British influence is clear, Guderian recognized that ideas on the use of tanks and other weapons must be adapted to the circumstances of the particular state. At some stage, a definite policy—a German policy—had to be adopted and pursued. To quote Guderian:

The task in the development of a weapon does not, however, consist in constantly adapting to changing views. Development is far more to be seen in the pursuit of a recognized goal, based on mature consideration, and unconcerned by transient opinions and currents and, moreover, continually to place the technical development which demands a lot of time on a long-term footing. Continuity is only to be attained when development remains under the control of one authority and when this authority enjoys the necessary full powers. As long as weapons are still in the early stages of their technical and tactical development, of their equipment and training, unified leadership is a matter of the greatest necessity.[5]

These administrative and organizational considerations may seem secondary, yet they were critical to the development and later success of the German tank arm. This can be appreciated by the massive disruption of Soviet tank doctrine as a consequence of Stalin's purges. In 1937 (the year Guderian's book was first published) Stalin had some of his most able senior officers murdered. Doctrinal assumptions and training that had flourished in the Soviet Union under Tukhachevskii were now rejected; continuity in training and development, identified by Guderian as so important, was disrupted, sacrificed to satisfy Stalin's ideological paranoia. Meanwhile, the Germans continually refined the theory and practice of armored warfare.

If continuity is essential, the question of how the tank arm will be deployed, and for what ends, is most important. In Guderian's words:

> Does one want to storm fortresses and permanently reinforced positions with them or does one want to employ them in open territory, in a strategic sense with a view to carrying out encirclement and outflanking operations, or are they to be used in a tactical sense with the aim of achieving a penetration and for countering enemy penetrations or encirclements, or, finally, are they merely to be used as armored machine gun platforms in close cooperation with infantry? Does one want to attempt quickly to resolve an imposed war of defense by a large-scale, concentrated operation of the main means of attack on the ground or does one want to bind these means of attack, having, in principle, renounced their inherent capability for rapid, wide-ranging movements, to the slow course of the infantry and artillery

battle and thereby conceding, from the very outset, the rapid decision of the battle and the war?[6]

French military thinkers insisted on allocating tanks to the infantry, something that Guderian regarded as a profound weakness because it meant that the tanks' greatest advantages—speed, firepower, and concentrated violence in the assault—could not be exploited. This was one reason for Guderian's rejection of French ideas. To achieve maximum penetration of an enemy's front, tanks must, Guderian believed, operate in dedicated armored formations. In all his publications and other forms of advocacy, Guderian devoted much time to exposing the weaknesses of the French doctrine and those in the German army who supported it.

To counter the view that tanks should be allocated to the infantry as support weapons and should not be used in large formations—divisions—operating independently, Guderian provided a theoretical illustration.[7] Imagine, he said, that there are two opposing armies, blue and red. Each side has 100 infantry divisions and 100 tank units. Red has allocated his tanks to the infantry divisions; blue has concentrated all his tanks in army-level formations. The total length of the front is 300 kilometers, of which 100 kilometers is secure from tanks, 100 kilometers is a hindrance to their movement, and the final 100 kilometers is ideally suited to tanks. Given that red has deployed two-thirds of his total armor in terrain that is not suitable for tanks, he is not making the most effective use of this weapon. Recognizing the nature of red's tank deployment, blue relies on a combination of terrain and well-sighted antitank guns to stop red's tanks should they move against him. Meanwhile, blue has deployed all his tanks on the part of the front that is suitable for tanks, offering the best chance to penetrate red's line. The outcome is that, on this part of the front, blue has achieved a twofold superiority in tanks. Guderian points out that this allocation of tanks to the infantry is an example of British tactics in 1916–1917, which ended in failure; however, when the tanks were used in concentrated form, this led to success at Cambrai. Another observation relevant to Guderian's example is that red faces a numerically superior enemy on a tank-suitable part of the front, but in the event of a blue tank attack, red may not have sufficient time to redeploy the remaining two-thirds of his armor where it is needed. The risk for red is that blue, having penetrated rapidly and in depth into red's rear echelons, could deliver a knockout blow *before* red recovers his balance. Moreover, should red decide to redeploy tanks to meet the blue breakthrough, those parts of his front where tank numbers have been reduced are now vulnerable, given the nature of the terrain, to attack by blue's infantry.

If tanks are allocated to infantry divisions, they have to wait for the horse-drawn artillery to be brought up, thus losing the advantage of speed and giving the enemy time to recover. The solution is for tanks to have their own artillery pulled by tracked vehicles, rather than being hampered by the much slower infantry. To quote Guderian:

> Making the tanks an organic part of all infantry divisions prevents the concentration of force in the decisive area. Large forces of tanks are placed on terrain on which they are unable to be deployed, or only in a very limited manner, and with losses. The tanks are forced to adapt to the slow combat conditions of horse-drawn artillery and to the marching speed of the allocated infantry. In short, the speed, and with it, the essential hope of achieving surprise and a penetrating battle success are killed off. The mass operation which, in view of the increasing power of antitank guns in all arms, undoubtedly has greater significance for the outcome of the battle than in 1917–1918, is prevented. The moving up and setting up of reserves is impossible and the capability to exploit the successes of the first encounter is denied. The enemy has time to move up reserves, to ensconce himself once again in positions to the rear, to avoid being encircled and to assemble his forces for a counterattack.[8]

To achieve what Guderian refers to as the decisively directed (*entscheidungssuchend*) outcome of the panzer assault, three conditions must be met. There must be (1) suitable terrain, (2) surprise, and (3) massed deployment in the necessary breadth and depth.[9] In World War II, ascertaining whether terrain was suitable was a much harder undertaking in the expanses of the east than in the west. Having served in World War I, many senior German officers were familiar with the terrain over which they would be deploying panzers in a war with France. Although Germany had deployed infantry divisions against the tsarist army, the scale of those engagements bore no resemblance to the proposals for Barbarossa, with its huge armored and motorized component that was expected to operate over a bigger area. Major terrain obstacles, such as the Pripet marsh-forest, were appreciated, but knowledge of local terrain was limited. Thus, both before and after the launch of Barbarossa, terrain reconnaissance and analysis were essential. The second element, surprise, is achieved by concentrating the necessary forces unobserved by the enemy and supplemented by deception measures and camouflage. To Guderian, the third element, massed concentrations of armor with sufficient breadth and depth, was the key component, since a massed break-in on an enemy position overwhelms the enemy's antitank defenses. In contrast, piecemeal deployment of tanks leads to their piecemeal destruction by antitank guns, or what Guderian identifies as the *Verzettelung der Panzerkräfte*.[10] This, in turn, leads to loss of the critical *Stoßkraft*, which, according to Guderian, "is the force which enables the attacker in the assault to bring his weapons within an effective distance of the enemy in order to destroy him. Only those troops in which this capability is inherent possess the necessary combat strength; that is, they are assault-prepared."[11] Panzers have the greatest assault power, and this capability mandates that operations should be based on the panzers' operational potential.

Piecemeal deployment also violates mass as a fundamental principle for all arms. This principle cannot, Guderian argues, be violated with impunity. In addition, the incorporation of mechanized infantry in panzer divisions has serious organizational and training implications that must be addressed in good time. To cite Guderian:

> This violation of one of the primary rules of the art of war can barely be accepted in peacetime because in a serious situation it will produce a bitter harvest. If one wants the mass deployment, the concentration of force on the decisive point then one must draw the organizational consequences in good time from this wish. Only when the panzer troops and their leaders have already learned in peacetime to fight in large formations can the mass deployment in war be successfully implemented. Improvisations among fast-moving mobile formations of troops, never mind the leadership, are considerably more difficult to conjure up out of nothing than is the case with the infantry.[12]

Once the assault has been initiated, Guderian envisages four encounters or battle lines (*Treffen*): (1) tying down enemy panzers and reserves and eliminating enemy headquarters and control centers (enemy vehicles are destroyed along the way, but tanks should not be involved in any battle); (2) destroying enemy artillery in the zone of operations, as well as the enemy's antitank weapons; (3) bringing up the infantry through the enemy's infantry zone and removing enemy infantry; and (4) bringing up large tank reserves, where available, to take on existing fronts. Guderian foresees the assault's development as follows:

> This entire, immense attack should simultaneously break into the enemy positions on a wide front, moving forward toward its objective in uninterrupted waves one after another. After the completion of the first combat missions, it is the mission of all battle lines to surge forward to be available for the forthcoming panzer battle. For this undoubtedly severe mission that awaits it, the first battle line will have to be made very strong whereas the second and third battle lines can be kept weaker. The strength allocation of the fourth battle line depends on the situation and the terrain. In the event that the wings of the assault can be secured, protection by means of antitank defense and other weapons will suffice. Exposed wings and flanks dictate protection mostly through echeloned tank forces in the rear.[13]

Guderian argued—and experience corroborated his view—that to maximize the penetrations achieved by the concentrated violence of mass armor, motorized infantry and motorized artillery should be integral and organic parts of the panzer division. Furthermore, the panzer division should incorporate a reconnaissance section, engineers, and antitank defense, all of which enhance the division's ability to operate independently and ahead of the nonmotorized infantry.

The main reconnaissance component of the panzer division was the Aufklärungsabteilung (AA), the reconnaissance section. This unit grew out of early trials and exercises using mock-up vehicles. These trials clearly demonstrated that mobile forces—tanks and motorized infantry—require high-speed reconnaissance forces capable of operating well ahead of the main forces and maintaining contact (Fühlung) with the enemy. In addition to operating ahead of the main forces, the AA must be able to operate for several days and, when necessary, redeploy itself very quickly in a new direction. These factors demand that the AA be self-sufficient and capable of observing without being observed; it should possess a large operational range and have excellent means of radio communication. In terms of armament, the AA must be sufficiently well equipped to engage, if necessary, similar enemy units. The Guderian view is that the AA is an outstanding military tool that can be used for operational reconnaissance tasks set by the army, as well as tactical tasks set by the division. Guderian concludes that the AA "is in terms of its origins, equipment, armament, training and leadership, an integral part of the panzer troops."[14]

Guderian envisages the next component, the *Panzerabwehrabteilung* (antitank section), as working alone or, better still, in conjunction with engineers, machine guns, and artillery to halt the advance of enemy tanks. In this role, these formations are known as *Sperrverbände*, and they are intended to function as an antitank screen. Guderian acknowledges that strong nerves and discipline are required in these units when they are under attack from enemy tanks, especially when the terrain favors tanks. Mechanized infantry is a crucial component of the panzer division. These units must be a permanent part of the division; they should be trained and incorporated in peacetime, and they must always be ready to move (*ausrückefähig*). The mission of mechanized infantry is to exploit rapidly the chaos and disruption caused by the armored penetration. These units require massive firepower, which in turn means a larger than usual component of machine guns and the necessary reserves of ammunition.

As a senior officer facing a large French army in the west and an even larger Soviet force in the east, Guderian had to consider, theoretically at least, the efficacy of his proposals for armored forces in light of these armies. Although he does not refer to France directly, Guderian strongly hints that he has France in mind when he says that this state is *rüstungsfrei*. In other words, unlike Germany, it is not burdened by the provisions of the Treaty of Versailles and is free to develop its armed forces according to its perceived needs. In the 1930s the two states most dedicated to the building of large-scale fortified positions were France and the Soviet Union, so it is reasonable to assume that Guderian is addressing the tactical problems associated with the Maginot and Stalin Lines. Guderian's assessment of the Maginot defenses assumes that terrain will be optimally exploited to ensure that enemy tanks are defeated by antitank weapons and artillery. Not addressed is how an attacking enemy might bypass these fortifications.

Guderian makes no specific reference to the Soviet Union, but when he considers the defensive options of a state that has no strong natural boundaries or anything resembling the Great Wall of China, he is, I suggest, looking in the direction of the Soviet Union. Here, Guderian presents his assessment of those options:

> For countries that are not protected by any aforementioned Chinese Wall, it follows that the necessity arises that they must have to

reckon with surprise, initial successes and more or less rapid and deep penetrations from an attacker. These penetrations will not primarily be conducted with infantry divisions, still less so with cavalry divisions. Rather, the attacker will for this purpose deploy his heavy assault panzers which will be followed by light armored forces and motorized support weapons of all types. Simultaneous with the land attack the air forces will be deployed in order to paralyze the defender's airpower, to delay the moving up of defensive forces on land—above all the panzer and motorized formations—and also to paralyze the command and control points. The effect of the attacker's air and armored forces will become all the more marked, the longer it takes the defender to mobilize his forces. If the defender has to limit the enemy penetration because he lacks the depth of territory permitting a drawing in of the attacker, then rapid moves and rapid deployment of strong, comparable forces, if not, at the very least, locally superior combat forces in the air and on the ground are necessary.[15]

Expounded here by Guderian is the very essence of German planning for and execution of Barbarossa in June 1941.[16]

Guderian provides more detail about the development of panzer doctrine and operational deployment in his autobiography. He confirms in this later work that, notwithstanding the limits imposed by Versailles, a great deal of useful experimental work was conducted. One of the first operational tests of the tank arm was its role in the Anschluß in March 1938. Despite the speed with which the operation was planned and the fact that nothing similar had not been attempted before, things went well. Most striking was the distances the armored formations could travel: troops of the 2nd Panzer Division covered 700 kilometers in forty-eight hours, and troops of the SS-Leibstandarte Adolf Hitler covered 1,000 kilometers in the same amount of time. This clearly demonstrated the speed and striking power of such formations. Although the engagement did not result in an exchange of fire, the deployment of German armor projected German power on land and influenced political decisions to Germany's advantage—analogous to the way the British Royal Navy projected British power on the high seas.

The speed and reach of the panzer units would play a role in later operations in both the west and the east—even, in the case of the latter, allowing for the bad roads. Maintenance was shown to be a weak link, and the necessary steps were taken to remedy these faults. One of the main conclusions drawn by Guderian was that "the theoretical assertions concerning the employment of panzer divisions were consistent with the operational tasks. March performances and speeds had exceeded expectations. The troops had their self-belief strengthened and the leadership had learned a great deal."[17]

Based on these mechanized marches, the way was now clear for the setting up of motorized corps. Also clearly demonstrated was the enduring force of the Clausewitzian maxim concerning friction in war. At every stage of an operation, problems, some foreseen and some unforeseen, can interfere. The Anschluß march highlighted such problems so that they could be dealt with, representing a new stage in the development of the German panzer arm and its readiness for later campaigns. For his part, Churchill claimed that the Germans had been bedeviled by problems and that the march was a disaster. Guderian directly challenged Churchill's account of the mechanized march, point by point, and convincingly concluded: "The same war machine which here 'had crossed the border rumbling and stumbling' [Churchill], had in 1940 in only slightly improved form been sufficient to overcome the obsolete armies of the Western powers in a short time."[18]

The impressive performance on display in the Anschluß operations was demonstrated again during the march into the Sudetenland. Guderian makes an important observation about the psychological impact of armored operations on an enemy that has no obvious answer to a mass panzer incursion and whose will to resist has been paralyzed, observing that the Czechoslovak army was "crushed without a battle."[19] The German incursion spearheaded by armor was a demonstration of power and efficiency that convinced the enemy to capitulate without a fight. This is a highly effective use of military power: it saves blood and treasure and ensures that the assets required by the victors are not destroyed.

The success of the Polish campaign demonstrated the efficacy of the doctrines and equipment developed by Guderian, but a far more demanding challenge was planning for an attack on the Anglo-French forces in the west. The architect of that bold and original plan was General von Manstein, and Guderian assured him that the plan would work as long as the mass of armor and motorized infantry was large enough.[20] What is remarkable about German planning at this stage in the war is that Halder, the chief of the army General Staff, wanted to use the tanks to secure a bridgehead and allow time for the slower infantry to catch up—what he called a "unified attack."[21] Such a proposal was anathema to Guderian, who saw this as squandering all the advantages conferred by the speed and Stoßkraft of the panzers. The panzers, argued Guderian (countering Halder), had to be deployed in concentrated form, with surprise, at the decisive point, and in sufficient depth so that there was no concern about flanks and the infantry could exploit the penetration.

At this juncture in his career, on the threshold of a remarkable military victory, Guderian pondered why the French—and, to a certain extent, the British—seemed so oblivious or even hostile to the advantages of mass armor and why the French set so much store by fortifications such as the Maginot Line. These reflections led Guderian to some of his most significant insights about the use of armored units in other armies and about the state of German military doctrine and leadership in particular:

> From this one had to conclude that the supreme French leadership had not recognized, or had not wanted to acknowledge, the significance of panzers for mobile warfare. In any case, all the exercises and large-scale training maneuvers of whose conduct I acquired any information, permitted the conclusion that the French leadership was determined to lead its troops in such a way that decisions based on a foundation of reliable knowledge should serve the purposes of secure movements and planned offensive and defensive measures. Every effort was made to achieve complete clarity concerning the deployment and breakdown of enemy forces before any decision to act was taken. If any decision was taken, so everything proceeded, almost one must say, in a manner that was schematic. This applied to the approach march, the preparation, preparatory fire and execution of an attack or to the installation of a defensive position. This striving for planned action in which nothing should be left to chance also led to the incorporation of the mobile force of the panzers into the organic structure of the army in a manner which did not violate the schema; that is, it led to the allocation of the panzers to the infantry divisions. Only a small fragment was organized for strategic deployment.[22]

What clearly emerges from the Guderian analysis is that the French army of 1940 was equipped with the tools of modern war—that is, tanks—but French evaluation of the advantages of increased speed, armored protection, and main armament lagged far behind the doctrinal insights appreciated by Guderian and others. France planned to use tanks more or less the same way it had in World War I, negating the technical changes that had taken place since 1918.

Other critical weaknesses in French doctrine are also evident. The insistence that no moves could or should be made without reliable information about the enemy—location and order of battle—was applicable to the static warfare of World War I, but there was no way to achieve anything close to the same degree of certainty when dealing with the highly mobile and aggressively led German army of World War II. Information derived under conditions of static warfare changes slowly, whereas information about a highly mobile enemy quickly loses reliability. In such conditions, a commander has to make decisions regardless of whether he has all the necessary information (which he often does not); this increases the pressure on the commander. In addition, the French attempt to eradicate uncertainty flies in the face of what Clausewitz teaches—and what has been endlessly vindicated: war is the realm of chance. Chance cannot be eradicated, but armies that are prepared for whatever opportunities arise can seize the moment. Doctrine and training are paramount: mastery of the fundamentals of war translates into better opportunities to exploit uncertainty. Chance favors the prepared.

Guderian's proposed deployment of concentrated armor meant that commanders at all levels had to make decisions based not only on their overall operational orders but also, with regard to local conditions, on their own initiative. To those staff officers in the British, French, German, and Soviet armies who had failed to grasp the essence of Guderian doctrine, large armored units operating way ahead of the infantry seemed too independent and likely to undermine command and control from the rear. Inevitably, they would have too much initiative. This is analogous to opposition to the raising of commando and special forces units in the British army, even when their efficacy had been demonstrated. Armored units operate in the enemy rear by tearing open gaps through which they can surge; airborne and commando units, delivered by glider or parachute, attack the enemy rear.

The other element of French doctrine that assisted the German attack was that the French High Command, still thinking in terms of the static conditions of World War I, could not envisage anything other than the Germans attacking in accordance with the Schlieffen Plan. This defensive mentality was demonstrated by the fact that neither the French nor the British made any move against Germany while most of its armored forces were deployed in Poland.

Soviet Military Thought, 1918–1941

Although it suited Hitler to encourage the idea that the Nationalso-zialistische Deutsche Arbeiterpartei (NSDAP; National Socialist German Workers' Party) was a revolutionary socialist party represented on the streets by the Sturmabteilung (SA), he understood that he required a group of well-trained and expert staff officers and military planners that could translate his directives and instructions into effective operations. The propaganda of a workers' army based on the SA served Hitler's purposes in his rise to power. Once power was firmly in his hands, this legacy of the street struggles became something of an embarrassing incubus that was exacerbated by SA leaders' strident demands for the creation of a truly revolutionary army. These demands posed a direct threat to the ethos and status of the regular army, caused serious alarm among senior officers, and threatened to destabilize German rearmament and war planning. One way or another, Hitler had to decide whether the National Socialist revolution would lead to the creation of new, revolutionary German armed forces or whether the professionalism of an established officer corps, with its tradition of analysis and deep planning, would be the preferred model. The problem was finally resolved during the night of the 30 June–1 July 1934, the so-called Night of the Long Knives, when Röhm and others were executed. For the time being, Hitler preferred professionalism to SA street fervor. Ten years later there would be a sadistic and very public reckoning with the professional German officer corps.

Hitler's sacrificing of the SA, one of the revolutionary founders of the NS state, to secure the loyalty of the German armed forces stands in complete contrast to what happened in the Soviet Union after Lenin's seizure of power. German officers—Guderian is a good example—were never denied access to the traditions and insights of Frederick the Great, Clausewitz, von Moltke, and Seeckt; they were free to adapt the teachings and experiences of their illustrious predecessors to the demands of modern war. The very code name Hitler chose for his invasion of the Soviet Union—Barbarossa—was an appeal to the past, not a rejection of it. In the Soviet Union, Marxism-Leninism and eventually Marxism-Leninism-Stalinism mandated either a complete rejection of tsarist military traditions or a suspicious view of the great Russian military leaders of the past: Potemkin, Suvorov, and Kutuzov. The wellspring of Soviet military thinking was an assertion made by Marx and Engels: "The history of all preexisting society is the history of class struggles."[23] More importantly, the Marx-Engels assertion that class struggle is the source of all wars and conflicts imposes a way of analyzing war that excludes elements of the unknown and chance and many of the insights on war that have accrued since the time of Thucydides.

Class struggle as the driving force of war was refined by Lenin and became one of the main influences on Soviet military doctrine. Thus, in his famous essay *Printsipy sotsializma i voina 1914–1915* (The Principles of Socialism and the War of 1914–1915), Lenin claimed there was an inevitable link between wars and class struggle and that wars would cease only when a classless society had been achieved. The claim that all wars arise from class struggle leads to the view, fully incorporated in Soviet military thought, that civil wars waged by an oppressed class against an oppressing class—slaves against slave owners, serfs against landowners, and hired labor against the bourgeoisie—are lawful, progressive, and necessary. Lenin then transferred his progressive view of civil wars to wars between states. To quote Lenin: "For example, were tomorrow Morocco to declare war on France, India on Britain and Persia or China on Russia and so on these would be 'just,' 'defensive' wars *irrespective* of who attacked first, and any socialist would sympathize with the victory of the oppressed, dependent, unequal states against the oppressive, slave-owning, rapacious 'great' powers."[24] This, in turn, led to the Soviet view of the just war, which is a war waged to secure liberation from oppressive forces and ultimately to bring about a classless society and the final victory of socialism. This view of class struggle provided a welcome justification for subversion and the fomenting of revolution. What happened in Germany in 1918 is one obvious example.

It is a matter of historical fact that struggle between various groups (classes) for power and economic advantage has occurred and continues to occur. However, Lenin's assertion that the dissolution of classes and class struggle would eradicate war as an institution in human affairs must be taken on faith—dubious faith—since it is flatly contradicted by some 2,000 years of recorded history and the equally dubious expectation that a classless society would be essentially strife free and would not generate the various forces that lead to war. Any strife-free human society would imply a totally new type of human being, one who lacked envy, greed, ambition, and lust for power and whose instinct for private property had been eradicated—that is, one who recognized no distinction between "yours" and "mine." The classless society and, with it, the abolition of war (if Lenin is to be believed) would also have serious implications for the pursuit of knowledge and human progress, both scientific and economic. These implications are clearly and demonstrably derived from Marxist-Leninist ideology as a whole, with its all-embracing expositions of human behavior, and not just from the Leninist view of war, which is just one part.

A strife-free society presupposes an unusual degree of intellectual and personal harmony. Intellectual harmony can reasonably be derived only from a general agreement that all the essential problems of man's existence have been solved. The very existence of dissenters, be they religious, philosophical, or ideological, is a direct threat to intellectual harmony, since dissent provides the breeding ground for internal conflict. (In this regard, it is noteworthy that a declaration that religious faith is absurd and irrational and that the socialist commonwealth is atheistic solves nothing.) Should dissenters be crushed or expelled as renegades from the socialist nest, affirming the age-old reliance on repression and violence? Even if such a conflict-free society could ever be established in the Soviet Union, its rulers must confront the possibility of external hostile forces. That is, they must plan for war and be prepared to conduct war at least as ably as their potential opponents; otherwise, they will succumb. Thus, they confirm the role of war in human affairs. It follows that complete security can be achieved only when all opposition to socialism has been eradicated. In other words, the first socialist commonwealth must wage war against all global opposition to eliminate all threats: total, merciless war must be waged against all nonsocialist states to eradicate war once and for all. This, I suggest, is the implicit and real meaning of "Workers of the world unite!"

To reiterate: the Marxist-Leninist view is that wars pursued by capitalist states are inherently wrong, whereas wars pursued for the liberation of the working class enjoy a unique moral, historical, and ideological position. Given that class war is based on a whole series of erroneous assumptions about the way societies function, especially in the economic sphere (which ultimately led to the demise of Soviet state and its post-1945 empire in eastern Europe), the Soviet study of war is bound to be skewed and distorted by the prism of Marxism-Leninism. Looking back at this Soviet view of war, one can see how deeply flawed it is. When the Soviet study or advocacy of war moves away from Marxism-Leninism, we may find areas worthy of serious study. The corrupting effects of ideology are evident in David Glantz's observation that Soviet "military science must accord with politically correct doctrine."[25] The problem of politically correct doctrine is evident in the claim that Soviet doctrine is based on scientifically founded views. But to be scientifically founded, a viewpoint must be fully consistent with Marxism-Leninism;

otherwise, it cannot be considered scientifically founded. Thus, if the whole analysis of war has to be based on the assumptions of class war, there can be no place for views that reject or question the role of class struggle in the study of war and the formulation of doctrine. Such views would be heretical and dangerous.

Caution is also required when encountering Marxist-Leninist terms such as *pravdivost'* (truthfulness or veracity). In the context of Marxism-Leninism, *pravdivost'* enjoys no independent, objective status. Anything so described must be consistent with Marxism-Leninism; otherwise, it cannot be *pravdivyi* (truthful). Terms such as *military science* also assume that the study of military matters is a science and that the subject being studied—complex human societies—behaves with the same regularity observed in matter and can be defined by something analogous to the laws of physics and chemistry. The study of war across the ages, beginning with Thucydides, the first major scholar on the subject, makes it possible to derive general principles about the nature of war, but it cannot provide complete certainty and predictability in the tactical, operational, and strategic realms. What can be observed are statistical tendencies that can help formulate military doctrine and planning. But these tendencies are of little utility if, for example, Stalin is confronted with clear and compelling evidence that an enemy attack is imminent and he refuses to take the warning seriously. Again, if those charged with the formulation of military doctrine are compelled, under pain of arrest, incarceration, and execution, to interpret all military problems, past, present, and future, through the ideological framework of Marxism-Leninism, regardless of inconsistencies, doctrinal insights will offer only problems, not solutions.

Marxist-Leninist ideology makes stupendous claims about the nature of the material world that are, in essence, acts of faith. This is especially true with regard to war, since all previous wars—or the bulk of them—are deemed to be rapacious and unjust, whereas the Soviet prosecution of war marks a new, progressive beginning and therefore demands a new justification and a new doctrine. This was the position confronting some of the main Soviet military thinkers and analysts in the 1920s and 1930s as they grappled with the aftermath of the civil war and the emergence of NS Germany.

Mikhail Frunze (1885–1925)

Frunze's essential contribution to Soviet military thought was to set out the main features of a unified military doctrine for the Red Army, which he did in an influential article published in 1921. Frunze began, perhaps not surprisingly, by attacking the legacy of the tsarist state, claiming that its repressive nature crushed all forms of initiative and hindered any advances in the realm of military thought. In Frunze's words: "All these deformities were especially clearly marked in the situation of our military art where intellectual curiosity was mercilessly nipped in the bud and initiative was stifled."[26] By contrast, Frunze believed, the new state had broken with the past and cleared the way for a serious investigation of military matters in a free and open manner. For the time being, there was some scope for theoretical speculation, but this relative latitudinarianism would not last. Had Frunze survived, he would have seen that tsarist obscurantism and censorship were mild, even benign, in comparison to the monstrosities that emerged in the 1930s.

Frunze prefaces his definition of the unified military doctrine with an examination of modern war. One of the features of modern war is that it involves millions of people, not just those serving in the armed forces, and it influences every aspect of social, political, and economic behavior. Moreover, modern wars are fought over vast territories, in the air, and on the oceans, and the weapons and technical means of waging war are constantly changing. Given these developments, Frunze concludes that the scale of modern war mandates greater unity, a high level of integration, and strict coordination in its prosecution: his trinity of *edinstvo* (unity), *tsel'nost'* (integrity), and *soglasovannost'* (coordination). Frunze also recognizes that achieving the requisite unity of thought and will is an exceptionally demanding and complicated task that can be accomplished only with carefully formulated policies. In other words, Frunze identifies the need for time and continuity, as Guderian would in the 1930s.

The unified military doctrine must also consider the nature of military operations and the nature of the threat—that is, whether the posture should be defensive or whether more active operations are required. Critically, the doctrine must be "a reflection of the united will of the social class in power."[27] Taking into account political and technical considerations, Frunze defines the term *unified military doctrine* as follows:

> It is the unified teaching accepted in the army of a given state
> establishing the forms of construction of a country's armed forces,
> the methods of combat training of the troops and the manner of
> leadership on the basis of the prevailing views in the state on the

character of the military tasks confronting it and the means for
resolving them which are derived from the class essence of the state
and the conditions of its productive forces.[28]

Frunze then seeks to develop the meaning of the term with reference to
the three main Western military powers: France, Britain, and Germany.
Frunze's view of France is that it lacks military vigor, which confirms the
overriding need for a unified doctrine. Even though Britain is primarily a
maritime power, Frunze sees the unified doctrine in its attempt to dominate
the oceans. However, the essential point remains: regardless of whether the
emphasis is on land or sea power, a state requires a unified military doctrine
that reflects its defensive requirements.

The seriousness with which military affairs are studied in Germany
clearly impresses Frunze. He notes the marked emphasis on offensive
operations, the vigorous search for solutions to military problems, and the
status and prestige enjoyed by the German General Staff. The results speak
for themselves. To quote Frunze: "The education and instruction of all troops
was conducted in that same spirit of offensive tactics and in the final analysis
prepared, in terms of its structure and training, a military force which later
on huge battlefields of the imperialist war revealed its outstanding military
qualities in the highest degree."[29] German military success, Frunze asserts,
is a direct consequence of the fact that the German army's training is based
on a unified military doctrine and that elements of this doctrine pervade
every aspect of the army. However, Frunze is quick to stifle any suggestion
that the Germans have some special gift for military affairs. Rather, the
difference is one of organization and a unified military doctrine, which
avoids any consideration of the source of this organizational talent and
the doctrine that flows from it. There is no doubt—despite the obligatory
Marxist-Leninist view that the 1914–1918 war was an imperialist one waged
by aggressive and rapacious capitalist states—that the German approach
to military training and organization is an attractive model for Frunze. He
concludes: "The very first clashes with the hostile armies demonstrated the
strategic and tactical soundness of the tenets of German doctrine."[30] These
views would have cost Frunze dearly in the 1930s or, had he survived, in the
post-1945 *Zhdanovshchina*.

Frunze's analysis leads him to some general conclusions about a unified
military doctrine. First, the military art in a given state is not a self-sufficient
entity but something that is wholly determined by the general conditions in

that state. Second, the character of the military doctrine in a given state is determined by the character "*of the general political line of the social class at its head.*"[31] Third, "*the fundamental condition of the vitality of military doctrine consists in the strict consistence with the general aims of the state and with those material and psychological resources which are at its disposal.*"[32] Fourth, one cannot invent a doctrine capable of being a vital organizational factor because, according to Frunze, all the main elements are a function of the milieu. The function of theoretical work is to seek out these elements, reduce them to a system, and bring them into line with the fundamental tenets of military science and the demands of military art. Fifth, the theoretical foundation of work in the Red Army must be studying the social environment and determining the nature of military tasks derived from the proletarian state and objectively and inextricably linked with its character.

In the early 1920s Frunze envisaged that the Western powers would attack Russia again, making the implementation of a unified military doctrine an urgent requirement. Frunze also called for the complete elimination of political discord from the Red Army. Ideologically hostile elements, he demanded, should be removed, and the command staff had to be fully sovietized. Only when the command stratum had fully internalized the new class ideology would it be possible to abolish the institution of military commissars. The fact that this institution was periodically withdrawn and then reintroduced at moments of crisis highlights the divide between the army and party and the fact that this tension was never really resolved. Frunze's call for reliable, Soviet-thinking officers had long-term consequences, since it marked a definite step toward imposing an ideological orthodoxy on the officer corps that would not encourage new ideas; in other words, it would re-create the conditions that, according to Frunze, had stifled military thought in tsarist Russia. Furthermore, and unbeknownst to him, Frunze was preparing the ground for the mass arrests and executions in 1937: one wonders how many senior army officers and victims of NKVD terror were confronted with Frunze's words by their interrogators.

Considering the questions of defense and offense, Frunze underlines the irreconcilable contradictions and hostility separating the new socialist state and the bourgeois states of the West and, moreover, points out that this situation can be resolved only by war. The options for defense or offense vary according to circumstances, but the aim is the "conquest of the entire bourgeois world" once the necessary material conditions are extant and Soviet power is suitably secure.[33] Quite apart from any rationale derived from class war, the need to take offensive action is stipulated in the military aphorism cited by Frunze: "Only he who musters the determination to attack will be victorious; the side that only defends is inevitably doomed to defeat."[34] And in Frunze's own words: "The working class will be compelled by the very course of the revolutionary, historical process to go over to the attack when a suitable opportunity for this emerges."[35]

Two key proposals in Frunze's essay are (1) that the vast expanse of Russia offers exceptional opportunities for withdrawing into the depths and conducting mobile operations, and (2) that partisan warfare—what Frunze calls *malaia voina* (small war)—can be used to disrupt the enemy's operations. Frunze's war of maneuver envisages operating over vast distances and on a major scale to achieve a strategic effect. *Malaia voina* is intended to counter a technically superior enemy by attacking lines of communication and taking full advantage of terrain (forests and marshes). A large part of the Finnish response to the Soviet invasion in 1939 was essentially *malaia voina*, and it proved highly effective.

Even allowing for the class-based perspective from which Frunze develops some of the main threads of his unified military doctrine, he recognizes the efficacy of German preparations for war, and much of what Frunze proposes for the Red Army seems to be derived from the German model. The German model also inspires confidence because it has proved to be astonishingly resilient, even if ultimately overwhelmed. Frunze's thoughts on the nature of a unified military doctrine also raise interesting questions for liberal democracies. Specifically, do highly centralized authoritarian and totalitarian states perform better in war than liberal democracies do? Must a liberal democracy become more centralized to survive a protracted struggle, inevitably undermining basic freedoms? There is something of a paradox here: A liberal democracy or even NS Germany would permit the discussion of military ideas, whereas censorship and terror in the Soviet Union put a stop to serious military discussion in 1937, with disastrous consequences. Yet the totalitarian state established under Stalin—of which the mass executions of Red Army officers in 1937–1938 were one small part—was resilient enough to survive Stalin's egregious errors *and* the German onslaught.

Vladimir Triandafillov (1894–1931)

First published in 1929, Triandafillov's *Kharakter operatsii sovremennykh armii* (The Character of the Operations of Modern Armies) has long been considered a major and comprehensive contribution to Soviet military thought.

In the introduction to the first edition, Triandafillov states that his aim is nothing more than an examination of the sum of all those elements that characterize the operations of modern armies. The extent of Triandafillov's analysis is indeed impressive, and he provides valuable insights into how a future war could be conducted.

Based on data available in the 1920s, he begins his analysis by considering the matériel foundation of armies and weapons; then he addresses a whole series of questions pertaining, *inter alia*, to the conduct of deep operations. Overall, his analysis bears the stamp of Marxism-Leninism, and Triandafillov provides candid insights into the nature of war waged by the Soviet state in pursuit of its ideological goals. Triandafillov also warns that, "since the material basis being examined in the present work is mainly characteristic *for the start* of a future war, all the author's tactical and operational assumptions and conclusions mainly pertain to the operations *of the first period of this war*."[36] In view of what actually occurred on all fronts during World War II, Triandafillov's qualification proved to be accurate. Regarding later periods, all that can be established are general trends. What this implies is that any analysis of the first phase of a future war is critical for both attacker and defender. Again, this was manifestly the case after 22 June 1941 and the eventual assault on Moscow.

Triandafillov's book was issued in three editions, the last two of which were published after his death in 1931. In view of the fact that his book was considered valuable because of "its correct [*pravil'naia*] Marxist methodology" (as stated in the introduction to the second edition),[37] one might assume that this protected the author. However, even if he wrote a book that satisfied the ideologically correct requirements of Marxism-Leninism, Triandafillov shows no signs of the intellectual slavishness that would become the norm after 1937 and do such damage to Soviet military thought. One cannot know whether Triandafillov would have been cut down by Stalin's Terror, but along with Frunze, Tukhachevskii, and others, he certainly falls into a category of Soviet military thinkers who regarded military professionalism as a virtue and as essential if Soviet goals were to be achieved. Military professionalism requires an independence of mind without which rigorous analysis becomes impossible and military theory cannot be formulated and distilled. In 1937, however, these Clausewitzian postulates, taken for granted in all other major armies, aroused Stalin's suspicion because they were perceived as a threat to his final consolidation of power.

A key question for the modern army is whether it should be a mass army, in excess of a million strong, or whether quantity should be sacrificed or reduced for quality. A small, professional army acquires a sense that it is special, that it is an elite force. From a Marxist-Leninist perspective, this is potentially dangerous because it risks Bonapartism. To achieve the goals envisaged by Triandafillov, large armies are required, but this leads to problems of quality and training. Triandafillov argues, "The idea of conquering modern states by small numbers of troops, even if motorized is naïve. Such an army, having penetrated into the depth of an enemy country, runs the risk of being isolated, if, at the same time it is not supported by a much stronger army."[38]

Countering the British military theorist Fuller, Triandafillov sees specific advantages in a large, mass army—the so-called nightmare army—because it possesses all the necessary technical means to solve the problems of modern war. According to Triandafillov, Fuller's misgivings about the nightmare army are prompted by fear of the inevitable proletarian revolution, a fear that arises from a lack of trust in the masses that have become class-conscious. In Triandafillov's rejection of Fuller, and in Triandafillov's less than convincing arguments about the nature of capitalist societies and their succumbing to fascism, there are ideas of merit that have special relevance for 1939–1945:

> The provision of the best conditions for the conduct of freedom of maneuver and of the broad tactical and operational art will not be achieved by returning to the numerically smaller armies of armchair strategists but by the corresponding increase in the mobility of million-strong armies by means of improving the technology of transport (the use of road transport, six-wheeled vehicles, a wider development of railway communications and so on). That country which is compelled out of political considerations to return to a numerically smaller army, as a result of a lack of trust in the masses, cannot reckon with the possibility of its being able to conduct a major war.[39]

This assessment points to the type of army that actually emerged from Germany's final renunciation of the Treaty of Versailles and Hitler's rise to power. The treaty provisions resulted in a much smaller German army and one that, at least for the time being, was denied a whole range of weapons. In other words, the Weimar German army bore some resemblance to the numerically small but professional army rejected by Triandafillov, even if it was temporarily denied the equipment envisaged by him. The provisions of Versailles notwithstanding, the German army was still able to study the nature of future war and conduct various exercises and small-scale trials. Guderian's advocacy of the panzer bears witness to the fact that the theoretical analysis was conducted at the highest level and that there was openness to new ideas from whatever source. This theoretical work illustrates that time spent in reconnaissance is never wasted. To put it another way, time spent considering the nature of future war is not wasted and is, in fact, one of the primary duties of a professional corps of staff officers. Such work was conducted in Germany even within the limits imposed by the Treaty of Versailles.

The theoretical work carried out by officers such as Guderian bore fruit when it eventually became possible to translate plans and ideas into realities with the construction, testing, and creation of panzer divisions. Critically, the ethos of military professionalism maintained during the Weimar years not only facilitated the rapid expansion of the German army (and other service arms) when the time came but also ensured a high standard of quality. This totally vindicates the requirement for a thoroughly professional corps of staff officers dedicated to studying all questions related to war. Thus, by 1939, Germany had built a large, high-quality, and well-led army—something not envisaged by either Fuller or Triandafillov. This state of affairs strongly implies that had Stalin not succumbed to ideological paranoia and violence in 1937 and torn apart the theoretical and practical development initiated in the 1920s, the Soviet Union would have been in an incomparably stronger position in 1941.

Conceptualizing the formation and professionalism of Western armies based on the belief that their soldiers are in some way "committed to capitalism," Triandafillov misconstrues or cannot grasp the reasons why men serve. Some soldiers serving in Western armies may grasp the fundamental differences between privately owned and state-owned means of production, but such men are not normally motivated to join the military by such bloodless, economic abstractions. Rather, they are motivated by a sense of duty, patriotism, and adventure, by the intense emotional experiences and comradeship offered by war. Even if one conceded that the motives for pursuing international revolution in accordance with Marx, Engels, and Lenin were somehow morally and intellectually superior to the pursuit of war out of a sense of patriotism and a desire for adventure, that motivation to serve in the *Raboche-Krest'ianskaia Krasnaia Armiia* (Workers-Peasant Red Army [RKKA]) confers no superiority when it comes to mastery of the art of war. What made the Wehrmacht so formidable was that it managed to fuse outstanding military professionalism with a commitment to the ideas of National Socialism. Here, we can see a conspicuous failing of Marxist-Leninist analysis, which had no obvious and convincing conceptual framework to accommodate or explain the masterful political manipulations of highly charismatic leaders such as Adolf Hitler and their rise to power.

The degree to which Triandafillov's Marxist-Leninist-based analysis misconstrues the nature of Western societies—and, above all, the Soviet Union's future opponent—is evident in his description of what he considers the main weaknesses of Western societies: "This, of course, does not mean that the bourgeoisie has succeeded in or will succeed in eradicating those preconditions determining the unreliability of the armed masses in capitalist countries. Class, national and other contradictions which are undermining the capitalist system will not only remain but in the course of a war will inevitably grow to an extreme limit of aggravation and will, in all probability, lead, and not in one country alone, to unavoidable social shocks."[40] This is wishful thinking born of Marxism-Leninism.

Triandafillov devotes much space to developing his ideas on the shock army (udarnaia armiia). His use of the term is based on the formation of the German army in World War I that advanced through Belgium to the Marne and the advance of the Red Army to the Vistula in 1920. A shock army is an army designed to advance on the main axis, and Triandafillov stipulates that it "must be organized in such a manner that it is able, using its own forces, to conduct a series of consecutive operations from start to finish. It must possess all the resources which would permit it to overcome any resistance on the part of the enemy both at the start as well as during the course of the operations being undertaken."[41] The demands on shock army commanders are considerable. They must grapple with changing circumstances after the start of the battle as the enemy reacts: the enemy gains strength, the density of the front increases, and hastily prepared defensive positions appear on the lines of advance.

With regard to the width of the front, Triandafillov, basing his analysis on the final stages of World War I, asserts that a modern defense is so resilient that it cannot be broken by attacks on a narrow sector of the front. The reason for this failure, according to Triandafillov, is that such a blow engages only an insignificant part of the enemy's forces, and enemy reserves will be used to create a new front to envelop and quarantine the attackers. Crucial to the defender's ability to counter a breakthrough is his use of the rail network to deploy reserves to the threatened sector. Given the defender's ability to respond in this manner, Triandafillov concludes that an attacker can achieve a successful penetration only where he is able to pin down large enemy forces and place himself in an operational situation that gives him an advantage over the defender.

However, even when a massive concentration of force is deployed on a narrow front, a major offensive success is unlikely, mainly because of the resilience of the defense and the defender's ability to withdraw his forces in good time. The way to break the defense is by a combination of blows, with consecutive operations carried out at great depth. The aim here is to encircle the enemy and destroy or capture his forces. Based on the mobility constraints on the western front in World War I, Triandafillov's proposals for breaking the defense are reasonable. Unfortunately, he makes no allowance for the increased speed and armament of tanks, and since Triandafillov does not envisage tanks taking a dominant role in an assault, he makes no allowance for the effect of mass armor in contrast to mass infantry. As was the case in the summer of 1940, the speed of the German advance meant that it was able to overwhelm the defenders before they could react. Again, Triandafillov's ideas about defensive operations—with special attention to reinforced zones and, above all, to the carrying capacity of the rail network—are silent on how these installations might be bypassed and how to counter the rail network's vulnerability to air attack. In fact, when he considers the costs of war—resources, high casualties, and loss of equipment—Triandafillov envisages a future war as being similar to World War I, but on a far more destructive scale. Nor does he see this as a war of maneuver. On the contrary:

> In the future it is necessary to expect the long-term growth in casualties. The phase of mobility in the world war cannot in this regard be considered to be characteristic for future operations. Quite the reverse in fact; the character of future battles in terms of the saturation of automatic fire, the correlation between the forces of the attack and defense, the scale of the use of airpower and chemical weapons will bear a much closer resemblance to those battles out of which were formed the operations of 1918 on the western front.[42]

Implicit in his remarks is the recognition that casualties were reduced in the mobile phase of World War I. When contemplating the defensive systems envisaged by Triandafillov, the options for the attacker are indeed sobering, but the problems are not insurmountable. To overcome these problems, the attacker must be original, innovative, bold, and willing to try new ideas and take risks; he must develop new ways to solve problems, including the use of psychological weapons, special forces, and sophisticated deception and trickery; he must have a command system that encourages leadership and initiative at all levels. This summary does not describe the state of the Red Army in 1939–1941. For all the difficulties envisaged in the deployment of shock formations (*udarnye gruppirovki*), Triandafillov argues that "deep and crushing blows remain the most decisive means of strategy in attaining the goals demanded by the war."[43] Confronted with the apparently insurmountable problems of deep operations, military planners may succumb to what Triandafillov calls "operational opportunism," by which he means the tendency to reject "active and deep blows" in pursuit of "the tactics of staying put and inflicting short-range attacks, operations characterized by the modish word 'attrition' (*izmor*)."[44] The correct way forward for operational art, argues Triandafillov, is not to limit voluntarily the depth of consecutive operations but to maximize all avenues in order to destroy the enemy. In his words: "The correct resolution of this question will inevitably be linked with the total exploitation of possibilities for the development of decisive blows at a maximum depth which are permitted by the physical and psychological condition of the troops and by the conditions arising from the restoration of roads and supply."[45] In other words: "The art of the strategist and the operational staff is correctly to perceive the limit in the forcing of human and material resources beyond which may lead to the breakdown of the troops, resulting not in victory but in defeat."[46]

One of the main reasons Triandafillov so forcefully advocates the concept of deep operations is that he considers them an effective means of achieving the revolutionary goals of Marxism-Leninism. Small states—those he dubs somewhat contemptuously "Lilliput states"—can be easily crushed, whereas larger states can be destabilized and weakened. Major blows against larger states can lead to "the creation of objectively favorable conditions for societal-political shocks in the enemy's country." Moreover, "deep and crushing blows remain one of the most reliable ways to transform a war into a *civil war*."[47]

Triandafillov's analyses of the "form of the blow" are remarkably prescient in terms of the German army's actions in 1941. Operating against an enemy with a wide front and an open rear, the correct approach is to deploy concentric advances that can lead to the destruction of enemy forces. Speed of the advance is essential here, and the role of large armored formations and mechanized infantry is obvious, since they can outstrip the nonmotorized infantry's ability to withdraw. When the enemy can be pushed back against a neutral border, sea, mountains, or impassable terrain such as marshes, one shock group (*udarnaia armiia*) will suffice. Whether using one or two shock groups, the aim is to destroy the enemy's manpower. In summarizing the theoretical requirements for the conduct of such operations—well-organized rear echelons, a high level of training, troops accustomed to rapid and deep movements, and a command stratum in charge of the situation, all of which secures a high level of tactical mobility—Triandafillov provides an accurate description of what the German army achieved in 1940–1941 and the Red Army emphatically did *not*.

As an orthodox Marxist-Leninist, Triandafillov attaches great importance to the role of agitprop. He also envisages the possibility that troops will be cut off from their main forces and will have to fight in encirclement. Thus, Triandafillov acknowledges that encirclement (*okruzhenie*) is a fact of modern war; unlike attitudes in the Red Army between 1941 and 1945, it is not something that should be regarded with suspicion by Soviet security forces. Overall, the conditions of this future war will impose enormous strain on the troops, requiring that they understand the nature of the struggle. The nature of a future war waged by the Soviet Union will be a revolutionary class war, necessitating that close attention be paid to the troops' political indoctrination before and during the war. Triandafillov concludes: "And only the army which knows for what it is fighting and knows that it is protecting its vital [*krovnye*] interests, is capable of that."[48] That Triandafillov can characterize these interests in terms of blood is most unusual for a Soviet military thinker espousing the Marxist-Leninist cult of class and class war, since there is a distinct echo of the themes of *Blut und Boden* in NS ideology.

Mindful perhaps of the role played by antitsarist subversion and agitation in undermining the Russian army in World War I, Triandafillov maintains that the same subversive activity must be conducted among enemy troops in any future war so as to exploit what he sees as the inevitable class, national, and other contradictions and, ideally, to provoke civil war. In addition, every effort must be made to win over the civilian population and explain to them the nature of capitalist exploitation, although Triandafillov makes no provision for the treatment of those civilians who remain skeptical of Marxist-Leninist promises about the socialist commonwealth. Such skeptics would be well advised to hide their views, given what Triandafillov envisages after the fighting is over: "A huge burden of work falls on the political apparatus of the army with regard to the sovietization of the territories recaptured from the enemy."[49] Sovietization is the process whereby all institutions in the new zones are brought into line with Marxist-Leninist ideology. It amounts to a thoroughgoing purge of all those in positions of power, influence, or authority who are deemed to be hostile, anti-Soviet elements. In practice, it meant mass arrest, deportation, incarceration, dispossession, and execution, the fate endured by Poland and the Baltic states after September 1939. Sovietization also anticipates, and provides a template for, NS Gleichschaltung.

Georgii Isserson (1898–1976)

The significance of Isserson's 1940 work Novye formy bor'by (Opyt issledovaniia sovremennykh voin) (New Forms of Combat [An Essay Researching Modern Wars]) for any study of Barbarossa, in particular, and for the development of deep operations, in general, is the author's clear and penetrating understanding of what the German army achieved in the invasion of Poland and the obvious dangers that operation, and subsequent developments in the French campaign, posed for the Soviet Union.

In his introduction, Isserson explains the implications of the "new forms of combat" in his title: "Every time when the development of productive forces creates new technical means, when societal relations and social conditions change, when politics brings forward new aims of struggle both the forms and methods of the conduct of war change."[50] Isserson then proceeds to explore the theoretical aspects of and problems arising from these new material changes in war, with brief reference to the Spanish Civil War and a more in-depth examination of the German-Polish war in September 1939.

In writing about the use of tanks in Spain, Isserson's analysis shows signs of being influenced by the German success with armored divisions in both Poland and, more recently, France (Isserson wrote his book in June–July 1940 and stated he would deal with the German invasion of France at a later date). Thus, he implies that the conclusion drawn by some Soviet military theorists about the future deployment of tanks based on what happened in Spain is premature. Although he is ostensibly addressing Fuller's assessment of the use of light Italian tanks in Spain, Isserson is also responding to those in the Soviet Union who have been too quick to draw the wrong conclusions:

> From the point of view concerning the perspectives of a large modern war and of the mass use of new means of fighting this conclusion was exceptionally shortsighted. In the general history of wars there

are few situations when a new means of waging war has immediately exerted a decisive influence on the character of a struggle since the art and ability to use it does not usually arise at the same time as the appearance of the weapon.[51]

This is intended as a warning to Soviet thinkers not to dismiss the mass use of tanks. Isserson's own views are clearly in the German direction, since he says that tanks were used in Spain in small groups or in isolation, so they were easily knocked out; as a result, the advantages of operational mass in the depths of the enemy's positions were not achieved. His observation on this matter is indisputable: "Generally, the experience is frequently important not in itself: far more important are the conclusions that can be drawn from it."[52] Isserson's basic point is that the war in Spain—or rather the use of tanks there—owed too much to World War I and thus offered no real insights into how tanks could best be used. According to Isserson, one must look to the war in Poland to see what is really possible.

Isserson's analysis of the German-Polish war is often eerily prescient with regard to what happened to the Soviet Union in 1941. Thus, he warns that because the German-Polish war was over so quickly—though he rather conveniently fails to mention the Soviet Union's role in the downfall of the Polish state—it can tell us nothing about how a war between two equal states or an all-embracing war—total war—would progress. Isserson's analysis concentrates on five factors: (1) the move leading to war; (2) the conditions giving rise to a war of maneuver; (3) the operational deployment and potential of modern means of war, particularly airpower and motorized-mechanized troops; (4) the development of maneuver in the war, up to attaining a decisive outcome; and (5) the means of conducting operations.

Isserson shares Triandafillov's view that the first phase of war is critical. With regard to the start of the German-Polish war, Isserson calls it "a new phenomenon in history."[53] In this case, the Poles were not unaware that the political relationship between Germany and Poland was deteriorating and that this might lead to war; even so, the German invasion caught the Polish side totally by surprise. The critical point here is that there was no obviously discernible mobilization, as had been the case in World War I. The war began with an *invasion*, not with a declaration of war followed by hostilities. Isserson's conclusions on this state of affairs have profound implications for what would eventually happen on 22 June 1941:

In the course of all these proceedings, the old tradition, according to which it is necessary to deliver a warning, before one launches any blow, is dispensed with. In general there is no declaration of war. The war is merely started by armed forces which have been deployed in advance. Mobilization and the concentration of forces do not relate to the period after the onset of a state of war, as was the case in 1914, but are conducted imperceptibly and gradually well before. It goes without saying that this cannot be entirely hidden. In varying degrees the scope of the buildup becomes known. However, only one step ever remains from the threat of war to the entry into a war. It gives rise to doubt whether in actual fact a military intervention is being prepared or not or whether it is only a threat. And while one side remains in a state of doubt, the other side which has taken a firm decision to enter into a war, continues the concentration of forces, until, finally, a huge armed force turns out to have been deployed on the border. After this it only remains to give the signal and the war is unleashed in all its force. The German-Polish war began in such a way. It revealed a new method of entry into a modern war and that was, in essence, the main strategic surprise [*glavnaia strategicheskaia vnezapnost'*] for the Poles. Only the fact that military operations had been opened, finally, resolved the doubts of Polish politicians who, more than anything, by their arrogance, had provoked the war but, who at the same time turned out to be those who were most of all caught unawares.[54]

When he turns to the series of errors made by the Polish General Staff, Isserson inadvertently highlights the future failures of Stalin's regime. If the Polish General Staff was guilty of staggering incomprehension and a fundamentally incorrect assessment of what was happening, resulting in Poland being taken by surprise, what can be said about Stalin and his staff in the period leading up to 22 June 1941?

Isserson identifies three major errors made by the Poles. First, they assumed that the bulk of German forces would be deployed in the west, in the expectation that the Anglo-French armies would attack Germany. Anglo-French guarantees to Poland were worthless—they had no intention of attacking Germany from the west—and the Poles' dissemination of misinformation about full mobilization, designed to alarm the Germans, was a bluff that the Germans called. (The Germans discerned the weakness behind the bluff, just as they would a year later with the promulgation of the TASS communiqué of 13 June 1941.) Second, the Poles failed to grasp the scale of German ambitions and believed the Germans would be content with Danzig. As a consequence, the Poles were caught unprepared. Third, the Poles assumed that Germany would be unable to mobilize all its forces at once, giving them time to react. To cite Isserson:

> In such a way, Germany's mobilized readiness and its entry into a war with all the forces immediately designated for this purpose remained unknown to the Polish General Staff. The Poles had not examined the strategic situation. And that meant that at the very least they lost the first phase of the war, and then the entire war. In this regard, for Poland, the war was lost even before it started.[55]

In examining these Polish failings, Isserson is also highlighting what would go wrong in the Soviet Union. Polish mobilization started too late, occurring in the confusion and chaos of the opening hours of war. From the outset, the Poles were at a huge disadvantage from which they could not recover. When Isserson asks how the Germans could concentrate such a vast army on the Polish border largely unnoticed, he raises a question that goes to the heart of Stalin's failure in 1941. A buildup that progresses in stages over a long period does not attract the same attention as a sudden large deployment of men and equipment. Even when it is noticeable, the question remains: does it signify war, or is it merely an attempt to apply diplomatic pressure? Isserson maintains that the Polish General Staff should have kept a constant eye on the German buildup in eastern Prussia, Danzig, Pomerania, Silesia, and Slovakia, noting "every new detail of concentration, periodically summarizing the established facts and drawing the necessary conclusions therefrom. If this did not happen, there is nothing surprising in the fact that one fine day Poland saw the huge armed forces of Germany deployed on its borders."[56]

The Polish General Staff's failure to see the storm clouds meant that the Polish air force was caught unawares and that the rail network, essential for mobilization, was effectively paralyzed by both German air attacks and the congestion resulting from the delayed mass mobilization of Polish reserves. The speed of the German advance meant that the Poles had no time to consolidate new lines of defense, and their unit cohesion disintegrated under attacks from the air and the deep thrusts of tanks. Command and control broke down, contact with the troops was lost, and there was a complete collapse of transport links in the rear. However, the main factor, according to Isserson, was that "the head of the armored formations penetrated deep into the body of the army [Polish]; between the retreating troops they penetrated into the deep rear, right up to the capital, way ahead of the retreating columns, everywhere entering into their rear and leaving them behind on all the most important lines right up to the Vistula and San."[57] Isserson shows a good grasp of what the German army had achieved, especially in the use of armor, as envisaged by Guderian:

> The independent use of armored and motorized divisions in order to solve operational tasks in the enemy's deep zone, way ahead of the front of the all-arms infantry formations for the first time received its practical use in the German-Polish war and immediately imparted a character profoundly different from the military operations of past wars. The theory of this question, as the essence of the new forms of a deep operation, was formulated in the years preceding. This conception stemmed from the very nature of the fast-moving means of war and only required the corresponding organization and exploitation.[58]

Such an intimate understanding of the Guderian doctrine suggests that Isserson either read Guderian's *Achtung-Panzer!* (1937) or, quite independently of Fuller and Guderian, realized the importance of the mass deployment of armor and mechanized infantry. In any case, and regardless of any familiarity with Guderian's ideas, Isserson provides an exceptionally clearheaded analysis of German doctrine and what became known after the Polish campaign as Blitzkrieg. Remarkably, for an analysis written by a Soviet military theorist in June 1940, Isserson's book is largely unencumbered by ideological incantations and deals essentially with the facts as they are known to the author. However, and perhaps not surprisingly, there are no references to or conclusions about the obvious role played by the Soviet-German Non-Aggression Pact in the crushing and dismembering of Poland.

Isserson's study is especially valuable for the student of Barbarossa and Soviet military doctrine because it demonstrates that there were high-quality military analysts in the Soviet Union who had identified the dangers posed by the new German doctrine of high-speed warfare not just for the hapless Poles and the Anglo-French armies but potentially for the Soviet Union. In fact, one might go further and argue that much of Isserson's book, especially as it concerns the failings of the Polish General Staff, is intended to warn

Stalin and the Soviet General Staff—albeit in the form of allegory—of the dangers posed by mass armored attacks, mechanized infantry, and superb ground-to-air cooperation. Isserson's advocacy of mass armor—echoing the Guderian maxim *Klotzen nicht Kleckern!* (concentrate, not dissipate)—is especially timely in view of the conclusions being drawn in certain Soviet quarters about the use of armor, which were in complete contrast to German thinking. Perhaps the most wounding part of Isserson's book, assuming Stalin ever read it, is the warnings about monitoring the buildup of enemy forces on a shared border, especially relevant after the carving up of the Polish state to avoid falling victim to *strategicheskaia vnezapnost'* (strategic surprise).

Weisung Nr. 21 and Planning for Barbarossa

From the German perspective, Molotov's visit to Berlin in November 1940 must be judged a failure, in diplomatic terms. Molotov proved to be impervious to Hitler's bullying and haranguing and was unimpressed by Hitler's attempts to push the Soviet Union in the direction of India. Molotov returned to brief his master in the Kremlin, and soon after, Hitler initiated detailed planning for *Unternehmen* Barbarossa with *Weisung Nr.* 21, which was issued on 18 December 1940.

Some preliminary work had already been completed on a campaign in the east before Hitler issued his directive. A draft plan, *Operationsentwurfost*, dated 5 August 1940, had been drawn up by Generalmajor Marcks. In that draft, Moscow is regarded as the economic, political, and intellectual center of the Soviet state, and it is assumed that the loss of Moscow would destroy the state's cohesion. Marcks believed that the attacking forces would have to be divided: one army group (Nord), consisting of fifteen panzer divisions, two motorized divisions, fifty infantry divisions, and one cavalry division, would attack north of the Pripet; another army group (Süd), consisting of five panzer divisions, six motorized divisions, and twenty-four infantry divisions, would attack south of the Pripet. Once the Pripet zone had been passed, a combined operation against the Soviet army would be possible. The main German effort would then be directed north of the Pripet against the bulk of the Red Army, the goal being the capture of Moscow. The missions of the weaker forces deployed south of the Pripet would be, first, to prevent a Soviet attack against Romania, the main concern being protection of the Romanian oil fields, and second, to prepare to cooperate with the main German force east of the Dnieper. Another contribution to the planning process was *Operationsstudie für einen Feldzug im Osten*, dated 7 December 1940 and drawn up by General von Sodenstern. Unlike Marcks, von Sodenstern envisaged three army groups (*Heeresgruppen*) being deployed. The aim of his operation was to paralyze the Soviet leadership by destroying the Soviet armies and seizing the large armaments industries located around Moscow and Leningrad. Elements of both drafts were eventually incorporated in the final invasion plan.

The stated aim of Hitler's Barbarossa directive was to defeat the Soviet Union in a rapid campaign before the war with Britain had been concluded. In other words, Hitler was committing Germany to a war on two fronts, based on the assumption that the Soviet Union could be defeated in short order. That Hitler was prepared to wage a two-front war but was unwilling to mount Operation Sea Lion betrays a curious mixture of recklessness and risk aversion. Regarding Sea Lion, Hitler was distinctly risk averse, despite the huge strategic advantages if the invasion of Britain were successful; yet with regard to the invasion of the Soviet Union, he exhibited a recklessness that ignored all objections placed before him. Defeat in Sea Lion certainly would have damaged Germany militarily and politically, but it would not have been fatal, whereas defeat in Russia and Ukraine, while Britain was still growing stronger, would have been fatal, at worst, or would have condemned Germany to a long war of attrition, at best. An additional risk was that the British would secure American involvement or that the United States would decide on its own to enter the fray based on national self-interest.

These same considerations featured in Hitler's final briefing to his senior army commanders, which took place on 14 June 1941. Guderian attended this meeting and provides the following record of what Hitler told his assembled generals:

> Hitler said that he could not defeat England. Therefore he had, he said, in order to achieve peace, to force a victorious conclusion of the war on the continent. In order to secure an unassailable position on the European continent, Russia had to be defeated, he said. Hitler's detailed expositions concerning the reasons which had led him to undertake a preventive war against Russia were not convincing. The tensions arising from the conquest of the Balkans by the Germans, the interference of the Russians in Finland, the occupation of the peripheral Baltic states were as little able to justify such a serious decision as were the ideological foundations of National Socialist Party doctrine and certain military intelligence concerning preparations

for an attack from the Russian side. As long as the war in the west had not been brought to a conclusion, any new military undertaking must lead to a war on two fronts and the Germany of Adolf Hitler was just as unprepared for that as had been the Germany of 1914.[59]

If any new military undertaking must lead to a war on two fronts, then such an outcome must also be implicit in the German conquest of the Balkans, Greece, and Crete and Soviet moves against the Baltic states, Bessarabia, and northern Bukovina, not to mention the joint German-Soviet invasion of Poland. Both Germany and the Soviet Union tried to improve their respective positions at the expense of the other, and it was this relentless, incremental acquisition of territorial assets and the pursuit of diplomatic advantages by both sides that contributed to the possibility of a war on two fronts for Germany.

On the one hand, Hitler's reasoning for moving against the Soviet Union before the war in the west had been concluded arose from his failure to mount Operation Sea Lion, but it also owes something to the westward expansion of the Soviet borders, a consequence of the Non-Aggression Pact. On the other hand, by not moving against Britain, he was effectively condemned to move against the Soviet Union. If he failed to move at all, he would concede the initiative to his enemies. The question here is why Hitler was prepared to attack the Soviet Union, which involved incomparably greater risks to Germany's strategic security, but not prepared to invade Britain. Perhaps the answer lies in Hitler's psychology and his willingness to succumb to the ideological-psychological self-portrait and visions outlined in *Mein Kampf*, regardless of any rational objections. Seeing himself as an instrument of destiny, as Germany's redeemer, Hitler believed that, unlike his generals, he was not bound by the limitations of time and space.

The operational burdens of Barbarossa fell, above all, on the army, with tactical and operational support from the Luftwaffe. The focus of German naval operations was Britain. The general operational aim of Barbarossa was to destroy the mass of the Red Army located in western Russia by the bold and deep deployment of panzers. Soviet air bases would be overrun at the beginning of the campaign to neutralize the Soviet air force and eliminate any opportunity to attack targets in Germany. The final aim of the entire operation was to establish a line running from the Volga to Arkhangelsk, isolating the Russian land mass in Asia. Any Soviet industry in the Urals would then be destroyed by air attacks.

The weight of the German advance was to be concentrated north of the Pripet marsh-forest zone with the deployment of two army groups: Army Group North, commanded by Generalfeldmarschall Ritter von Leeb and supported by Luftflotte 1, and Army Group Center (Mitte), commanded by Generalfeldmarschall von Bock and supported by Luftflotte 2. Army Group South, commanded by Generalfeldmarschall von Rundstedt and supported by Luftflotte 4, was to be deployed south of the Pripet marsh-forest. The primary mission of Army Group Center was to destroy the enemy in Belorussia with the deployment of armored and mechanized forces. Here, the necessary conditions existed for the deployment of strong motorized forces to the north, which would eventually, and in cooperation with the troops of Army Group North, operating on the Leningrad axis, destroy enemy forces in the Baltic states. Once these goals had been achieved, resulting in the occupation of Leningrad and Kronstadt, offensive operations would be resumed, with the aim of capturing Moscow. The mission of Army Group South was to move on a general axis from Lublin to Kiev and destroy enemy forces along the Dnieper, securing the all-important crossings over that river. A vital task for the 11th Army, part of Army Group South, was to prevent any attacks on the Romanian oil fields. Primary goals were the early seizure of the economically important Donetsk basin in the south and the speedy attainment of Moscow in the north. Important for later decisions once the invasion was under way was Hitler's clear statement that "the seizure of this city [Moscow] constitutes politically and economically a decisive success and, furthermore, the loss of the most important network of railway junctions."[60]

Translating Hitler's directive into a detailed operational plan now fell to the various staff officers who had been indoctrinated concerning Hitler's intentions. The military planning problems they faced were formidable. They had to deploy huge armies to the eastern border regions; undertake a vast program, known as *Aufbau Ost*, dedicated to building the necessary military infrastructure (roads, railway upgrades, bridges, defense installations, airfields, hangars, fuel and ammunition storage dumps); and concoct a thoroughly prepared and well-coordinated deception plan to hide the real aim of all this activity. Hitler had specified that all preparations had to be undertaken by 15 May 1941. Once the start date of Barbarossa had been set for 22 June 1941, this provided the time frame for the final transport deployment phase—*Höchstleistungsfahrplan*—to be initiated from 23 May 1941.

One of the remarkable aspects of planning for Barbarossa—and one that is not widely recognized—is that during the war games undertaken as part of the preparation, some senior German officers remained unconvinced of the wisdom of the mass deployment of armored forces. Guderian, for example, points out that the infantry generals—one assumes not all of them—wanted to initiate the offensive with infantry rather than armor. To these proposals Guderian forcefully objected:

> The tank generals, on the other hand, set great store on the fact that from the very beginning the tanks should be in the front-most line precisely because they saw the offensive power of this arm of service and expected a rapid and deep penetration and strived immediately to exploit this initial success created by the speed of engines. In France, they had experienced that the reverse of this procedure had at the very moment of success led to the roads being full of the endless, horse-drawn columns of the infantry divisions which hindered the movement of tanks. For the tank generals, it also came down to getting the panzer divisions in the front-most line in those sectors in which a penetration was being sought, and there, where other tasks were to be to solved, for example, the capture of a fortress, to deploy the infantry divisions.[61]

This is also a classic statement of the Blitzkrieg concept. Once the tanks had achieved a penetration and advanced at high speed, they paralyzed the enemy rear. Soviet divisions would find themselves operating against enemy infantry divisions pressing from the border and large armored forces behind them. Their choice would be to retreat and avoid encirclement or to stand and fight with enemy infantry to the front and enemy tanks and motorized infantry to the rear. The question is, how should a Soviet commander react to this development? In these circumstances, retreating to the rear enables the enemy infantry to advance, maintaining pressure on and close contact with the Soviet forces, causing them to lose cohesion in the retreat and, ideally, depriving them of the time needed to establish a new defensive line. This facilitates the breakdown of command and control and eventually results in the complete loss of unit cohesion, causing units to split up into groups of stragglers and okruzhentsy. One way to react to this situation is to advance to meet the enemy infantry. This maintains order and cohesion and has the potential to disrupt the enemy infantry's advance and sever its links with the advancing tanks.

Terrain and Weather in the Barbarossa
Zone of Operations

Terrain, the physical environment in which an operation takes place, has both tactical and strategic consequences. Forests, mountains, lakes, rivers, oceans, marshes, deserts, jungles, taiga, subarctic tundra, open steppes, and man-made structures (towns and cities) exert a permanent influence on the conduct of all military operations. On land, the terrain determines the use of armor and infantry and the way they are commanded; it sets limits—and creates opportunities—for operational planning and execution. What is regarded as a terrain obstacle to one side may be seen as a terrain opportunity to the other. Examples in World War II include the mass deployment of German armor through the heavily forested Ardennes in 1940, the Japanese axis of attack against British forces in Singapore in 1941–1942, and the deployment of raiding groups—the Long-Range Desert Group and the SAS—by the British across terrain considered impassable by the Italians and Germans in North Africa. Weather is another consideration that affects operations on land, at sea, and in the air. It is one of the prime factors contributing to what Clausewitz calls friction in war; it is a multiplier of uncertainty that influences every level of command. On the Eastern Front, terrain and weather reduced the operational efficiency of both sides, testing their soldiers and equipment to destruction.

Compared with operations in Poland and the west, the impact of terrain on the Barbarossa zone was exacerbated by the breadth and depth of the area over which operations were conducted. In such spatial circumstances, terrain becomes a function of time because it can retard the speed of any advance (the same holds true for weather). Furthermore, the greater the distance penetrated by the invading Germans, the longer the lines of communication and resupply had to be. Even under summer conditions, these greater distances led to a loss of time. The impact of bad weather and, later, partisan raids rendered resupply a nightmare. The main terrain features affecting and determining the conduct of military operations in the Barbarossa zone were rivers, large primeval forests, marshes, poor roads, major cities, and towns.

Rivers were major obstacles. They included the Western Bug[62] (approximately 800 kilometers long); the Southern Bug (790 kilometers); the Neman (957 kilometers); the Shchar; the Svisloch' (343 kilometers), which flowed through the Minsk and Mogilev districts of Belorussia, and another river of the same name (137 kilometers) in the Grodenskii district of Belorussia; the

San (444 kilometers), a tributary of the Vistula; the Oka (1,480 kilometers), a tributary of the Volga; the Zel'vianka; the Düna; the Susha; the Moskva (502 kilometers), a tributary of the Oka and linked to the Volga by a canal; and the Dnieper (2,285 kilometers), one of Russia's main rivers. The Dnieper also had wide and substantial tributaries that were famous rivers in their own right, such as the Berezina (587 kilometers) and the Desna (1,126 kilometers), which flowed into the Dnieper about 6 kilometers above Kiev. Most of these rivers also had smaller tributaries that created their own networks and thus presented additional obstacles to movement. Whether defender or attacker, the retention, seizure, and, when necessary, destruction of bridges over these rivers were critical.

If existing bridges could not be captured intact, rivers had to be crossed in assault boats, particularly during a contested crossing. Later, it might be possible to repair existing bridges or build new ones. If existing bridges had been damaged, acceptable crossing points—those where the west banks were not too steep—had to be found. Depending on the depth of forestation along the riverbanks, suitable sites were not always available. In addition, naturally occurring sites that could accommodate vehicle crossings would be known to the enemy, who might be able to take timely countermeasures, such as pre-registering guns and preparing ambushes in depth on both sides of the river.

The problems associated with contested river crossings are evident from Guderian's account of the forcing of the upper Dnieper by his Panzergruppe 2, part of Army Group Center, in July 1941. It also illustrates the nature of operational command in the context of Blitzkrieg. The problem was straightforward: should Guderian attempt to force the Dnieper with armored forces alone, or should he delay the crossing and wait for the German infantry forces to catch up? A crucial consideration was that it would take the German infantry some fourteen days to reach the river—time the Soviet defenders would put to good use to widen and deepen the defenses. It also meant that the battle for Smolensk would be that much more costly in terms of lives. Loss of time, the pressing need to achieve operational objectives, and, above all, Guderian's confidence in his men decided the matter. To quote Guderian:

> I was fully aware of the seriousness of the decision. I had reckoned with the danger of a strong reaction against the open flanks on all three of the panzer corps that would arise after the crossing of the Dnieper. In spite of this I was so imbued with the importance of the

tasks with which I had been charged and that they could be achieved and, at the same time, so convinced of the undiminished operational capabilities and attacking power of my panzer troops that I ordered the immediate assault across the Dnieper and the continuation of the moves against Smolensk.[63]

Guderian notes that Generalfeldmarschall von Kluge was against the operation, but he eventually succumbed to Guderian's reasoning, although not without chiding, "Your operations always hang on a silken thread!"[64] Guderian's boldness paid off. The Dnieper was crossed on 10 and 11 July 1941, and the advance on Smolensk was resumed. Smolensk fell to the 29th Infantry Division (Motorized) on 16 July 1941, and with it, a major operational objective was achieved.

Large forested areas are a major feature of Ukraine, Belorussia, and Russia. Although they could be traversed, the existing tracks were vulnerable to ambush; in addition, they channeled movement and provided cover for enemy formations, both regular and irregular. They also provided refuge for scattered and encircled Soviet units trying to reach their own lines and eventually served as bases—some of them very large—for partisans. Marshes and boggy ground are also found throughout the area, and even in summer, when water levels subside and the land becomes partially desiccated, these features can delay movement. The experiences of German troops in Army Group North, heading for Leningrad, illustrate the problem:

> The slogan "Open the gates to Leningrad" had its magical effect, and weariness was forgotten and unit after unit rolled toward the new objective. The road was good, and it was hoped that the sixty miles could be covered in a few hours. At the entrance to the swampy area southwest of Lake Samros hopes were dashed when the road became a swampy path of the worst type. Progress became increasingly difficult, and before dusk tanks that had tried to skirt especially bad spots and those that tried to drive through swampy ponds by force were stuck fast. After hours of work by every officer and man to make the way passable by the use of tree trunks, boughs, planks, and the last available fascine mats, the first moor was crossed.[65]

The main marsh feature influencing the conduct of operations in the Barbarossa zone, and one to which German planners gave a great deal of thought, was the Pripet marsh-forest. This approximately 100,000-square-kilometer (38,000-square-mile) area, known as the *Poles'e* in Russian, occupies the southern part of Belorussia, northwestern Ukraine, and a small part of eastern Poland and western Russia. It effectively divides any invading force from the west. To describe the Pripet zone as a marsh or a swamp, as German and English documents often do, is somewhat misleading. It is, in fact, a vast area of forests, marshes, and small rivers with open spaces and other areas that are largely free of inundation during high summer. Elevation differences throughout the area are typically in the range of five to ten meters. There are also some settlements and scattered villages. The question for German planners was whether the Pripet zone should be bypassed completely or whether German units should move through it to secure the flank of Army Group South. In one German document relating to Barbarossa, there is a somewhat enigmatic statement that the Pripet marshes "are not totally *taboo*."[66] This reference suggests that operations in the Pripet zone had not been ruled out at that stage of planning. The case for moving through the Pripet was militarily and practically sound. Although some German planners believed the region was impassable, experiences during World War I and the Russo-Polish war in the 1920s clearly demonstrated that troops and equipment could move through the terrain. German officers with knowledge of the area warned "against stating and believing this marshy area to be operationally unsuitable—above all for the Russians—and believing that this area could be passed by unchallenged."[67] Their advice prevailed, and the German units encountered substantial Soviet resistance and had to adapt very quickly to the demanding combat and terrain conditions.

Large urban areas in the zone of operations are important terrain features for a number of reasons. First, they tend to be situated astride major river and rail routes. They are also likely to have airports or airfields. Thus, their capture denies the enemy the use of communications assets that are essential to his defense. Second, depending on their size, they may be major administrative centers, the loss of which damages the prestige and eliminates the presence and influence of the Communist Party, a critical consideration with regard to Moscow. Third, if a large urban area is bypassed, it must at some stage be either invested or occupied to eliminate any threat to the occupying army's rear.

The one feature that was built specifically to cater to defense was the Stalin Line. It consisted of a series of reinforced regions (*ukreplennye raiony*) built in depth and intended to delay any enemy advance from the west.

When Soviet borders moved westward after the invasion of Poland and the annexation of the Baltic states, work on the Stalin Line was discontinued; new defensive lines to the west were initiated, but they were not ready by the start of Barbarossa.[68] Inspiration for the Stalin Line may owe something to the Maginot Line, but as Viktor Suvorov has pointed out, Slavs have a long history of using large obstacles to impede an invader. One of the main obstacles was the *zaseka*, or abatis, which Suvorov describes as follows:

> An abatis is a strip of forest in which the trees are chopped down to a level higher than human height in such a way that that the trunk remains connected to the stump. The top of the trees are piled up crosswise in the direction of the enemy and fastened to the ground by stakes. The thin branches are broken off and the thick ones are sharpened. The depth of the abatis is tens of meters where the enemy's appearance is all but ruled out. However, on the most likely lines of enemy movement, the depth of the abatises reaches astonishing proportions: 40–50 kilometers of impenetrable obstacles, strengthened with palisades, large stakes, wolf pits, terrible traps capable of breaking a horse's legs and snares of the most cunning construction. The abatis zone of the Russian state stretched for hundreds of kilometers and the great abatis feature, created in the sixteenth century, was more than 1,500 kilometers. Fortresses and city fortresses were built behind the abatis area. The abatises were scrupulously protected by light, mobile detachments. These light detachments would inflict surprise attacks on the enemy without getting involved in any protracted engagement. Then they would disappear in the multitude of labyrinths. Any attempts by the enemy to pursue them cost the enemy dear. In the abatis zone there were passages which could only be used by their creator. Those unfamiliar with the passages in the abatis area were led into ambushes and traps.[69]

The abatis was built to counter or delay any invasion of Russia from the south, so it had little relevance for the German invasion. However, the Stalin Line and the large-scale defenses built with conscripted labor that were intended to stop the German advance on Moscow drew on the tradition of the seventeenth-century *zasechnaia cherta*.

Three weather factors influenced the conduct of operations in the Barbarossa zone: (1) the high summer heat and dust; (2) the autumnal and vernal rains and mud—what the Germans call the *Schlammperiode* (mud period) and the Russians call the *rasputitsa* (literally, when roads and tracks fall away); and (3) winter proper, with heavy snow and prolonged spells of subzero temperatures punctuated by intermittent thaws.

High summer heat is physically demanding even for very fit infantry troops, and its effects are exacerbated in sandy terrain, where there is an absence of potable water. A particular scourge of high summer, however, is dust, which puts an exceptional strain on vehicle engines, tanks, and prime movers, resulting in delays for maintenance and replacement. To quote Guderian: "Men, weapons and engines suffered in equal measure from this plague which lasted for weeks on end. The engine blocks of the tanks, in particular, became so worn by sand that their performance dramatically sank."[70] This extraordinary wear and tear meant that tank engines had to be replaced, stressing an already overstretched supply chain.

Even before the onset of the full *rasputitsa*, spells of heavy rain caused flash flooding, washing away tracks and dramatically slowing down movement by foot and in vehicles. Guderian notes that on 4 September 1941 it took him four and a half hours to cover seventy-five kilometers.[71] On 11 September 1941, after a night of heavy rain, Guderian's four-wheel-drive, cross-country vehicle got bogged down and had to be recovered by an artillery prime mover. Once he got moving again, his vehicle could manage only ten kilometers an hour. Guderian assessed the situation as follows:

> At 1830 hours [12 September 1941] I was at my battle headquarters. On 10 September I had covered 165 km in 10½ hours and on 11 September I covered 130 km in 10½ hours. The water-logged roads rendered any faster movement out of the question. These time-consuming trips provided me with sufficient insight into the forthcoming difficulties that awaited us. Only he who has himself experienced existence in these mud canals up to the front-line units can form any idea of the demands being made on the troops and equipment, and can correctly judge the situation and draw the relevant conclusions from events. That the heads of our military had no practical experience in this regard and were not initially willing to ascribe any belief to our reports, bore bitter fruit and cost us incalculable losses and many avoidable reverses.[72]

When the first snowfall came—occurring in Guderian's sector during the night of 6–7 October 1941—the snow soon melted, adding to the misery of mud and filth enveloping everything. Wheeled vehicles had to be towed by tracked prime movers, and all kinds of measures had to be improvised, including dropping ropes and chains suitable for towing from aircraft. According to Guderian, supplies of Glysantin for radiators, which had been requested eight weeks previously, had not arrived, nor had winter clothing.

On the other side of the front, things were not much better, although the rasputitsa helped the Russian defense. Vasilii Grossman recorded in his 1941 war diaries: "Nobody has seen such mud. True enough this is rain, snow and sleet, a liquid, bottomless swamp, black dough churned up by thousands of thousands of boots, wheels and caterpillar tracks. But again, everyone is pleased: the Germans are being delayed by our hellish autumn, in the air and on land."[73]

Adding weight to Guderian's judgments about the impact of the weather, especially in his arguments with Hitler, is the fact that he is a senior commander who has seen for himself the conditions on the ground and has a clear understanding of the limitations of both men and machines. When a regimental commander of the 3rd Panzer Division tells Guderian that he has only ten operational tanks at his disposal, Guderian notes, "These numbers give a shattering picture of the requirements of the troops for rest and maintenance. They prove that the brave men had given everything in order to carry out the tasks that had been set."[74] But the Russian rasputitsa and the disruption it caused were merely a prelude to the real ordeal—the ferocious violence of snow, ice, and wind that was about to fall on Germans and Russians alike in the winter of 1941–1942.

The exceptionally severe weather's effect on operations in northern Russia during the winter of 1941–1942 constitutes a vital part of the history of Barbarossa and subsequent campaigns on the Eastern Front, most notably Stalingrad and those in the winters of 1943–1944 and 1944–1945. Obviously, German preparations for the winter campaign of 1941–1942 were largely and woefully inadequate, especially with regard to equipping the infantry, their vehicles, and the armored formations. However, according to Guderian, the SS and Luftwaffe units were well provided for, and he does not blame Hitler for the lack of proper winter clothing.[75]

Exposure to prolonged cold (low temperatures plus wind chill) places severe physical demands on infantry soldiers. Their clothing must be adequate, ideally consisting of many thin layers that can be removed as heat is generated by exercise and then replaced to prevent rapid cooling. Footwear must allow for the layering of socks or equivalents and should provide a suitable grip on frozen surfaces. Soldiers require adequate high-calorie rations to meet the body's demands for energy. Access to potable water can also be a problem, since water sources freeze and ice has to be melted. The soldier's personal water bottle should be insulated or carried close to the body to prevent or delay freezing. Adequate water intake may not seem to be a problem in cold weather, but moving through deep snow causes perspiration and can lead to dehydration if water losses are not replaced. Soldiers may suffer from lethargy, which in cold weather can have fatal consequences. Once the thermometer falls below minus 20°C, soldiers cannot be expected to maintain optimal efficiency. The combination of cold and physical stress reduces alertness and can have a soporific effect. Overcome by sleep, the victim dies of cold in his sleep: the so-called white death. There are other physical consequences of cold. For instance, defecation becomes dangerous because feces can freeze in the anal orifice immediately before elimination. Soldiers thus have to defecate under shelter and dispose of their waste in strictly designated areas so that it can be quickly buried after the spring thaw and reduce the risk of fecal contamination.

In any case, the Russian winter was killing Germans, as recorded by Grossman in his diary:

> There are severe frosts and hard crunching snow. The icy air catches your breath. One's nostrils stick together and one's teeth ache. On the main roads of our offensive there are frozen Germans: their corpses are untouched. They were not killed by us; they were killed by the frost. Pranksters set the frozen Germans up on their legs, on all fours and create intricate, fantastic sculptured groups. The frozen corpses stand with raised fists and hands open wide. Several of them look as if they are running with their heads pressed down on their shoulders. They wear thin boots, thin overcoats and paper-thin jerseys which do not retain any warmth. At night, during bright moonlight, the snow fields appear blue and the dark corpses of the frozen German soldiers set out by the pranksters stand in the blue snow.[76]

Evidence of the extreme cold is conveyed by Grossman's description of the blue-tinged ice and snow, which occurs only at very low temperatures.

Even in extreme cold, soldiers are required to perform sentry duty and to man weapon and observation posts out in the open or under minimal shelter. Therefore, some kind of rotation system must be devised so that periods spent in the cold alternate with periods spent in heated shelters, improvised or otherwise. Extreme cold weather also affects weapons of all

Table 1.1. Winter Temperatures Recorded in von Wiedebach-Nostitz's Diary,
November 1941–January 1942

Date	Temperature
14 November 1941	–10°C
5 December 1941	–25°C ↓ –30°C
7 December 1941	–15°C
8 December 1941	+1–3°C
25 December 1941	–15°C
26 December 1941	–20°C
27 December 1941	–26°C ↓ –33°C
28–30 December 1941	–30°C ↑ – 25°C
1 January 1942	–30°C
2–3 January 1942	–48°C
3–4 January 1942	–44°C
6 January 1942	0°C ↓ –15°C
9 January 1942	–15°C
18 January 1942	–30°C
19 January 1942	–30°C
21 January 1942	–40°C

types. Firing pins in rifles will shatter, as will springs in the magazines of pistols and handheld submachine guns, rendering them effectively useless. Machine guns are also vulnerable to jams and stoppages from ice. Deep snow neutralizes the impact of hand grenades and infantry mortar shells and dramatically reduces the fragmentation effect of artillery shells. Extreme cold weather can also wreak havoc with artillery fire control; in this case, trajectory and other ballistic data used by German artillery formations were based on meteorological conditions typical in central Europe.

There is no doubt that even by Russian standards, the winter of 1941–1942 was exceptionally severe. There are numerous references to cold weather in Guderian's memoir. For instance, he records that the temperature fell to minus 15°C on 12 November 1941 and to minus 22°C the next day.[77] Yet, he notes, the soldiers were still wearing light trousers, chains for tanks had not arrived, and guns sights on tanks were obscured because of the cold. On 4 December 1941 the temperature fell to minus 35°C; the lowest temperature he recorded was minus 50°C.[78] Temperatures almost as severe were recorded by Gefreiter von Wiedebach-Nostitz in his diary (see table 1.1). According to a study by the US Army's Center of Military History, based on the experiences of senior German commanders: "In the area northwest of Moscow the mean temperature during January 1942 was –32°F., and the 26th of the month in the same area saw the lowest recorded temperature of the entire Russian campaign: −63°F [equivalent to about minus 53°C]."[79] These severe cold spells are known as the *Kreshchenskie morozy* (Epiphany frosts), since they often occur around the time the Russian Orthodox Church celebrates Epiphany.

It falls to Heinz Guderian, a commander famed for his audacity and celerity and who made regular visits to his frontline troops, to convey some idea of what his soldiers endured amid clothing, equipment, and ration shortages during that dreadful winter of 1941–1942:

> My onward journey took me to the reconnaissance section and from there on to the 33rd Rifle Regiment of the 4th Panzer Division and for the night to XXIV Panzer-Korps. Only he who has seen the endless expanses of the snow-covered Russian lands in this winter of our misery, over which the icy wind swept and blew across every piece of uneven ground, only he who, for hours and hours on end, has driven across no-man's-land in order to encounter the sparse, all too sparse, positions of badly clothed and badly fed men, who by contrast to this, has seen the well-fed, fresh Siberians, exceptionally well equipped for the winter, is able correctly to judge the serious consequences that now ensued.[80]

Harsh terrain and brutally demanding weather in the high summer and in the depths of the Russian winter, never mind the Soviet counteroffensive, stopped the German advance on Moscow. But the same weather that had exacted such a cruel toll on the Wehrmacht and worked to halt Operation Typhoon now assisted the German defenders as they sat out the winter.

As a rule, Clausewitz is consistently sagacious and rigorously empirical in his analyses of war, so the Prussian master's claim that weather is of little import in military operations is somewhat shocking: "It is rarer still for weather to be a decisive factor. As a rule only fog makes any difference."[81] The obvious and profound impact of weather on German and Soviet military operations in the second half of 1941 and thereafter makes a mockery of Clausewitz's bizarre claim.[82]

Planning for Occupation, Control, Exploitation, and Extermination

Planning for the policies to be pursued by the German occupation forces in the newly conquered territories ran parallel with the strictly military-operational planning for Barbarossa. These plans, policies, and directives pertained to a number of specific areas: the agricultural and economic exploitation of the east in support of the German war effort; security measures to be adopted by the German occupation forces with regard to the treatment of partisans and the response to any manifestations of rebellion; specific policies toward Jews and, after the invasion, reports based on the work of the Einsatzgruppen in the rear areas; general statements of the NS ideological position; and policies for the treatment of Soviet prisoners of war. Many of the relevant documents were cited in support of the prosecution's case at Nürnberg. Access to new sources now clarifies a number of German and Soviet policies whose full significance was not realized at the time and even now may not be completely obvious. For example, a critical part of German planning for the occupation regime involved hiding the real nature of German intentions with regard to the Soviet collective farm system from the inhabitants of the occupied territories.

Agricultural Exploitation

German planners intensively studied how best to exploit the economic and agricultural resources of the Soviet Union, and by the end of April 1941, preliminary agreement had been reached concerning the organizational structure in the eastern territories.[83] Three main groups would be established: Group M (pertaining to army requirements and armaments), Group L (handling all matters involving foodstuffs and agriculture), and Group W (dealing with the commercial economy, including raw materials and production concerns). Once certain areas had been occupied, the plan was to establish five inspectorates; their locations and code names are shown in table 1.2. Based on rail nodes and close to major rivers—the Dnieper, Don, and Volga—these inspectorates would provide an efficient model for the rapid accumulation and transportation of raw materials, goods, and slave labor.

The culmination of German planning is *Wirtschaftspolitische Richtlinien für Wirtschaftsorganisation Ost, Gruppe Landwirtschaft* (Economic-Political Guidelines for Economic Organization East, Agricultural Group), dated 23 May 1941.[84] This document (referred to here as Document 126-EC) lays out the various German policy positions and is exceptionally important in terms of grasping the nature of Germany's plans for the conquered territories: its scope and aims are grandiose; its methodology is meticulous and carefully targeted; its implementation is pitiless.

A serious problem confronting German planners before the start of

Table 1.2. German Inspectorates to Be Established in the Soviet Union after the Invasion

Inspectorate Number	Code Name	Proposed Locations
1	Leningrad (Holstein)	Vilna
		Riga
		Reval
		Leningrad
		Murmansk
		Vologda (branch)
		Arkhangelsk (branch)
2	Moscow (Sachsen)	Minsk
		Moscow
		Tula
		Gorky
		Briansk (branch)
		Iaroslavl' (branch)
		Rubinsk (branch)
3	Kiev (Baden)	Lemberg
		Kiev
		Kishinev
		Odessa
		Kharkov
		Dnepropetrovsk
		Stalino
		Rostov
		Stalingrad
		Sevastopol (branch)
		Kerch (branch)
		Voronezh (branch)
		Kursk (branch)
4	Baku (Westfalen)	Krasnodar
		Grozny
		Tibilisi
		Baku
		Batumi (branch)
5	Reserve	To be deployed as necessary

Source: Document 1157-PS, in *Trial of the Major War Criminals before the International Military Tribunal Nuremberg, 14 November 1945–1 October 1946*, Blue Series, 42 vols. (Nuremberg, Germany: n.p., 1949), XXVII:35.

Barbarossa was the absence of reliable information about Soviet agriculture and the economy. After 1917, the Soviet regime created a system of censorship that not only targeted literature and the arts but also exercised tight control over the release of all social, economic, and agricultural data. Thus, the authors of Document 126-EC, in trying to draw up a preliminary assessment of total agricultural production in the Soviet Union, had to rely on statistics released by the tsarist government for the period 1909–1913. These data revealed that immediately before the start of World War I, Russia produced the biggest agricultural surpluses in the world. For example, about one-third of the total grain traded on world markets came from Russia (11 million tonnes). By the end of the 1930s, total grain exports had fallen to 1 million to 2 million tonnes. Whereas the amount of Soviet grain exported could be verified by market data, other Soviet claims had to be viewed with profound suspicion because they could not be confirmed, and Soviet statistics often functioned as an extension of agitprop to demonstrate the superiority of the Soviet economic model based on state control of all assets.

Critically absent from the German analysis is any mention of the catastrophic effects of forced collectivization on Soviet agriculture (effects that continued to blight agricultural production, especially grain, in the Soviet Union until its collapse in 1991). In Ukraine, for example, party-planned genocide in the early 1930s led to the death of about 6 million people in the Holodomor, with an additional 4 million to 5 million dying of disease and hypothermia and in insurrections that were put down by the Red Army and the NKVD. This same sort of ruthlessness would, in due course, be associated with the SD and the *Einsatzgruppen* and would be inflicted on Ukraine, Belorussia, and Russia. The genocide in Ukraine and the wider effects of collectivization not only reduced the working population—those with the skill and knowledge to grow food—but also led to the mass slaughter of livestock by peasants as a desperate protest. The obvious result here was that general agricultural production fell below what the fertile regions were capable of achieving. Even without taking into account the effects of forced collectivization, the authors of Document 126-EC pointed out: "It can be assumed that the recent harvests, despite the expansion of land under cultivation, are not greater than the period before World War I."[85] It followed that the quality of nutrition in the Soviet Union had not improved since 1909–1913 and, if anything, had deteriorated. The authors also observed that Russian surpluses in grain were determined not by a bigger harvest but by the level of domestic consumption. Thus, a reduction of about "30 kg per head of the population (220 kg instead 250 kg) and a reduction of horse fodder by 25 percent will produce an export surplus which almost reaches peacetime levels."[86] This policy of reducing consumption among the civilian population was "the key element on which our measures and agricultural policy is to be based."[87]

German policy in this area was facilitated by the fact that in the Russian landmass, the surplus regions in the south and southeast were separated from the beneficiary-recipient regions in the forest zones of the north. As a result, any incipient black-market transfer of food could easily be interdicted by the occupation forces—something that was much harder to achieve in Poland, France, and Belgium. The authors of Document 126-EC are clear about the policy to be pursued: "The sealing off of the Black Earth region must under all circumstances make, more or less, large surpluses available to us in these regions. *The consequence of this policy is that the entire forest zone, including the essential industrial centers of Moscow and Petersburg, will not be supplied.*"[88] In other words, these northern regions would starve. The southern regions were also well placed to transport surpluses by virtue of their access to the Black Sea and the Volga, and such considerations may have influenced Hitler's final deliberations for *Fall Blau* (Case Blue).

The need to separate the surplus zone from the beneficiary-recipient zone led to the adoption of four policies. First, the industrial regions of the north, Moscow, Petersburg, and Siberia would be abandoned, saving 5 million to 10 million tonnes in agricultural products. Second, an exception to this policy would be the oil-producing region of Transcaucasia, which also produced wool, manganese, copper, silk, and tea; it would continue to be supplied, not merely because of these valuable resources but also "for special political and agricultural reasons."[89] These political reasons were not specified, but this area comprised the Muslim republics that were hostile to the Soviet Union, so it is likely the Germans hoped to exploit this discontent to serve their own military aims. Third, there would be no other exceptions to this policy. Fourth, the sole industries maintained would be those in the Donetsk region.

The authors of this policy—which, they stressed, had approval from "the highest offices"—envisaged a number of consequences. In the forest zone, which would no longer receive surpluses, agricultural behavior would revert to that which had characterized the period of World War I and wartime communism. Production for the market would cease, dairy production would collapse, and subsistence agriculture would become the norm. Document 126-EC refers to this process as *Naturalisierung*. Apart from securing enough food to supply German troops stationed in the region, the Germans had no interest in it. The authors of Document 126-EC spell out what these policies will mean:

> The population here will use their land according to the old ways in order to secure their food. Any expectation that there will be any surpluses in grain and so on is pointless. Only after many years could these extensive areas be intensively cultivated so that real surpluses could be gained. The population of these regions, in particular the population of the cities, will encounter the greatest hunger. The situation will arise in which the population will have to be directed to the spaces of Siberia. Since any form of rail transport is out of the question, this problem will become exceptionally difficult.[90]

The other German fear was that once surpluses of food were no longer delivered to these areas, the peasants would have no choice but to start slaughtering livestock in order to survive. Therefore, the German planners proposed to move quickly and seize all livestock before the local inhabitants grasped the full significance of the termination of food deliveries. As the planners noted, this meant that the meat derived from the slaughtered animals had to be conserved as soon as possible by canning. Thus, all reserves of tin in Russia must be seized.

Variations of these policies would be applied to the Baltic states and Belorussia. The Baltic states would be treated in the same way as the new districts (*Gaue*) in the east, whereas Belorussia's primary value to Germany was its timber. In addition, there were plans to secure the entire Soviet fishing fleet for German purposes.

The German planners also identified a problem that had confronted the Communist Party as it planned forced collectivization: because the surplus zones would deliver their produce only in return for consumer goods produced largely in the forest zone, it was imperative that all available consumer goods be transferred to Germany, thus giving it a monopoly in the exchange of agricultural goods from the south. This policy aim was no different from that adopted in both tsarist and Soviet Russia. The peasant was forced to pay high prices for consumer goods, as well as taxes, to raise the delivery of grain surpluses. To ensure the long-term future of Germany, it was desirable that the consumer goods industries in the forest zone cease to function, so that the German monopoly in the production of consumer goods could be used in the same way.

In one of the most important passages in Document 126-EC, the planners drew together the various implications of their policies:

> From all this it follows that the German administration in this territory [the forest zone] may well endeavor to mitigate the consequences of the starvation that will undoubtedly occur and to accelerate the reversion process to subsistence agriculture. One can endeavor to cultivate these areas more intensively in the sense of an expansion of the land given over to potato production and to cultivate other fruits which are important for consumption giving higher yields. Starvation cannot be averted in this manner. Many tens of millions of people in this area will become superfluous and will die or will have to emigrate to Siberia. *Attempts to save the population there from starvation by bringing in surpluses from the Black Earth zone can only be carried out at the cost of supplying Europe. Such measures undermine Germany's resilience in the war and undermine Germany's and Europe's ability to withstand the blockade. There must be absolute clarity in this matter.*[91]

As far as the planners were concerned, such measures were justified by the assertion that, regardless of its political structure, Russia had always been an enemy of Europe. Any form of market economy or rationing for this area was explicitly ruled out from the outset.

The German planners' food-seizure policies leading to mass starvation may not have been based exclusively on NS racial ideology. They may well have been inspired, in part, by the food-requisitioning policies (*prodrazverstka*) adopted by the Soviet regime during the civil war—seizures that led to a disastrous famine in 1921–1922. The Communist Party later used mass starvation to target Ukraine in the 1930s. Thus, reasoned the Germans, if the Communist Party could cause millions of Soviet citizens to starve to death, why should an invader be obliged to feed populations in the occupied territories? Similar reasoning may have played a role in the callous treatment of Soviet prisoners of war.

To maximize the prodigious fertility of the Black Earth zone, German officials—*Landwirtschaftsführer*—would be appointed and instructed to familiarize themselves with local conditions as soon as possible. Speed was essential, since the stated intention was to ensure that German armies in the east would be self-sufficient with regard to food in the third year of the war (1942). Some two-thirds of all food required by the Wehrmacht was expected to come from the eastern territories. Total requirements were estimated at 1 million tonnes of grain, 1.2 million to 1.5 million tonnes of oats, 450,000 tonnes of meat, and 100,000 tonnes of fat, as well as hay, straw, fruits, vegetables, fish, sugar, cereals, and pulses.[92] The eventual aim was to eliminate Germany's dependence on foodstuffs from overseas. In the long term, with guaranteed food security, Germany would be in a position to challenge the United States.

Attachments to the German-Soviet trade agreement concluded in January 1941 provide some idea of the agricultural goods and raw materials the German occupation regime hoped to derive from the Soviet Union. Total deliveries of agricultural goods to be shipped to Germany amounted to 2.5 million tonnes and included 1.1 million tonnes of wheat, 200,000 tonnes of rye, 900,000 tonnes of barley and maize, 200,000 tonnes of oats, and 100,000 tonnes of leguminous products. Other foodstuffs included 100,000 tonnes of pork. The Soviet side also agreed to provide 10 million tonnes of timber.[93] Planned deliveries of industrial raw materials included 85,000 tonnes of shale oil and 982,000 tonnes of refined oil products. Other deliveries involved large and valuable amounts of iridium (48 kilograms) and platinum (2,192 kilograms).[94] Iridium is a highly heat- and corrosion-resistant metal that combines with platinum to form alloys that have weapons applications. Platinum functions as a major catalyst in a number of industrial processes, such as hydrogenation, that were essential to Germany's war economy. Platinum is derived largely as a by-product of nickel mining, which explains the Germans' determination not to succumb to Soviet pressure to relinquish any interest in the Finnish nickel mines in Petsamo. Iridium and platinum were also crucial for the emerging jet engine and rocket technologies being developed in the late 1930s.

To secure agricultural production and win the so-called *Erzeugungsschlacht* (production battle), the German planners insisted on retaining the agricultural system and infrastructure established by the Soviet Communist Party—the *kolkhoz* and the *sovkhoz*. Thus, the planners argued, there could be no question of reprivatizing the land. Nor would any land seizures by the peasants, such as occurred in 1917–1918, be tolerated. German reasoning was perfectly sound.[95] First, the bulk of the equipment needed to farm the land, along with the seeds and stock, was concentrated on the collective farms. Second, reprivatization would result in a massive increase in small farms and plots, making the task of the German farm overseers impossible and leading to a reduction in the amount of agricultural produce secured by the German occupation administration. The planners were well aware of the Soviet peasantry's loathing of the collective farm system, as well as the widespread expectation that, with the arrival of the German army, the collective farms would be abolished. The planners, however, were quite clear about what needed to be done: *"Any attempt to dissolve the large-scale concerns must therefore be combated with the harshest measures."*[96] There was a third reason (not highlighted in Document 126-EC) why it made good sense for the Germans to retain the concentrated form of Soviet food production. Given that German planners anticipated armed resistance to German rule and the onset of partisan warfare, tightly controlled food production and distribution would limit the amount of foodstuffs available to the partisans. In contrast, abolition of the collective farms, resulting in the creation of hundreds of thousands of small farms, would work to the partisans' advantage.[97]

Two conflicting elements were at work in the Germans' intention to retain the collective farm infrastructure to serve German ends. German food requirements clearly took priority over propaganda appeals based on the abolition of collective farms. On the one hand, if the war in the east could be brought to a swift conclusion (and Document 126-EC does envisage a scaling down of German troops in the third year of the war), the Germans could ignore the wishes of the Soviet peasants who had been dispossessed by the Soviet state and, not surprisingly, were eager to recover stolen assets. On the other hand, if the Soviet system did not collapse in 1942, the bitterness and resentment engendered by the Germans' exploitation of the collective farms would work against the occupation regime. Russians, Belorussians, and Ukrainians dispossessed in the 1930s would see no difference between Hitler and Stalin. Any belated concessions by the German occupation regime, such as occurred after the fall of Stalingrad, would look like a sign of weakness and work to the advantage of the Soviet side.

These German planning stipulations regarding the retention of the Soviet system of collectivized agriculture explain why the Germans did not dissolve the collective farms. In terms of propaganda, doing so would have been enormously popular and deeply damaging to the Soviet state. It also would have put Britain in a difficult position, since, by virtue of its alliance with the Soviet Union, Britain would be seen as supporting the detested agricultural system. The Germans undoubtedly hinted that the collective farms would be abolished, but these vague promises were never intended to be honored.

A letter sent by Professor Dr. Wolodymyr Kubijowytsch, leader of the Ukrainian Central Committee, to Hans Frank, governor of the General-gouvernement, dated 25 February 1943, exposes the double game being played by the Germans.[98] The provisions of Document 126-EC could not be clearer: the German occupation regime encouraged the belief that the collective farm system established by the Soviet Communist Party would be abolished while doing everything possible to strengthen its grip. It is quite clear from this letter that the reprivatization of farmland matters a great deal to the Ukrainian population. To quote Kubijowytsch: "The problem of reprivatization is of fundamental significance for the further shaping of German-Ukrainian relationships. On the German victory in the east the entire Ukrainian people have pinned the hope that at this juncture the entire remnants of the Bolshevik regime would finally be removed."[99] Kubijowytsch's reasons for pressing Frank on the abolition of the collective farms are based on the understanding that nationalization renders the farmworkers little more than slaves with no long-term interest in the productivity of the land. Why should they toil when the fruits of their labors are taken from them and they enjoy no secure tenure in landownership? This is the fundamental problem undermining state ownership of the means of production, and it is one the Soviet state tried to resolve by coercion and violence. The German occupiers were no different.

In his letter, Kubijowytsch politely but firmly points to an inconsistency in the German position:

> The Ukrainian population received with complete gratitude Your Excellency's proclamation of 1 August 1941 in which you, Herr Generalgouvernor, in principle resolved this question, establishing reprivatization as a guideline for the state's agricultural policy. Now, however, the attitude of many officials is as if the matter of reprivatization is once more being called into question and is as if there would be no place for private property in the new social order. This state of affairs is being very skillfully exploited by enemy rumor-propaganda. The rumor, being very actively spread, that the reason private property has so far not been reintroduced is that a large resettling of Ukrainians from Galicia to the east can be expected.[100]

Adding weight to these rumors was the fact that properties were being standardized in terms of size, farms were being surveyed, and what were, in effect, taxes were being levied. These measures were fully consistent with the provisions of Document 126-EC.

Kubijowytsch also complained about the brutality and violence being directed against Ukrainians by the German occupation forces. That behavior may well have been the inevitable manifestation of the violence that informed all German occupation policies, but in late February 1943, it also may have been prompted by an unease among senior Nazi officials in the occupied territories. Their new empire in the East was under threat—Stalingrad had just fallen—and they believed that any manifestations of opposition to German rule—real, potential, or imagined—had to be resolved by terror and violence, not by concessions. The master does not make concessions because he enjoys the privileges and prerogatives of the *Herrenvolk* (on this point, the authors of Document 126-EC are emphatic). If there was a perception that the empire was in jeopardy, the issue of food security would become even more urgent, and the imposition of coercive measures on the occupied peoples would be essential to maintain order. There could be no consideration of reprivatization.

However, the NS regime was not insensible of the need to maintain the fiction that the Germans were liberators from Bolshevism. A key problem here, and one identified by Alfred Rosenberg (who exerted considerable influence on the planning for Barbarossa, especially as it affected German policies toward nationality groups), was establishing priorities for the occupation regime. Once the military subjection of the Soviet Union had been achieved, emphasis would shift to the inevitable administrative and agricultural difficulties that would arise. Rosenberg believed that military subjection would happen quickly; like his master, he took the view that the multiethnicity of the Soviet state would render it vulnerable in the event of war and accelerate its collapse. Thus, Rosenberg asks what he considers a serious question: "Should the nature of the occupation be determined by purely military or economic requirements or are, for the expansion of the occupation, political considerations to play a part in the future shaping of the territories from the start?"[101]

If the Soviet state succumbed quickly to the German invaders, a rapid transition to a purely administrative regime concentrating on the primary tasks of economic and agricultural exploitation would at least be feasible. But Rosenberg saw potential problems arising from the abolition of private property by the Soviet state: "It is also not improbable that this question [private property] could have practical consequences immediately after the occupation of the territory. A spontaneous move on the part of the totally uneducated rural population with a possible unauthorized dissolution of the collective farm economy could lead to unforeseen material damage."[102] In other words, efficient exploitation of the region's agricultural resources meant there could be no unplanned, anarchic destruction of the collective farms. Politically and ideologically, it made good sense to declare that the collective farm system would be abolished under German occupation. However, from the point of view of ensuring maximum exploitation of the region's agricultural resources, the immediate abolition of the collective farms and the ensuing chaos would be disastrous, as it would unleash a destructive peasant rebellion, a *bunt*, or an anarchic free-for-all. The obvious solution was to give tacit, vague assurances that at some stage the collective farms would be abolished. This is the policy that was eventually adopted.

German agricultural policies for the occupied territories were later set out in *Erlaß des Reichsministers für die besetzten Gebiete* (Decree of the Reichsminister for the Occupied Territories), dated 16 February 1942. This decree, which was clearly intended to allay any fears about German motives, was published in *Das Recht der besetzten Gebiete* (The Law of the Occupied Territories [1943]), a collection of orders, decrees, and rules pertaining to the administration of agriculture. The authors provide assurances that the Bolshevist system of agriculture will gradually be abolished to allow an orderly transition to a system based on a "cooperative" or "independent" farming model. The authors state: "First of all the constitution of the *kolkhoz* is to be rescinded and the collective farms, with immediate effect, are to be transformed into cooperative farms."[103] In fact, the changes being proposed by the German occupation regime were little more than window dressing. These farms would no longer be referred to as collective farms, but the basic principles of operation would remain the same: "The cooperative farms shall function according to the guidelines of the German administration."[104] Fully consistent with the German determination to control all agricultural production, the network of *sovkhozy* and machine tractor stations would be taken over and run by the German administration. Even when promises were made that certain levels of individual ownership would be permitted, all such proposals would be subject to German approval.

Despite what appear to be various belated concessions to individual farming and abolition of the Soviet agricultural system, the policies in *Das Recht der besetzten Gebiete* were an attempt to deceive the farmers in the occupied territories. The policies were fully consistent with those contained in Document 126-EC, though without the indifference to the possible loss of tens of millions of lives. Any promises of change were intended primarily to bring stability to the agricultural sector so that German war needs could be met with a minimum of unrest. The brutal truth—which would have been apparent to the more astute farmers and certainly to Professor Kubi-jowytsch—was that the peasants were now being controlled and exploited by masters who were every bit as rapacious as their Soviet overseers.

Clearly, the German occupation regime intended to maximize the agricultural exploitation of the Soviet Union based on a model of genocide established by the Communist Party. This is one example of the many parallels between NS Germany and the Soviet Union, and it underlines the dreadful fate that befell Ukrainians, Belorussians, and Russians, who were caught between the two totalitarian states. The worst fate was reserved for the Russians (Großrussentum), who would be driven into the forest zone and the collective farms occupied by Kleinrussen.

The general principles to be adopted in all dealings with Russians—a version of modern slavery—were made explicit:

> The men [Landwirtschaftsführer] must always be clear about the fact that they will only ever be able to assert themselves against the population when they act firmly, to the point and pitilessly. Russians invariably want leadership. Orders and instructions must be sufficiently short, concise, clear and precise so that they do not give rise to any discussions among the Russians: these must be nipped in the bud. Only in this way can Russians be successfully led.[105]

Further details of the leadership qualities demanded of the Landwirtschafts-führer are the subject of a lengthy exposition in Document 089-USSR, dated 1 June 1941. This document was drawn up in the same office—and, it can be assumed, by the same German official, Staatssekretär Herbert Backe—responsible for Document 126-EC. According to the contents list, Document 089-USSR is divided into part A, which is devoted to general policy, and part B, which is devoted to special concerns. In addition to Backe's twelve principles pertaining to the Landwirtschaftsführer assigned to the eastern territories, part A contains sections on taking over and running the kolkhoz, sovkhoz, and machine tractor stations, as well as general guidelines for the acquisition of agricultural products and delivery deadlines.

Significantly, these twelve principles were the only part of the larger document that the Soviet side later submitted as a prosecution exhibit to the International Military Tribunal. Of course, it is possible that the twelve principles were the sole surviving part of the document and that the remaining sections were lost or destroyed. However, one must consider the possibility that the Soviet side withheld the rest of the document because an open discussion of its contents in the courtroom would have revealed too much about the generally appalling state of Soviet agriculture and the genocidal methods used by the Communist Party to impose collectivization in the early 1930s. For example, three sections of part A dealt with the collective farm system. If the content of these omitted sections of Document 089-USSR were comparable in analytical depth and breadth to that of Document 126-EC, the Soviet side would have good reason to want to suppress Backe's assessment of the Soviet collective farm system.

Backe's twelve principles, especially as they concern leadership, develop some of the conclusions first set out in Document 126-EC and constitute something of a leadership manual. Thus, Backe instructs the appointees: "At this juncture you are all being given a unique opportunity to get stuck in, to put your ability, your know-how and operational ability to the test. For centuries England employed young men in responsible posts in its empire giving them the chance to develop their leadership qualities."[106] Not for the first time, German policy in the east drew on the British Empire for inspiration. From the Soviet perspective, the fact that Nazi policies in the occupied territories were at least partly inspired by British imperialism would be a highly convenient bit of propaganda in the emerging Cold War (by 1946, the alliance with the Anglo-Americans engendered by fighting a common foe was falling apart).

There are indications that other prosecutors—Anglo-American, French, or Soviet—may have excised material prejudicial to the Soviet Union. For instance, the Decree of the Reichsminister for the Occupied Territories was submitted as a prosecution exhibit during the Nürnberg trials of the major war criminals, but a comparison of the full text published in *Das Recht der besetzten Gebiete* and that submitted at Nürnberg (which purports to be taken in full from the same German publication) shows that substantial parts were missing.[107] To begin with, approximately 50 percent of the introduction was absent. In the original, the authors, Dr. Schiller and Dr. Szogs, provide a damning and accurate assessment of the manner in which Soviet collectivization was carried out. They note: "By means of compulsion and terror the Bolsheviks coerced the peasants into the collective farm system and were only able to maintain it by force."[108] They also state, quite correctly, that the Soviet collective farm system was incompetently managed and organized, largely because it was run by unqualified, party-appointed outsiders; in addition, the peasants were reduced to penury. Schiller and Szogs also refer to the genocide in the 1930s: "There were years in which the peasants went hungry or even, as in 1933, perished in their millions from starvation."[109] They point out, again quite correctly, that "the able peasants were exterminated by the Bolsheviks as 'kulaks' or exiled."[110] That the German occupation regime's overriding concern was to avoid a collapse of the Soviet agricultural system in order to maximize agricultural production for the benefit of Germany was clear enough; also obvious was its indifference to the mass death from starvation caused by its policies of agricultural exploitation. However, that does not detract from the fact that the German planners presented an accurate statement of what happened to peasants in the 1930s and that those parts of the German occupation decree were cut from the prosecution evidence submitted at Nürnberg. These cuts—and others—are significant because they raise questions about whether Soviet prosecutors should have taken part in deliberations concerning German mass murder and genocide, especially in view of what happened in Soviet-controlled Ukraine.[111]

The cool, merciless appraisal of German aims and ambitions set out in Documents 126-EC and 089-USSR reveals that the men chosen to administer these policies were far removed from the unimaginative party apparatchiks who simply followed orders. As the German planners recognized, the task facing the *Landwirtschaftsführer* was enormous. They would have to operate over vast areas with generally poor communications, and they could expect little in the way of orders from superiors on how to proceed; they would have to create their own administrative structure from nothing. The planners stressed that the men chosen for these posts must be capable of working alone and making decisions without seeking authority from remote headquarters in the rear areas. Those who lacked the necessary initiative and enthusiasm were unsuitable. In effect, these men had to combine the functions of colonial administrator, imperial policeman, soldier, agriculturalist, and supreme ruler and, when necessary, be willing to exercise powers of life and death over their empires.

Security and Punitive Measures

Of all the orders and decrees emanating from Hitler's headquarters, and certainly among those that pertain to the planning for Barbarossa and that survived the end of the Third Reich, very few have been subjected to such detailed scrutiny as the *Erlaß über die Ausübung der Kriegsgerichtsbarkeit im Gebiet Barbarossa und über besondere Maßnahmen der Truppe* (Barbarossa Jurisdiction Decree) of 13 May 1941 and the *Richtlinien für die Behandlung politischer Kommissare* (Commissar Order) of 6 June 1941.[112] During the Nürnberg trials, the prosecution relied heavily on these two documents to argue the essential and even unique criminality of the NS regime, a position that has been reiterated ever since.

The controversy surrounding the Commissar Order shows no signs of abating. One of the main shortcomings in discussions of the planning and implementation of the Commissar Order is the failure explicitly to acknowledge the nature of the Soviet regime that created the institution of commissars and how these functionaries conducted themselves. It is too often forgotten or ignored that the military commissars constituted one of the main terror strata of the Soviet state and operated in accordance with the Soviet ideological worldview. The failure to acknowledge openly the nature of the Soviet regime means that the military commissars have acquired a victim status that is not entirely merited. A legal-historical analysis of the NS regime's treatment of this ideological stratum based solely on Western legal norms and customs ignores the ideological nature of the Soviet regime and its behavior and results, first, in a thoroughly distorted picture of the Soviet state. Second, it avoids the question of how to deal with members of an ideological caste who were known *not* to be bound by the very customs and rules of war established by international law—customs and rules that were nevertheless applied to judge Germany's prosecution of the war. The Commissar Order is the subject of a longer and more detailed examination in chapter 2, while the main focus in this section is the Barbarossa Jurisdiction Decree.

The Barbarossa Jurisdiction Decree arose from what the planners, chief among them Hitler, argued would be the special features of the war on the Eastern Front.[113] In the preamble they cite the vast operational area and the nature of the enemy, which means that the troops must assume some measure of direct and immediate responsibility for dealing with threats from the civilian population, matters that would normally be the preserve of the military courts and their staff. The decree's guidelines are universal in scope: they apply not only to the front but also to the army's rear areas and to those areas under German occupation and administration. In detail, the Barbarossa Jurisdiction Decree attends to three specific concerns: offenses committed by enemy civilians, offenses committed by members of the Wehrmacht and other formations against the indigenous population, and the responsibilities of troop commanders.

By far, the most far-reaching provision for the prosecution of the war on the Eastern Front was this stipulation: "Responsibility for handling offenses committed by enemy civilians on the part of military courts and courts-martial is removed until further notice."[114] This allowed soldiers at the front to dispense summary justice and gave a free hand to the *Einsatzgruppen* operating in the rear. Although the *Einsatzgruppen* were not directly referred to in the Barbarossa Jurisdiction Decree, these units were covered by use of the word *Gefolge* (entourage or accompanying units). The provision for the reestablishment of normal military jurisdiction in pacified areas was meaningless, since it would not (could not) occur until after the *Einsatzgruppen* had carried out their planned mass murder and would have impeded the rough and summary punishment of partisans and *Freischärler* (guerrillas or irregulars). The inclusion of this particular clause, I suggest, was intended to deceive senior officers who were alarmed by the implications of the Barbarossa Jurisdiction Decree and to encourage them to believe that suspension of the normal functioning of courts-martial was a temporary measure when, in fact, it was the standard policy of the occupation regime throughout the Eastern Front.

The central theme in responding to acts of violence directed against the Wehrmacht and other formations by enemy civilians was swift retribution. The *Freischärler* were to be eliminated on the spot or in flight, and army officers could decide whether suspicious persons should be shot. Collective punishment (*kollektive Gewaltmaßnahmen*) could also be inflicted on entire villages from which German forces were attacked when it was not possible to identify the individuals responsible.

The ideological basis for the severity of the Barbarossa Jurisdiction Decree is clearly revealed in the following statement: "When making a judgment of such deeds any procedural measures are to take into account that the collapse in 1918 and the later time of suffering of the German people and the struggle against National Socialism with its countless sacrifices made in blood could be decisively traced back to Bolshevik influence and that no German has forgotten this."[115] Thus, apart from anything else, the war in the east was a war of revenge.

Section III of the Barbarossa Jurisdiction Decree imposes clear obligations on troop commanders to ensure that all subordinate units are indoctrinated into the provisions of section I (swift and ruthless measures), that all legal advisers are fully informed, and that "only such verdicts that are consistent with the political views of the leadership are to be upheld."[116] There is, in other words, a presumption that members of the Wehrmacht and others who perform acts that would normally merit military-legal sanctions should not be considered guilty of any wrongdoing.

That Generalfeldmarschall Wilhelm Keitel and his master were well aware of the criminal provisions of the Barbarossa Jurisdiction Decree is evident from Keitel's order dated 27 July 1941—the invasion was now well under way—that all copies of the original May order, as well as the later order, be destroyed. However, this bonfire of documents had no effect on the Barbarossa Jurisdiction Decree itself, as Keitel made clear: "The force and validity of the decree shall not be affected by the destruction of the copies. Troop commanders remain personally responsible, in accordance with the requirements of section III, for the fact that officers and legal advisers are informed in good time and that only such verdicts that are consistent with the political views of the leadership are to be upheld."[117] This left no room for German commanders in the field to evade their duties as prescribed.

Another important document with implications for both German security and agricultural policies in the east is the record of a meeting attended by Hitler, Rosenberg, Lammers, Göring, and Keitel on 16 July 1941.[118] The value of Document 221-L, which was probably compiled by Martin Bormann, lies in the brutal clarity with which Hitler states the policies to be adopted in the occupied territories in the east. The primary aim of these policies was the full Germanization of large swathes of territory and the complete removal of any military threat to German power as far east as the Urals. Since these policies were based on the Hitler triad of domination, administration, and exploitation, they had to remain hidden until it was too late for them to be opposed successfully. In propaganda terms, this meant that Germany's actions had to be presented as necessary to occupy, to bring order to, and to secure the territories. In other words, Germany should be presented to the world as a liberator and a defender of civilization, not as a conqueror and exploiter. Hitler states: "It should therefore not be recognizable that all these measures are the start of moves towards a final resolution. Nevertheless we shall carry out all the necessary measures—shootings and resettlements—and so on and will be able to do them regardless."[119] This duplicitous policy also clarifies the German attitude toward collective farms in the occupied territories: encourage the belief that reprivatization will occur, but take all the necessary steps to consolidate the German stranglehold over agricultural production. Hitler also confirms that Galicia is to be Germanized, indicating that the rumors noted by Kubijowytsch in his letter were not unfounded.

In Document 221-L Hitler asserts that the sole bearer of arms in the occupied territories is to be the German soldier, even if arming some of the conquered peoples appears to be expedient: "Only the German soldier may be permitted to bear arms: not the Slav, not the Czech, not the Cossack or the Ukrainian!"[120] Clearly, this policy position could be asserted only after the Soviet Union had been destroyed, but as the Blitzkrieg gave way to a war of attrition, manpower became critical, and Hitler's rulings that indigenous peoples were not to be trained and armed were abandoned. A year later, during the Stalingrad battle, *Hilfswillige* were attached to German divisions, and plans to arm Cossacks and Tartars and to raise Turkic battalions were well advanced.

A variation on the use of peoples in the occupied areas was advocated by Keitel, who not unreasonably pointed out that there was insufficient German manpower to guard every dwelling and station and that local people had to be conscripted to carry out such tasks. However, the terms of employment proposed by Keitel were unlikely to lead to a flood of volunteers: "The inhabitants must know that any person who fails to discharge his task will be shot and that they shall be liable to arrest for any misconduct."[121]

Document 221-L was cited during the Nürnberg trials. The prosecutor, noting the Germanization policy, stated: "It [Document 221-L] is important also for its disclosure of the utterly fraudulent character of the whole Nazi propaganda program. It shows how the conspirators sought to deceive the entire world; how they pretended to pursue one course of action when their aims and purposes were to follow precisely the opposite course."[122] The literal meaning of *propaganda* is not lies and distortion; the modern view is that propaganda is a combination of lies, half-truths, distortions, plausible lies, and omissions designed to support certain policy goals. Joseph Goebbels was one of its master practitioners, and the NS regime certainly pursued a duplicitous policy, as the prosecutor claims. However, Hitler and his plotters were not guilty of behaving any differently from other leaders of government, whatever their ideological and political leanings. Moreover, at the time these trials were taking place (1946–1947), Soviet propaganda in the territories, now occupied by the Red Army, was clearly intended to deceive the entire world. Behind a façade of democracy and sham elections, dissent and civil society were being crushed, church leaders were being persecuted, and the primacy of communist parties was being asserted by violence and terror—the process of sovietization.

Document 221-L was also potentially embarrassing to the British, since Hitler argues that Germany must learn from British policies in India and apply them to the administration of the German empire in the east. Moreover, he proposes that after Göring has relocated all his training bases to the east, even the Ju-52 transport aircraft can be used to bomb insurgents—once again adopting methods used by the British to police their empire. The British had no qualms about bombing recalcitrant tribes in Iraq and on the northwest frontier, which may have given Hitler ideas about how he should treat his new subjects.

Decrees demanding violence continued to be issued after the invasion began. One month after the start of Barbarossa, Hitler strengthened the punitive regime against resistance to German occupation forces on the Eastern Front. Quite apart from Hitler's unshakable belief that extreme repression was the only way to maintain order, the sheer size of the operational area demanded such measures. As Hitler argued: "The relevant army commanders are to be made responsible for the peace in their areas with the troops at their disposal. The army commanders are to find the means in order to maintain order in their security zones not by submitting requests for additional security forces but in the application of suitably draconian measures."[123]

Some three months later, in a decree issued on 16 September 1941, Keitel noted that since the start of the German invasion, all kinds of communist resistance movements, encouraged by Moscow, had emerged in the German-occupied territories. The Keitel decree also confirmed that although the Germans were publicly willing to encourage various nationalist groups, they were aware that opposition to the Soviet state did not automatically translate into support for the German occupation forces and that nationalist groups also constituted a threat to German rule. The response to the emergence of these communist and nationalist bands was—no surprise here—even more violence and brutality. Keitel proposed five specific guidelines: (1) All manifestations of rebellion against German rule must be attributed to communist incitement. (2) To crush any incipient rebellion, it is insufficient to kill just one person. In those cases in which a German soldier dies, the killing of some fifty to a hundred communists must be considered a measured response. In this regard, Keitel recommended that "the method in which these sentences are carried out must increase the deterrent effect."[124] Keitel expressly proscribed the use of milder sentences initially; extreme ruthlessness was to be the fundamental principle from the outset. (3) "Political relations between Germany and the relevant country are not decisive for the behavior of the military occupation authorities."[125] This provided further evidence that anticommunist nationalist groups would not enjoy any special favors. (4) The use of any indigenous forces in the application of repressive measures is forbidden, since this would pose a threat to German troops. (5) The death penalty alone can maintain peace and security.

Hitler's and Keitel's demands that field commanders take ruthless measures against any and all resistance undoubtedly played a part in the orders issued by Generalfeldmarschall von Reichenau, commander of the 6th Army, and General von Manstein, commander of the 11th Army, on 10 October and 20 November 1941, respectively. Von Reichenau's order, which was presented as a US exhibit during the Nürnberg trials, was an attachment to an order issued by the 12th Infantry Division on 17 November 1941. The 12th Infantry's original order stipulated various measures to be taken to protect the troops against partisans and sabotage. Von Reichenau's earlier order stressed the urgency of such measures.

The 12th Infantry Division document is important because it highlights one of the fundamental policies adopted by the German occupation forces and one that alarmed the NKVD: the appointment of a *starosta*, or village elder, which was broadly analogous to the principle of appointing a *Judenrat*, or Jewish council. The *starosta* was ordered to draw up a list of villagers and to notify the German occupation forces of the presence of any strangers or visitors. The aim was to use local people to police their neighbors and to hold them responsible for security lapses and acts of sabotage. There was also a provision for collective punishments. The policy was one of divide and rule. *Starostas* were targeted by the partisans because they were assumed to be actively collaborating with the Germans. The implication of this policy was that, despite German successes, groups of Red Army stragglers (some of which were very large) were cause for concern in the German rear areas. Thus, the 12th Infantry Division order stipulated that all Russian soldiers in uniform or in civilian clothes who had not reported to the German authorities by 20 November 1941 would be shot as partisans. In addition, it required that the shooting or hanging of any partisans, those who helped them, and those found to be in possession of weapons would take place wherever they were caught—the objective being, one assumes, to maximize the deterrent effect.

Considered by Hitler to be a model for how to proceed on the Eastern Front, von Reichenau's order was copied and widely circulated. In the introduction he states: "The most fundamental aim of the campaign against the Jewish-Bolshevist system is the complete smashing of the means of power and the eradication of the Asiatic influence within the circle of European culture."[126] In this war, according to von Reichenau, the German soldier was the "bearer of a merciless national idea and an avenger of all the bestialities that have been inflicted on Germany and related peoples."[127] Von Reichenau was prompted to formulate this order by what he considered the outrageous resistance on the part of Russians and others to the idea that the inhabitants of the occupied areas must unconditionally submit to German authority. Any kind of resistance not only was futile but also merited savage retribution. In von Reichenau's view, the war involved the total physical destruction of the Soviet state as well as its symbols and cultural influences. Thus, he asserts, "Neither historical nor cultural considerations play any role herewith."[128] Given this crusade advocated by von Reichenau and others, the German troops were encouraged to destroy churches and other artistic artifacts, to plunder, and to behave, in other words, like the Communist Party did in its campaigns against the Russian Orthodox Church and its wars against the national culture of Ukraine.

Very little separates von Reichenau's order from that issued by the 11th Army's commander. In fact, much of von Manstein's order appears to be a direct borrowing from von Reichenau: the Jewish-Bolshevist system must be eradicated once and for all; the German soldier in the east is the bearer of a national idea and the avenger of the cruelties (unspecified) inflicted on the German people. Von Manstein also recites the by now familiar litany of grievances: resistance to the German invasion has not been crushed, sporadic attacks on German soldiers are increasing, and these attacks are starting to show signs of a directing hand.

Von Manstein shows himself to be breathtakingly cynical. Bolshevik attacks in the rear area are, he says, destroying the harvest and factories, leading the urban population to starvation. Any concerns about the urban population are then completely undermined when von Manstein stresses that because of the dire situation with regard to rations and foodstuffs, German troops must be sustained by whatever they can secure from the east, and any surpluses must be placed at the disposal of the homeland—Germany. Regardless of whether he is familiar with the detailed plans drawn up by Göring's ministry for the agricultural exploitation of the occupied territories, it is reasonable to assume that von Manstein has been indoctrinated and that he is aware of the consequences of the actions he is advocating: "Particularly in the enemy cities a large part of the civilian population will have to starve."[129] The same inconsistency is revealed when von Manstein insists that various soldierly virtues must be upheld and that a certain correct attitude must be adopted toward civilians and prisoners of war, even while the official German policy is to maximize agricultural exploitation and abandon Soviet prisoners to starvation.

Von Manstein fully grasps the Leninist idea that those who are not with us are against us. Thus, Russians, Ukrainians, and Tartars who refused to acknowledge the new order must, if necessary, be compelled to accept it. Overall, the policies advocated by von Manstein for the occupied territories showed no understanding of human nature; they failed to acknowledge that people who have been terrorized into submission by violence and by public hangings and shootings, who have had their animals and seed stolen by hungry soldiers or by the more organized methods of plunder being pioneered by Göring's *Landwirtschaftsführer*, are unlikely to exhibit personal initiative or to internalize German policies. German planners were well aware that Soviet agricultural policies had been a catastrophe, yet they still seemed to believe, as von Manstein did, that the Germans could pursue the same policies. The default solution to all German problems was violence.

With regard to Jewish populations in the east, violence was not the default solution but the main solution: it was systematic, shrouded in bureaucratese and evasion, planned in detail, pitiless and cruel in execution, and carefully recorded. The process of isolation—the use of ghettos—started soon after the defeat of Poland, a country that had the largest Jewish population in Europe in 1939; of the approximately 3.5 million Polish Jews, about 350,000 lived in Warsaw and 200,000 lived in Lodz.[130] Just over 2 million lived in the zone occupied by Germany, and the rest, along with some refugees, were located in the Soviet occupation zone. In 1939 the Jewish population of the Soviet Union numbered approximately 3 million; this rose to about 5 million after the annexations of Bessarabia and the Baltic states.[131] All these Jews were now in jeopardy from Himmler's death squads.

Before the *Einsatzgruppen* set to work in the Soviet Union, there may have been some room for interpretation when it came to Alfred Rosenberg's words: "For Europe the Jewish question is only finally solved when the last Jew has left the continent of Europe."[132] But soon after 22 June 1941, the significance of these words was clear enough. Some 2,000 to 2,200 Jews were murdered in Belostok on 27 June 1941, a minor massacre compared with what followed in Minsk, Berdichev, and Kiev. One feature of these mass shootings, clearly documented by Vasilii Grossman, was that they gave free rein to sadists and the depraved to torture, mock, rape, plunder, and beat the victims, regardless of sex, age, or infirmity, before ending lives.

Thus, in his documentary essay "Ubiistvo evreev v Berdicheve" (The Murder of the Jews in Berdichev), Grossman records that German troops derived great pleasure from tormenting and killing Jews in cruel and sadistic ways: Jews were taken to the local tannery and forced to jump into large pits full of the acrid by-products of the tanning process. Jewish men were forced to pray and seek forgiveness for sins committed against Germans; then they were locked in the synagogue and burned alive. Jewish women were forced to strip naked and swim back and forth across one of the local rivers until, exhausted and cold, they drowned.[133]

Soon after the arrival of German troops in western parts of the Soviet Union, Jews were isolated from the rest of the population. This measure was largely intended to concentrate Jews so that they were easily accessible to their executioners when the time came to murder them. However, from the German point of view, a not undesirable secondary function of this isolation was that it destroyed any sense of solidarity between Jews and their fellow Soviet citizens, increasing the psychological pressure on an already bewildered Jewish population, creating a sense of helplessness, and convincing them that resistance was futile. Among non-Jews, some of whom associated Jews with the hated Stalinist regime, this isolation encouraged their collaboration with the Germans in the hope of deriving material benefit from the dispossession of Jews. Collaborators in Poland, Belorussia, Ukraine, Estonia, Lithuania, Latvia, and Russia indisputably made significant contributions to the prosecution of the Holocaust.

A report on the postinvasion "cleansing work" (Säuberungsarbeit) of Einsatzgruppe A in Ostland (the new designation for the territory comprising Estonia, Latvia, and Lithuania), probably written in early 1942, provides a detailed account of just one small part of Hitler's grand genocide. In the report it is noted that a total of 229,052 Jews have been executed in Ostland so far. Highlighted here is a curious feature of NS ideology: Jews are regarded as part of the eastern Untermenschentum, yet their success in business and in many other aspects of culture is readily acknowledged. Indeed, the report states that not all Jews are to be killed because they are essential to the local economy. The Einsatzgruppe A report also notes that as of December 1941, approximately 19,000 "partisans and criminals—mainly Jews that is—have been shot."[134] Given the Germans' very loose definitions of partisans and criminals, these killings clearly point to the Wehrmacht's complicity in tasks formally allocated to the Einsatzgruppen. There is no doubt that the Wehrmacht played a major role in killing Jews (though these activities were often camouflaged as antipartisan operations), making the German army complicit in NS crimes. To quote Christian Hartmann: "For including the Wehrmacht in the murder of Jews the partisan war was far more important. By placing the fight against partisans on a par with extermination of Jews military tasks were increasingly blended with the exterminatory strategy of NS racial ideology."[135] This policy is also summed up in the slogan *Wo der Partisan ist, ist der Jude, und wo der Jude ist, ist der Partisan* (where the partisan is, there's the Jew, and where the Jew is, there's the partisan).[136] Such attitudes are also clearly documented by Waitman Wade Beorn, who shows that for some German units, Jew hunts were part of the occupation regime and were justified as antipartisan operations.[137]

Soviet prisoners of war were another group that experienced the full force of the German regime in the east. Denied the legal protections that Anglo-American prisoners took for granted, they perished in large numbers, especially from the start of Barbarossa until the end of the winter of 1941–1942. By the end of World War II, it is estimated that up to 5.75 million Soviet soldiers had been captured by the Wehrmacht and that as many as 2.6 million to 3.3 million of them died in German captivity.[138] After capture, prisoners were forced to undertake long and exhausting marches to the rear areas. Many died from starvation, thirst, arbitrary shootings, disease (dysentery, typhus, tuberculosis), beatings and other forms of random violence, medical neglect, and loss of the will to live; exposed to the full force of the Russian winter, and lacking proper shelter and adequate food and clothing, they died of the cold in large numbers. It should be borne in mind that death by cold does not occur only in the very low temperatures of winter. It can also occur from a combination of the rain and wind of the autumnal *rasputitsa*, even though temperatures are above freezing. Hartmann is quite right to describe the death of so many Soviet prisoners of war in German captivity as "one of the greatest crimes of military history."[139]

The Armenian genocide, the Holodomor (Ukrainians), the *Nanjing datusha* (Great Nanking Massacre in China), the Katyn (Poles), the Holocaust (Jews), the Hongerwinter (Dutch), the killing fields of Cambodia, and China's Great Leap Forward all instantly identify a genocide, mass murder, or horrendous suffering inflicted on a specific group of people. Yet the death of approximately 3 million Red Army soldiers in German captivity remains a crime without a name that provides instant recognition of what has taken place, in the way the genocide of the Jews is immediately recognized by just one word: Holocaust. To identify the truly dreadful fate of Soviet prisoners of war, I suggest the German word Höllenqual (the torments or agony of hell), a word that conveys a sense of the physical and psychological suffering of the Soviet prisoners while en route to and held in the German camps. Important to note is that both German and Soviet officials neglected their duties to these men: the Germans because they subjected so many captured Soviet soldiers to cruel and prolonged suffering and death (especially by hunger), and Soviet officialdom, essentially Stalin, because he slandered his men as cowards and deserters for being captured (Order № 270) and then denied them and their families the support to which they were entitled. Nor did the eventual liberation of the surviving Soviet prisoners of war put an end to their suffering. Suspected of being traitors and deserters merely because they had been captured, they were subjected to prolonged filtration by SMERSH interrogators. Even if they managed to withstand this exhausting filtration process, they were marked men and women for the rest of their lives.

Conclusion

Hitler boasted during a planning meeting on 3 February 1941 that when Barbarossa started, the world would hold its breath and be transfixed: *Wenn Barbarossa steigt, hält die Welt den Atem an und verhält sich still.* This was no idle threat. Everything about Barbarossa was on a grand scale: the size of the armies, the concentration of armored and mechanized forces, the dazzling air strikes, the deception, Hitler's unwavering and relentless ambition, and the four years of violence that ensued. When, across a front stretching from the Arctic Circle to the Black Sea, the three German army groups—North (commanded by Generalfeldmarschall Ritter von Leeb), Center (commanded by Generalfeldmarschall von Bock), and South (commanded by Generalfeldmarschall von Rundstedt)—crossed their start lines after first light on Sunday, 22 June 1941, and invaded the Soviet Union, months of rumors, counterrumors, dissembling, and speculation about German-Soviet relations ended in spectacular fashion. The start of Barbarossa revealed to the world the full dimensions of Germany's indefatigable planning and preparation, redolent of the fictional Martians in *The War of the Worlds* (1898).

The shock effect was enormous. Paralyzed by months of indecision arising from Stalin's dangerous wishful thinking, Red Army units were overrun, outflanked, encircled, and destroyed. There is also plausible evidence that Stalin lost his nerve in those first hours and days after the invasion. One of the latest recitations concerning Stalin's behavior in the immediate aftermath of the German invasion lends weight to the claim that he buckled under the strain and had to be coaxed back to his post by Molotov and Beria. Simon Montefiore suggests that the critical period for Stalin occurred between 28 June and 1 July 1941.[140] The denial of any collapse by Stalin comes from *Federal'naia sluzhba bezopasnosti* (FSB; Federal Security Service) archivists. Relying on a logbook covering the period 21 to 28 June 1941 in which the dates and times of Stalin's visitors were recorded, they argue, not unconvincingly, that the record clearly shows that Stalin was at work during the period in question.[141] The FSB position on this matter is clear:

> Historians, publicists, writers, political and military memoirists illuminate the first days of the war in various ways. The reaction to the start of war and the behavior in the unfolding situation of the state-political leadership of the Soviet Union and, naturally, above all I. V. Stalin is of particular interest to readers. In works of literature, newspaper articles and memoir publications which were published in the period leading up to the fiftieth anniversary of the victory and additionally in documentary films which were shown on Russian and foreign television screens in connection with this epoch-making event there were episodes of impermissible liberties and sometimes, quite simply, irresponsible interpretations of concrete historical facts. In particular, it is asserted that after Germany had attacked the USSR Stalin, from the first hours of the aggression and for several days thereafter, was in a state of shock; that he was rendered prostrate and withdrew to his dacha, receiving nobody. Hence the conclusion is drawn that at such a critical moment the head of the party and state abandoned the Soviet people and country to the vagaries of fate.[142]

The diary entries cited by FSB archivists and their arguments do not, however, effectively rebut accusations that Stalin evinced cowardice. They merely modify the chronology. For example, there are no entries for 29 and 30 June 1941, and the entries resume on 1 July. This is the critical period noted by Montefiore.

Even if one accepts the view that Stalin did not suffer a psychological collapse when he learned of the German invasion, the obvious choice to address the Soviet people at such a moment of supreme danger was Stalin, not Molotov. Stalin finally did so on 3 July 1941—eleven days later—but that was too late. Stalin's delay amounted to a dereliction of duty, even an act of cowardice. As that dreadful summer unfolded, Soviet commanders, officers, noncommissioned officers, and soldiers would face the possibility of being demoted, incarcerated, or shot on the flimsiest of evidence, always being held to a higher standard of military and ideological conduct than that shown by Stalin, the man who had done so much to cause the catastrophe.

When confronted with an existential crisis, Stalin's default position was to adopt the methods used in the civil war. Evidence of this is provided by the reintroduction of the Institution of Commissars, as specified in the decree dated 16 July 1941,[143] and by Order № 270, issued on 16 August 1941. The reversion to the Institution of Commissars confirmed that Stalin did not trust the Red Army and was prepared to put ideological-political considerations ahead of military ones in this fight for survival. The presence of commissars was utterly unwelcome to commanders who were desperately trying to master the chaos and impose some semblance of command and control when everything around them seemed to be collapsing.[144] The thinking behind Order № 270 was apparently much the same. It was one of the most vicious and vindictive orders ever issued by Stalin, and its detrimental effects undoubtedly would have been far more severe had the Wehrmacht not pursued such brutal policies against Soviet prisoners of war and the civilian population.

Despite pockets of stubborn Red Army resistance that helped delay the German advance, German successes were relentless. The fate of Minsk, Berdichev, Smolensk, Orel, and Kiev; the assault and investment of Leningrad; and moves to the south and in Crimea created an atmosphere of despair and hopelessness that threatened to overwhelm the psyches of all but the toughest Soviet commanders and soldiers. Grossman, whose mother would perish soon after the fall of Berdichev, expressed the sense of doom and evil that was stalking Russia: "We are on the move. The roads are empty. Trenches have been dug everywhere, there are massive ditches, defense installations, antitank obstacles and not a single soldier. The whole place is deserted: quiet and deserted. But there is much terror in this silence and autumnal peace."[145]

The campaigns of Blitzkrieg against France and Poland could not, however, prepare the Wehrmacht for what German commanders and soldiers would encounter in Russia. Despite the depth of penetration achieved by the German panzers after 22 June 1941 (e.g., von Manstein's formation reached Dünaburg, a distance of 300 kilometers from its start line, in four days and five hours[146]), the huge number of prisoners captured, and the destruction of Soviet divisions, the Red Army demonstrated a power of recovery that at first baffled and then alarmed German commanders. The Wehrmacht was subjected to a rate of attrition in men and equipment for which it was not prepared and from which it could not easily recover. One of the more impressive achievements of the Soviet regime amid the chaos of the German invasion was the relocation of some 1,523 major industrial enterprises—all vital to the war effort—far into the rear, often in remote and uninhabited regions. It required a total of 1.5 million train wagons and placed unimaginable strain on the carrying capacity of the rail network, but it allowed the Soviet Union to retain part of its industrial base.[147]

By the start of October 1941, Guderian records that some of his commanders were at the end of their tethers: "For the first time in the course of this demanding campaign Eberbach [Oberst] left me with an impression of exhaustion, and it was not the physical exhaustion but the psychologically shattered state that could be seen."[148] In fact, the signs of exhaustion that Guderian detected in one of his best commanders became evident soon after the start of Barbarossa. Even before the autumn and winter battles, German soldiers were showing signs of acute physical and psychological exhaustion brought on in part by the relentless pace of operations, along with Red Army resistance. In 1941 the Red Army lacked the military professionalism of the Wehrmacht, but this was often partially offset by a stubbornness in defense (which often appeared irrational to the German soldiers), cunning, and a capacity for self-sacrifice that was most unwelcome to the Germans. Even when major Soviet units were encircled and destroyed, the scattered remnants posed a major threat to the German rear. Having escaped from encirclement, these soldiers formed partisan bands or crossed the lines to rejoin the Red Army, and they were no longer in awe of German arms.

Other factors exacerbated the psychological shocks and stresses of war. Coming from a state with an advanced industrial economy, German soldiers perceived the Soviet Union as alien and unnervingly primitive.[149] These perceptions cannot be blamed solely on NS racial ideology. The image of modernity projected by Soviet agitprop was a deception. Major industrial centers had been built at dreadful cost and would now play a decisive role in the war, but the damage done to rural Russia and agriculture had been immense, reducing the standard of living to below pre-1917 levels. The Soviet image of peace and plenty remained unchallenged only as long as the Soviet Union remained closed to the outside world. Once the borders had been breached, German soldiers could not help but notice the difference between rural life in Russia and that in Germany and western Europe. Combined with NS ideology, empirical reality reinforced the view of the Soviet Union as barbarous and backward. Yet somehow, this backward people was capable of producing an outstanding battle tank—the T34—in huge quantities. This sense of the alien and the primitive was also magnified by the sheer expanse of the Russian lands and the feeling that the Germans were not only at war with the people but also under attack by the terrain—the vast forests, rivers, and marshes—and even the weather. One unsettling Russian innovation in the summer of 1941 was the use of forest fires to cause panic and drive German soldiers into prepared killing zones:

> Not only the physical, but the psychological impact of such fires was severe. The crackling of burning trees, the acrid gray-black smoke, the increasingly unbearable heat, and the feeling of uncertainty put troops under a severe strain. Fleeing before towering sheets of flame, men would fight through mile after mile of burning forest only to be confronted by enemy bunkers and fortified positions. Ammunition dumps blew sky high and gave the impression that fierce battles were raging to the rear.[150]

The overall effect was one of insecurity and anxiety: behind every tree a *Heckenschütze* could be hiding; every surrendering Red Army soldier might be carrying a hidden grenade with which to kill his captors; every track through the forests led to a potential ambush; and every civilian or child could be a partisan spy or *diversant*. This fear of the unknown was a situational factor that predisposed German soldiers to react with extreme violence on any pretext.

The near-total surprise achieved by the Wehrmacht across the entire front represented complete vindication of Isserson's analysis of the German-Polish campaign and the latent dangers it posed for the Soviet Union. Isserson, however, proved to be a prophet without honor in his own land, and the Soviet Union would now pay a dreadful price for Stalin's vacillation and the judicial murder of so many talented commanders four years previously.

2 The Commissar Order
Reflections on an Enduring Controversy

In the struggle against Bolshevism one cannot reckon with the fact that the enemy will behave in accordance with humanitarian principles or those of international law. In particular, one must expect a hate-filled, cruel and inhuman treatment of our prisoners from political commissars of all types, as the actual bearers of resistance.

—*Guidelines for the Treatment of Political Commissars, OKW, 6 June 1941*

Certainly, the killing of defenseless prisoners of war belongs to one of the blackest moments in the history of the German army but in the final analysis the Bolshevik military commissars were not little innocents but the architects of, and accomplices to, numerous horrific purges against high-ranking Soviet officers, and were in war and in peace the brutal political slave-drivers of the Red Army. In the general view of the noncommunist world they were a particular type of enemy that were considered to be capable of everything other than the faithful observance of the currently accepted rules of war. In support of this view numerous instances from contemporary anti-Bolshevist literature can be cited.

—Heinrich Uhlig[1]

Three legal approaches to the planning and implementation of the Commissar Order can be formulated. The first, favored by a majority of historians and legal scholars, is to regard the Commissar Order as a unique piece of Nazi malevolence for which there were no mitigating circumstances. The second is to make some concessions regarding the nature of the Soviet state but categorically to insist on the criminality—even the unique criminality—of the Commissar Order and that the military commissars were entitled to the full protection of the Hague and Geneva Conventions. The third approach, the one I favor, is to raise the possibility that because the military commissars, like the NKVD with which they closely cooperated, were an integral part of the Soviet terror apparatus, operating outside the customs and rules of war established by international law, their entitlement to protection under the Hague and Geneva Conventions is not a given. In the context of Western norms, the wholesale execution of captured commissars would not have been justified, but clearly there are questions about how these ideological functionaries should have been treated. In any case, Western norms did not apply on the Eastern Front: the norm there was lawlessness. The rejection of Western norms by both the Nazi and the Soviet regimes before and after 22 June 1941 is the framework in which the Commissar Order must, in my opinion, be judged. If the Commissar Order and the Barbarossa Jurisdiction Decree are cited as legal abominations by exclusive reference to the NS regime, without any reference to the nature of the Soviet regime, the result is a seriously flawed historical analysis. I also contend that, by the totalitarian standards of these two regimes, the Commissar Order was far from unique; if anything, it was fairly routine and bears a striking resemblance, in terms of ideological assumptions but not implementation, to the Soviet decision to execute Polish prisoners of war in NKVD camps in the spring of 1940.

Introduction

Targeting a specific ideological stratum of the Soviet military machine, the Commissar Order was the logical outcome of the Barbarossa Jurisdiction Decree, which itself arose from a perception of the unique struggle to be waged in the east. Undoubtedly inspired by his virulent hatred of communism, Hitler declared his intention to issue what eventually became known as the Commissar Order on 31 March 1941. The final version of the order, which was ready on 6 June 1941, is short and unequivocal. It is founded on four assumptions: (1) that the commissars were representatives of a distinct ideological group and waged war according to the tenets of Bolshevism (Marxism-Leninism), thus denying them the protection of international law; (2) that because the commissars had already demonstrated a capacity for extreme brutality, there was a very real risk that German prisoners would not be treated in accordance with international law, making preemptive brutality directed against the commissars essential and justified to protect German soldiers;[2] (3) that by forcing Red Army soldiers to fight when they might otherwise surrender, commissars increased German casualties; and (4) that even in captivity, commissars posed a security threat because they would engage in anti-German agitation and propaganda. Thus, in most circumstances in which German soldiers would encounter commissars, as envisaged by the German planners, execution by shooting was the appropriate action. Further, the Commissar Order stipulates that political commissars of all types are to be eliminated. This potentially includes any Soviet officials in Red Army formations who serve a political agitation function; it could also include soldiers who are members of the party and the Komsomol since, by virtue of their membership, they would be expected to set an example of ideological commitment and loyalty and to engage in agitation work.

The drafting, dissemination, and execution of the Barbarossa Jurisdiction Decree and the Commissar Order constituted a major part of the prosecution's case against senior German officers during the Nürnberg International Military Tribunal and were cited in paragraph 37 of the first count of the indictment.[3] Among those indicted under the provisions of the High Command case were Generalfeldmarschall Wilhelm von Leeb, Generalfeldmarschall Hugo Sperrle, Generalfeldmarschall Erich von Manstein, Generalfeldmarschall Georg von Küchler, Generaloberst Herman Hoth, General der Artillerie Walter Warlimont, and Generaloberstabsrichter (Generalleutnant) Rudolf Lehmann.

On the witness stand, the German defendants who had been largely responsible for drafting the Commissar Order attempted to distance themselves, but they were far from convincing and were exposed by the prosecution. Lehmann, one of the principal drafters, along with Warlimont, now asserted that "the order cannot be justified."[4] Von Leeb stated that he considered the order "contrary to international law" and then claimed that, in any case, very few commissars had actually been shot.[5] General Reinhardt also tried to convince the court that he was hostile to the Commissar Order, calling it "repugnant" and stating that "a commissar was a soldier who wore a uniform and who carried arms and fought like anybody else."[6] Reinhardt's belated sense of repugnance lacked conviction, since German officers who condemned the Commissar Order after 1945 showed no signs of outrage at the measures Hitler took to deal with, among others, Ernst Röhm, leader of the SA and a former army officer, in 1934. Senior German army officers welcomed Hitler's order to remove (murder) the leader of their main organizational rival for professional status, and they expressed their gratitude after Röhm and others were killed. For example, General Werner von Blomberg, the defense minister at the time of the killings, thanked Hitler for his actions on behalf of the German army. The army's complicity in the killings—victims included senior officers—meant that its much-vaunted sense of honor and tradition had already been severely compromised well before the drafting of the Commissar Order. Having given their blessing to the killings, German officers looked the other way when Hitler's execution squads went into action. Therefore, the German officer corps could easily be co-opted to carry out Hitler's later orders, including the Barbarossa Jurisdiction Decree and the Commissar Order.[7]

Under cross-examination, von Manstein stated that the Commissar Order was "against the honor of a soldier" and that, "in practice, the order was not carried out." He also asserted that "the troops, who inwardly disliked the order intensely, certainly did not look for commissars amongst the prisoners."[8] However, by the time he got around to writing his autobiography, von Manstein's position had changed, and he was far less conciliatory about the status of commissars. If anything, his position had moved closer to Hitler's thinking. For example, von Manstein now argued, unlike many of the other defendants, that in terms of international law, military commissars could not be considered soldiers. He likened them to Gauleiters. On the witness stand, Warlimont advocated something similar. When pressed about the precise status of the commissars, he asserted that they were paramilitaries.[9] Von Manstein also pointed out that commissars could not be granted "the status of noncombatants, as was enjoyed, for example, by medical personnel, army chaplains and war correspondents."[10] According to von Manstein, in their purely ideological capacity as agents of state surveillance, the commissars imparted "an extreme brutality to the battle and a character which totally contradicted all previous conceptions of the soldierly conduct of battle," and he accused them of waging war by methods "which stood in flagrant contradiction to the provisions of the Hague Convention."[11]

Some weight is lent to von Manstein's claims about commissars and partisans, and at least some consideration must be given to them, by the terms of Articles 1, 2, and 3 of the regulations annexed to the Hague Convention and dated 18 October 1907. These three articles apply not just to regular armies but also to militias and volunteer corps. Under Article 1, four conditions are applicable to militias and volunteer corps: these units

(1) "must be commanded by a person responsible for his subordinates," (2) "must have a fixed distinctive sign recognizable at a distance," (3) "must carry arms openly," and (4) "must conduct their operations in accordance with the laws and customs of war." The issue here is whether Soviet partisan units and detachments fall under these provisions. Partisan detachments are commanded by appointed persons, often NKVD or NKGB officials, but it is unclear whether the other three conditions are met. NKVD orders specifying that partisan detachments carry out acts of terrorism are not consistent with Article 1, and the killing of German-appointed *starostas* is clearly proscribed. Carrying weapons openly in areas where the partisans are generally secure from attack, and carrying concealed weapons in German-occupied territory prior to an attack, also violates Article 1.

Dual command—exercised by a military commissar and an army officer—was unique to the Red Army and complicated the stipulation that militias and volunteer corps "must be commanded by a person responsible for his subordinates." In those periods when Red Army officers enjoyed sole command (*edinonachalie*), they were responsible for subordinates, but in conditions of dual command, military commissars and officers shared responsibility. One effect of dual command was to enhance the status of the commissar at the expense of the officer; in German eyes, this justified the Commissar Order, since the commissar's enhanced role could be interpreted to mean that ideological prerogatives took priority over international law and the customs and rules of war.

The wording "in accordance with the laws and customs of war" posed something of a problem for the Soviet Union, since these laws and customs constitute a body of knowledge, wisdom, and legal reasoning that goes back at least to Saint Augustine and thus long predates the emergence of the Soviet state. The revolutionary nature of that state and its abandonment of the accrued wisdom of the past in the name of a workers' state made its willingness to follow the provisions of the Hague and Geneva Conventions somewhat problematic, since these legal instruments were the products of liberal, bourgeois, capitalist states that Soviet ideologues considered reactionary and predatory and destined to be crushed and eclipsed by the rise of global communism. The key question here—one clearly answered by von Manstein—was whether the appointment of military commissars who were to be guided at all times by a Marxist-Leninist, revolutionary code that rejected many principles of Western jurisprudence was consistent with the laws and customs of war, or whether it violated those laws and customs.

Article 21 of the 1929 Convention Relative to the Treatment of Prisoners has potential relevance for commissars, since it introduces a category of "persons of equivalent status."[12] Article 21 also requires that at the outbreak of hostilities, "belligerents shall be required reciprocally to inform each other of the titles and ranks in use in their respective armed forces, with the view of ensuring equality of treatment between the corresponding ranks of officers and persons of equivalent status." I do not know whether any such exchange of information took place between NS Germany and the Soviet Union, but I suggest it is highly unlikely. In the German view, commissars were not persons of equivalent status to anyone in the Wehrmacht, whereas if the Soviet side accepted the category of persons of equivalent status, it would, in effect, be recognizing part of a legal instrument derived from Western legal reasoning.

If commissars were indeed persons of equivalent status (contra von Manstein) and did enjoy the protection afforded by Article 21, they would also be bound by the obligations imposed by the convention. Therefore, Soviet commissars would have to behave in a way that was consistent with the laws and customs of war, not Soviet *revoliutsionnyi poriadok* or the incitement of class war and hatred. If they joined Soviet partisan detachments, they would have to refrain from taking part in NKVD-ordered acts of terrorism (killing *starostas*, for example). It is noteworthy that some Soviet commissars, aware of the Commissar Order, removed their badges of rank as a precaution in the event they were captured; thus, they were violating both Soviet law (Stalin declared them traitors) and paragraph 2, Article 1, of the Hague Convention.

The German View of the Commissar Order

The Commissar Order—its ideological background, origin, mode of dissemination, and implementation by the Wehrmacht's frontline units—has been extensively studied in Germany since at least the 1950s. German historians such as Heinrich Uhlig,[13] Hans-Adolf Jacobsen, Christian Streit, Christian Gerlach, Joachim Hoffmann, Manfred Messerschmidt, Ernst Nolte, Helmut Krausnick, and Jürgen Förster have all written about this order. Most of them have challenged the general assertion in autobiographies and divisional histories that, by and large, commissars were killed in battle rather than being executed after capture. One of the most recent studies (2008) is Felix Römer's *Der Kommissarbefehl: Wehrmacht und NS-Verbrechen an der Ostfront 1941/42* (The Commissar Order: Wehrmacht and NS Crimes on the Eastern Front 1941/1942), which is based on an exceptionally detailed examination and thorough analysis of all the extant files of German divisions. Römer's forensic analysis effectively settles the question, initiated by Christian Streit in *Keine Kameraden* (1978), regarding whether the Wehrmacht was complicit in the prosecution of the Commissar Order.[14] The critical components of Römer's analysis are the ideological assumptions on which the Commissar Order was based, what he regards as the incontestably criminal nature of the order, the degree to which a majority of officers at all levels supported the order's ideological assumptions and policies, and a statistical analysis of the number of commissars shot from 22 June 1941 to 6 May 1942, when the Commissar Order was finally rescinded.

Central to Römer's study is the assertion that commissars were demonized owing to the NS Weltanschauung and Hitler's hatred of communism. The language of both the Barbarossa Jurisdiction Decree and the Commissar Order justifies this claim of demonization. The Commissar Order itself and the recollections of German commanders remove all doubt about the kind of war Hitler intended to wage on the Eastern Front, and Römer and his colleagues have amply documented not only the nature of Hitler's ideological crusade but also its impact on the military planning for Barbarossa.

A number of problems do arise, however, from Römer's analysis. He argues that even from the contemporary perspective, there can be no doubt about the illegality of the guidelines issued for the treatment of commissars. He states: "Finally it was obviously the case [*war es unübersehbar*] that the Soviet political officers met all the requirements that were specified in the Hague War Convention with regard to regular combatants according to which they in the event of capture could lay claim to exactly the same rights accorded to prisoners of war just like all other members of the Red Army."[15] The immediate problem is, first, whether political commissars actually enjoyed the various provisions of the Hague Convention and, second, whether Römer's begged question—"like all other members of the Red Army"—can be accepted. That is, were political commissars members of the Red Army, or were they political functionaries attached to the Red Army? It is here that von Manstein's assessment of the military commissar's status, referred to by Römer, must be addressed in some detail, if only to demonstrate that von Manstein is fundamentally wrong or not, as the case may be.

One of the more serious accusations that can be leveled at German historians, including Römer, is that, despite their technical and presentational competence, their various analyses are severely hampered by reference to an exclusively National-Socialist context. Clearly, studies that investigate the mixture of war aims and methods and politics of NS Germany operate in that context. However, very few of these studies make any effort to ascertain the reasons underlying Hitler's *Weltanschauungskrieg* (ideological war between states), the sources nourishing it, and why it commanded such influence throughout the Wehrmacht. The demonization of the Bolshevik regime and the relentless hostility toward the Soviet state and everything it stood for—propagation of class war, extermination of class enemies, and world revolution—are not ideological fabrications: they are reactions to the clear and obvious threat posed by the Soviet state and the policies it pursued after the Bolshevik seizure of power in 1917.

Class war and world revolution, as formulated by Lenin, were implacably opposed to any form of national identity or patriotism, and Lenin and his Bolsheviks made no secret of their hatred of the nation-state and its unique culture and history. Thus, Lenin states: "Bourgeois nationalism and proletarian internationalism—they are two irreconcilably hostile slogans which correspond to the two great class camps of the whole capitalist world and which express two policies (moreover: two worldviews) in the national question." And he goes on: "We say yes to any struggle against any national oppression. To any struggle *for* any kind of national development, *for* 'national culture' in general, we say unconditionally no."[16] That Lenin was formulating class war, hatred of national identity, and world revolution in 1913 (and well before) shows that the idea of an ideological war between states (*Weltanschauungskrieg*) was not founded by the NS regime; it was something to which the NS regime was reacting. Subversion was also critical to the Leninist view of class war and world revolution, and Lenin clearly set out the methods for undermining a state from within in one of his most important works, *Chto delat'*? (What Is to Be Done? [1902]). After 1917–1918, the Marxist-Leninist ideology of class war, world revolution, and fear of subversion all helped provoke a violent nationalist counterreaction in Germany.

NS propaganda alone, however effective, could not have produced a willingness to subscribe to *Weltanschauungskrieg* and the policies described by Römer and others. This is indicated by one German soldier's recollections, which were far from uncommon: "We acted from conviction, in the belief in a good and just cause!"[17] Molotov made much the same claim on behalf of the Soviet Union in a radio address delivered at 1215 on 22 June 1941, telling his audience, "Our cause is just; the enemy will be destroyed; victory shall be ours."[18] The widespread belief that sooner or later there would have to be a reckoning with the Soviet Union cannot be ascribed solely to NS propaganda:

it was based on the knowledge—the Non-Aggression Pact notwithstanding—that the Soviet Union posed a threat to Germany, which it clearly did, and that at some stage the Soviet Union might attack Germany. Seeing the Soviet Union as a threat that justified military measures was not self-serving. Römer tries to explain the hatred of Bolshevism by reference to the collapse of 1918 and what became known as the Stab-in-the-Back Legend (Dolchstoßlegende), but these alone cannot explain the Wehrmacht's commitment to destroy the Soviet state. Marxism-Leninism, class war (the horrors of the civil war and the Red Terror), genocide in Ukraine, world revolution, and the Great Terror convinced a great many Germans, both civilian and military, that the Soviet Union endangered German survival. In passing, Churchill's own implacable and virulent hatred of Bolshevism can be noted.[19]

Again, Römer cites the provisions of the Barbarossa Jurisdiction Decree and the Commissar Order without examining in any depth why the drafters proceeded from the assumption that commissars and other political functionaries were criminals who were not entitled to the protection of international legal instruments. When, for example, Hitler and the German planners attribute Soviet atrocities and brutal behavior in Galicia, Lithuania, and Latvia to the ideological caste to which members of the NKVD and the commissars belong, it is necessary for Römer to clarify whether he considers these accusations to be true or false. In the context of his repeated use of the phrase "criminal orders" in parentheses (verbrecherische Befehle), it is imperative that Römer acknowledge as true the allegations of criminal behavior made by Hitler and his commanders against the Soviet state. Otherwise, the explicit failure of any analysis of the orders to acknowledge the veracity of these accusations implies that Hitler and his commanders were lying to justify their criminal orders, that Hitler's virulent hatred of Bolshevism was completely irrational and baseless, and that there were no grounds for considering the Soviet state dangerous.

If German allegations of Soviet atrocities in the Baltic states and elsewhere were not based on lies, irrational hatred, ideology, and propaganda—that is, if the allegations had substance—then the interpretation of the origin and passage of various orders, such as the Barbarossa Jurisdiction Decree and the Commissar Order, through NS institutions, must be modified. If a state (NS Germany) intends to wage war against another state that exterminates class enemies (including prisoners of war) in accordance with its ideology of class war (the Soviet Union), should the attacking state consider itself bound by the established conventions protecting prisoners of war—"the laws and customs of war," in the words of the Hague Convention—or can it consider itself released from these conventions and permitted preemptively to kill the class-war killers before the class-war killers kill the attacker's soldiers? Such speculation is not irrelevant, since Polish prisoners of war captured by the Red Army in 1939 were regarded as class enemies and were murdered in the spring of 1940. At no stage in his analysis does Römer consider the possibility that the Soviet Union was guilty of war crimes and that any number of "criminal orders" were drafted by Soviet agencies, chief among them the NKVD. The assumption made by Römer—and he is by no means alone—is that the various orders issued by Hitler and his planners were not only criminal but also uniquely criminal, and moreover, that this assumption is so obvious and self-evident that no examination of its reliability is required. The failure to highlight, in detail, the criminal behavior of the Soviet state in the period leading up to 22 June 1941 leaves the false impression that the Soviet Union was an innocent bystander when, in fact, it was guilty of monstrous crimes, including genocide and mass murder, and did itself issue, as Römer would put it, "criminal orders" (verbrecherische Befehle).

Römer's analysis of the origins of the Barbarossa Jurisdiction Decree and the Commissar Order meet all the required standards of objectivity, but since he confines himself exclusively to the NS state as the source of the two orders, with no reference to any external influences, he implies that the orders emanated exclusively from the essence of the NS regime itself, when in fact the orders have much in common with those issued in the Soviet Union. This touches on a problem that, for all the technical and analytical competence of German historians, continues to bedevil German historiography when dealing with the period between 1933 and 1945. Römer is essentially correct that postwar German memoirists, among them von Manstein and Guderian, have played down the significance and implementation of the Barbarossa Jurisdiction Decree and the Commissar Order. But too many German historians have been willing to ignore the influence of the totalitarian ideology of Marxism-Leninism—Bolshevism, in NS jargon—on the formulation of NS policies and have failed to consider the possibility that criminal orders issued in the Soviet state and outright state terror against so-called enemies of the people (vragi naroda) played any role in the genesis of NS orders, which they unequivocally condemn as criminal and often as uniquely criminal.

That terror was deployed against enemies during the Red Terror was clear enough to foreign observers. Nor could it plausibly be attributed to the excesses of the class struggle. It was Bolshevik policy, and Lenin had no intention of dispensing with terror. In 1922, in a directive to Dmitrii Kurskii, the commissar of justice, Lenin ordered Kurskii "to adduce a principled and politically correct—and not merely a legally narrow—statute setting out the *essence* and *justification* of terror, its necessity and boundaries."[20] Lenin stipulated that the statute's basis for the use of terror must be as broad as possible, "since only a revolutionary sense of justice and a revolutionary conscience will put in place the conditions for its application, as widely or as narrowly, in practice."[21] In other words, the Bolshevik regime arrogated to itself the right to use terror in all possible circumstances, such that any person, class, ethnicity, nationality, or group could be targeted. Moreover, party prosecutors and functionaries, relying on their highly flexible "revolutionary sense of justice" and "revolutionary conscience," would determine the categories for arrest. Though intended primarily to authorize the use of terror against internal victims, nothing in Lenin's directive proscribes the use of terror against non-Soviet citizens. Lenin's order to Kurskii is a legal landmark. To quote Richard Pipes: "For the first time in legal history, the function of legal proceedings was defined to be not dispensing justice but terrorizing the population."[22]

Acknowledging that Soviet behavior could have inspired NS policies (at least in part) would undermine the obsessively held view in Germany that the NS regime was sui generis and that any arguments contradicting this tacit, politically correct assertion are somehow immoral or, at best, of dubious provenance and thus can be disregarded.[23] German historians who make the case that the NS state has to be examined alongside the Soviet Union, and that criminal acts committed by the NS regime have parallels with policies and crimes of the Soviet Union, are likely to be ostracized and suffer professionally. The *Historikerstreit* in the mid-1980s showed what can happen to those who challenge the conventional wisdom. To escape these sanctions, German historians must examine the NS state as if it were a completely isolated phenomenon, something that emerged ex nihilo without any clues to its origins. Regarding the NS state as some kind of immaculate ideological conception extrudes the subject from the realm of historical analysis and relegates it to the realm of demonology.

German historians who concentrate exclusively on the NS regime as the sole factor in NS crimes—rejecting any suggestion that the NS regime shared anything in common with the Soviet Union—have nevertheless produced some highly competent and technical analyses of the NS state. However, these often brilliant analyses are flawed precisely because they are based on the self-imposed, never-to-be-challenged assumption that NS Germany was and shall remain for all time *Ungeheuer Nr. 1*. Relentlessly excavating and examining every available body part, they lay out the innards of the NS state as if performing a giant postmortem, but the focus on such detail hides a reluctance to consider an important question: was NS Germany some creation that emerged spontaneously and independently of any other political entity, or must the genesis of the NS state be examined alongside the emergence of other political entities—the Soviet Union—in order to apprehend the processes determining the Commissar Order?[24]

In Römer's view, there is no real basis for German soldiers and planners to see the military commissars as anything other than soldiers; any other position is clear evidence of NS ideology and the propaganda of demonization and is relentlessly asserted. For instance, Römer describes Generaloberst Georg von Küchler, commander of 18th Army, as "a determined advocate of the commissar guidelines."[25] Among von Küchler's views that Römer deems unacceptable are that Russian soldiers would pretend to be dead and then attack and that the commissars would mete out savage treatment to *Volksdeutsche*. Feigning death was a tactic adopted by Japanese soldiers, and it resulted in robust countermeasures by US marines. It is also true that *Volksdeutsche* and others were brutally treated by the Soviet occupation forces after the annexation of the Baltic states. Von Küchler's hope that eliminating the commissar caste will cause the Soviet system to collapse operates on the same principle as *sovetizatsiia*. It is reasonable to assume that senior German officers had read translations of books by Frunze, Triandafillov, Isserson, and Tukhachevskii and that this knowledge added to their belief that the Commissar Order was necessary, since they would have noted the fanaticism when dealing with class enemies and counterrevolutionaries. Tukhachevskii's role in the savage suppression of the Kronstadt rebellion and the Tambov peasant uprising, and his advocacy of merciless measures against "enemies of the people" would have been well known to senior German commanders, some of whom were familiar with the Red Terror. Tukhachevskii's ideas on how to deal with enemies of the Soviet regime were also set out in his 1926 essay *Bor'ba s kontrrevoliutsonnymi vosstanaiiami* (The Fight against Counterrevolutionary Insurrections).

There are other reasons why German commanders were willing to accept the Commissar Order. First, many of the senior commanders had experienced the collapse of 1918 (specifically referred to in the Barbarossa

Jurisdiction Decree). Second, they had been front commanders during World War I, and some of them had seen the horrors of the Russian Civil War themselves or had been fully briefed about events (there was some contact with Soviet officers after the civil war). There is also every reason to believe that the experiences of World War I had hardened German attitudes toward communism and encouraged the use of violence. But if that were true of German commanders, it must also be true of British and French soldiers who participated in World War I or intervened in the civil war. Russian soldiers had endured World War I and then fought for the Reds or the Whites in the civil war. The civil war was conducted with the utmost savagery and brutality by the Reds, who fully accepted that because they were trying to build a socialist utopia based on what they considered to be the superior insights of Marxism-Leninism, they were not obliged to consider bourgeois notions of law, rights, and justice ("the laws and customs of war," in the words of the Hague Convention). The experiences of Red commanders in the civil war inured them to the routine use of violence and mass murder and prepared the way for genocide in the 1930s.[26] Hitler and his commanders were well aware of events in the Soviet Union, and it is entirely plausible that detailed knowledge of this violence, inspired by the class ideology of Marxism-Leninism, influenced the drafting of the Barbarossa Jurisdiction Decree and the Commissar Order. That it failed to exert some influence strikes me as thoroughly implausible.

For his part, Lenin removed all doubt about what class war and class struggle would mean for those who opposed the cause of the proletariat or were deemed its enemies. In 1918, as Germany was threatened with revolution, he let it be known that "the revolutionary dictatorship of the proletariat is power, won and maintained by the violence of the proletariat over the bourgeoisie, power *unconstrained by any laws.*"[27] Thus, the revolutionaries were free to pursue any policies they chose to further the cause of revolution; they were bound by no laws, customs, or established practices of earlier ages. In the name of revolution and class war, all abominations were justified.

Lenin advocated the total repudiation of all moral and legal obligations entered into by the tsarist state. In international legal terms, this marked the implementation of the *clausula rebus sic stantibus* (at this point in affairs) doctrine on a comprehensive scale that is without precedent in interstate relations before or after 1917. It requires no great leap of the imagination to apprehend that Lenin's *mirovozzrenie* (worldview) of class hatred and class war, with some minor modifications, prepared the way for Hitler's *Weltanschauungs-*

krieg on behalf of the *Herrenvolk*. Like Lenin and Stalin, Hitler had no intention of letting any laws constrain the pursuit of his ambitions.

Von Küchler's hope that the Soviet regime would collapse is dismissed by Römer: "This utopian expectation was unmistakably based on ideological stereotypes. For in Küchler's statements the common idea resonated that in the Soviet Union Bolshevism represented unloved and alien rule; that the indigenous, leaderless peoples had been violently suppressed by a small caste from beyond the country and that they were only waiting for its removal."[28] It is by no means clear that von Küchler's views of the Soviet Union were based on any utopian assessment. The brute facts, of which Römer is surely aware, are that a small conspiratorial group seized power, imposed a murderous regime, and then laid the foundations for the world's first totalitarian state—the Soviet Union. The civil war, war communism, the Holodomor, and the Great Terror all justify von Küchler's view that the Soviet regime was unloved, to put it mildly. Whether the killing of commissars would accelerate the fall of the Soviet Union is not clear, but the claim that the Bolshevik regime was unloved beyond its immediate cadre and circle of beneficiaries is accurate and far from utopian. If Römer believes that von Küchler's assessment of the Soviet Union was wrong—that the Bolshevik regime was in fact widely liked—then he has to explain how that view is reasonable, given the violence inflicted by the Bolshevik regime on its internal and, by 1940, external enemies (the Baltic states and eastern Poland). A reasonable view of the Soviet state in 1940 is that it was a totalitarian state ready to exterminate millions of people as class enemies. Any claim that the Soviet Union adhered to generally accepted norms of international (essentially Western) law would itself be grotesquely utopian. That von Küchler's view of the Soviet Union was based on stereotypes or that he accepted the NS regime's image of the Soviet state does not render the stereotypical view irrelevant. Stereotypes have an empirical basis. If the perception that the Soviet Union was a one-party state that had already killed millions of so-called enemies of the people and class enemies by 1941 and ruled by terror is stereotypical, it also happens to be supported by the historical record. That German commanders supported the Barbarossa Jurisdiction Decree and the Commissar Order based on this historical record may not remove the stamp of criminality from these two orders. However, this is irrelevant when it comes to assessing the truth of the German view that the Soviet state was led by ideological fanatics who, well before 1941, had demonstrated an unprecedented capacity for mass murder, class terror, and genocide.

Römer expends a great deal of energy trying to demonstrate that the Wehrmacht view of the military commissars and politruks was based on NS ideological constructs, not on any kind of observable and verifiable behavior. Thus, Römer dismisses the Wehrmacht position that commissars were ideological fanatics, claiming that "canonized ideological ideas" informed this image of the enemy.[29] Even if the assessment criteria being used by German officers were based on "canonized ideological ideas," the question arises whether these ideas were necessarily wrong or false. An aspiring Soviet commissar became a commissar precisely because he was a "convinced and inflexible fanatic" and accepted the murderous policies of the Soviet regime as the norm.[30] As a commissar, he became an agent of the party and was expected to carry out its orders without question. If German officers were driven and inspired by "clichés of a typical commissar,"[31] then it must be noted that commissars, politruks, party members, NKVD officials (especially members of the special sections), and members of the Komsomol all unconditionally accepted the Communist Party clichés about class war and enemies of the people. If radicalization in the use of violence arises through "the normative force of the acts of violence themselves which have already been carried out before one ascends the next stages of escalation,"[32] this applies with equal force to the criminal orders of the NKVD and its role in genocide, mass murder, and the exploitation of slave labor.[33]

The 16 July 1941 statute that introduced the institution of military commissars in the RKKA—though, strictly speaking, this was a *reintroduction*—amply confirms the exceptionally close relationship among the commissars, the Communist Party, and the NKVD and the ruthlessness with which commissars were expected to operate in support of party policy. For example, paragraph 8 stipulates that the military commissar is "to wage a merciless struggle against cowards, panic-mongers and deserters, applying revolutionary order and military discipline with a firm hand. Coordinating his activities with the organs of the 3rd Directorate of the People's Commissariat for Defense, the military commissar is obliged to eradicate any manifestation of treason."[34] The significance of this coordination and cooperation requirement—analogous to Wehrmacht cooperation with the RSHA (*Reichssicherheitshauptamt*; the main terror and police agency of the NS regime)—arises from the organizational changes initiated by Stalin in February 1941. The NKVD was divided into two commissariats: the NKVD (headed by Beria) and the NKGB (headed by Merkulov). As a consequence of these changes, the Third Directorate inherited the functions of the Special

Section of the Main Directorate of State Security of the NKVD. About a month after the start of the war, Stalin made additional changes. The organs of the Third Directorate were transformed into special sections, and the Third Directorate itself became the Directorate of Special Sections. Stalin appointed Viktor Abakumov as its head. (In 1943 SMERSH, the counterintelligence agency, was formed on the basis of the Directorate of Special Sections, with Abakumov as its head.) Eventually, on 20 July 1941, the NKGB and NKVD were amalgamated into a single commissariat, the NKVD, led by Beria. That the Third Directorate referred to in the 16 July statute was abolished by Stalin's resolution of 17 July 1941 did not materially affect the function of military commissars, who now worked with the special sections and their directorate. Both the military commissars and the special sections were required to impose revolutionary order, and members of both institutions were expected to carry out summary executions when necessary. Christian Streit writes: "The commissars were incorporated into the army as supervisory and advisory organs of the CPSU. In accordance with international law they had to be seen as combatants and treated just like other prisoners of war."[35] This explanation is not entirely adequate. First, the commissars' role was far more than supervisory and advisory, as the statute of 16 July 1941 makes clear. They were, like the NKVD, with which they cooperated, agents of retribution. Second, commissars represented a new type of combatant, an ideologue-combatant, for which there were no clear-cut, unambiguous provisions in international law in 1941.

The NS regime's view of Bolshevism—its belief in the "danger of world Bolshevism"—is dismissed by Römer as merely a "propagandistic incantation."[36] Unfortunately, this cursory dismissal is not consistent with the ideological worldview of Marxism-Leninism, its demonstrable commitment to world revolution, and the Soviet state's equally demonstrable and demonstrated habit of invading and annexing states in pursuit of its interests. Römer's statement that the threat posed by Bolshevism is based on some kind of "propagandistic incantation" is itself a potentially propagandistic incantation whose purpose is to represent the Soviet state as a victim of unjustified ideological slurs. If, as Römer claims, the deeply entrenched German assessment of the commissars is based on the construct of the *Feindbild* (enemy image), the same is true of the *Feindbild* held by the political commissars and the NKVD, whose worldview is dominated by class enemies.[37] The various euphemisms used in German files to refer to the killing of real or imagined enemies carried out in accordance with the Commissar Order—for example, *erledigt* (dealt with), liquidiert (liquidated), umgelegt (bumped off), unschädlich gemacht (taken care of), auf der Flucht erschossen (shot while trying to escape), angetroffen (apprehended), gesondert abgeschoben (separately deported), behandelt (dealt with), and gut behandelt (dealt with well)—are not specific to the NS regime.[38] They have their euphemistic counterparts in the bureaucratese of the NKVD.

The thinking that led to the Barbarossa Jurisdiction Decree and the Commissar Order cannot be dismissed merely as stereotypical and lacking any empirical basis unless one can refute the stereotypical thinking and assumptions on which, according to Römer, the two orders were based. If it turns out that Hitler and his commanders were right—that the Soviet Union was indeed a murderous and bloody tyranny—the question arises whether, in those circumstances, orders like the Barbarossa Jurisdiction Decree and the Commissar Order can ever be justified. If the answer is an overwhelming no under any and all circumstances, then those who reject such orders must explain how one belligerent party can wage war against another belligerent party who wages war on the basis of class war (i.e., the Soviet state conflates class war with war between states), which, according to Marx, Engels, and Lenin, represents a superior stage in man's political development and thus cannot be bound by bourgeois notions of justice, such as a presumption of innocence. Soviet leaders—among them Lenin, Trotskii, Stalin, Latsis, Zinoviev, Kirov, and Dzerzhinskii—all adhered to the view that enemies real or imagined should be exterminated. Extermination was the default position. Zinoviev stated: "To dispose of our enemies, we will have to create our own socialist terror. For this we will have to train 90 million of the 100 million Russians and have them all on our side. We have nothing to say to the other 10 million; we'll have to get rid of them."[39] Thus, to dismiss the two orders as inherently criminal—as Römer does in his favored and ubiquitous trope verbrecherische Befehle—without any preliminary examination of the empirical basis that informs them, begs the question. It shows that Römer has predetermined the outcome: the two orders are self-evidently criminal because they were derived from Hitler; as far as Römer is concerned, that settles the matter. Not to proceed from this assumption is to imply that the NS regime was not unique and that the Barbarossa Jurisdiction Decree and the Commissar Order may be no worse than similar orders issued in the Soviet Union before 1941.

Interrogations of Soviet prisoners were one of the main sources of information about the status and role of military commissars in the Red Army. Although there was some risk that Soviet prisoners would tell their German interrogators whatever they thought the Germans wanted to hear,

Römer's dismissal of these statements as implausible, simply because they were broadly consistent with German assumptions, is unconvincing. Römer finds it expedient to cast doubt on Soviet prisoner-of-war statements because they do indeed provide a thoroughly negative view of the commissar caste. He justifies his approach as follows: "As far as posing the question of this examination is concerned, what is decisive is not the veracity inherent in the German information but what on the German side is considered to be the truth and possibly became in the future an influence on motives and relevant for behavior."[40] This is an extraordinary admission on Römer's part.

According to Römer, the truth and accuracy of the information available to German intelligence officers and others are not decisive, opening the possibility that German views of the commissar caste were based on lies and distortions. If the German intelligence officers based their assumptions on, among other things, the interrogations of Soviet prisoners, and if this information were correct, that in itself might not justify the implementation of the Commissar Order, but it would corroborate the German view that commissars were ideological fanatics who were consumed by class hatred, and it would provide some justification for addressing the threat posed by the commissars. That being the case, the German files may well create a picture of the commissars that the intelligence officers not only *considered* to be true but also *was* true. Nor does the fact, according to Römer, that the intelligence files create a "stereotypical enemy image" of the commissars pose a problem,[41] for reasons that have already been explained with regard to von Küchler's views.

Römer's willingness to accord second-class status to the intelligence reports and to imply that they were not necessarily true assessments of the commissars is somewhat at odds with his own assessment of the files and records kept by Wehrmacht formations on the Eastern Front. Earlier in his book he concludes that regardless of how they were created and handed down, the files possess a high degree of authenticity and can be relied on. To quote Römer:

> The operational files were not the forum for the propagandistic tampering in dealing with military reality but were the place where one took stock of the situation. *Their very function guarantees their authentic character.* The files served as a means of internal reporting and were functional media for operational communication within the military apparatus. *Their veracity was a military requirement.* In particular this applied to the consistency between the levels of command.[42]

Römer wants it both ways: he accepts that accuracy and veracity were operational requirements—indeed, for purposes of his study, accuracy and veracity are absolute preconditions—yet the massive and near-unanimous body of documents prepared by German intelligence officers about the nature of commissars, based on Soviet prisoner interrogations, is deemed suspect.

It should be noted that Soviet sources also glorify the role of commissars and other political functionaries, especially in the civil war (see below). If this propaganda created a false picture of commissars that the Germans took as accurate, that is not the Germans' fault. The other factor to be considered here is that it is reasonable to assume that some German staff officers and planners read works by Frunze, Tukhachevskii, Shpanov, Triandafillov, and Isserson, and that the whole ideological nature of communism and class war would have been apparent, especially in works by Triandafillov.

German misgivings about commissars were reinforced by the executions carried out in haste by the NKVD before its units fled east. That these executions occurred is beyond doubt. Römer's position on the truth of German perceptions of commissars is complicated when he cites German eyewitness reports of commissar brutality.[43] That this behavior was observed by Germans confirmed what Soviet prisoners had been telling their interrogators. Yet Römer has a different explanation:

> Of course such perceptions were for a considerable part determined by the existing images of the enemy and only became certainties by the fact that they were brought into line with the news about the activity of commissars which were in circulation. It is precisely such projections as these that present particularly compelling evidence for the great influence of these ideas on the perception of the war among German troops. In individual cases these observations were, to be sure, also confirmed by the statements of captured political officers from whom corresponding admissions had been forced under interrogation. For example, in the 123rd Infantry Division, in February 1942, a captured politruk admitted when being questioned "to having forced Red Army soldiers forward with drawn pistol during an attack."[44]

This explanation illustrates further inconsistencies in Römer's reading and interpretation of primary source material. As Römer himself notes, the vast majority of the files he examined showed that the Wehrmacht regarded commissars as virulent ideological enemies who tyrannized Soviet soldiers and hardened their resistance. Having cited German eyewitness accounts that corroborated the statements of Soviet prisoners, Römer then casts doubt on the reliability of these German observations. But if German soldiers had observed Soviet commissars behaving in the way they described, why should they not be believed—bear in mind here Römer's own observations on the requirement for veracity (Wahrhaftigkeit)—especially when they were confirmed by Soviet prisoners? When soldiers on both sides agree on events, Römer's claims that the German soldiers were somehow seeing only what they wanted to see are implausible.[45]

In August 1941 the German 9th Army applied the provisions of the Commissar Order to members of the NKVD. Römer explains the German thinking behind this widening of the order's application:

> On the German side the NKVD was generally accepted as the most important executive organ of the Bolshevik terror apparatus and was, among other things, held definitively responsible for carrying out the prison massacres in the initial phase of the campaign. On the basis of the propagandistically fostered associations with the crimes of the Bolshevik regime it was not difficult to convey a sense that radical behavior toward the members of the formations was required.[46]

Römer creates the impression that the German view of the NKVD is essentially the result of German propaganda and that the perception of the NKVD as "the most important executive organ of the Bolshevik terror apparatus" may be in error or false. This interpretation becomes clearer when Römer refers to "the propagandistically fostered associations with the crimes of the Bolshevik regime" to justify harsh measures against the NKVD. Römer's phrase "the propagandistically fostered associations with the crimes of the Bolshevik regime" can be read in two ways. First, it can be read literally to mean that the association between the NKVD and the crimes of the Bolshevik regime is merely conjecture, and there is no way of knowing whether it is true or false. Second, given the widely accepted meaning of propaganda as state mendacity and disinformation, it can be read to mean that the German view of the NKVD's role in the Bolshevik state is also mendacious. The only way to remove this implied ambiguity is to ask whether these German views—that the NKVD is "the most important executive organ of the Bolshevik terror apparatus" and that the NKVD is associated with the crimes of the Bolshevik regime—are correct, rather than implying that these views may be the by-products of NS lies and that any policies based on them—such as widening the provisions of the Commissar Order to apply to the NKVD—are further evidence of Wehrmacht war crimes.

Potentially fatal for Römer's assessment of German attitudes toward commissars is the fact that a great deal of modern research supports the negative views of Soviet commissars found in the German files. The conflict between ideological functionaries or commissars and soldiers is also a major plot driver in much of Soviet-Russian war literature.[47] Römer, however, identifies the challenge:

> The question whether the German views are actually in accord with the state of today's knowledge is, to be sure, hardly relevant for the existing examination. The decisive point was that the command headquarters of the Eastern Army regarded their knowledge concerning the role of the commissars as proven, permitted them to have some influence on their thinking and drew conclusions for their actions, as, *inter alia*, was evident in the conception of German propaganda.[48]

That the latest research on the commissars' reception in the Red Army is irrelevant is a reasonable point. Any challenge to Römer's assessment of Wehrmacht attitudes toward military commissars and politruks as being based on ignorance, willful denial, and the Weltanschauung of National Socialism, and his claim that the Commissar Order was uniquely criminal, must be able to demonstrate that Wehrmacht planners and intelligence officers could have concluded, based on sources available to them before the start of Barbarossa, that the commissars did indeed represent a threat as envisioned by the Commissar Order. Factors influencing German attitudes toward the Soviet state and especially the political caste of functionaries to which the commissars belonged were numerous and, in some cases, well documented. The primary source material includes firsthand knowledge of the savagery and class violence carried out after 1917, the Red Terror, and especially the civil war; the genocide in Ukraine; and the Great Terror, as well as published works on Soviet military doctrine and Lenin's own works. Russian émigré literature also provides detailed insights into the way party functionaries and the state security apparatus (Cheka, OGPU, NKVD) behaved, especially during the civil war. Two obvious and important sources in this regard are a report entitled *Cheka: Materialy* (The Cheka: Documentary Material), which was compiled by the Central Committee of the Socialist Revolutionary Party and published in Berlin in 1922, and Sergei Melgunov's *Krasnyi terror v Rossii* (Red Terror in Russia), published in 1924.

Moreover, comprehensive and detailed accounts of what Pipes calls "the Communist holocaust of 1918–1920" were provided by German journalists reporting from Russia.[49] Articles published in the Berlin *Lokalanzeiger* provided graphic accounts of executions of "enemies of the people." As Pipes correctly observes, the methods used in the Red Terror anticipate the modus operandi of Nazi execution squads. In the 1930s the role of the NKVD in Spain would not have passed unnoticed. The Red Terror (*Terror Rojo*) in that country bore the indelible stamp of the Soviet precedent—systematic and planned killing of class enemies—and resulted in various atrocities, such as the execution of some 1,000 to 2,000 prisoners at Paracuellos de Jamara in 1936. In a portent of how the Soviet state reacted to the discovery of the graves of executed Polish prisoners of war in 1943 (it blamed the Germans), Soviet planes shot down the plane carrying Dr. Georges Henry, an official of the International Red Cross, to France and blamed the Nationalists. At the time, Henry was in possession of his detailed report on the Paracuellos killings. With regard to Spain, Walter Warlimont served as a military envoy to General Franco and led the German Volunteer Corps in Spain, so he would have been well informed about the terror tactics and the purges being conducted by the NKVD against ideological enemies. The period of cooperation between the NKVD and the Gestapo after September 1939 also provided detailed knowledge of NKVD methods and what could be expected.

One other source, perhaps not immediately obvious, is the substantial body of Soviet-Russian literary works published before 1941 in which the violence and the leading role of party officials and military commissars in the civil war are glorified. Some of these works were instantly canonized as the truth about the civil war, such as *Chapaev* (1923) by Dmitrii Furmanov, who served as a military commissar; *Zheleznyi potok* (The Iron Flood [1924]) by Alexander Serafimovich; and *Razgrom* (The Rout [1927]) by Alexander Fadeev. The best known example is Mikhail Sholokhov's epic novel *Tikhii Don* (The Quiet Don [1928–1940]), a work that attracted a lot of interest inside and outside of the Soviet Union and for which the author was awarded the Nobel Prize in 1966. One of the main characters, Bunchuk, a party fanatic, justifies the summary execution of a captured officer by Red Army soldiers: "It is necessary to kill them, to exterminate them without mercy! They would show us no mercy, and well, we don't need it either, and there's no reason to spare them. To hell with them! We have to remove this filth from the face of the earth! And generally, without any sentimentality once it's a matter of the fate of the revolution."[50] Bunchuk is then posted to the revolutionary tribunal, where he is in charge of carrying out executions. There is no question of bourgeois justice obstructing the work of the *revolutionary* tribunal. The party chairman tells Bunchuk that they must preserve their "humanity" (!), but "from necessity we must physically exterminate counterrevolutionaries."[51] Thereafter, much as the NKVD would later execute thousands of enemies of the people in the Great Terror, the victims are forced to dig their own graves and then shot, accused of being "enemies of the revolution." Bunchuk sees his work as "exterminating human filth." "How many of these vermin," he asks, "these lice, have I executed? A louse, that's an insect that eats into your body."[52] As far as Bunchuk is concerned, the extermination of enemies of the people is a necessary step for the creation of the new Soviet socialist order and is fully justified by the postulates of *revolutionary*, class-based justice. The language used by Bunchuk to characterize the enemies of the people—they are variously called lice, human filth, vermin, insects, and counterrevolutionaries—accurately reflects the language used by Lenin and other party leaders to describe any opposition to Soviet power, internal or external.[53] To this hate list can be added the standard ideological denunciation *nemetsko-fashistskii* (German fascist) favored by Soviet propagandists, which prefigures and serves the same purpose as the NS construct *jüdisch-bolschewistisch* (Jewish Bolshevik), found in German orders.

The problem concerning the application of the Commissar Order is complicated by the way the Soviet state treated its own soldiers and commissars. For example, once it became known that the Germans were executing commissars, the commissars (very sensibly) removed their badges. Unfortunately for them, this was condemned as an act of treachery and cowardice by Stalin in his notorious Order № 270. Between 22 June and 1 December 1941, a total of 14,473 Soviet soldiers were executed by their own side for cowardice and other crimes.[54] Under the conditions at the front and in the immediate rear areas, there would have been no time for thorough investigations.

A not insignificant question is whether there was any difference between Germans' shooting commissars in accordance with the Commissar Order and the large-scale executions of Soviet soldiers by the NKVD in accordance with Stalin's malevolent orders. Some might claim that Stalin was killing his own and that these executions were strictly an internal Soviet matter—although huge numbers of Ukrainians, Belorussians, Latvians, Lithuanians, and Estonians emphatically rejected any notion of being Stalin's "own" and regarded Stalin's crimes as being directed against their specific nationalities. In this case, one would be expected to ignore murderous Soviet behavior before and during the war and to discount it as a factor in German planning. And as far as the Commissar Order was concerned, the Germans would be held to a higher legal standard than their Soviet antagonists.

One is left with the conclusion that what really engages some German historians is not so much that commissars were executed but that they were executed by *Germans*. For example, where there is clear and compelling evidence of arbitrary executions carried out by the NKVD on a greater scale than that carried out by the Wehrmacht, too many German historians do not seem overwhelmingly engaged and, as far as one can tell, show no signs of being enraged. The Wehrmacht's killing of commissars cannot be assessed and condemned inside a box. It may well be that when waging war against an enemy that is willing to execute and murder its own soldiers and civilians on the flimsiest of pretexts, the smart move is to treat captured political paramilitaries and partisans humanely to highlight the differences between the two sides and encourage defections. However, when planning a war against a state that has demonstrated a total ruthlessness against its own citizens, co-opted or willing, and has absolutely no compunction in killing millions of so-called class enemies, it is reasonable to assume that one's own soldiers who fall into the hands of that state's functionaries will be handled with the same ruthlessness. How, then, does one proceed? This legal and moral conundrum was identified by von Leeb on the witness stand at Nürnberg. Regarding the legality of the Commissar Order, he stated: "From the legal point of view, it didn't seem to me to be very convincing that the commissars were not soldiers because, after all, they were uniformed, and they were divided up into formations." But then he added: "And for the rest, with regard to the activity of the commissars as described by Hitler, this was very soon confirmed. It turned out that in no way did the commissars in their turn adhere to international law. It was frequently shown that they were deeply hated and frequently they were betrayed by their own troops."[55]

So, under such circumstances, what constitutes the proper treatment of commissars? Does one permit one's own captured soldiers to be shot and tortured, taking the rather detached, legalistic, Western-centric view that this merely confirms what was known or suspected beforehand,[56] or does one behave in a manner that is consistent with the Roman view, *si fueris Romae, Romano vivito more* (when in Rome, do as Romans do)? Any army that goes to war against an enemy that tortures and executes prisoners, and fails to take ruthless countermeasures, will soon find that orders regarding the humane treatment of captured prisoners will be disobeyed. Not surprisingly, soldiers tend to have a sense of humor failure when they encounter the mutilated bodies of their comrades. Their rage can be partially controlled by military discipline, but the ability of discipline to control the desire for revenge has its limits.

This is well illustrated by German soldiers' reaction to the more flexible approach demanded by some senior German commanders for the conduct of antipartisan operations in 1942. These policy proposals had little chance of success because the German soldier had the perception—by no means the result of NS ideology or orders—that he was operating "in areas where the writ of no state ran."[57] The partisans rarely took prisoners and, like the Germans, ignored international law.[58] In this situation, German soldiers considered themselves to be in a legal no-man's-land where both sides operated in accordance with the principle that "everything is permitted." Appeals from senior officers for a more enlightened and flexible approach, something akin to a hearts-and-minds policy, were more or less doomed to fail. To quote Christian Hartmann: "It was precisely on the basis of this experience, on the dynamics of mutual brutalization, that the well-intentioned advice and orders of those generals and staff officers who themselves did not have to undergo the immediate experience of this war, broke apart."[59]

Thus, Verwilderung—the concern expressed in the Barbarossa Jurisdiction Decree—can also occur when soldiers sense they are being sacrificed in the pursuit of standards that are not observed by the enemy. As far as I know, no army in history has reacted to the possibility or the fact of its soldiers being tortured and shot as prisoners with abstract notions of justice and equanimity. Even when it is impossible to apprehend those directly responsible for atrocities, reprisals against those deemed likely to have committed the atrocities, or those who aided and abetted the perpetrators or merely had some sympathy for them, can satisfy the overwhelming need for revenge. As far as those seeking vengeance are concerned, the fact that their victims may be innocent of any wrongdoing is irrelevant. Revenge demands blood; revenge is good for morale. Reprisals, in other words, may be psychologically necessary because they satisfy the atavistic need for blood and allow soldiers to cope with the horrors of war, especially the mutilated bodies of comrades. It goes without saying that once the cycle of atrocities and reprisals starts, it becomes the norm, as was the case on the Eastern Front. In such circumstances, neither side has any interest in the esoteric and legal-academic niceties of proportionality governing the use of reprisals. These generalities apply to every documented war—the Peloponnesian War, the Roman campaigns against the

German tribes, the Mongol conquest of the Russian lands, the Thirty Years' War, Britain's Army of Retribution in Afghanistan, Barbarossa—and they continued to complicate military operations, especially counterinsurgency operations, after 1945, as has been amply demonstrated in Malaya, Vietnam, Algeria, Northern Ireland, the Soviet invasion of Afghanistan (1979–1989), Iraq, and Afghanistan again from 2001.

Statistical Assessment of the Number of Military Commissars Executed under the Commissar Order

The most important part of Römer's study of the Commissar Order is his attempt, based on extant files, to determine the number of commissars executed. Thus, it can be demonstrated that for the period during which the Commissar Order was in effect—22 June 1941 to May 1942—a minimum of 3,430 executions were carried out.[60] There is also a high probability that an additional 380 were executed; the files indicate that of these 380, 287 were reported captured, and there is no further reference to them. Römer assumes that this signifies their execution, which was also the most likely fate of the remaining 93. Overall, based on German files, the total number of executions amounts to just under 3,500. Taking other probable executions into account, the total figure rises to "just under 4,000 victims."[61]

Furthermore, executions took place in different areas. Of the total proven executions (3,430), about two-thirds, or 2,257, occurred in the front zone.[62] The remaining one-third of executions—1,173—occurred in the rear areas and were carried out by the security divisions. Significantly, more than half the executions that took place in the rear areas—669—were carried out by just *one* unit: the 403 Security Division, which operated in the rear of Army Group Center. This completely undermines Guderian's claim that the Commissar Order was not carried out (Guderian's Panzergruppe 2 also belonged to Army Group Center).[63] The 403 Security Division had very good records, leading Römer to conclude that the number of commissars executed in the rear areas must have been higher than 1,173 and, therefore, that the total number of commissars executed in both front and rear areas must be higher as well.[64]

Other factors indicate that the number of executions was probably higher. For example, very few intelligence officers made a distinction between commissar and politruk.[65] Civilian political functionaries (party members) might also be treated according to the Commissar Order. Thus, in the area of Guderian's Panzergruppe 2, 37 commissars were dealt with from 22 June to 19 July 1941. These 37, which included civilians, were lumped together in the report as "commissars."[66] The important point in this part of Römer's analysis is that if the number of executions carried out by the 403 Security Division reflected the standard, the total number must be higher than 3,430. He concludes:

> Proceeding from the minimum number of approaching 4,000 proven cases in the files, the actual number of victims of the Commissar Order in the front and rear zones can probably be estimated to be a high four-figure number, but is unlikely to be a five-figure number or, if so, only just. Of these numbers, in my opinion, at the very least, a half of the executions can be allocated to the rear areas, in particular to the prisoner-of-war camps, whereas the front formations could be credited with the preponderance of the commissar shootings in the first months of the campaign only. At the front, therefore, probably about five to ten percent of the deployed Soviet political officers were executed by German front-line units.[67]

Thus, the number of executions moves from a definite 3,430 to a possible maximum of 10,000, although this upper figure is unlikely. A plausible number would be in the range of 6,000 to 7,000.

One final point concerns how many commissars were killed by German units after capture, in accordance with the Commissar Order (at the front or in the rear), and how many died from other causes. Waitman Beorn, citing Hartmann's use of Soviet statistics,[68] states: "More than 100,000 serving political officers in the Red Army were lost during the war, according to Soviet statistics; 57,608 were killed as a result of military action, and an amazing 47,126 were 'missing.' The vast majority of these missing were likely executed in accordance with the Kommissarbefehl."[69] Whereas Römer provides a detailed assessment of the number of commissars killed as a consequence of the Commissar Order, based on German records, Beorn has obviously not read these records or has ignored them. The number of executions ranges from a definite 3,430 to a maximum of 10,000, although this upper figure is, as Römer concedes, highly unlikely. Thus, Beorn has no grounds for making the inflated claim, based on the numbers of missing provided by Hartmann, that "the vast majority of these missing were likely executed in accoradance with the Kommissarbefehl." That 42,126 (not the 47,126 incorrectly attributed to Hartmann by Beorn) were posted as missing is not evidence that the "vast majority" were executed in accordance with the Commissar Order, certainly not in the light of Römer's exhaustive mining of the records. It should also be pointed out that "missing" is a standard category when determining the casualty returns of an army (killed, wounded, and missing), and it can cover a number of possibilities: killed in action without recovery of a corpse (which might have been blown to pieces, completely burned, or decomposed), desertion (and, in the case of the Eastern Front, joining a partisan band), capture, and suicide (a real option for commissars facing capture). Beorn implies that Hartmann accepts Beorn's view that the "missing" were likely executed, but it is quite clear that Hartmann does not. Hartmann argues that the statistics of killed and missing commissars raises further questions: How many commissars fell into German hands? How many were identified as commissars? How many Red Army soldiers were shot as commissars, even though they were not?[70] One cannot reliably conclude that the 42,126 commissars listed as missing were shot in accordance with the Commissar Order.

The Commissar Order and the Katyn Memorandum

During the Nürnberg proceedings, the prosecution asserted that the Commissar Order "was one of the most obviously malevolent, vicious, and criminal orders ever issued by any army of any time."[71] In the immediate aftermath of World War II, this was not an unreasonable assertion, but the prosecution's concession that the Commissar Order was only *one* such order invites comparison with other examples. This is required, in my opinion, not only because the Soviet state issued similar orders with very similar ideologically prophylactic assumptions but also because the Soviet state was sitting in judgment of Germany, even though it was guilty (though not publicly admitted) of the same behavior.[72] The obvious document supporting this assertion is Beria's memorandum to Stalin dated 5 March 1940 (hereafter referred to as the Katyn Memorandum).

In the Katyn Memorandum, Beria makes the case for the mass shooting of Polish prisoners of war captured by the Red Army after its invasion of Poland in collusion with its then German ally in September 1939. He informs Stalin that former officers of the Polish army, members of the intelligence agencies, members of Polish nationalist and counterrevolutionary parties, participants in insurgent organizations, deserters, and others are being held in NKVD camps in western Ukraine and Belorussia and that "all of them are sworn enemies of Soviet power and consumed by hatred of the Soviet system."[73] As evidence of this conclusion, Beria states that the prisoners are engaging in anti-Soviet agitation; if released, they will take up arms against the Soviet

Union; the core instigators are former officers; and more than 97 percent of the prisoners are of Polish nationality. Having provided the number of prisoners being held and their occupations, Beria recommends that because "they are all inveterate, incorrigible enemies of Soviet power," they should all be shot.[74] To avoid alerting the prisoners to what awaits them and thus avert mass unrest, the detainees are not to be summoned to hear any charges against them. Their first and sole summons will be to meet their executioner.

The Katyn Memorandum anticipates the approach of the Commissar Order. In the case of the latter, a class of individuals has been identified as sworn enemies whose existence on the battlefield and in the prison camp (where, it is assumed, they will continue to agitate against the Germans) is deemed sufficiently threatening to warrant shooting them soon after capture. During the High Command case, the prosecution made much of the following extract in the Commissar Order: "As a matter of principle, when deliberating the question of 'guilty or not guilty' the personal impression received by the commissar's outlook and attitude should be considered of greater importance than the facts of the case for which there may not be proof."[75]

The principle here is that when a German officer or a member of the SD judged a Soviet commissar to be a threat (guilty), execution was the correct procedure. It is important to note that this sort of prophylactic terror was exactly the same method used by the NKVD to select victims for arrest and execution. In essence, there was no difference between the Commissar Order and the Katyn Memorandum, which advocated the execution of Polish prisoners of war because they posed a threat to Soviet interests. The Polish prisoners were to be executed not because of what they had done but because of what they might do when they were liberated. Another element of the Katyn Memorandum is that it was directed almost exclusively against Poles, thus combining racial-ethnic murder and class murder. Poles were to be executed, first, because they were Poles, and second, because they were sworn class enemies. This racial and class hatred of Poles was nothing new in NKVD policies. As Timothy Snyder points out: "The most persecuted European national minority in the second half of the 1930s was not the four hundred thousand or so German Jews (the number declining because of emigration) but the six hundred thousand or so Soviet Poles (the number declining because of executions)."[76] Moreover, the deportation of Volga Germans and Crimean Tartars was based on the same racial-ethnic and class criteria applied to Poles.

In light of the similar assumptions underlying the Katyn Memorandum and the Commissar Order and the ruthlessness with which their provisions were implemented, the question arises whether the Germans were influenced by the NKVD's mass murder of Poles at Katyn and other sites. For example, were the Germans aware that the mass murders had taken place in the spring of 1940?[77] It is entirely possible that the Germans knew that the NKVD was arresting, deporting, and executing people in the Soviet occupation zone. The German intelligence services had agent networks in the Soviet zone—something known to the NKVD and Stalin—that would have informed the Germans about these sovietization operations, and it is possible that, despite its best efforts, the NKVD could not hide the scale of these operations. For example, from September 1939 to June 1941, the NKVD repressed some 500,000 Polish citizens in the Soviet occupation zone: 315,000 were deported, 110,000 arrested, and 30,000 executed; 25,000 died in custody.[78] In addition, it is known that meetings between the NKVD and the Gestapo took place. Such meetings would have been the obvious forum for the two agencies to discuss and even coordinate their operations against the Poles. Hans Frank, head of the Generalgouvernement, gave the order for the AB Aktion (Außerordentliche Befriedungsaktion; extraordinary pacification operation) to kill selected Poles on 2 March 1940, just three days before Beria sent the Katyn Memorandum to Stalin. This is an interesting coincidence, to say the least.

Snyder does not believe that there was any coordination between the German and Soviet agencies.[79] However, he acknowledges that deportations and shootings were taking place concurrently throughout both occupation zones, providing strong circumstantial evidence *for* German-Soviet coordination and an exchange of information, not evidence *against* it.[80] Coordination would have been a sound practical measure, since it would ensure that Polish enemies were targeted by the Germans and their Soviet counterparts at more or less the same time in both zones. An exchange of information and coordination would also be consistent with, and was in fact required by, paragraph 2 of the Secret Confidential Protocol annexed to the German-Soviet Friendship and Border Treaty dated 28 September 1939: "Both parties shall not permit any Polish agitation on their territories whatsoever which operates against the territory of another country. They [both parties] shall liquidate any such incipient agitation on their territories and will inform each other concerning measures expedient for this purpose."[81] Allen Paul marshals effective evidence of close cooperation between the Gestapo and the NKVD, and he has not overlooked the significance of the secret protocols annexed to the German-Soviet Friendship and Border Treaty. Moreover, it is known that Gestapo and NKVD officials had meetings in Kraków, Lwów, and Zakopane. Ivan Aleksandrovich Serov, head of the NKVD in Ukraine from September 1939 until February 1941, took part in these meetings. To quote Paul: "These sessions had a two-fold purpose: first, to coordinate so-called resettlement policies in the German and Soviet spheres, as well as other plans to eliminate the Polish intelligentsia, and second, to devise effective policies for combating the Polish underground."[82]

If German planners knew or had good reason to believe that Soviet agencies had murdered large numbers of Polish prisoners of war some six months after they were captured and that a similar fate awaited German prisoners, this may have convinced them that it was reasonable to kill those who were most likely to take such arbitrary action—specifically, the military commissars and politruks. In this regard, an observation made by Tadeusz Bór-Komorowski, head of the Polish Home Army, is germane: "Apparently the NKVD methods for combating our Underground were greatly admired by the Gestapo, and it was suggested they should be adopted in the German zone."[83] Why should these methods, adopted against a stratum of Polish society deemed to be dangerous by the Gestapo, not be deployed against a stratum of the Soviet regime deemed to be an equally serious threat to German interests?

Another point of comparison between the Katyn Memorandum and the Commissar Order is that they both ignore any customary or legally binding tradition regarding the proper treatment of prisoners. For example, when Captain Berezhkov, the NKVD officer in charge of the Starobelsk camp, requested a copy of what he called the Doctors' Geneva Convention (1929), to provide him with some practical guidance for camp administration, he was bluntly informed: "The Doctors' Geneva Convention is not the document by which you shall be guided in your practical work. In your work you are to follow the instructions of the Directorate of the NKVD for Prisoners of War."[84] In spirit and substance, this instruction from Moscow center was no different from those parts of the Commissar Order and the Barbarossa Jurisdiction Decree stating that established international norms did not apply to commissars and politruks. Eventually, 3,820 Poles from the Starobelsk camp were executed.

The reasons behind the NKVD's assertion that its own directives took precedence over international laws and norms are not difficult to discern. The aim was to deny Polish prisoners their status as prisoners of war.

Declassified NKVD documents clearly point in this direction. First, one can consider the draft statute on how to treat prisoners of war dated 19 September 1939, two days after the Red Army had invaded eastern Poland. Striking are the provisions of paragraph 1(a), which define prisoners of war (among other considerations) as those "who openly bear weapons and observe the customs and rules of war established by international law."[85] This wording, which incorporates key points annexed to the Hague Convention, clearly precludes the mass execution of prisoners of war. The inclusion of key provisions from the Hague Convention in this draft statute also reveals that the Soviet drafters were well aware that, regardless whether the Soviet Union had signed all the relevant international legal instruments, it was bound by the customs and rules of war. Nevertheless, by the time the Soviet state finally adopted an internal special statute concerning prisoners of war on 1 July 1941, that specific wording—"the customs and rules of war established by international law"—was not included.[86] Thus, despite public concessions to the Hague and Geneva Conventions made during the war, the Soviet regime reserved the right *not* to be bound by the customs and rules of war. The Katyn executions in 1940 were one early example of this policy (which is why the 1939 draft statute was never adopted); the execution, incarceration, and deportation of Cossacks—forcibly repatriated by the British—in 1945 were another.

Polish prisoners of war were well aware that their Soviet captors were not abiding by international norms. Thus, a group of Polish doctors and pharmacists, citing the Geneva Convention, protested their imprisonment and requested that they be sent to neutral states or discharged and allowed to return to their places of permanent residence.[87] A group of Polish colonels also challenged Soviet procedures and asked for clarification of their status. If the Soviet Union considered them prisoners of war, they demanded that they be treated "on the basis of the rules regarding prisoners of war accepted by all governments."[88] This was an obvious reference to the Hague and Geneva Conventions. If, however, the officers were regarded as arrestees, they demanded that they be informed of their crimes and formally charged. Finally, they asked whether they were being detained or interned; because they were being held on Polish territory, the implication was that the Red Army had no right to be there and that the detention of Polish officers was illegal. Russian scholars support the Polish view, pointing out: "The Polish officers correctly protested against their detention in captivity insofar as no state of war had ever been declared between their homeland and the USSR."[89]

This is important because, in the Soviet prisoner of war statute dated 1 July 1941, only those persons serving in the armed forces of a nation "in a state of war with the Soviet Union" are recognized as prisoners of war.[90]

Soviet attempts to deny Polish officers and others the status of prisoners of war are strongly implied in the Katyn Memorandum itself. In his preamble Beria refers to "*former* Polish officers" (*byvshie pol'skie ofitsery*)—a status that is not covered by the Hague and Geneva Conventions. Soldiers do not become "former" soldiers merely because they have been captured; captured soldiers retain their rank and status and are still soldiers, albeit captured ones. The consequence of regarding captured Poles as former soldiers was that it effectively denied them protection under the Hague and Geneva Conventions—protection to which they were entitled. More important, the creation of this new status—former soldier—prepared the way for NKVD directives and orders to be the sole legal or quasi-legal instruments covering the treatment of prisoners, as was made clear to Berezhkov.[91] In effect, Polish prisoners would be treated in accordance with the ideological worldview of the Soviet state and its secret police. This ideological vendetta was pursued not just against Polish soldiers but also against Polish civilians. In a report dated 4 December 1939, clergy, landowners, officials, and police officers were listed as prisoners of war.[92] Such persons are not recognized as prisoners of war in the Hague and Geneva Conventions, and imputing such status to them was a violation of "the customs and rules of war established by international law." Significantly, despite Beria's use of "former" to characterize the Polish prisoners, thus denying them their rightful status as prisoners of war and preparing the way for their mass execution, the wording "former Polish officers" or "former prisoners of war" was not used in internal Soviet documents relating to Katyn generated from the late 1950s onward.[93] Many of these documents arose from the pressing need, as far as the Soviet Union was concerned, to counter Western claims in books and documentaries that the Soviet secret police, not the Germans, had carried out these murders. Even in documents whose drafters were clearly hostile to accusations of Soviet guilt, the victims are referred to as "Polish officers" or "Polish prisoners of war," thus clearly recognizing their status as prisoners of war.

The designation "former" was by no means confined to captured Polish officers. Red Army soldiers who were captured by the Germans were routinely referred to as *byvshie Krasnoarmeitsy* (former Red Army soldiers), suggesting—and confirmed by Soviet practice—that the Soviet state regarded its captured soldiers differently from the way the Western Allies regarded their soldiers in German or Japanese captivity. If captured Red Army soldiers lost their status in the eyes of the Soviet regime, the same must be true—and even more so—for captured military commissars, whose capture represented a personal failure and almost a betrayal of the Soviet state by members of a privileged caste. Thus, the military commissars found themselves in a far worse situation than did the soldiers of the Red Army: the NS regime planned for their elimination on capture, and their own side disowned them for having been captured. Here is the problem: If a captured military commissar is no longer recognized as such by the Soviet state, what exactly is his status in the context of the Hague and Geneva Conventions? Furthermore, in the event that commissars are indeed protected by these conventions, do their provisions apply regardless of the ideological principles of the Soviet state? If the Soviet state is entitled to demand that the Germans protect captured Soviet soldiers and commissars, the Soviet state is also obliged to ensure that its captured soldiers are looked after. Abandoning captured soldiers and commissars out of ideological considerations may not deserve the same punishment as the German perpetrators, but it undermines—to put it mildly—Soviet expressions of outrage at the Nürnberg hearings. Given that the Soviet regime abandoned and disowned its captured soldiers and commissars as traitors and considered them "former" members of the Red Army, was it not at least partly complicit in their treatment by the Germans?

Conclusion

Römer's judgement of the Commissar Order is unequivocal: "The Commissar Order was therefore nothing other than a methodical, ideologically motivated program of murder carried out against a narrowly circumscribed group of members of enemy forces."[94] Indeed it was, and the NKVD's murder squads inflicted exactly the same measures—"a methodical, ideologically motivated program of murder carried out against a narrowly circumscribed group of members of enemy forces"—on Polish prisoners of war in the spring of 1940. Or to cite Robert Conquest on the significance of the Katyn murders: "We have here a clear-cut example of a mass execution carried out, without trial and in complete secrecy, as a routine administrative measure—and in peacetime."[95]

During the Nürnberg proceedings the prosecution stated, "The mere passing down of this order [Commissar Order] was a criminal act."[96] That being the case, NKVD officials who drafted and transmitted Beria's orders were also committing a "criminal act." Thus, the Commissar Order cannot be considered to be sui generis; it must be seen as part of a corpus of murder and extermination decrees promulgated not only by NS Germany but also by its more successful competitor in mass murder and genocide, the Soviet Union. In some ways, the magnitude of the NKVD's crimes against the Poles was greater than that of the German crimes committed under the Commissar Order. The intensity of the murders was far greater—the Poles were all murdered in a matter of weeks, after being held captive for six months—and the number of Polish victims exceeded the number of commissars shot by the Germans by a considerable margin. The NKVD murdered a minimum of 21,857 Polish prisoners of war, and the real figure may be even higher. Moreover, whereas there remains—in my opinion—some doubt about the precise status of Soviet military commissars and whether they were entitled to the protections of the Hague and Geneva Conventions, no such doubt exists about the Polish prisoners of war: they were not shot down in battle; they were murdered in captivity six months after their capture because they were considered incorrigible class enemies.

There is another component that the aftermath of the Commissar Order shares with the Katyn Memorandum. Römer asserts that studying the Commissar Order is an important part of the German recollection of World War II.[97] The same is absolutely true of Polish scholars' attempts to uncover what happened at Katyn and elsewhere. At no time did state-sanctioned censorship prevent West German and, more recently, German scholars from studying the Commissar Order. In contrast, up until 1990, Polish scholars were denied access to the relevant files held in the Soviet Union. Moreover, from April 1943, when the mass graves were first discovered, until 1990, Soviet officials and their Western apologists scorned the suggestion that the Polish prisoners of war had been murdered on Stalin's orders, dismissing such accusations as Cold War propaganda.

The Katyn murders were the subject of examination by the Nürnberg court between 1 and 2 July 1946. Reading the proceedings, one gets the impression that the court, though conscious of its legal responsibilities, was not overly concerned about pressing the matter. In striking contrast was its determination to exhaust all avenues of examination with regard to the Barbarossa Jurisdiction Decree and the Commissar Order. When the defense counsel, Dr. Laternser, asked the president of the court to put the question of responsibility for the Katyn case to the prosecution, he received the following response: "I do not propose to answer questions of that sort."[98]

Even though no firm conclusions were reached about ultimate responsibility for the Katyn murders, the Soviet prosecutor made every effort to lay blame on the Germans, claiming that the killings had been carried out by a special unit, Construction Battalion 537. With the benefit of hindsight, it is clear that the Soviet prosecution mounted a well-planned campaign to deceive the court and shift suspicion away from the Soviet Union. One of the main witnesses was Oberst Friedrich Ahrens, commander of Signals Regiment 537. Ahrens's unit was stationed in a building called the Dnieper hotel, which by Soviet standards was well equipped and included a rifle range; it was also suspected of being a rest home for members of the NKVD. Interestingly, Document 054-USSR names Construction Battalion 537 as the German unit responsible for the executions, not Signals Regiment 537, as stated by Ahrens. This strikes me as a cunning and deliberate error intended to avoid suspicion that the Soviet side was presenting false evidence. The citation of Construction Battalion 537 contained the right balance of error (Construction Battalion rather than Signals Regiment) and accuracy (the unit number 537), which is often the case with intelligence reports, thus making it more likely to be accepted as credible. "Construction Battalion" was a piece of bait for the defense. Of the two pieces of data, the numerical designation probably carried more weight, since there was indeed a German unit with that number: Signals Regiment 537.

Under cross-examination, Ahrens stated that in 1942 he had heard rumors about mass shootings in the area. Further, Oberst von Gersdorff, the chief of intelligence at Army Group Center, had told Ahrens that he "knew all about this matter."[99] The local couple who had shared the rumors with Ahrens were identified as beekeepers, and Smirnov, the Soviet prosecutor, repeatedly asked about their names. Given the zeal with which the NKVD and SMERSH pursued the filtration of civilians who had lived through the German occupation, it is clear that the Soviet prosecutor's attempts to elicit the beekeepers' names had no other purpose but to silence them for good or have them arrested under the catchall provisions of Article 58 of the Criminal Code of the RSFSR for spreading counterrevolutionary rumors or anti-Soviet propaganda.

Some procedural anomalies also occurred. The court accepted as reliable evidence a Soviet report that claimed 11,000 Poles had been murdered in the autumn of 1941.[100] However, one of the striking facts about the 1946 investigation into the Katyn murders was that no representative of the post-1945 Polish government was allowed to cross-examine either German or Soviet witnesses. Thus, the country whose soldiers and civilians had been murdered at Katyn were forced to rely on the legal services of the very state that had carried out the murders. Some Poles—certainly those who had spent the war in the Soviet Union and now constituted the Polish administration controlled by the Soviet occupation forces—probably accepted the Soviet version that the killings had been the work of the Germans, or if they had any doubts, they kept quiet. But given Stalin's prevarication when confronted by the Polish government-in-exile's persistent demands during the war, there were other Poles who drew the right conclusions. Their suspicions were ignored.

Even now, well into the twenty-first century, not all the archival material on the Katyn murders is in the public domain. For example, of a reported 183 volumes dealing with Katyn held in the Russian Federation, 35 volumes remained classified in 2011.[101] The only plausible reason for these documents still being classified is that they contain information that the government of the Russian Federation does not want released. If this material is eventually declassified and is found to contain nothing new, then one must suspect that any compromising material was removed and destroyed before its release (otherwise, there would have been no need for it to remain classified). Another reason to keep these files classified is that Beria and Stalin, having concluded that the Katyn murders had gone smoothly, were planning additional mass killings of Polish prisoners and that the remaining files confirm these plans. Such a program would have been a logical and consistent extension of the mass murders of Poles carried out in the 1930s and of the provisions contained in Order № 00447. If the Katyn murders were intended to be merely the first tranche in a rolling program of mass murder, were any mass shootings of Poles subsequent to Katyn actually carried out? Could the still-classified documents contain evidence of these additional shootings? It is possible that Gorbachev ordered the release of the Katyn files in the last months of the Soviet Union's existence because those graves had already been exhumed by the Germans in 1943, and, after nearly fifty years, it was no longer politically possible to keep issuing point-blank denials. If, however, more Poles were the victims of mass murder subsequent to Katyn—and to date, no one knows for sure whether this happened or where the victims were killed and buried—there has been no pressure on the government of the Russian Federation to release any material. The best way to hide a secret is to hide the fact that there is a secret, and the smart move would be to keep any relevant material out of the public domain. This suggests that the eventual release of the Katyn files was intended not to acknowledge the Katyn murders but rather to be an act of closure, to draw attention away from other killings that might have taken place after Katyn. One obvious question that arises is, if the mass graves had not been found by the Germans in 1943, would the Soviet government (Gorbachev) and the successor state, the Russian Federation, have ever acknowledged the murders and the NKVD's responsibility? Thus, the full story of the Katyn murders, which is an integral and critical part of the complex of German-Soviet and German-Soviet-Polish relations in the period leading up to Barbarossa, still has not been told, unlike the history of the Commissar Order.

The mass deportations, manhunts, and mass shootings inflicted on the Poles after the Nazi and Soviet regimes dismembered the Polish state in 1939 were highly effective and required close cooperation between the Nazi and Soviet occupation forces. This close cooperation was a direct result of the diplomatic relations between Nazi Germany and the Soviet Union. These relations are the subject of the next chapter.

3 Dance of the Snakes
Soviet and German Diplomacy, August 1939–June 1941

And if pacts of mutual security were made, they were entered into by the two parties only in order to meet some temporary difficulty, and remained in force only so long as there was no other weapon available. When the chance came, the one who first seized it boldly, catching his enemy off his guard, enjoyed a revenge that was all the sweeter from having been taken, not openly, but because of a breach of faith.

> Thucydides, History of the
> Peloponnesian War

Just take foreign policy. Not in a single country even the most democratic and bourgeois is it conducted openly. Everywhere the deception of the masses, in democratic France, Switzerland, America and England, is a hundred times more widespread and more refined than in other countries. Soviet power in a revolutionary manner has torn away the shroud of secrecy from foreign policy.

> V. I. Lenin, "Proletarskaia revoliutsiia i
> renegat Kautskii" (1918)

I repeat, the great alibi for the deal with the Nazis—the gaining of time—is a base myth, a fairy tale, a cynical propaganda lie.

> Viktor Kravchenko, I Chose Freedom

Concluded in August 1939, the Soviet-German Non-Aggression Pact (Molotov-Ribbentrop Pact) initiated one of the most tortuous, notorious, and duplicitous periods in twentieth-century diplomacy. For that reason, apart from its impact on Europe, it is an endlessly absorbing subject. The master practitioners of lies, deception, prevarication, ruthlessness, treachery, and backstabbing—whether they be Tiberius, Nero, Commodus, or Machiavelli—command our attention. Soviet-German diplomacy in this period fulfills all expectations. The pact represented a spectacular—if temporary—rapprochement between two sworn and bitter ideological enemies, and it took most contemporary political observers by surprise—evidence, perhaps, of how little Western academics and politicians (with one obvious exception) understood the real nature of National Socialism and Marxism-Leninism-Stalinism. It also marked the countdown to the start of World War II and the German invasion of the Soviet Union in June 1941. Relying primarily on the collection of declassified Soviet documents that was first published in 1998, this chapter summarizes and analyzes the state of Soviet-German diplomacy and provides the necessary diplomatic context for the military preparations for Barbarossa.

Introduction

The moment Hitler secured and finally consolidated his power base inside Germany—which was completed with the eradication of Ernst Röhm (among others) on the night of 30 June–1 July 1934—the countdown to *Unternehmen* Barbarossa began. Meanwhile, there was much to be done. By 1939, a decade after the Wall Street crash (1929) that had sent Western economies into depression, Germany's fortunes had been transformed. Germany had freed itself from the hated constraints of the Treaty of Versailles and, under Hitler, had achieved a string of dazzling diplomatic and military successes: the Anglo-German naval treaty (1934); the reoccupation of the Rhineland (1936); the Berlin Olympics (1936), which had showcased the regime; Austria's incorporation into the Reich (1938); the overwhelming of Czechoslovakia (1938–1939); a highly successful involvement in the Spanish Civil War; the eclipsing of Italy as the leading challenger to the ethos of the liberal democracies; and the humiliation of the British and French.

At this stage, Poland was Germany's key problem, and the effective start of the snake dance that ended with Hitler's lunging at his rival's neck on 22 June 1941 was the signing of the Soviet-German Non-Aggression Pact. Both parties were driven by the brutal, hardheaded pursuit of self-interest and were little bothered by the ideological contradictions and the confusion this agreement caused among their respective supporters. Germany regarded the Soviet Union as peopled by subhumans, and the Soviet Union regarded its National Socialist opponent as the enemy of all decent proletarians and one that had to be vanquished.

The dramatic change in German fortunes and status—Germany's apparent defiance of the laws governing economic depression, which had blighted the liberal democracies, and its rearmament programs—had hardly passed unnoticed in the Soviet Union. In fact, from the very creation of the Soviet state, its intelligence agencies had been focused on Germany. Ideologically, in the 1920s it was fervently hoped and believed that Germany would be the catalyst for a socialist revolution that would dispossess the capitalist order, sweeping through western Europe like a steppe fire. These ideological aspirations notwithstanding, the Treaty of Rapallo (1922) provided for close military cooperation between the two states and accelerated and intensified the Soviet intelligence agencies' interest in German policy. With Stalin's consolidation of power, the propaganda of proletarian world revolution remained, and the struggle against what was now called fascism intensified. Practical considerations were not neglected, however.

Throughout the 1930s the Soviet Union sought to portray itself as the only reliable, humane, and progressive alternative to the liberal democracies, which, torn by class hatred, had seemingly encouraged Hitler's voracious appetite. Domestically, the Soviet people were subjected to a nonstop barrage of propaganda aimed at exposing the evils of fascism. There is no doubt that Hitler and the Nazis were public enemy number one for the Soviet media. Thus, anything less than outright hostility was out of the question. As Viktor Kravchenko observes: "The villainy of Hitler had become in our land almost as sacred an article of faith as the virtue of Stalin."[1]

The Non-Aggression Pact

The announcement of the Non-Aggression Pact was prefaced by various statements in *Pravda* (21 August 1939) on a new trade-credit agreement between the two states. Political and diplomatic observers would have noticed that no explanation was offered for the strained relations between the two states prior to the trade agreement, and there was no mention of which side had made the first move to deal with this situation. Strikingly out of place to readers of the Soviet press would have been the use of *germanskii* instead of the customary *fashistskii* to refer to Germany. Finally announced in *Pravda* on 24 August 1939, the Non-Aggression Pact was justified, as far as the Soviet side was concerned, by the history of cooperation between the Soviet Union and Germany; this latest treaty was consistent with that tradition. The announcement noted that differences in ideology between two states were not a barrier to good relations, and it blamed other states—implicitly France and Britain—for the previous hostility between Germany and the Soviet Union. The world was stunned by the news that Hitler and Stalin had concluded such an agreement, and the staggering hypocrisy and volte-face were superbly captured in a famous David Low cartoon published in the *London Evening Standard* on 20 September 1939. In his memoir, Kravchenko reports that news of the pact left people "stunned, bewildered and groggy with disbelief."[2]

The Non-Aggression Pact provided for the destruction of Poland and gave some assurances to Hitler that his eastern territories would be secure from any Soviet attack when he moved west against France, Belgium, and Holland in the summer of 1940. Unknown until after the war, though suspected in some quarters, was the existence of secret protocols annexed to the pact, which complicated German-Soviet relations until Hitler finally abandoned the pretense of nonaggression. This means that the pact cannot be studied in isolation, since its overall interpretation is modified and shaped by other documents.

The Non-Aggression Pact itself is a short document consisting of seven articles. Articles I, III, and VI merit some clarification.[3] Under Article I, both states agree to refrain "from any violence, from any aggressive operation and from any attack in relation to one another, independently or jointly with other powers." Refraining from any physical attack is clear enough, but how widely should the notion of an "aggressive operation" be interpreted? Secret orders issued by Hitler to start planning for Barbarossa eventually led to intelligence-gathering operations in the form of reconnaissance flights—the open violation of Soviet airspace. These flights could not be hidden, and their purpose all too obviously constituted aggressive operations. German support for and training of various nationalist groups, as well as the infiltration of German agents across the border, also clearly fell into the category of aggressive operations. The Soviet intelligence agencies were well aware of these activities, but the Soviet Union did not effectively challenge the Germans. Technically, the German side could have argued that Ukrainian nationalist groups and émigré Russians being recruited by the Abwehr did not constitute a power (*derzhava*), but the Germans' behavior clearly violated the spirit of the Non-Aggression Pact and, at the very least, indicated hostility toward Soviet interests.

Article III states that both parties will "remain in contact with one another for consultation in order to inform one another concerning questions touching upon their common interests." Since these interests are not defined, it implies that German-Soviet interests may include areas that neither party wishes to be in the public domain. It is worth noting that the pact is conspicuously silent on the question whether Germany and the Soviet Union should act together in pursuit of their common interests, one of which was the elimination of the Polish state.

Article VI specifies that the pact will remain in force for ten years; thereafter, it will automatically be renewed for another five years, unless one of the parties declares within one year before the expiration date that it intends to withdraw from the pact. A state that commits to a non-aggression treaty creates a set of conditions from which it is not easily disencumbered. Thus, if all the parties have observed the terms of the treaty, why would one party wish to terminate it? At the very least, doing so would be interpreted as a slight or rebuff by the other side. History supports this view. When the Anglo-Japanese naval treaty that had served Britain so well in World War I was due for renewal in 1921, Britain, under pressure from the United States, did not renew the treaty. The Japanese were deeply offended, and the consequences were far-reaching for both Britain and the United States.

With regard to the German-Soviet Non-Aggression Pact, the requirement that a party formally declare its intent to withdraw poses a problem for any party contemplating aggression. Declaring an intent to withdraw from the pact might well be construed by the other side as evidence of hostile intentions. The inclusion of this provision suggests two conclusions. First, the side contemplating aggression (in this case, Germany) would have every reason to attack without warning and certainly without the declaration required by Article VI. Second, given that, by the end of the summer of 1940, Hitler's war machine had demonstrated its prowess, Germany had every incentive to move against the Soviet Union sooner rather than later. Assuming that the Soviet Union could be defeated quickly, Germany could then return to the problem of Britain. Ten years of nonaggression worked in favor of the Soviet Union and Britain but against Germany, since it would permit a whole range of training and reorganizational tasks to be carried out by Zhukov, thus making the Soviet Union a far more formidable foe. Nor would Britain waste this time. The ten-year time frame does not mean that Stalin required ten years to complete the necessary reforms, but it suggests that whatever hostile plans Stalin may or may not have harbored against Germany (the Stalin attack thesis), he wanted the pact to survive beyond 22 June 1941.

The Secret Supplementary Protocol

The real meaning of the wording in Article III—"concerning questions touching upon their common interests"—is clarified with admirable brutality, despite the officialese, in the secret supplementary protocol (23 August 1939) annexed to the pact.[4] This protocol sets out the mutual interests of both states in eastern Europe. For example, Finland, Estonia, Latvia, and Lithuania are to be subjected to "territorial-political reconstruction," and the same fate is to be visited upon the unsuspecting Poles. The boundary between the German and Soviet spheres of interest in Poland is cited as the line following the Narev, Vistula, and San Rivers. The Soviet interest in Bessarabia is affirmed, and Germany declares that it has no interests in these districts. On 28 August 1939 the boundary line separating the German and Soviet spheres of interest in Poland was amended to follow the Pissa, Narev, Vistula, and San Rivers.[5]

This secret protocol confirms that NS Germany cannot be held solely responsible for starting World War II. The possibility that Hitler would have attacked Poland without an agreement with Stalin is irrelevant. The two states actively cooperated to destroy the Polish state. Likewise, their intentions toward Finland and the Baltic states were clear and were confirmed by subsequent events. Finland was the victim of Soviet aggression; the hapless Baltic states were occupied and sovietized, with all that meant for its populations. The language used in the secret protocol—"in the event of a territorial-political reconstruction of the districts comprising the Polish state"—does not indicate that such a situation *could* arise as a result of unforeseen circumstances. It is a declaration of intent: it *will* happen because NS Germany and the Soviet Union *are going to make it happen.*[6]

Despite the Soviet prosecution's desperate attempt to prevent any discussion of the Non-Aggression Pact and, above all, the secret protocol, the German defense at Nürnberg managed to underline the role played by the Soviet Union in dismembering Poland. On 1 April 1946 Dr. Seidl, one of the defense counsels, opened the session by asking von Ribbentrop whether he was familiar with certain wording—read aloud by Seidl—from the secret pact concluded between Germany and the Soviet Union on 23 August 1939.

Seidl then went on to read an extract from an affidavit given by Dr. Friedrich Gaus, a legal adviser who had been part of the German delegation involved in negotiations in Moscow.[7] At this juncture, General Rudenko, one of the Soviet prosecutors, told the chairman of the court: "I do not wish to discuss this affidavit [by Gaus], as I attach no importance whatsoever to it."[8] There is no formal record that Rudenko's objection to the reading of the affidavit was dismissed, but clearly, it was; the reasons are not indicated.

Listening to the Gaus affidavit must have been a very unpleasant experience for the Soviet delegation. Gaus confirmed the existence of a secret protocol and provided an accurate summary of its contents: "Besides the Non-Aggression Pact there were negotiations for quite some time on a separate secret document which according to my recollection was called a 'secret agreement' or 'secret additional agreement' and the terms of which were aimed at a demarcation of the mutual spheres of interest in the European territories situated between the two countries."[9] Gaus also provided an accurate recollection of the main details of the secret protocol dealing with the spheres of interest, and the contents of his affidavit were more or less confirmed by the full version, which is now in the public domain. On the witness stand, von Ribbentrop left no doubt about the consequences of the secret protocol for Poland:

> I should like to emphasize that there was not the slightest doubt in either Stalin's or Hitler's mind that, if the negotiations with Poland came to naught, the territories that had been taken from the two great powers by force of arms could also be retaken by force of arms. In keeping with this understanding, the eastern territories were occupied by Soviet troops and the western territories by German troops after victory. *There is no doubt that Stalin can never accuse Germany of an aggression or of an aggressive war for her action in Poland. If it is considered an aggression, then both sides are guilty of it.*[10]

Von Ribbentrop's point is unassailable.

The secret protocol also emerged as a theme in Seidl's cross-examination of Ernst von Weizsäcker on 21 May 1946. Once again, Rudenko tried to prevent any discussion of this subject, but he was overruled. Von Weizsäcker acknowledged that he had read the secret protocol. However, when Seidl tried to read aloud the secret addendum, the court informed him that this document was inadmissible. In fact, Rudenko stated that it was "a forged document and cannot have any probative value whatsoever."[11] Even though

Seidl was denied the chance to submit further evidence, von Weizsäcker provided sufficient and convincing details about the pact and the secret protocol from memory, reinforcing Gaus's testimony of 1 April 1946. The most important point made by von Weizsäcker was that "this secret agreement included a complete redirection of Poland's destiny."[12]

The Friendship and Border Treaty

By the end of September 1939, Britain and France were at war with Germany. The Polish state, as earlier envisaged by Germany and the Soviet Union, had been subjected to "territorial-political reconstruction" by the two aggressors and had effectively ceased to exist. Germany and the Soviet Union now set out their position with regard to the new status quo in another German-Soviet treaty dated 28 September 1939 (the Friendship and Border Treaty). Annexed to this treaty were three protocols, two of which were designated secret. The preamble to the Friendship and Border Treaty reads as follows: "After the collapse of the former Polish state the government of the USSR and the German government envisage their task as exclusively to reestablish peace and order on this territory and to secure for the national groups living there a peaceful existence consistent with their national characteristics."[13] Evasive and mendacious, the wording of this preamble is an example of how both states used bureaucratese to hide their real aims. The obvious point is that the Polish state did not just collapse as a result of some unexpected and unexplained catastrophe about which Germany and the Soviet Union knew nothing. Poland was the victim of two acts of aggression: one by Germany (1 September 1939) and one by the Soviet Union (17 September 1939). At the time this preamble was written, both occupying powers had served notice of how they intended to behave, and the German interpretation of "peaceful existence consistent with their national characteristics" did not apply to the bulk of Poles and emphatically not to Poland's large Jewish population. Likewise, the Soviet understanding of that phrase did not apply to Poles and members of other national groups deemed to be class enemies. In fact, the ability to deal with enemies based on race, culture, or class is implied in Article II: "Both Parties acknowledge the border of mutual state interests established in Article I to be final and shall remove any interference of third powers in this decision." This provision rejects any British or French claim to an interest in the fate of the former Polish state; indeed, it rejects the right of any international nongovernmental organization such as the International Red Cross to intercede on behalf of persecuted groups. In other words, the German occupation forces (army, SD, Gestapo, SS, and *Einsatzgruppen*) were free, within their zone of occupation, to hunt down, arrest, enslave, deport, and exterminate their enemies as determined by Nazi ideology. Likewise, the Soviet occupation forces (Red Army and NKVD) had a free hand to do the same, within their zone of occupation, to their class enemies. With just a few lines of text, Poland had been converted into a huge experimental death camp. In view of what would happen to Poland's Jewish population, and what was already happening, the use of "final" (*okonchatel'nhyi* in Russian) in Article II has decidedly sinister overtones.

The first of the three protocols annexed to the Friendship and Border Treaty, referred to as a confidential protocol (*doveritel'nyi protokol*), is straight-forward.[14] The Soviet party agrees that it will not impede German citizens in its zone who wish to relocate to the German zone. This transfer of people is to take place with the assistance of the authorized and competent German agencies. The German party agrees to reciprocate with regard to "persons of Ukrainian or Belorussian origin" (which could include individuals of various nationalities). Any persons of Ukrainian or Belorussian origin who had not already left the German zone of Poland likely had no wish to do so because they fled the Soviet zone of Poland when the Red Army invaded. In essence, this confidential protocol is a proposal, in somewhat camouflaged form, that the two parties exchange persons who may be of interest to their respective security agencies. There may be an implicit threat of blackmail from the Soviet side, to the effect that ethnic Germans (*Volksdeutsche*) who were caught unprepared by the Soviet invasion of eastern Poland will be allowed to leave the Soviet zone only if persons of interest to the NKVD are handed over.

The first of the two secret protocols amends the supplementary secret protocol annexed to the original Non-Aggression Pact, stating, "the terri-tory of the Lithuanian state shall be included in the sphere of interests of the USSR since, on the other hand, the Liublin province and parts of the Warsaw province shall be included in the sphere of German interests."[15] In this protocol, the Soviet side refers ominously to "special measures for the preservation of its interests" in Lithuania. These measures include identify-ing, incarcerating, and deporting all persons hostile to the Soviet presence in Lithuania. The second secret protocol is aimed specifically at Poles: "Both parties shall not permit any Polish agitation on their territories whatsoever which operates against the territory of another country. They [both parties] shall liquidate any such incipient agitation on their territories and will inform each other concerning measures expedient for this purpose."[16] To the NKVD, Polish agitation was not confined to Poles asserting their Polish identity, nationalism, or grievances against Germany and the Soviet Union; it included any person *who might succumb to such behavior*. In keeping with NKVD measures against what were perceived as manifestations of Polish nationalism in the Soviet Union (Order № 00447, for example), the antiagitation measure was aimed at both real and potential enemies. The mass murder of Poles carried out by the NKVD from March 1940 onward at Katyn and other sites was based on this assumption. In light of this second secret protocol, the obvious question is whether the Soviet side ever informed its German counterpart of this mass murder.

Soviet Moves against Estonia, Latvia, Lithuania, Bessarabia, and Northern Bukovina

The German-Soviet Non-Aggression Pact not only led to the destruction of the Polish state and the opening moves of World War II; it also led, in due course, to Soviet actions against the Baltic states. Likewise, the Soviet invasion of Finland was part of the general Soviet expansion and a consequence of the German-Soviet pact. Soon after the signing of the Non-Aggression Pact, the Soviet Union moved to conclude a series of mutual assistance treaties with Estonia (27 September 1939), Latvia (2 October 1939), and Lithuania (3 October 1939). Whatever their justified misgivings about such treaties, the three states signed them: Estonia signed on 28 September, Latvia signed on 5 October, and Lithuania signed on 10 October. The treaties included military assistance clauses in the event of aggression by another European power; realistically, this could have referred only to Germany, although it was undoubtedly presented as a move against Britain and France. The military assistance clauses provided for the stationing of Soviet troops on the territories of all three states—the real purpose of any treaty. This amounted to up to 25,000 troops in Estonia, 20,000 troops in Latvia, and 25,000 troops in Lithuania. With the Red Army came the NKVD, which prepared for the moment when the three Baltic states would be formally annexed by the Soviet Union. At first, the Soviet presence was low-key and intended to provide some reassurances that it was not a threat. However, that changed on 30 May 1940, when the Soviet Ministry of Foreign Affairs accused Lithuania of not observing the terms of the mutual assistance pact and of adopting a hostile attitude toward Soviet military personnel.[17]

On 14 June 1940 Molotov summoned the Lithuanian foreign minister, Juozas Urbšys, and informed him that the Soviet Union intended to deploy an extra nine to twelve divisions in Lithuania, including in Kaunas.[18] Molotov's tone was bullying and aggressive: his demands amounted to an ultimatum, since he insisted that they were nonnegotiable. The Soviet record of the meeting reveals the naked threats and pressure applied to the Lithuanian foreign minister. Urbšys attempted to ascertain whether the Soviet army would interfere in the internal affairs of Lithuania, but he was answered with barely concealed contempt by Molotov. The Soviet demands also included the removal and replacement of the Lithuanian cabinet, which was deemed hostile to Soviet interests, and envisaged legal measures against Lithuanian officials such as Minister of Internal Affairs Kazimir Skučas. What awaited Lithuania after the Red Army and the NKVD had deployed in force was evident in Molotov's reply when Urbšys pointed out that there was no legal basis for bringing Skučas or others before a Lithuanian court. According to the record of the meeting, Molotov countered: "First of all it is essential to arrest them and put them before a court and the legal clauses will be found. Indeed, Soviet legal experts could help in this after they had studied the Lithuanian legal code."[19] In plain English: bring in the guilty individual, and he will have a fair trial. Molotov's threats of immediate Soviet action had the desired effect: Urbšys duly reported that the entire Lithuanian cabinet had retired and been replaced.

Similar meetings took place between Molotov and representatives of the Latvian and Estonian governments.[20] In the Soviet view, Latvia and Estonia were more recalcitrant, since the two states had concluded an earlier military alliance, the Baltic Entente, which Moscow regarded as threatening but also saw as an opportunity to achieve its ends. Molotov believed that even though Lithuania was not a member of the pact between Latvia and Estonia, that pact was nevertheless serving to unite all three Baltic states in a military alliance against the Soviet Union. Once again, Molotov insisted that the present Latvian government should resign and let it be known that additional Soviet troops would be deployed in Latvia. The meeting between the Latvian emissary in Moscow, Fricis Kotsinsh, and Molotov on 16 June 1940 revealed that the Soviet side was instigating incidents on the border to step up pressure on the Latvian government. For example, Kotsinsh informed Molotov that on the previous evening, a group of armed men had crossed the Latvian-Soviet border from the Soviet side and attacked two border posts. As a result, several border guards were killed and the posts' buildings were burned.[21] Molotov also summoned the Estonian emissary, August Rei, and delivered much the same tirade, informing him that additional troops would be deployed in Estonia.[22]

To supervise the measures undertaken in all three Baltic states, as demanded by Molotov, the Soviet government sent V. G. Dekanozov to Lithuania, A. Zhdanov to Estonia, and A. Vyshinskii to Latvia. In the words of the Russian archivists: "In close contact with the local communist parties they supervised the entire process of the political transformation which took place in June [1940] and which led to the creation of Soviet republics and their incorporation into the USSR."[23] To destroy the independence of Estonia, Latvia, and Lithuania, the Soviet Union used a combination of patient subversion and the threat of naked force at the appropriate moment. It comes as no surprise that these methods had much in common with Hitler's moves against Austria, Czechoslovakia, and, aided and abetted by the Soviet Union, Poland. The presence of communists in all three Baltic states was exploited by the Soviet regime, just as Hitler had earlier exploited the presence of ethnic Germans (Volksdeutsche) in Czechoslovakia and Poland to browbeat the national governments. The Soviet orchestration of border incidents, as reported by Kotsinsh, was the sort of Aktion pioneered by the Germans as a pretext for armed intervention (the well-known Gleiwitz incident, for example, on the German-Polish border).

One must be clear about the meaning of the "political transformation" of the Baltic states. Nationalists, landowners, and all other persons deemed hostile to the Soviet state would be removed from their posts, according to lists drawn up in advance by the NKVD. Arrests, executions, and deportations would follow. The new political class in the three states would be drawn from members of their respective communist parties, carefully vetted and supervised by their Soviet advisers. All institutions in the three states would then be completely sovietized. The treatment of the three Baltic states became the standard Soviet model for internal subversion, terror, and military intervention to sovietize eastern Europe after the defeat of NS Germany. It is worth noting that Estonia, Latvia, and Lithuania regained their independence only after the collapse of the Soviet Union in 1991 and that they are once again facing a security threat from Moscow and the Russian Federation. Rulers and ideologies come and go, but geography remains the same.

The Soviet case and complaint against Lithuania were made very clear in a TASS communiqué dated 16 June 1940. It included additional details that Molotov apparently did not mention in his meeting with Urbšys. In the communiqué, the Lithuanian authorities were accused of abducting Soviet military personnel stationed in Lithuania in accordance with the Soviet-Lithuanian Mutual Assistance Treaty. There is no obvious reason why the Lithuanian authorities would engage in such politically suicidal behavior. The Lithuanian government was also accused of arresting its own citizens—those who provided essential services to the Soviet garrisons, such as laundry and canteens—and sending them to concentration camps. According to TASS, the nature of these individuals' work implied that they fell into the Marxist category of the "working class," thus providing some spurious justification for the Soviet state's intervention on behalf of the oppressed. The authors of the TASS communiqué had no doubt about the intent of the Lithuanian authorities:

> These totally unprovoked and unrestrained repressions against
> Lithuanian citizens engaged in the provision of essential services
> for Soviet units are aimed not only at making the presence of Soviet
> military units in Lithuania impossible but are also intended to incite
> hostility toward Soviet military personnel in Lithuania and to prepare
> the way for attacking these units.
>
> All these facts indicate that the Lithuanian government is grossly
> violating the Treaty of Mutual Assistance concluded by it with the
> Soviet Union and preparing to attack the Soviet garrison located in
> Lithuania on the basis of this Treaty.[24]

Also cited as an aggressive move by the Lithuanian government was its participation in the Baltic Entente with Latvia and Estonia. As far as Moscow was concerned, this alliance was clearly aimed against the Soviet Union. Therefore, in the words of the communiqué, Lithuania had "grossly violated" the Treaty of Mutual Assistance, especially Article VI. Another complaint was that contact among the General Staffs of Estonia, Latvia, and Lithuania had taken place and been kept secret from the Soviet Union. The Soviet Union also demanded that Skučas, the minister of internal affairs, and Augustus Povilaitis, claimed by the Soviet side to be the head of the political police, be indicted "as the primary culprits of the provocative actions against the Soviet garrison in Lithuania."[25] However, Molotov's thoughts on due process and how to manipulate the Lithuanian legal code, which he had outlined to Urbšys, were omitted. The Soviet protest also demanded that the entire Lithuanian government be replaced. Moreover, Soviet troops were to be granted unobstructed passage throughout Lithuania and would be deployed in the most important centers and in the numbers necessary to allow implementation of the treaty. This final demand was, in essence, a notification that, one way or another (with or without Lithuanian assistance or compliance), Lithuania would be occupied by the Red Army.

Soviet moves against the Baltic states—their de facto occupation by the Red Army—at a time when Germany was bringing its highly successful military campaign in the west to a conclusion, changed the map in this part of the world in ways that were not to Germany's advantage. Furthermore, the fact that these changes were implemented while Germany was otherwise engaged may have hardened Hitler's determination to seek a reckoning with the Soviet Union before Britain had been diplomatically or militarily neutralized. In a 17 June 1940 meeting between Molotov and the German ambassador in Moscow, von Schulenburg, Molotov, having sweetly congratulated Germany on its military success in the west, justified Soviet moves in the Baltic states as being intended to prevent any British or French intrigue in the region.[26] With all the finesse and poise of a professional diplomat, von Schulenburg informed Molotov that the whole affair was solely between the Soviet Union and the Baltic states. Militarily, of course, this could not be the case, since the changes strengthened the Soviet position relative to Germany's. Diplomatically, there were problems ahead. Lithuanian president Antanas Smetona had fled to Germany, and the new Lithuanian government, under pressure from their Soviet masters, might request that he be returned. Another matter raised in this meeting was that entire Lithuanian units were crossing the border to escape Soviet forces. Molotov indicated that the Soviet Union would, if requested by the Lithuanian government, deploy Soviet border guards.

The entry of Soviet troops into the Baltic states prompted a great deal of speculation in the worldwide media, which meant that the Soviet propaganda apparatus had to attempt to counter the rumors. This became a pattern over the next year as German-Soviet relations deteriorated. One line of speculation making the rounds was that Soviet troops had been deployed because of dissatisfaction or unease with the Germans' military success in the west. In response to claims that some 100 to 150 Soviet divisions had been deployed in the Baltic states, TASS asserted that the total number in all three states amounted to only 18 to 20 divisions.[27] This official number is clearly inconsistent with what Molotov told Urbšys (Lithuania), Kotsinsh (Latvia), and Rei (Estonia). Molotov had earlier told Urbšys that an additional

9 to 12 divisions (3 to 4 corps) would be deployed in Lithuania.[28] He told Kotsinsh that there would be 2 Soviet corps in Latvia,[29] and he told Rei that 2 to 3 corps of Soviet troops would be deployed in Estonia.[30] Thus, a total of about 40 Soviet divisions would be deployed in all three states, in addition to the Soviet units already stationed there. Bear in mind that the military assistance clauses already provided for the stationing of 70,000 Soviet troops in the three states. So the overall number of Soviet troops after the Molotov ultimatums could be 50 or more divisions, more than double the official figure claimed by TASS. From the Soviet point of view, the most worrying aspect of Western and Japanese press speculation was that the commentators saw the Soviet deployments as a weakening of the Non-Aggression Pact. Trying to neutralize such speculation had consequences for the Soviet side, since the more determinedly TASS and other Soviet sources denied any rift between the Soviet Union and Germany—insisting that all was in order—the more they were compelled to praise the pact and intensify the language (the hyperbole) of mutual respect and cooperation, thus offering a whole range of hostages to fortune. Not only did this eventually, and spectacularly, damage Stalin's reputation at home and abroad, but it also effectively delayed the start of an honest assessment of Soviet-German diplomacy in 1939–1941 and more or less until 1989–1991 and after. Although the TASS communiqué of 13 June 1941 (see appendix C) is by far the best known, most cited, and most infamous example of the Soviet denial of problems with Germany, the process of prevarication and denial started well before 13 June 1941.

The next move against Germany was the successful Soviet attempt to recover Bessarabia and to secure northern Bukovina. The role played by the secret supplementary protocol attached to the Non-Aggression Pact was critical, since the Soviet interest in southeastern Europe and Bessarabia had been conceded, and the Germans had declared their "complete lack of political interest in these regions" (Article 3). In the summer of 1940 this article started to cause problems because, among other reasons, political interests could not be separated from economic and military interests. This was clearly understood by both sides, even though it was not made wholly explicit in the secret supplementary protocol. Thus, Germany could not be indifferent to the Soviet intention to seize Bessarabia and northern Bukovina. Nor could the Soviet side permit itself to be marginalized in any discussions of, or solutions to, the Balkans question. The German ambassador in Rome, Mackensen, had told Gelfand, the Soviet chargé d'affaires in Rome, that the Balkans question could be solved peacefully. On this basis, Molotov sought assurances from von Schulenburg that (1) the provisions of Article 3 still applied; (2) the Balkans question would be resolved by the three powers (Germany, the Soviet Union, and Italy) and that Article III of the Non-Aggression Pact, requiring consultation on common interests, still applied; and (3) the German government stood by Mackensen's statement to Gelfand.[31]

The impossibility of divorcing political problems from economic ones (which should have been a given for two states espousing some form of socialism) was evident in von Schulenburg's concern that any solution to the Bessarabia problem would cause chaos in Romania, disrupting the Germans' desperately needed supply of oil and other products from that country. Regardless of these German concerns, Molotov emphasized that the issue of Bessarabia and northern Bukovina was "exceptionally urgent," hinting that military moves were imminent.[32]

Von Schulenburg delivered the German response to Soviet concerns about Bessarabia and Bukovina (the Soviet record shows that Germany referred to Bukovina, not merely to *northern* Bukovina) to Molotov on 25 June 1940. He made four points: Germany fully recognized the USSR's rights to Bessarabia; Germany, having vital economic interests in Romania, desired a peaceful solution to the problem; Germany regarded the question of Bukovina as a new one, without which the solution of the Bessarabian question would be greatly facilitated; and Germany was concerned about the fate of Germans in Bessarabia and Bukovina (not just northern Bukovina) and hoped their resettlement would be resolved by the Soviet Union "in the spirit of the agreement concerning the resettlement of Germans from Volyna."[33]

Concerning Bukovina, Molotov's view was that the bulk of the population was Ukrainian and that the Soviet government's request was "correct and opportune since at the present time all Ukraine, with a minor exception, had already been united, but that the Soviet Union, not considering the matter to be topical, had not put the question to Hungary concerning Carpathian Russians."[34] The Soviet Union was using ethnicity to justify the seizure of territory, just as Hitler did (under the pretext of protecting ethnic minorities). The announcement that the Soviet Union did not consider the question of the Carpathian Russians to be topical echoed Hitler's claims, since no sooner had he devoured some state than he declared he had no more territorial demands (for the time being). Germany was now on the receiving end of its own methods. Von Schulenburg used 1925 population data to try to convince Molotov that Ukrainians did not constitute a majority in Bukovina, but Molotov dismissed those data as being designed to benefit Romania.

Von Schulenburg's requests for delays, a peaceful solution, and separation of the Bessarabia issue from the Soviet claim to northern Bukovina were ignored. Molotov was not bluffing when he insisted that a solution was urgent. On 26 June 1940 Gheorghe Davidescu, the Romanian ambassador in Moscow, was summoned to a meeting with Molotov and bluntly informed that the Soviet Union required the return of Bessarabia. The Soviet demand, as Molotov claimed and clarified, arose from a deep injustice:

> In 1918, Romania, exploiting Russia's military weakness violently seized a part of its territory from the Soviet Union (Russia)—Bessarabia—and so violated the age-old unity of Bessarabia, predominantly populated by Ukrainians, with the Ukrainian Soviet Republic.
>
> The Soviet Union has never reconciled itself to the fact of the violent seizure of Bessarabia about which the Government of the Soviet Union has repeatedly and openly declared to the entire world.[35]

Molotov's justification for the return of Bessarabia was not based on any interpretation of class solidarity or concern for the welfare of suppressed proletarians, as one might expect. It was based on ethnicity, just as Hitler used the presence of ethnic Germans in Czechoslovakia to foment trouble and justify intervention. Nor was Molotov content with recovering Bessarabia; he wanted northern Bukovina as well. Once again, the demand was based on a naked appeal to ethnicity. According to Molotov, the return of Bessarabia was "organically linked to the transfer to the Soviet Union of that part of Bukovina of which the overwhelming majority of the population was linked with Soviet Ukraine as a community sharing a historical fate and as a community of shared language and national composition."[36] Molotov then claimed that the transfer of northern Bukovina would partially, though obviously inadequately, compensate "for the massive damage which was inflicted on the Soviet Union and the population of Bessarabia by the twenty-two year domination of Romania in Bessarabia."[37] Molotov's dubious legal reasoning and distortion of historical facts, never mind his sheer brazenness, rival any of the outrageous demands made by Hitler in the 1930s.

Whether playing for time or disingenuously interpreting the Soviet demands, the Romanian ambassador informed Molotov that the Romanian government was prepared to enter into detailed negotiations. Such a ploy got Romania nowhere. Molotov's response was brutally pragmatic: if, he told Davidescu, the Romanian government found the Soviet proposals agreeable, there could be no obvious objection to the immediate deployment of Soviet troops. One of Davidescu's objections to Molotov's timetable centered on the specific procedure for the transfer of territory "and the juridical forms of implementing the given measures."[38] Davidescu was quite right to want to ascertain the procedure for evacuating various Romanian officials and public servants before the entry of Soviet troops, whereas Molotov wanted to deploy Soviet troops immediately and sort out what the Soviet side regarded as minor matters later, in accordance with Moscow's interests. Behind Molotov's desire for speed was the very real fear that any delay between Romania's acceptance of—capitulation to—Soviet demands and the deployment of Soviet troops would increase the risk of organized, armed resistance to Soviet intervention and the destruction of vital infrastructure. From the Soviet point of view, speed was of the essence.

With the acquisition of Bessarabia and northern Bukovina, the Soviet Union next sought to resolve a territorial problem in Lithuania. Under the terms of the secret supplementary protocol (28 September 1939), "as soon as the government of the USSR has taken special measures on Lithuanian territory in order to secure its interests, then, with the aim of implementing a simple and natural boundary, the present German-Lithuanian border shall be amended such that the Lithuanian territory which is situated to the southeast of the line indicated on the map, shall be allocated to Germany."[39] The immediate problem was that moves were afoot to incorporate Lithuania into the Soviet state, and German possession of this territory (Mariampol) would be an obstacle to that. Thus, Stalin and Molotov formally requested that Germany consider the possibility of relinquishing this small piece of territory.[40] The matter was raised again by Molotov on 23 August, the first anniversary of the signing of the Non-Aggression Pact.[41] As a precedent of Soviet goodwill, the fact that the Soviet Union had solved the question of the Suvalskii district in Germany's favor was cited.

Meanwhile, on 11 August 1940 Molotov delivered a diplomatic note to von Schulenburg announcing that, based on their requests (naturally, there was no question of coercion), the Soviet Union had agreed formally to incorporate Estonia, Latvia, and Lithuania into the Soviet Union. The note stated: "In such a way Lithuania, Latvia and Estonia are now constituent parts of the Union of Soviet Socialist Republics on the basis of complete equality with the other Soviet Socialist Republics with all the rights and obligations issuing therefrom."[42] The immediate consequence was that the three Baltic states' separate diplomatic relations with other states now ceased. Germany was requested to close down its consulates by 25 August 1940.

Having successfully seized the territory of the three Baltic states, the Soviet Union now moved to seize their assets abroad. To this end, the Soviet Union demanded, via its embassy in London, that all gold belonging to Estonia, Latvia, and Lithuania and held by British banks be transferred to the Soviet Union. In a note to Maiskii, the Soviet ambassador in London, Moscow pointed out, "The gold referred to was acquired from the Lithuanian, Latvian and Estonian banks by the State Bank [Gosbank] of the USSR on the basis of a sale-purchase agreement and was subject to being transferred to the deposit of the USSR State Bank without any doubt on the strength of obligations sent by the telegraph instructions of Lithuanian, Latvian and Estonian banks to the Bank of England dated 13 July 1940."[43] Maiskii was informed that, despite three reminders, the Bank of England had so far refused to hand over the gold. The ambassador was ordered to visit Halifax and demand that the gold be transferred to Gosbank. Here we see another affinity between the Soviet Union and the NS state. Nazi ravings about Jews never got in the way of stealing Jewish gold (and other assets). Likewise, this unseemly lusting after the Baltic states' gold shows that the Soviet Union would not permit ideology to get in the way of good old-fashioned greed and, when the opportunity arose, theft: *pecunia non olet* (money does not smell). Assets held by ethnic Germans in the Baltic states were also a source of friction between Germany and the Soviet Union, as evidenced by the Molotov–von Schulenburg meeting that took place on 23 August 1940. Soviet intentions in the three states were clear: all privately owned assets were to be nationalized.

On 12 August 1940 Molotov addressed the question of compensating Germany for the loss of territory in Lithuania (Mariampol). From the outset, the Soviet side rejected the idea of territorial concessions to compensate Germany, since "this could not be carried out without inflicting great moral damage to the USSR."[44] As far as Molotov was concerned, militating against territorial concessions was the fact that any such territory had already been subjected to "new procedures, corresponding to the state structure of the USSR," and "a reconstruction of [the] municipal and rural population had been accomplished."[45] In other words, Lithuania had been totally sovietized: all private property and other assets had been seized, and all those deemed to be hostile, anti-Soviet elements—including former members of the armed forces, politicians critical of the Soviet state, and landowners—had already been arrested and deported, or were liable to be. Conceding territory that had been subjected to such a brutal and ideological reconfiguration—the total destruction of civil society—could have had severe propaganda consequences for the Soviet Union.

Molotov also pointed out that no moral damage would be inflicted on Germany by renouncing this territory, since it was not part of Germany. Another factor, and one that probably worried the Soviet Union more than it did Germany, was that "any such new amendment to the officially declared borders between Germany and the Soviet Union would provide sustenance to hostile elements for them to wage a campaign to cause serious friction between our two countries and instability in their mutual relations."[46] Molotov then reminded Germany that in the process of redefining the borders between the two states, the Soviet Union had conceded the Suvalskii district to Germany, without any compensation. This was all leading up to the main point: to compensate Germany for conceding Mariampol—referred to here, and subsequently, by both sides as kusochek Litvy (a small piece of Lithuania)—the Soviet Union offered 3.86 million gold dollars, which, it was pointed out, amounted to half of what the United States had paid the tsarist government for Alaska. Alternatively, the Soviet regime offered to pay the compensation in goods.

The matter of compensation was eventually formalized in a secret protocol dated 10 January 1941. It stipulated that Germany would renounce any claims to the relevant part of Lithuanian territory and would receive 7.5 million gold dollars, which was equivalent to 31.5 million German Reichsmarks.[47] The secret protocol was linked to a new treaty providing for the exchange of goods between Germany and the Soviet Union. The treaty covered the period from 11 February 1941 to 1 August 1942, during which time the Soviet Union agreed to deliver goods to Germany valued at 620 million to 640 million Reichsmarks. For its part, Germany agreed to deliver to the Soviet Union goods and tools of the same value.

It seems to me that the issue of Soviet compensation for Germany's abandonment of its claim to a small part of Lithuania goes beyond straightforward remuneration. Molotov knew his August 1940 offer would not result in immediate acceptance or rejection by the German side. I suggest that from the moment the offer of compensation was made, the aim was to tie the secret protocol (10 January 1941) to the new economic treaty. From the Soviet perspective, the new treaty was designed to test the Germans; if they signed the treaty, this would indicate to Stalin that Germany would remain committed to the Non-Aggression Pact at least until 1 August 1942, thus buying more time. Article 2 of the treaty supports this view: "It has been established, moreover, that the Soviet side shall be able in the period of the operation of the present agreement to place orders with delivery dates advancing after 1 August 1942."[48] Earlier, at the 6 January 1941 meeting between Molotov and von Schulenburg, Molotov had wanted the repayment schedule to extend for two years (January 1941–January 1943), whereas Karl Schnurre, the trade specialist at the German embassy in Moscow, made it clear that the German side wanted to resolve the matter as soon as possible.[49] Therefore, it is likely that the Soviet option of ordering goods that might be delivered beyond 1 August 1942 was a way to extend the period of economic cooperation. It is plausible, in my opinion, that the real purpose of this treaty and the compensation for the *kusochek* of Lithuanian territory was to convince Germany that its interests would be best served by cooperating with the Soviet Union. It is possible that Stalin persuaded himself that, out of fear of suffering economic damage, Germany would not attack the Soviet Union any time before August 1942. Naturally, such reasoning would have suited Hitler's purposes.

Ongoing German-Soviet Discord

Tensions over the Balkans reemerged some two weeks after the first anniversary of the Non-Aggression Pact when von Schulenburg handed Molotov a written summary of the Vienna negotiations. Molotov immediately accused the German side of being disloyal, since Article III of the pact stipulated that both sides were obliged to keep the other informed about common interests. Decisions made in Vienna, Molotov asserted, fell into that category, and the Soviet Union had been informed only after the fact. Molotov pointed out that when he had sought confirmation that a statement made by the German ambassador in Rome—that the Balkans question could be solved by Germany, Italy, and the Soviet Union—was the position of the German government, that confirmation had not been forthcoming. For its part, the Soviet Union had kept Germany fully informed of its intentions regarding Bessarabia and Bukovina. Molotov stressed that although the Soviet move against Bukovina had been confined to the northern part, he expected German support for Soviet interests in southern Bukovina as well.[50] Molotov was clearly alarmed by the international press coverage, which noted the absence of the Soviet side at the Vienna negotiations.

Molotov responded in greater and more critical detail to von Schulenburg's note of 9 September 1940 when the two men met again on 21 September. The thrust of Molotov's oral and written assertions was that the German government had failed to observe the provisions of Article III of the Non-Aggression Pact regarding consultation (Molotov also offered to discuss amending or repealing Article III). Von Schulenburg's immediate response was that since the conclusion of the pact in August 1939, the Soviet Union had made no claims with regard to Romania, and Soviet claims involving all of Bukovina represented a new factor that might lead to Romanian resistance. What really alarmed Molotov was the guarantee given to Romania, which he perceived—quite rightly—as being aimed against the Soviet Union and led, once again, to press speculation on precisely this point.

The detailed Soviet response to the German position was set out in a lengthy memorandum that was passed on to von Schulenburg.[51] The German position, it noted, was that after the Bessarabian question had been dealt with, Germany and the Soviet Union had no other common interests with regard to Hungary and Romania in the context of Article III of the Non-Aggression Pact. The Soviet view was that such a position contradicted Article III, since it ignored the parties' obligation to consult on what constituted their common interests. The disagreement over this article stemmed from the fact that each side, according to its circumstances and interests, saw an interest as being either static (resolved) or dynamic (still to be resolved and offering further opportunities). The German view of the Soviet interest in Bessarabia, as highlighted in the Soviet complaint, was static: the Bessarabian issue arose, it was dealt with, and the matter was closed. With regard to the Soviet interest in Romania, it could be seen as dynamic and subject to change (Bukovina, north and south, for example). Given the high strategic stakes, any move made by any party, whether apparently benign or obviously malign, ran the risk of changing what was understood as a common interest by either side. The other consequence amply demonstrated by this situation was that making and acting on territorial claims can become a habit that inevitably gives rise to conflict between two such rapacious powers.

On matters concrete, the Soviet side claimed that the transfer of a sizable part of Transylvania to Hungary, as well as guarantees given to Romania by Germany and Italy, undoubtedly fell within the scope of the consultation clause (as did negotiations over the Danube basin). The other Soviet complaint was that information was provided *post factum*—in other words, it was a fait accompli. Given that the Soviet Union had seized Bessarabia and northern Bukovina, assurances that it "did not intend to threaten the territorial inviolability of Romania" did not inspire confidence.[52] The nature of the German guarantee to Romania was especially alarming, since it gave rise to international press speculation that all was not well between Germany and the Soviet Union. This was a major theme in many of the exchanges between von Schulenburg and Molotov, and the Soviet side perceived it as an attempt by Western papers and governments to incite war between Germany and the Soviet Union. The real Soviet fear was that such attempts might succeed.

Germany duly informed the Soviet regime about the conclusion of the Tripartite Pact (the so-called Axis Pact), but no gloss could hide the fact that this pact, presented by Germany, Italy, and Japan as being directed against Western warmongers—Britain and various elements in the United States—had serious consequences for the Soviet Union. That Italy was a signatory to the Axis Pact was somewhat irrelevant, confirmed by the abysmal performance of the Italian army. The main development was that two potentially powerful enemies—Germany and Japan, both on Soviet borders—had come together. This certainly had implications for the British in the Far East and the naval base at Singapore, but it also represented a threat to the Soviet Union. Soviet unease was revealed by Molotov's requests for a copy of the treaty and any secret protocols attached to it. Upholding the finest traditions of his diplomatic calling, Werner von Tippelskirch, the German chargé d'affaires, refrained from pointing out that secret protocols were meant to be kept secret, and he merely agreed to pass on the request. Molotov also noted that various agencies were reporting that an agreement had been concluded between Germany and Finland, allowing German troops stationed in Norway to cross Finnish territory. Molotov requested a copy of that treaty and any secret protocols, basing these demands on Articles III and IV of the German-Soviet Non-Aggression Pact.

Meetings in October between von Schulenburg and Molotov revealed a series of issues that led to friction between the two sides. The composition of the Danube Basin Commission was one such matter. Germany wanted to include Italy, whereas Molotov pointed out, quite correctly, that Italy was not a Danube state and did not deserve to be a member of the commission, let alone enjoy the same rights as the Soviet Union.[53] Von Schulenburg agreed that Italy's inclusion was an anomaly, but given its present relations with Germany and the fact that Italy had been using the Danube for the last twelve years, it was not possible to exclude Italy from the commission. The Soviet side eventually gave in, but it had no illusions about Italy's role—it was essentially a German puppet—and it seems highly unlikely that the Italian position would carry much clout. Agreeing to the German request provided leverage for the Soviet side to extract a concession from Germany in the future. For his part, von Schulenburg was concerned that various issues associated with German nationals and ethnic Germans in the Baltic states and Bessarabia were not being properly handled by the Soviet side. One critical issue was that Germans were not being compensated for the nationalization of assets. Another problem was that Germans who were being evacuated were subjected to exceptionally high levels of taxation. According to von Schulenburg: "The taxes were so great that were they to be paid nothing would be left to the Germans. Moreover, the Germans have already paid taxes to the Romanians."[54] Another sign of trouble was the arrest of the German nonpermanent consul in Arensburg, of which Molotov claimed to have no knowledge. The deployment of German ground and air forces to Romania, connected (publicly, at least) with the defense of the Romanian oil fields, also alarmed Molotov and gave rise to accusations that, once again, the German side had failed to inform the Soviet Union in a timely manner.[55]

The highlight of the October meetings was a letter from von Ribbentrop to Stalin, which von Schulenburg passed on to Molotov on 17 October 1940. Von Ribbentrop's letter contained, among other things, an invitation for Molotov to visit Berlin. But it also set out Berlin's view of the war, the world, and the current state of German-Soviet relations. Timing is always important in diplomatic matters, and the question is why the Germans sought a face-to-face meeting with Molotov in Berlin at this time. Von Ribbentrop justified the meeting by claiming that, now and again, such meetings are inevitable. Indeed they are, and although this meeting may have been intended, on its face, to resolve some of the problems already noted, its other function was to shore up the "special relationship" between the two states at the very moment Hitler had decided to proceed with Barbarossa.

The unresolved war between Britain and Germany featured prominently in von Ribbentrop's letter, and the British were duly castigated for their attempt to lure the Soviet Union into a coalition against Germany. Von Ribbentrop accused the British of being perfidious in their relations with France and claimed that the British were using the French as their sword on the Continent. British military performance also left much to be desired. To quote von Ribbentrop: "Our troops have routed the British everywhere where they have encountered them in battle. The German soldier has everywhere demonstrated his superiority."[56] German successes justified this view, but Stalin might have perceived a threat in von Ribbentrop's exuberance. In fact, by laying out the scale of German military successes, von Ribbentrop was, in effect, telling the Soviet Union that it should discount the possibility of an alliance with Britain because Britain was finished, and in any case, an Anglo-Soviet alliance would never be able to withstand the might of German arms. One obvious flaw in von Ribbentrop's assessment of British military performance was that he ignored the defeat of the Luftwaffe in the summer of 1940. Furthermore, the longer an invasion was delayed, the stronger British defenses became. Any German invasion attempt that failed after Dunkirk was unlikely to succeed in the spring or summer of 1941. This German failure clearly had implications for the Soviet Union. In the event Germany was unable to deal with Britain, what would be its next major move—to the Mediterranean and Africa, or to eastern and southeastern Europe?

German moves in the Balkans had rattled the Soviet Union, as the exchanges between von Schulenburg and Molotov revealed. The lack of consultation was explained by the fast-moving situation and the need to forestall any British sabotage. Von Ribbentrop was far less convincing in downplaying the significance of the Axis Pact. It was, he said, "the logical continuation of the long-standing foreign policy conception of the German government on the strength of which German-Soviet and German-Japanese friendly cooperation may exist alongside without mutual hindrance."[57] These Bismarckian overtones, with their implicitly pro-Russian slant, could not hide the differences between Germany and the Soviet Union, which had been put to one side for the time being and were now complicated by Japan's alliance with Germany and Italy.

The fundamental contradictions and intractable nature of the German-Soviet relationship clearly emerged during Molotov's visit to Berlin in November, when he met with von Ribbentrop, Göring, and Hitler. Before Molotov was introduced to Hitler, von Ribbentrop prepared the way by setting out the nature of German-Soviet relations and returning to some of the points raised in the earlier letter to Stalin. He began with a summary of the war so far, insisting that Germany had already won the war and lecturing Molotov: "No state in the world is in a position to alter the situation created as a result of Germany's victories."[58] With regard to Britain, he was emphatic: "We are now experiencing the beginning of the end of the British Empire. Britain has been smashed and the matter of her recognizing this defeat is only a matter of time."[59] The impression conveyed by von Ribbentrop was that all Germany's efforts were now being aimed at the final defeat of Britain, which was somewhat inconsistent with the claim that Britain had already been smashed. It did not escape Molotov that much of this boasting was aimed at the Soviet Union. According to von Ribbentrop, Germany's position in Europe was unassailable: "The Axis rules absolutely supreme over a significant part of Europe both in military and political respects."[60] During this preliminary meeting, von Ribbentrop tried to persuade Molotov (or perhaps bully him into believing) that the Soviet Union's interests were in the south—a theme Hitler would return to with a vengeance during his meeting with the Soviet foreign minister. The German hope here was that the Soviet Union would succumb to the temptation to attack the British position in India. Von Ribbentrop's assurances to Molotov that Germany had no interest in this region must have seemed open to question, given earlier assurances that Germany had no political interest in Romania.

Turkey would play a major role in the German attempt to turn the Soviet Union south toward India. The selected lever was the 1936 Montreux Convention, which gave Turkey effective control over the passage of civilian and military shipping through the Dardanelles, the Bosporus, and the Sea of Marmara. Unlike Germany, the Soviet Union had signed the convention, but it now wanted to renegotiate the terms or replace it completely. As a concession to his guest, von Ribbentrop agreed that it was completely natural that the Soviet Union, as a Black Sea state, should enjoy special rights to this part of the world. "It is," he claimed, "completely absurd that other states enjoyed equal rights with the USSR or with other Black Sea states."[61] The obvious target here was Britain and her naval interests. In principle, von Ribbentrop's proposal may have sounded reassuring to Molotov, but surely he recalled that von Schulenburg had earlier insisted that even though Italy was not a Danube state, it should have equal rights with the Soviet Union. When it suited Germany, it was willing to grant special rights, implying that Germany was the final arbiter of who got what and that whatever privileges Germany bestowed on its allies, Germany was free to withdraw. German blandishments notwithstanding, von Ribbentrop's proposals were a clumsy attempt to signal that in the sphere of German-Soviet relations, Germany was primus inter pares.

Molotov also had some hardheaded questions concerning the meaning of the "new order" in Europe and the "great East Asian space." Von Ribbentrop dodged the issue, claiming that these issues posed no threat to Soviet interests, but they clearly introduced new factors into German-Soviet relations. What now was the status of the Non-Aggression Pact in light of these developments? Molotov argued that the spheres of interest established in 1939 "had been exhausted in the course of events of 1939–1940 with the exception of the Finnish question."[62] He was substantially correct, since the map of Europe had been radically changed by German military and political successes since the invasion of Poland. The critical question here was whether the central provision of the Non-Aggression Pact still applied if the spheres of interest established in 1939 had been exhausted or radically changed. The mutual nonaggression provisions of the 1939 pact assumed, and were based on, the status obtaining in Europe in August–September 1939. If these conditions changed, did this invalidate the mutual nonaggression provisions? Stalin certainly recognized the danger that the Germans might interpret Molotov's stance as meaning just that. Having received a summary of the Molotov–von Ribbentrop meeting, Stalin replied that it was necessary to say that the protocol to the pact was redundant, "but not the agreement [itself], since the expression 'the exhaustion of the agreement' could be understood by the Germans to mean the exhaustion of the Non-Aggression Treaty, which would, of course, be incorrect."[63]

When Molotov met Hitler on 12 November 1940, Hitler began by telling his guest, "It is difficult to establish the course of future development. Questions concerning future conflicts depend on personal factors which are decisive in political life."[64] What Hitler meant was that the future might be difficult to discern, but personal factors, such as Hitler's will and ambition, would triumph, since he was a world historical figure, a prime mover in the world's political life, not just Germany's. Hitler was the secular god who determined whether nations would exist, and Molotov and his master would be well advised to bear that in mind. Judging by the summary of the meeting Molotov sent to Stalin, the Soviet foreign minister was not overwhelmed by this master-of-the-universe rhetoric. Yet, despite the view articulated in NS ideology and, above all, in *Mein Kampf* that war is an inevitable and ineradicable element in the life of states, Hitler informed Molotov that he sought to remove friction and conflict from German-Soviet relations. Was Hitler proposing that diplomacy replace war, or did he see diplomacy as just one phase of war, a short-term, pragmatic solution to a problem that would eventually have to be resolved by force of arms?

Alert to Soviet concerns about German moves in Romania, Hitler insisted that these actions had been unforeseen. The Soviet record of the meeting notes the following: "It is clear," Hitler asserted, "that in connection with such a huge expansion of the war (the Germans) were compelled to enter into those regions which were necessary for defense but which did not interest Germany either politically or economically."[65] Hitler's separation of the political and economic dimension from the purely defensive was utterly implausible, since the decisive factor in Romania was a secure supply of oil, without which Germany, as a continental power blockaded by the Royal Navy, could not continue to prosecute the war. Any move by the Soviet Union that threatened German access to this oil, such as the seizure of Bessarabia and northern Bukovina, would constitute a political, economic, and military threat and thus be a source of conflict. Hitler also sought to allay Soviet fears about German expansion to the east (a central policy articulated in *Mein Kampf*). The Soviet minutes record the following:

> Germany needs territory but as a consequence of the war it has completely secured enough territory for more than a hundred years. Germany requires additions to her colonies but she can get these in Central Africa, in regions that are of no interest to the USSR (it is a matter of old German colonies with several amendments). Certain raw materials are also required and moreover that question needs to be solved as soon as possible. Meeting these demands in no way infringes upon Russian interests, since, on the other hand, one can conceive of the future development of Russia without any injury to German interests.[66]

During this phase of the meeting, Hitler, as recorded in the Soviet minutes, coined the phrase "blood creates rights,"[67] which meant that the spilling of German blood in a war caused by British and French refusal to meet German demands must be paid for. This expression is consistent with the NS ideological view of Germany's world mission and can be interpreted to mean that blood confers special rights, such as liberation from legal, moral, and cultural norms in the *Kampf* (struggle) for survival and domination. For Molotov, this provided food for thought: if the current targets of this blood-based creed were Britain and France—fellow western Europeans that Hitler acknowledged as the founders of great cultures and civilizations—what could the inhabitants of the Russian lands expect when the hour arrived?

Hitler foresaw a greatly increased US role in world affairs. He argued that the United States was not fighting for Britain but was endeavoring to seize its own legacy and replace the British Empire. The rise of the United States had to be countered, and toward this end, Hitler argued for something like a European version of the Monroe Doctrine (1823) that would include Europe and Africa, although this, he said, was a matter not for 1940 but for 1970 or 2000.[68]

Molotov was not carried away by Hitler's grand strategic visions and, at the appropriate moment, turned toward more immediate matters: Finland; the Axis Pact, and the new order in Europe. Concerning Finland, Molotov's view was that this was the sole area of German-Soviet relations that had violated the 1939 agreement. As for the Axis Pact, it had clear implications for the Balkans, and these issues had to be resolved. Hitler was vague on what would constitute a new order in Europe, and possibly for good reason. A new order would be predicated on either equal rights for all participating states or a leadership role for one state. That one state would effectively be the master of the new order and would dominate the continent of Europe. Would the Soviet Union be subordinate to Germany, or would it enjoy an equal partnership? Various pacts and trade agreements between Germany and the Soviet Union could provide short-term advantages for both states, but a permanent new order in Europe was fraught with problems. Neither Germany nor the Soviet Union would accept inferior status, and equal status would result in permanent tensions that would eventually exhaust the two states' capacity and willingness to make concessions in order to avoid war.

A theme in all of Molotov's meetings with Hitler and others in Berlin was that the British defeat was merely a matter of time. Göring, the head of the Luftwaffe, assured Molotov that Royal Air Force attacks on Berlin were causing few problems and no major damage. According to Göring, at this time of year, the prevailing winds blew from the west, which prevented British bombers from reaching Berlin. This was a bizarre explanation, since winds from the west would assist British bombers on their flight to Berlin. Headwinds on the return journey would increase fuel consumption, but this would be partly compensated by the fact that, having dropped their bomb loads, the planes would be lighter. That Göring devotes so much time to downplaying the impact of British bombing on the German capital (it is noteworthy that he says nothing about British air attacks farther west) suggests that the effects were not so negligible. Even if British bombing was largely ineffective at this stage of the war, the fact that the British were bombing cities and other targets inside Germany and German-occupied Europe at all was proof that Britain was not out of the war.[69]

Göring, privy to Hitler's plans to attack the Soviet Union, made his own contribution to attempts to deceive Molotov about the state of German-

Soviet relations. He told his guest that Germany "has conducted a complete reorientation of foreign policy" and that this reorientation was "the final and irreversible decision of the German government."[70] This highlights one of the flaws and strengths of Nazi foreign policy, especially in its dealings with the Soviet Union. As articulated by nineteenth-century British statesman Lord Palmerston, states have permanent interests, not permanent friends. In part, permanent interests arise from, and are imposed by, geography. For that reason, geographic factors limit what can be achieved by diplomacy and political meddling. The German reorientation could not be "irreversible." Located on the fringe of northwestern Europe, England, for example, has always looked to the seas, not to the continental landmass of Europe. For Germany, Russia—whether in its tsarist or Soviet manifestation—must always figure in German diplomatic and military considerations. The fundamental truth is that two great peoples, the Russians and the Germans, have interests that, more likely than not, will bring them into conflict. The politics may change, but the underlying conflicts of interest remain. For short-term purposes, the fundamental nature of a relationship between states can be ignored, much as Blitzkrieg can obviate the need for total war. The German-Soviet Non-Aggression Pact is a superb example of a hastily improvised diplomatic response to a problem. It startled the generally conservative diplomacy of Britain and France precisely because, in diplomatic terms, the Non-Aggression Pact was not conservative. It was created by two revolutionary regimes that violated the established, perhaps too comfortable, norms of diplomacy and did not play by the rules. However much military utility Hitler and Stalin derived from the pact, and however much pleasure they derived from the discomfiture of Britain and France, the pact could not remove the deep-seated ideological and military rivalry between NS Germany and the Soviet Union. Between them, Germany and the Soviet Union might have carried out a revolution in diplomatic affairs. However, given the geographic factors and the irreconcilable nature of the two regimes, Göring's assertion that Germany had totally and irreversibly reoriented its policies toward the Soviet Union could not be true.

Complications were evident in the delivery of goods and raw materials between the two states. For its part, the Soviet Union met delivery timetables, but the German side was behind schedule. Göring explained that these delays arose from war damage in the occupied territories, which, given the brevity of the campaign, was not plausible. The crux of this delivery problem was revealed in the Soviet request for a certain type of armored plate, which, according to Göring, could not be produced owing to unspecified technical reasons. Göring suspected—and Molotov realized that Göring suspected—that the Soviet side actually wanted to acquire a sample of armored plate for analysis. In return for raw materials, the Soviet regime was hoping to harvest German industrial secrets (industrial espionage, in other words). When Molotov asked Göring to clarify what was regarded as secret, he was clearly probing the nature and extent of this secrecy, which was useful information in itself.

At the start of his second meeting with Molotov on 13 November 1940 (which lasted three and a half hours), Hitler rejected the Soviet claim that Germany had not observed the pact with regard to Finland. Hitler tried to argue his case by reference to Bukovina. Bukovina represented, Hitler claimed, a new factor that had been accommodated and for which allowances could be made. He then stated, "In relation to Finland, Germany occupies a totally analogous position."[71] In support of an apparently pro-Soviet position, Hitler admitted he had ordered that shipping deliveries to Finland be detained, conceding to Molotov that "he had no right to do that."[72] This was not entirely pro-Soviet behavior; it merely underlined that Hitler would act outside the law—any law—if need be. This clearly had implications for German-Soviet treaties as well. Hitler repeated the earlier position on Finland set out by von Ribbentrop: German interests in Finland and Romania were purely economic—timber and nickel from Finland, oil from Romania.

Hitler stressed Germany's need to prevent the Baltic from becoming a zone of military operations and cited the threat posed by British long-range bombers and fighters, which could reach Finnish ports. At this juncture, one wonders whether Molotov recalled that Göring had assured him that British bombers could not reach Berlin because of the prevailing winds from the west. Clearly, if British bombers could reach Finnish ports, they could reach the German capital. Hitler's insistence on the British threat to Finland and to the Baltic area in general—the justification for Germany's military interest—did not impress Molotov, as indicated by the Soviet record of the meeting:

> Molotov said that he did not understand why the question of a war in the Baltic Sea was being so vigorously asserted. Last year the situation was much more complicated and there was no mention of any war. Germany had managed to defeat France, not to mention Belgium, Holland, Denmark and Norway, and in addition considers Britain

to be defeated. So from where now does the danger of a war in the Baltic Sea arise? Germany is bound to conduct that policy in relation to the interests of the USSR provided for in last year's treaty, a policy which it conducted last year without any reservations. Nothing more is required.[73]

The basic point asserted by Molotov was that Finland constituted a new factor. The British threat was illusory, a flimsy pretext for German action in Finland.

Likewise, Hitler used the British threat to justify the movement of German troops into Romania (he apparently forgot that he considered the British defeated). The most striking thing about this meeting, and also evident in Molotov's dealings with von Ribbentrop and Göring, was the contrast in styles. Hitler used weak arguments to bolster some policy position. When that failed, he moved to another subject or tried to present the subject in terms of decades in the future. Thus, when prevaricating about the great Asian sphere, Hitler claimed it had a central Asian element "which stretches to the south, securing an exit to the open sea, and is envisaged by Germany as a sphere of Russian interests."[74] According to Hitler, achieving this goal would require some 50 to 100 years. When Hitler could convince his interlocutors to suspend their disbelief and their critical faculties, or when he ranted and raved, he could secure his diplomatic aims. Confronted, however, with a stubborn and determined negotiator like Molotov, who was not bewitched by Hitler's man-of-destiny pose and would not allow himself to be diverted from Soviet interests—Finland and the defense guarantee given to Romania by Germany and Italy without consulting the Soviet Union—Hitler was unable to get his way. One senses the existence of insurmountable differences that were not amenable to any stable or permanent diplomatic solution.

These differences emerged in Molotov's second meeting with von Ribbentrop, which, despite Göring's insistence that the Royal Air Force could not reach Berlin, took place in von Ribbentrop's air-raid shelter between 2100 and 2400 hours because of a British air raid. Von Ribbentrop's opening move was to raise the possibility of closer cooperation between the Axis and the Soviet Union. The Soviet record notes that von Ribbentrop recited the articles of a short draft agreement that made the brazen claim (among a fair number attributable to von Ribbentrop) that the Axis's aim in drawing up the agreement was to "prevent the war from becoming a global conflict."[75] He hoped the Soviet Union would cooperate with the Axis to meet this aim and that the parties could resolve their differences "in a friendly spirit" and would not support any alliances aimed at any other party. Von Ribbentrop proposed that the agreement be valid for ten years, with provisions for the addition of secret supplementary protocols. The proposed agreement was, in reality, an attempt to divert Soviet attention to the south, toward the Indian Ocean and India itself, in the hope that the Soviet Union would then become embroiled in a conflict with Britain.

On the issue of Turkey, Molotov made three points: (1) the Soviet Union needed to reach an agreement with Turkey regarding the straits; (2) the Soviet Union rejected the Montreux Convention, and (3) British attacks through the straits had to be prevented.[76] Obviously, both Germany and the Soviet Union were exploiting the threat posed by Britain. Hitler claimed the British were finished, yet he used the British threat to justify German moves in Finland and Romania. Von Ribbentrop was playing the same double game as his master. When it suited him, he told Molotov that the British were finished, yet he claimed that certain questions could not be resolved because the war was not yet over. The Soviet notes attribute the following to von Ribbentrop: "At that moment when Britain acknowledges that she is defeated and sues for peace Germany will limit her economic interests and German troops will be withdrawn from Romania. Ribbentrop wants to repeat, once again, that Germany has no territorial interests there."[77] This would not have been much comfort to Molotov.

For his part, Molotov used past British naval incursions into the Black Sea and this supposedly ongoing threat to secure more concessions from Bulgaria and Turkey. Any British threat in the Black Sea was illusory, and Molotov knew it. Mockingly, he pointed out that if Germany were engaged in a life-and-death struggle against Britain, and Germany were more or less victorious, what was Britain fighting for, "her death"? As far as the Soviet Union was concerned, the real threat in the Black Sea was Germany. This might explain why Molotov instructed von Ribbentrop that he "must agree with the position that Germany is not a Black Sea power."[78] Molotov deliberately overstated the danger to Soviet security in the straits to justify the presence of Soviet troops in Bulgaria, which had nothing to do with a British threat and *everything* to do with countering German influence in the Balkans. This was Molotov's main reason for telling von Ribbentrop that the Soviet Union could not be indifferent to what happened in Romania and Bulgaria. Farther north, the same Soviet concerns emerged, which was why Molotov wanted to know whether Germany was still committed to the idea of Swedish neutrality. In both the south and the north, German moves were a potential military threat. The invitation for the Soviet Union to join the Axis was just another German trap.

Molotov addressed the German proposal for the creation of a pact of four on 25 November 1940 in Moscow. In fact, there were two separate items on the meeting agenda. The other involved economic cooperation, which had more or less ground to a halt. Von Schulenburg, accompanied by Schnurre, attempted to get things moving. The stumbling block concerned grain deliveries. Germany required a delivery of 2.5 million tonnes, a figure that included grain normally received from the Baltic states and Bessarabia. Schnurre also raised the issues of compensation for the cellulose processing plant in Keksgolm, a part of Finland that had been ceded to the Soviet Union; compensation for ethnic Germans and German citizens in the Baltic states; and repayment of the Czech credit loan to buy machine tools, which had been delivered in full by Skoda. During these discussions with Schnurre, it came out that Finland had agreed to supply Germany with 60 percent of the nickel ore mined in Petsamo, an agreement that, as far as Molotov was concerned, infringed on a Soviet interest in that part of the world. On the question of the provision of Finnish nickel ore, Schnurre argued that deliveries were covered by a German-Finnish agreement "concluded not for 1940 or 1941 but for an indefinite period."[79] The German position was that Molotov should not try to change the period over which the ore was to be delivered. Molotov more or less dismissed the agreement by noting he had not seen it and therefore the Soviet Union could offer no guarantees. The real issue here was not about Finnish nickel ore, although that was clearly important to Germany. Molotov and Schnurre were trying to assert the primacy of their respective interests in Finland. Apparently, German-Soviet diplomatic relations had started to break down during or after Molotov's visit to Berlin, and the process of deterioration was accelerating.

That German-Soviet relations were deteriorating or attitudes were hardening is suggested by the Soviet conditions for joining the Axis: (1) the withdrawal of German troops from Finland, since this was a Soviet sphere of influence (the Soviet Union would guarantee the supply of nickel ore and timber); (2) the conclusion of a mutual-assistance pact with Bulgaria and the long-term lease of naval and military bases; (3) recognition that the area south of Batumi and Baku toward the Persian Gulf was a center of Soviet interests; and (4) Japan's renunciation of its concessionary rights to coal and oil on North Sakhalin.[80] Molotov also proposed various secret supplementary protocols.

Flinty silence was the German response to these Soviet conditions. Eventually, on 17 January 1941, Molotov expressed irritation at the German side's failure to reply, as well as concern about German behavior. He wrote in a note to von Schulenburg:

> According to all information German troops have been concentrated in Romania in large numbers and have already been prepared for entry into Bulgaria, having as their aim the occupation of Bulgaria, Greece and the Straits. There can be no doubt that Britain will endeavor to prevent the operations of German troops and occupy the Straits and, in alliance with Turkey, commence military operations against Bulgaria, so transforming Bulgaria into a war zone. The Soviet government has on several occasions stated to the German government that it considers the territory of Bulgaria and both Straits to be a security zone of the USSR in view of which it cannot remain unconcerned in relation to events threatening the security interests of the USSR.
>
> In view of the above the Soviet government considers itself duty bound to warn that the appearance of any foreign armed forces on the territory of Bulgaria and on both Straits shall be considered to be a violation of the security interests of the USSR.[81]

The German government's response to the Soviet proposals was delivered on 23 January 1941. Von Schulenburg stressed that German actions in Bulgaria were contingency moves in the event it became necessary to act against the British, whereas Molotov stated that the Soviet Union wanted to prevent the Black Sea region from becoming a war zone. This is an excellent example of a well-established problem in international diplomacy: Measures taken by one state to enhance its security are interpreted by another state as a threat, leading to countermeasures. This evokes another security response, and the cycle of measures and countermeasures escalates, provoking the very conflict that such measures were designed to prevent. As the Soviet record of the meeting shows, von Schulenburg somewhat disingenuously tried to link German and Soviet behavior, claiming that "the interests of the USSR and Germany run parallel. Germany also has no interest in the transformation of the Black Sea into a theater of military operations. . . . In his opinion, the response of the German government speaks for the fact that a precondition for the entry of German troops into Bulgaria would be an attempt by Britain to establish herself in Greece."[82] So, at the end of January 1941, the British—written off by von Ribbentrop, Hitler, and Göring in November 1940—were far from vanquished. In fact, they were prompting all kinds of fears about their intentions in Greece. Once again, the British provided a suitable pretext for German and Soviet moves, presenting opportunities for each side to deceive the other.

The Endgame

Starting in March 1941, there were signs of strain in German-Soviet relations. The main sources of friction were familiar ones, but there were new ones as well: Bulgaria, the Baltic states, German access to Finnish nickel ore, and accusations that TASS journalists were engaging in anti-German propaganda by amplifying parts of the Soviet government's statement on Bulgaria.[83] On 1 March von Schulenburg notified Molotov that Germany would be deploying troops in Bulgaria to counter British moves in Greece. As expected, Molotov condemned the deployment as a threat to Soviet security interests.[84] In the Baltic states the matter of the resettlement of German nationals and the issue of compensation were still unresolved. There were also signs that the NKVD was conducting sweeps and arresting those deemed to be anti-Soviet elements. Thus, 300 ethnic Germans had been arrested by the NKVD in Kovno, another 43 in Riga, and 41 in Tallin.[85] German requests that its diplomatic representatives be permitted to remain in the Baltic states were denied on the pretext that no exception could be made for Germany.[86] In the same spirit, Germany refused to issue extra visas for Soviet officials to travel to Paris.[87] On the question of German access to Finnish nickel ore, the Soviet side clearly rejected any German claim that the delivery of ore was for an indefinite period and confined itself to meeting deliveries for "the time span of the Soviet-German Non-Aggression Pact."[88] Later assurances that the Soviet side would take into account the two agreements concluded between Germany and Finland on 24 July and 16 September 1940 meant very little.[89]

The British ambassador in Moscow, Sir Stafford Cripps, drew certain conclusions based on his various sources. In an off-the-record briefing to British and American journalists, some of whom, such as Walter Duranty, were well-known Soviet sympathizers who could be relied on to pass the word, Cripps let it be known that "Soviet-German relations are definitely deteriorating and Vyshinskii's statement on the Bulgarian question was a markedly open expression of Soviet dissatisfaction with Germany. A *Soviet-*

German war is inevitable. Many reliable diplomatic sources from Berlin are reporting that Germany is planning to attack the Soviet Union this year, probably, in the summer."[90] The British were certainly not disinterested bystanders, and they had obvious motives for sending this message to their Soviet hosts, but the diplomatic pointers were clear enough. Strains in the German-Soviet relationship could no longer be hidden.

Behind the scenes, there was also clear evidence of hardening attitudes and mutual recriminations. On 4 April 1941 Molotov informed von Schulenburg that the Soviet Union was going to conclude a five-year nonaggression pact with Yugoslavia. Von Schulenburg was not impressed by this news and observed (rather late in the day, in view of German behavior) that such a pact would only increase tensions. He also pointed to a series of anti-German incidents inside Yugoslavia: the German envoy had been hissed in Belgrade, the German military attaché had been beaten up, and—obviously unable to recall *Kristallnacht*—German shops had been smashed.[91] Further evidence of German-Soviet friction was the fact that Germans scheduled for resettlement in Germany were being arrested in the Baltic states.

Meanwhile, Stalin was looking elsewhere for diplomatic successes—specifically, he hoped to conclude a Soviet-Japanese neutrality pact. The Soviet record of the meeting between Stalin and Matsuoka, the Japanese ambassador, reveals Stalin's highly successful and deceptive pose of friendliness and openness. The Soviet transcript recorded the following Stalin gem for posterity:

> Further, Comrade Stalin said that he had listened with great pleasure to Matsuoka, who had talked honestly and directly about what he wanted. He had listened with pleasure since in our time, and not only in our time, one very rarely encountered a diplomat who would speak openly about what was on his mind. As is well known, Talleyrand in Napoleon's time said that a diplomat had been given a tongue in order to hide his thoughts. We, Russian Bolsheviks, see things differently and think that it is possible in the diplomatic arena to be sincere and honest.[92]

The meeting with Matsuoka also hinted that Stalin was well aware of the growing military threat posed by Germany. He told Matsuoka that any four-power pact (Germany, the Soviet Union, Italy, and Japan) would be one of mutual assistance and that, "if Germany does need assistance, this means that the four-power pact is still not ready."[93] The wording is misleading, since it was the Soviet side's various conditions for joining any four-power pact that had prompted Germany to reject a pact of mutual assistance. Recall, too, that one of the Soviet Union's stipulations for joining the other three powers in a new pact was Japan's renunciation of any concessions to coal and oil in northern Sakhalin. Yet here, in his discussion with Matsuoka, Stalin's tone was far more conciliatory. The main Soviet fear about Sakhalin, analogous to its fear about the Black Sea, was that Japan possessed too many choke holds on Soviet naval access to the Pacific. In any event, the Soviet-Japanese neutrality pact was finally concluded on 13 April 1941.

German-Soviet relations continued to deteriorate throughout May. By now, Hitler's assurances that Germany had no territorial or political interests in the Balkans, assiduously passed on by von Schulenburg, were not being taken seriously in Moscow. Von Schulenburg reported that Hitler was angered by the neutrality pact concluded between the Soviet Union and Yugoslavia and irritated by recent Soviet statements: "These statements from the Soviet government create the impression that the Soviet Union is trying to prevent Germany from exercising her vital interests, to prevent Germany's striving to conquer Britain."[94] One unwelcome consequence of the Soviet-Yugoslav pact, as far as von Schulenburg was concerned, was the obvious joy it gave Churchill. The change in tone toward Britain was apparent: the conquest of Britain, which Hitler, Göring, and von Ribbentrop had assured Molotov in November 1940 was a *certainty*, had now become a *striving* to conquer Britain. Worse still were the rumors in Britain of a war between the Soviet Union and Germany, which had been circulating since January. When asked by Dekanozov to identify the source of these rumors, von Schulenburg evaded the question. However, the Soviet transcript notes: "In any case, in Schulenburg's opinion, rumors of a forthcoming war between the Soviet Union and Germany are explosive and they have to be countered, their force broken."[95] In a follow-up meeting with Dekanozov on 9 May 1941, the Soviet deputy minister wasted no time in reciting a series of Soviet grievances: German guarantees to Romania, German troops in Bulgaria, German procrastination over ratification of a border treaty involving the Igorka River–Baltic Sea boundary, and the still unresolved dispute over access to Finnish nickel ore in Petsamo.[96]

The main subject of the meeting that took place on 12 May 1941 appeared to be a joint communiqué to quash rumors about a conflict between Germany and the Soviet Union. Yet the most significant development was the change in attitude toward Britain and its refusal to sue for peace. For example, von

Schulenburg now conceded that even if British air raids were causing negligible damage in Berlin, fairly serious damage was being inflicted on Bremen, Kiel, and Hamburg.[97] The Soviet transcript states: "In his opinion, moreover, the time is not that far off when they (the belligerent parties) must come to an agreement and then the disasters and destruction being caused to the cities of both countries will cease."[98] This assessment by von Schulenburg represented a dramatic shift in stated German attitudes toward Britain. Gone was the boasting by Hitler and Göring that Britain was doomed; in its place was a willingness to consider some kind of an agreement. This shift in the German position was clearly aimed at the Soviet Union, since an agreement with Britain would remove the possibility of a war on two fronts for Germany in the event of a German attack on the Soviet Union. Von Schulenburg's announcement of this shift might have had something to do with Rudolf Hess's flight to Britain on 10 May 1941, since it played on the very real Soviet fears that Hess had gone to Britain to negotiate some kind of a deal.

In fact, Dekanozov prepared a preliminary report on the Hess affair indicating that the central worry was indeed that Hess's trip was related to an agreement between Germany and Britain.[99] Although some of the papers and documents relating to the Hess affair are still not in the public domain, the one question that can be reasonably posed and possibly answered is who actually benefited from Hess's actions. The obvious answer is Britain. By flying to Britain, Hess caused huge diplomatic embarrassment to the NS regime. Even if he had no intimate knowledge of the planning for Barbarossa, he might have picked up some information in party circles, so there was a risk that German planning would be compromised at this very late stage and that the British—naturally, in the spirit of unsullied interest—would pass on any material they obtained to Stalin. British historian Alan Clark claims that Hess did in fact provide information about Barbarossa to the British.[100] The timing of the flight was also perfect, since it occurred during a period of worsening German-Soviet relations and fueled Stalin's suspicions that the Germans were planning another sensational nonaggression pact, this time with Britain, as a prelude to attacking the Soviet Union. If that happened, Germany would be liberated from the threat of a war on two fronts, and the Soviet Union would have to confront Germany alone. Allan Bullock notes that the British, much to Hitler's surprise, did not exploit the propaganda advantage of Hess's arrival.[101] The low-key British approach, I suggest, was quite deliberate and calculated to arouse Stalin's paranoia that something dark and unseemly was happening between Germany and Britain. The goal was either to draw Stalin closer to Britain or perhaps to bring matters to a head between Germany and the Soviet Union.

The final moves, public and private, in the diplomatic game between Germany and the Soviet Union had something of an unreal quality. On 13 June 1941, nine days before the charade came to an abrupt end, TASS issued a communiqué that encapsulated the fear, uncertainty, prevarication, and wishful thinking that now gripped Stalin. The communiqué was prompted by a maelstrom of rumors that a war between the Soviet Union and Germany was imminent. The wording of the communiqué leaves little doubt that, publicly at any rate, the Soviet Union considered the British ambassador to Moscow, Sir Stafford Cripps, responsible for these rumors. Cripps's earlier off-the-record briefing probably helped ensure this Soviet finger-pointing, but Cripps was obviously a scapegoat. Seasoned diplomatic observers would not have been fooled.

Both openly and behind the scenes, the attempt to counter the rumors was not convincing. Any diplomat or military attaché who had been following the border changes in territories occupied by Germany and the Soviet Union since September 1939, never mind subsequent German and Soviet moves in Bulgaria and Romania, would have noted that the use of "borders" in the TASS communiqué now meant something quite different. Thus, the communiqué's acknowledgment that German units returning from operations in the Balkans were now being deployed in the eastern and northeastern regions of Germany—contiguous to Soviet territory—raised the question of why these units were being sent there. In this context, von Schulenburg's hint that Germany might conclude a deal with Britain undercut or rendered redundant the German disinformation line that these deployments were in preparation for an invasion of Britain. It also weakened speculation by TASS that these deployments had nothing to do with Soviet-German relations. The communiqué raised the question of why the Soviet Union had not submitted a formal request for clarification and made the response public. Nor was it the case—as Molotov made clear to von Schulenburg—that the German side had unswervingly observed the provisions of the Non-Aggression Pact. This was a hostage to fortune, since when the German attack came, it lent some credence to the German claim that Germany had honored the pact—TASS said so only last week, after all—but the Soviet Union had not. Soviet misery and humiliation were compounded by the German response to the TASS statement: a damning and contemptuous silence.

The TASS claim that all was in order was demonstrably undermined by the Soviet record of a meeting between von Schulenburg and Vyshinskii on 14 June 1941, the day after the TASS communiqué was written and the day its text was published in *Izvestiia*, among other outlets. After all this time, there are still unresolved problems involving the Baltic states, especially the resettlement of Germans. However, the matter that catches the eye is the departure of a number of aristocrats and eminent Poles for Germany. Von Schulenburg, on behalf of the kings of Sweden and Italy, submitted a request for a list of names to Vyshinskii. Even though the German ambassador stressed—possibly too much—that Germany had no interest in this matter and was merely passing on the request of others, one must suspect an ulterior motive. Vyshinskii's response to this inquiry was to point out that, with the promulgation of the Supreme Soviet decree of 29 November 1939, these Poles were Soviet citizens, and there was no reason for the request to be processed. I suspect that the request for information about these Poles was related to the mass murders at Katyn and other sites in March 1940. Royal families tend to have many international links and relatives abroad, and it is possible that the Swedish and Italians had heard rumors of the executions. Vyshinskii was in charge of the sovietization of Latvia, which included the deportation and execution of anti-Soviet elements. He was clearly dissembling, since he would have been well aware of the implications of von Schulenburg's inquiry. The Soviet record of the meeting concludes with an ominous observation: "It is important to note that Schulenburg uttered not a single word about the TASS report of 14.04."[102] The date cited in the record—14 April—is a typographical error, given that the meeting took place on 14 June 1941.

In one of his last meetings with von Schulenburg on 21 June 1941, Molotov raised the issue of the TASS communiqué, noting that it had not been published in Germany. Von Schulenburg offered no explanation and studiously avoided any discussion of its contents. When pressed about German troop deployments, von Schulenburg replied that, according to Hitler, the concentrations of German troops on the Soviet border were "precautionary measures."[103] Von Schulenburg was also handed a memorandum detailing violations of Soviet airspace.

Accompanied by Gustav Hilger, von Schulenburg delivered the declaration of war to Molotov at 0530 hours on 22 June 1941, giving Molotov a taste of the same poison he had delivered to the hapless Kotsinsh, the Latvian envoy, a year ago. "In view of the intolerable further threats which have been created for the eastern German borders as a consequence of the massed concentration and preparation of all the armed forces of the Red Army, the German government considers itself compelled immediately to take military countermeasures."[104] When Molotov asked what the note meant, von Schulenburg replied that is was the start of war. Because the Russian language has no definite or indefinite article, it is not clear whether the Russian *nachalo voiny* means the start of "a war"—that is, something unforeseen and unexpected—or the start of "the war"—that is, the war Germany had long been planning and that Stalin had sought to avert and, when that was no longer possible, willfully to deny.

Later that day, Molotov addressed the Soviet people over the radio, a task that Stalin should have undertaken himself at such a dangerous moment. What emerges clearly in Molotov's speech, as well as in Stalin's own radio address on 3 July 1941, is the outrage born of the knowledge that Stalin and Molotov, both master schemers and plotters, have been totally outmaneuvered and outwitted by Hitler. Speculation about the Germans' hostile intent in the international press and the clumsy denials in the TASS communiqué a week previously, not to mention the disregarded intelligence summaries, all helped expose Stalin's grotesque miscalculations about Hitler's intentions. The international humiliation inflicted on Stalin and Molotov by Hitler is palpable. On behalf of his shell-shocked boss, Molotov—who had colluded with von Ribbentrop to destroy Poland, imposed the cruel deception of treaties of friendship on the Baltic states, and used all kinds of spurious pretexts to justify the seizure of Bessarabia and northern Bukovina—in a fit of self-righteous rage, now declared that the German invasion was "an act of treachery unparalleled in the history of civilized peoples," launched in spite of the Non-Aggression Pact.[105] All Molotov's pitiful complaining about German violation of the pact and his instant and reflexive recourse to ideological insults such as "fascist" (rather neatly drawing attention to the fact that the Soviet Union had concluded a Non-Aggression Pact with *fascist* Germany) could not hide the fact that Hitler had acted with consummate skill, delivering Stalin and Molotov a master class in duplicity and treachery.

Conclusion

From the very beginning of what appeared to be a rapprochement between the Soviet Union and Germany in August 1939, the two parties relentlessly sought to maximize their territorial, economic, and military gains at the expense of the other party. This was done openly, if there was no other option; preferably, it was done covertly. In 1939 Poland, partitioned by the two totalitarian states, ceased to exist. In 1940 the Soviet Union seized Bessarabia and northern Bukovina while keeping an edacious eye focused on southern Bukovina. Later, the Soviet Union forcibly incorporated Estonia, Latvia, and Lithuania into the USSR and then brutally sovietized them. German moves in Romania and Bulgaria and the punitive military action against Yugoslavia were aimed primarily at the Soviet Union, regardless of whether these operations were also intended to thwart British ambitions in the Balkans. Disputes over access to Finnish nickel ore, never-ending negotiations over borders, and protestations from von Schulenburg that German nationals in the Baltic states were being dispossessed of assets without compensation all added to the expanding mix of mutual distrust and suspicion.

November 1940, the occasion of Molotov's visit to Berlin, was when the contradictions in German-Soviet relations become irreconcilable. The documents cited here suggest that both parties knew it. The contrast between the Soviet Union's response to the real or perceived infringement of its interests in the diplomatic sphere and its response to the alarming signs of a German military buildup on its western borders is stark. While the diplomatic relationship lasted, Molotov demonstrated a clear-headed grasp of the essential details, never losing sight of Soviet interests and stubbornly refusing to be diverted by von Ribbentrop or Hitler. Diplomatically, the Soviet Union was alert to all the dangers, using every opportunity to avert or counter them; militarily, it was paralyzed, even though some in its intelligence agencies recognized the danger. The fate of Austria, Czechoslovakia, and Poland is instructive. Even forceful diplomacy (and Anglo-French diplomacy was not forceful) is doomed to fail if it is not based on a willingness to act. All the signs were there: diplomatic posturing alone would fail to deter Hitler, who respected only the efficacy of violence. Stalin believed he had the measure of the snake, but the snake bit him.

4 The Soviet Intelligence Assessment of German Military Intentions, 1939–1941

The profession of arms calls above all for clear-headed thinking, and any self-deception must sooner or later exact a bitter revenge. Bullets and shells are not to be deflected from their trajectory by chatter.

Bruno H. Jahn, Die Weisheit des Soldaten, 1937

There is a point in any mystery when the shape of the answer becomes suddenly clear.

Peter Wright, Spycatcher, 1987

Stalin was exceptionally well informed about German preparations for an attack against the Soviet Union. For example, Churchill gave him advance warning of a German attack, and Soviet agents in Germany and Japan confirmed the information provided by Churchill. Basic intelligence tradecraft conducted by the NKGB, NKVD, and Soviet General Staff also produced a detailed picture of German military intentions. Even though German army and SS formations achieved complete tactical surprise along the entire front on 22 June 1941, the long and sustained military buildup of men and equipment—a huge logistical operation carried out over many months—could not escape detection and had been carefully monitored by the various Soviet intelligence agencies. It is only very recently that substantial amounts of material about Soviet intelligence assessments of the threat have been declassified and made available to historians. This material—and there is almost certainly more to come—fills in huge gaps in the historical record, especially on the Soviet side, concerning what was known about the military planning for Barbarossa. In one sense, this new information answers many questions about the efficacy of Soviet intelligence. Clearly, its officers and agent handlers were doing a very good job. Yet it also makes Stalin's failure to take robust countermeasures, when confronted with an avalanche of raw data, numbers, and clear hostile intent, all the more perplexing.

Introduction

The German invasion of Poland demonstrated the efficacy of the Blitzkrieg doctrine. Nine months later, the doctrinal success of Blitzkrieg was once again confirmed when France, the Netherlands, and Belgium were overwhelmed and British arms suffered one of its most humiliating defeats. On 17 September 1939 the Red Army, acting on the basis of secret protocols annexed to the Non-Aggression Pact, invaded Poland. After the dismembering of Poland, the close contact between the German army and the Red Army, various civilian agencies, and the security agencies of both states meant that, despite the serpentine niceties of diplomacy, both parties had a heightened interest in any kind of military or security-related activity in the other side's zone of occupation. German interest was prompted by the emerging requirements of Barbarossa, whereas Soviet interest and fear were initially inflamed by the stunning success of German arms in the west.

The Soviet documents that are now available pertaining to the period from the defeat of France to 22 June 1941 make it possible to reconstruct a detailed picture of what the various Soviet agencies knew about German military intentions. Most Soviet intelligence assessments are derived from NKGB agent reports and sources, NKVD monitoring of the new border zones, the Soviet General Staff, and diplomatic channels. As German intelligence agencies accelerated their infiltration of lone agents and reconnaissance groups across the Soviet border, especially in the first half of 1941, armed clashes between NKVD border units and German agents resulted in casualties on both sides. Interrogations of captured agents and deserters supplement the overall picture. Among the stream of Soviet intelligence assessments from all sources, some stand out as critical for the clear picture they provide of the relentless German buildup through the second half of 1940 and the first half of 1941. I call these major signposts on the road to 22 June 1941 critical intelligence assessments (CIAs), and they are analyzed here in chronological order.

June 1940

Soviet analysts were alarmed or even mesmerized by the success of German operations in the west, and they exhausted all options to identify why the Western Allies were so comprehensively and rapidly defeated. One obvious starting point is the memorandum sent to Stalin by I. I. Proskurov, the chief of staff of the Intelligence Directorate of the Soviet General Staff at the beginning of June 1940. The memorandum consists of three summaries, one of which was based on an exchange of views between the German military attaché in Tokyo, Oberst Gerhard Matsky, and the assistant German military attaché in Moscow, Oberstleutnant Heygendorff, concerning the lessons to be derived from the campaigns in Poland and the west.

The source report based on this exchange of views notes that Matsky had spent two weeks attached to the headquarters of a German unit and had witnessed the offensive against Belgium, Holland, and northern France. Matsky's assessment of German offensive operations was highly favorable: "Operations on the Western Front developed with such power and speed that the enemy's defensive plans were overturned. The paratroopers and airborne assault units gave an especially good account of themselves."[1] The Rotterdam airport was overwhelmed by a drop of 15,000 parachutists and air-landed troops armed with light weapons. Critical for German operations was the crossing of the Albert Canal. To avoid heavy losses it was imperative that the bridges be captured intact. Once again, the specially and intensively trained German airborne units demonstrated their unique value. The *Fallschirmjäger* managed to seize the bridges before they could be blown, and Heygendorff notes that the German airborne units were reinforced by soldiers who were delivered there by other means. Proskurov comments: "concerning these *other* means Heygendorff did not want to speak in any detail."[2] Heygendorff's reference is almost certainly to the German special forces units, the Brandenburg zbV 800, whose contribution to the success of the German assault was considerable. They were able to capture the bridges by various tricks and ruses and hold them until relieved. Based on the absolute precondition of holding the bridges or, if necessary, destroying them to deny their use by the enemy, the enemy's defenses had been breached. The consequences were decisive, since the German armored units could now cross the Albert Canal and attack the enemy rear, causing massive disruption and dislocation.

Another critical element in the German plan was the capture of fortifications in Belgium, especially the fortress Eben Emael, which was seized by glider and parachute troops. What emerges from Heygendorff's observations is that German trials and experiments in Czechoslovakia had yielded a whole new range of explosive methods for breaching such fortifications; these methods were then deployed against the Belgian forts and reinforced zones. According to Heygendorff, "without the capitulation of Czechoslovakia the capture of Lvov would have been impossible and now one can also say that the Maginot Line itself poses no insuperable obstacle for us."[3] Heygendorff provides no precise details about the new explosive devices—citing military secrecy—but they were later revealed to be beehive charges designed to concentrate the explosive force in a very narrow direction to achieve maximum cutting and destructive effect. The combination of new weapons and tactics was devastating. Matsky states, "The garrisons of the Belgian forts were so psychologically weakened by the power of the attack and the use of these new combat methods that it was impossible for them to offer any further resistance."[4] Airpower was also decisive:

> The suppression and demoralization of the enemy was further facilitated by the constant air attacks to which the most important installations and roads were subjected. As bombs we are now using bombs of the heaviest type, 1,700 kg. These bombs are fitted with a siren which produces a deafening row when falling. This had a hugely demoralizing effect on enemy troops. When these sorts of bombs were dropped on any troops, they lost any will to continue the battle.[5]

Matsky argues that the French made a critical error: instead of launching a major counterattack, they made a series of minor attacks and thus dissipated their forces, which were then defeated piecemeal. Another reason for German success was the major reorganization of the German army after the Polish campaign. To quote Matsky: "Thanks to this work during these several months, we changed this entire motley group which our army was during the Polish campaign into a uniform, cohesive army in which strict discipline dominated and with which we were able to achieve our current successes."[6]

The ideas exchanged between Matsky and Heygendorff raised a number of serious challenges for the Red Army. First, the Red Army had to question whether it enjoyed the same level of technical competence and leadership, and if not, what could be done about it. Second, the success of the German armored divisions en masse suggested that major armored formations should be retained. Third, high levels of all-arms cooperation, especially between the air force and the army, were essential. Fourth, high-speed, all-arms warfare meant that commanders at all levels had to make decisions without recourse to superior command. This, in turn, required highly trained command strata at all levels, especially among junior leaders, with an emphasis on initiative, risk taking, and mastery of all phases of war. Fifth, the Germans' new methods and means of overcoming reinforced regions and strong defensive positions—such as shape-charged explosives, airborne assault units, and special forces—caused the Red Army to question whether too much reliance could be placed on, say, the Stalin Line. Static defensive positions such as the Maginot Line conceded too much initiative to the enemy, since fixed positions that could be reconnoitred and studied to find ways to breach or bypass them. When the emphasis is on a mobile and fluid defense behind a defensive screen, the enemy does not possess a clearly defined target, and the risks and uncertainties of any offensive operation are greater. Furthermore, a mobile defense in depth retains a high degree of initiative. Unfortunately, when such planning and tactical initiative are largely negated by political and ideological control, the advantages of a mobile and fluid defense are lost, and greater reliance is placed on reinforced positions. The Matsky-Heygendorff dialogue reveals not only that the German armed forces were at the cutting edge of military equipment and doctrine but also that the German troops' technical competence and leadership were at the highest level. Thus, the editorial board's statement in the introduction to the two volumes of 1941 god concerning Soviet knowledge about German troops does not strike me as relevant: "One can note that in the standard intelligence information there is an absence of data concerning the qualitative training of German soldiers and officers and their high combat level."[7] The Germans would not have been able to bypass the Belgian and Dutch defensive systems and overwhelm the British and French so quickly without exceptionally high levels of military training and technical mastery.

Early signs of German troop deployments toward the east can be noted in two reports from June 1940. They observe that more troops are being deployed to the border with Lithuania, the German garrison in Königsberg is being reinforced, the pace of moblization in eastern Prussia is being accelerated, and Romanian mountain rifle units have been deployed to the north. This last deployment is seen as a move to cover the mountain passes from the north to the south at the point where the Soviet and Slovakian borders meet.[8] A later report, dated 21 June 1940, draws similar conclusions, although there is no sense of any alarm. General-Lieutenant Proskurov concludes: "Germany continues to strengthen its units in the border zone with Lithuania. This concentration of troops apparently shows no signs of being on a major level."[9]

In contrast with Proskurov's lack of concern about German deployments, General-Colonel Pavlov, commander of the Belorussian Special Military District, saw a severe security threat from units of the Lithuanian, Latvian, and Estonian armies. In a memorandum to Timoshenko, Pavlov submitted a number of proposals, including that the armies of all three states be disarmed and the weapons sent to the Soviet Union. Pavlov then suggested that the three armies' officer corps be purged and reinforced with Soviet command personnel (essentially military commissars). In the event of war, he recommended that the Lithuanian and Estonian armies be used outside the Belorussian Special Military District, possibly against the Romanians, Afghans, or Japanese. This second recommendation goes to the heart of the Soviet Union's legitimacy (or lack thereof) in the Baltic states, which would be brutally exposed after 22 June 1941 in Ukraine and Belorussia and in 1942 in the steppe republics and the Caucasus. In light of the fate of the Polish officer corps and other members of the Polish professional classes at Katyn and other sites in March–April 1940, Pavlov's recommendation to purge the officer corps had ominous implications for the officers themselves and their families. With regard to the Latvian army, Pavlov urged that it be entirely disarmed. He also advocated disarming the populations of all three countries and recommended that those who failed to hand over any weapons should be shot.[10]

July 1940

Before turning to some of the more routine intelligence reports, it is worth examining a memorandum from the Fifth Section of the NKGB dated 9 July 1940 and written by its head, Fitin, which was circulated to Beria, Stalin, Molotov, Voroshilov, and Timoshenko. Its value is that it gives a very good idea of the multifarious data crossing the desks of intelligence professionals and highlights the critical problem of assessing the weight and importance of information from different sources.

Fitin's intelligence report comprises seven serials. Serial 1 states that the former (abdicated) British king, Edward, maintains contacts with Hitler and "is conducting negotiations with Hitler on the question of forming a new British government [and] the conclusion of peace with Hitler on condition of a military alliance against the Soviet Union."[11] In serial 2 it is noted that major offensive operations are under way against Britain. Serial 3 contains the remarks of the German and Italian military attachés in Bucharest, according to whom "in the future Bessarabia and Soviet Moldavia will be taken from the USSR."[12] Serials 4–6 are exclusively concerned with German construction work and troop deployments in the east. For instance, they state that, in the part of Poland bordering the Soviet Union, the Germans are laying down "strategic highways."[13] In addition, a cement factory in Bohemia now works in three shifts, and Skoda factories are producing steel frames for gun positions being built in Poland. The final serial notes that, in the protectorate, registration is under way of all officers and other ranks with knowledge of Russian, Serbian, Croatian, Bulgarian, and Romanian. More worrying, perhaps, is the observation that the German military authorities are bringing together what Fitin refers to as White Guards and providing them with military training. Related to this training program is the observation that "the Ukrainian White emigration has received instructions to intensify its anti-Soviet propaganda."[14]

Despite the apparent inconsistencies between serials 1 and 2—the former British king is negotiating with Hitler, yet German offensive operations against Britain have been intensified—there is a consistent anti-Soviet trend in these serials. Remarks made by military attachés are not necessarily decisive, but they may warrant extra weight when considered alongside the physical evidence of road building and fortifications close to the Soviet border. Why, for example, does Germany require a network of strategic roads in this area? The very use of the word "strategic" implies a threat. Especially alarming, I suggest, is the fact that the Germans are providing military training to White Guards. The conclusion to be drawn here is that any training is likely to emphasize intelligence gathering, which would imply attempts to infiltrate agents across the border. The identification of Russian-speaking officers also suggests a heightened intelligence interest in the Soviet Union. Although stepping up anti-Soviet propaganda might not serve an immediate military purpose, it is certainly consistent with rumors that the Germans have territorial ambitions regarding Ukraine or wish to destabilize Soviet rule. None of these serials mandates a dramatic response, but they are straws in the wind and certainly require that the Soviet regime pay attention to activities taking place on its borders and in eastern Germany and not be distracted by the Luftwaffe's struggle for aerial supremacy over the south of England in the summer of 1940.[15]

Three days after Fitin's memorandum landed on Stalin's desk, the NKVD Border Troops Directorate in Ukraine reported on Romanian attitudes and government measures undertaken after Bessarabia and northern Buko-vina became part of the Soviet Union. The Russian word for this process is *prisoedinenie*, which can be translated into English as the somewhat neutral "joining," but a more accurate translation would be "annexation." Among Romanians, the mood was hostile toward the Soviet Union, and they were not reconciled to the new status quo. Thus, the report's author points out:

> Among the officer stratum and indeed among a part of the rank and file of the Romanian army which has withdrawn across the River Prut there is the widely disseminated opinion that the liberation of Bessarabia and the northern part of Bukovina is a matter of time and that the Romanian government intends once again, with the help of Germany and Italy, to recover these regions from the Soviet Union by military force.[16]

The author stresses that these and similar views have been "confirmed by other sources."[17]

There is evidence that the situation on the Romanian side of the Prut was highly volatile. The same report notes that on 29 June 1940, Romanian soldiers who had crossed the Prut circulated rumors that units of the Red Army were following behind them. Local civilians who gathered to wel-come the Red Army in the town of Dorokhoi were fired on by Romanian soldiers. Though not explicitly stated, the majority of those welcoming the Red Army were probably Jews, given that pogroms against them were ini-tiated at that time. The authors state: "According to information received from the 97th Border Detachment the Romanians are terrorizing the local population, organizing pogroms of the Jewish population in the towns of Dorokhoi, Seret, IAssy and Galats."[18] In addition, on orders of the Romanian High Command, reservist soldiers—Ukrainians and Jews—who had been brought back across the Prut and expressed a wish to return to Bessarabia and northern Bukovina were executed.[19]

A series of reports throughout July 1940 all point to an ongoing buildup of German forces along various parts of the Soviet border. A report dated 13 July 1940 notes the arrival of German tank and infantry units in the border zone in the direction of Peremyshl'. Table 4.1 provides an idea of their de-ployment and composition. Although the report's compiler, General-Major Petrov, did not draw this conclusion, the deployment of five infantry regi-ments in Krosno—36th, 134th, 289th, 438th, and 647th—implied that there might be five infantry divisions deployed in the area. For example, the 134th

Table 4.1. German Troop Deployments Relative to Peremyshl', as Recorded by Border Troops of the Ukraine SSR, 13 July 1940

Town	Orientation	Type of Unit	Unit Designation
Krosno	65 km SE of Peremyshl'	Infantry regiment	36th, 134th, 289th, 438th, 647th
Iaroslav	20 km N of Peremyshl'	Infantry and artillery regiments	39th Infantry Regiment, 116th Artillery Regiment
Zheshuv	60 km SW of Peremyshl'	Infantry, artillery, and antiaircraft regiments	129th Infantry, Artillery, and Antiaircraft Regiments
Pshevorsk	40 km SW of Peremyshl'	Infantry and artillery regiments, machine gun battalion	192nd Infantry Regiment, 44th Heavy Artillery Regiment, 16th Machine Gun Battalion
Iaroslav	—	3 tank echelons	Unknown (70 tanks)
Liublin	100 km SW of Brest-Litovsk	Tank unit	Unknown
Lantset	45 km SW of Peremyshl'	HQ (3 generals and 30 officers)	Unknown

Source: № 53, "Zapiska zamestitelia nachal'nika pogranvoisk NKVD SSSR nachal'niku 5 otdela GUGB NKVD SSSR Fitinu o perebroskakh i kontsentratsii germanskikh voisk, 13 iiulia 1940 g.," 1941 god, 1:114–115.

Infantry Regiment was part of the 44th Infantry Division, suggesting that other formations of this division were in the area or that the 134th Infantry Regiment was an advance party. If the other infantry regiments were also advance parties, that would represent a significant deployment of infantry. The fact that three generals—divisions were typically commanded by generals—and thirty other officers, most likely key headquarters personnel, were known to be in Lantset was consistent with the arrival of at least three and possibly five infantry divisions. The known presence of the 39th Infantry and 116th Artillery Regiments in Iaroslav and the known presence of the 129th Infantry, 129th Antiaircraft, and 129th Artillery Regiments in Zheshuv also implied the presence or imminent arrival of the rest of their respective divisions.

Petrov also provides some idea of the construction work being undertaken by the Germans in this region. Trenches were being dug and mines were being laid, and about 2,500 soldiers with excavators were being used. By the start of July, Petrov reports, the construction of major highway roads from Krakow to Tarnuv, Tarnuv to Iaroslav, and Iaroslav to Zasane had been completed.[20]

The first of the CIAs, dated 20 July 1940, was an early attempt to synthesize a number of prior reports to provide an overview of German behavior on the other side of the Soviet border. It is important not only because it identifies the number of German divisions but also because Golikov makes this central observation: "After the capitulation of France the German High Command set about transferring its troops from the west to the east and southeast a significant proportion of which were deployed to East Prussia and to the territory of the former Poland and Austria."[21] The scale of this deployment was underlined by the fact that, according to Golikov, "Over the period from 19 June to 14 July 1940 the agent networks of the 5th Directorate and the intelligence sections of the Western Special Military District and the Kiev Special Military District recorded a total of 860 special troop trains heading from the west in easterly and southeasterly directions."[22] In the former Polish territories facing the Western Special Military District, three infantry divisions and a tank regiment had arrived, and up to five infantry divisions and an unknown number of cavalry units had arrived opposite the border of the Kiev Special Military District. The total German deployment is summarized in table 4.2.

The various Germans units identified by Soviet agencies as arriving in eastern Prussia from 15 June to 15 July 1940—not including units whose

Table 4.2. Deployment of German Troops Facing the Western Special Military District (ZAPOVO), the Kiev Special Military District (KOVO), and in Austria, 16 July 1940

Location	Infantry Divisions	Tanks	Cavalry Regiments
ZAPOVO	13 (+ 7 in Warsaw*)	1 regiment	2
KOVO	15	1 unit	3
Austria	10–11	2 divisions	—
Total	45–46	2 divisions	5

Source: № 60, 1941 god, 1:122.
*Subject to confirmation by Soviet agencies.

deployment could not be identified—constituted a substantial buildup. They included sixteen infantry regiments, five of which were motorized; four cavalry regiments; one infantry division (unidentified); and at least eight major troop trains and miscellaneous tank units, among them a ten-kilometer-long tank column seen on 7 July.[23] Much the same picture was reported in Poland. Units observed included eleven infantry regiments, three artillery regiments, and a total of 394 troop trains. In addition, 200 motorcyclists arrived in Warsaw on 27 June. Over the period 1–7 July, seven infantry divisions arrived in Warsaw and the surrounding area, and from 6 to 9 July, the following units and equipment arrived in Krakow: a motorized infantry regiment, 33 antitank guns, 220 field guns, 90 antiaircraft guns, 180 tanks, and 6 armored trains.[24]

The details provided in these summaries suggest that Soviet intelligence agencies had competent agents in place. The problem for Golikov and his colleagues was how to explain this deployment. According to the German military attaché in Moscow, these movements represented the return of German units to their original locations. In other words, as far as the German military attaché was concerned—or what he wanted his Soviet hosts to believe—they were routine transfers that should not be construed as hostile acts against the Soviet Union. At this stage, it was possible, or even plausible, that the German explanation could be taken at face value. The essential task was to identify the moment when transfers of German troops and equipment to the east ceased to be routine and acquired an altogether different character.

Stalin's reaction to Golikov's report is not known. However, Beria summarized some of the material in a memorandum that he sent to Stalin and Molotov sometime in July. The introductory paragraph of Beria's memorandum is clear and unequivocal: "Reports have been received *concerning*

German military preparations directed against the Soviet Union from two NKVD USSR agents who have returned from a mission to the German-occupied territory of the former Poland."[25] As evidence that German measures were directed against the Soviet Union, Beria cited the construction of fortifications in the territories bordering the Soviet Union, the laying down of strategic road highways, and the deployment of military units to Germany's eastern borders.

August 1940

Sometimes, what appear to be minor or even irrelevant intelligence serials in a report are in fact very revealing. Among the stream of German troops and equipment observed by NKVD border troops in Ukraine, some senior German officers were visiting the populated areas close to the Soviet border, where they could observe Soviet territory. The military planning implications of these visits were clear. Meanwhile, two NKVD border detachments, the 92nd and the 93rd, were reporting changes in German security measures. German border detachments were being strengthened by day and by night. The report states, "Border protection is mainly being strengthened in those regions where building of fortifications is taking place. Related to the strengthening of the border protection is the fact the Germans are reinforcing the personnel in the border cordons and also setting up new ones."[26] Strengthening of the border zone, along with the ongoing transfer of units and construction work, can only be construed as an attempt by the Germans to prevent the penetration of their border regions by Soviet agents, since they wish to hide the nature and scale of their activities.

Among the various intelligence reports are elements of wishful thinking. For instance, a summary of information from the Soviet resident in Kaunus, prepared by Beria and sent to Stalin and Molotov, claims there are severe food shortages in Germany. On Soviet-German relations, one report states: "Throughout various social groups in Germany there is a solid body of opinion that holds the view that a confrontation between Germany and the Soviet Union is unavoidable. Related to this is the view that Germany will be compelled to act against the Soviet Union since a second winter at war will further exacerbate the condition of German workers and will give rise to a revolutionary upsurge."[27] This report fails to appreciate, first, the National Socialists' grip on all institutions and the power they enjoyed in Germany and the occupied territories and, second and critically, the huge level of support enjoyed by Hitler. The fantasy of a German workers' rebellion against Hitler arose from interpreting events in Germany as if they should conform to some kind of Marxist-Leninist-Stalinist template. Whether Stalin or the cynical Beria and Molotov accepted this fantasy at face value is unknown, but the possibility of a German workers' uprising in the winter of 1940–1941 might have sustained Stalin's belief that he still had time on his hands. Reporting that a German-Soviet confrontation was inevitable was certainly consistent with other intelligence data, but it could be undermined by ideological abstractions. The critical part of Beria's summary is the conclusion: "The concentrated buildup of German troops in the east and especially in Galicia continues. Some 40 divisions are concentrated along the entire eastern border of Germany."[28]

A number of high-quality and detailed intelligence reports in August must have added to the woes of Soviet planners who, whatever their official position, had to deeply alarmed by the incoming data. The first of these reports is dated 15 August 1940, and it provides a detailed, consolidated summary of (1) the deployment of German troops on the Soviet border (as of 1 August), (2) military construction work in the border region, (3) the presence of military aerodromes, and (4) the construction of barracks.

German deployments are comprehensively logged in twenty-three serials. The overall effect is to indicate a huge redeployment of men and equipment. For example, serial 5 states: "At the beginning of July of this year, German units passed through the town of Raiovets in the direction of the town of Kholm. There were up to about 100 motorcyclists with sidecars. On each motorcycle there were 3 soldiers armed with rifles and machine guns. Further, a column of about 50 vehicles carrying weapons of some sort, covered by tarpaulin, passed through."[29]

A huge influx of German troops was recorded between 8 and 17 July. According to serial 14, there were "up to 200,000 troops, approximately 5 divisions," the bulk of which were infantry.[30] Serial 18 reports that between 12 and 17 July, all civilian passenger travel on trains between Warsaw and Malkino and Brest was stopped because of the volume of troops being transferred. Serial 20 notes: "Over the course of 120 kilometers from the Soviet border there are German troops in almost every village, and an especially large concentration of German troops in the area from the village of Kupka to the town of Tarnograd."[31] From the point of view of an intelligence analyst, another detail in serial 20 would be significant: "Starting on 9 July and lasting until 17 July 1940 approximately 2,000 vehicles with various items of military equipment, among the equipment, 69 vehicles of pontoon troops with 28 large pontoon boats, a field hospital of 123 vehicles and 23 motorcyclists, passed through Liublin from Warsaw in the direction of Kholm and Liubartov."[32] The deployment of river-crossing equipment and large pontoon boats might not confirm hostile intent in itself, but it reveals forward planning—specifically, that in any advance to the east, river obstacles such as the Bug and the San would have to be crossed. Serial 21 is also alarming:

> In the town of Sandomir, some 20 kilometers from Peremyshl' up
> to about 2 divisions of German troops comprising various arms of
> service are located. On 18 July of this year 550 tanks were recorded
> on the town square of Sandomir. All the town's streets were full of
> troops. At the same time there were about 6 freight trains, loaded
> with military equipment and tanks, standing at the Sandomir railway
> station. In the area of the station there were heavy artillery guns.[33]

The same serial states: "On the very same day [20 July 1940] six German officers, moving along the bank of the river San, observed Soviet territory with binoculars and took photographs."[34]

Parallel with the deployment of ground forces, the Germans were making sustained efforts to enlarge and improve various airfields. At the Warsaw aerodrome there were now twelve reinforced concrete hangars measuring thirty by seventy meters. Another six hangars had been constructed on the nearby civilian airfield. Each of these airfields had two fuel storage tanks, each with a capacity of 80,000 liters. The Liublin and Krakow aerodromes had also been upgraded and militarized.

Two reports dated 16 August 1940, both from the NKVD Transport Directorate, provide much the same picture. The matter-of-fact introduction, virtually the same in the two reports, states the problem: "According to information received from the undercover network of the NKVD road-transport section of the Brest and Lvov railways, German troops continue to be concentrated in the border zone close to the Soviet Union."[35] The NKVD agent reports that the Germans have conscripted peasants to dig trenches close to the river Bug at night: "The trenches are camouflaged and telephone cable is laid throughout the field," and "German machine gun units are located along the river Bug."[36]

As German reinforcements flooded into the border regions, there seemed to be a marked increase in the activity of various nationalist groups. Given the nature of the German internal security regime, these were almost certainly not spontaneous manifestations of anti-Soviet hostility; they were most likely actively supported and encouraged by the Abwehr. According to the NKVD agent, the Germans were recruiting Ukrainians who promoted their nationalist agenda. The agent quoted the comments of one Ukrainian activist: "As soon as we finish the war with Britain, we'll march off to liberate Ukraine from the Soviets and we'll create an independent Ukraine."[37] The agent also reported a large demonstration:

> On the 14 July [1940], in the towns of Peremyshl' and Zhuravitsy, led by a representative of the National Socialist party, there was a large meeting of Ukrainian nationalists at which the participants swore an oath of loyalty to Hitler. On that day the towns of Peremyshl' and Zhuravitsy were bedecked with yellow-blue Petliurov flags. After the oath had been given there was a parade. The demonstrators marched through the town in columns. During the procession anti-Soviet slogans were shouted from the ranks of the demonstrators.[38]

In the second of the two reports, the agent notes: "Soldiers are being transported from the French front to the Soviet border under the pretext of being sent on leave, but the soldiers are not sent on leave."[39] There was additional evidence of the Germans creating nationalist units from among Polish prisoners of war, such as "the 3rd Polish Infantry Legion."[40] Generally speaking, the reporting of these nationalist sentiments among Poles, Ukrainians, and Romanians was factual and, by Soviet standards, relatively neutral. However, NKVD officers would have been well aware that Ukrainians, Belorussians, Estonians, Latvians, and Lithuanians had good reason to work with the Germans. Any neutrality was essentially a form of internal censorship adopted by NKVD officers because the reasons for the profound resentment and bitter hatred of the Soviet state—the Holodomor and the targeting of Polish nationalists in the 1930s—could not be mentioned, even in top-secret internal reports.

In a third report from the NKVD Transport Directorate, dated 23 August 1940, there are signs that the Germans are exploiting the resentment of Ukrainian nationalists. According to the report's sources, "the Germans are actively organizing Ukrainians in order to fight the Soviet Union under the slogan 'an independent Ukraine' and that allegedly a national army made up of Ukrainians has already been created."[41] The precise wording used to describe this new-model Ukraine is *Samostiinaia Ukraina*, which can be translated as "separate Ukraine." The distinction between a "separate" (*samostiinaia*) and an "independent" (*nezavisimaia*) Ukraine may be significant, because the former does not necessarily mean the latter. An independent Ukraine would be outside German control, whereas a separate Ukraine, outside the Soviet Union but subject to overall German control, would be far more desirable from the point of view of German territorial ambitions in the east. The source also reports: "Germans are forming Ukrainian legions—the Sicheviki—and the Ukrainian nationalist organization is also conducting negotiations with the Germans about the creation of a secret transit location for the deployment of Ukrainians to Germany via Hungary."[42]

Compiled by Timoshenko and Voroshilov, the second CIA is dated 19 August 1940, and it deals with the necessary strategic deployment of Soviet forces in the west and east for the years 1940 and 1941. This assessment is divided into six main headings: (1) the most probable enemies, (2) the armed forces of the probable enemies, (3) the enemies' probable operational plans, (4) the fundamentals of strategic deployment, (5) the fundamentals of strategic deployment, and (6) the fundamentals of strategic deployment in the east.

The CIA begins with a stark warning of the present and growing danger to the Soviet Union: "The unfolding political situation in Europe is creating the probability of an armed confrontation on our western borders."[43] The main and most powerful enemy in the west was Germany, and as Timoshenko and Voroshilov acknowledged, any conflict with Germany was likely to embroil Finland, Romania, and possibly Hungary—all seeking revenge—in a war with the Soviet Union. At this stage, Italy was regarded as an indirect threat. Iran's and Afghanistan's position toward the Soviet Union was assessed as one of "armed neutrality." Turkey, incited by Germany, was acknowledged as a possible enemy. The preliminary conclusions were stark and uncompromising: "Consequently, the Soviet Union must be ready for a war on two fronts: in the west against Germany, supported by Italy, Finland and Romania, and possibly Turkey, and in the east against Japan as an open enemy or as an enemy occupying a position of armed neutrality and always able to cross over into open conflict."[44]

The Soviet General Staff maintained that the political situation in western Europe made it possible for the Germans to transfer "the greater part of their forces against our western borders."[45] The "greater part" was assessed as 173 of the total available divisions, broken down as follows: 138 infantry divisions, 15 tank divisions, 10 motorized divisions, 5 light divisions, 3 airborne divisions, and up to 12,000 aircraft. The total strength of German ground and air forces as assessed by the Soviet General Staff is presented

Table 4.3. Soviet General Staff Assessment of German Land and Air Forces, 19 August 1940

Type of Division	Total
Infantry	200
Tank	15
Light *	5–7
Infantry (motorized)	10
Mountain	8
Airborne†	2–3
Total divisions	240–243
Total aircraft	13,900
Total tanks (all types)	9,000–10,000
Total men under arms	8 million

Source: Data derived from № 95, 1941 god, 1:181.
*German infantry divisions designated Jäger (light infantry).
†Includes air-landing, glider, and parachute units.

in table 4.3. That Timoshenko and Voroshilov could conceive of the Germans deploying the bulk of their forces against the Soviet Union while still waging an unresolved war against Britain was tacit acknowledgment that the war with Britain was meant to divert attention from Germany's main strategic ambition in the east—war with the Soviet Union. When the possible contributions of Germany's allies were taken into account, the picture was daunting. The total combined forces ranged against the Soviet Union in the west are shown in table 4.4.

Having assessed the likely forces to be deployed against the Soviet Union in the west, Timoshenko and Shaposhnikov directed their attention to the Japanese threat. They estimated that the total Japanese forces that could be deployed against the Soviet Far East amounted to 39 infantry divisions, 2,500 aircraft, 1,200 tanks, and 4,000 guns.[46] Thus, if the Soviet Union found

Table 4.4. Soviet General Staff Assessment of Probable Enemy Land and Air Forces Deployed against the Soviet Western Front, 19 August 1940

State	Infantry Divisions	Tanks	Aircraft
Germany	173	10,000	12,000
Finland	15	0	400
Romania	30	250	900
Hungary	15	300	600
Total	233	10,550	13,900

Source: Data derived from № 95, 1941 god, 1:182.

itself embroiled in a war on two fronts, it could expect to face a total of 270 infantry divisions, 11,750 tanks, and 16,400 aircraft.[47]

In terms of assessing the probable operational plans of the enemy (that is, the Germans), the Soviet General Staff had no primary source material (material acquired from espionage). Thus, the task facing the Soviet General Staff was a daunting one. They had to bring together all the information available from various agents' reports and diplomatic sources, knowledge gleaned from recent German campaigns in the west, advances in technology and doctrine, their own intimate knowledge of the strengths and weaknesses of the Red Army, and their own personal experiences. In the Soviet context, the ideological incubus of Marxism-Leninism and revolutionary enthusiasm were extra distractions, distorting the analysts' vision and leading them away from cool and rational appraisal.

Two German attack options were considered. The first option envisaged a main German thrust to the north from the mouth of the San River, with the aim of striking and developing the main forces from eastern Prussia through Lithuania in the direction of Riga and Kovno and then further to Dvinsk and Polotsk, or along the Kovno–Vil'no line and on to Minsk. It was estimated that the Germans would deploy up to 123 infantry divisions and about 10 tank divisions, supported by the greater part of their aircraft. At the same time, there might be a series of German strikes on the Belostok front and Brest, with the aim of developing the attack in the direction of Baranovichi and Minsk. Against Riga, Timoshenko and Voroshilov considered the possibility of a German amphibious landing from the Baltic Sea in the region of Libava, to threaten the flanks and rear of the Soviet armies operating in the area of the lower Neman. In addition to a German strike from eastern Prussia, there was a real possibility of a simultaneous strike from Kholm, Grubeshov, Tomashev, and Iaroslav in the direction of Dubno and Brody, with the eventual aim of breaking into the rear of the Lvov formation (Red Army) and taking western Ukraine. It was estimated that the Germans would deploy up to 50 infantry divisions and 5 tank divisions in this operation, with the main formation in the region of Kholm, Tomashev, and Liublin. In the event Finland entered the war with Germany, an attack against Leningrad from the northwest could not be ruled out. In the south, an attack by Romanian units supported by the German army could be expected from northern Romania in the direction of Zhmerinka. The second option envisaged a concentration of German forces south of the mouth of the San, with the aim of taking Ukraine—the main blow being against Kiev—and, in

Table 4.5. Total Deployment of Soviet Forces Needed to Cover the Soviet Union's Northern, Southern, and Far Eastern (Japan) Borders, 19 August 1940

Arm of Service	Total
Rifle divisions	37
Cavalry divisions	10
Independent rifle brigades	3
Airborne brigades	3
Tank brigades	10
Aviation regiments*	65

Source: № 95, 1941 god, 1:185.
*Includes the air defenses available to Moscow, Baku, and Leningrad.

the long term, taking the Caucasus. In this operation, the Germans would deploy 110 to 120 infantry divisions and the bulk of their tank and air forces, leaving about 50 to 60 infantry divisions and some tanks and aircraft in the north. Having summarized these options, Timoshenko and Shaposhnikov concluded: "*the first operational variant is the fundamental and by far the most politically advantageous one for Germany and consequently the most likely; that is the deployment of the main German forces to the north of the mouth of the river San.*"[48]

When considering where to concentrate the bulk of Soviet forces in the event of a war on two fronts, Timoshenko and Shaposhnikov concluded that the bulk must be concentrated on the Western Front. On the Eastern Front, they recommended, "it is necessary to designate such forces which would be able to guarantee the stability of the situation."[49] Elsewhere, only minimal forces—sufficient to cover the borders—would be deployed. The total deployment of forces envisaged for the northern, southern, and far eastern

Table 4.6. Total Deployment of Soviet Forces Needed to Cover the Soviet Union's Western Front, 19 August 1940

Arm of Service	Total
Rifle divisions	143*
Motorized divisions	8
Tank divisions	18
Cavalry divisions	10
Total divisions	179
Independent tank brigades	14
Aviation regiments	172 (10,320 aircraft)

Source: № 95, 1941 god, 1:185.
*Of these, 23 would require 15 to 30 days to be fully operational, and another 6 were national divisions from the Baltic states.

Table 4.7. Allocation of Forces to the Armies of the Western Front, 19 August 1940

Unit	3rd Army	4th Army	10th Army	13th Army
Rifle divisions	6	10	15	6
Tank brigades	1	2	3	—
Motorized divisions	—	—	1	—
Cavalry divisions	—	—	3	—
River flotilla	—	1 (Pinskaia)	—	—

Source: № 95, 1941 god, 1:186.

borders is shown in table 4.5. The total deployment of forces envisaged for defense of the crucial Western Front is shown in table 4.6

Having established that the main German blow would most likely be directed north of the mouth of the San, Timoshenko and Voroshilov stipulated that, apart from an active defense to cover western Ukraine: "*The main task of our troops must be to inflict a defeat on the German troops concentrated in Eastern Prussia and in the Warsaw region and by an ancillary blow to defeat the enemy formation in the region of Ivangorod, Liublin, Grubeshov, Tomashev and Sandomir.*"[50]

In the west, the three designated fronts were the Western Front, the North-Western Front, and the South-Western Front. The Western Front, by far the most critical, consisted of the 3rd, 4th, 10th, and 13th Armies. Units allocated to these armies are shown in table 4.7. The total forces available to the command of the Western Front, with the addition of other units after mobilization, are shown in table 4.8.

The mission of the Western Front was defined as follows:

> The fundamental mission of the Western Front is by means of a blow to the north of the river Bug and in the general line toward Allenstein and jointly with the armies of the North-Western Front to inflict a decisive defeat on the German armies being concentrated on the territory of Eastern Prussia, to seize the latter and to proceed further to the lower reaches of the river Vistula. Simultaneously, by a strike of the left-flank army and in the general direction toward Ivangorod, jointly with the armies of South-Western Front to inflict a defeat on the enemy Ivangorod-Liublin formation and also to proceed to the river Vistula.[51]

This CIA is silent concerning the circumstances in which this overall plan would be initiated, and it offers no justification for proceeding to the Vistula or explanation of what would happen after that goal was achieved. The

Table 4.8. Total Forces Available to the Command of the Western Front

Formation	Total
Rifle divisions	41
Motorized divisions	2
Tank divisions	5
Cavalry divisions	3
Independent tank brigades	4
Aviation regiments	74

Source: № 95, 1941 god, 1:186.

question is: was this plan essentially a defensive response to any German aggression, or were there circumstances in which the Soviet High Command would consider acting preemptively in the face of clear and compelling evidence of growing German aggression?

The strength of the North-Western Front, with a similar mission to enter and occupy eastern Prussia, is shown in table 4.9. The total forces available to the command of the North-Western Front, with the addition of other units after mobilization, are shown in table 4.10.

The mission of the South-Western Front was stated as follows:

> The fundamental mission of the South-Western Front is by means of active defense in the Carpathians and along the border with Romania to cover the Western Ukraine and Bessarabia and, simultaneously, by a blow from the front, Mosty-Velikie, Rava-Russka, Seniava in the general direction of Liublin and operating jointly with the left-flank army of the Western Front to inflict a defeat on the Ivangorod-Liublin enemy formation and to proceed to, and to reinforce on, the middle reaches of the Vistula river.[52]

The South-Western Front consisted of the 5th, 6th, 9th, 12th, and 18th Armies; its strength is shown in table 4.11. The total forces available to the

Table 4.9. Allocation of Forces to the Armies of the North-Western Front, 19 August 1940

Unit	8th Army	11th Army
Rifle divisions	10	11
Tank divisions	2	—
Tank brigades	1	1
Motorized divisions	1	1

Source: № 95, 1941 god, 1:185.

Table 4.10. Total Forces Available to the Command of the North-Western Front

Formation	Total
Rifle divisions	31
Motorized divisions	2
Tank divisions	4
Independent tank brigades	3
Aviation regiments	20 (1,200 aircraft)

Source: № 95, 1941 god, 1:186.

command of the South-Western Front, with the addition of other units after mobilization, are shown in table 4.12.

In the event the Soviet Union had to fight a war on two fronts (west and east), the 46th Rifle Division, one mechanized corps consisting of two tank divisions, and one motorized division from the Trans-Baikal Military District would be transferred to the west. The total forces allocated for operations in the east were as follows: twenty-six rifle divisions, four cavalry divisions, three independent rifle brigades, eight tank brigades, and forty-three aviation regiments (number of aircraft not indicated).[53] The two main fronts were the Trans-Baikal Front and the Far Eastern Front, operating in conjunction with the Pacific Ocean Fleet. As in the west, decisive blows were planned against the Japanese, but the deployment plan was silent on whether the attacks would be initiated preemptively or in response to Japanese-initiated aggression.

On both fronts, specific operational tasks were allocated to the Soviet air arm: conducting joint operations with ground forces against major enemy formations; dealing with enemy aircraft; working with naval aircraft against the enemy in the Baltic Sea and thwarting any attempts to land on the coast; striking German airfields, especially in eastern Prussia; interdicting enemy

Table 4.11. Breakdown of Divisions and Other Units in the Armies of the South-Western Front

Unit	5th Army	6th Army	9th Army	12th Army	18th Army
Rifle divisions	5	10	6	6	4
Tank divisions	1	—	4	—	—
Tank brigades	—	1	1	1	—
Cavalry divisions	—	2	5	—	—
Motorized divisions	—	—	2	—	—

Source: Data derived from № 95, 1941 god, 1:187–188.

Table 4.12. Total Forces Available to the Command of the South-Western Front

Formation	Total
Rifle divisions	40
Motorized divisions	3
Tank divisions	7
Independent tank brigades	4
Cavalry divisions	7
Aviation regiments	58 (3,480 aircraft)

Source: № 95, 1941 god, 1:188.

troop movements; and attacking major enemy installations. Logical and reasonable as these plans were, they showed no awareness of the revolutionary changes in air warfare brought about by both the British and German air forces in the west. The real question was whether the Soviet air arm had sufficient numbers of modern aircraft and trained personnel to mount a credible response to the Luftwaffe. That question was brutally and clearly answered on and after 22 June 1941, but operational requirements should have been modified before that day of reckoning. Quite apart from the quality of German pilots and planes, German air and land operations had highlighted the utility of surprise, and here, the Soviet air force had options.

A realistic assessment of the limitations of the Soviet air force suggested that it would be treated very harshly by the Luftwaffe, especially in air-to-air encounters. Therefore, the best way to destroy large numbers of German aircraft was not in the air but on the ground.[54] For example, the Soviet plan called for air attacks against German aerodromes in eastern Prussia. However, the value of such attacks would be greatly reduced once hostilities started, suggesting that a preemptive strike could achieve major results. The other advantage, especially for the inexperienced Soviet air force, was that attacking German aircraft on the ground negated the Luftwaffe's superior skill and experience. Provided large numbers of Soviet aircraft could find the airfields and achieve tactical surprise, they could inflict serious damage on the Luftwaffe and severely disrupt the German air and ground plan. The implications for Soviet ground forces would have been enormous, relieving them from air attacks and permitting effective counterattacks. Critical considerations in any preemptive strike would be timing and secrecy: strike too soon, and large numbers of German aircraft might not be destroyed; strike too late, and the Germans might have time to launch their own surprise attacks. The best moment to attack would be when Soviet agents indicated the German airfields were close to capacity. Of course, Stalin's attitude ruled out any such preemptive strike, but implicit in the plan to attack the German aerodromes in eastern Prussia was the question of timing: should these air strikes be launched after the Germans had already attacked, thus reducing their value, or should they be launched beforehand, with the aim of achieving a knockout blow? I suggest that when Timoshenko and Voroshilov included the task of attacking German air bases, "above all in Eastern Prussia,"[55] they calculated that their master might consider the option of a preemptive strike.

September 1940

The plan for the strategic deployment of Soviet forces in the west and east was considered by the General Military Council when it convened on 16 August 1940. At that time, the possible main lines of an enemy advance were amended, along with the corresponding operations of the Red Army. These changes were worked out under the leadership of the chief of staff of the General Staff, General Meretskov, who took up his post on 19 August 1940. The revised document was ready on 18 September, and Stalin gave further instructions about the main line of advance on 5 October. The final version was ratified on 15 October, and from then until February 1941, it was subjected to only minor revisions. Once Zhukov took over as chief of staff in February 1941, the document underwent substantial changes, resulting in new versions.

The Meretskov document (dated 18 September 1940), which must be considered a CIA, recognized Germany as the main enemy, and the introductory paragraph remained unchanged. There were two variants of the western deployment. The first envisaged a deployment to the south of Brest-Litovsk, "with the aim by means of a powerful blow in the direction of Liublin and Krakow and on to Breslau in the first phase of the war to cut Germany's links with the Balkans, to deprive her of her most important economic sources and to exert a decisive influence on the Balkan states on questions of whether they should participate in the war or [the second variant] move north of Brest-Litovsk with the task of inflicting a defeat on the main German armies within the confines of Eastern Prussia and to seize the latter."[56] Meretskov notes that although any decision concerning a deployment "will depend on that political situation that obtains by the start of the war," both variations must be worked out.[57] With regard to the South-Western Front, an additional long-term consideration was that after the Vistula had been reached, a blow along the Kel'tse-Petrokov axis and on to Krakow must be delivered to seize the Kel'tse-Petrokov region, and then proceed to the river Pilitsa and the upper reaches of the river Oder.

The second variant envisaged that eastern Prussia would be captured: "The destruction of the Germans in Eastern Prussia and the seizure of the latter shall have exceptional economic and above all political implications for Germany, which will inevitably influence the further course of the war with Germany."[58] Balanced against the possibility of a victorious conclusion was the awareness of several potential problems: Germany would offer exceptionally tough resistance, the terrain in eastern Prussia would severely complicate the conduct of offensive operations, and the whole area was exceptionally well prepared for defense, especially in terms of engineering installations and roads. The sober conclusion drawn by Meretskov was that "the battle on this front may lead to protracted engagements, will tie down our main forces and will not secure the necessary and rapid effect such that it will make inevitable, and will accelerate, the entry of the Balkan states into the war against us."[59]

Like the August deployment plan, the Meretskov version is silent about timing: should these plans be implemented in response to German aggression, or should they be undertaken to forestall any German moves? It might be an exaggeration to say that the silence on this matter is deafening, but the lack of consideration of this question, even among such a small group of recipients, is striking.

Two additional reports, one dated 19 September and the other dated 25 September, underline the profound concerns expressed in the CIAs. A report to Golikov from the head of the intelligence section of ZAPOVO provides detailed evidence of the ongoing German buildup. Most of the serials provide the numbers of various German regiments, and a divisional headquarters in Rembertov is identified. A significant discovery was the arrival of up to 1,000 air force personnel—they are specifically referred to as pilots (let-chiki)—on 3 September in Sedlets. Details of large-scale exercises involving three divisions are given, their aim being to practice launching an offensive against enemy defensive positions. The report notes that, for purposes of the exercise, the enemy "occupied defensive positions close to our border."[60] According to the report, four German naval vessels—one of them an aircraft carrier—had docked in the port of Gdynia. German engineering projects also provided some clues to future intentions: a narrow-gauge railway line was being changed to wide gauge, a new aerodrome was being built south of the village of Voronets, and large-scale barracks construction was under way. Major Il'nitskii, the report's author and deputy head of the intelligence section of the Western Special Military District, comes to three central conclusions: First, and indisputably, "the deployment of German troops to the territories of Eastern Prussia and the Generalgouvernement continues."[61] Second, German troop deployments were particularly important for assessing German intentions and establishing an order of battle; the presence of the German 1st, 24th, 224th, 361st, and 368th Infantry Regiments was confirmed in Königsberg, the 71st Infantry Regiment was known to be in Sokolov, and the 212th and 431st Infantry Regiments were in Lodz. Though lacking precise detail, the third conclusion had serious implications: "The Germans continue to prepare the theater along all operational lines, building barracks accommodations and aerodromes, using both service personnel and the local population as labor."[62]

In the intelligence report dated 25 September 1940, Captain Benenson, an officer in the Transport Directorate of the NKVD, notes that the Germans are building machine gun posts along the border with the Soviet Union: "This line of reinforcements is being camouflaged by the Germans, all work takes place only at night and no person is permitted to enter the construction zone without special passes."[63] In common with other reports, Benenson's confirms the huge building program being undertaken by the Germans. He also notes the presence of Ukrainian nationalists and reports, "Agitators from among the number of Ukrainian nationalists are driving around the villages of the Generalgouvernement, actively promoting the creation of Ukrainian nationalist organizations under the slogan of a struggle with the Soviet Union and for the creation of a *Samostiinaia Ukraina*."[64] Particularly alarming—and surely an indicator of malign intent—were details about the Germans raising Ukrainian nationalist regiments. The following rumor was making the rounds: "After the war with Britain these regiments will be used in military operations against the Soviet Union for the creation of a *Samostiinaia Ukraina*."[65]

October 1940

Standing out among the intelligence summaries in October 1940 are the Timoshenko-Meretskov memorandum to Stalin, two intelligence reports on Germany (one from Golikov's office), and a report from Beria.

Sometime after 5 October, Timoshenko and Meretskov responded to Stalin's instructions concerning the deployment plan for Soviet forces in

1940–1941, seeking confirmation. They stressed that the likelihood of a war on two fronts was a fundamental part of the deployment plan and that the main theater of operations would be the west; therefore, the main Soviet forces must be concentrated there. The total forces allocated to the west, based on current availability, were as follows: 142 rifle divisions, 7 motor-rifle divisions, 16 tank divisions, 10 cavalry divisions, 15 tank brigades, and 159 aviation regiments. Forces allocated to the east consisted of 24 rifle divisions, 4 motor-rifle divisions, 2 tank divisions, 4 cavalry divisions, 8 tank brigades, and 43 aviation regiments. For operations in the Transcaucasian region and central Asia, the following forces were allocated: 11 rifle divisions, 6 cavalry divisions, 2 tank brigades, and 27 aviation regiments (including those allocated for the air defense of Moscow). There was a real sense of urgency in this memorandum, evident in the recommendations to accelerate fortification work on the north and northwestern borders, build more aerodromes, and expand the rail network in the southwest. Moreover, Timoshenko and Meretskov were quite clear about "the superiority of the probable enemy in the air arm" and recommended raising the total Soviet air strength to 20,000 aircraft, which would require forming an additional 100 aviation regiments in 1941 (60 percent bombers and 40 percent fighters). All would be deployed in the west. Whether aircrews could acquire anything close to the mastery enjoyed by their opponents in the time available was another question. The demand that the main transport agency of the Soviet Union prepare a detailed rail schedule for deployment added to the sense of urgency. Such comprehensive measures suggest that the Soviet General Staff and even Stalin recognized the full significance of the numerous intelligence reports about the German buildup. Stalin's complete instructions, dated 5 October 1940, are not available, so one cannot say whether he considered any preemptive operations. Certainly, given Timoshenko and Meretskov's point about the Germans' obvious air superiority, serious consideration of preemptive operations—essentially, attacking the German planes on the ground—was warranted.[66]

Golikov's memorandum to Timoshenko (dated 10 October 1940) is a summary of high-grade information, with reference to providing Germany with fuel. In his preamble, Golikov stresses the reliability of his source: "The source has repeatedly provided timely and quite correct information on questions known to the German embassy in Moscow. On the strength of this and on the basis of the present material, ascertaining serious shifts toward deterioration in relations between Germany and the Soviet Union and the possibility that Germany will not be able to meet its contractual deliveries, deserves serious attention."[67] The summary focuses on six areas: Germany's economic relations with the Soviet Union, the provision of oil products to Germany, activities of Ukrainian nationalists in Berlin, independent information concerning British air raids on Berlin, the use of Soviet fruit for planting in Germany, and rumors concerning Britain's capitulation.

For his summary of economic relations, Golikov appears to be relying on a source in the German embassy in Moscow. Gustav Hilger, an official at the embassy, had received a top-secret letter from the German Ministry of Foreign Affairs. Golikov's source had the letter in his possession for several minutes and was able to provide a general overview: On returning to Germany, the German trade delegation discovered that the question of whether to provide supplementary deliveries of goods to the Soviet Union, as required by the parties' agreement, had not been resolved. Worse still, the Germans could not meet the conditions of the agreement. At this stage, according to the source, any changes in the agreement would require the consent of a number of German agencies and, almost certainly, would have to be approved by Hitler. There was a perception in Berlin that the Soviet side has already started to reduce the rate of delivery of various goods. Regardless of whether the deliveries suddenly stopped—causing something of a scandal—or were gradually reduced, a crisis in German-Soviet relations was at hand. The cause of this crisis, according to the source, would most likely be orders by either Hitler or Göring that German industry give the highest priority to the army, "even in the event that this makes it impossible to fulfill obligations concerning deliveries to the Soviet Union."[68] The danger was that if the war continued through the winter, the agreed-on deadlines between Soviet importers and German firms would not be met. This danger was exacerbated by the British air raids, which were causing considerable alarm. The German assessment of the situation was that Soviet deliveries would cease in order to pressure Germany to meet its obligations.

According to the source, Germany was well provided for in terms of oil products. However, the bulk of Germany's oil storage facilities were located in the west, where they could be reached by enemy aircraft. With regard to petrol and lubricants, the situation was satisfactory, but the availability of diesel products for engines was less satisfactory. Various synthetic products were being used to compensate for the deficiencies. Oil deliveries from Estonia, required by the German navy, had ceased, and the German ambassador had requested that they be resumed.

The source reported that there had been a marked increase in the activity of Ukrainian organizations in Germany, especially the Ukrainian Mittel-stellen in Berlin. Ukrainians were also being given preferential treatment in the Generalgouvernement and were acquiring government posts, especially in the police force. They were also fast-tracked for German citizenship.

The most important part of Golikov's summary was not rumors of British capitulation (hardly credible after the major defeat inflicted on the Luft-waffe in the summer of 1940) or the Germans' acquisition of cold-resistant fruit seeds. It was the fact that the Germans placed the highest priority of supplying the German army, even if it meant violating the terms of the trade agreement with the Soviet Union. These priorities implied that any agreement was perceived as a purely temporary measure.

The penultimate summary of interest in October 1940 (dated 25 October) is based on the report of an agent from the NKVD Transport Directorate. Its detail is impressive. Like other reports, it notes the ongoing arrival of German men and equipment. For instance, at the end of September there was a large delivery of pontoon units, with boats and bridges. According to one NKVD agent, "On the territory of a brick factory German soldiers are burying white, metallic plates to which are led cables. The significance of these plates has not been discovered."[69] Reaffirming Ukrainian disaffec-tion, the source reports: "Members of Ukrainian nationalist organizations render all kinds of help to German troops and willingly register for service in military formations. After work they receive military training under the supervision of German officers."[70] Among German troops there were rumors of an imminent war with the Soviet Union and that Germans and Ukrainians would create a *Samostiinaia Ukraina*.

These rumors of war could not be dismissed out of hand, but they had to be treated with caution. How much weight should be attributed to them? One of Beria's sources inside the German Economics Ministry—code name *Korsikanets* (Corsican)—confirms the likelihood of a war between Germany and the Soviet Union: "In the beginning of the next year Germany will ini-tiate a war with the Soviet Union. The preparatory move toward the start of military operations against the Soviet Union will be the occupation of Ro-mania by the Germans preparations for which are under way now and must, allegedly, be implemented in the course of the next months."[71] *Korsikanets* is quite specific about German war aims: "The aim of the war is to remove the European parts of the Soviet Union—Leningrad to the Black Sea—from the Soviet Union and to create a state completely dependent on Germany. On the remaining part of the Soviet Union, according to these plans, a government with a friendly disposition toward Germany must be created."[72] *Korsikanets* had been informed by a senior officer that Germany would start a war against the Soviet Union in about six months.[73] When high-level sources inside the German establishment provide more or less the same information as that derived from German soldiers, a pattern emerges. Over time, this pattern achieves an alarming level of consistency and clearly invites an appropriate evidence-based response.

November 1940

Reports of the German buildup continued to circulate throughout November, but the one that deserves attention is a document originating from the Special Section of the GUGB NKVD concerning measures to interdict German agents. German agents were recruited mainly from the western districts of Ukraine and Belorussia, and they were being used to undermine the effectiveness of Red Army units by encouraging treachery. The Germans tended to send lone agents and groups, who were identified as follows:

1. Qualified intelligence agents belonging to the Organization of Ukrainian Nationalists, who possessed "great experience in operating against us, with an excellent knowledge of our territory and with a large number of contacts."

2. Poles who were members of illegal nationalist formations in Germany with links to the Polish counterrevolutionary underground on Soviet territory (such persons were frequently installed as the leaders of organizations serving German intelligence).

3. Service personnel of the former Polish army returning from German captivity who were recruited upon their discharge from prisoner-of-war camps (the implication being that working for German intelligence had secured their discharge).

4. Poles and Ukrainians returning from France who were working there before the German-Polish war (1939).

5. "Fugitives from the western districts of the Ukraine SSR and Belorussian SSR, participants in various counterrevolutionary formations, criminal-bandit elements and, additionally, those persons fleeing the Soviet Union with the aim of avoiding conscription into the Red Army."

6. Poles and Jews forcibly conscripted to work in the German border zone on the construction of defense installations.

7. German army deserters who were captured and recruited by German border intelligence detachments (though this was admittedly an infrequent occurrence).[74]

The danger posed by members of nationalist groups was fully consistent with the many NKVD agent reports about the rise of the *Organizatsiia Ukrainskikh Natsionalistov* (Organization of Ukrainian Nationalists [OUN]). Members of the OUN were a serious threat not merely because they were qualified agents—they had received thorough training in one of the Abwehr schools—but above all because they had excellent knowledge of the local terrain and contacts in the area. They were also highly motivated. Given the scale of Soviet persecution of any person deemed to be a Polish or Ukrainian nationalist in the 1930s, the high number of Poles and Ukrainians in the OUN was hardly surprising. The NKVD recommendations for dealing with this threat consisted of standard tradecraft practices: investigate those soldiers who revealed any defeatist sentiments, and pay particular attention to the families and acquaintances of those known to have left Soviet territory.

This report fails to mention that a key problem for the counterintelligence agencies on both sides of the border was terrain. Vast expanses of forests and numerous rivers clearly favor agent infiltration and exfiltration. The main crossing points can be monitored, and regular patrols can impede infiltration-exfiltration to some extent, but the NKVD faced a daunting task. In those circumstances when it did not have the manpower to place all suspects under surveillance, mass deportation offered an effective solution. Another countermethod omitted from this document was to penetrate organizations such as the OUN and disrupt them from the inside.

December 1940

Among the noteworthy intelligence summaries for this month are an agent report from *Litseist* (Lyceum student) dated 14 December, an NKVD report dated 27 December, and a deployment plan prepared by the Kiev Special Military District in November–December 1940 that must be regarded as a critical intelligence assessment.

The importance of the *Litseist* material is that, despite substantial and robust evidence of a hostile German intent toward the Soviet Union, the *Litseist* summary can be cited to show that Germany still regards Britain as its main enemy and that any conclusion that Germany is preparing to attack the Soviet Union is exaggerated. *Litseist* advances two considerations for his

Soviet handlers to ponder. First, Germany will do everything in its power "to avoid a war on two fronts and only special circumstances can compel her to take that course of action."[75] Although Germany desires general political control in Europe, it also wants to prevent any alliances among other states that would weaken central Europe. Second, citing Hitler, *Litseist* asserts that Germany's sole enemy is Britain and that Germany must maintain good relations with Russia. According to *Litseist*, "the position adopted by TASS does not reveal a reciprocal desire from the Soviet side to interpret events in its own interests."[76] *Litseist* also maintains that the purpose of the fortification work in the east, what he refers to as the "eastern rampart," is to encourage the Soviet Union to adopt a friendlier attitude toward Germany. But would Germany really devote so much effort to such a task, and what happens if the Soviet Union fails to see where its best interests lie? The eastern rampart is clearly a threat. If diplomatic efforts fail, the eastern rampart can be used as a base from which to compel Soviet compliance with German ambitions. Is the *Litseist* report a statistical outlier to be disregarded in the intelligence assessment calculus, or does it explain the real reason for the large-scale deployment of German troops and matériel to the east? The lot of an intelligence analyst is not an easy one, especially in the Soviet Union; this one must have thought that the old Russian saw about the weight of Monomakh's crown applied to him.

The intelligence summary of the Road-Transport Section of the NKVD provides critical information about aerodromes. It reports that five new aerodromes are under construction in the area of Warsaw, and the Warsaw airport, damaged during the German-Polish war, has now been fully repaired:

> These aerodromes are all being built to a single plan, without hangars, close to forests and with very large landing strips. On the two opposite sides roads have been laid in order to bring up aviation fuel. From the main highway, leading to the landing strip, there are about 4–5 concrete tracks along which the aircraft are taken away from the airfield and concealed in the forest. Fuel for the aircraft is kept in fuel storage tanks each with a capacity of 50,000 liters which are dug into the ground on a concrete base. These tanks are covered with earth to a depth of 30 centimeters.[77]

The most likely source of this detailed information was one of the conscripted laborers. Regardless of the source, it was valuable information.

Why did the Germans need all these new airfields? They clearly had no role in an invasion of Britain. Furthermore, knowledge of the locations of these new airfields, along with information about their all-important fuel storage facilities and capacity, meant that Soviet air force planners could prepare for a preemptive strike. Once they ascertained the types of Luftwaffe aircraft that would be based on these fields, they could make some assumptions about operational range and likely targets across the Soviet border and take the necessary defensive and offensives measures.

This report also provides valuable information about German attitudes and policies inside the Generalgouvernement. First, it notes that the Germans have initiated the mass requisitioning of foodstuffs—the seizure of grain, potatoes, meat, and fat—and that this is carried out with brutality. Second, Poles living in villages close to the border have been warned that they will be deported to the Polish heartland: "In place of the Poles, these villages are to be resettled by *Volksdeutsche* (Germans, inhabitants of the former Poland who have acquired German citizenship)."[78] Here, we have just one example of the ethnic cleansing, violence, and mass deportations implemented by the Germans in the occupied territories—a primary cause of the violence directed against Germans in Czechoslovakia and Poland after the end of World War II.[79]

The report also provides clear evidence that Polish Jews were starting to feel the full, cruel weight of Nazi policy:

> Throughout the towns massive roundups of Poles and Jews are being conducted. Those who do not have a permanent place of work are detained and sent to a camp.
>
> In the camps there is a high mortality rate. The prisoners are beaten. A so-called "ghetto" has been organized in Warsaw for the Jewish population. A special region of the city has been allocated for the ghetto, which is surrounded by a brick wall. Entry to, and exit from, the ghetto is forbidden and the exits are guarded by groups of police. At the present time there are about 410,000 Jews living in the ghetto who have been moved from all regions of the city. Apart from Warsaw, ghettos have also been organized in major separate locations. The population of the ghetto receives only about 125 gr. of bread a day and as a consequence of this the mortality rate among the Jews is particularly high.
>
> Ukrainians, Belorussians and Russians—who are not subject to any

limitations—consort freely with the Germans, and enjoy a privileged position.[80]

Among the Polish population of Warsaw, rumors were circulating that Hitler intended to create a Polish protectorate with a new Polish army. The army would be led by Polish officers released from German captivity, and the soldiers would wear Polish uniforms. This army would be used in a war against the Soviet Union and to seize western Belorussia and Ukraine.

The third CIA of 1940 bears witness to a marked shift in emphasis and a growing awareness of the fragile nature of German-Soviet relations, as well as the consequences if those relations should collapse. To quote Purkaev, chief of staff of the Kiev Special Military District:

> One can assume that the Non-Aggression Pact between the Soviet Union and Germany and the same between the Soviet Union and Italy are going to guarantee peace on our western borders for the immediate future.
>
> The deployment of German troops in Romania and Finland, the deployment of more than 100 divisions toward the borders of the Soviet Union and the direction of political and strategic efforts in the Balkans (the group of General Blaskowitz and the group of General Reichenau); the existence of a Tripartite Pact (Axis) involving Germany, Italy and Japan and the appearance of Italian divisions in Romania, has to be seen not only as measures directed against Britain, but also as *measures the point of which could be directed against the Soviet Union.*
>
> Any German assault on the Soviet Union would be most likely to occur in a situation in which Germany had emerged as the victor in its struggle with Britain and would maintain its dominant economic and military influence in the Balkans.
>
> Such a situation in the Balkans will create favorable conditions for Germany to (a) exploit cooperation with its European ally, Italy; (b) exploit the military-economic resources of the Balkan states (above all oil) and their armed forces (in the first instance Hungary and Romania) and the exploitation of a staging area for the invasion of the agriculturally and industrially rich territory of the Ukrainian SSR.
>
> Proceeding from this assumption it is necessary to assess the focal point of German forces as being directed against the South-Western Front. *Here one must expect the main blow of the enemy's combined forces.*[81]

Table 4.13. Soviet Assessment of the Number of German Aerodromes and Landing Strips Capable of Supporting German Operations against the Soviet South-Western Front, December 1940

Location	Aerodromes	Landing Strips
Generalgouvernement (Poland)	57	—
Germany (to Dresden meridian)	12	16
Czech Republic and Slovakia	64	50
Hungary	39	—
Romania	54	53
Total	226	119

Source: № 224, 1941 god, 1:489.

These introductory paragraphs show a clear and cool appraisal of what was happening and an awareness of the threat posed by Germany, despite all the attempts by German diplomacy to mislead the Soviet side. However, one must question whether Purkaev really believed that the primary aim of the massive German buildup had anything to do with an aggressive posture toward Britain.

One of the most important elements of this appraisal is the very detailed knowledge of enemy aerodromes and their preparation, which could be used to support a German offensive. The geographic extent of the network is shown in table 4.13. In assessing the landing capacity of these sites, the Soviet planners assumed that one aerodrome could accommodate 30 aircraft and that 50 percent of the landing strips were suitable for high-speed aircraft. Thus, within 600 kilometers of the borders of the Soviet Union, the enemy could locate up to 8,500 aircraft. They noted the presence of 53 aerodromes and 24 landing strips within 100 kilometers of the Soviet border, which they calculated would provide landing capacity for 4,000 aircraft. That 4,000 figure is higher than the total obtained by applying the same assumptions used to estimate the capacity of 226 aerodromes and 60 landing strips ([226 + 60] × 30 aircraft = 8,580). Thus, 53 aerodromes and 24 landing strips would be able to hold a total of 2,310 aircraft (77 × 30), mainly fighters and light bombers.

The intelligence data also indicated the main locations of the enemy aerodrome network, which meant that consideration should have been given to attacking these bases *before* the Germans launched their own attack. However, that part of the air plan did not go into effect until the *first day of operations*. It was envisaged that on day one, two consecutive raids would be launched on enemy aerodromes located in a zone at a depth of 150 to 160 kilometers. The forces used would consist of sixteen long-range bomber regiments, thirty medium bomber regiments, and ten fighter aviation regiments. The strike would be repeated on the second, third, and fourth days. On the fourth day, the long-range bombers would attack enemy aerodromes at a depth of 400 kilometers.[82] Once again, the plan was silent about whether this would be a preemptive strike or a retaliatory strike.

January 1941

Reports by Soviet agents and NKVD intelligence summaries for January all head in the same direction. In a report from Germany dated 4 January 1941, the agent states that another source has confirmed Hitler's top-secret order for an attack on the Soviet Union. The agent notes that preparations for such an attack had begun much earlier but were delayed by British resistance. The general assumption had been that once the British were neutralized, Germany would be free to turn its attention to the east. But the source has warned that Germany's ongoing sale of equipment to the Soviet Union, its apparent acceptance of the Soviet occupation of Bukovina, and its decision to ignore Soviet propaganda in Bulgaria should not fool anyone: Hitler has hostile intentions toward the Soviet Union. Moreover, Hitler is convinced that because the condition of the Red Army is so poor, he will be successful in any war.[83]

Generalfeldmarschall Walther von Brauchitsch's visit to the town of Sanok on 9 December 1940, accompanied by three generals, was a notable event picked up by the border troops of the NKVD. The visit of such a high-ranking German officer to the border region might be seen as routine, but given the Germans' efforts to fortify the border zone and the vast amounts of men and equipment deployed there, the visit should be interpreted as confirmation of the Germans' intense interest in the region. Various details in this report stand out. For example, in the second half of December, all quarters and barns in populated areas within twelve kilometers of the border were requisitioned by the Germans for troop accommodations.[84] Along the railway line thirty kilometers northeast of Warsaw, along the Warsaw–Min'sk–Mazovetski route, air defenses had been concentrated, suggesting a possible air attack that was not likely to come from Britain's Royal Air Force.

Two NKVD reports, dated 18 and 29 January 1941, provide clear evidence of agents recruited by the Germans who were active on Soviet territory. Both reports focus on Germany's interest in Soviet aviation and motor vehicle fuels and note that the agents were instructed to acquire samples used in civil and military aviation and ascertain whether different fuels were used in summer and winter. This German interest was confirmed by captured agents in December 1940 and January 1941. Two such German agents, I. I. Zhuk and A. A. Sosnovskii, confirmed that they had been ordered by German intelligence to acquire and send to Germany "samples of Soviet petroleum products used in transport and industry."[85] None of those detained could explain the Germans' interest in acquiring these samples. Soviet intelligence officers were also perplexed, and Fitin sought Golikov's opinion on why the Germans wanted the fuel samples.[86]

Beria's memorandum to Stalin and Molotov dated 21 January 1941, based on a source in the German Air Ministry, summarized Göring's argument that, in view of the problems caused by the war with Britain, some agreement should be sought between Germany and Britain and the United States. True or not, such a report would have alarmed Stalin; he would have perceived such an agreement as a move against the Soviet Union and a variation of the Axis Pact—though a far more dangerous one. Meanwhile, Beria reported that Göring had ordered a comprehensive aerial photographic survey of the Soviet Union's border regions, including Leningrad.

February 1941

Among the reports for February 1941 were further alarming signs of German military planning directed against the Soviet Union: an NKGB source report, NKVD summaries, and two clear warnings about likely start dates for a German invasion.

The NKGB memorandum to Stalin and Molotov, dated 8 February 1941, assesses German preparations for war against the Soviet Union, the Soviet-German trade agreement, and various data about the economic situation in Germany. The introductory paragraph offers a blunt warning: "A number of indices point to the fact that the German military command is conducting systematic preparations for a war against the Soviet Union."[87] According to *Korsikanets* (see above), the aim of the war is to seize the European part of the Soviet Union from Leningrad to the Black Sea and create a state that is entirely dependent on Germany. On the remaining part of the Soviet Union, a state that is well disposed toward Germany will be created.

Merkulov's summary provides details about the availability of raw materials in Germany. For example, there was a shortage of cobalt, and three-quarters of Germany's rubber was already being produced synthetically. Regarding oil, requirements for 1941 could be met from existing reserves and augmented by foreign oil purchases. The critical product was grain: if the Soviet Union did not maintain deliveries, bread rationing would be necessary. The situation in Germany was exacerbated by the fact that, owing to the acute food shortage in Belgium, Germany would have to deliver 20,000 tonnes of grain. Merkulov's summary also highlights a problem that would plague the German war economy: an acute labor shortage. This manpower shortage would eventually have horrendous implications for Soviet civilians; large numbers of them would be forcibly conscripted by the German occupation forces and deported to Germany, where they would be subjected to appalling conditions and used as slave labor. In fact, the effects of this acute labor shortage were already being felt by civilians in Poland and the protectorate who were being forcibly conscripted.

The two NKVD reports, dated 14 and 27 February 1941, were both based on material gathered by the Transport Directorate of the NKVD. Once again, they show the scale of the relentless German buildup. The earlier report begins with the standard, all-too-familiar opening: "According to reports from our undercover agents the regrouping of German forces in the regions bordering the Soviet Union continues."[88] It notes that large numbers of German troops were being withdrawn from the border with the Lithuanian republic "and are allegedly being redeployed to the Anglo-German front."[89] The NKVD reported that, subject to confirmation, a newly formed Ukrainian volunteer corps had established its headquarters in Liublino, and elements from this group had already undergone tactical training. Worse still, from a Soviet perspective, was the fact that a Belorussian volunteer corps, known as *Liberation*, was being formed in Warsaw, and so far, 7,000 volunteers had registered. The formation of various nationalist corps and legions, all with a marked hostility to the Soviet state, could lead to only one plausible conclusion: these units were going to be deployed at some stage against the Soviet Union, most likely alongside regular German units. Again, from a Soviet perspective, these units were regarded as counterrevolutionaries, White Guards, and all sorts of motley anti-Soviet elements. But inside these nationalist formations, the reason for their creation was quite clear: to liberate their homelands—Ukraine, Belorussia, Estonia, Latvia, and Lithuania—from Soviet occupation and oppression. With German support (or even without it), these formations posed a clear threat to Soviet interests. Germany, the creator of these nationalist legions, was supposed to be bound by its Non-Aggression Pact with the Soviet Union. German behavior was also inconsistent with the spirit and possibly the substance of the second supplementary protocol annexed to the German-Soviet Friendship and Border Treaty.

Further alarming signs were the scale and structure of the new aero-dromes and the speed with which they were being built. Unconfirmed re-ports indicated that military aerodromes were being built with *underground hangars* located no more than twenty-five to fifty kilometers from the border. The best guess was that, with the deployment of 300 laborers and the use of 100–200 vehicles, it would take seventy-five days to build one such aero-drome.[90] The Germans were also trying to increase the railway capacity. The military implications of such work were clear, and it had nothing to do with the ongoing war with Britain.

The NKVD was well informed about what was happening inside the Gen-eralgouvernement. Food products were being requisitioned from the rural population. The monthly ration allocated to the rural population was 200 grams of sugar, 150 grams of jam, and 300 grams of flour. Sugar, coffee, and tea could no longer be purchased. The urban population received 100 kilograms of coal per family per month; the rural population received no fuel. The Germans were also conducting a census of the population in the border regions, with the aim of forcibly deporting the inhabitants to the German heartland. One consequence of these plans, noted in the report, was a widespread desire to move across the Soviet border to avoid deportation. This constituted a security threat, since it was reasonable to assume that German agents would be among those seeking sanctuary. The NKVD also found evidence of armed revolt against German rule. In the first days of Jan-uary 1941, many members of the Gestapo had been killed during a rebellion that was eventually put down by the Gestapo and Ukrainian nationalists. Desertion from German units was also reported, including seventy deserters in January 1941. Other indicators that something serious was afoot included this report: "In the sector Zheshov–Iaslo–Shutsku the railway line has been completely militarized. The running of the line is carried out exclusively by German soldiers. The territory adjacent to this sector has been converted into a reinforced zone. Access to this zone by the civilian population is forbidden."[91] Likewise, all railway bridges in the Zheshov-Peremyshl' sector were guarded; the whole area was patrolled by German troops, and blackout measures were being enforced. There was additional alarming evidence of the role of nationalist units in German military planning:

> The rumors circulating about a forthcoming war between Germany
> and the USSR have led to an increase in activity of Ukrainian
> nationalist organizations. Ukrainian legions, formed by a special

commission of German officers, are being incorporated into the manpower of the German army.

In all Ukrainian schools the geography of a Separate Ukraine is being presented. In Krakow a map of a Separate Ukraine is being displayed in prominent places for public inspection. Territory of the Ukrainian SSR, including Kiev, Kharkov and other cities forms part of the map of a Separate Ukraine.

According to rumors 200 active Ukrainian nationalists from Krakow have allegedly gone to Berlin where in special courses they will be trained as the leading officials of a Separate Ukraine. No information about the personal composition of those Ukrainian nationalists who have traveled to Berlin is available.[92]

The agent source report from the NKGB reinforces the general picture. Reporting from Zurich, the Soviet agent *Dora* claims that the Germans have now amassed 150 divisions on the Soviet border and that the end of May 1941 is the most likely start date for the German attack.[93] The summary of the Soviet General Staff, based on the work of its illegal *rezidentura* (agents operating in another country), also makes for alarming reading. The source, code-named *Al'ta*, stresses that in German military circles, the war against the Soviet Union is expected to start this year—with 20 May 1941 given as the date of the invasion. The source identifies the main lines of advance of the German armies and notes that Russian-speaking German officers and noncommissioned officers are being concentrated in headquarters. In addition, trains suited to the wide-gauge lines in Russia are being built.[94]

March 1941

The reports for March 1941 show a definite intensification of trends already observed: German preparations for an attack on the Soviet Union are now well advanced. In total, there are four summaries from the NKGB, two assessments prepared by the Soviet General Staff, and a remarkable assessment of German military morale.

The first of the NKGB assessments, dated 6 March 1941, is based on information provided by the now familiar source *Korsikanets*. It offers important insights into German military thinking:

Among the higher levels of the German command structure the possibility of turning the military front to the east against the Soviet

Union is allegedly being discussed very seriously. These plans are allegedly based to a considerable degree on the exceptionally serious food situation that obtains in Germany and the occupied territories. In Belgium, for example, a real famine has started.

. . . The same interlocutor reports that the chief of the General Staff headquarters (ground forces) Generaloberst Halder is calculating on the unconditional success and rapid occupation by German troops, above all of Ukraine where, in Halder's assessment successful operations will be expedited by the good condition of rail and road communications. The same Halder also considers the occupation of Baku and its oil installations to be a straightforward mission in which the Germans could allegedly restore very quickly any damage inflicted by military operations. Halder considers that the Red Army will not be able to render suitable resistance to a Blitzkrieg offensive carried out by German troops and that the Russians will not even be able to destroy reserves.[95]

Halder's purely military view of the Germans' likely success is contrasted with an analysis by civilian officials:

According to information received from an official of the German committee responsible for the Four Year Plan, the committee has completed its deliberations about the economic effect in the event of a German attack against the Soviet Union. The committee has come to negative conclusions in the sense that given normal economic relations between Germany and the Soviet Union, Germany gains considerably more in the economic relationship than would be the case were Soviet territories to be occupied.[96]

Merkulov notes that any German move against Britain has been delayed; this was confirmed by the fact that the trading ban imposed on German ships had been lifted, and trade with South America could resume. The essential question was where Germany would strike next. According to the Soviet agent's German interlocutor, there would be a move against Turkey, followed by military operations against the Soviet Union, and finally an invasion of the British Isles. The latest Soviet plan for the mobilization of Soviet forces reflected the General Staff's view that the critical zone of operations was the west. The familiar introductory wording of earlier plans had become more specific, even unequivocal: "The developing political situation in Europe compels us to pay *exceptional attention to the defense of our western borders*."[97] This was supported by the NKGB report based on information from *Korsikanets*, who revealed that the Germans were making a major effort to complete an air photographic survey of the western parts of the Soviet Union.[98]

The NKGB report dated 27 March 1941 points to the Germans' heightened security regime in the border region.[99] Civilian travel on trains was now impossible without a special pass. Nighttime movements of German troops had increased, and all trains were blacked out. There were other seemingly insignificant signs of impending conflict. For instance, all cattle in the border regions had been registered by the Germans, and the animals' slaughter and sale required the permission of the occupation regime. When food is scarce, control of food is an effective way to control the population. This might also be seen as an antipartisan measure designed to deny them any kind of material support. The Soviet agent also reported that large numbers of young Germans (aged seventeen to eighteen) were present in Warsaw.

Among the flood of data about German troop movements and units were summaries of the rumors circulating among the civilian population. The words of a Polish telephonist were reported in detail. She claimed to know, from German officers who had visited her, that Germany was preparing for a war with the Soviet Union. According to a railway coupler: "The Germans, you know, will soon be attacking the Soviet Union, and to this end everything among them is ready."[100] In the Generalgouvernement there were rumors that Germany would attack the Soviet Union, with the aim of seizing Ukraine, and that the Soviet Union had delivered an ultimatum to the German government concerning the withdrawal of German troops from Bulgaria.

The two Soviet General Staff assessments were both prepared by Golikov and revealed detailed knowledge of the German armed forces, their current dispositions (as of March 1941), and changes to units and weapons, including small arms, tanks, and guns. The most notable change identified by Golikov was that, between 1 October 1940 and 1 March 1941, the total aircraft available to the Luftwaffe had almost doubled (a 74 percent increase). The full scale of German aircraft production is presented in table 4.14.

One of the most striking points about the deployment of German aircraft was its concentration in the west (see table 4.15). From these deployments Golikov concluded, "One should expect an intensification of German air force operations against the metropolitan areas of Britain, against her

Table 4.14. Number of Aircraft Available to the Luftwaffe as of 1 October 1940 and 1 March 1941

Aircraft Type	1 October 1940	1 March 1941
Bomber	2,100	4,090 (+ 1,990)
Dive-bomber	700	1,850 (+ 1,150)
Reconnaissance	900	1,220 (+ 320)
Fighter	2,000	3,820 (+ 1,820)
Naval aviation	300	350 (+ 50)
Other types	5,900	9,370 (+ 3,470)
Total	11,900	20,700 (+ 8,800)

Source: № 316, "Spetssoobshchenie razvedupravleniia genshtaba Krasnoi Armii o napravlenii razvitiia vooruzhennykh sil Germanii i izmeneniiakh v ikh sostoianii, № 660279ss, 11 marta 1941 g.," 1941 god, 1:746–747.

maritime communications, her fleet and an intensification of operations against the British navy in the Mediterranean."[101] This huge increase in the deployment of aircraft in the west, coupled with the stability of aircraft deployments on the Soviet border, did indeed suggest that, for the foreseeable future, Britain and British interests were the main targets, not the Soviet Union. What this analysis did not take into account, however, was that an obvious buildup of aircraft on airfields close to the Soviet border would have caused great alarm among Soviet observers. Moreover, unlike infantry and tank divisions, aircraft can be deployed quickly. There was no need for the aircraft to be in place three months (or even one month) before an air assault against the Soviet Union. However, the aerodromes, hangars, fuel depots, and other support infrastructure had to be prepared well in advance so that the aircraft could be received immediately before the countdown to the start date. The later this happened the better, since it would reduce—but not entirely eliminate—the time available to the enemy to take any counteractions (possibly a preemptive strike). Thus, one might see the huge German deployment of aircraft in the west (targeting Britain) and in Italy (targeting British interests in the Mediterranean) as deliberately calculated to provoke precisely the assessment Golikov provided to Stalin. At this stage in the German move east, the critical indicators were the deployment of heavy equipment and infantry, the relentless increase in the number of aerodromes and airstrips, and, as already reported by Soviet agents, the intensification of German reconnaissance flights over the Soviet Union.

Golikov's analysis of the aerodrome network in eastern Prussia and on the territory of the Generalgouvernement supports the view that the immediate

Table 4.15. Deployment of German Aircraft as of 1 October 1940 and 1 March 1941

Deployment Location	1 October 1940	1 March 1941
Western Front*	4,000	8,030
On the Soviet border	700	700
Germany	400	400
Czech Republic, Moravia, and Slovakia	600	400
Italy, Romania, and Bulgaria	—	1,450
Total	5,700	10,980

Source: № 316, 1941 god, 1:748.

*Golikov's use of na zapadnom fronte (on the Western Front) is potentially misleading when study-ing a military system that uses the word "front" to refer to conglomerations of armies. However, given Golikov's conclusions, his use of the term can be taken to mean the Anglo-German zone of conflict in western Europe.

task was the expansion and completion of infrastructure.[102] He notes that before September 1939, there was a total of 55 aerodromes and 28 landing strips in eastern Prussia and 100 aerodromes and 124 landing strips in what is now the Generalgouvernement. Thus, the Luftwaffe had a combined total of 307 aerodromes and landing strips available. Based on the Soviet General Staff's assumption that each site could accommodate 30 aircraft (mainly fighters and fighter-bombers), the total capacity would be 9,210 aircraft (307 × 30). Golikov's own figures show that from 1 October 1940 to 1 March 1941, the number of German aircraft stationed on the borders with the Soviet Union remained stable at 700 aircraft (which would require about 24 sites). Yet, as Golikov points out, the Germans were relentlessly raising their existing capacity by building new aerodromes, landing strips, fuel storage facilities (some underground), and other related infrastructure, despite the presence of only 700 aircraft. Approximately 25 new aerodromes and 20 landing strips were being built throughout eastern Prussia and the Generalgouvernement, which would accommodate an extra 1,350 aircraft (45 × 30). Sixteen of these new aerodromes and landing strips were being built close to the boundaries between the Western Special Military District and the Kiev Special Military District, with a capacity of 480 aircraft (16 × 30). Assuming that the Germans' expansion of their aerodrome program was not some monstrous bluff, there could be only one plausible explana-tion: at some stage, this network would be used to accommodate aircraft—reconnaissance planes, fighters, fighter-bombers, and bombers—whose targets were located in the Soviet Union.

Golikov's analysis of the redeployment of German infantry and tank

Table 4.16. Changes in Disposition of the German Army from 1 September 1940 to 1 March 1941

Location	1 September 1940				1 March 1941			
	Infantry	Motorized	Tank	Total	Infantry	Motorized	Tank	Total
Western Europe	89	7	6	102 (45%)	86	1	5	92 (35%)
Eastern Europe	62	3	7	72 (32%)	52	5	4	61 (23%)
Southeastern Europe	20	—	2	22 (9%)	50	4	8	62 (24%)
Reserve	30	—	2	32	8	5	—	13
Reformed	—	—	—	— 14%	25	5	5	35 (18%)
Total	201	10	17	228	221	20	22	263

Source: № 316, 1941 god, 1:747.

divisions showed a shift from the west toward eastern and southeastern Europe, as indicated in table 4.16. This shift was consistent with the extra time required for the buildup of tanks and infantry compared with the air arm. Thus, the large number of German aircraft retained in the west was not a decisive indication that German strategic ambitions were directed against Britain.

For reasons that will become apparent, Golikov's second intelligence assessment, dated 20 March 1941, was something of a milestone en route to 22 June 1941. Golikov begins by stating the following: "The majority of agent data concerning the possibilities of war with the Soviet Union in the spring of 1941 are derived from Anglo-American sources *whose tasks at the present day are undoubtedly a striving to bring about a deterioration in relations between the USSR and Germany.*"[103] But the majority of information and data clearly pointing to Germany's aggressive intentions toward the Soviet Union were not derived from Anglo-American sources. Soviet agents under deep cover, NKVD border units, and NKVD officers tasked with the routine analysis of troop movements and, in the case of Golikov himself, the major expansion of the aerodrome network in the east had provided compelling evidence, certainly by the date of Golikov's report, that Germany's intentions were hostile. Having dismissed the Anglo-American sources as mischief makers, Golikov then cites some sixteen paragraphs of statements (some from open sources) that support the conclusion that German intentions were hostile. Thus, Golikov reports that British and American sources talked openly about German preparations for an attack on the Soviet Union; that the Japanese military attaché declared that, after finishing the war against Britain, Hitler intended to attack the Soviet Union; that German and Italian guarantees given to Romania about the status of its borders were aimed at the Soviet Union; and that, according to one source cited by Golikov, "*One can expect a conflict between Germany and the Soviet Union in May 1941.*"[104] In addition, "*The Swedish military attaché as corroboration of information concerning preparation for an attack against the Soviet Union in the spring of 1941 emphasized that the information had been received from a military person and was based on a top-secret order from Hitler which was only known to a limited circle of responsible persons.*"[105] There is more along these lines. Having reviewed the serials contained in the intelligence assessment, Golikov reaches the following conclusions:

1. On the basis of all the statements and all the operational variations cited above for spring of this year I consider the most likely period for the start

of a war against the Soviet Union will be the moment after victory over Britain or after the conclusion of peace with her that would be honorable for Germany.

2. It is necessary to assess the rumors and documents which speak of the inevitability this spring of a war against the USSR as disinformation originating from British and even perhaps from German intelligence.[106]

Diplomatic gossip, isolated remarks picked up by military attachés, and various press reports were not necessarily hard evidence of German intent. But when qualified Soviet sources repeatedly identified troop movements that were consistent with rumors and information from other sources that Germany's intentions were not peaceful, hard decisions were required at the highest level. Golikov's conclusions bore the stamp of Stalinist expectations: Golikov told his master what he expected to hear. After the war, while working on his book V Moskovskoi bitve (In the Moscow Battle), Golikov requested access to some of the intelligence summaries he had prepared. About the conclusions in his summary dated 20 March 1941, Golikov stated, "They have no significance."[107]

The morale and behavior of German soldiers attracted a lot of attention from the NKVD, which was looking for clues to how well the German army would fight. A March 1941 report offers a snapshot of the German army that was very much at odds with an army thoroughly imbued with professional pride and conscious of its recent achievements. The report cites instances of desertion and what the author refers to as "general, moral decay."[108] It attributes this breakdown in military discipline to a deterioration in the provision of material goods caused by a protracted war, frequent moves from one front to another, and the effects of British air raids. The report cites cases of troops being executed: "On 30 September 1940 a machine gun battalion from the Bzhozuv garrison made up of Austrians and Bavarians refused to take the oath and be deployed to the front. The battalion was disbanded and on the sentence of a court-martial 75 soldiers were shot."[109]

In December 1940, in the port of Kiel, the crew of a U-boat refused to put to sea, and the German sailors and officers were arrested. According to the report, two senior officers committed suicide after receiving news that their families had been killed in British air raids; it also cited many examples of soldiers deserting. Interestingly, most of these disciplinary offenses occurred among soldiers who were returning to their units from leave. Disciplinary offenses are a fact of life in any army, so the problem for the NKVD analyst was how much weight to give these incidents, relative to the size of the enemy army. Imputing too much weight to such offenses while ignoring the huge buildup of men and matériel would be misleading.[110]

April 1941

Despite the best intentions of their authors, the intelligence summaries and agent source reports from April 1941 onward reflected a sense of urgency that even Stalin's hostility to the obvious could not entirely dispel.

Korsikanets and Starshina continued to provide valuable and timely material to their handlers. The NKGB source report based on material sent by Zakhar, dated 2 April 1941, begins with a clear warning: "Starshina met Korsikanets. Starshina reported that the plan for the attack on the Soviet Union had now been completely prepared and worked out by his organization."[111]

More important, the agents provided precise details about the likely targets of the Luftwaffe's attack. Since Soviet industry was dispersed over such a wide area and therefore could not be destroyed in a short period, the Luftwaffe's initial plan was to attack the railway networks linking the industrial centers and the main strategic locations. The main targets were the railway foci in the central part of the Soviet Union. More specifically, in the first phase, the Germans planned to paralyze the following railway communications: Tula–Orel–Kursk–Khar'kov, Kiev–Gomel', the line south via Elets', and the line south via Riazhsk.[112] The aim was to cut the economic arteries in a northeasterly direction and prevent the deployment of reserves from east to west. Among other first-wave targets reported by Starshina were power stations, the Donets basin, and the engine and ball-bearing plants and aviation industries in Moscow. Highly valuable for any possible Soviet preemptive air strike was Starshina's unambiguous statement that "air bases [German] in the Krakow area are to be one of the main departure points for the air attacks launched against the Soviet Union."[113] Critical and urgent was Starshina's knowledge from various documents that preparations for the attack on the Soviet Union were complete; however, he did not know whether Hitler had made a final decision. On the timing of any German invasion, Korsikanets provided a small but significant piece of information. One of his interlocutors had informed him of the decision to import all rubber from the east via the sea, not via the Soviet Union, regardless of the threat from the British navy. Korsikanets saw the cessation of shipments via the Soviet Union as an indicator of preparation for an attack. Litseist reported being told by a German officer, an Oberst Blau: "During this war we have managed by means of the colossal movements of troops to hide the real intentions of the German command."[114]

Starshina himself was not entirely convinced that the invasion would occur, but he relayed the opinion of another well-placed source, a German major: "The undertaking against the Soviet Union has now been finally determined and the attack will soon follow."[115] This anonymous major, who had contacts in the German General Staff, also provided some detail about the Germans' ground attack plan. There would be a rapid and sudden blow on Ukraine and then on to the east. Simultaneously, there would be a strike north. The army coming from the north would link up with the army coming from the south, surrounding and cutting off the Soviet armies. Such a plan was also broadly consistent with the German measures to reinforce and widen the defense installations on their side of the border. Any large-scale Soviet move west would encounter these fortified positions (with rivers to their front) and would also run the risk of being cut off by the two German armies in its rear. According to this report, the preferred start date for the German invasion was May, not June, and any move against Yugoslavia would delay the start date by four weeks. The Luftwaffe feared that a delay might result in a lost opportunity, presumably because the element of surprise would be forfeited. The Luftwaffe planners also calculated that, as far as the air plan was concerned, May was the better month, since the state of Soviet aerodromes at that time of year would complicate their use by the Soviet air force.

A source report prepared by the Soviet General Staff provides a startling example of the institutional paranoia and indecision that gripped certain parts of the Soviet intelligence establishment with regard to German intentions. The first part of this assessment could not be clearer about the threat posed by Germany:

> The concentration of German troops along the entire border with the Soviet Union from the Black to the Baltic Seas, the unconcealed revanchist statements of Romania about northern Bukovina, the deployment of "instructors" to Finland, the well-disposed attitude to the mobilization carried out in Sweden, the latest deployment of troops from the west to the Generalgouvernement and, finally, the fact that the Balkan countries have been turned into allied states means that the idea that Germany has military intentions against our country cannot be excluded, even more so were Germany to succeed in establishing herself on the shores of the Adriatic and Aegean Seas.[116]

Having produced this assessment, the author, Golikov, then tried to under-mine its conclusions: "However, bearing in mind that this information orig-inates from German sources and received its widest possible dissemination at a time of active German diplomacy in the Balkans, one can assume that Germany when preparing its next move in the Balkans is making good the shortage of real forces by exerting psychological pressure."[117]

If, having satisfied himself in the first part of his appraisal that the de-ployment of German troops and equipment along the entire Soviet border indicates hostile intent, Golikov has to explain why the fact that these sources are mainly German (if, in fact, they are) overrides his own earlier conclusions. The logical conclusion—or certainly one that should be con-sidered—is not that the earlier appraisal can be dismissed but that, taken together with diplomatic rumors, it acquires additional weight, not less. The Golikov assessment strikes me as a good example of reliable evidence being adduced (if it were not reliable, Golikov would not have cited it), only to be dismissed as unreliable or erroneous for reasons other than those required by a strictly data-based and probability-assessed intelligence analysis.

The same stark warnings of the German buildup, though without Go-likov's unconvincing caveats and prevarications, are contained in a report from the Ukraine NKVD and one from the NKGB, both dated 9 April 1941. The warnings could hardly be clearer: "According to information which is derived from various sources, it is evident that from the beginning of 1941 and particularly very recently major redeployments of troops from Germany to the territory of the Generalgouvernement and toward the borders of the Soviet Union are being carried out by the German command."[118] Ever alert to ideological dangers caused by what it sees as the curse of national identity, the NKVD notes that in Peremyshl' there was plenty of talk about German preparations for war with the Soviet Union. Loudspeakers had been set up in the streets, and there was open agitation against the Soviet Union. The threat from Ukrainian nationalism was explicit: "Ukrainian nationalists conduct open agitation for a joint action with German troops against the Soviet Union under the slogan 'Liberation of Ukrainian Land from the Soviets.'"[119]

The NKGB also clearly recognizes the danger and significance of the German buildup: "From information derived from undercover agents and the statements of those who have violated the borders it can be ascertained that the concentration of German army units on the border of the Soviet Union continues. At the same time, the high tempo of the construction of defense installations, aerodromes, strategic railway, branch lines and tarmac and graded roads continues."[120] This introduction is supported by a wealth of detail that leaves little doubt that a massive expansion of military infrastructure is under way and has been for some time. The Germans must realize that the Soviet side knows about their aerodrome-building program and might be tempted to act before the Luftwaffe does. German defensive measures must therefore be seen as an indicator of hostile intent.

A memorandum drawn up by the Ukraine NKGB on or after 15 April 1941 and sent to Nikita Khrushchev, then the first secretary of the Ukraine Communist Party, must be considered a CIA. The initial warning is stark and uncompromising: "According to information from undercover agents and the investigation of files of deserters it can be ascertained that the Germans are intensifying their preparations for war against the Soviet Union for which purposes they are concentrating troops on our border, are building roads and reinforced positions and are moving up ammunition."[121] Adding weight to this report was the fact that a German plane, a JU-86, had been brought down by Soviet air defenses while on a reconnaissance flight, and maps and cameras had been found on board.[122]

Even allowing for the objectively demonstrated buildup of German divisions on the border, the Soviet Union's greatest fear seems to be that Germany might use disaffected nationalist elements and the OUN in Ukraine as a fifth column in the event of an attack. The report's author concedes that the OUN constitutes a serious threat, since it is well armed. Particularly alarming, from the Soviet standpoint: "The so-called 'revolutionary center' of the OUN, led by Stepan Bandera, without waiting for war, is already now organizing active opposition to measures undertaken by the Soviet authorities and in all kinds of ways is terrorizing the population of the western districts of Ukraine."[123] Examples of party officials being killed are also cited. This clearly constitutes a threat to Soviet power:

> During the day the illegals hide in the forests, wandering along the roads. In the evenings they appear in the villages and find shelter in the houses of kulaks and among the families of the repressed and even in their own houses. The population of several villages are terrorized to such a degree that even those people who are well disposed to Soviet power are frightened to inform on the illegals.[124]

The hard core of the OUN was estimated to consist of about 1,000 illegals.[125] Meshik, the report's author, recommended four measures for dealing with the OUN. First, the Soviet law concerning traitors should be applied to the members of anti-Soviet organizations found, illegally, in the western regions of the Ukrainian republic. Such a proposal failed to consider that an illegal might be a citizen of another state who just happened to be in the Soviet Union illegally. Second, all the families of illegals should be repressed (to use the Soviet term), and all their property confiscated. Third, "the families of arrested members of the OUN are to be deported to the remote regions of the Soviet Union." Fourth, to prevent them from providing shelter to the OUN, all kulaks should be deported to the remote regions of the Soviet Union, and their property should be transferred to the collective farms.[126] The first measure could have been implemented almost immediately, but there is no indication whether any arrests took place before 22 June 1941 or whether any were being planned. Such actions could have been counterproductive, since news of them would have reached OUN leaders across the border, adding weight to their claims that they were fighting a war of liberation from Soviet oppression. Meshik's recommendations were the classic prophylactic measures adopted by the Soviet state to deal with national minorities, and they clearly owed much to earlier decrees, such as Nikolai Ezhov's Order № 00447 (1937).

Two reports dated 16 April 1941, one from the Ukraine NKGB and the other prepared by Golikov on behalf of the Soviet General Staff, provide critical indicators of preparations for hostilities. The NKGB report begins with the familiar warning about the German buildup and then points out that a special order issued by the German High Command prohibited all contact between the local population and the troops, and locals were not permitted access to unit lines. Tightening of security in the border zone was also indicated by a 6 April order, published in the local press, that as of 12 April, all civilian rail travel was forbidden. Preventing speculators was the reason cited for this measure, "but the population does not believe this and considers that this is linked to the preparation for the attack against the Soviet Union."[127] The ubiquitous Ukrainian nationalist threat was high on the list of NKGB and NKVD concerns: "In connection with the concentration of German troops close to the Soviet border one part of the Ukrainian nationalists is hoping that it will march off with the Germans and will, with their assistance, create a great, separate Ukraine."[128]

According to Golikov, during the first fifteen days of April, the size of the German deployment on the eastern border increased with the arrival of three infantry and two motorized divisions, 17,000 armed Ukrainian nationalists, and one regiment of paratroopers. Thus, the Germans now had seventy-eight divisions of all types in eastern Prussia and the General-gouvernement.[129] In at least six regions, concentrations of pontoon bridges, river-crossing equipment, and various wooden bridges had been observed. Golikov's sources were also very well informed about the scale of German ammunition and fuel deliveries. Since the beginning of 1941, a total of 6,995 wagons of ammunition (including 16 with aviation bombs) and 993 wagons with fuel had been recorded.[130] Fifty-seven percent of the total ammunition shipments and 34 percent of the total fuel shipments had been delivered to Ostrov, and 1,640 wagons of ammunition (23 percent) had been delivered to Sedlets. High concentrations of fuel had been delivered to Biala-Podliaska (220 wagons, or 22 percent) and Zamost'e (236 wagons, or 24 percent). Ostrov appears to be the central depot for these deliveries—an important finding that requires an explanation: Ostrov, Sedlets, Zamost'e, and Biala-Podliaska would be prime targets in any Soviet air attack. Golikov also confirms the travel ban for civilians and the evacuation of the families of German military personnel from Warsaw and places east of the city to the German heartland. Having cited this detailed and comprehensive evidence of German activity, Golikov merely states the obvious: the German buildup is continuing. Remarkable is the absence of any rational assessment of why the Germans are concentrating so many men and so much matériel in the regions of the Soviet border.

Where Golikov fears to tread, the Soviet military attaché in Berlin, General-Major Vasilii Ivanovich Tupikov, most certainly does not. Among all the Soviet documents dealing with this period in Soviet-German military relations that are in the public domain, Tupikov's memorandum to Golikov, dated 25–26 April 1941, stands out as one of the most clear-sighted analyses available, and it is undoubtedly a CIA on the road to 22 June 1941. This memorandum is just one of many Tupikov sent to Golikov after his appointment as attaché, and one can assume that his other assessments of Stalin's (and others') response to the obvious are far from flattering.

The critical question identified by Tupikov is straightforward enough: is there any evidence of Germany's preparing for a war with the Soviet Union, and if so, when would such a war start? In providing his assessment of German intentions to Golikov, Tupikov hints that his report might be unwelcome: "If it seems to you that with this exposition of my views I am stating the obvious then I shall in no way be dismayed."[131] To begin with, Tupikov sees the recent neutrality pact between the Soviet Union and Japan as "an indicator of the course of German policy aimed at the Soviet Union."[132]

To this end, Tupikov points out that Matsuoka's arrival was preceded by a number of rumors: that a war between Germany and the Soviet Union was inevitable; that there was evidence of a German buildup in the east; that Germany had openly disregarded Soviet interests in the Balkans; and that Matsuoka's visit to Moscow was, supposedly, of very little significance. However, the visit itself was accompanied by new levels of propaganda that war was inevitable, that negotiations between Germany and Japan represented the establishment of contact between the two nations and a simultaneous move against the Soviet Union, and that the concentration of German troops in the east was ongoing. From his perspective in Berlin, Tupikov argues that the Soviet-Japanese pact stunned the Germans, but they still tried to impose an interpretation that suited Germany and the Axis powers. The German version of the pact, according to Tupikov, was that the Soviet Union now had something like dominion status in relation to the Axis Pact. "On the strength of this," concludes Tupikov, "the question of any confrontation is one of times and dates which are not that far removed, since, being so dependent on normal relations with us, Germany would hardly consider it possible to plan for a long period of stability in German-Soviet relations on the basis of an anti-Soviet policy."[133]

The essence of Tupikov's interpretation is that even though Germany benefits from its trade relationship with the Soviet Union, Germany has decided that the same benefits can be derived from war, occupation, and exploitation, and a move in that direction is imminent. In support of this interpretation, Tupikov notes that Germany spends all its money on food "but maintains an army of such a size, which, apart from our theater of operations, can be used nowhere."[134] Moreover, the buildup of troops is occurring not in the west but in the east. Critically, Tupikov understands that in terms of training, morale, and equipment, the German army is reaching its peak, and that peak cannot be maintained indefinitely: at some point, the archer, having drawn the bow, must release the arrow. In the Balkans, Tupikov asserts, Germany "seeks out and pursues its interests, directly, clearly and in an anti-Soviet manner, most of all, in an openly anti-Soviet manner and even there, as in Finland, where these interests, apart from being militarily anti-Soviet, are absent."[135]

At the start of this remarkable memorandum, Tupikov makes it clear to Golikov that although his conclusions are based on a variety of sources, they are merely "grains of an answer to a fundamental question."[136] Nevertheless, Tupikov's conclusions could not be clearer or more alarming for his masters.

Table 4.17. German Divisions and Deployment, November 1940–April 1941

Formation	Number of Divisions		
	15 November 1940	15 January 1941	25 April 1941
Western	90	90	75
Eastern	70	80	95
Balkans	—	—	50
Italian-African	—	—	8–10
Inside Germany	65	75	45
Total	225	245	273–275

Source: № 412, 1941 god, 2:118.

The first two conclusions are critical and carry the most weight. First, the Soviet Union is now the prime target of German military planning. Second, the time frame for this confrontation is possibly very short and "*without a doubt within the current year.*"[137] The third of Tupikov's conclusions is the least threatening to the Soviet Union. Although it anticipates pressure being applied to Sweden and Turkey, there is a possibility that Germany might pursue its operations in the Middle East, which would weaken its European formations.

Attached to Tupikov's memorandum is an assessment by Golikov of the total number of German divisions as of 25 April 1941 (see table 4.17). The obvious conclusion is that there has been a marked increase in troop levels in the east, and the buildup has not stopped. Of the 275 divisions available to the five formations, 145 divisions, or 53 percent of the total, are now located in the east and the Balkans.

By now, some individuals at the highest level of the Soviet military establishment are coming to the same conclusions as Tupikov. One indication of this is Zhukov's 29 April directive to the Moscow Military District, in which he orders that the 231st and 224th Rifle Divisions, with a full complement of equipment and good-quality military personnel, be sent to reinforce the Western Special Military District. This move is to be completed by 10 May 1941.[138] Buried among the minutiae of this staff directive is further evidence that, despite all the Soviet propaganda concerning multiethnic solidarity and internationalism, members of national minorities—the *natsmeny*—are deemed unreliable and untrustworthy. Zhukov's order could not be clearer:

> Red Army soldiers—natives of the western districts of the Ukraine
> SSR and Belorussian SSR (of all nationalities), the conscription cohort

of the autumn of 1940 and those arriving in April–May 1941, and, additionally, those among the personnel of the two divisions being sent who are of Lithuanian, Estonian, German, Polish, Bulgarian and Greek nationality are to be transferred to other units in the district and are to be replaced by an allocation of a corresponding number of the best conscripts who arrived in the district in the months of March and May this year.[139]

These transferees would be well aware of why they were being separated from the Russians, and they would not be moved by calls to fight for a political system that regarded them as pariahs. The transfer of the *natsmeny*, especially the removal of Belorussians and Ukrainians from the western districts, can also be seen as a counterintelligence response to the possibility that there were OUN members among the Soviet units. This might partially neutralize the OUN, but it would also affect the *natsmeny* psychologically. Once the catastrophe started, they would find it much easier to surrender, desert, and, as events would show, actively collaborate with the German invaders.

Further evidence that Zhukov was now deeply alarmed and desperately trying to make up for lost time was his order to Pavlov sometime in April 1941. He instructed Pavlov to work out an operational plan for the deployment of the armies of the Western Special Military District. In doing so, Pavlov was "to be guided by the following factors," the first of which was: "It can be assumed that the Non-Aggression Pacts between the USSR and Germany and between the USSR and Italy at the present time shall secure the state of peace on our western borders. The USSR does not plan to attack Germany or Italy. These states, apparently, are also not planning to attack the USSR in the near future."[140] Having made this concession to his master, Zhukov then admitted to Pavlov that there were grounds for concern: the German occupation of Bulgaria, wars in Yugoslavia and Greece, the Germans' suspicious behavior in Finland and Romania, the concentration of considerable German forces on the Soviet border (by the end of April 1941, estimated to be 1.2 million to 1.5 million men in the Generalgouvernement alone[141]), and the Axis Pact, which could be directed against the Soviet Union. This order is a very important document. It suggests that Zhukov, among others, was going along with Stalin's views on German intentions, yet doing everything he could within this framework of official denial to avert the impending disaster.

May 1941

Evidence of official denial, on the one hand, and growing alarm, on the other, are the central themes in some of the intelligence summaries for May 1941.

Stalin and Molotov received an NKGB intelligence report, based on the work of its agents and dated 5 May 1941, that contains a whole series of individual observations, and they all point one way. In the Generalgouvernement, it notes, military preparations are conducted without any attempt to hide them, and German soldiers talk of a war with the Soviet Union as a decision that has already been made. The role of the Ukrainian fifth column is cited as a factor that will enable Germany to seize Ukraine. Other indicators include the following: since the end of April, all schools have been closed and turned into military hospitals; all Red Cross teams have been called up; all private vehicles have been requisitioned; and a full nighttime blackout has been ordered. In addition, German officers are studying Russian, and they have been issued topographic maps of the border regions of the Soviet Union. In the immediate border zone, some 35,000 Jews have been conscripted to dig foundations under the supervision of the Todt organization, and all the inhabitants in the region of Rodoma have been deported from 250 villages.[142]

Along with the huge concentrations of infantry and tank divisions, the exhaustive efforts to build aerodromes and landing strips were raising profound concerns about German intentions. NKVD agents identified two main concentrations of aerodrome networks: one in Zamost'e, and another in Liublin. These airfields, some of which were still under construction, pointed to a major deployment of aircraft at some later stage. In the village of Mokre (Zamost'e), there were three hangars, each with a capacity of ten aircraft, and six underground fuel storage facilities, each with a capacity of 100,000 liters. A total of seven aerodromes and two landing strips had been identified in Zamost'e; based on the estimate of 30 planes per site, that would amount to 270 aircraft.[143] Existing Polish aerodromes in the Liublin area were being repaired and expanded, and additional aerodromes and associated infrastructure were being built in at least nine other sites.

Two Soviet General Staff memoranda dated 15 May 1941 (one of them a CIA) reveal that not all members of that august body were singing from the same hymn sheet. The first, authored by Golikov, shows his characteristic prevarication; the second, though coauthored by Timoshenko and Zhukov, bears the unmistakable stamp of the victor of Khalkin-Gol.

Golikov's introduction, though objectively accurate, is potentially misleading: "The regrouping of German troops over the first half of May [1941] is characterized by a continuing strengthening of formations against the USSR along the entire western and southwestern border, including Romania as well, and by a further strengthening of forces for operations against Britain in the Near East, in Africa and in Norway."[144] The question here is why such a massive deployment of German troops would be seen as anything other than a clear expression of hostile intent against the Soviet Union at a time when no state of war existed between the two states. Golikov's linking of German actions against the British with a possible attack against the Soviet Union is misleading precisely because it suggests uncertainty in German planning, even though the main conclusion of Golikov's report—"The increase in German troops on the border with the USSR continues. The main regions of concentration are: the southern part of the Generalgouvernement, Slovakia and the northern part of Moldavia"—suggests the opposite.[145] Germany was indeed at war with Britain, but the buildup on the Soviet borders indicated that the Germans were planning to break their self-imposed taboo of a war on two fronts.

Of all the countless intelligence reports and summaries that had passed over Stalin's desk, none spelled out the grave risk facing the Soviet Union in the middle of May 1941 better than the Timoshenko-Zhukov memorandum. The memorandum laid before Stalin certain plans "in the event of war with Germany and its allies." Timoshenko and Zhukov were prodding the *vozhd'*. As one would expect, the memorandum is a wealth of detail about the state of the German armed forces and its allies, but the dire warning concerns not so much the number of German divisions deployed but the fact that, as pointed out by Tupikov, the German armed forces expect a release of energy soon. Germany is ready, and this is clearly recognized by Timoshenko and Zhukov: "Bearing in mind that at the present time Germany maintains its army in a totally mobilized state, with all its rear echelon support services deployed, it has the opportunity to steal a march on us in operational deployment and launch a sudden attack."[146] If one could cite the one moment when the threat of a German surprise attack was laid out before Stalin with brutal and logical clarity, this memorandum might well be it.

The succeeding paragraph shows the same clarity and awareness of danger as it spells out what needs to be done:

> In order to avert this (and to rout the German army), I consider it essential that the operational initiative in no way be conceded to the

German command and to forestall the enemy in deployment and to attack the German army at that moment when it finds itself in the process of deployment and will not manage to organize its front and the interoperability of its arms of service.[147]

This assessment is clearly inviting Stalin to consider a preemptive land and air strike against the Germans. In fact, Timoshenko and Zhukov state this clearly after setting out the tasks for the fronts: "In order to secure the execution of the plan outlined above it is essential to implement the following measures in good time *since without these measures inflicting a surprise attack on the enemy from both air and land will be impossible.*"[148] These measures—the same ones Zhukov would take when planning for Uranus some eighteen months later—envisaged the following: total and concealed mobilization of troops under the pretext of an exercise call-up, a concealed deployment of troops much closer to the western border, a concealed concentration of planes from remote districts and the immediate preparation of the air support infrastructure, and the *gradual* deployment (emphasis in the original), under the pretext of training, of the rear echelons and medical services.[149] The recommendation concerning the deployment of aircraft recognized that aircraft cannot be deployed within range of targets until the necessary infrastructure is in place to receive them. This is exactly what the Germans had been doing in eastern Prussia and the Generalgouvernement over the last year: airfields and infrastructure first; planes later—much later.[150]

June 1941

In the immediate aftermath of the Germans' success against the Anglo-French alliance in June 1940, any indications that their strategic ambitions were now being directed toward the east could be argued away by claiming that Germany had learned its lesson: a war on two fronts led to disaster. By 1 June 1941, that explanation carried little or no weight. As events moved to their climax, the evidence for an invasion continued to flood in; time seemed to accelerate.

At the beginning of June, Golikov received two reports from an agent, code-named *Ramzai*, in Tokyo.[151] The agent reported that the German invasion was scheduled to be launched in the second half of June and cited various indirect indicators to support this claim: the technical department of the German air force had been ordered to return, no sensitive messages were being sent via the Soviet Union, and the transportation of rubber through the Soviet Union had been reduced to an absolute minimum. The second report revealed the German view of the Soviet defensive system: the Germans considered the lack of an extensive defense in depth as a great tactical error, since it would help smash the Red Army in the first major encounter.

Events in Romania were also alarming. Two reports drawn up by the Soviet General Staff provide clear evidence that the Romanian army was being mobilized. Schools had been told to accelerate their examination schedules so that by 10 June 1941, school buildings could be used as barracks and hospitals.[152] The second report notes: "Mobilization in Romania is confirmed by many sources. Those in the age range from 18 to 42 years are being called up. The call-up is being conducted via telegram. At the same time cavalry personnel and vehicles are being mobilized."[153] All normal civilian travel and shipment of goods by rail had been suspended, and the network was being used to move German troops to Moldavia and northern Dobrudzha. The report's conclusion betrays a sense of urgency: "Bearing in mind, accordingly, Romanian moblization as a means of the long-term strengthening of the German right flank in Europe, it is necessary to devote PARTICULAR ATTENTION [OSOBOE VNIMANIE] to the ongoing concentration of German troops on the territory of Poland."[154]

Additional NKVD and NKGB reports provide some idea of the violation of the Soviet borders by land and by air. From October 1940 to 10 June 1941, 185 German aircraft violated Soviet airspace. According to Beria, from 1 May to 10 June 1941 there were 91 violations of Soviet airspace, an increase that was consistent with final preparations for a German attack.[155] Some of these flights were well inside the Soviet Union—from 100 to 200 kilometers—and their profile showed an interest in defensive installations and troop concentrations.

The Germans were also making great efforts to infiltrate agents across the border, as shown in table 4.18. The figures in the table were derived from a report submitted by Beria. In his report, Beria states that the total number of detentions for 1 January–10 June 1941 was 2,080; however, when he provides the number of detentions per month, the total is only 1,780. The discrepancy is not explained. Encounters between German agents and NKVD border guards frequently resulted in the exchange of fire, and over this period, 36 German agents were killed and 25 wounded.[156] Beria provides no figures for killed and wounded NKVD border guards. Indicative of the imminence of a German invasion was the fact that many of the agents captured and killed

Table 4.18. Number Detained by the NKVD while Crossing the Soviet Border,
1 January–10 June 1941

Month	Number Detained
January	503
February	175
March	381
April	260
May	353
June (1–10)	108
Total	1,780
Average per month	336

Source: № 544, 1941 god, 2:350.

were equipped with radios, weapons, and grenades. The NKGB report dated 20 June 1941 also suggests that the invasion was imminent. German agents who had been deployed for up to ten to fifteen days had been told that, in the event the German army crossed the border, they were to report to any German unit before returning to Germany.[157]

In the seven days leading up to 22 June 1941, the "grains of an answer to a fundamental question," to use Tupikov's expression, had become a mountain of sand: the answer to the fundamental question was quite clear. The final countdown began on 15 June when an NKGB source with links to Göring reported, "Germany will initiate military operations against the Soviet Union on about 15 June."[158] One day later, the Soviet ambassador in London, Maiskii, informed Moscow that he had received a detailed report from the British foreign secretary about the mass deployment of German and Romanian divisions along the Soviet borders.[159] Whatever TASS might publicly hint about the intentions of the perfidious Albion, this warning confirmed the mass of material gathered independently by the NKVD and NKGB. That alone made the London warning—and others—valuable.

On 17 June 1941 an NKGB source working in the German Air Ministry provided a clear warning of imminent danger: "All German military preparations for an attack against the USSR are now completely finished and the blow is to be expected at any moment."[160] Stalin's response to Merkulov was blunt and blasphemous, and it underlined his determination to see no evil in Hitler's moves. It has since become something of a classic counter-intelligence faux pas: "To Comrade Merkulov: You can tell your source in the headquarters of the German Air Ministry to fuck off to his whore of a mother. He's no source; he's a *disinformer*."[161] A day later, compounding his offense, Merkulov informed Stalin, Beria, and Molotov that all was not well in the German embassy in Moscow:

> According to information available to the NKGB SSSR a great deal of nervousness and sense of disquiet have been observed among the officials of the German embassy staff in Moscow over recent days. This arises from the general conviction among the embassy staff that mutual relations between Germany and the Soviet Union have deteriorated to such an extent that in the immediate days ahead a war is due to start between the two.[162]

The final—and at this stage, almost irrelevant—confirmation of what was about to be unleashed came in the early hours of 22 June 1941. At 0310, two hours and twenty minutes before Schulenburg delivered his ultimatum to Molotov in Moscow, the Ukraine NKGB reported that it had picked up a German deserter, one Alfred Germanovich Liskov, serving in the 221st Engineer Regiment, 15th Division. The previous evening, Liskov had been informed by his company commander that the next day, after an artillery bombardment, the unit would cross the river Bug. Liskov told the NKGB that, as a supporter of the Soviet Union, he had decided to inform the Soviet authorities.[163]

Even allowing for Stalin's determination not to see the obvious, the final orders dispatched from Moscow could not hide the panic and confusion. In a directive to his subordinate armies, Pavlov passed on the information from Moscow that a surprise German attack was possible sometime on 22–23 June. Various standard measures to ensure that the units were fully battle-ready were ordered, but the essence of this directive was that Soviet troops "were not to succumb to any provocative acts whatsoever which could cause serious complications."[164] At the same time, Soviet commanders were directed to prepare to repel the invaders. This shamefully and deliberately incoherent order, which had Stalin's hands all over it, was bound to cause confusion and uncertainty rather than operational clarity, and effective and decisive action.

Further clarification of what the Soviet side knew about German intentions before 22 June 1941 is contained in the postinvasion report of NKVD intelligence officer Major Aleksei Kravtsov, head of the operational center of the intelligence headquarters attached to the Western Front (*Zapadnyi front*). The report covers the period before and after the start of the German invasion, and like so many other documents, it reveals the consequences of Moscow's (Stalin's) determination, despite the evidence, to see no evil. As early as March 1941, one of the operational center's sources, a *sekretnyi sotrudnik* (secret coworker or collaborator—often abbreviated to *seksot* in Russian) code-named Felix, reported that the Germans had concentrated more than a hundred infantry divisions and eight to ten tank divisions in eastern Prussia and Poland.[165] The information had been obtained from a German officer working in the German headquarters in Warsaw. Felix was summoned by his handlers, chastised for providing disinformation, and duly instructed that the total number of German divisions was only twenty-five to forty.

A month later, two *rezidenty*, code-named Visla and Arnold, provided even more alarming information. Arnold reported that White Guard organizations were stepping up their anti-Soviet agitation in Warsaw, Lodz, and Prague, mainly through the Russian, Belorussian, and Ukrainian National Committees. The same month, Arnold and other *rezidenty* claimed that up to 1.5 million German troops were now deployed along the Soviet border. When this figure was passed on, the head of the intelligence section was not impressed: "Only the Lomzha operational center could be expected to come up with such nonsense."[166]

Without being summoned, and ahead of his scheduled meeting on 20 June, Arnold presented himself to his controllers on 28 May and offered four additional pieces of information: (1) the Germans were preparing an offensive, and the war against the Soviet Union would begin in the middle of June; (2) the Germans had concentrated 1.5 million to 2 million troops on the Eastern Front; (3) up to 10,000 White Guard saboteurs had been deployed to carry out acts of sabotage before the start of the war; and (4) the Germans planned to capture Minsk on D+8 and Moscow on D+21.[167] Summoned for further questioning in Minsk, Arnold was told that his "material was not true and that it was an invention of British intelligence."[168] Arnold stuck to his guns: "You can shoot me but I answer for the truthfulness of this information with my head. I have discharged my duty to the Soviet state and you can believe me or not, it's up to you. The war will start in the middle of June."[169] Kravtsov openly admitted that the information received from Arnold was heavily edited before being passed on to Moscow; five days had been allocated to this task. At the start of June 1941, as reported by Arnold, small groups of saboteurs were being deployed. Some of them were apprehended by the 87th Border Detachment, located in the area of Lomzha. These deployments were a clear indication of an imminent attack.[170]

Conclusion

By 1 June 1941, and certainly no later than that, Soviet intelligence agencies—the intelligence section of the Soviet General Staff, the NKGB, and the NKVD—had built up a detailed picture of German military intentions. Their sources were wide and varied and included information from undercover agents and contacts, diplomatic gossip and exchanges, rumors, inferences drawn from what was and was not published in the foreign press, lapses in German security, and basic intelligence gathering, such as train and port spotting and convoy observation.

Between June 1940 and June 1941, the information received from these sources indicated a sustained and massive buildup of infrastructure required to accommodate, train, and provision a very large army. Tank divisions required field workshops, fuel depots, and tank parks. Both infantry and tank divisions required prodigious amounts of ammunition—millions of rounds of small-arms ammunition, hand grenades, infantry mortar shells, and ammunition for artillery and tank guns. Equipment had to be moved, stored, and defended. Such requirements mandated the construction of new roads, depots, and defensive installations. Critical among this construction boom was the Germans' well-organized effort to build the necessary infrastructure to support aircraft: aerodromes, landing strips, underground fuel storage tanks, and the associated deception and camouflage measures. Deception and camouflage were, in the last months, reinforced by travel restrictions, blackout regulations, deportations of civilians, and an intensified security regime.

The German High Command was well aware that large-scale troop deployments to the east would be picked up by the Soviet intelligence services, and it would need to provide some convincing explanations to allay Soviet suspicions. In a memorandum dated 6 September 1940, Jodl advised the Abwehr that the Soviet side must not be given the impression that any kind of offensive was being prepared; the deployments should lead them to believe that "we are able to protect our interests—especially those in the Balkans—with strong forces at any time against any Russian sudden move."[171] In other words, the focal point was to the south and southeast, not to the east. Again, aware that the Soviet intelligence agencies would be seeking answers, Jodl proposed the following detailed deceptions: (1) Camouflage the total strength of German troops in the east and attribute the huge changes in the troops stationed there to transfers to training camps and regroupings. (2) Create the impression that the main weight of this deployment was to the south and that relatively small forces were being sent north. (3) Exaggerate, if need be, the scale of equipment in the formations, especially in tank divisions (the idea here was to create the impression that these tank divisions' objectives were not to the east and northeast). (4) Create the impression that, with the conclusion of the campaign in the west, antiaircraft protection would be increased in the east and strengthened by captured French equipment (in other words, create the impression that the Germans saw no obvious threat there, so they were using inferior French equipment rather than first-line German equipment). (5) To hide the real purpose of infrastructure enhancement (rails, roads, and airfields), explain that this work was part of a routine reconstruction program in the newly acquired eastern territories and served, above all, the economy.

Naturally, despite the Germans' best efforts to hide what was taking place, Soviet intelligence agencies learned a great deal. For instance, certain military equipment has a definite signature: pontoons and boats are used to cross rivers. Therefore, the concentration of this type of equipment, along with improvised bridges, close to the rivers Bug and San was worrisome and led to an obvious question: were the Germans planning to force the river at some stage? Likewise, why were the Germans devoting so much effort to expanding the existing network of airfields and building new ones? Another security problem for the Germans was how to explain and justify this huge buildup to their own men. Some German soldiers accepted at face value the explanation that this was all intended to cover up Hitler's plans to invade the British Isles. Others were not so easily deceived, and their discussions of these rumors were picked up by NKVD agents and informers.

There is no doubt that the NKVD was obsessed with any manifestation of Polish and Ukrainian nationalism. So the fact that the Germans were training and supporting nationalist formations such as *Samostiinaia Ukraina* and OUN, exploiting their grievances while tacitly encouraging them to think in terms of future independence, caused deep concern in NKVD circles. The NKVD correctly identified these groups not as just a fifth column that could assist the German invaders but as the heart of a future, organized anti-Soviet political power in Ukraine.

Table 4.19 lists some of the indicators being picked up by Soviet intelligence agencies. Discrete and disparate intelligence items were reported, collated, analyzed, and synthesized to produce a clear picture—or at least as clear a picture as possible—of enemy intentions. These syntheses resulted in high-level intelligence memoranda and intelligence reports circulated only

Table 4.19. Indicators of Probable German Military Action against the Soviet Union, 1940–1941

Indicator	Date	Significance
Air reconnaissance flights with increasing range and frequency	1940–1941	High
Deportation of civilians from border zones	1941	High
Increasing aerodrome construction and infrastructure	1940–1941	High
Deployment of large volume of aircraft	Second quarter 1941	Very high
Increased road and rail construction	1940–1941	High
Heightened security regime (curfews and blackouts)	1941	Medium
Travel restrictions in border zones	1941	Medium
Unusually high concentrations of tank and infantry divisions	1940–1941	High
Active anti-Soviet propaganda and disinformation	1940–1941	Medium
Infiltration of agents across the border	1940–1941	Medium → high
Recruitment and training of nationalist organizations	1940–1941	Medium → high
Full mobilization of German and allied armies	1941	Extremely high
Diplomatic rumors	1940–1941	Low → high
Undercover agent reports	1940–1941	Medium → high
Interrogation of deserters and captured agents	1940–1941	Medium → high
Warnings from foreign governments	1940–1941	Medium → high
Identification of signature equipment (pontoons)	1940–1941	Medium → high
Support for allied states acting against the Soviet Union	1940–1941	Medium → high
Rumors of war in Germany and elsewhere	1940–1941	Low → high
Increase in shipping movements	1940–1941	Medium → high
Large-scale conversion of buildings to hospitals	1940–1941	High
Issuance of topographic maps of Soviet border areas	1941	High
Reports of Germans studying Russian	1940–1941	Medium
Failure by May 1941 to launch an invasion of Britain	1941	High
Securing of samples of Soviet vehicle and aviation fuels	1940–1941	High
Fuel and food rationing	1940–1941	Medium

Note: The use of the arrow symbol (→) indicates a change in significance over the period in question. Some of the indicators, taken on their own, do not necessarily point to hostile intent; however, taken together, especially with total mobilization and other signs of aggressive intent (e.g., the infiltration of agents and open support for the OUN), they lead to that conclusion. Any intelligence officer who rejected that view—and ultimately, that meant Stalin—had some explaining to do.

Table 4.20. Summary of Major Soviet Intelligence Assessments Indicating a German Invasion of the Soviet Union, 20 July 1940–22 June 1941

Date	Agency/Person	Subject of Assessment
20 July 1940	Golikov, Soviet General Staff	German buildup*
July 1940	Beria to Stalin and Molotov	German moves aimed at USSR
19 September 1940	ZAPOVO to Golikov	German buildup
25 September 1940	NKVD Transport Directorate	Ukrainian nationalism threat
5 October 1940	Timoshenko and Meretskov to Stalin	Germany the main threat
December 1940	KOVO to Soviet General Staff	German buildup*
21 February 1941	Agent report from Dora	Invasion at end of May
6 March 1941	Agent report from Korsikanets	German invasion plans
11 March 1941	Soviet General Staff	Defense of western borders
20 March 1941	Golikov, Soviet General Staff	German invasion plans
April 1941	Zhukov's order to Pavlov	Defense of ZAPOVO
2 April 1941	Agent reports from Korsikanets and Starshina	Luftwaffe air plan (targets)
15 April 1941	NKGB Ukraine to Khrushchev	German buildup and OUN threat*
16 April 1941	Golikov, Soviet General Staff	German buildup
25–26 April 1941	Tupikov, Soviet military attaché	Analysis of German plans and danger
29 April 1941	Zhukov to Moscow Military District	Mobilization and dangers posed by natsmeny
15 May 1941	Timoshenko and Zhukov to Stalin	Clear and imminent danger*
1 June 1941	Agent report from Ramzai	Invasion in second half of June
7 June 1941	Golikov, Soviet General Staff	Mobilization of Romanian army
15 June 1941	NKGB source report	Invasion by 15 June 1941
17 June 1941	NKGB source in Germany	Invasion imminent (mocked by Stalin)
18 June 1941	NKGB to Stalin	German embassy staff leaving
22 June 1941	Родина-Мать зовет! (Mother Russia calls!)	Великая Отечественная война (The Great Fatherland War)

*Considered a critical intelligence assessment.

to Stalin and his immediate inner circle. There was a relentless accumulation of hard intelligence assessments, and table 4.20 lists those I consider preeminent in terms of 22 June 1941.

The recommendations in these reports were clearly taken seriously by someone, as demonstrated by a number of countermeasures initiated before 22 June 1941: strengthening of the Western, Kiev, Baltic, and Odessa Special Military Districts; expansion of railway capacity; Stalin's address to Red Army graduates on 5 May 1941; Zhukov's order to the Moscow Military District; detailed mobilization plans; insistence that the west would be the main theater of operations; deportations from the Baltic states and the Moldavian republic (13 June 1941); action against the OUN; increased aircraft production; and action against German agents in the border regions.

Soviet intelligence agencies had done everything asked of them. They had collected as much information as possible from a wide range of sources and evaluated this material in a thoroughly professional and objective manner. The Soviet military attaché in Berlin, General-Major Tupikov, and the newly appointed chief of the General Staff of the Red Army, General Zhukov, clearly grasped the dangers. In most reports, attention to small and often significant details was apparent. That Stalin did not appreciate these efforts of his subordinates was another matter.

Zhukov covers the period immediately before and after the start of the war in chapters 9 and 10 of his memoirs, published in 1969. However, his account is generally disappointing, and he ignores many of the critical questions. In a passage probably intended for publication in 1969 but first published only in 1998, Zhukov reveals Stalin's state of mind before the German invasion and his refusal to contemplate the seriousness of the situation. According to Zhukov, Stalin was not the only wishful thinker; Molotov, Zhdanov, Malenkov, Voroshilov, Khrushchev, and Kalinin all agreed with Stalin's analysis that Hitler would not risk a war on two fronts. Zhukov also confirms Stalin's reluctance to take any preparatory measures, lest the Germans be provoked. One of Zhukov's more interesting revelations is that Stalin permitted the Germans to search the border zone, purportedly for the graves of German soldiers killed in World War I. Zhukov was not fooled: "It was clear that the Germans were not looking for graves but for the weak spots in our border zone and were studying the nature of the terrain for their forthcoming operations."[172]

In his counterintelligence thriller published in 1974, *V avguste 1944* (In August 1944), Soviet writer Vladimir Bogomolov depicts a SMERSH team's efforts to track down a dangerous German spy ring. The novel is rich in counterintelligence jargon, and one of the terms used by Bogomolov—the "moment of truth" (*moment istiny*)—represents the essence of the problem facing Soviet intelligence agencies as they attempted to discern the meaning of German behavior from June 1940 onward. The moment of truth occurs when all the disparate, discrete, and often contradictory pieces of information point to only one realistic conclusion—in this case, that Hitler either planned to invade the Soviet Union or intended to present a credible threat of an invasion in order to extract concessions. Why Stalin failed to draw the necessary conclusions—to recognize the moment of truth—despite some desperate attempts at one minute to midnight by Zhukov and others, is considered in chapter 9.

Group photo of the leadership cadre of Einsatzgruppe A. This formation, along
with other Einsatzgruppen, was responsible for the mass shootings of Jews.
Einsatzgruppe A operated in the northern part of the Soviet Union from the summer
of 1941 to the autumn of 1944. Left to right: Obersturmführer Dr. Heinrich
Bosse, Hauptsturmführer Harry Zöller, Untersturmführer Heinrich Amann,
Sturmbannführer Otto Kraus, Hauptsturmführer Georg Fuhrmann, unknown
Hauptsturmführer, Obersturmbannführer Karl Tschierchky, Hauptsturmführer
Kurt Junker, Untersturmführer Eberhard Büttner, Untersturmführer Willi Thilo,
unknown Obersturmbannführer, Obersturmführer Karl Pierre, and Obersturmführer
Franz Dietmann. (Bundesarchiv, B 162 Bild-05598, photo by o. Ang.)

JU-52 transport aircraft supplying the Demiansk Kessel, winter 1941–1942. (Bundesarchiv, Bild 101I-003-3445-33, photo by Ullrich)

A captured female Soviet soldier, referred to by the Germans as Flintenweiber. Note the terrain, which offered plenty of cover for the remnants of scattered Red Army units and, eventually, partisans. (Bundesarchiv, Bild 101I-010-0919-34, photo by Georg Schmidt)

The same female soldier is now joined by other Soviet prisoners. (Bundesarchiv, Bild 101I-010-0919-37, photo by Georg Schmidt)

The misery and humiliation of surrender: these soldiers were subjected to brutal treatment in the German camps and regarded as traitors by the Soviet state. (Bundesarchiv, Bild 101I-010-0919-39, photo by Georg Schmidt)

German and Soviet soldiers meet in Poland on 20 September 1939, as that country is being dismembered by both states. (Bundesarchiv, Bild 101I-121-0008-25, photo by Max Ehlert)

Mark III assault gun of the Waffen SS Division Totenkopf, June–July 1941. The dust wreaked havoc with vehicle engines. (Bundesarchiv, Bild 101I-136-0882-13, photo by Albert Cusian)

The Jewish ghetto Litzmannstadt, 1941. The sign reads: "Jewish Residential Area. No Entry." The restricted entry to what purports to be a "residential area" confirms the suspicion that this is actually a prison. (Bundesarchiv, Bild 101I-133-0703-30, photo by Zermin)

Generaloberst Heinz Guderian, central Russia, 1941. The legendary tank commander led from the front and inspired deep loyalty among his soldiers. (Bundesarchiv, Bild 101I-139-1112-17, photo by Ludwig Knobloch)

Whether in the Wehrmacht or the Red Army, horses endured a wretched existence. (Bundesarchiv, Bild 101I-215-0366-03A, photo by Geller)

Generaloberst Erich von Manstein, architect of the 1940 German invasion of France and conqueror of the Crimea, spring 1942. (Bundesarchiv, Bild 101I-231-0718-12A, photo by o. Ang.)

German soldiers in an improvised defensive line constructed from snow blocks, December 1941, near Orel. Sited according to the principles of mutual fire support, these positions could nevertheless be infiltrated by Red Army fighting patrols at night. (Bundesarchiv, Bild 101I-287-0872-04, photo by Koll)

German soldiers in an improvised snow-block shelter near Orel, December 1941. Snow-block shelters, snow caves, and snow trenches can be relatively comfortable, since they provide protection from the wind. (Bundesarchiv, Bild 101I-287-0872-05, photo by Koll)

This photograph, taken in the winter of 1941–1942, illustrates the terrain over which German and Soviet troops had to operate. The problem of drifting is evident. Without snowshoes or cross-country skis, movement was exhausting. (Bundesarchiv, Bild 101I-287-0872-24, photo by Koll)

Executed partisans, one woman and two men, in Orel, winter 1941–1942. The Russian caption reads: "Such is the end of partisans." (Bundesarchiv, Bild 101I-287-0872-29A, photo by Koll)

German machine gun position in open terrain near Orel, winter 1941–1942. Note the use of captured Soviet weapons. (Bundesarchiv,Bild 101I-287-0885-29A, photo by Karl Müller)

Russian female prisoner of war captured in October 1941. (Bundesarchiv, Bild 101I-449-0779-20, photo by Benno Wundshammer)

Refugee children, September 1941. (Bundesarchiv, Bild 101III-Baumann-077-07, photo by Ernst Baumann)

Waffen SS soldier with a female prisoner of war inspecting a captured semiautomatic rifle, the Tokarev-40, September 1941. (Bundesarchiv, Bild 101III-Baumann-077-10, photo by Ernst Baumann)

Waffen SS trench positions, 1941. (Bundesarchiv, Bild 101III-Exter-071-10A, photo by Exter)

Taken by an SS propaganda company photographer in 1940, this picture records the miserable fate of Volksdeutsche who were resettled in Poland, almost certainly sent from the Soviet occupation zone to the German occupation zone. This little girl's face tells a universal tale about war in the twentieth century: the mass deportation of civilians. (Bundesarchiv, Bild 101III-Wisniewski-020-38A, photo by Wisniewski)

Troops of the Waffen SS Division Das Reich crossing a bridge over the river Desna, September 1941. The sign reads: "Desna Bridge 'For the Last Race,' Built by Engineer Battalion 48." (Bundesarchiv, Bild 101III-Zschaeckel-150-26, photo by Friedrich Zschäckel)

SS-Obersturmführer Fritz Rentrop with Ritterkreuz (Knight's Cross), winter 1941. (Bundesarchiv, Bild 101III-Zschaeckel-159-15, photo by Friedrich Zschäckel)

Dr. Hans Frank, Generalgouveneur of the German occupation zone, attending a police parade in Krakow, Poland, circa 1939–1940. Frank was condemned as a war criminal at Nürnberg and executed on 16 October 1946. (Bundesarchiv, Bild 121-0270, photo by o. Ang.)

NKVD prison in Lemberg. When unable to evacuate prisoners to the rear because of the speed of the German advance, the NKVD executed them in situ. (Bundesarchiv, Bild 146-1979-039-03, photo by Hübner)

Road and rail bridges over the Dnieper River in Kiev, 1942. This photograph provides some idea of the size of this formidable natural obstacle. (Bundesarchiv, Bild 146-2005-0071, photo by Kress)

Orders being issued to Russian farmers, August 1941. The children's faces tell us all we need to know. (Bundesarchiv, Bild 183-B09519, photo by Röder)

SS-Obergruppenführer and General der Polizei Reinhard Heydrich, 29 January 1942 (nine days after the Wannsee conference). Along with Hitler and Himmler, Heydrich was one of the main architects of the Endlösung (Final Solution). Heydrich was attacked by British-trained agents of the Special Operations Executive (SOE) on 27 May 1942, and he died of his wounds on 4 June. (Bundesarchiv, Bild 183-B20373, photo by Friedrich Franz Bauer)

Herbert Backe, one of Göring's chief agricultural planners, in the uniform of an SS-Obergruppenführer, 2 June 1942. (Bundesarchiv, Bild 183-J02034, photo by o. Ang.)

Stalin—"the scum of the earth," in the words of the famous Low cartoon—meets von Ribbentrop—the foreign minister of "the bloody assassin of the workers"—23 August 1939. (Bundesarchiv, Bild 183-H27337, photo by o. Ang.)

SS-Brigadeführer Otto Ohlendorf, commander of Einsatzgruppe D. Ohlendorf was condemned as a war criminal and executed on 8 June 1951. (Bundesarchiv, Bild 183-J08517, photo by Schwarz)

Excavation of the mass graves of Polish officers buried in the Katyn forest fifteen kilometers northwest of Smolensk, April 1943. (Bundesarchiv, Bild 183-J21201, photo by o. Ang.)

Soviet officers captured at Minsk, July 1941. (Bundesarchiv, Bild 183-L19481, photo by Bauer)

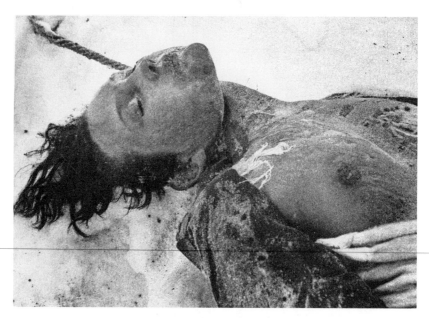

The body of Zoia Kosmodemianskaia, who was tortured and then hanged as a partisan, on 29 November 1941, by the Germans on the approach to Moscow. (Bundesarchiv, Bild 183-R0130-325, photo by Strunnikov)

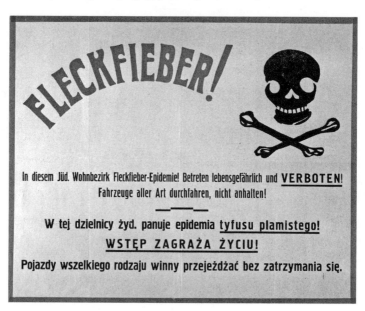

Poster warning of the dangers of typhus, 1941. The poster reads: "There is a typhus epidemic in this Jewish residential area. Entry is life-threatening and FORBIDDEN! Vehicles of all types are to drive through and not stop!" (Bundesarchiv, Plak 003-037-084, designed by o. Ang.)

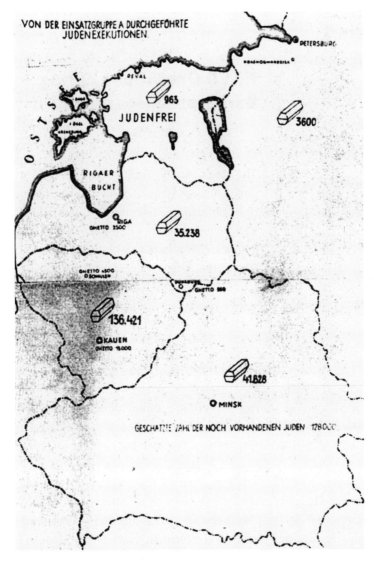

Executions of Jews carried out by Einsatzgruppe A in the Baltic states and Belorussia after the start of Barbarossa. Cited as evidence during the Nürnberg War Crimes Tribunal, the map was part of an official report; the report was undated but was most likely written in the autumn of 1941. Areas where all the Jews have been executed are deemed to be judenfrei (Jew free). Numbers executed are shown next to the coffin symbols. (Document 2273-PS, in Trial of the Major War Criminals before the International Military Tribunal Nuremberg, 14 November 1945–1 October 1946, Blue Series, 42 vols. [Nuremberg, Germany: n.p., 1949], XXX:77)

5 NKVD Operations during Barbarossa, 1941–1942

> The fundamental mission of the Special Sections
> and the troop subunits of the NKVD consists in the
> most rapid imposition of firm, revolutionary order
> in the rear echelons of divisions, corps, armies and
> fronts and in a decisive struggle against deserters,
> those spreading panic and cowards.
>
> *Isai Babich, deputy chief of*
> *the Special Section of the NKVD of*
> *the North-Western Front*

No sooner had the Red Army invaded eastern Poland in September 1939 than the NKVD initiated a wave of arrests as part of its program of sovietizing the newly occupied territories. West of the demarcation line, Hitler's security agencies were pursuing much the same policy of arrests and roundups. Throughout this period there was considerable cooperation between the Gestapo and the NKVD, and a number of meetings took place between representatives of the two organizations. It was during this period of cooperation and liaison that Polish prisoners were murdered at Katyn and other sites. Meanwhile, the NKVD and its various directorates were providing a steady stream of reliable data and information about the buildup of German military forces and infrastructure. So perhaps some NKVD officers drew the necessary conclusions and were not caught entirely unawares, unlike their master. The eventual German invasion placed enormous strains on the NKVD. This chapter examines how the NKVD coped with the demands of internal security and counterintelligence and the range of punitive measures adopted to stabilize the situation in the face of the German advance.

Introduction

The declassified documents pertaining to NKVD functions in the period from 22 June 1941 to the end of December 1941 fall into several distinct categories. To begin with, the outbreak of war prompted a number of administrative and bureaucratic reorganizational measures at the highest level of the Soviet state, and these measures had a major impact on NKVD operations. One obvious measure intended to make intelligence gathering and related activities more effective was the merger of the NKVD and the NKGB on 20 July 1941 into a unified body, now known as the NKVD.[1] Internal security measures, which included countering desertion, protecting railways and transport, evacuating the industrial plant, and dealing with panic mongers and the filtration of Red Army soldiers suspected of being German agents, were basic NKVD tasks. After Stalin issued his Order № 270, these tasks acquired new urgency. Another critical NKVD mission was the detention of enemy spies and parachutists. At the same time, the NKVD was training and organizing partisan, sabotage, and reconnaissance teams for dispatch across the German lines. The NKVD had always paid great attention to any manifestation of national identity, but it became obsessed with this task in wartime, correctly identifying nationalism as a potentially deadly threat to the Soviet state. During the latter half of 1941, mainly at the behest of Lavrentii Beria, mass deportations of ethnic Germans, especially those from the Volga region, were carried out. Later in the war, other nationalities would suffer the same fate. The NKVD was also one of several Soviet institutions that played a part in the arrest, interrogation, and eventual execution of General Pavlov and his colleagues, whom Stalin held responsible for the early German successes. Even in October 1941, when it seemed that Moscow might fall to the Germans, Stalin was still obsessed with revenge killings. On the basis of another Beria recommendation, twenty-five prisoners, most of whom were senior officers, were executed in Kuibyshev.

There are lacunae in the published documentation. For example, there is nothing related to the mass executions of prisoners hastily carried out by the NKVD in Ukrainian towns as the Germans approached. However, even though certain documents and attachments have not yet been declassified, the available material provides an exceptionally detailed account of the NKVD's role in this early part of the war.

Internal Security

In an NKGB directive issued on 22 June 1941, Merkulov tried to respond to the challenges now facing the NKGB and the NKVD. By the morning of the day of the invasion, the present and ongoing threat posed by German special forces and nationalist sabotage groups was all too clear, and Merkulov ordered that the most important parts of the industrial-military infrastructure (railway junctions, stations, bridges, radio-telephone and telegraph posts, and aerodromes) be protected. Merkulov also ordered that "operational measures to interdict any attempts on the part of hostile elements to inflict damage on the Soviet Union" be taken.[2] The nature of the threat, according to Merkulov, arose from crimes against the state in the form of espionage, terrorism, sabotage, uprisings, banditry, and calls for strikes and counter-revolutionary sabotage. Significant here is that the threat posed by internal enemies of the regime seemed to cause greater alarm than the actions of the invading Germans. Among the Soviet leadership there was a real fear that the regime was not as secure as the propaganda claimed. The demand that the NKGB resort to "operational measures" means, I suggest, that when in doubt, all resistance or *potential resistance* should be eliminated.

Two days later, Merkulov went into greater detail about the most urgent tasks facing the intelligence agencies. He stipulated the following immediate measures: (1) accelerate the tempo of the evacuation of all arrestees, "in the first instance from those regions in which the situation is intense";[3] (2) remove all archival material not essential for immediate operational tasks to the rear; (3) take all measures to ensure that cipher material did not fall into enemy hands; (4) do not abandon positions, under any circumstances, unless ordered to do so by a superior authority; (5) work with the NKVD to deal with "enemy parachute assaults, sabotage and bandit-insurgent groups and organized counterrevolutionary elements";[4] (6) form well-armed detachments to deal with any manifestations of anti-Soviet behavior; (7) maintain contact with other agencies of the NKGB; (8) uncover informers in the agent network and "instruct the agent network that in the eventuality of our troops withdrawing, agents are to penetrate the depths of enemy troop dispositions and carry out subversive and sabotage work";[5] (9) inform NKGB headquarters about the situation in the provinces no less than twice a day; and (10) crush all signs of panic and confusion among the ranks of the NKGB.

Most of these measures are what one would expect under the circumstances. The one that stands out is the requirement to evacuate all prisoners to the rear, since the historical evidence shows that where this was not possible, they were executed in situ. The precedent for executing prisoners who could not be evacuated in time had, in fact, been set during the civil war, and the mass killings are well documented.[6] Such ruthless measures were provided for in the order to put all Soviet penal institutions on a war footing, which was issued on 22 June 1941.[7] The principle of neutralizing all enemies, potential or otherwise, underpinned all these measures. Thus, all scheduled releases of "counterrevolutionaries, bandits, recidivists and other dangerous criminals" were canceled,[8] and the right to send and receive correspondence was withdrawn. This heightened security regime also applied to the so-called Polish contingents. Although the NKGB and NKVD dispensed with bureaucratic niceties when necessary, putting penal institutions on a war footing meant that the prisoners were effectively under military jurisdiction. Therefore, prisoners being held in areas likely to be overrun by the Germans (Belorussia, Ukraine, the Baltic states) could be regarded as active or potentially active enemy agents and thus executed if it was impossible to remove them to the rear. Operating on the same principle, the agencies of the NKGB and NKVD were targeting whole categories of undesirables in Moscow and the surrounding district. Subject to immediate arrest were Trotskyites, members of religious sects, pacifists, and various unspecified anti-Soviet elements.[9]

Proceeding from the authority conferred on him by the Supreme Soviet decree that placed Moscow on a military footing, the commander of the Moscow garrison, General-Lieutenant Zakharkin, introduced additional measures to ensure social order and the security of the state. The workday was scheduled to start at 0830 hours, and parks, theaters, and other places of entertainment were to close at 2245 hours. The same closing time applied to restaurants, cafés, laundries, and barbershops. Entry into Moscow (which was pass-controlled) was forbidden for people who were not registered as being domiciled there; however, exceptions were made for those who lived outside the city and worked in Moscow. All photography and filming inside the city was forbidden unless approved by the commander of the Moscow garrison. Likewise, all pedestrian and light vehicle traffic was forbidden between midnight and four in the morning. Exceptions to this order were pass-controlled.[10]

Information control was also essential. The Soviet state placed extraordinary emphasis on the efficacy of its own agitation and propaganda apparatus, regarding it as essential not only for controlling its "infosphere" but also for winning what today we might call the information war. The war tested this information control, since events at the front could not be controlled by the Soviet regime—certainly not in 1941—and rumors were generated quickly and spread with astonishing speed. This explains the extraordinary venom with which panic mongers and rumor spreaders were characterized in official documents throughout the war.

Some measure of the official displeasure caused by rumors can be seen in an NKGB directive drafted by Merkulov: "According to precise information available to the NKGB of the USSR, German intelligence agencies, with the aim of disorganizing the rear areas by means of their agent network, are disseminating rumors about the approach of German troops in order to create panic among the population, mainly in the region contiguous to the front line." Merkulov recommended that all those who spread rumors be arrested and brought before a military tribunal.[11] That recommendation was acted on, since a decree of the Supreme Soviet stipulated that those spreading false rumors and causing panic among the population were liable to a two- to five-year prison sentence.[12]

That rumors were deemed a serious problem is clear in a memorandum (dated 27 June 1941) sent by an NKGB team in Zhitomir. It notes that since the start of the German invasion, there has been a huge influx of refugees from the western districts of Ukraine, and rumors are circulating that the towns of Lvov, Lutsk, and Rovno have been totally destroyed. According to an NKGB informer code-named Zhukov, a certain individual named Go-zhenko has been wandering the streets and spreading rumors that Kiev is burning and the Germans know where to drop their bombs. According to the NKGB source, Gozhenko was very pleased when he saw German planes overhead.[13] Another disgruntled inhabitant reportedly said: "For 23 years they have been drinking our blood, deceiving the people, taking our last piece of bread. Such a bunch of liars cannot remain in power."[14] Yet another dissatisfied Soviet citizen, Chernobul'skii, told an informer: "The Germans are strong, they are occupying one town after another."[15] Chernobul'skii also offered some cynical remarks about Molotov's wife. The report notes that there was a constant stream of such remarks. The source of these rumors was not just refugees. German radio broadcasts in Russian undoubtedly fueled the rumors.

In highly controlled information environments, rumors are inevitable, and official rage is a reflection of the frustration over the inability to stop them. One possible way to stop or, more realistically, control the spread of rumors is to control access to news. Thus, the Politburo resolution dated 25 June 1941, mandating that the general population hand over all radio receivers and radio transmitters, was a logical step.[16] It was also an important counterintelligence measure, since such receivers and transmitters could be exploited by enemy intelligence agencies. However, the main purpose of these measures was to ensure that the people got their news and information about the war from official Soviet sources, not the German enemy or even the Western Allies. Indeed, the same thinking underpinned the formation of the Sovetskoe Informatsionnoe Biuro (Soviet Information Bureau) on 24 June 1941. The aim of what became known as the Sovinformbiuro was to control the dissemination of information concerning international events, military operations, and life inside the country. This meant controlling print and broadcast media, as well as organizing "counterpropaganda against German and other enemy propaganda,"[17] which probably explained the presence of Filipp Ivanovich Golikov, head of the GRU (*Gosudarstvennoe razvedyvatel'noe upravlenie*; State Intelligence Directorate), on the organizational committee.

The Soviet regime was prepared to deal severely with those who spread rumors, as evidenced by various proposals for the treatment of those accused of treason. What made these measures especially cruel was that they targeted family members and relatives, as well as the prime suspects. An order drafted by Merkulov and Abakumov and dated 28 June 1941 stipulated that the families of those who were guilty of treason or flight abroad were subject to prosecution.[18] Such measures amounted to collective punishment and were applicable regardless of whether the families assisted in a crime or had any knowledge of it. The FSB archivists acknowledged the illegality and harshness of these measures, noting, "The violations of the law inhering in the above document consist in the fact that it directed the investigating agencies in their investigation of a specific category of matters to be guided not by the criminal procedural law but by an instruction of the NKVD of the USSR."[19] This observation merely stated the obvious in order to negate the obvious. Furthermore, it confirmed the all-powerful role played by the NKVD—as well as its predecessors and successors—in the life of the Soviet state, and it exposed the sham nature of Soviet normative legal documents when the leader wanted to override them (there was no rule of law—just the rule of arbitrary laws and decrees). It also demonstrated that the NKVD, as one of the essential parts of the Soviet terror apparatus, was a law unto itself. This legal situation would be intolerable enough in peacetime. In time of war, when multiple cloaks of secrecy were used to hide the work of the intelligence agencies and could be plausibly justified as essential, the state enjoyed the power of life and death over the population.

The Merkulov-Abakumov decree was bolstered by what was, in Soviet hierarchical terms, an even more significant move in the direction of ruthlessness and collective punishment: a joint directive issued by Stalin and Molotov on 29 June 1941.[20] This decree likely played a major role in putting the Soviet Union on a war footing, although its importance has been somewhat overstated.[21] It also prepared the way for one of the most infamous orders Stalin ever issued: Order № 270. In wording, themes, and demands for action, the Stalin-Molotov decree clearly adumbrates the much harsher, even sadistic provisions of Order № 270.

Order № 270 was issued on 16 August 1941 and was circulated in written form only to higher formations; lower formations received the order orally. The full text of the order was first published in 1988. Although Stalin began by paying tribute to some Red Army units, any praise was merely a minor and insignificant concessionary preamble to the main part of the document. Given the way Red Army units and soldiers were treated by the filtration squads of the NKVD, Stalin's praise for those fighting their way out of *okruzhenie* (encirclement) was cynical and duplicitous. Those commanders who had been captured by the Germans or had surrendered— specifically, General-Lieutenant Kachalov, General-Lieutenant Ponedelin, and General-Major Kirillov—Stalin singled out as cowards, deserters, and incompetents who had betrayed their units and the Soviet Union. The two most striking provisions of Order № 270 are not the demand for the instant, on-the-spot execution of deserters (no surprises here in Stalin's imperium) but the stipulation that the families of deserters and cowards be arrested and deprived of state benefits and assistance and Stalin's countenance of the mass execution of Soviet units showing any sign of surrendering. Denial of state benefits to families, especially in times of scarcity and rationing, was not far short of a death sentence; it was a cruel blow for the women trying to hold their families together while the men were at the front. That Stalin could sanction the mass destruction of Soviet units that *might* surrender reveals a contempt for the lives of his own soldiers, and it hardly seems consistent with the outrage directed against, for example, the Commissar Order.

The Merkulov-Abakumov decree and Stalin's Order № 270 arose in the desperate circumstances of the late summer of 1941—circumstances that were directly attributable to Stalin's failure to see the danger posed by Hitler.

This meant that scapegoats had to be found to account for the German military success, much as traitors and enemies of the people had been blamed in the 1930s for Soviet industrial and agricultural shortcomings. Here, the Soviet intelligence agencies played a major role in identifying those who could plausibly be held responsible for the disasters. A prime candidate for the desired retributive and propitiatory measures was General Dmitrii Pavlov, commander of the Western Special Military District and the Western Front, who was arrested in the first week of July 1941.

The Arrest, Interrogation, and Execution of General Dmitrii Pavlov

The record of Pavlov's interrogation, which took place on 7 July 1941, and the subsequent interrogator's report confirm that Pavlov had been targeted for arrest and eventual execution. Regardless of any objective reasons for the failure to stop the German advance, Pavlov would be held responsible. The assumption was that Pavlov was at fault, and it was his duty to cooperate with the interrogator to demonstrate what had already been decided by the Central Committee: that Pavlov was guilty. This peculiarity of Soviet jurisprudence stems from the ideological view of the infallibility of the Communist Party. The perverse consequence of this view is that prisoners who attempt to defend themselves—in Pavlov's case, from accusations of treachery—confirm the accusation by the very act of not cooperating with the interrogator. Their resistance can only mean that they have something to hide and, worse still, that they are asserting an individual point of view against the omniscience of the party and its collectively imposed wisdom.

In response to the accusation that he was a traitor, Pavlov maintained that the reasons for the defeat of the troops under his command were beyond his control. This led the investigator to claim that Pavlov's "behavior in the course of a number of years was treasonous, and that this was especially evident in deeds, which came to light during your command of the Western front."[22] This was the first clue that the charges against Pavlov had been fabricated, based on the same standards used during the purges. Significantly, the investigator did not present this evidence, and Pavlov did not demand to see it.

Pavlov's account of the last hours before the German attack was fully consistent with the passive Soviet position adopted on Stalin's orders, despite clear indications that some form of German military operation was imminent. Pavlov reported that, over the last thirty-six hours, there had been a nonstop flow of German motorized and mechanized units into the Suval'skii salient, and the Germans were removing barbed wire obstacles. However, he was told not to panic and not to respond to any provocation. He was also ordered to assemble his headquarters. Such orders placed Pavlov and all other commanders in an intolerable position. They had no clear order to act in the event of a German move or, indeed, any clear order not to act. This confusion was exacerbated by the use of ambiguous words such as "provocation." If a Soviet commander reacted to German actions, he was liable to face sanctions for succumbing to provocation. If, however, the so-called provocation turned out to be something serious and the commander failed to act, he would face sanctions for not acting. This ambiguity arose from Stalin's indecision, even at this late hour.

Pavlov's summary of his actions and discussions with subordinate commanders was consistent with the measures available to him within the framework of not succumbing to provocation. The interrogator mounted no informed or serious challenge to Pavlov's account of his actions. At this stage, the interrogation was a probing operation in which the interrogator hoped to find some weakness that could be exploited.

Some vulnerabilities were uncovered in the actions of Korobkov, commander of the 4th Army. Korobkov had lost contact with some of his units, and there were signs that he was being overwhelmed by fast-moving events. The most serious concern was the general inadequacy of communications. However, the overall picture presented by Pavlov was of Soviet units being overwhelmed on land and in the air by the Germans. In Pavlov's own words:

> Assessing the entire situation, I judged that the headquarters of the 3rd Army had left Grodno and transferred to Luno but the enemy was not applying any especial pressure or pursuit of 3rd Army. On the left flank of 10th Army the enemy with great effort was exploiting his success and squeezing our units. On the remaining sectors of the 10th Army all attempts by the enemy to mount an offensive had been repulsed. In the 4th Army there was a sense of complete confusion on the part of the commanders, control of the troops had been lost and the enemy was rapidly exploiting his success, with his axis of advance along the Bobruisk-Brest highway.[23]

Pavlov's interrogation confirmed the devastating effectiveness of the German assault. In coordinated and simultaneous air attacks against Soviet aerodromes, the Luftwaffe destroyed some 300 planes in Pavlov's operational area. Planes located at border aerodromes were unable to get airborne in a timely manner because the pilots were not trained for night flying, a remarkable and damning admission. There were also signs that discipline was breaking down in some Soviet units. To counter these lapses, Pavlov ordered executions, if necessary, to stop unauthorized withdrawals.

One of Pavlov's problems was that the interrogator had no grasp of the situation faced by the Soviet commanders, who had been taken by surprise for reasons that were beyond their control. Unable to breach Pavlov's account, the interrogator resorted to accusations of treachery that predated the German invasion. To quote the interrogator: "The investigation has established that you participated in a conspiracy as early as 1935 and that even at that time intended to betray the Motherland in any future war. Your present situation at the front confirms the information available to the investigation."[24] Apparently, Pavlov was never confronted with this material; its evidentiary basis was merely asserted. The interrogator's claims raise two obvious questions: if Pavlov had been involved in a conspiracy in 1935, why was he not arrested sooner, and why was he permitted to serve in the high-prestige enterprise of the Spanish Civil War?

The document setting out the reasons for Pavlov's arrest—a resolution of the 3rd Directorate of the People's Commissar for Defense dated 6 July 1941—is a typical example of the bizarre assertions and fabrications used in the 1930s. Based on the material submitted to him, the investigating officer's preliminary findings were that Pavlov had links with anarchists and that he had appeased members of the right deviation. Being a prisoner of the Germans from 1916 to 1919 was also a stain on his record.[25] Accusations from 1928 onward became more serious. Pavlov was accused of a mixture of incompetence, duplicity, and treachery. In battle and on exercises, he failed to appreciate the importance of reconnaissance, and according to the investigator, he got involved in party work to gain access to military secrets (which presumably implied some competence in reconnaissance work). Praising the German army was also held against him. Fatal accusations involved Pavlov's being "closely linked to enemies of the people,"[26] including those who had been executed in the prewar purges of the Red Army: Ieronim Petrovich Uborevich (shot in 1937); Pavel Petrovich Rulev, accused of being part of a "military-fascist conspiracy" (died during the investigation); Boris Iosifovich Bobrov, chief of staff of the Belorussian Military District, accused of being "an active participant in an anti-Soviet, military-terrorist conspiracy" (shot in 1937); Andrei Leont'evich Karpushin-Zorin, deputy chief of staff of the Belorussian Military District, accused of being part of an anti-Soviet military conspiracy (shot in 1937); and Vladimir Ivanovich Mal'tsev, head of the 8th Section of the headquarters of the Belorussian Military District, accused of being part of an anti-Soviet military conspiracy (shot in 1938).[27] Worse still for Pavlov was that, according to the investigator, other members of this alleged anti-Soviet conspiracy had "exposed Pavlov as a participant in this conspiracy."[28] Among them were Semen Petrovich Uritskii, former head of the Intelligence Directorate of the Red Army (shot in 1938); Ian Karlovich Berzin, former head of the Intelligence Directorate of the Red Army and military adviser in the Spanish Civil War (shot in 1938); Ivan Panfilovich Belov, former commander of the Leningrad, Moscow, and Belorussian Military Districts (shot in 1938); Petr Aleksandrovich Smirnov, army commissar (shot in 1939); and Nikolai Polikarpovich Rozhin, chief of staff of the 21st Mechanized Brigade (shot in 1937).

In his arrest statement, Uritskii claimed that Pavlov became part of the conspiracy on the recommendation of Uborevich, and the aim in Spain had been to topple the Republican government. Unbelievably damning for Pavlov was the following statement from Uritskii: "In March 1937 I received information from Pavlov about the conspiratorial work in which he described his treacherous work in some detail. From foreign Trotskyites and units of anarchists he had created a single tank company."[29] Uritskii continued: "In response to this letter I sent Pavlov through the conspirator Vorob'ev a letter in which, expressing approval of his treacherous work, I recommended expanding his conspiratorial links, and not just confining himself to Trotskyites and anarchists but to inveigle socialists."[30]

In other damning testimony, Berzin claimed that Pavlov had been recommended as a conspirator before Berzin left Moscow for Spain. Interestingly, also implicated in the conspiracy was Semen Moiseevich Krivoshein, who had been appointed commander of the 29th Tank Brigade after serving in Spain and, beginning in 1940, commanded the 15th Motor Rifle Division, followed by the 3rd Tank Division. In his autobiography, Heinz Guderian refers to a meeting he had with a Brigadier General Krivoshein during a ceremony on 22 September 1939 to mark the formal handover of the Brest fortress to the Red Army at the end of the Polish campaign.[31] This might not have been the same Krivoshein, but the fact that both Berzin and Guderian refer to him as a tank officer suggests that it was the same man. Berzin testified: "I ordered Pavlov to continue the treacherous work, which had earlier been carried out by Krivoshein both in the area of training tank crews, sending out untrained tank crews to the front, and in the combat use of tank units which he carried out."[32] That Krivoshein was so heavily implicated in the alleged conspiracy yet somehow survived raises all kinds of questions that may never be answered. Despite his dubious connections to plotters and enemies of the people, the Krivoshein linked to Pavlov lived until 1978, revealing the highly arbitrary nature of Soviet law and the complete freedom of Soviet agencies to pursue their ideological vendettas. This also strongly suggests that Pavlov's guilt had been predetermined, making him a scapegoat for the Red Army's failures.

The prosecutor had no doubt that Pavlov was guilty. According to Belov, Pavlov had confirmed his participation in the conspiracy. Likewise, Smirnov stated that he knew from Uborevich that Pavlov was a conspirator.[33] Pavel Matveevich Arman, another veteran of the Spanish Civil War, testified that Pavlov had pursued a treacherous line aimed at the defeat of the Republican Army. According to Arman, Pavlov "encouraged cowards and Trotskyites who were undeservedly put forward for decorations, adopted a condescending attitude toward the Spanish soldiers, whipping up nationalist antipathies among them."[34] The case against Arman was dropped on 21 June 1939. Boltin, the commissar of Pavlov's detachment, also weighed in, claiming that while stationed in a villa, a German translation of Trotsky's book My Life had been found and immediately burned. Pavlov's response had been to reproach Boltin: "One of Trotsky's books has been found here and you burnt it. You've done the wrong thing, you should have let people read it."[35] The outcome of all this evidence was that Pavlov was arrested under the terms of Articles 58-1(b) and 11 of the Criminal Code and Articles 145 and 158 of the Criminal Procedural Code.

A comparison of the record of Pavlov's interrogation and the interrogator's report indicates that the interrogator had his own agenda—or, rather, he had been briefed on what was required. The interrogation was carried out by the same individual who wrote the interrogator's report, Senior Battalion Commissar Pavlovskii, chief of the investigative unit of the 3rd Directorate NKO USSR. Although it is clear from Pavlov's interrogation record that the main accusation was one of treachery and vague and unsubstantiated assertions of his involvement in conspiracies, at no stage was Pavlov, at least according to the record, ever confronted with any evidence of this alleged activity by the interrogator. The interrogation report, in which Pavlovskii recommends Pavlov's arrest, bears no resemblance to the formal record of the interrogation. There are no verbatim extracts from Pavlov explaining military operations on and after 22 June 1941; there is no reference to the order that commanders should not panic and, critically, should not succumb to German provocations; there is no mention of delays in the provision of replacement radios, despite urgent requests to Moscow; and there is nothing in the record to indicate that the various accusations and statements made by Uborevich and others were ever placed before Pavlov or that he had an opportunity to rebut them. Nor is it clear that Pavlov's interrogation record was attached to the interrogation report, thus removing any chance of independent oversight (which, in the Soviet case, would have been an unrealistic expectation anyway).

Having interrogated Pavlov, Pavlovskii recovered the files of Uborevich and others and wrote a report that included material derived from prisoners who, during the purges, would have been subjected to the full range of NKVD torture techniques—sleep deprivation, face slapping, relay interrogations, prolonged beatings, mock executions, and dehydration—to extract confessions. With regard to confessions and the gathering of evidence, the ethos of the NKVD is summed up by this advice given to an NKVD interrogator: "If the accused will not sign the record of the arrest which you have written, beat him until he signs."[36] What in most jurisdictions would be flagrant procedural inconsistencies and failures were, in the Soviet legal system, the norm.

The decree of the State Defense Committee confirming the arrest of Pavlov and other commanders and ordering that they be brought before a military tribunal was issued on 16 July 1941 and signed by Stalin, the committee chairman. The wording and general line of the document conformed to Stalin's standard pattern. Praise for Soviet units that were doing their duty and bravely resisting the Germans was part of the ritual formula intended to highlight the differences between them and the accused and to pave the way for the arrestees' ideological, quasi-legalistic condemnation. That these men had been arrested meant that they were guilty; the presumption of innocent until proved guilty is a bourgeois concept. Stalin's language reflected the Soviet view that arrest necessarily implies guilt. Unbothered by qualifiers such as "alleged," Stalin leaves no doubt about the outcome:

> The panic monger, the coward and the deserter are worse than the enemy since they not only undermine our cause but tarnish the honor of the Red Army. Reprisals against panic mongers, cowards and deserters as well as the reestablishment of military discipline are therefore our holy duty if we wish to protect the great calling of the warrior of the Red Army from being sullied.

Proceeding on this basis, the State Defense Committee, acting on representations made by the supreme commanders and commanders of the fronts and armies, has arrested and brought before a court of a military tribunal on charges of shaming the calling of a commander, cowardice, inaction, lack of control, breakdown in command of the troops, handing over weapons to the enemy without a fight and arbitrary abandonment of positions the following officers.[37]

Those named in Stalin's resolution were General Pavlov, former commander of the Western Front; General-Major Klimovskikh, former chief of staff of the Western Front; General-Major Grigor'ev, former chief of communications of the Western Front; General-Major Korobkov, former commander of the 4th Army (Western Front); General-Major Kosobutskii, former commander of the 41st Rifle Corps of the North-Western Front; General-Major Salikhov, former commander of the 60th Mountain Rifle Division; regimental commissar Kurochkin, former deputy commander of the 60th Mountain Rifle Division; General-Major Galaktionov, former commander of the 30th Mountain Rifle Division of the Southern Front; and regimental commissar Eliseev, former deputy commander of the 30th Mountain Rifle Division.[38] Stalin also ordered that the resolution be read out in all the subunits of the Red Army and the air force.

Five days later, on 21 July 1941, Pavlovskii recommended that the case against Pavlov, Klimovskikh, Grigor'ev, and Korobkov be combined and treated as a single case. The main charge against all four was "the conduct of treasonous activity at the front."[39] The formal indictment, which was also issued on 21 July, contained the first set of specific charges against the four men.

Concerning Pavlov, it was asserted that, driven by treachery, he had brought about the breakdown in command and control of the troops and the surrender of weapons to the enemy without a battle, making it possible for the enemy to break through the front. Accusations based on the testimony of Uborevich and others were now given some shape, however spurious:

> The arrestee Pavlov, being a participant in an anti-Soviet military conspiracy as early as 1936 and being in Spain, betrayed the interests of the Republicans. In command of the Western Special Military District he failed to act.
>
> Pavlov acknowledges his guilt from the fact that in the interests of

conspiratorial aims he failed to prepare the command stratum which had been entrusted to him for military operations, weakening the mobilization preparation of the troops in the district and that out of a thirst for revenge for the fact that the conspiracy had been routed, opened the front to the enemy.

As a participant in this conspiracy, Pavlov is exposed by the testimonies of Uritskii, Berzin, Belov, Rozhin and Meretskov.[40]

The most striking aspect of this part of the indictment is that no reliable evidence was ever presented that would have justified an arrest, never mind a formal charge. There was no evidence that Pavlov had formally accepted his responsibility for the alleged crimes, and even if there had been a signed acknowledgment, the methods used to acquire it, given the modus operandi of the NKVD, would have rendered it worthless: those who did not sign were beaten. Evidence of Pavlov's guilt was derived not from any signed confession or the presentation of reliable evidence but from assertions that Pavlov had failed to act in the period immediately before the invasion and in the chaos of the first few days thereafter. Not taken into account were the operational constraints imposed on Pavlov and all other commanders by Stalin's indecision and by fears of provoking the Germans. And, as noted previously, there was no reference to Pavlov's detailed exposition of the course of military operations obtained during his interrogation, an omission that strengthens the suspicion that the verdict was decided before the interrogation.

It is reasonable to assume that the same investigative methods were used against Pavlov's former colleagues. Klimovskikh, for example, was indicted based on statements attributed to Mikhail Efimovich Simonov, a divisional commissar who was arrested in 1938 for being part of a "military-fascist conspiracy" and shot.[41] The fact that Klimovskikh was also an officer in the tsarist Russian army probably did not help his case. Significant in the case against Klimovskikh—he was accused of criminal inaction—was the claim that he had been exposed by the testimony of Pavlov and Grigor'ev.[42] Given that Pavlov did not incriminate Klimovskikh in his interrogation and that no specific document was produced to support such a claim—the full record of Klimovskikh's and Grigo'rev's interrogation, for example—one must suspect that the investigator fabricated the accusations against Klimovskikh. The main charge against Grigor'ev was that he failed to organize proper communications; rather conveniently, he too was indicted on the basis of Pavlov's and Klimovskikh's testimony. Korobkov, another former officer in the tsarist Russian army, was indicted because he lost control of his troops and did nothing to control outbreaks of cowardice and panic.

Events moved quickly. The hearing against Pavlov and his codefendants was held in the early-morning hours of 22 July 1941, commencing at twenty minutes after midnight and concluding at 0325. The nocturnal setting and the fact that the chairman was Vasilii Ul'rikh—a major player in the purges of Red Army officers—must have removed any doubt about how this process would end. The defendants' only option was to stand their ground and fight. Pavlov rejected the accusation regarding his involvement in a conspiracy, and he showed no sign of admitting military incompetence:

> I recognize my guilt in not managing to have checked the execution of my order to Korobkov, the commander of the 4th Army concerning the evacuation of troops from Brest. As early as the beginning of June I issued the order for the withdrawal of units from Brest to the camps. Korobkov failed to carry out my order as a result of which three divisions were destroyed by the enemy when leaving the city.
>
> I recognize my guilt in having interpreted the directive of the General Staff of the RKKA in my own way and of not having set it in motion earlier; that is before the enemy offensive. I knew that the enemy was about to attack but I was being assured from Moscow that all was in order and I was ordered to keep calm and not to panic. I cannot name the surname of the person who told me this.[43]

Pavlov's statement was far from an admission of guilt. That he interpreted the directive in his own way was perfectly reasonable in light of what was happening along his front, and he had every right to trust a senior commander (Korobkov) to carry out orders. Damning for Stalin was Pavlov's claim that he was being assured by Moscow that all was in order. If Pavlov knew an attack was imminent, it should not have escaped the notice of his superiors.

Parts of the published record of this hearing have been removed. For example, when Ul'rikh asked Pavlov to confirm testimony he had given a few hours earlier on 21 July, Pavlov refused to do so. In his words: "I gave it while in a bad condition. I request that the testimonies that be believed are the ones given by me in the preliminary investigation on 7 July 1941."[44] Given that this later testimony was not published, and in view of Pavlov's rather oblique reference to being in a "bad condition," one is tempted to conclude that he was subjected to the standard physical interrogation measures used by the NKVD and that he wanted to withdraw that coerced testimony. Referring to the accusation about being part of a conspiracy, Pavlov stated: "The first time I leaned about the aims and tasks of any conspiracy was from Meretskov in 1937, when I was still in Spain."[45] This extract from Pavlov's testimony—made only hours earlier, probably late in the evening of 21 July—was also omitted from the formal indictment prepared by Pavlovskii, which, as noted earlier, included no published attachments. The indictment merely noted that Pavlov's participation in some conspiracy was revealed (allegedly) by the testimony of Uritskii, Berzin, Belov, Rozhin, and Meretskov, not that Pavlov admitted to being part of a conspiracy.

As the hearing progressed, Ul'rikh brought up additional extracts of testimony that Pavlov later refuted. For example, when Pavlov denied any involvement in anti-Soviet plots, Ul'rikh reminded him: "Several hours ago you said something completely different, and in particular about your hostile activities."[46] Ul'rikh then quoted Pavlov's earlier testimony: "On page 82 of the first volume you say: 'The aims and tasks of the conspiracy which were expounded to me by Meretskov came down to changing the leadership of the army, having placed people useful to the conspirators, such as Uborevich and Tukhachevskii, at its head.'"[47] But at the hearing, Pavlov denied that any such conversation ever took place. Although the documentary evidence against Pavlov was supposedly considerable, other than these extracts cited by Ul'rikh, very little is in the public domain. That Ul'rikh refers to page 82 of a first volume leaves little doubt that the amount of still classified material on Pavlov may be substantial. Other examples support this view. According to Ul'rikh, Pavlov stated during the preliminary hearing: "After I returned from Spain and in conversation with Meretskov about the conspiracy we decided in the interests of protecting the anti-Soviet activity from failing temporarily to suspend our activity, to go deep underground and to present ourselves according to the line at work only in a positive light."[48] For this extract, Ul'rikh cited page 83 of the first volume. Pavlov maintained that the investigator had recorded things differently. Similarly, Ul'rikh read the following from Pavlov's earlier testimony (page 86): "The whole time we maintained constant contact with Meretskov. The latter in his many conversations with me [Pavlov] systematically expressed his defeatist views, tried to prove the inevitable defeat of the Red Army in the forthcoming war with Germany. From the very start of German military operations in the West Meretskov said the Germans don't feel like attacking us but in the event of a German attack on the Soviet Union and the victory of the German army it will not be any worse for us."[49] Pavlov admitted that this exchange took place.

Ul'rikh next turned to the question of armaments. According to the record (page 88), Pavlov had stated the following: "In order to deceive the party and the government, I know precisely that the General Staff has raised the orders for wartime tanks, vehicles and tractors about 10 times. The General Staff justified this increase by the lack of capacity, whereas at the same time the capacity that could be provided by industry was considerably lower. . . . By means of this plan Meretskov intended to confuse all the calculations for deliveries of tanks, tractors and vehicles to the army in time of war."[50] Pavlov confirmed this testimony.

The record of the session shows that Ul'rikh presented additional testimony of Pavlov's alleged treacherous behavior from page 89 of the first volume, although nothing was cited verbatim. At this point, Pavlov rejected any treacherous intent concerning communications, pointing out that they were the responsibility of the chief of staff. Ul'rikh also accused Pavlov of failing to ensure that the reinforced regions were properly prepared. According to testimony by Klimovskikh (citing page 25 of volume 2): "Work on the construction of the reinforced regions was progressing extraordinarily slowly. By the start of military operations out of a total of 600 fire positions only 189 had been equipped, and not completely."[51] Pavlov agreed with this assessment and pointed out that he had informed the Central Committee of this situation in May 1941.

Ul'rikh then referred to the concluding part of Pavlov's 21 July testimony and claimed he had said the following (page 92 of volume 1):

> Having been embittered by the circumstance that many Red Army commanders who had been close to me were arrested and condemned, I selected the most reliable means to exact revenge, organizing the defeat of the Red Army in the war with Germany. . . . I partially managed to achieve that which Tukhachevskii and Uborevich failed to achieve in their time; that is, to open up the front to the Germans.[52]

In his rejection of the above statement, Pavlov denied being embittered and denied any connection with former heads of the Red Army. Significantly, he revealed that the preliminary investigation had lasted fifteen days (most likely resulting in a considerable amount of documentary material) and that he had been interrogated about a conspiracy. In response to Ul'rikh's question whether he would confirm his testimony from 11 July, Pavlov replied: "This was also forced testimony."[53] In other words, Pavlov was stating that he had been subjected to torture.

Undeterred by the accusation of torture, Ul'rikh continued to cite Pavlov's testimony from 11 July. According to Ul'rikh, Pavlov had stated the following (page 65 of volume 1): "The main reason for the defeat on the Western Front was my treasonous activity as a participant in a treasonous organization although that to a considerable degree was furthered by other objective conditions which I indicated during my interrogation of 9 July."[54] Pavlov also rejected this testimony on the grounds that it had been coerced.

Pavlov reiterated his suspicion that a German attack was imminent and its confirmation by the intelligence agencies. Pavlov then maintained that, despite assurances from Moscow that there was no cause for alarm, he gave the order to raise combat readiness and to occupy positions. When questioned by Orlov, one of Ul'rikh's assistants, about why Minsk had been "abandoned to the vagaries of fate" on 26 June 1941, Pavlov pointed out that the party administration had been already abandoned the city on 24 June.[55]

Ul'rikh next directed his attention to Klimovskikh, who admitting making errors in the conduct of his professional duties. Klimovskikh stated that although he knew the Germans were concentrating troops, he had been misinformed by Pavlov, who claimed the German tanks were light versions.[56] Klimovskikh also accepted some responsibility for what happened in the aftermath of the German attack: "The enemy's first blow on our troops was so devastating that it caused total confusion among the front command staff. In his capacity as front commander Pavlov was guilty, I, as the chief of staff of the front, Grigor'ev, the head of communications, the head of artillery and other commanders."[57] Like Pavlov, Klimovskikh denied any involvement in an anti-Soviet conspiracy.

Grigor'ev also provided clear evidence of torture during interrogations. When Ul'rikh asked whether he could confirm his testimony, Grigor'ev vouched for his own handwritten statements but rejected the rest, claiming coercion.[58] From this phase of the court hearing, it emerged that Grigor'ev had been interrogated on 5 July 1941 and thereafter. Orlov also cited testimony taken from a fourth volume of documents, further proof that a lot of material is still classified.

Korobkov mounted a particularly spirited defense. The only failure for which he was prepared to take responsibility was his inability "to determine the precise start of military operations."[59] Especially damning for Stalin and

Timoshenko was Korobkov's testimony that he did not receive Timoshenko's order until 0400 hours, by which time his formations were already under attack. He also rejected Pavlov's claim that he had ordered Korobkov to withdraw units from Brest: "I personally never saw any order."[60]

The four accused men were given the opportunity to make concluding statements to the court, which amounted to a recitation of their main points. Two points stand out—one by Pavlov and one by Korobkov. Pavlov concluded his statement with this assertion: "We at the present time find ourselves on the stand not because we have committed any crimes during the period of military operations but because we made insufficient preparations for war in peacetime."[61] Korobkov ended with a damning indictment of the highest levels of the Soviet leadership: "The forces were unequal: the enemy excelled us in all respects."[62]

The verdict was not long in coming. The charges of cowardice, inaction, and panic were upheld, and all four men were collectively held responsible for allowing the Germans to break through on one of the main axes. All four were sentenced to be shot, and their property confiscated. There was no right of appeal. The court also recommended that the Presidium of the Supreme Soviet be petitioned to strip Pavlov, Klimovskikh, and Korobkov of all awards and medals.[63]

The available documentary evidence concerning the arrest, interrogation, and conviction of these four men confirms that whatever their professional failings, Pavlov, Klimovskikh, Grigor'ev, and Korobkov were arrested and executed essentially to provide high-profile scapegoats for Stalin's own disastrous failings. It is likely that all four men were tortured and subjected to other forms of physical coercion. In these matters, Soviet institutions are not entitled to the benefit of the doubt. That Ul'rikh and his minions were prepared to accept evidence secured by such means is evidence enough that the hearing was merely a gruesome ritual whose outcome had been predetermined. Ul'rikh did his master's bidding and gave Stalin the verdict he required.[64]

Pavlov, Klimovskikh, Grigor'ev, and Korobkov were not the only senior Soviet commanders to be executed in the second half of 1941. In an instruction dated 18 October, Beria ordered the execution of twenty-five prisoners being held in Kuibyshev. Their crimes are summarized below.[65]

General-Colonel Grigorii Mikhailovich Shtern was head of the Air Defense Directorate. He was arrested on 7 June 1941 and accused of participating in an anti-Soviet military conspiracy, conducting work designed to undermine the defense of the Soviet Union, and plotting a coup d'état. Shtern was executed without trial on 28 October 1941.

Aleksandr Dmitrievich Loktionov was commander of the Baltic Special Military District. He was arrested on 19 June 1941 and accused of taking part in an anti-Soviet conspiracy. Loktionov was executed without trial on 28 October 1941.

Iakov Vladimirovich Smushkevich was a general-lieutenant in the air force. At the time of his arrest on 7 June 1941, he was assistant head of the General Staff, with responsibility for aviation. He was charged with being a member of an anti-Soviet military conspiracy, undermining the defense of the Soviet Union, and working for foreign intelligence agencies. Smushkevich was executed without trial on 28 October 1941.

Georgii Kos'mich Savchenko was a general-major in the artillery. At the time of his arrest on 19 June 1941, he was the deputy chief of the Red Army's artillery directorate. He was charged with being a participant in an anti-Soviet military conspiracy and an agent of German intelligence. Savchenko was executed without trial on 28 October 1941.

Pavel Vasil'evich Rychagov was a general-lieutenant in the air force. He was a Hero of the Soviet Union and had served in the Spanish Civil War. At the time of his arrest on 24 June 1941, he was a deputy in the People's Commissariat of Defense. Rychagov was arrested under the provisions of Articles 58-1b, 58-7, 58-8, and 58-11 of the Criminal Code and was executed without trial on 28 October 1941.

Ivan Filimonovich Sakrier was a divisional engineer and, at the time of his arrest, was the deputy chief responsible for armaments and supply of the main directorate of the air force of the Red Army. He was arrested on 21 April 1941 and accused of being a member of an anti-Soviet organization. Sakrier was executed without trial on 28 October 1941.

Colonel Ivan Ivanovich Zasosov was the temporary chairman of the artillery committee of the main artillery directorate of the Red Army. He was arrested on 5 July 1941 and charged with participating in an anti-Soviet conspiracy operating within the Red Army and of attempting to disrupt the equipping of the Red Army. Zasosov was executed without trial on 28 October 1941.

General-Major Pavel Semenovich Volodin was chief of staff of the air force. He was arrested on 27 June 1941 and charged with participating in an anti-Soviet conspiracy operating within the Red Army and of attempting to undermine the defensive capacity of the Soviet Union. Volodin was executed without trial on 28 October 1941.

General-Lieutenant Ivan Iosifovich Proskurov was commander of the 7th Air Army. He was arrested on 27 June 1941 and charged with being a member of an anti-Soviet organization. Proskurov was executed without trial on 28 October 1941.

Stepan Osipovich Sklizkov was a brigadier engineer commander and head of the small-arms artillery directorate of the Red Army. He was arrested on 28 June 1941 and charged with being a member of an anti-Soviet organization, undermining the production of small arms, and spying for German intelligence. Sklizkov was executed without trial on 28 October 1941.

General-Lieutenant Fedor Konstantinovich Arzhenukhin was head of the air force academy for command and navigation personnel. He was arrested on 28 June 1941 and charged with being a member of an anti-Soviet organization, conducting subversive activities designed to disrupt the capacity of the air force, and supplying German intelligence with information. Arzhenukhin was executed without trial on 28 October 1941.

General-Major Matvei Maksimovich Kaiukov was working at the Commissariat for Defense when he was arrested on 29 June 1941 and charged with being a member of an anti-Soviet organization and, since 1938, disrupting the equipping of the Red Army. Kaiukov was executed without trial on 28 October 1941.

Mikhail Nikolaevich Sobornov, a military engineer, was head of the experimental section of the Technical Council of the People's Commissariat for Armaments. He was arrested on 2 July 1941 for his involvement in an anti-Soviet conspiracy whose aim was to overthrow the Soviet power and remove the leaders of the party and the government. He was also accused of conducting work intended to disrupt the supply of modern weapons to the Red Army. Sobornov was executed without trial on 28 October 1941.

Iakov Grigor'evich Taubin was a small-arms and weapons designer. He designed the world's first automatic mortar and was awarded the Order of Lenin for his work. He was arrested on 16 May 1941 and charged with being a member of an anti-Soviet organization and disrupting the supply of armaments to the Red Army. Taubin was executed without trial on 28 October 1941.

David Aronovich Rozov was a deputy of the People's Commissariat for Trade. He was arrested on 28 March 1940 and charged with being a member of an anti-Soviet organization and spying for foreign states. Rozov was executed without trial on 28 October 1941.

Zinaida Petrovna Rozova-Egorova was a student who was studying languages at the time of her arrest on 28 March 1940. She was charged with being a member of an anti-Soviet, Trotskyite organization and spying for Germany. Rozova-Egorova was executed without trial on 28 October 1941.

Filipp Isaevich Goloshchekin was the main arbitrator attached to the Council of People's Commissars. He was arrested on 13 October 1939 for participating in an anti-Soviet, rightist, Trotskyite organization; recruiting new members; and expressing terrorist intentions against the Soviet government. Goloshchekin was executed without trial on 28 October 1941.

Dmitrii Aleksandrovich Bulatov was the first secretary of the Omsk regional committee of the Communist Party. He was arrested on 29 January 1938 and charged with being one of the leaders of an anti-Soviet, rightist, Trotskyite organization; carrying out activities to disrupt livestock production; and preparing terrorist acts against the leaders of the party and the government. Bulatov was executed without trial on 28 October 1941.

Major Mariia Petrovna Nesterenko was a military pilot. She was arrested on 25 June 1941 and accused of knowing about the criminal activity and Trotskyite links of her husband, Pavel Vasil'evich Rychagov. Nesterenko was executed without trial on 28 October 1941.

Aleksandrova Ivanova Fibikh was the wife of Georgii Kos'mich Savchenko. She was arrested on 19 June 1941 for being the wife of a traitor and because she failed to inform Soviet agencies of his criminal contacts with enemies of the people. Fibikh was executed without trial on 28 October 1941.

Samuil Gertsovich Vainshtein was a deputy in the People's Commissariat for the Fishing Industry. He was arrested on 16 June 1939 and accused of participating in a rightist, Trotskyite organization; working for Polish intelligence; and disrupting the food production industry of the Soviet Union. Vainshtein was executed without trial on 1 November 1941.

Il'ia L'vovich Belakhov was the director of the Institute of Cosmetics and Hygiene. He was arrested on 10 June 1939 and charged with being a member of an anti-Soviet organization and conducting subversive measures against the party and the government. Belakhov was executed without trial on 1 November 1941.

Anna Iakovlevna Slezberg was the head of a subsidiary of the Commissariat
of the Food Industry of the Soviet Union. She was arrested on 17 June
1939 and accused of belonging to a rightist, Trotskyite organization.
Slezberg was executed without trial on 1 November 1941.

Evgenii Viktorovich Dunaevskii, described as a literary functionary, was
arrested on 19 February 1939 and accused of working for British intelligence. Dunaevskii was executed without trial on 6 November 1941.

Mikhail Sergeevich Kedrov, a former member of the Cheka, was the director
of a military sanatorium at the time of his arrest on 16 April 1939. He
was accused of being a member of an anti-Soviet organization. Kedrov
was executed without trial on 1 November 1941.

The arrest of senior military commanders and military specialists in the
first half of 1941 and immediately after the German invasion suggests that
the process of finding scapegoats for Soviet military failures was under
way *before* the Germans invaded and *before* Pavlov was arrested.[66] In turn,
this implies that there were suspicions at the highest levels of the Soviet
government—Stalin, Beria, and Molotov—that the Germans were planning an attack. But Stalin was unwilling to act, and senior military figures
had already been targeted for liquidation. The most striking aspect of the
executions of Shtern and the others is the bizarre and implausible reasons
given for their arrest—very much in keeping with the reasons cited during
the Great Terror. Accusations that these people were part of Trotskyite conspiracies or agents of foreign intelligence services were pure fabrications,
as Stalin, Beria, and Molotov well knew. If there had been grounds for these
accusations, Stalin's willingness to act on them would only highlight his
disastrous failure to act on the evidence of German military intentions
from much more diverse and reliable sources. Also, the fact that Shtern,
Loktionov, Smushkevich, Savchenko, Sakrier, and Taubin were all arrested
before 22 June 1941 indicates some kind of preemptive move on Stalin's part
to keep these officers assisting the invader, which means that Stalin must
have known about or at least suspected Hitler's intentions. Instead, Stalin
took the easy option. Unable or unwilling to draw the necessary conclusions
from the information provided by his intelligence agencies, and fearful
of provoking Hitler, Stalin lashed out at the very people the Soviet Union
needed in its time of crisis.

Partisans: The People's Avengers

Stalin's paranoia—which was nearly fatal to Soviet military readiness—was also a prime cause of the dismantling of the well-trained cadre of partisan warfare experts and the infrastructure needed to sustain these partisan networks behind enemy lines. The theoretical and practical problems of partisan warfare had already been addressed by the Soviet military thinkers Frunze and Tukhachevskii in the 1920s and 1930s. In fact, the efficacy of partisans and other irregulars had been well and clearly demonstrated in the Peninsular War, the first Great Patriotic War, the American Civil War, the Soviet Civil War in the 1920s, and, very painfully for the Red Army, the Winter War against Finland. Any misgivings Stalin had about partisan units in the latter half of the 1930s were cast aside after 22 June 1941, and a major effort was launched to rebuild the training schools, organize and equip networks, and recruit the necessary personnel. The bulk of this work fell to the NKVD.

In his radio address to the Soviet Union on 3 July 1941, Stalin identified partisan warfare as one of the immediate measures to be taken to counter the German invaders:

> In the regions occupied by the enemy it is necessary to create partisan detachments, on horse and foot, to form sabotage groups in order to fight enemy units, so as to ignite partisan warfare everywhere, to blow up bridges and roads, to wreck telephone and telegraph communications, to set forests, dumps and supply lines ablaze. In the territories which have been seized it shall be necessary to ensure intolerable conditions for the enemy and all his accomplices, to hunt them down and to destroy them at every opportunity and to disrupt all their measures.[67]

Further impetus to the creation of partisan detachments was a resolution of the Central Committee issued on 18 July 1941. Its assumption was that people in the German-occupied areas would remain loyal to Soviet power and its institutions. As events proved, this was not a reliable assumption. The resolution contained four general measures. First, only the most reliable people would be deployed—party members and Komsomol—and each group would consist of two to five members; in addition, none of the groups would have knowledge of the other groups. Second, in those regions threatened with enemy occupation, the necessary steps to form groups must be taken sooner rather than later. Such steps involved the provision of equipment, weapons, and rations. Members of the NKVD and NKGB would play a leading role. Third, party organizations were responsible for the selection of personnel. Fourth, party organizations were obliged to inform the Central Committee of the names of those selected to lead partisan groups.[68] Obviously, if the partisan warfare infrastructure set up in peacetime had not been disbanded, the partisan threat would have been far more disruptive of German operations and, critically, would have occurred much sooner. Expecting party organizations to take these measures in the face of imminent occupation was unrealistic.

That there were serious shortcomings was evident from events in the Kalinin district. To begin with, partisan groups and detachments were being assembled hurriedly, often in a matter of hours; most of their members did not know one another and were not used to handling weapons or explosives. These groups often lacked local guides and were not issued maps and compasses (although even if they had been, there was no guarantee they would know how to use them, since effective navigation skills require training and thorough familiarity with these instruments). Levels of training and briefing were inadequate, and the groups had no clear idea what they were supposed to do. Very little consideration had been given to providing clothing and rations. Major Tokarev, head of the NKGB in the Kalinin district, concluded: "As a result of the shortcomings indicated, sabotage groups and partisan detachments being deployed into the enemy rear are not fully able to carry out the tasks they have been set and may fall into enemy hands and be shot."[69]

Tokarev made a series of recommendations, all of which were based on principles adopted before the war.[70] Most critical were the selection and training of the right personnel and their equipment: (1) Personnel for partisan groups should be derived primarily from members of the NKVD and NKGB, members of the Communist Party and Komsomol, and others known to be loyal to the Soviet state. (Comment: Clearly, members of the NKGB and NKVD had the necessary background, training, and expertise, but recruiting only such people weakened the assertion of a monolithic Soviet entity. Not all Soviet citizens were loyal to the Soviet state, and members of the NKVD and NKGB did not consider themselves bound by international law, which contributed to the brutality with which partisan warfare was conducted.) (2) Weapons and supply dumps must be organized in good time. (Comment: That was a given, but it would be much harder to achieve under the pressures of war.) (3) Training and equipping these groups should take place in army units. (Comment: Given the speed of the German advance and the ensuing chaos, it was not clear how Red Army units would be able to manage the additional—and to them, unwelcome—tasks of equipping and training partisans.) (4) All partisan groups should include drivers. (Comment: The Red Army needed all available drivers.) (5) Leaders of these groups must conduct thorough reconnaissance of targets and terrain before any mission. (Comment: The fact that this basic procedure had to be stipulated underlined the lack of training.) (6) Reliable methods of conspiratorial communication must be worked out in good time (e.g., the use of apartments). It was also essential to maintain good communications with areas not occupied by the enemy. (Comment: These measure were essential for any subversive organization, but they would be exceptionally difficult to carry out in wartime.) (7) Group leaders should be briefed about politically unreliable persons who may remain in the enemy rear and in the zone of partisan operations. (Comment: The existence of such people proved that Soviet solidarity could not be taken for granted, and their identification suggested that they might be targeted for liquidation, if necessary.) (8) Personnel in the partisan group should be instructed how to uncover traitors infiltrating the group. (Comment: Infiltration by enemy agents was a serious problem and a highly effective countermeasure against partisans.) (9) Detachments and groups should be briefed on their tasks, and each group should devise an operational plan for its area. (Comment: This was essential but severely time-contingent.) (10) Guides should be used when crossing the lines, and any crossing must be approved by local Red Army commanders and the special sections. (Comment: This was standard procedure.) (11) The formation of partisan detachments and sabotage groups must take place in contact with and under the control of local party agencies. (Comment: This showed that although party agencies saw the obvious advantages of partisan warfare, they feared losing control and the potential dangers if partisan groups enjoyed too much operational independence.)

Even before the Central Committee resolution, the NKGB in Belorussia had started to organize partisan networks. By 26 June 1941, fourteen partisan detachments with a total of 1,162 personnel had been set up—539 were members of the NKGB, and 623 came from the NKVD and police.[71] The operational areas, sizes, and commanders of these groups are shown in table 5.1. Their main weapons were pistols and rifles, along with two to three machine guns per group. Mindful perhaps that groups operating behind the lines were beyond its immediate control, the Central Committee

Table 5.1. Status of Partisan Detachments in Belorussia, 26 June 1941

Operational Area	Personnel	Detachment Commander
Slutskii region	100	Captain Vasilevskii, NKGB
Lepel'skii region	101	Senior Lieutenant Sulima, NKGB
Dzerzhinskii region	51	Senior Lieutenant Starinov, NKGB
Osipovicheskii region	101	Captain Rubinov, Border Troops
Chervenskii region	50	Captain Zaitsev, NKGB
Berezinskii region	96	Lieutenant Iurin, NKGB
Belynichskii region	50	Junior Lieutenant Liakhov, NKGB
Krichevskii region	50	Lieutenant Simakhin, NKGB
Mogilevskii region	101	Lieutenant Pribyl', NKGB
Vitebskii region	53	Senior Lieutenant Pasmanik
Shklovskii region	93	Senior Lieutenant Koba
Bykhovskii region	103	Police Lieutenant Kuzmenok
Orshanskii region	102	Police Captain Kozhemiakin
Bobruiskii region	111	Lieutenant Morozkin, NKGB

Source: OGB, 1941/1, № 368, 188–189.

of the Belorussian Communist Party allocated one party representative to each group. The effectiveness of these partisan detachments was illustrated by the first batch of information provided by Lieutenant Iurin's detachment operating in the Berezinskii region. In an encounter with an enemy column numbering about 200 Germans on 3 July 1941, Iurin's detachment reportedly killed 150 of the enemy and caused the rest to flee.[72]

An additional ten groups with about ninety members, composed of NKGB leaders and party officials, were formed and sent to the districts of Poles'e, Vitebsk, Minsk, and Gomel'. These districts were strategically important, and during the civil war they had been the site of much partisan activity. Other groups were formed to attack enemy aerodromes and to locate formations of the Western Front with which contact had been lost.

Additional measures were taken to set up rezidentury in areas vulnerable to occupation. The primary mission of these groups was sabotage and terrorism. A total of eight rezidentury were set up in the Vitebsk district. Typically, each group was controlled by a rezident with a small circle of contacts. For example, the first rezident, Stepan Il'ich Azarov, was in contact with only three people. Azarov had his own apartment and false documents and had been supplied with 40 Mills hand grenades, 16 kilos of ammonal, and 100 meters of detonation cord. The location of this equipment was known only to Azarov. All the rezidentury operated on the Leninist cell principle and thus were unable to compromise other groups in the event they were uncovered by German counterintelligence agencies. Alongside these preparations for behind-the-lines operations, the NKGB suspected 1,123 people of being spies, insurgents, and counterrevolutionaries in just the eastern districts of Belorussia. Of these, 434 had their cases referred to a military tribunal.[73]

A memorandum written by P. K. Ponomarenko, the secretary of the Central Committee of the Belorussian Communist Party and a member of the Military Council of the Western Front, provided additional details about partisan operations and the general situation in Belorussia in mid-July 1941. For example, he reported that as soon as the order had been given, cattle were moved away from the collective farms; a total 350,000 head of cattle had now been moved across the Dnieper and Dvina Rivers, thus vindicating the fears of the German planners who had hoped to exploit Soviet agricultural resources. Ponomarenko also reported that some 150,000 women and children were working on defenses along the Dnieper.

According to Ponomarenko, there was a mood of defiance among the collective farm workers, and they were requesting weapons so that they could fight the Germans. Everywhere, he claimed, partisan groups were being set up without any prompting. On its face, this spontaneous emergence of partisan groups seemed encouraging, but it was fraught with danger for Soviet power. There was no guarantee that these groups would be loyal to Soviet institutions, and even if they were nominally loyal, armed groups left to their own devices could develop independent habits that would bring them into conflict with Moscow. This explains why the Belorussian Communist Party attached a responsible party official to each of the partisan groups in Belorussia.

Ponomarenko also provided more details of partisan successes. Referring to the operation carried out by Iurin's detachment, he reported that the German survivors of the ambush "were destroyed one at time by the peasants."[74] Such behavior suggested a policy of the premeditated killing of German prisoners. Another partisan detachment surprised a German column of tanks in a forest and burned them. Ponomarenko also reported that enemy parachutists were being killed by the peasants, and as a consequence, they were being dropped far less frequently.

From Moscow's point of view, the most alarming part of Ponomarenko's report was the Germans' treatment of the peasants: "On arriving in a village the German soldiers and officers shake the hands of the most respected peasants, hand out chocolate to the children and give the women some 2–3 meters of calico, mainly in prerevolutionary colors."[75] Worse still were the promises being made by the Germans: each peasant would receive land,

and the products of his labor would be his property; no taxes would be levied, nor would there be any forced loans; the Stakhanovite press would be smashed; and the cross, icons, churches, and mosques would be returned to believers. When the Germans asked one peasant what authority he wanted, he replied, "One that would leave our village alone."[76] This was not exactly a ringing endorsement of Soviet power or, for that matter, an expression of confidence in the promises of the invaders.

There were also signs that the sense of *Soviet* identity was in jeopardy. For instance, Ponomarenko pointed out a rural-urban divide: "In conclusion I must emphasize the exceptional fearlessness, steadfastness and irreconcilable opposition on the part of the collective farm workers to the enemy, unlike a certain service class in the cities which thinks of nothing other than saving its skin. This can be explained to a considerable degree by the large Jewish stratum in the cities. They are in the grip of an animal fear of Hitler and instead of fighting, they flee."[77] This reflected an ominous and latent development. On the one hand, as noted by Ponomarenko, German propaganda identified Jews and Bolsheviks as one, yet on the other hand, Jews were being criticized by a senior Soviet official for fleeing. Such flight strengthened German propaganda—they flee because they fear retribution—but it also inspired accusations that the Jews left it to others to fight the Germans. So even if a Belorussian peasant was not enamored of the Germans or the Bolshevik regime, the knowledge that Jews had fled, whereas he had stayed, made him receptive to German blandishments and susceptible to German policies of divide and rule.

By early August, the head of the first section of the intelligence department of the NKVD in Belorussia, Senior Lieutenant Grigorii Semykin, reported that 35 sabotage *rezidentury* comprising a total of 131 persons had been left behind in territory now occupied by the Germans. Dispositions are shown in tables 5.2 and 5.3.

Meanwhile, as in Belorussia, a huge effort had been under way in Ukraine since the start of the war to organize partisan detachments. One of the immediate and first-line responses to the Germans was the formation of so-called destroyer battalions (*istrebitel'nye batal'ony*). Their operational principle bore some resemblance to that of American militia units during the Independence War. Members would go about their day-to-day affairs but be ready to respond to enemy action at short notice when summoned. Over the period August–September, destroyer battalions in the Sumsk, Poltava, Dnepropetrovsk, and Zaporozh'e districts detained 49 enemy parachutists,

Table 5.2. Numerical Strength of NKVD Sabotage Residencies Operating in Belorussia, 8 August 1941

District	Number of Residencies	Personnel
Vitebsk	15	58
Mogilev	15	57
Pinsk	3	11
Minsk	2	5
Total	35	131

Source: № 480, "Iz spravki razvedotdela NKVD Belorusskoi SSR o chislennom sostave diversionnykh rezidentur v tylu protivnika, 8 avgusta 1941 g.," OGB, 1941/1, 466.

26 enemy rocket signalers, 427 counterrevolutionaries, and 1,975 deserters.[78] Destroyer battalions were typically led by police officers, reservists from the Red Army, and those who had served as partisans during the civil war. From July to September 1941 a total of 648 destroyer battalions were formed, numbering about 118,000 persons. Their disposition, numerical strength, and weapons are shown in table 5.4.

The recruitment and equipping of such large numbers amid the chaos of an invasion was an impressive administrative achievement. However, by October 1941, the number of destroyer battalions and personnel had dropped sharply, mainly because of the manpower requirements of the Red Army and the evacuation of plant and qualified personnel to the east. The total number of destroyer battalions now stood at 142, with 26,001 personnel (see table 5.5).

Destroyer battalions formed the basis of partisan detachments, and some

Table 5.3. Numerical Strength of NKVD Sabotage Groups Operating in Belorussia, 8 August 1941

Raion*	Number of Groups	Personnel
Vitebsk town and area	13	51
Orsha town and area	2	7
Mogilev town and area	15	57
Pinskii raion	1	3
Leninskii raion	1	4
Luninetskii raion	1	4
Starodorozhskii raion	1	3
Liubanskii and Gluskii raiony	1	2
Total	35	131

Source: OGB, 1941/1, № 480, 467.
*An administrative, not geographical, region.

Table 5.4. Disposition, Numerical Strength, and Weapons of Destroyer Battalions in Ukraine, July–September 1941

District	Number of Destroyer Battalions	Personnel	Rifles	SMGs*	HMGs†	Grenades	Revolvers
					Weapons		
Kiev	62	3,912	11,547	39	—	465	—
Dnepropetrovsk	30	6,579	9,313	110	—	1,330	—
Odessa	51	11,225	6,149	89	4	—	134
Zaporozh'e	38	7,006	6,556	64	3	1,090	—
Sumsk	32	6,073	1,800	43	1	117	114
Voroshilovgrad	36	8,006	2,243	66	4	—	—
Kharkov	42	8,400	8,675	85	—	600	—
Nikolaev	33	6,156	11,600	48	6	—	—
Poltava	44	9,520	3,306	141	—	1,100	125
Chernigov	39	7,292	9,313	110	7	—	—
Stalinsk	33	6,570	3,645	62	—	—	125
Kamenets-Podolsk	38	8,111	6,000	74	—	—	—
Vinitsk	44	9,136	6,149	89	—	—	134
Zhitomir	35	6,540	4,000	—	—	—	—
Izmailsk	22	4,397	697	13	2	237	219
Tarnopolsk	36	4,600	691	2	—	—	—
Kirovograd	33	4,500	4,392	60	—	—	—
Total	648	118,023	96,076	1,095	27	4,939	851

Source: OGB, 1941/2, № 596, 175.

*Handheld submachine guns.

†Larger-caliber machine guns, typically mounted on bipods or tripods.

Table 5.5. Disposition and Numerical Strength of Destroyer Battalions in Ukraine, 1 October 1941

District	Number of Destroyer Battalions	Personnel
Voroshilovgrad	36	8,006
Stalinsk	33	6,870
Sumsk	6	300
Khar'kov	38	7,600
Dnepropetrovsk	4	600
Zaporozh'e	25	2,625
Total	142	26,001

Source: OGB, 1941/2, № 596, 176.

125 battalions were used to create 6,236 detachments with a total manpower of approximately 19,765.[79] The partisans were armed mainly at the expense of the destroyer battalions, from Red Army and NKVD sources. Those selected for partisan detachments underwent a five-day training program that focused on weapons (their own and the enemy's), navigation, and the use of explosives. It was soon discovered that large partisan units were too unwieldy, so they were disbanded. Small, independent detachments with 20 to 25 members became the norm. From July to September 1941 a total of 122 partisan detachments, numbering some 5,809 personnel, and 69 sabotage groups, with 743 individual operatives (in addition to 1,725 other members, or about 20 to 25 per group), were deployed behind German lines throughout the districts of Ukraine. Their dispositions are shown in table 5.6. In addition to these forces, 192 partisan detachments, numbering 5,440 personnel, were left behind in the enemy's rear in the regions (raiony) of the Sumsk, Dnepropetrovsk, Kiev, Nikolaev, and Kirovograd districts (oblasti).[80] Thus, the number of partisans operating in the German rear in Ukraine totaled about 13,717. For an area the size of Ukraine, this was not a huge number. However, the mere existence of these groups and the fact that they made their presence known by acts of sabotage and revenge killings of German-appointed officials created the impression of ubiquity and the sense that, despite the Germans' success, Soviet power had not been completely eliminated.[81]

Sergei Savchenko, an official in Ukraine's NKVD, acknowledged that owing to the absence of regular communications between the controllers and the partisan groups, it was not possible to obtain a complete picture of partisan operations in the rear areas. However, he was able to provide some preliminary results for July–September 1941:

Table 5.6. Deployment of Partisan Detachments and Sabotage Groups in Ukraine, July–September 1941

District	Partisan Detachments Number	Personnel	Sabotage Groups and Individuals Groups	Individuals
Sumsk	7	43	32	266
Chernigov	2	34	—	81
Voroshilovgrad	8	239	—	—
Stalinsk	7	135	13	39
Poltava	2	41	—	93
Dnepropetrovsk	13	358	—	66
Zaporozh'e	14	1,008	4	82
Khar'kov	13	297	3	9
Odessa	3	56	10	61
Kamenets-Podol'sk	1	52	—	—
Nikolaev	—	—	1	5
Zhitomir	3	220	5	26
Kirovograd	—	—	—	9
4th Section, NKVD	49	3,328	1	6
Total	122	5,809	69	743

Source: OGB, 1941/2, № 596, 179.

Killed: 13 German officers, 1,132 other ranks, 20 German officials (1,165).

Captured: 133 agents, saboteurs, and scouts; 4 German officers; 28 other ranks (165).

Detained: 49 pilots and parachutists, 26 spies, 2,057 deserters (2,132). It is assumed that the deserters were Red Army personnel.

Destroyed: 15 grain dumps, 73 tanks, 3 guns.[82]

These raw numbers were supplemented by details of various operations. Thus, on 12 August 1941 a group of six partisans attacked the village of Snovidovichi, caused the police unit made up of Ukrainian nationalists to flee, and captured an individual named Bogachev who was in possession of a German order appointing him the commandant of Kiev and a resolution of the Snovidovichi national committee concerning the execution of twenty-two village activists. The partisan group executed Bogachev.[83] On the night of 29 August 1941 a group of six partisans accompanied by a Red Army subunit attacked a German garrison in the village of Grigorovka. Seventy-five Germans were killed and nine prisoners were taken, including three officers.[84] On 31 July 1941 a sabotage group destroyed a bridge over the river Trosianitsa and organized the killing of the German-appointed starosta (village elder), a

Table 5.7. Disposition and Numerical Strength of Partisan Detachments Operating in the Orlov District

Region	Detachment(s)	Total Strength
Novozybkovsk	1	75
Zlynkovsk	2	140
Klintsovsk	4	225*
Klimovsk	2	116
Pogarsk	3	80
Krasnogorsk	1	60
Staodubsk	1	200
Ponurovsk	1	60
Mglinsk	1	51
Pochepsk	1	45
Pognedinsk	1	90
Dubrovsk	1	100
Kletiansk	1	103
Gordeevsk	1	56
Total	21	1,401

Source: OGB, 1941/2, № 540, 40–41.
*Numbers are provided for only two detachments.

man named Lisovskii, described as a kulak.[85] On 17 August 1941 a group of six partisans captured and executed the German-appointed *starosta* and the commander of a mounted patrol near the village of Rudnia Makarovskaia.[86] One of the more successful raids was carried out in the village of Dich in the Sumsk district. After learning that there were some 200 drunk German soldiers and officers in the village, the head of the NKVD's regional section, Lieutenant Kharchenko, organized a raid, and 130 Germans were killed.[87]

A similar picture of mass organization of partisan detachments and hasty improvisation can be seen in other parts of the Soviet Union, on the Briansk Front, and in Leningrad and Moscow and their environs. On 8 September 1941, for example, the secretary of the Orlov district committee of the Communist Party informed the Military Council of the Briansk Front about the scale of partisan operations. At that time, there were thirty-six partisan detachments operating in enemy-occupied territory, comprising 1,632 partisans.[88] Based on the available data, the disposition and strength of twenty-one of these partisan detachments are shown in table 5.7. Partisan detachments already operating in the occupied regions were supplemented by others from Soviet-held territory. A total of 240 partisans in seven detachments were deployed via Trubchevsk, and another 120 partisans in six detachments were deployed via Zhiriatino.[89] Meanwhile, additional

Table 5.8. Disposition and Strength of Partisan Detachments in the Orlov District Being Prepared for Deployment

Location	Number of Detachments	Total Strength
Ordzhonikidzegrad (raion)	8	298
Briansk (town)	1	167
Komarich (raion)	3	104
Zhukov (raion)	1	60
Vygonich (raion)	2	22
Zhiriatino (raion)	3	54
Navlinsk (raion)	1	40
Sevsk (raion)	1	50
Suzemsk (raion)	3	46
Brasovsk (raion)	1	110
Khvastovich (raion)	1	74
Diat'kov (raion)	2	90*
Total	27	1,115

Source: OGB, 1941/2, № 540, 42–45.
*This figure refers to only the first detachment. No figure was given for the second detachment.

detachments were being assembled and prepared for deployment. Their disposition and strength are indicated in table 5.8.

A total of 13 sabotage groups, with a numerical strength of 101, had already been deployed. In one case, four members of a group deployed to the Pogarsk raion were dismissed for "cowardice and . . . sent to the ranks of the RKKA."[90] Another 48 sabotage groups and lone operatives, totaling 364 individuals, had been deployed to those parts of the Orlov district that were not yet occupied by the Germans as contingency measures. According to one Soviet source, the partisans in the Orlov district had achieved a whole series of successes by mid-July 1942. Among other things, they had retained control of 490 populated areas; killed 23,838 German soldiers and officers, wounded 6,958, and captured 236; destroyed 47 planes and 52 tanks; and derailed 63 rail columns.[91]

Combating Enemy Parachutists

Quick to establish partisan detachments, the NKGB and NKVD were well aware of the vulnerability of the Soviet rear to the same sort of sabotage operations. In this regard, German airborne troops—glider-borne, air-landed, and parachutists—evoked real concern among the internal security formations of the NKVD. (Much the same could be said about British reactions as the country waited for a German invasion in the summer of 1940.)

German airborne forces and the special forces of the Brandenburg zbV had demonstrated their effectiveness in seizing important military objectives. Parachute drops were also an ideal way to supply nationalist formations close to the front and in remote parts of the Soviet Union. The seriousness of the threat and the urgency with which it had to be combated were evident in the Politburo resolution of 24 June 1941. The immediate and first line of defense against these German airborne units were destroyer battalions, consisting of 100 to 200 men recruited from the Communist Party and the Komsomol. They were commanded by NKVD officials and members of the police force.[92] At first, these measures were useful, but the critical problem was identifying key potential targets and then devising an effective system of reporting their location so that reaction forces could be deployed quickly.

Beria responded to this Politburo resolution with his typical energy and efficiency. Recognizing that effective command and control measures were essential, he appointed General-Major G. A. Petrov, a senior NKVD officer, to take charge. Critically, he identified good communication links as fundamental. The heads of destroyer battalions were ordered to form liaison groups in collective farms and various other enterprises, and it fell to the liaison groups to inform the destroyer battalions about the presence of enemy airborne troops. The heads of destroyer battalions were also required to identify key targets in their areas and ensure that the necessary security measures were taken. Forestry workers, shepherds, collective farm workers, road repairmen, and railway employees were all enlisted as observers and instructed to report any sightings of airborne landings. Alert to the possibility that anti-Soviet elements might make false reports of airborne landings, Beria stipulated that all sightings must be verified.[93]

Related to the threat posed by German airborne troops and night air attacks was the presence of signal'shchiki in the Soviet rear. These enemy agents or anti-Soviet elements were equipped with rocket flares to highlight targets for nighttime air attacks. These rockets could also be used to indicate possible drop zones. The NKGB planned to provide rocket flares to its own people in the German-occupied territories and instruct them to use these rockets at their discretion during Soviet air attacks. Given that there was no contact between the NKGB and the signal'shchiki in the German-occupied territories, and in the absence of some forewarning of a Soviet raid and a predetermined color sequence for the rocket flares, it is unclear how these individuals could be of any real use. The most likely (but unstated) goal was not to provide signals to Soviet planes but to create the impression of a Soviet presence among the German occupation forces and show that Soviet agents were active. Firing off rocket flares behind the German lines, especially in or close to settlements, was potentially fatal not just for the individual *signal'shchik* but also for the settlement, since this sort of behavior would invite wholesale German reprisals. Such reprisals would suit NKVD-NKGB purposes, fueling resistance to the German occupation, and this may have been the thinking behind the whole project.[94]

A later report specified the key problems in combating German airborne landings. First, likely targets had to be identified (and prioritized). Second, there had to be detailed knowledge of suitable drop zones and landing sites in the area; this was especially important in large forested areas. Third, an effective system of air observation had to be established, and observer groups had to be equipped with the necessary communications. Fourth, reaction to German landings must be swift. All command staff were expected to read the pamphlet *Kak borot'sia s vozdushnymi desantami vraga* (How to Combat Enemy Airborne Landings).[95]

Railway Security

Railway infrastructure occupied a major place in the defense of the Soviet Union and therefore had obvious security implications. The NKVD was the primary security provider, responsible for ensuring that enemy attempts to disrupt the rail network were interdicted. In fact, these tasks applied to all other forms of transport as well: maritime, rivers, air, and road. In addition, the NKVD was responsible for ensuring that rolling stock was used effectively, that accidents were forestalled, and that proper timetables were in place—in other words, ensuring the smooth running and exploitation of the rail network.

Attention was focused on three main areas: the secure and safe passage of trains, route security and protection of railway infrastructure, and operational investigations and security. As in all areas of the Soviet state, great care was taken to vet personnel and weed out anti-Soviet elements. The selection of staff and workers was to be based on "the principle of political trust and sufficient experience."[96] After the inspection of a train, a document had to be completed that indicated the names of the staff responsible for the inspection; the names of the persons inspecting the right and left sides had to be recorded, as well as the name of the fitter. Anything that went wrong—an accident, trains allowed to pass or sent in the wrong direction—would trigger an NKVD investigation, based on a presumption of sabotage or wrecking. With regard to route security, the overwhelming emphasis—even to the exclusion of the staff's technical abilities—was on that Soviet ideological staple, vigilance (*bditel'nost'*).

Operational security on the Soviet rail network was intended to uncover enemy spies, saboteurs, various criminals, and Red Army deserters. At railway stations, particular attention was paid to porters, buffets, hairdressers, left-luggage compartments, and any places that provided temporary accommodation. Detailed instructions were issued for checking trains. Passengers who had joined the train on its journey were deemed to be of special interest, as were evacuees who were not part of an organized evacuation.[97] The overall procedures for railway security were well thought out and exceptionally thorough, revealing a complete grasp of potential problems. The weak link—which was perhaps unavoidable—was the sheer volume of specific tasks and the lack of fully trained personnel to carry them out. This remained a permanent security problem. On the assumption that basic security measures would protect the main rail assets, the most effective way to interdict suspicious persons, especially in a state obsessed with documentation, was the routine and assiduous checking of documents.

Deportation of National Minorities

One of the main themes of Soviet wartime propaganda was the essential unity of the *Soviet* people, who were united in the struggle against the German invaders. Soviet unity was a feature of Molotov's speech on 22 June 1941 and Stalin's on 3 July 1941. Behind the scenes, however, Stalin and Beria and other officials harbored no illusions about the solidarity of the various nationalities and ethnic groups that made up the Soviet people. They pursued policies that left little doubt that they considered whole groups of Soviet people, especially the national minorities, "socially or ideologically dangerous and hostile elements"—a phrase used in many Soviet reports. In the first half of 1941 and the early part of 1942, Soviet citizens who were ethnic Finns and Germans were the main targets of Stalin and Beria. Mass deportation was the standard procedure, and Finns and Germans were deported from Leningrad, Moscow, Saratov, Zaporozh'e, Voronezh, Kuibyshev, and the Volga region. Later in the war, Crimean Tartars and Chechens, among others, were subjected to mass deportation.

The mass deportation of real and *potential* enemies of the Soviet state had in fact been widely practiced before the German invasion and was a standard procedure in the sovietization of newly occupied territory.[98] From September

1939 to June 1941 there were mass deportations of Poles and, after the Soviet Union's seizure and annexation of the three Baltic states, of Estonians, Lithuanians, and Latvians. When the Red Army reconquered the Baltic states in 1944–1945, the deportation of so-called hostile elements resumed. On the eve of the war, the NKGB deported various categories of undesirables, just under 14,000 from Moldova (see table 5.9). Bearing in mind that categories 6–11 pertain to the families of those arrested, and assuming that a typical family consisted of four to five members, the numbers deported were likely much higher than those cited. The profile of the arrestees and deportees underlined the class-based criteria and assumptions on which NKGB and NKVD operations were planned. The profile also bore a marked resemblance to that of the Poles murdered at Katyn and other sites a year previously. Thus, it is reasonable to assume that a proportion of those listed in table 5.9 were executed immediately after arrest or that they were executed later, in NKGB and NKVD detention centers and prisons in regions threatened by the Germans, because they could not be evacuated to the rear areas.

On 30 August 1941 Merkulov submitted a memorandum to Beria in which he set out draft proposals for the removal of Finns and Germans from the Leningrad district. The deportations affected eight raiony within the Leningrad district. In each raion a troika had been appointed to oversee the deportation program, and these troikas reported to a district troika. The total numbers envisaged for deportation were 88,700 Finns and 6,500 Germans, based on a 1939 census.[99] Merkulov proposed that all families targeted for deportation be instructed to take food, clothing, bedding, small domestic utensils, and minor agricultural items with them. The total weight allowance per family was not to exceed 600 kilograms (1,322 pounds). Merkulov clarified that this was not an "administrative eviction but a forced evacuation."[100] Given the potential opposition, it would require the presence of armed guards and the participation of party activists and organizations. Those resisting deportation would be arrested. The operation was scheduled to be completed by 7 September 1941, and the final destination of the deportees was Kazakhstan. Merkulov felt some urgency to act since he informed Beria that Germans and Finns were hiding in the forest, awaiting the arrival of the German army, whereas Russians were converging on Leningrad. One of the striking things about this entire operation—something it shared with other deportations, especially that of the Jews by the SS—was that it placed a critical strain on the entire railway and transport infrastructure at a time when every available railcar was required for troop and equipment deployments.

Table 5.9. Persons Characterized as Counterrevolutionary and Criminal Elements and Deported by the Moldovan NKGB, 13 June 1941

№	Category of Arrestees and Deportees	Number Arrested	Number Deported
1	Counterrevolutionaries and nationalists	1,681	—
2	Police officers, guards, and prison warders	389	—
3	Major landowners, traders, and merchants	1,719	—
4	Former officers of the Polish, Romanian, and White armies	268	—
5	Fugitives from the USSR	249	—
6	Families of those in category 1	—	5,353
7	Families of those in category 2	—	1,124
8	Families of those in category 3	—	5,764
9	Families of those in category 4	—	623
10	Families of those in category 5	—	604
11	Families of leaders of counterrevolutionary and nationalists organizations condemned to death	—	113
12	Arrivals from Romania but not returned there	36	101
13	Prostitutes registered with the former Romanian police	2	119
14	Criminal elements	163	84
	Total	4,507	13,885

Source: № 584, "Iz dokladnoi zapiski NKGB Moldavskoi SSR v NKGB SSSR, 19 iiunia 1941 g.," 1941 god, 2:394.

Deporting Germans from Leningrad was just the start. In early September 1941 Stalin ordered that all Germans resident in Moscow and the Moscow district—a total of 8,617 people—be deported. An additional 21,400 Germans were to be deported from the Rostov district. The main destinations were, once again, the remote parts of Kazakhstan, the aim being to send these people to existing collective farms, which, in effect, meant abandoning them to a wretched and bare subsistence existence on the steppe. Ominously, Stalin's resolution states: "In the absence of any corpus of habitable buildings and administrative infrastructure in the areas of settlement the construction work is to be carried out by the efforts of the deportees."[101]

The results of the operation were reported on 20 September 1941 and can be summarized as follows: The total number of Germans in Moscow and the Moscow district was ascertained to be 11,567 persons. Of these, 8,449 people were deported—3,524 from Moscow and 4,925 from the Moscow district—and 1,142 were arrested. An additional 356 persons were scheduled to be deported on 22 September. The NKVD allowed the remaining 1,620

Germans to stay in Moscow: 912 of them were the heads of families that were not German, 364 were elderly or invalids, 100 were family members of Red Army soldiers who were not deemed to be suspicious, 97 were not deported for operational reasons of the NKVD, and 147 were major specialists who were not deported at the request of commissariats. Ten people were known to have evaded deportation.[102] This illustrates another administrative feature shared by the NKVD and its Nazi counterparts: those deemed to be enemies of the state but who possessed valuable skills were not deported. Even the SS was forced to recognize that its exploitation regime in the occupied territories could not entirely dispense with skilled Jewish artisans and professionals.

By far the biggest NKVD deportation operation being planned in August and September 1941 envisaged the deportation of the entire population of the German Volga Republic (401,746) and all Germans from the districts of Saratov (54,389) and Stalingrad (23,756)—a staggering total of 479,841 Germans.[103] The primary destinations of the deportees were the northeastern districts of Kazakhstan, the *raiony* of Krasnoiarsk and the Altai, and the districts of Omsk and Novosibirsk. Deportees were permitted to take some food, domestic goods, and minor agricultural tools, and they were expected, if necessary, to construct their own dwellings. No German was to be spared Beria's ethnic cleansing operation: "All Germans without exception are subject to deportation, inhabitants of cities and in rural areas, including all members of the VKP (b) and the VLKSM [Komsomol]."[104]

The thoroughly spurious justification for these brutal measures was made clear in a decree of the Supreme Soviet dated 28 August 1941. The first three paragraphs of this decree expose the ideological and criminal nature of the entire deportation:

> According to reliable information received by the military authorities there are *thousands and tens of thousands of saboteurs and spies among the German population living in the Volga regions* who on the receipt of a signal given from Germany are to bring about explosions in the regions of the Volga populated by Germans.
>
> None of the Germans living in the Volga regions has reported anything concerning the presence of such a huge number of saboteurs and spies among the Volga Germans. Therefore the German population of the Volga regions are hiding among them enemies of the Soviet people and Soviet power.

In the event that acts of sabotage occur, carried out by German
saboteurs and spies in the German Volga Republic or in the adjacent
regions, on orders from Germany, there will be bloodshed, then
the Soviet government in accordance with the laws of wartime will
be forced to take punitive measures against the entire German
population of the Volga region.[105]

It is unclear how the Soviet authorities knew about the existence of these
tens of thousands of German saboteurs and spies, and no documents were
attached to this decree that might support such inflated claims. If these
German agents did indeed exist, they were unlikely to reveal their presence
and purposes to the uninitiated and thus run the risk of compromising the
success of any planned sabotage. Moreover, deporting thousands of people
based on the claim that they *must* know there are saboteurs among them
and that they are guilty of some crime because they have failed to report
the locations and plans of these saboteurs is such an obviously crude and
fallacious justification that it exposes the real reason these hapless people
were being deported. Deportation en masse was being conducted on the
principle, well established in Soviet law, that because *some* of these Germans
might be agents of Hitler's Germany, and because it was not possible to
separate the agents from the nonagents, *all Germans* in the Volga regions
(and other parts of the Soviet Union) were presumed to be potential or actual
saboteurs. All distinctions between guilty and innocent were eradicated
and replaced by the sole category of potentially guilty. Since all Germans
in the Volga regions were *potential* agents of the invader, according to this
ideological reasoning, all Germans were *guilty*.

Mass deportations clearly had the potential to arouse resistance among
the deportees. The question was, who would be responsible for any bloodshed—the NKVD or the deportees? The two officials who drafted the decree
had no doubt: the deportees (and the tens of thousands of elusive German
agents) would be responsible. Any opposition to deportation thus justified
punitive measures on the basis of wartime laws against the entire German
population in the Volga regions. References to the laws of war were mere
window dressing to cover the criminal nature of the deportations. There
are no laws of war that would allow a state to take such actions. Reprisals
against the entire German population constituted collective punishment—
Germans were guilty merely for being German—and clearly violated legal
instruments such as the Geneva Convention—instruments the Soviet state

was eager to apply to German violators in 1945–1946. Soviet application of
the principle of collective punishment to Volga Germans was no different
from NS application of collective punishment to residents of the German-
occupied territories and enshrined in the Barbarossa Jurisdiction Decree
and the Commissar Order.[106]

In all, 7,170 families, or 26,245 people, were deported from the Stalingrad district from 3 to 16 September 1941.[107] Their final destination was
Astrakhan'. In anticipation of the destruction of assets similar to that which
occurred during forced collectivization, firefighting teams were deployed to
grain silos, livestock yards, and agricultural enterprises in areas with heavy
concentrations of Germans. Blocking detachments comprising police, special detachments, and destroyer battalions were deployed on all crossroads
throughout the area.

During this forced deportation, only fifty-eight counterrevolutionaries
were arrested, and there was no counterrevolutionary activity from Germans—at least no shootings or explosions.[108] Some of the acts of anti-
Soviet behavior involved rumors, one of which was that the Germans would
be taken out to sea and drowned.[109] This rumor was undoubtedly based
on events that occurred during the civil war. For example, when a strike
by workers and soldiers in Astrakhan was put down by the Cheka in 1919,
captured strikers were loaded onto barges and thrown into the Volga with
stones around their necks. Others were shot. It is estimated that some 2,000
to 4,000 strikers were shot or drowned.[110] In view of the claim that tens of
thousands of German saboteurs and spies were waiting for the signal from
Berlin to unleash murder and mayhem, the numbers arrested by the NKVD
were pitifully exiguous. One would have expected these counterrevolutionary organizations, if they existed, to disrupt the deportations, yet nothing
happened. Therefore, the most plausible explanation is that these tens of
thousands of saboteurs and spies were NKVD concoctions.

In keeping with the original order, all ethnic German members of the
NKVD in the Stalingrad district—a total of twenty-three—were discharged
and expelled from the district.[111] Thus, when doing so was expedient, the
Soviet state persecuted its own citizens on grounds of class and race (or
ethnicity), unlike the NS regime, which was obsessed solely with race. The
authors of the report note: "Among the workers, officials and collective farm
workers of Stalingrad and the [Stalingrad] district the measures taken to
deport the Germans have been greeted positively."[112] Such a response by
one group of Soviet citizens to the forced deportation of their fellow Soviet

citizens did not exactly support the notion of Soviet solidarity. Barely three months into a struggle for survival, the Soviet regime felt compelled forcibly to deport tens of thousands of Soviet citizens of German ethnicity from all parts of the Soviet Union. Clearly, the Soviet regime did not trust them and did not regard them as fraternal comrades in the socialist commonwealth. Those who approved of such measures showed very little understanding of what had happened; if one group of Soviet citizens could be treated that way, they all could be: Ukrainians, Estonians, Lithuanians, Latvians, Romanians, and Poles before the war; Finns and Germans today; Tartars and Chechens tomorrow. New enemies of the people can always be found when needed.

In an operation that lasted from 3 to 20 September 1941, all Germans were finally and forcibly deported from the Volga regions. The scale of this operation was revealed in Beria's final report to the State Defense Committee, dated 21 September 1941 (see table 5.10). Beria also reported that a total of 1,097 persons had been left behind for various reasons, including orphans and their guardians, invalids, those who were ill, and those who absconded. Beria's report provides further evidence of the similarities between the NKVD and the SS and *Einsatzgruppen*. For example, he states: "10,000 collective farm workers from the Saratov and Stalingrad districts have been moved to the populated areas *which have been liberated from German deportees.*"[113] The italicized text is identical in spirit and content to the wording in SS documents reporting, with professional pride and satisfaction, that whole areas from which Jews have been deported or eliminated in mass-murder operations are now judged to be *judenrein* or *judenfrei*. The same sense of professional pride in a job well done is evident in a report submitted by a Moscow NKVD official, Mikhail Zhuravlev, on the deportation of Germans from the Moscow district: "The resettlement of persons of German nationality from the regions [raiony] of the Moscow district has been completed."[114] Moscow has been fully cleansed of Germans.

The removal of Germans from the German Volga Republic was not the end of the mass deportations. Over the next two months, Beria and his deputies submitted draft proposals for the deportation of Germans from other parts of the Soviet Union:

1. Germans were to be arrested and deported from the Krasnodar, Ordzhonikidze krai, Tula district, Kabardino-Balkarskii, and North Ossetian Autonomous Republic, numbering about 141,240 people (21 September 1941).[115]

2. Germans were to be deported from the Zaporozh'e, Stalinsk, and Voroshilovgrad districts, totaling about 109,487 people: 63,000 from Zaporozh'e, 41,000 from Stalinsk, and 5,487 from Voroshilovgrad. Over the period 2–5 September 1941, 7,091 had already been arrested for being "anti-Soviet elements," and the entire German male population—13,484 people—had been taken under guard to work in the gulag (22 September 1941).[116]

3. Germans were to be deported from the Voronezh district. The number of deportees was not given, and the operation was to be completed by 22 October 1941 (11 October 1941). In this and subsequent orders, and based on the standard NKVD application of collective punishment, Beria stipulated the following: "Before the start of the operation explanatory work shall be conducted jointly with the Soviet party activists and the deportees shall be warned that in the event that any individual members of families attempt to violate the deportation order that full responsibility shall be borne by the head of the family."[117]

4. Germans were to be deported from the Gor'kov district. The number of deportees was not given, and the operation was to be completed by 23 October 1941 (15 October 1941).[118]

5. Germans were to be deported from the Dagestan and Chechen-Ingush Autonomous Soviet Socialist Republics (ASSRs). The number of deportees was not given, and the operation was to be completed by 30 October 1941 (24 October 1941).[119]

6. Germans were to be deported from the Kalmytsk ASSR. The number of deportees was not given, and the operation was to be completed by 10 November 1941 (3 November 1941).[120]

7. Germans were to be deported from the Kuibyshev district. The number of deportees was not given, and the operation was to be completed by 5 December 1941 (26 November 1941).[121]

The mass deportation of various ethnic groups who were citizens of the Soviet Union—in 1941, overwhelmingly ethnic Germans—shows that whatever the official propaganda about Soviet unity and the existence of a Soviet *Rodina* (Motherland), the Soviet leadership and its security agency, the NKVD, regarded all non-Russian nationalities with profound suspicion. Nowhere in the available documents is there any awareness that non-Russians' reluctance to consider themselves *Soviet* rather than, say, Estonian or Belorussian might be due to the Soviet state. The default position of NKVD

Table 5.10. Germans Deported from the Volga German Republic and the Saratov and Stalingrad Districts, September 1941

Area	Germans Subject to Deportation		Germans Actually Deported	
	Families	Individuals	Families	Individuals
Volga Republic	82,608	374,225	81,771	376,717
Saratov district	11,319	43,101	11,388	46,706
Stalingrad district	6,541	24,656	7,170	26,245
Total	100,468	441,982	100,329	449,668

Source: № 570, "Dokladnaia zapiska NKVD SSSR № 2639/B v Gosudarstvennyi Komitet Oborony SSSR ob itogakh pereseleniia nemtsev iz byvshei Respubliki Nemtsev Povol'zh'ia, Saratovskoi i Stalingradskoi oblastei, 21 sentiabria 1941 g.," OGB, 1941/2, 124.

functionaries was always that any hostility to the Soviet state could only mean that those holding such views were socially hostile or counterrevolutionary elements who must be dealt with accordingly.

Conclusion

By the start of the German invasion in June 1941, the NKVD was firmly established as one of the central components of the Soviet state. Under the general rubric of state security, its functions expanded enormously, making the NKVD the main instrument of totalitarian control in the Soviet Union. In wartime it was the only Soviet organization with the administrative structure, experience, personnel, and equipment to handle the huge range of tasks that fell to its senior commanders.

Internal security now included many additional tasks. A serious NKVD concern was that nationalists, counterrevolutionaries, hostile and anti-Soviet elements, and criminals—in short, any person with a grudge against the Soviet state—would exploit the chaos of war to settle scores and that these grudges would be exploited by German intelligence agencies, as indeed they were. Even allowing for the institutional and ideological paranoia of Soviet officials when confronted with manifestations of nationalism, the threat posed by nationalists and other disaffected groups was not insignificant. They were partisans and saboteurs in waiting. In the first half of 1941 the NKVD also played a major role in policing the scattered remnants of Soviet soldiers who had been cut off from their units. This was an administrative and security nightmare, since the chaotic retreat provided ideal conditions for the German intelligence agencies to infiltrate its agents and spies. NKVD special sections now had to subject Red Army soldiers to filtration, a task that acquired greater importance as the war progressed, especially with the liberation of German-occupied territory. When necessary—and these powers were not used sparingly—the NKVD played the lead role in arresting and executing soldiers of all ranks. General Pavlov and his colleagues were some of the first senior officers to be executed.

With its reach into every facet of Soviet life, the NKVD was also the sole organization that could raise, equip, and supervise partisan detachments and sabotage groups. The disruption caused by Stalin's purges of the partisan units could not be easily remedied in the middle of a war—preparation and training of partisans are peacetime tasks—but the institutional drive and energy of the effort were impressive. Nevertheless, despite the calls for all-out partisan warfare, the concept of a well-armed and well-equipped partisan network behind German lines could only be partially realized. To begin with, the main task was to encourage and nourish the spirit of resistance to German occupation. Killing the German-appointed starostas and minor acts of sabotage were one solution, since they gave the impression of a Soviet presence and led to German reprisals that could be exploited. Large-scale partisan operations would come later.

The NKVD also played a major role in the scorched-earth policy (politika/ strategiia vyzhennoi zemli) initiated by Stalin in his 3 July speech and designed to destroy major assets or goods that could be useful to the invading Germans. For all the spurious and cynical Soviet patriotism in his speech, this policy's moral and legal basis was far from clear. Hartmann, for example, asserts that the Soviet sabotage squads were destroying their own land and installations.[122] However, it should be pointed out that large numbers of Belorussians and other national groups rejected the claims made by the Soviet power. In view of the dreadful suffering inflicted on the various national groups constituting the Soviet state and, in the case of Ukraine, the genocide carried out less than a decade earlier, Stalin's claims that the Germans sought, among other things, "the destruction of the national culture and national statehood of Russians, Ukrainians, Belorussians, Lithuanians, Latvians, Estonians, Uzbeks, Tartars, Moldavians, Georgians, Armenians, Azerbaijanis and the other free peoples of the Soviet Union"[123]—the same antinational policies pursued by the Soviet regime since 1918—must have induced a state of suppressed rage and disgust among some of these national groups. Stalin's volte-face, no different in principle from Hitler's tearing up of the Non-Aggression Pact, exemplified the essential and open hypocrisy of raw and unfettered power and the lawlessness on which the Soviet regime was founded and acted.

Land, assets, installations, and, above all, people do not suddenly become "Soviet" merely because a totalitarian regime in Moscow invades and annexes territory. For their part, the Germans were simply the latest set of occupiers. For these reasons, Hartmann's view that the Soviet side enjoyed some allegedly higher moral right to engage in a scorched-earth policy is erroneous and objectionable.[124] It is objectionable on four counts: (1) The entire Soviet state was based on the principle of expropriation by violence and dispossession of so-called exploiters, for which there was no mandate of any kind. The dispossessed survivors did not recognize this dispossession, which is why they fervently hoped and expected that the Germans would abolish the Soviet collective farm system and restore private property rights. This rejection of Soviet appropriation applied not only to those who had been dispossessed in Belorussia and Ukraine but also to the inhabitants of the recently annexed Baltic states, Bessarabia, and northern Bukovina. (2) By destroying assets and infrastructure to which it had no lawful or reasonable claim, and by virtue of its status as an occupying power, the Soviet Union behaved no better than Germany and encouraged the Germans—who needed no encouragement—to do the same thing, starting in the winter of 1941–1942. This later evolved into a fully organized and systematic German scorched-earth policy (*Politik der verbrannten Erde*). (3) Even if the Soviet regime in Moscow could demonstrate that assets and resources derived from one part of the imperium had objectively improved the material conditions of people elsewhere—in Estonia, for example—the fact that the Estonians' consent was neither sought nor given meant that these improvements had been imposed by an occupying power and carried out primarily to serve the interests of the occupying power. (4) The destruction and removal of assets condemned the people who could not escape German occupation to massive hardship, demonstrating that the Soviet state had no interest in the well-being of people it claimed were Soviet citizens. Having abandoned any duty of care, or not considering itself bound by any duty of care in the first place, the Soviet state lost any claim to exercise legitimate authority over the lives of people it had left to their own fate. The Soviet state reacted to the plight of Red Army soldiers captured by the Wehrmacht with exactly the same callous indifference and cruelty.

Deportation measures enacted against German minorities were justified by the dire security situation: tens of thousands of German agents were supposedly using the Germans of the Volga regions as cover, merely waiting for the right moment to unleash sabotage. No plausible evidence to substantiate these claims has ever been produced. Ethnic Germans and other national minorities were deported en masse not because of what they had done but because of what they *might do*. Moreover, the principle of collective guilt was applied throughout these deportation operations: the actions of individuals rendered all liable to punishment. These were the same principles underpinning the German Barbarossa Jurisdiction Decree and the Commissar Order. That the Soviet state and its primary enforcement agency, the NKVD, deported tens of thousands of ethnic Germans in 1941, and targeted other national groups for the same treatment later in the war, removes any doubt about the totalitarian nature of the Soviet state. In peace and in war, the NKVD, like the SS and SD in NS Germany, functioned as a state within a state, accountable only to the rages, psychopathic vendettas, and orders of its master.

6 20th Panzer Division and the Diary of Gefreiter H. C. von Wiedebach-Nostitz

Precisely at 0230 hours, with the civilian population not having any idea at all, the whole village is set ablaze. Within 5 minutes it is engulfed in bright flames. Roused from their sleep and terrified, the inhabitants run outside screaming. All they can do is to save their naked lives. It is a grim scene. Then we also abandon the village; our route taking us through other burning villages. The entire region is lit up bright red; the snow reflects the red glow. Here we are once again assembled with SS and police units who are still holding up the advancing enemy.

Gefreiter H. C. von Wiedebach-Nostitz

The histories of German divisions that served on the Eastern Front are some of the best sources for German operations, especially those that were written some twenty to thirty years after the war, when many of the veterans were still alive. However, a divisional history is an account of a major formation, anything from 12,000 to 16,000 soldiers, and absent exceptional circumstances that merit a detailed treatment, these histories cannot deal with the fate of individual soldiers or very small units and their actions. Taking part in arduous and prolonged operations, most soldiers have neither the time nor the inclination to maintain a regular diary. When the immediate danger of battle has passed, the priorities are food, warmth, and rest. Any free time available for writing is usually spent writing letters home, not compiling a personal record of operations. To date, the best study of the 20th Panzer Division is Rolf Hinze's *Hitze, Frost und Pulverdampf: Der Schicksalsweg der 20. Panzer-Division* (Heat, Frost, and the Smoke of Battle: The Fate and Path of the 20th Panzer Division [1981]). Additional material is available in the short history of the division's Infantry Regiment 59—*Infanterie-Regiment 59 später Pz. Gren. Regiment 1934–1945* (circa 1983). This account summarizes the regiment's history, from its formation in peacetime until the final German capitulation in 1945. However, the section that deals with the start of Barbarossa and ends with the winter battles of 1941–1942 is very short and lacks detail. The von Wiedebach-Nostitz diary clearly fills a gap, since it is an in-depth account of the German invasion from the first day up to 19 January 1942, when von Wiedebach-Nostitz was wounded and evacuated.

Introduction: 20th Panzer Division, October 1940–April 1942

The headquarters of 20th Panzer Division was assembled on 15 October 1940. It was formed from the 59th and 112th Rifle Regiments, with a total of four infantry battalions. The main tank component of the division consisted of Panzer Regiment 21, with three battalions. Other mobile elements were an armored reconnaissance section and a motorcyclist battalion. A motorized artillery unit, Artillery Regiment 92, provided artillery support. The division also included a signals section, an engineer battalion, a dedicated antitank section, and the supply units common to divisions of all types: medical services, along with bakery and butchery companies. During its existence, the division would have four commanders; the first was Generalmajor Horst Stumpff, who assumed command on 13 November 1940. The breakdown of units in 20th Panzer Division is shown in table 6.1.

Once the various components of the division had been assembled, a program of intense and thorough training was initiated, lasting throughout the winter of 1940–1941. The emphasis was naturally on mobile warfare, and it was based on the now tried and tested doctrines pioneered by Guderian and von Manstein. Even allowing for the special requirements of mobile warfare, the emphasis continued to be the mastering of all phases of war—attack, defense, pursuit, and patrolling—such that the division, like other German divisions, possessed a breadth and depth of training. Mastery of the basics ensured that the soldiers would be able to adapt to the vagaries and uncertainties of modern war, as units on the Eastern Front were disbanded and re-formed, losses mounted, and fuel and equipment shortages occurred. In fact, equipment failure was a central theme in von Wiedebach-Nostitz's diary, since a large percentage of 20th Panzer Division's wheeled, armored vehicles were Panhards, French armored reconnaissance vehicles that proved to be very unreliable in the terrain of the Eastern Front.

Table 6.1. Units of 20th Panzer Division and Command Appointments

Formation and Subunit	Commander
20th Panzer Division	Generalmajor Stumpff
Panzer Regiment (PzR) 21	Oberstleutnant Schmidt
1st Bat PzR 21	Oberstleutnant von Gersdorff
2nd Bat PzR 21	Major Straub
3rd Bat PzR 21	Major Freiherr von Bülow
20th Schützen Brigade	Oberst von Bismarck
Schützenregiment 59	Oberst Weichardt
1st Bat Schützenregiment 59	Hauptmann Nebe
2nd Bat Schützenregiment 59	Major Kempchen
Schützenregiment 112	Oberstleutnant Simon
1st Bat Schützenregiment 112	Major von Petersdorff
2nd Bat Schützenregiment 112	Major von Reckleben
Kradschützen Bat 20	Oberst Mowitz
Artillery Regiment (AR) (Mot.) 92	Oberstleutnant Zierold
1st Bat AR (Mot.) 92	Hauptmann Kuhlmann
2nd Bat AR (Mot.) 92	Hauptmann Brandt
3rd Bat AR (Mot.) 92	Major Hempell
Panzer Aufklärungs-Abteilung 92	Hauptmann Bentele
Panzer Nachrichten Abteilung 92	Hauptmann Hoffmann
Panzer Pionier Bat 92	Major Oelze
Panzer Jäger Abteilung 92	Hauptmann Dippel
Division Nachschub-Führer 92	Major Spenner

Source: Rolf Hinze, Hitze, Frost und Pulverdampf: Der Schicksalsweg der 20. Panzer-Division [1981] (Meerbusch: Dr. Rolf Hinze, 1996), 14–15.

Before he addresses the operational history of 20th Panzer Division on the Eastern Front, Rolf Hinze asserts that, unlike the previous campaigns in the west, the planning for Barbarossa lacked precise knowledge of ground and river conditions, roads, attitudes of the population, concentration of forces, and defensive lines.[1] Later, he argues that "on the German side hardly anyone was informed about conditions in the USSR."[2] These are unusual assertions, given that the German army would have possessed a great deal of knowledge about the area, derived from the officers who had served there, especially in Ukraine, during and after World War I. Moreover, the exchanges made possible by the Treaty of Rapallo would have provided additional opportunities to assess the factors essential for planning. In his own memoir, Guderian notes that part of the planning for Barbarossa involved a detailed study of previous campaigns against Russia. Up-to-date information also would have been available from the comprehensive air reconnaissance undertaken by the Luftwaffe. Likewise, given the scale of the German intelligence effort to ascertain information and enlist the assistance of disaffected Soviet citizens—a major concern for the NKVD—Hinze's claim of ignorance of the population's attitude is not persuasive. Hinze also ignores the copious information about the Red Army—doctrine, training, morale, combat performance—derived from the Finns in the Winter War (1939–1940).

Throughout several German memoirs and divisional histories covering the first phase of Barbarossa, it is clear that Soviet cities and the evidence of Soviet rule did not make a good impression on German soldiers. Advance elements of 20th Panzer Division entered Minsk on 29 June 1941, and even allowing for the impact of Nazi indoctrination, their view of Soviet society was far from flattering:

> One or two days previously, Minsk must have been subjected to a major air attack by the Luftwaffe. Ruins were all that remained. With the exception of the large party building alongside the Lenin memorial, all the party buildings, schools, tenement blocks and state-owned, food-dispensing outlets were destroyed. Dead Red Army soldiers lay on the roadsides. Nobody bothered about them. Nothing better could characterize the apathy and crushed nature of the population than this attitude toward its own dead. By contrast, the mob was very eager to drag away anything of use from the ruins, especially food and items of clothing from the warehouses. Women, carrying huge bundles, almost collapsing under the load, stole into the side streets.[3]

In open country where there was good visibility, the German armored units were almost impossible to stop. In close country, however, and in terrain more suited to infantry and where visibility was restricted—built-up areas, narrow streets, wooded areas affording good cover—German tanks were vulnerable to attack from Soviet infantry armed with Molotov cocktails and grenades. They might not be able to destroy the tanks, but immobilization was almost as good. In such circumstances, Soviet infantry would climb onto the German tanks and try to drop grenades and incendiary devices down the hatches, or they would attack the vehicles' fuel tanks. A German tank commander described the methods adopted by the Soviet infantry:

> My tank was moving along a track in the deeply rutted trail of which lay a Russian. Another 20 meters or so and the tracks of my tank would have crushed him. He remained lying there quite cold-bloodedly

until my tank reached him. Then he rolled over to one side such that he was under the oil sump. The tank rolled over him without anything happening to him. Like lightning, he jumped up and attempted to climb up onto my tank from the rear. Pistol in hand, I shot him.[4]

The Soviet infantry's methods of dealing with German armor, as well as its effective deployment of snipers and well-organized ambushes based on improvised obstacles and mines, strongly suggest that, had this sort of warfare been retained, as advocated by Frunze, the German advance would have suffered far more serious consequences. Indeed, the problem of resupply was already becoming critical in late summer, even without any partisan attacks, causing delays and enforced halts. Hinze, for example, notes that by the end of July 1941, the tanks were showing signs of wear and tear. The deeper the German army penetrated into Soviet territory, the more complicated its supply chain became. The autumnal rains that lay ahead would be followed by snow, frost, and black ice, creating nightmarish problems for the already hard-pressed supply officers. Whereas the German army experienced serious resupply problems as it moved closer to Moscow, the Red Army was able to rely on the good road network in the Moscow area and shorter lines of communication.

Accumulating snow, freezing, and rapid thawing followed by sudden, steep falls in temperature affected every aspect of the battle. Attritional losses sustained in the prewinter battles were now being compounded by the effects of cold. For example, 20th Panzer Division's losses from 22 June to 18 September 1941 amounted to 929 dead, 2,402 wounded, and 50 missing—a total of 3,381.[5] The onset of the Russian winter brought a marked increase in cold-related injuries. From 1 to 5 December 1941, 20th Panzer Division's main casualty-clearing station reported 294 cases of frostbite: 205 cases of first-degree, 52 cases of second-degree, and 37 cases of third-degree frostbite.[6] Extreme, sustained frost rendered the construction of bunkers and the digging of trenches a thankless task, since the frost had penetrated seventy centimeters cm below the ground's surface by 7 December.[7] Positions now had to be constructed from snow and ice. Although they offered cover from view and protection from small-arms fire and wind, no heating of any kind was possible.

One of the characteristics of the 1941–1942 winter battles was the determination of both sides to possess and retain buildings and villages. Villages were important for two reasons: they provided shelter from the relentless and bitter cold and access to food, and they were often located at road junctions, so control of the village meant control of roads and rail links. Any usable roads or tracks in and out of these villages were under permanent observation, were preregistered for artillery and mortar fire, and were covered by antitank guns and machine guns. Mines were used at certain choke points. The only way to approach a village unseen required a cross-country march over, and often through, deep snow, relying on compass bearings. Such marches were utterly exhausting, since all the heavy equipment—machine guns, ammunition, and any other support weapons—had to be dragged on improvised sledges or carried. Like the Germans, the Soviet troops made full use of the long, cold winter nights to send out reconnaissance and fighting patrols. Typically, the patrols would start as soon as night fell and last until first light the next day. Lacking sufficient manpower to form a continuous front, German winter defenses were based on a series of strongpoints, with gaps covered, ideally, by fire. Such a defensive layout made it possible for Soviet fighting patrols to infiltrate the gaps and attack German positions in the rear. Another winter tactic used by the Red Army was the construction of snow tunnels to approach German positions, although this resulted in heavy losses.[8]

Mindful of German attempts to approach villages unseen over rough country, the Soviet units deployed listening posts well forward of their main position. From a defensive point of view, this was an essential measure; however, if the Germans could identify the position and manage to kill the occupants of the forward post, they would be able to mount a surprise attack on the village. Soldiers who were stuck out on remote listening posts would talk to one another to relieve the boredom, and they would smoke. Their voices and the strong smell of Russian tobacco, makhorka, would be enough to betray the position. Clear nights favored navigation but increased the risk of being seen, especially by snipers exploiting the good visibility. Bad weather—snowstorms and fog—covered the approach but made control much more difficult.

Deep snow limited mobility, which meant that any encounter with the enemy would be decided not by flanking movements but by the speed with which each side reacted and the amount of fire that could be brought to bear. The patrol point would typically carry a machine pistol, allowing immediate automatic fire in response to any contact. Grenades would also be used. The immediate fire provided by machine pistols would then be supplemented by the heavier fire of the MG 34 (later the MG 42), whose gunner would be located at the center of the patrol. Success required exceptionally high-quality leadership, mastery of fieldcraft, tactical awareness, navigation, and, once in contact with the enemy, boldness. As soon as a village had been captured, it was essential to move in heavy weapons—mortars and antitank guns—as quickly as possible. In these circumstances, captured enemy weapons and the ability to use them were crucial.

Defense of the Rusa position was 20th Panzer Division's crucial engagement during the winter battles, and this defensive success owed much to the personal example and leadership of Generalmajor Wilhelm Ritter von Thoma, who assumed command of the division on 14 October 1941. Von Thoma made regular visits to the forward positions, encouraging and inspiring his exhausted and freezing soldiers. To the uninitiated, the commander's presence at forward positions might seem of little consequence, yet for the troops, it was essential. It maintained discipline, order, and morale and inspired confidence and professionalism. Von Thoma's corps commander, his immediate superior, delivered the following verdict:

> I am completely clear that without your 20th Panzer Division the situation would not have been held. True enough, you had other means but your personal involvement was *decisive*. You are overwhelmingly to be thanked for the "Rusa miracle." Over the last days I have indeed on several occasions given you a piece of my mind. But don't reproach me for being soft-hearted. I have never before encountered such a good Panzer Division.[9]

As the spring thaw set in, the encircled Soviet troops tried to get through the German lines. Some of these infiltration attempts led to major engagements. In early April about 350 Russians managed to break into the position of Infantry Regiment 95 and had to be cleaned out in a counterattack. Hinze records that during these breakout attempts, large numbers of Soviet officers were captured.[10] These breakout attempts and cleanup operations marked the end of the winter battles and a pause before the start of summer operations in 1942.

Overview: The Diary of Gefreiter von Wiedebach-Nostitz

Hans Caspar von Wiedebach-Nostitz was born in Wiesa on 13 April 1921. Having completed his *Abitur* (secondary education certificate, required to pursue higher education), he embarked on a career in agriculture. Whether he volunteered for or was conscripted into military service is not known, but he served in the 2nd Panzer Aufklärung Abteilung 92, a reconnaissance unit of 20th Panzer Division. He was wounded in January 1942 and spent thirteen months in a military hospital. After being medically discharged, he resumed his agricultural career in Silesia. Following the failed attempt to assassinate Hitler on 20 July 1944, von Wiedebach-Nostitz, along with others whose attitude toward the NS regime had aroused suspicion, was returned to military service, even though he had earlier been declared unfit due to the wound received in Russia. He spent some time as a prisoner of the American forces and once again returned to agriculture after being released. However, large numbers of farmers driven out by the Allied policy of deportation and ethnic cleansing of Germans from Czechoslovakia and Poland were also seeking work in this area, so von Wiedebach-Nostitz relocated to what was then West Germany. After what the Germans call the *Wende* (literally, the change or the turn)—that is, the collapse of the East German communist regime in 1989—von Wiedebach-Nostitz and his wife returned to the eastern part of the now reunified Germany. He died in 1996.

His diary covers the first eight months of *Unternehmen Barbarossa*, providing an almost continuous daily record of operations after the invasion. The original diary was compiled in the summer of 1942, when von Wiedebach-Nostitz was recovering in Germany from injuries received in a mine explosion. He wrote his diary in a small notebook, which his widow later transcribed. My translation is based on her typescript.

The diary portrays the author's sense of pride and excitement over his involvement in the invasion, the frustrations caused by frequent breakdowns of the French Panhard armored cars, the delays arising from ammunition and fuel shortages, the obsession with food, the military successes and the encirclement of tens of thousands of Soviet prisoners, the stalling of the Blitzkrieg in the snow and ice before Moscow, and the dreadful engagements in the brutally harsh Russian winter of 1941–1942. Inevitably, the fear, uncertainty, and hazards of war have a personal impact on von Wiedebach-Nostitz. Badly mauled by the Germans, the Red Army is not defeated; it somehow manages to fight on, causing German losses in manpower that cannot be made good. His comrades are killed and wounded.

The sense of duty and comradeship, highlighted throughout the diary, helps explain how the German troops managed to withstand not just the Russian winter but also the Soviet counteroffensive. In all armies, these are critical factors, but in the German army of World War II, regardless of whether the enemy was Anglo-American or Soviet, these qualities were evident to an exceptional degree. It is in moments of supreme crisis, such as that confronting the German army in the winter of 1941–1942 (and on the Volga a year later), that these factors are decisive. A sense of duty and comradeship permeated the army from top to bottom—from the outstanding bravery and leadership of Generalmajor Ritter von Thoma down to the rank and file of 20th Panzer Division, such as Gefreiter Hans-Albrecht Piderit, Leutnant Tomasius, Leutnant von Riedesel, Gefreiter Joachim Goldmann, Leutnant Behr, and Unteroffizier Wohlfeil, who were all killed in action.

In this regard, it strikes me as significant that von Wiedebach-Nostitz concludes his diary with a summary of the duties of the German soldier and that he stresses comradeship, duty, and obedience. Obedience should not be misconstrued to mean something secured by a harsh disciplinary regime—a common and erroneous criticism of the German army in both world wars. Obedience is a function of trusting superiors who demonstrate competence, discharge their duties professionally, and command respect. Thus, when von Wiedebach-Nostitz describes Leutnant Behr as "exemplary and daring" and "respected"; Leutnant Tomasius as a "distinguished, upright and exemplary officer"; and Leutnant von Riedesel as an example of "self-control, reliability, uprightness and comradeship," he signals the high regard with which these junior officers were held and identifies one of the primary sources of German military success.

Von Wiedebach-Nostitz's Diary Concerning the Campaign in Russia: From Arnstadt, 17 June 1941, to Reinerz, 17 February 1942

Arnstadt–Lötzen, 17–21 June 1941

On Monday the final preparations regarding equipment and vehicles are under way. Every person has his hands full. Even though we have been feverishly working for months on end, there are piles of things to get done on the final day. This is in the very nature of things. Each one of us is busy with his tasks and, as regards vehicles, equipment and one's own matters the smallest details have to be taken care of, things which later will turn out to be irreplaceable. Now, matters are starting to get serious, something that the commander made clear the previous week at an equipment roll call. The worst thing however is that there is a fault with the gearbox of our tank. At the very last minute, people are sent to Magdeburg who, during Monday night, are supposed to remove the gearbox. Finally, the gearboxes arrive from Magdeburg and the long-awaited ones from Paris. I spend the last evening enjoyably with G. A. Piderit and with the kind Sauerlander locals. Then we finish off the rest of the work.

17 June 1941—On Tuesday before midday we enjoy a swim with the company. Then we have some free time. For two hours I try to ring home but without any success. We don't think too much about the future and in actual fact we are more concerned about what lies immediately ahead. We look forward to the uncertainty, to the new experiences.

Pit and I have our final midday meal with the Sauerlanders. Then we make our good-byes and leave behind the comfortable lodging with all its fittings to hand. For some time to come we shall not be seeing any bed.

Finally, at 1700 all the vehicles set off and accompanied by the inhabitants of Arnstadt, make for the station. Our tank is being towed and the gearbox is at the rear on top of the engine. Loading and securing of the vehicles on the rail wagons proceeds quickly. The weather is magnificent and lasts throughout the journey.

18 June 1941—At 0003 the train loaded with vehicles and carriages, about 50 wagons, sets off. As the train moves off into the night we have no idea where it will be taking us. Early on Wednesday it moves past Potsdam and we move into the Berlin–Grunewald area. Unfortunately, we cannot inform our families. I climb onto the top of our tank and on top from the aerial I am able to see Berlin for the last time, as we leave the city via the north ring. During a halt we try with the help of a crane to place the gearbox inside the tank. At the very least it weighs 2–3 hundredweight and the tank does not leave much room on the platform. In the end we give up trying to fit the gearbox.

Uncertainty as to where we are going remains. Finally, in the evening we arrive in Posen, having headed to Posen via Frankfurt and Schwiebus. The train is changed. We quickly get ourselves some coffee from the kitchen wagon and then the journey continues. Some destroyed bridges can be seen, otherwise there are no more signs of the Polish campaign. On the same evening the train stops at Gnesen and Thorn. We sit on the rear of our tank and examine the area and the setting sun. Beneath us the wheels clatter over the track and it is quite clear to us that we are moving toward East Prussia. In order to get to our sleeping car we have to climb over about 30 loaded platforms while the train moves, and jump over buffers and finally make our way along the outside of the closed cars to the entrance.

19 June 1941—When we wake up on Thursday morning, the train has stopped in Allenstein. Here, too, the train is merely changed. Then the journey resumes. An uninterrupted line of transport trains comes toward us from the other direction. Toward midday we reach the end of our journey: Lötzen. The whole area is swarming with soldiers. The unloading takes place quickly. Seven tanks including ours are towed away to a free space close to a huge lake. Here, the gearboxes that we have brought with us are due to be inserted as quickly as possible. The remaining company moves out to some remote village. We are here in the Masurian Lakes, a magnificent locality. While we are busy with block and tackle and jacks the sun burns. We remove our shirts and the top half of our bodies are black with oil.

20 June 1941—In the evening we bathe in the lake, spend some time sitting together and then sleep in some barn. The following day brings more heat and work but we manage to get everything done by evening. The vehicle runs faultlessly again and we drive off to our company that is located in some estate. Toward one o'clock in the morning we finally get to sleep.

21 June 1941—Early on Saturday morning there is a lecture conducted by Oberleutnant Kischnik and Leutnant Behr concerning conduct on operations, especially dealing with the technicalities of driving and then the peculiarities of the Russian armed forces: uniforms, tanks and types of aircraft. At midday the section drives off for about 100 kilometers to the forming-up area of the 20th Panzer Division which is located in the former Lithuania. How enormous is the difference of this area from Germany: dirty ruined houses, ragged population, neglected land and pitiful livestock. Later on, none of this would catch our attention. In the evening the vehicles are serviced, tents are erected and fires lighted. All that would later become a habit.

Late evening, on the longest day of the year, at a company briefing, we learn of the Führer's proclamation.[11] We are conscious of the historical nature of this moment. Early tomorrow morning at 0300 hours it was due to become a reality. In the distance one could hear the constant noise of rattling chains of moving tanks and the noise of engines.

Ostpreußen–Minsk–Vitebsk–Wehlich–Prechistaia

22 June 1941—Even before 0300 we are awakened by Luftwaffe squadrons. In the distance antiaircraft batteries can be heard. Unfortunately, we are not permitted to be among the first to cross the border along with the

others. An encounter with strong enemy forces is expected. Assault guns are in the lead. In the afternoon we are already hearing that the enemy has withdrawn. On the very first day our divisions have already managed to push forward over 100 kilometers.

At last our marching orders arrive. The section sets off at 1500 hours and we are soon crossing the border. I am in my seat in the rear, in Feldwebel Fiebig's vehicle. Behind us is Unteroffizier Kullack, with Pit manning the machine gun. We get on to the main advance road which is used by 2–3 divisions. It is the only good road in this area. In the main, two columns move along side by side. There is practically no room for oncoming traffic. There are hardly any signs of battle to be seen. We drive through the first small town (Kulavin?).

During a halt the signaller in the first reconnaissance troop is killed. Leutnant Behr, who requires an immediate replacement since he has a task to complete, takes me to his vehicle. Everything is in disarray. I have to leave nearly all my things behind. We are detached to divisional headquarters; we leave the detachment and follow on after the divisional headquarters. The town of Oliba is almost totally destroyed. A burnt-out Russian tank stands on the street. Meanwhile the Russians are also trying to start forest fires. These are my first impressions of the war.

A thick layer of dust lies all over the street, making our black uniforms look like a miller's jacket. Leutnant Behr, Kay and I are standing on top of the tank with a firm grasp on the antenna. As it gets dark I sit on the front on the left wing in order to help our driver to find his way and to maintain contact. The roads are also becoming noticeably worse as we move through the town of Oniskus, which is ablaze. Everywhere there are burnt-out vehicles and tanks on the street. Only as late as 0230 hours do we stop for a short pause with the divisional headquarters that we have caught up. For the first time we sleep on the bare ground with a blanket. That too is going to become a habit for us.

24 June 1941—At the present time the first commandment is to keep moving and to keep pushing ahead. After an hour's sleep the vehicles are refueled and then we move on, with Generalleutnant Stumpf in his Kübelwagen and followed by the personnel wagon with radio. In the afternoon we arrive in the area of Wilm and get something to eat at divisional headquarters. We are able to wash off the dust of the first hot days in a small stream and to take a bath. Toward evening the Panzer Regiment passes which with us

had captured Wilm and was now moving on toward Minsk. We deeply regret not being allowed to be with the advance section which is constantly pushing forward. Here we get hold of a bicycle that is fixed to the tank and a hundredweight of butter. After we have helped ourselves to some of the butter, the rest is passed on.

In the night shots are exchanged above me. Later it turns out that it was our own people. In the excitement and the lack of all-around view these sorts of things are happening more often.

25 June 1941—Early on Wednesday the divisional HQ's vehicles move onto a road and we continue our journey. Once again we are on a more or less properly constructed road and we can drive in fourth gear. However our Panhard starts to show its shortcomings. They become just about noticeable when the vehicle jumps gear or when moving slowly the clutch slips. Toward midday we stop for a rest in a village with the ruins of a castle. In the afternoon we reach Osmin, a small town behind Wilm. There is a stop here due to traffic jams. Tanks, lorries, vehicles, armored tracked vehicles, motorcycles, partly as units and partly as single vehicles. Everything here is in total confusion. Each vehicle tries to move on as quickly as possible. Every stop is used to get anything drinkable from any available kitchen. Three times a day the kitchens make tea. This little town makes a strange impression on us: dirty, wretched people, some Jews, can be seen with furniture, sacks and boxes and so on, moving through the streets. They take what they can from abandoned official buildings and rooms. There are not yet any German police there to rap their knuckles. But we do what we can to organize a box with about 100 pieces of chicken that is soon cooked, roasted and swimming in sauce.

Russian fighters and Iliushin bombers often attack us but they hardly achieve anything and are soon driven away by our light antiaircraft guns that are set up everywhere. And then once again the column moves off. We travel the entire afternoon once again until late into the night. On the journey, for miles on end, we sleep at the rear on the motor. But someone must always sit on the wing, taking note of junctions and making sure that we are heading the right way and wake up the driver who fell asleep during a stop.

26 June 1941—Only when the sun is once more in the sky is there an hour's rest and then the head of the column moves off. It seems that we are never able to catch them up. We are off the proper road again. The wheels spin in

deep sand, throwing up large columns of dust that covers everything. In a pine forest there's a whole, half-plundered Russian supply column. As always we have hardly any time to organize anything. At midday the divisional HQ calls a halt and we are able to bathe for a while in a small lake. A Russian is found in a bush who pretends to be completely dead. We try to get him to talk but he remains silent, moves no muscle and is then shot. After we have moved on we pass two destroyed Panhards. Generaloberst Schmidt who is taking part in the reconnaissance journey must make his way to the rear with the crews. Toward evening we are looking for a place to set up the divisional HQ on the road to Minsk, at which point we almost got caught up in an exchange of fire, which, as we ascertained later, had accidentally taken place between the 7th and 20th Panzer Divisions.

27 June 1941—Finally, early on Friday morning there's an opportunity to catch up on some sleep. In the afternoon we drive on to the HQ of the advance detachment. The Russians who just before the encirclement are located near Minsk put down artillery fire on the road. Therefore the HQ must move further to the rear.

28 June 1941—Early on Saturday we undertake a security patrol unhampered by the enemy. And together with the general we set off once again. The half-encircled Russians mount a tenacious defense. On our side we suffer the first real heavy casualties. Some of our tanks remain bogged down in a swamp. In the evening it starts to rain heavily. We get washed out with our tents, as it were, and have to sleep all rolled up in the tank.

29 June 1941—In spite of the fact that the roads have been rendered soft by the rain our tanks entered Minsk yesterday evening. We also resume our march with the divisional HQ. Bloated Russian corpses, Russian antitank guns, artillery and horses lie shot up on the route. A few kilometers on there is the completely destroyed reconnaissance squad from our company. The crew of the first vehicles are dead and partly burned. Those in the rear vehicle with Leutnant Kiesling were able to get away: a gruesome sight.

Toward midday we are coming toward Minsk, which is the first large city that we have seen. Almost 80% of it is destroyed. Only the suburbs are still standing. There are giant luxury buildings and factories among wretched wooden huts with poor plaster work, no guttering. Everything is dirty and untidy. The city has still not been completely cleared of enemy. Everywhere snipers are being flushed out and shot.

We are once more with the general on a main road which is full of standing vehicles when suddenly a heavy Russian tank comes around the bend in the road and comes rattling toward us. Vehicles disappear into side streets. We disappear into our tank and start firing off the first shots of our 2.5-cm gun that fail to penetrate the enemy armor. The tank drives past us and receives a direct hit, however, before it can fire and remains standing. The mounted infantry and the crew are smoked out. Late that evening our section is also hit by a shell from an antiaircraft gun. Leutnant Behr and I once again sleep on the rear of the tank and observe the burning Russian combat vehicles. The exploding ammunition produces giant columns of fire and the neighboring buildings are also set alight.

30 June 1941—We remain in Minsk on Monday and Tuesday. The first thing that we can secure is a large demijohn full of fruit juice extract which of course is fastened to the tank. A large radio factory is plundered by our people. We can take nothing away at all. I get myself some white linen and then a pair of rubber boots. Who knows what use I will be able to make of them. There are boxes full of biscuits, also chocolate and eggs and masses of Russian cigarettes. I ride around Minsk on our bike and take a look at the city.

1 July 1941—We are still here on Tuesday. We are next to a Russian military school that is quite modern. We find a great deal of Russian equipment here. Today, we can write home for the first time. This opportunity is immediately made use of. We want to pass on our impressions and experiences and are proud to be part of all this.

2 July 1941—Early on Wednesday we once again leave Minsk with the general. For the moment the direction of travel is northwest. We travel once more via Radosowice where the 3rd echelon is working. Here there are repair teams with our old tanks and they are inserting a new gearbox. Fortunately, I can grab hold of my things. I am very pleased about this. Then we turn off and head further to the north. Today we cover another 100 kilometers and we travel throughout the night. Here we find ourselves in a very lonely region: huge fields give way to giant forests, bush-covered steppe and marsh. We can be pleased with the fact that the weather is dry. Despite that, we have

real difficulty in getting through a number of places. There's plenty of work for the sappers.

3 July 1941—On Thursday after a rest for 2 hours we move out again. Early on I sleep a bit in the tank while we are on the move. At midday we arrive at divisional HQ and then set off to secure the location and remain here until the following morning. Peasants, attracted by our gramophone, bring milk and eggs. During the night we sleep in the tent.

4 July 1941—We are ready to move once again on Friday morning and we leave the HQ with the general and arrive at the Düna bridge, just before Lepel, which has been blown. The engineers have to build an emergency bridge. Hundreds of vehicles have to wait hours on end and then one at a time, and separated by large distances, they can cross over. Everywhere the Russians are mounting strong resistance. We come across three radio wagons of KFZ 17 of our HQ section that have been shot up. Today, as well, we manage to put many kilometers behind us. The general often disappears with his adjutant in the personnel wagon when it seems to get somewhat hot.

Late in the afternoon we reach the battle HQ of the advance section which is situated not far from Ulla. Here the Russians are holding out tenaciously. The town is leveled by our artillery and finally taken. However the river crossing has not yet been forced. The bridge has been blown here as well.

In the evening we move back a bit in order to wait for the divisional HQ. It does not arrive until the following day since it, too, was delayed near the Lepel crossing. So we spend the night alone with the general in the middle of the land. The midges torment us so much that I am kept awake all night. We capture two Russians who have been creeping about in the area. They are shot in the morning. Early on Saturday the divisional HQ finally arrives. We move into a nearby village. Then the vehicles are serviced and refueled, always the first task. Oil is replenished and small faults with the vehicles are dealt with. Now we have time to wash, which is done in a bucket that has been "organized" and is part of the tank's permanent equipment, along with the tent that is untied and erected in a few minutes. Then a fire is made, tea brewed and food cooked. The rest of the time is of course used for sleeping. Today we sleep the whole afternoon and also on Sunday to midday. In the evening everyone is sitting comfortably by the fire, the gramophone is playing or "Bommel" (Leutnant Behr) plays his lute and we are drinking Russian wine as well—which, mind you, is very heavy—or a bottle of vodka.

7 July 1941—Things were much the same on Monday. Today I write home though unfortunately I received nothing in the post. The crossing over the Düna is due to be forced today. Precisely at 1000 hours the Stukas appear and the artillery starts up. Then the engineers launch a diversionary attack on another position with boats. Immediately a pontoon bridge is built and the advance detachment crosses over but encounters strong resistance. The situation here does not look favorable.

At midday we set off with the general. In Ulla we bump into Leutnant Thomasius's reconnaissance squad where Pit is. I learn that Hauptfeldwebel K has been killed. Then we cross on the pontoon bridge that bends lightly under the weight of our tank. And now we follow on after the advance detachment on an open stretch. Oberst von Bismarck, the commander of the advance detachment, who is everywhere when there is any shooting, has also here, with the tanks and infantry, broken the resistance. The Russians have withdrawn on the flanks and the advance detachment pushes forward almost to the gates of Vitebsk. By evening we have also managed to advance about 60 kilometers. Then we turn around and head back to the crossing. Suddenly we encounter two lorries full of Russians whom we fire at. The Russians abandon their vehicles. Unfortunately, in all of this we have shot our bike to pieces.

9 July 1941—Meanwhile, it is morning again. After an hour's rest on the crossing we set off once again to the front. Damage to our fuel pump is soon repaired, then we continue for about another 20 kilometers. In the afternoon we finally arrive at divisional HQ after we have once more been delayed by the damaged fuel pump. This is a chronic failing on our Panhard that is caused by the awful dust and dirt in the fuel tank. We are comfortably situated in a small wood about 20 kilometers before Vitebsk. Vitebsk has almost been totally destroyed by our artillery. The rest is destroyed by the Russians themselves.

10 July 1941—On the following morning our reconnaissance troop and we are given the task of driving to Gendak to establish contact with our detachment which has taken the town and is defending it. This is the only good

tarmacked road that I have seen in Russia; that is the road from Vitebsk to Gendak. I have established radio communication and it works more or less. I send two calls. At midday we are back again.

11 July 1941—We can rest until midday on Friday. We note that the front left wheel on the armored car right up to the last layer is shattered. In the afternoon we want to head off to a settlement of Vitebsk. Swaying, we very carefully make our way there. Then Unteroffizier Faust (?) has to go in his vehicle to the 3rd echelon in Ulla in order to get a spring. In the evening there is once again magnificent weather. We sit on the beach of the Düna by the fire next to our tanks. We roast bread and chicken and drink some wine from Vitebsk. We sit there late into the night, talking.

Practically every day we experience Russian air attacks. Paratroops are supposed to have landed at Ulla with the aim of destroying the bridge. But nothing comes of it.

On Saturday toward 1000 hours the second armored car arrives with our spring and we immediately set about putting it in. After about three hours this difficult matter is dealt with. Then we eat at midday and afterward we all head off to the Düna. On floating tree trunks we can let ourselves be carried along. It is very hot.

In the afternoon we are off again. We make a detour around Vitebsk because all the bridges have been destroyed. Toward evening X returns. I must head back to the company. I hear that on 1 July 1941 I have become a Gefreiter. I also get some mail from home. The first I have received.

Once again the fuel pump has broken down. This is a constant worry. The carburetor gets flooded, the vehicle moves for about 20 meters and stops once more. Fortunately our 1st Squad is passing by. Meanwhile, it has got dark so we get some sleep first.

On the following morning the damage is repaired, then I have to leave "Bommel's" reconnaissance squad which is a bit of a blow. We've got really accustomed to one another through the common journeys and experiences. I drive with them to the Düna bridge and there with the 2nd Troop wait for Feldwebel Schneider in order then to return to my old recovery vehicle which, once again fitted out with clutch and gearbox, is on the Gendak-Vitebsk road. We bathe and swim the day in the river Düna. In the evening there is the miserable journey back to the recovery vehicle and my old tank that looks somewhat savage. I also have to search all over for my radio equipment.

14 July 1941—The next day we get down to things early on. The engine and gearbox are due to be removed and on top of all that it's boiling hot, it saps the body of any energy but the work has to be done. Once again we have to work with a crane and block and tackle. But by evening the main part of the work has been done. Once again I sleep next to my tank under a ground sheet. One sees the Russian houses only from the outside.

15 July 1941—On Tuesday we are to work on clearing up and so on. Of course, during the test drive all kinds of things are to be changed but then we soon get going. The next place is Vitebsk: it looks like a wasteland of piles of rubble. We come across some wine in a broken wine press. Then we push on over the railway bridge. We spend the night next to some of our other vehicles that are also out of action. In the evening we roast a piece of veal. The next day when we are under way we notice that the gearbox is slipping once again, just like the clutch, which, as we later find out, was incorrectly installed. Despite repeated tow start attempts and the most painstaking examination, the vehicle cannot be got going. So we at least move on a little further. At midday 20 eggs and 11 chickens are "acquired," the latter being plucked and drawn by Russian women. This gives us a hearty midday meal. Here we encounter the worst roads that I have ever seen: one deep hole after another. Our armored vehicle pitches like a ship in heavy swell. On occasions it hits them so hard that one has to take care that the heavy turret hatch does not fall on one's head, when you're having a crap, or that you don't get any broken ribs. Gas masks, cooking utensils or pistols fall all over the place, clattering on the metal floor, and on the exterior our old ration box jumps up: it is an empty grenade box that has been tied on the outside. In the evening we rest in some farmstead and sleep in the tent.

17 July 1941—On Thursday we go rocking off once more. This whole region is more or less dried-out marshland. We have constant problems with our carburetor. Frequently the fuel in the pipe has to be sucked out by mouth. Today, I am already feeling sick from doing this.

Today, getting on for midday, so as to have a good feed, we kill fish in the river Düna with explosive charges and hand grenades. Toward midday we arrive in Velich, where we immediately refuel from a Russian armored ship that is on the river Düna. Finally we manage to roast our fish. We have to stay here in Velich, Berger and I so as to replace a spring that was broken on the journey here.

18 July 1941—After a night spent in the vehicle we get down to work that demands a lot of sweat and energy. First, I have to acquire a spring from the maintenance company. Since there are no original springs on hand we have to make do with a German spring and finally after effort we manage to insert the thing. There is not much to eat here, above all very little bread. I acquire about 2 kilos of heavy Russian cheese.

19 July 1941—On the following day, toward midday we set off, Berger and I, into the wilderness, always following our divisional shield sign and the sign of our section. Once again we end up on a dreadful track which takes us more or less through ancient woodland or bush-covered steppe. Very rarely do we encounter vehicles. This is a route, which a few weeks later, becomes almost impassable owing to partisans. We have barely covered a few kilometers when the rack with the filled fuel cans and canisters gets torn off to one side. We have to fix it temporarily with bits of rope.

All the same we cover 80 kilometers today, even though we drive very carefully and I first of all precisely examine every dangerous position so as to give Berger exact instructions, since if we get stuck here there is nobody to pull us out. We get bread, eggs and milk from the peasants. In a village we make a stop with some other vehicles that are there. Faults with the carburetor, springs and the gear change still have to be rectified.

20 July 1941—Early on Sunday we get going again. Today, the route is not much better either. Marshy potholes and smooth, steep slopes and so on have to be negotiated. Most of the time, we travel in first gear. This uses up about 90 liters of fuel for every 100 kilometers. No matter, we generally get on okay. Toward midday we encounter 2 tanks of the 1st Company with which we travel together through the ancient wood. Toward 1300 hours we stop in a village where milk and bread are once again acquired from the peasants. In the afternoon we have to tow the store sergeant's vehicle; that of course ruins our clutch. Toward night we move into a village where there is some exchange of fire with partisans.

21 July 1941—On Monday the road gets a bit better yet it takes us nearly all morning to cover 30 kilometers since we meet the fuel column of practically the whole division that has to drive many miles to the rear, since the resupply does not get forward. Toward midday we arrive at the company location in Pashchislaia and report to Oberleutnant Kischnik. All the news

is exchanged. I see Bommel once again. He is no longer at division but has been relieved by Leutnant Thomasius. After four weeks I am now once more with the company.

In the Area to the North of Smolensk

We had already banked on and feared being unable to catch up with the head of the division until Moscow, since it was moving forward so quickly, and it would have more or less worked out like that had this not become possible due to considerations arising from the general conduct of the battle. However, the area between the point and the army was becoming ever bigger. Resupply, above all fuel and ammunition, were not getting forward; above all, the infantry was unable to fill the gaps that quickly and so close the *Kessel* which had been formed by the tank corps. Our division had marched without a break, everywhere ruthlessly breaking the enemy resistance and covered this tremendous distance in 4 weeks, continually in battle. As a consequence, it had created an important precondition for the successful outcome of the Smolensk *Kessel* and had got there ahead of the Russians, who, coming from the north and east, wanted to prevent that. Now we had the mission to hold this position against numerically superior forces until we were relieved by the infantry.

22 July 1941—The day-to-day routine of company duty is of course somewhat unusual. Once again there's falling in, and today an inspection of gas masks and weapons. The entire division is situated here in this region, waiting for fuel and rations. Cattle are acquired from the company and slaughtered and bread is baked. On the following day there is an inspection of vehicles and equipment. Here, of course, I have once again met Pit and Goldmann. Using people who no longer have any tanks and some from the resupply columns, the company has formed assault groups that travel on Russian vehicles and have a Russian antitank gun. The motorcycle squadron is reduced to a few motorcyclists. I am now part of the radio reconnaissance group.

24 July 1941—Toward midday our armored vehicle is told off once again to divisional headquarters with which we cover about 20 kilometers. The road throws up huge spirals of dust and the sun is burning hot. The divisional headquarters remains on the start line and we stay there as security and are able to observe a tank attack that runs into uncustomary resistance. We sleep the night in the tent.

On Thursday we have some free time. Toward midday a piece of beef is pot roasted and coffee prepared from beans. Once again we have guard duty. I have some time today and I write to Astel, Irmel and Usche. Our section rolls on past and assumes guard duty as well.

25 July 1941—Early, at 0800 hours we drive off with the general to the brigade battle position. Seventeen Russian tanks shot up by antitank guns and 88mm guns are on the route. Everywhere the Russians are launching heavy attacks; they are already encircled many miles deep. Once more we have problems on our armored vehicle with the gearbox, clutch and fuel pipe.

26 July 1941—In the night we are stood to: enemy tanks are said to have broken through. Nothing happens and we go back to sleep. Since our vehicle is not functioning properly we have to return to the company.

27 July 1941—The whole day is spent working on the vehicle until finally a fault in the carburetor is found. At this juncture there is a carburetor fire which fortunately can be extinguished. However, the gearbox and clutch are once again completely useless and so we can remove the motor and gearbox. There's not much hope on this crate. However, we are not the only ones; there are other vehicles which are continually in need of repair. In the evening I get some mail and some news about Karl-Georg's wound which happened on the second day of the operation and not that far from us, I reply immediately. In the night I have guard duty.

28 July 1941—On Monday there are once again strong Russian air attacks. Overhead 7 bombers are shot down. Our Stukas attack. There is plenty of activity from the artillery to be sure but somewhat impeded by a lack of ammunition. The Russians have managed to push forward with a reinforcement of 16 divisions which are cornered by us and are said to be encircled by the forces attacking from the south. Toward evening the section moves off. We remain behind in order to wait for the 1st Squad. We have to get out: some Russians are moving about but they manage to get away.

29 July 1941—The Panzer regiment passes through on Tuesday morning and occupies a position. The front has come back by a few kilometers. The headquarters of the Rifle Regiment and Oberst von Bismarck are with us. We also see General von Richthofen. The Russians mount attacks every morning

and evening. Assault guns are brought up. We are hard at it today; once more on the motor, clutch and gearbox. Once again we sleep in the shed.

30 July 1941—In the morning we are woken by artillery strikes. A comrade who leaves the shed is hit by a shell splinter in his heart. We bury him. Then we move off with our vehicles into a village out of range of the Russian artillery where our vehicle is being made ready. Now it runs perfectly. The sun burns mercilessly. Today, at midday, we fry potatoes and onions. I have a bath in a stream and wash my shirt. In the afternoon we head back to where the supply units are. The commander is wounded and the company is now commanded by Leutnant Behr and Oberleutnant Kischnik commands the section.

31 July 1941—I fetch the mail the next day: there are letters dated 28 and 30 June. I send some Russian soap home. Then we are paid and various matters attended to. In the night we again sleep in the tent.

1 August 1941—Early on Friday morning we are given a task by the company. We load up an assault group and drive about 18 kilometers. Today, for the first time in the campaign we encounter infantry and artillery being towed. These men have covered the distances in huge marches. We regret that we were unable to have taken part in the heavy battles that have taken place. It is evening by the time we move with the section into a village for security. In the night I have guard duty. We get some bread made so as to improve the rations.

2 August 1941—On Saturday there is a section muster parade. Promotions and decorations are handed out. Afterward, we move off to some village. Our vehicle and we are by a lake. In the afternoon we carry out a short reconnaissance trip. Here the encircled Russians hide in the woods, starving and restrained by the commissars. In the evening I bathe in the lake. We sleep in a small house close to the vehicle. For the time being Leutnant Furch is our reconnaissance troop commander.

3 August 1941—On Sunday, after a brief bathe we also conduct another reconnaissance trip. In the afternoon when we are once again in the lake, one of our comrades drowns. I manage to recover his body from water about 4–5 meters deep. He has suffered a heart attack and is dead. In the evening I get

some mail from Karl-Georg, M. Hoch, Monika and Frau Piderit. Today we eat fish which we have caught and honey which we've managed to get hold of.

4 August 1941—Early on Monday morning at 0830 hours everything is made ready for a reconnaissance trip. We scoured the entire divisional front line. We pass divisional headquarters and once again get stuck in mud. Two artillery prime movers are required to pull us out. The road is covered by a layer of dust at least 20 cm thick which, when one drives over it, is transformed into impenetrable mud. On Tuesday [5 August 1941] we wash our clothes. In the afternoon there is a muster parade.

6 August 1941—On the next day, after a swim, we carry out another administration trip. We acquire 25 eggs and blueberries. In the evening there are fried eggs and potatoes.

7 August 1941—Thursday—the last day in my old vehicle—is also a rest day. We bathe in the evening and then sit for a long while on the bank of the lake.

8 August 1941—On the following morning there is a reorganization of the section: 1st Company hands over all its vehicles which we take over with some men from 1st Company. Leutnant Behr wants to take me in his vehicle. He leaves it up to me. This is not an easy decision. Nevertheless, I decide to go with him. We also acquire a vehicle from the 1st Company. So today we drive off. After I have cleared out all my things we move out with Schneider in the armored command vehicle.

9 August 1941—During the night there is torrential rain. In the morning we enter a Russian house where we make tea in a samovar. We work the whole day. We cannibalize the old vehicle and put mountings on the one we now have for our fuel racks and so on. I sort through the radio equipment. Throughout the whole day, vehicles of 20th Panzer Division return. We spend the night in the tent again.

10 August 1941—On Sunday morning we drive to the maintenance company where I get a foot-activated trigger fitted for the gun. Toward midday we make some potato fritters that taste superb. Then I wrote home. There are countless vehicles of our division here that have been finished off by Russia's roads. We only return by evening and by the same route in fact by

which we came from Velich. We stop after about 15 kilometers and sleep outside in the wood.

11 August 1941—The next morning we set off really early and make it back to our company toward midday, in the village where Berger and I made a stop on 19 July. Our vehicle stands next to an empty barn. We make ourselves comfortable inside.

12 August 1941—Our division is now supposed to have about a week's rest so as to assemble all its units and above all to overhaul and to repair all its vehicles and tanks.

13 August 1941—At this time our section is dissolved and we are attached to Motorcyclist Battalion 20 of Major Wolff who inspected us at the same time. Once again Oberleutnant Kischnik assumes command of our company.

14–16 August 1941—We are also working on our vehicles. There are various muster parades, we wash our things and so on and live otherwise quite comfortably. In the evenings we roast our potatoes, which was actually forbidden and we often cook some good soup. I am often with Pit and Goldmann together. Here there is also an opportunity to bathe of which I make the most. It is already quite cold in the nights. Once again I get some news from home and I am really happy about hearing of Karl-Georg's Iron Cross.

17–18 August 1941—On Sunday there is a vehicle muster parade. In the afternoon we receive some chocolate and wine. At this time I twice have guard duty. I acquire some chocolate for our reconnaissance troop and various other things for our vehicles. The reconnaissance squads are once again divided up. Unteroffizier Schnuke is allocated a squad.

On Monday preparations are made for the march out. In the evening the vehicles are on the roads. Already parts of our division, which have to take the same route, come along continually.

Via Velikie-Luki to Torpech and Demiansk

19 August 1941—Before midday on Tuesday we are still here. Pit and I are quite happy together. Only in the afternoon do we move out to Velich.

However we use the better road which takes a detour and we drive into the night. We move into a village. We don't put up our tents. I sleep with a ground sheet and blanket on the ground.

20 August 1941—At 0345 hours on Wednesday we are up. We refuel and everything is made ready. On the journey ahead we go through Velich and then head off further to the north on a relatively good road, a distance of about 150 kilometers. But once again our engine is not running properly: the brake discs are rattling and some water has got into the engine block. Toward evening we move into an area close to Motorcyclist Battalion 20. We service the vehicle, refuel, set up the tent, and eat. Then it starts to rain.

21 August 1941—Although we were due to move out at 0200 hours in the night we nevertheless stay another day there. We set off with our vehicle to the 1st Squad who are supposed to insert a new engine for us. We work until nightfall.

22 August 1941—The company moves out very early on Friday. We have finished work on our motor, let it run, but it is still causing problems. After a number of trial starts it finally runs normally. Meanwhile, evening has fallen. During guard duty in the night I acquire two dishes of honey from the beehives. We really like the full honeycombs.

23 August 1941—We get going very early. Our vehicle is in the lead. Behind us are several trucks and 1st Squad. Later on we leave these vehicles behind and push on alone and continually overtake columns.

Also, on one occasion, we look over a medium-sized apple tree. Finally we make it to our lot. Along the way we also meet the company's office wagon and collect some mail. I have also received a letter from Karl-Georg. We pass by a captured Russian reinforced line with antitank ditches and minefields. Bommel is also traveling with us again. The column stops for a while in the afternoon, continuing the journey once again toward evening. Meanwhile, we have time to press out our honey that gives us two full dishes. Today, we make another wild night journey. Vehicles frequently end up in ditches and have to be pulled out again. In the distance one sees burning villages. Today, we hear that three company vehicles were knocked out and that seven men were killed, among them Leutnant Verch. The wounded were killed by the

Russians. Late in the night we finally arrive in our start line position. Only very recently there must have been a Russian headquarters here which we establish from signals cable, trenches and other equipment.

24 August 1941—We are woken as early as 0300 hours. I climb out from underneath our vehicle where I have been sleeping. Today is Sunday. Leutnant Behr sets off very early with three armed vehicles to secure the area. We also then have to move out about 2 kilometers forward and dig trenches. Afterward, as so often, I listen to music on my radio from Germany. It is organ music from 0800–0820. Pit who is still here tells me about his reconnaissance patrol on Saturday. Not far from us there stands a 3.7-cm gun, which shoots at Russian targets, trucks and so on, at a range of about 1,500 to 2,000 meters. We are able to observe the amazing hit results.

The Russians are now encircled between the infantry located near Velikie-Luki and us. Now we to try divide the *Kessel* and drive on to Velikie-Luki. In order to hold up the Russians continually breaking through, several vehicles are sent forward. Our vehicle is in the lead. Pit's vehicle is behind us. Some of the vehicles have used up all their ammunition. The Russians are everywhere, as if sown all over the place. When we are on the position where the Russians are running across, there is of course a lot of heavy fire from machine guns and heavy guns. I am also firing my pistol at the Russians from behind the turret hatch. While I get the order to drive to the rear, I change the gear from the front, I let the clutch go and the vehicle brakes. To the front there's the sound of a detonation on a vehicle that sounds much louder than the sound of our 2.5-cm gun. I detect a strong blast of air and the inside of the vehicle is filled with gunpowder smoke. To begin with I have no idea what's happening: then it is clear that our vehicle has been hit. Inside, Kublitz and Key have been thrown all over the place by the air pressure. The former calls out to me "reverse." So I drive on but the steering to the left no longer works. I am stuck on the edge of a trench. When I see that the two of them have left the vehicle, I grab my weapon holster that I always have ready at hand and jump in the trench. In answer to my question about Z I hear that he is presumably dead. We enter the trench embankment and return to battalion headquarters, where we report what has happened.

Afterward, we return in Pit's vehicle to the site of the incident and look at the whole mess. At the front of the vehicle a plate has been smashed by the impact of a heavy mortar shell and the fire hatch and gun have been ripped off. Nothing can be done with the gun. Now we clear all the things out of the vehicle, wrap them in tent sheets and head off in a truck to battalion headquarters. I have also been able to salvage my honey. We are finished for today. Key and I sort out the things belonging to Z and hand them over. The vehicle is towed away in the afternoon. The plate at the front is unscrewed and Z is removed. Then we bury him. In the evening, Oberleutnant Kischnik holds a memorial service with the whole company on the edge of the grave. We say good-bye to our comrade. It is only in the evening when I am falling asleep among my things outside that I am able to reflect on the day's experience for the first time. I will never forget it for the rest of my life. With gratitude I perceive the miraculous hand of God that protected me and which will further watch over me.

25 August 1941—On Monday Key and I load up things onto the ammunition truck and then we soon head off into the *Kessel* and onto Velikie-Luki. We stop in a village. I don't have much time, since I have been sent off to some motorcyclists: we are to get a hold of some trucks which have been abandoned by the Russians but we are soon ordered to return. A short while later, things get going again. This time I am traveling with Leutnant Behr on the tank. We take some prisoners but we are unable to get the trucks to work. On the other hand Leutnant Behr and I find the armored command vehicle belonging to a Russian marshal. We know this from the new uniform that's inside. The vehicle is an 8-cylinder Buick. Everything else in the vehicle is of course secured. I get my hands on some superb bathing trunks and a rubber inflatable pillow. Then we tow the vehicle away with the Panhard. It only has a minor fault in the carburetor. In the afternoon I am then detailed to a weapons vehicle. No sooner have I moved my things across than we are given a new task. Another batch of Russia trucks are acquired and prisoners taken. In the evening we are once again deployed and take up a guard position for the night. We are relieved by the guard. The *Kessel* in which the Russians are encircled is outlined by tracer ammunition and trails of light.

26 August 1941—At 0400 hours, toward morning, we return to the company but also take some more prisoners. We have just finished breakfast when the order comes to get ready to move. With Leutnant Behr's reconnaissance troop to which we have been attached, we advance straight into the *Kessel*. I get my hands on a set of periscope binoculars from a Russian truck. The motorcyclists are also now following on behind, under command of Leutnant Kischnik who travels in the armored command vehicle. We are approaching

Velikie-Luki. From all sides—from foxholes, bushes and houses—Russians appear, surrendering. We check them over and then send them to the rear. Vehicles, guns and all kinds of equipment, which have been abandoned by the Russians, are all over the place. We come upon the infantry who have been here for about 4 weeks, could not get any further and have suffered heavy losses, until such time as we managed to cut off the Russians opposing them. Not far from Velikie-Luki in a village we make a 2-hour midday halt. Then we set off with the company that has meanwhile assembled to the east through the smashed Russian *Kessel*. The whole place is a scene of destruction. We see a German K4 which has had its turret torn off by a Russian antiaircraft shell. Toward evening we stop in a new start line position with Motorcyclist Battalion 20. We do not get any sleep on this night either since we have security duty and are attached to the guard.

27 August 1941—Any hopes of getting even a couple days' rest here are disappointed when the order comes at 0400 hours to get ready to move. Today we are supposed to be heading toward Urozel. Leutnant Behr assumes command of the point reconnaissance troop and our reconnaissance troop assumes the lead of the advance guard and then things get moving. We drive on reasonably good roads, and then again through an area of forest. The road bends a lot and often crosses bridges. Everywhere we encounter Russian trenches and small bunkers. After we have covered about 20 kilometers we come upon the enemy, infantry, who soon scatter when they come under fire from our machine guns. After a short while an advance reconnaissance troop comes back to us. They encountered the enemy in a village and managed to leave behind a Russian truck which they set ablaze. Now we move together toward the village. Most of the houses are on fire. Here one dare not get out of the vehicle. Snipers are everywhere, behind bushes and in trees. Many Russians put up a heroic defense in their trenches. Grenades, thrown by our motorcyclists into their foxholes, are thrown back out by them again. Finally, they are flushed out. We only have 20 minutes for a midday halt. Meanwhile, the company has arrived but we are on the move again. Leutnant Behr who is once again at the head of the reconnaissance troop does not get far. The first vehicle is knocked out by a Russian antitank gun, the other two, which had almost been burnt out, since the Russians had thrown Molotov cocktails at them, retreat. Two men are wounded. Thereupon a major attack gets under way. We drive on the street, armored vehicles to the left and right beside us; behind them the motorcyclists on

foot, led by Major Wolff. To our rear Oberstleutnant von Bismarck and Ober-leutnant Kischnik are traveling in the Kübelwagen. Leutnant Behr is also with them. We push through the wood to a village that is being set on fire by our combat vehicles, while resistance is being offered. The Russians have dug trenches everywhere along the streets from which they throw Molotov cocktails. Now things are not working out so well for them. They creep off into the woods, though a combat vehicle has started to burn and one man has been wounded who is now loaded on to our vehicle. We take him back a bit, to a military ambulance where the commander's armored command vehicle is also located. There I see something dreadful. Leutnant Behr and Unteroffizier Wohlfeil are lying in the vehicle: they are both dead. That has finished me for today: I can't take anymore. All of us were profoundly shaken. Unteroffizier Wohlfeil received a fatal shot to the stomach from a sniper shooting from the wood, and when Leutnant Behr was about to go to his assistance, he received a fatal shot to the head. At first, we can hardly grasp that this exemplary and daring soldier has been so suddenly torn away from us. He was always a selfless comrade, trusted by all. Through his natural character he always maintained a cheerful and evenness of mood and was therefore respected and honored by the whole company.

The combat vehicles and other vehicles turn around in order to get on the line of advance on the road which has now taken another course. We remain here for a while as security, and somewhat later form up in the marching column which then comes to a halt after a few meters. It starts to rain and we have to sleep bunched up in the vehicle. Only very slowly do my thoughts sort themselves out, thoughts that are still occupied with the horrendous events of the last few hours.

28 August 1941—Very early on Thursday morning we have to do something about the track that has become sodden from the rain. Afterward, our re-connaissance troop is detailed as security for the location in which we are now located, while the other columns move off. Before midday our vehicle is sent to divisional headquarters with a report. A part of our company is also here. Here we have some time to wash, to eat and collect some mail. Then we have to head back. The route is dreadfully wet and soft and much effort is required to get back, and on one occasion we have to get ourselves pulled out. Everywhere the sappers have to build corduroy roads. In the evening we conduct a small reconnaissance trip and then sleep in the tent that is packed full of warm hay.

29 August 1941—We also conduct a reconnaissance journey on Friday morning and then we manage to cook ourselves some potatoes at midday. We receive an order over the radio to abandon our security post and in the afternoon we follow on after the battalion. In the evening we are located with the headquarters and we sleep in a shed.

30 August 1941—Very early on Saturday we set off again, constantly overtaking columns and struggling with the sodden roads. Frequently, one vehicle has to pull out the other. Toward midday we get on to a better road and then well on the way to Toropez. In a short break we take a look at a beautiful Orthodox church which has been converted into a grain silo. Later we push on to our company with which we stop close to Toropez.

31 August 1941—Sunday is a rest day. We have time to wash, fry some potatoes and to write. I meet Pit once again with whom I spend part of the day. In the evening there are company orders and then Oberleutnant Kischnik pays tribute to the memory of Leutnant Behr and our other fallen comrades.

1–2 September 1941—The company sets off in the morning. The line of march is supposed to be in the direction of Kalinin. I have been attached to Alfred Wirsig's vehicle as radio operator. We are to stay here and wait for the 1st Squad, since our vehicle is still not in order. Apart from us there are two other armored vehicles here. We all sleep together in a large Russian tent. Midday and evenings we all cook together.

3 September 1941—On Wednesday we have to go back over about 20 kilometers of the old track, which is now completely waterlogged in order to pull out an armored vehicle which has got stuck. We are unable to do it. Twice our own vehicle sinks up to the springs in mud and it is only with great difficulty that we manage to get back to Toropez. We have all kinds of things to do to our vehicle which we complete in the next few days and then we wait for the 1st Squad.

7 September 1941—On Sunday we come under serious Russian air attacks. The bombs fall in a area of about 50 meters from us, such that splinters come flying toward us. We crept into and under our vehicles. The 1st Squad finally arrives today, and our company also returns. It stops in a village about 8 kilometers from Toropez.

8 September 1941—On Monday we work on the vehicle. The water pump is repaired and we get a hole caused by an antitank shell welded in the tank maintenance workshop in Toropez. In Toropez I meet Goldmann's brother who is with the 19th Panzer Division. He then visits his brother.

9 September 1941—On the next day Oberleutnant Kischnik comes to us and informs us that the company is to be disbanded. All that is left is a remnants echelon. The armored cars and trucks are to be allocated to the artillery and rifle regiment. We are off to the divisional headquarters. Then the Oberleutnant awards us the tank combat badge certificate [*Panzerkampfabzeichenurkunde*]. Once again he summarizes all the shared experiences and provides an overview of the company's achievements. In the afternoon we drive off to the company. Our vehicle is attached to Reconnaissance Squad B.

10 September 1941—Today everything is made ready and completed for the journey to divisional headquarters. At midday there is a muster parade to mark the departure. The Oberleutnant shakes everyone's hand. It is painful for him that his proud company is to be disbanded. We all hope to see one another again in Germany. We spend the night with the company.

11 September 1941—On Thursday things get moving early. There is beautiful weather today and the road is fairly good. We have only covered about 15 kilometers when a spring on one of the front wheels breaks. Now this means that we can drive only slowly and today we make about 70 kilometers. We sleep in a small barn.

12 September 1941—It is somewhat uncomfortable the next day. There is a definite feel of autumn in the air. In the night it is already very cold. Today we travel via Pholm, a small town that has not been touched by the war. In Pholm we meet Leutnant Tomasius's reconnaissance squad where Pit is as well. After a short stop we continue our journey, for nearly the whole day. I sit with Goldmann in the rear of our vehicle during the journey. In the evening we refuel each vehicle with about 250 liters and then stop in a village. For the first time we sleep in a Russian dwelling.

13 September 1941—The journey continues the next day. We drive over hilly terrain with pretty churches. Everywhere the bridges have been blown. We pass antitank ditches and fortifications with barbed wire. Here the

defending Russians were also encircled. Two tank and 2 infantry divisions are marching on this stretch of road. In the afternoon we encounter vehicles belonging to divisional headquarters that are returning. In Demiansk we meet the Fauck and Weichert reconnaissance squads. This means that our division is coming back again. We are close to an antiaircraft gun that today has just brought down a Russian plane. At night I once again sleep on the vehicle and I have 2 hours of guard duty because of the partisans who are active in this area.

14 September 1941—It is Sunday again. Before midday I have time to write and to listen to the radio on my receiver. Toward evening the 19th Panzer Division rolls back once again toward Pholm, while the 20th Panzer Division strikes out in another direction toward Vitebsk. After we have reported to divisional headquarters, they refuse to accept us. We don't know immediately what we should do. Then we head straight back to the vehicle which we had to leave because of the damaged spring. Here we spend the night in a house while outside it is raining once again.

15 September 1941—On Monday we have to go back a couple of kilometers in order to fetch a tank which ended up in a trench in the night. Once we have got it back on the road, we get going. Today, the road is terribly jammed and waterlogged. There is no option for us other than to remain in the middle of the column and spend the night in the vehicle.

16–18 September 1941—Slowly we are able extricate ourselves from the endless column and arrive in Pholm toward midday, where we first of all make ourselves comfortable in a house. We sort out rations and fuel in the town. For the time being we are here for 2 days. Nobody bothers about us and we ponder our situation. We decide to return to the company once again. Finally, we get our vehicle as ready as we can for the journey. It is also raining again on Thursday. When leaving the farmstead we once again get stuck in a ditch and we only manage to get out at midday. Only with difficulty do we manage to cover the 15 kilometers in nonstop rain to the village where we have already spent a night. We decide to cannibalize the reconnaissance squad's third vehicle and leave it, since because of the spring and other faults it can go no further. We set ourselves up well in the house, light a fire, cook potatoes and have a good sleep.

19 September 1941—On Friday we still have some work to do on the vehicle. We acquire some eggs and milk in the village and have to stay another night here.

20 September 1941—Early on Saturday we get going again in the direction of Toropez, but there is an indescribable amount of mud that almost always reaches the vehicle's springs. Often we sink even deeper. We encounter many vehicles that are bogged down. The drivers have to wait until someone pulls them out and we often have to get ourselves pulled out. We make about 20 kilometers, since we hear that the road gets even worse and that there are partisans in the next village. At midday we have something to eat for the first time, then we decide to head back to Pholm, since the vehicles because of the many problems are not fully battle-ready and apart from that one of the machine guns won't work. So our vehicles wade through the swamp and toward evening we are once again in our old quarters in Pholm where the girl prepares some tea for us and we have a good sleep.

21 September 1941—On Sunday morning we hear the bad news. After a briefing with Leutnant Tomasius and Leutnant Piderit we are to hand over a vehicle to each one in order to make up the reconnaissance squad. Leutnant Tomasius wants to push on via Vitebsk with the division to the central front and Leutnant Piderit wants to go to Toropez to the 1st Company with his reconnaissance squad. We are also to go to Toropez by truck to the skeleton echelon. With great reluctance we hand over the vehicles which have become our mobile home during the campaign. Now we have become homeless infantry.

Getting on to midday we get going in a shaky, clapped-out 6-cylinder Renault truck. We have only made 200 meters and we stop. The driver works away for about half an hour, then the journey resumes perhaps for another 500 meters or so. The engine is working on four cylinders and the vehicle gets stuck in every puddle. Then of course everyone has to get out and push. When the vehicle gets going again the driver drives like a madman so that those of us in the back of the vehicle fly about half a meter in the air every time the vehicle goes over a hole. The journey continues like this until evening. We spend the night in the village where we have been twice before. Goldmann and I are on guard all night.

22 September 1941—Today is just the same as yesterday. Finally we catch a large prime mover that can at last tow us. The next night we stay in a village where there are antipartisan units. We are once again on guard.

23–24 September 1941—The next day we finally reach Toropez. The prime mover uncouples our vehicle and a Panhard from the 1st Company tows us into the village where our company is.

In the Remnants Echelon at Toropez

23–24 September 1941 (continued)—As a consequence of the great loss of vehicles which the 20th Panzer Division had suffered from the constant operations and most recently the bad roads toward Demiansk, the division had to set aside a great part of its men who were brought together in the remnants echelon. At this present time the Panzer regiment alone had only 30 to 40 of its original 200 vehicles. It was much the same with us, though Oberleutnant von Heydebreck, the head of the 1st Panzer AA 92, had managed to repair a number of the old vehicles and took on the remaining vehicles of our company. Why the 19th and 20th Panzer Divisions took the route to Pholm and Demiansk was not clear to anyone. At the very least they lost several vehicles. These two divisions now set off via Vitebsk to the central sector. We stayed in the remnants echelon at Toropez. On Monday after we had luckily reached the company, we managed to set ourselves up rather comfortably in a house. We have covered our straw dump with Russian tent sheets. On Tuesday we furnish the quarters. In the afternoon there is machine gun fire in a Russian antitank ditch.

25 September 1941—On Wednesday there are classes. This garrison-style duty strikes us as very odd in these Russian surroundings. In the afternoon we drive to the cinema in Toropez. We watch *The Gas Man*.[12]

26 September 1941—The next few days pass much the same. We have a lot of work to do on our personal equipment, washing and so on. We especially like making fried potatoes, potato fritters and boiled potatoes with tinned vegetables. We always suffer from a shortage of bread. I also spend a great deal of time with Goldmann. It is already very autumnal and it gets dark early. I am reading *The Wild Huntsman* by the light of a petrol lamp.[13]

29 September 1941—On Monday we have radio training once more. In the afternoon there is a clothing inspection. Finally, we get some mail and also a pile of illustrated magazines that can be read by the light of a petrol lamp.

30 September 1941—On Tuesday we are back on the training ground for the first time. In the afternoon there is shooting. I have guard duty again and have time to write a comprehensive letter home.

1–2 October 1941—We are due to be loaded up in the next few days, allegedly to the Smolensk region. On Thursday we pack up well. I have a lot of kit: 2 kit bags, 2 tent bundles and a writing case. Later, I must see to it that I am able to get these prepared items sent home as soon as possible.

3 October 1941—Some vehicles are on the road to Smolensk. The headquarters will also soon be loaded up. We have all day.

4 October 1941—Only on Sunday do we march out with part of our baggage to Toropez, to the loading station. We spend all day loading up and getting set up. In our goods wagon—it's a Russian one—there are bunk beds, desks and a table. We also get hold of an oven. In our wagon it is quite comfortable.

5 October 1941—On Sunday we move to Velikie-Luki. Our wagons have no brakes so that when starting and stopping they jerk. Here the station has been severely damaged by German bombers. There are burnt-out ammunition trains. The stretch is often destroyed by partisans so that the locomotive has to travel with a captured Russian tank.

6 October 1941—In the night the train travels on further to Nevel. We are met by the Spanish Blue Division wearing German uniforms and which is being entrained here.[14] The journey continues further via Guodek. Just as in Velikie-Luki we recognize much familiar terrain again. In the night we arrive in Vitebsk. Here we see the first German rail network.

7–8 October 1941—Our train stops in Vitebsk until Tuesday midday. Then the journey resumes. The train travels throughout the night and early on Wednesday at about 1000 hours arrives in Smolensk. Everywhere one sees destroyed Russian tanks. There are many burnt-out Russian freight trains at the station, parts of tanks and aircraft. There are knocked-out German tanks here as well, mainly from the 19th and 20th Panzer Divisions. From here we drive about 8 kilometers by truck in a southeasterly direction to the village of Autochovka. Our company is supposed to be here. Here we are welcomed by Oberleutnant Kischnik, who has meanwhile been in Germany. We are once again allocated to training classes. I am with the signallers.

9 October 1941—The Russians have to give everything a thorough clean and we comfortably settle in. There is plenty of alcohol here so that once again, just as in the times before, there's a real booze-up. On Thursday–Friday night I have guard duty. In the night Russian bombers attack Smolensk. Bombs fall not far from us. Our antiaircraft guns create some pretty fireworks.

10 October 1941—On Friday there is a major battalion muster parade. In his address, the battalion commander, Major Wolff, mentions the great successes of our division in July and August and likewise the recently accomplished battles of annihilation and declared that the matter would soon be decided and that we would be going back to Germany. At that time nobody doubted it at all, but it turned out differently and so many comrades would never see home again.

11 October 1941—Saturday passes with classes and pay parade. Potato fritters are again made in the evening.

12 October 1941—On Sunday we drive to Smolensk in the trucks which have stayed with us, where we can take a bath which is a real blessing. In the afternoon we watch a kitschy film.

13 October 1941—An NCOs course begins on Monday in which Goldmann and I take part. The course mainly consists of drill, fieldcraft, muster parades and instruction in NCO-specific themes and so on. The course is taken by Leutnant Tomasius and the instructors are Oberfunkmeister[15] Klingmann and Unteroffizier K. On Monday there is a group church attendance in Smolensk. We have already had many days of snow and cold. Now and again it thaws.

19 October 1941—The next Sunday we are back in Smolensk to take a bath. In the evening we drove off to see a function put on by Saarbrücken Radio Station.

22 October 1941—On Wednesday it is Oberleutnant Kischnik's birthday. We wake him with a song and present arms. He makes a short speech. One night, at 0200 hours there is a masked ball.

26 October 1941—On this Sunday as well we are back in Smolensk for a bath. The course eventually comes to an end. On Friday there are preparations for the inspection which takes place between 1300 and 1700 hours. Leaving the good food and punch behind, mind you, is somewhat depressing.

2 November 1941—On Sunday all course participants go their separate ways and everything is rearranged. I remain with the signallers in the quarters. Goldmann also stays here. Unfortunately Pit has to go. He was also in the course for about a week. We are also having beds built and lights and radios are also being installed. Things are getting quieter. On a couple of occasions we have instruction duty.

4 November 1941—On Tuesday there is pistol and machine gun shooting. As always I meet all the requirements. In the afternoon there is a check of weapons. On Tuesday I am the duty NCO and I am on guard, while in the company there is a bit of a booze-up. During the night we get called out. Oberleutnant Kischnik—drunk—is sitting on some old Russian nag. After we have fallen in he shouts: "Greetings Guard!" All about there is a snowstorm.

14 November 1941—The next Sunday we are back in Smolensk once more. We watch *Frau Luna*.[16] In the evening we have chicken to eat. Otherwise, every evening we either make fried potatoes or fritters since there's not enough bread. The average temperature is now about minus 10 degrees. The first cases of lice infection are being noted, though luckily not with us. Major Wolff is setting up a new company which will be off to the front. Several men from our company have been attached to it. We have to hand over several items, among them our pistols, which we do not like having to do. The situation around Moscow is said to be not looking too good.

16 November 1941—The next Sunday we watch the film *Willi Forsts Operette* once again which we really like.[17] The cooks put on some good food for the company from beef and flour. There's also some cake for each of us.

18 November 1941—On Tuesday I am once again the duty NCO. The next day we learn that the entire remnants echelon is to be set up to operate as infantry, including our company. There is already great excitement. All the preparations are under way. But only 3 groups leave the company. They go to Wolff's heavy battalion.

21–27 November 1941—On Friday the instruction finally comes to an end. Remembrance Sunday is a rest day. At midday I prepare cutlets with roast potatoes. In the evening there is roast goose with homemade Silesian dumplings. On Monday exercises resume again. On Wednesday I am again duty NCO. On Thursday there is a meeting of the junior leaders in the canteen which is conducted by Oberleutnant Kischnik with an interesting game plan.

28–29 November 1941—On Friday there is shooting on the range, though it is already quite cold. I am the clerk. In the evening another warning order arrives. Everything is to be ready by Sunday. Everything is being feverishly packed; excess equipment is sent to Smolensk, including among it my periscope-binoculars. I have already sent other items home in parcels. Every effort is made to get some good food; two pigs are slaughtered. As a hardworking assistant one can acquire a decent piece of meat. While this is going on the bigwigs are having a booze-up in the canteen so that the good supplies of food do not perish. On Saturday evening we have a magnificent sauna, something that refreshes the body wonderfully.

30 November 1941—Today is the first day of Advent and we have decorated our barracks room and put up an Advent wreath. Today, of course, we often have to think of home and years past. At midday Goldmann and I make Silesian dumplings. The following days are quiet. Now, all of us are waiting for the movement order. I am writing lots of Christmas letters home. At this time I have received a couple of parcels from home.

4 December 1941—The warning order to get ready finally arrives on Thursday. Once again there is feverish activity all over the place. The company is split into separate groups which move out one after the other owing to transport problems with the railway network.

5 December 1941—The movement order itself finally arrives on Friday. We are part of the first group, so we are the first to move out. For the last time

we eat from plates and are well aware what we are losing with our comfortable home. The girl will probably get everything clean for us; get the clothes washed and potatoes cooked. Apart from that it is minus 25 degrees outside. This morning there was company muster parade. Pit, among others, received the Iron Cross for which I heartily congratulate him. Who would have thought how the twists of fate would turn.

Smolensk–Kaluga

5 December 1941 (continued)—No sooner are we on the way to Smolensk, where the Mercedes diesel truck is supposed to be taking us, when the whole carry-on starts. The fuel feed pipe is constantly freezing so that it takes us about 6 hours to cover the 8 kilometers, most of which we travel on the road. There is an icy wind blowing today and we get a foretaste of what we are due to experience. In the town we have driven off for another 2 kilometers when I have to fetch, apart from a rucksack, a petrol lamp and a box of grenades that has come undone on the way. I have to stay behind and have to spend a lot of time looking for the armory where my comrades have gone. We are very grateful for the room with straw and a hot stove since the temperature has already dropped to minus 30 degrees. Here, rations that must last for 8 days are issued and then we get our heads down.

6 December 1941—We are up at about 0800 hours the next morning. We stay here until late afternoon and then our baggage is loaded up at the station by truck on which some of us travel. We want to go on foot on the assumption that it is not too far. At about 1500 hours we set off with Unteroffizier K to the main station. However, there is nobody there. The waiting rooms are full to bursting. Nobody here knows anything about our people. It has already got dark but there is nothing more for us to do other than to go to Station East. It is about 9 kilometers away. It takes us about two and a half hours since our nailed boots slip backward a lot on the smooth, packed-down snow. Also, our equipment bears down on us: we are carrying rations, cooking utensils, hand grenades, rifles, respirators, blankets and tents. After a long spell of searching we eventually find Leutnant von Riedesel and the other comrades in an old railway wagon all packed in tightly together. We sleep—very warm and well—in a nearby railway workers' barracks.

7 December 1941—Today is Sunday again. We give ourselves a thorough wash and look for some wood to light a fire (it is about minus 15 degrees).

About 1100 hours a hospital train arrives which takes us to Rosslavl'. In one of the wagons there is only one stove which does not provide much warmth. We arrive at about 1900 hours. We get set up well in a large waiting hall. It is not very warm here. We get some very good hot soup and coffee from the Red Cross.

8 December 1941—It feels somewhat warm on Monday morning: it's only about 1–3 degrees. During the night it snowed. We stay here for a bit and I have time to write home. At about 1600 hours we pick up another hospital train that takes us about 100 kilometers. We get set up well in the next station.

9 December 1941—At about 1000 hours on Tuesday there is another train that can take us. We get our hands on gutter pipes for a chimney; then we're off. On this occasion we make long stops and this is how the night passes. It is very uncomfortable; there's not much straw and with only one stove it is very cold.

10 December 1941—The next morning we are in Suchmitschki. The train is uncoupled and we stop here for about 24 hours. With a few comrades I get a rations sled, some straw as well and a second stove is secured. We only start to continue our journey at about 2200 hours in the evening.

11 December 1941—On Thursday we arrive in Kaluga not much before morning. We stop here. In one of the station workshops we can take a hot shower. Then at midday the train sets off for Maloyarosslavits where we arrive at about 1700 hours. Here we meet Major Wolff's heavy battalion and the comrades of our company who have already taken part in some hard operations. In the same night however we are supposed to return to Kaluga where the 20th Panzer Division is supposed to assemble.

12 December 1941—Toward morning we are once more in Kaluga. Today there is a thaw, something of an exception. We march about 3 kilometers with 3rd Company, Motorcyclist Battalion 20 to quarters. It is a tall, modern, stone-built building the plumbing and central heating of which is of course totally kaput. Nobody knows anything about the whereabouts of a remnants echelon. Nobody knows where we are supposed to be going and what will happen to us. To start with, we assume that our company will follow on behind.

13 December 1941—The following days are thoroughly comfortable. We have got ourselves a stove and we also have electric light. We have time for reading and writing. We go to the town, take a bath and go to the cinema which is close by.

15–18 December 1941—The town is almost completely unscathed and of all the towns makes the best impression of the towns which we have so far seen. By Russian standards the Russian population itself looks to a marked degree well clothed and fed. We also come across shops in Kaluga in which there are only sour gherkins and matches. We also pay a visit to a Russian teahouse that has a strong stink of makhorka, the Russia tobacco. We spend the days after in much the same way.

19–20 December 1941—On Saturday four of us go to a nearby village to get straw and potatoes which we send to our quarters on a sled. Next we want to push on a bit further to get a Christmas tree from somewhere. We have to go a few kilometers through snow a meter deep. Eventually we end up, without finding anything, on the large road to the south of Kaluga when suddenly we encounter lines of German soldiers who have blocked off the road. We hear that the Russians have broken through about 20 kilometers away. Whereupon, we drive back to Kaluga in a truck.

21 December 1941—Very early the next day, we hear a long spell of 8.8 gunfire and a lot of noise on the roads. There is almost an atmosphere of panic in the town. Early on the Russians have reached the edge of the town where a severe engagement is under way. Many vehicles are trying to leave the town. Machine guns and antitank guns are set up on the most important streets. Units are continually being deployed out of the town; sometime later a police regiment as well. The Russians are slowly forced out of the town.

The Last Operation
21 December 1941 (continued)—Meanwhile, Leutnant von Riedesel had reported to Major Wolff who along with his headquarters was located in the town. We had already packed our few things and now we receive the order that we are to be temporarily deployed and, indeed, to be under command of Major Wolff. We are told that it is a matter of only 2 or 3 Russian regiments which will soon be destroyed. So, therefore, we think that we will only be deployed for about 2 or 3 days at the most and so only take our essential

things with us. We only have our rifles but no steel helmet or ammunition pouches and immediately move out to R [unidentified] where we arrive as it is getting dark, and secure the village. For the time being, the Russians are still not here. Goldmann, Siebenwisch and I conduct a reconnaissance to the end of the village. The night is very dark and because of the unfavorable nature of the terrain is impenetrable.

22 December 1941—The next day—it is a Monday—passes relatively quietly. During the night one could see several houses burning in Kaluga. The whole sky is colored red and the flashes of light from machine guns and antiaircraft guns. Sometimes the Stalin organs fire, though without any obvious fire plan.

23 December 1941—We also undertake another reconnaissance mission on Tuesday, though there are still no Russians to be seen here. The day also passes quietly. In the evening we are to build snow huts so that we can sleep outside. It is pretty cold. Goldmann and I have built a snow hut in which we sleep. We understand one another very well and often discuss things that are of concern to us if we are outside alone.

24 December 1941—On Wednesday afternoon we change positions and move to a village on the other side of the gully in a southwesterly direction. We are told that today the infantry will relieve us. Today is Christmas Eve. From 1700–1800 hours Goldmann and I are outside on security duty and despite Kaluga, which is burning, our thoughts at this time keep going back to home and to years past. Later, in the warm quarters, I write in my diary. Then we are relieved and we head back to R where we are fed. Today there's some chocolate and schnapps. From there we cross over the river Oka back to Kaluga. In the course of all this, we lose our bottle of schnapps, which I want to look for. Meanwhile it has become dark and I lose contact with the company. I then go to our old quarters in Kaluga from where I intend to seek out the company the next day. I get here at about 2200 hours and meet several comrades. As a Christmas present I receive an Advent parcel and a letter from home. So we light ourselves another candle and celebrate for another two hours. Leutnant von Riedesel is also here. I write another letter home. Only at 0100 hours do we get to sleep, dead tired.

For many days German convoys have been returning through Kaluga. We are able to observe them; above all they are constantly on the go and disappear in a wood on the road in the direction of Iuchnov. From these observations and rumors doing the rounds it is becoming clear to us that here the entire front—previously situated about 80 kilometers to the front of Kaluga—is being drawn back; and that the Russians with strong forces have broken through the advancing German troops and cannot be stopped, since for the time being there still exists no unified front line. We hear that not so long ago the Führer assumed supreme command of the army and that a few days ago he was in Kaluga and that among certain authorities and administrative officials had to sort things out. A little later we note this in the rations with regard to the provision of tobacco, chocolate and so on. The 137th Infantry Division has now assumed responsibility for the defense of Kaluga. Hitherto defense of the town had been very inconsistent. Everything that was there has been taken. Even the bakery and butcher companies were deployed. However, we are told that Kaluga will definitely be held, which for the time being poses no difficulty since there are indeed plenty of heavy weapons on hand.

25 December 1941—This is the first day off. Very early on we go down to the river Oka where our company has taken up a position. Here we have relatively comfortable quarters with a Christmas tree. Here we are on security duty. We quite often come under fire from the gun of a Russian 52-ton tank. It starts to snow once again. It is minus 15°C.

26 December 1941—The next day we clean our quarters. All the superfluous junk gets thrown out. Beds are acquired from other houses. It is minus 20°C. From white bed sheets and so on we make camouflage clothing. In the afternoon we dig out a position.

27 December 1941—Saturday passes much as the day before. It is minus 26 degrees Centigrade. The Russians are slowly being pushed back. In the night we are once again outside in pairs. It is bitterly cold: minus 33°C.

28–30 December 1941—Sunday also passes without incident. We've got our hands on some chickens which are boiled and roasted. During Sunday–Monday night I am woken up at midnight. Two other comrades and I are to report to the company battle headquarters and to leave the town on sled columns. It is rumored that Kaluga will shortly be given up. From the company battle headquarters we set off with some comrades—there is perhaps about 40 of us—to our old quarters in Kaluga. It is about a 3-kilometer march. Having arrived here, we are due to receive rations within a quarter of an hour. Various miscellaneous items of baggage are to be fetched that are located in a dark room on the fourth floor. Everything and everyone is bumping into one another on the narrow stairs and in the pitch black. Due to a slight mishap I get down about 5 minutes late. There is nobody to be seen. I have two heavy pouches, a sack with rations for 5 men for 2 days and I don't know where to go. I set off immediately and soon meet several comrades who have missed the RV. Each one has a load of kit. The only option is for us to go to battalion headquarters, which is however lower down on the exit from the town and situated on the river Oka, about another 3 kilometers back. In spite of the approximately minus 30°C we are sweating and cursing. We often have to lay the kit down. Finally, we make contact—everything here is in the process of moving out. There is a constant stream of vehicles leaving the town but nobody knows anything of our sledge company. After much lengthy and uneasy searching it becomes clear to us that our people cannot be here. So, for better or for worse we have to load ourselves up and return to the old quarters. We slide all over the place on the smooth-trodden snow and we have to keep laying the load down. On a street corner, in the middle of the town, a German truck is burning. Suddenly there is an incoming shell from a heavy Russian mortar. Several others follow. We have to take cover for several minutes. Getting on to about five o'clock in the morning we finally arrive. We get a fire going in a small stove and rest until first light. We then ask after our comrades. We hear that the sledge squad has already set off. However, a remnant squad has remained here. We have a bit more time, but we should return to the company again. I put on my overalls and rubber boots in anticipation of what might come. It is minus 25°C. Toward 1000 hours we get going again and report to Leutnant von Riedesel. I am actually very happy to be among the comrades once again. Goldmann is also pleased that I am there again. We are again in quarters and the whole company is together. We have no idea what will become of us today but we think that we shall soon be leaving the town. Up until about 1600 hours we remain here on the town's main arterial road. Vehicle columns are continually leaving the town; the artillery is also limbering up and moving out. Finally we learn what is to happen to us. Oberleutnant Rohrbecher, who also belongs to the remnants echelon, has now assumed command of our company. We are under command of Major Wolff.

Of all things our company must take over the rear guard tonight and be the last ones to leave the town. On the southeast exit of the town we are to occupy an ice bridge on the river Oka until such time as we receive the order, via a rocket flare signal, to move out.

The whole thing looks somewhat tricky, since nobody knows, indeed, what the Russians will get up to, possibly cutting off the retreat. We are already waiting impatiently to get going. While we move out to the ice bridge in order to take up the position, the last vehicle columns and units leave the town. It is about 1800 hours.

Our machine guns are brought on to the ice bridge and then it's a question of waiting in this awful cold (minus 30°C), standing around for hours on end outside. All the company vehicles have already left the town with our packs. Only sledges wait for us in the town; they are intended for any wounded. At about 2145 hours the last infantry company which had been on the other side of the river crosses the bridge, which is then blown. Also, wagons and trains in the station, still partly loaded with rations, are blown. What could still be taken has already been grabbed by the infantry. Part of a clothing depot is also sent skyward, and likewise, of course, all the vehicles left behind. As on the previous days, the Russians are constantly bombarding us with fire from heavy mortars or tanks.

At about 2300 hours the exchanges of fire with Russian advance parties and reconnaissance patrols start. One group has already withdrawn. The Russians move slowly over the river. At about 2400 hours the Russians start to attack. Now our time has come. Leutnant von Riedesel fires a red flare and we slowly leave our position. Bullets are already flying down the streets. Without mishap we reach our sledges and abandon the town. The Russians are continually bombarding the exit out of the town but are unable to cause us any harm.

About 4 kilometers behind the town we meet the supply section of our company. Machine guns and ammunition have to be pulled along on sledges, something that requires a lot of effort. My rubber boots are superb when walking. After about 10 kilometers we arrive in a village where we stop for 20 minutes. Nobody can get in any of the houses: they are all occupied, so we have to wait outside in the cold; then we push on through the pitch-black wood. Eventually we come to a bigger village, which is also packed full of columns. It is 0600 hours. We look for a place to rest in some house or other. Here, too, everything is jam-packed. There's only about a square meter for lying down. We are able to sleep for about 2 hours. Then the company assembles again and moves out. Our march destination for today is Svol, which, having covered about 20 kilometers, we reach by last light. This location is also almost completely jam-packed. We manage to find a couple of spots where we can throw ourselves down; the main things are to find a bit of warmth and somewhere to get one's head down. The next day is New Year's Eve. Today we have a rest day, so during the night we can sleep right through. On New Year's Eve evening, things are quite comfortable: there's food, wine, cognac, cigars and cigarettes. We sit together for a long time until dog-tired we sleep in the New Year.

1 January 1942—At 0700 in the morning we fall in. Oberleutnant Rohrbecher tells us that we have to push forward again. We leave our heavy stuff behind, just taking a ration bag, blanket and cape with us. Several people—mainly a Feldwebel and so on—who are allegedly ill remain behind. By midday we arrive back in the village where we rested. It is minus 30°C. The village possesses a large and attractive monastery and a church. Therefore we call the village the monastery village. Here we are colocated with SS and tank formations which are still to be deployed in the sector. For the time being, the enemy is to be held here. Nevertheless, there is a constant stream of dead and wounded being brought back. In the night we are once again on guard.

2–3 January 1942—On Friday—it is minus 48°C—things are relatively quiet. I have some time to wash. In the evening we go to an engineer battalion on security duty. In the night it is once again appallingly cold: minus 44°C. We stop in a school which I take a closer look at on Saturday. It is quite modern and equipped with all the teaching aids typical of a senior school. In the library we find the works of Stalin and Lenin. Today, I sew myself some head protection and a wristwatch strap from leather. Toward evening we move off about 10 kilometers along the road to Kaluga. We are subjected to some sporadic Russian artillery fire. It is minus 40°C. We settle down in a small village in the middle of a wood. During the night, on guard duty it is very cold, too cold for sleeping. When moving about our socks freeze in the boots. Hoarfrost and icicles form on our headgear.

4 January 1942—On Sunday morning there is beautiful weather. We conduct a reconnaissance mission with Leutnant von Riedesel. It is difficult to make out the front. We have to wade through deep snow, carrying the machine gun on our backs. One sees lots of Russian fighters.[18] During the night we are doubled up on guard with the machine gun.

5 January 1942—The following day is relatively quiet. We have slowly warmed up our hut. Outside it has become slightly warmer.

6 January 1942—On Tuesday, at about 1100 hours, we head back to the monastery village. Here, in the afternoon, we meet the second company of the motorcyclist battalion. There's a midday meal on the street. When we learn that we have once again to move out on security duty, the mood becomes pretty bad. After a long, arduous march of about 3–4 hours through deep snow we finally arrive in a village toward 2100 hours. After a long wait we finally get to some house where we make ourselves comfortable and then we can eat for the first time. Goldmann and I are the first on guard duty again. The temperature is once again minus 15°C, whereas about 3 hours ago it was about zero degrees.

7 January 1942—The next day we move into another house and we eat a whole load of potatoes with salt. Otherwise the food is quite good. There are plenty of cigarettes and schnapps. The following night we finally get some rest and sleep for eleven hours.

8 January 1942—On Thursday we mount a reconnaissance mission. We are back by midday. Today our company receives the order to reinforce the infantry in a village about 6 kilometers away. We are away at 1400 hours. Each group has its sledge on which are stored the essential equipment. We arrive as it's getting dark and move into a large brick building. Apart from the normal cooking stove in the large space there is another stone and iron stove inside as well. There are also various sewing machines here. Probably a Jew had worked here as a tailor. Later, under the potatoes we find 4 plucked and drawn geese. In the night each one of us has to occupy the machine gun position for 5 hours. I am with Goldmann again. Just before midday, after a Russian attack has been repulsed, no person is to be seen in the night. The dead Mongols lay half-dressed in the snow.

9 January 1942—The next day passes quickly. We try to get as much sleep as we possibly can. Now, we often sleep on the stove. We work on the bunkers and positions. It is minus 15°C.

10 January 1942—The next night it snows. There's a snowstorm and it is pitch black so that outside we have to focus our eyes, but there are no Russians

to be seen. Everywhere on the horizon villages are seen burning. Today we come across a whole procession of Russian civilians with children and the whole family crossing the deep snow, trying to run away. We send them back. It is a grim fate that has befallen these people.

11 January 1942—There is clear weather on Sunday. We conduct a reconnaissance patrol with the task of setting alight a large haystack between us and the enemy on a large observable plain. On the return leg we come under small-arms fire but everything works out well.

12 January 1942—The next night an enemy reconnaissance patrol appears which, having abandoned its skis, barely manages to escape. With Leutnant von Riedesel we build a temporary barbed-wire obstacle. Otherwise the day is quiet. In the evening comes the all-too-familiar warning order to move out. We had really set ourselves up well in the village. Once again, we also found a whole load of honey in the house which we eat up. At about 2000 hours things get going. We are to return to the battalion. Through a misfortune we are held back in the night, spending the night in another village.

13–15 January 1942—The next day we find the route back to the battalion. Today, our fate, as we already foresaw, comes to pass. We are finally incorporated in Major Wolff's battalion and in a platoon under Leutnant von Riedesel in 3rd Company under Oberleutnant Milch. We want to try everything to get back to Oberleutnant Kischnik. In the night we sleep eleven hours. In the day and at night we man the machine guns outside.

16 January 1942—On Thursday we once again build a machine gun position in the wood and we have to carry beams and clear the snow which already lies about 70–80 cm high.

17 January 1942—However, early the next morning at about 0500 hours, we have to abandon the village, having spent the whole night outside manning the machine gun position again. On the march out we have to carry most of our equipment since we have too few sledges. We move into a village about 4 kilometers back. After a brief sleep we have to go to the position which is situated in a shed and set back a bit from the village. The Russians have already started to push forward. The straw and grain stores in front of us are set alight. Once again, our group has been assigned the task of being the last

one to leave the village. We build ourselves a small stove in the shed. In the evening I get an awful toothache that I successfully suppress with tablets. At about 2130 hours we leave the shed and head back to the village where we once again occupy the position. The bulk of the Wolff batalion soon moves out.

18–19 January 1942—Precisely at 0230 hours, with the civilian population not having any idea at all, the whole village is set ablaze. Within 5 minutes it is engulfed in bright flames. Roused from their sleep and terrified, the inhabitants run outside screaming. All they can do is to save their naked lives. It is a grim scene.[19] Then we also abandon the village, our route taking us through other burning villages. The entire region is lit up bright red; the snow reflects the red glow. Here we are once again assembled with SS and police units who are still holding up the advancing enemy. We have about 10 kilometers to march. At about 0530 hours we arrive in a village that is already completely full. Tightly packed together, all we can do is to warm ourselves up for a bit. We are hardly able to eat anything. Yesterday, all we were able to eat were rolls toasted on some tin in the shed. Now we have to go outside and build another position. We are relieved only hours later. We go to some house where we can finally get something hot to eat and get about 2 hours sleep.

At 1230 hours we have to go out once again to the position. I am once again together with Goldmann. Now, the Russians have already advanced to the edge of the wood in front of us and are bombarding our position. Only three hours later are we able to return to the village where, in places, we can only move by crawling. But even now we can hardly do anything to get ourselves warm. Shortly after, we are stood to; we are all out once again. Our heavy mortars are bombarding the Russian positions. Goldmann and I move to the village exit. There is little of the enemy to be seen but bullets are constantly whistling past, one of which strikes the roof of the first house. It must have been an incendiary round. After a short while the roof is on fire. We help to get the horses out of the stalls. The best people can do is to rescue the most necessary things, since the whole house is already ablaze. Inside the machine gun ammunition detonates in the flames.

The blaze, in all probability, must have been the signal for the Russians. At about 1600 hours they attack. The situation is very bad for us. The positions to the left of the village exit are slowly being cut off by the Russians. Only the men in the next position are able to get back, crawling on all fours, our squad among them. Moreover, with the onset of darkness, we are standing in the light of the burning house. With loads of shouts of "urrah," the

Russians press forward to the entrance to the village. We retreat back by several houses. The houses in which the Russians are situated are now set alight, so that they are now in the light and we are in darkness. In such a way the individual Russians can easily be shot down with rifle fire. Individual houses are shot up by fire from antitank guns. This way we check the Russians and slowly force them back again. Then we break contact with the withdrawing enemy. It is minus 30°C. The battalion is assembled and toward 2100 hours, having left a rear guard, heads out. We are happy that we are under way. At least we can get moving and we don't have to stand around the whole time in the dreadful cold. We have about 10 kilometers to cover. All about us many villages are on fire. We are in a trap. It is high time we get out of here before the Russians encircle us. We stop in a large village with a large modern school. Since the battle our company has 9 men posted missing, 4 wounded. Apart from that we are missing various machine guns and a large part of the ammunition. In the night we are able to sleep a bit but we have to go outside on guard duty for 2 hours. I have to stuff a new batch of dry hay in my rubber boots and let my footcloths and socks get a bit of air, then my feet are once more warm and dry.

This is the last day that I am due to spend with my comrades on operations, with Leutnant von Riedesel and Goldmann. We have become accustomed to experiencing everything together and to talk about everything that interested us and to understand each other. There could not be a purer form of comradeship and it was this comradeship that kept us permanently alert and prevented belief in the homeland becoming weakened.

The Russians had soon followed on after us and with daybreak the battle for the west side of the village resumed and within the next hours the Russians had already succeeded in occupying the west exit of the village. During the morning we get our machine guns and ammunition boxes in order. Later, Oberleutnant Nische arrives in the battalion with a radio wagon of the 20th Panzer Division in order to maintain radio contact with the division. We hear that Oberleutnant von Heydebreck has been killed and that Oberleutnant Kischnik has assumed command of that company.

At about 1100 hours there's a midday meal. Then our group receives a task: we are to support the sapper platoon located in the southeast part of the village. In the afternoon, they have the task of setting the village alight. Then at about 1700 hours the battalion is due to leave the village on a track through the woods.

We set off marching, to start with through the village; then we have to

cover 800 meters of open road to the far end of the village. To our astonish-
ment, we can already see, from some way off, that this part of the village
is on fire. One house after another starts to emit smoke until bright flames
flare up. We are now on the open part of the road: the Unteroffizier is in the
lead and I am on Goldmann's right side. Suddenly there is a terrible bang
ripping out the earth from underneath us. For a moment I see nothing but
black, dense smoke around me and I detect a powerful blow against my
right foot. Within perhaps half a second or so I find myself in the snow a
couple of meters beside the road. At the same time what has happened is
quite clear to me. The first thing I do is to make sure that everything in my
body is in order, including the right foot, which is unbelievably painful but
the boot itself is intact. Now, for the first time, I see the most dreadful thing
that causes me to stop worrying about myself. My comrade, Goldmann, is
lying on the road. He bore the full force of the mine and has almost completely lost his left leg and endured very severe wounds. For all of us this is
incomprehensible. But help is the main thing we think about now. A sledge
is quickly on hand which gets us to the next medical NCO. All he can do
is to apply an emergency dressing to Goldmann. Then we have to push
further to the rear. Rifles and respirators have already been left behind. We
can also say good-bye to our comrades here. We have about 7 kilometers to
cover. Goldmann, wrapped in blankets, lies in the horse-drawn sledge, in a
terrible state. But for all that he is freezing. All the same the temperature is
minus 25°C. Now we think of the most obvious thing. We both think about
soon getting back home and I promise Goldmann that, in any event, I shall
inform his mother or brother. He has completely resigned himself to his
fate, the very picture of manliness and soldierly virtue. We only hope that
we are able to remain together.

At the next battalion headquarters post Goldmann's wound is dressed.
Meanwhile, it is the afternoon, about 1430 hours. Goldmann is in dreadful
pain. He hardly complains and only thinks of his mother. Then we drive
about another 2 kilometers to the regimental headquarters. Here Goldmann
is once again examined by the regimental medical officer. It is slowly getting
dark and Goldmann soon falls asleep. He must have been unconscious for
about an hour. The doctor gives him a cardiac injection and then tries to
resuscitate him artificially for some time and then gives up. After a while
Goldmann's things are removed, his identity disks, wallet and so on; and
then he is carried out. Afterward, it slowly dawns on me that today I have
lost my best friend and comrade, who will never again see his homeland

or his mother of whom we have so often spoken. However, now that I have been fortunate I resolve to make it my duty to take his last greetings and possessions home with me in order to pass them on to his mother who was always in his thoughts.

Medical Evacuation: Destination Germany

We are due to be shipped out on the same evening, since the regimental medical officer is to leave here the next day. Everything moves very fast. By about 2100 hours the regimental medical officer has had 2 sledges secured in which we 6 wounded are due to return. My foot starts to cause me a lot of pain. The rubber boot is cut off. I assume that it is merely sprained. Now I notice a lot of small and large holes in my overcoat: they must have come from the mine splinters. Toward 2100 hours we move out at first via some river. We have a journey of about 17 kilometers ahead of us, mainly through forest. Everywhere villages are ablaze, the sign of the retreat. Anyhow, we make it unseen to Svissy. Afterward, our sledge is twice unhitched. We have to wait about half an hour outside the casualty-clearing station until the lazy medical orderlies are out of bed. Today, once again it is below minus 30°C. It is about midnight when we finally get to rest in some house. Everything is spinning in my head and it takes a long time for me to fall asleep.

20–21 January 1942—The next day we are due to get going again. The whole casualty-clearing station is moving out. We are loaded up onto recovery vehicles of the 127th Infantry Division. At 0900 hours we are off. I have to wrap up my foot, which is very painful and sensitive, very carefully. We have about 20 kilometers to cover which we drive on concrete. I sleep for a large part of the way. Having arrived on the main Rosslavl-Moscow highway, we are unloaded for a short while. Then in the afternoon we push on another 17 kilometers to Iuchnov, to a large assembly point. Hundreds of wounded are lying there. Many have been waiting several days for connecting transport. Already on the next day I am able to move on. It is minus 40°C. We travel in vehicles that belong to the State Railway to Aleksandrovskoe. Once again it is terribly cold. We are always looking forward to a warm resting place. We have covered about 90 kilometers in 5 hours.

22–23 January 1942—Also on Thursday morning, before midday, I have the good fortune to be able to get going again. On this occasion we travel the 90 kilometers in 2 hours by ambulances to Rosslavl'. We also stay here on Friday. The food is good. There is often chocolate and cigarettes. My foot is only bandaged.

24 January 1942—The next day, while it is still dark, we travel the 120 kilometers to Smolensk in the State Railway vehicles in 3 hours. Here again, we end up in a giant assembly point which is just as lice-ridden and filthy. These places are just breeding grounds for lice. Still on Sunday we are taken to the station in ambulances and loaded into goods wagons, which are cold and dark. At first the stove will not heat up very well. We lie freezing on sacks full of wood shavings. The severely wounded are in a bad way. We are unable to rest or to sleep. The waiting is worst of all.

25–27 January 1942—The train finally moves out on Sunday. Ahead of us we now have a journey of 4 weeks. The train also stops for a long time in Orscha. We are always waiting for a locomotive. Once again, the food here is good but the care is wretched. Things move on a bit quicker from Minsk. Russia will not gladly let us go, but from now on the journey moves ever closer to the homeland without stopping. The temperatures are no longer so low and the depth of snow is not so great. When we reach Brest-Litovsk the care gets better. We are now inside Poland.

28 January 1942—Just before Warsaw the train turns to the south and we cross the Lysa-Gora. In a small town we are received by an infantry orchestra and one sees more Germans. We often receive biscuits and cigarettes. By nightfall on Saturday the train stops in Krakov. Now this phase of the journey is over. It lasted 14 days: the rail transport from Smolensk to Krakov lasted a week. As we are being taken out of the train and loaded onto ambulances to be taken to the hospital we know that we have left behind the last exertions of the Russian winter; that we will now be taken care of; and that we can get ourselves treated.

31 January 1942—In the reserve section of Military Hospital 3 we are finally unloaded. Today, a new life begins for us in which we move from out of the nomadic existence, where each one of us had to fend for himself, and are once again to become civilized people in civilized surroundings.
It is almost an inconceivable blessing finally to be rid of the heavy, burdensome, filthy things and to take a bath. That's the first thing. Then we go into a large hall, in white beds, get something to eat in bed and so on and once

more have an orderly life. Fortunately, I have retained all my most important possessions, such as my watch, wallet, diary and money. First of all I write home from where I have had no news for a long time and also to where I have not been able to send anything.

1 February 1942—On Sunday an X-ray reveals that my heel bone is broken. Now I know that I shall soon be going to Germany and that the injury will not be healed in 14 days. A splint is fitted to my right leg which causes a lot of discomfort. So I spend the days this way and slowly become accustomed to bed and civilization.

5 February 1942—On Thursday I am loaded up for a move to Germany, since the doctor can do no more for me. Unfortunately, I have to leave my black uniform behind. A nightshirt is my sole piece of clothing. We get into a superb hospital train that soon takes us over the German border. Already by Friday morning we are in Gleiwitz. It is a real blessing once again to be able to see German villages and towns. Everywhere, the lightly wounded are being unloaded. The following night we travel through Breslau and Glatz and finally arrive midday Saturday in Bad Reinerz, where we are unloaded. I am here together with a Reichenbacher [inhabitant of Bad Reinerz?], Hoffmann, with whom I get on very well. Here in Reinerz, everything is in the depths of winter, but compared to Russia the climate strikes me as very mild. We are taken to some house in Bad Silesia, which for us is very quiet and comfortable. The quality of care and food is also good. Here also, I immediately write home and eagerly await some news, as I have heard nothing from home since November. As soon as Tuesday I receive a telegram informing me that at home everything is well and on Friday I receive a large parcel. Contact has once again been established.

16 February 1942—On Monday I receive the very first visit from my parents. It is a wonderful reunion in great gratitude for my miraculous, wonderful safe-keeping during the long period of uncertainty while in that dreadful Russia.

17–18 February 1942—On Tuesday in the afternoon I am transferred to the Saint Elizabeth Hospital under the care of Dr. Tudika. I end up in a large room with two beds where I am to remain for a long time until I am fully recovered, which takes a lot longer than I thought it would. During the first three weeks I am fitted with a traction bandage that causes a lot of pain. Later, the pain goes and I have time, more than sufficient time for thinking, writing letters and so on. I can now catch up on all the things I have missed. Body and soul can be fully healed. Lastly, my thoughts always return to Russia where the rest of the 20th Panzer Division still stands in the thick of the battle.

Since the middle of January the rest of my old company has also been there, operating as black-uniformed infantry under the command of Oberleutnant Kischnik and helping to stem the Russian advance. Among them the hard winter operation relentlessly demands its sacrifices as well. On 18 February 1942 my true and best comrade, Hans-Albrecht Piderit, is killed. The news of his death has a profound effect on me not only because since the time we were recruits we were good friends at home but also because in Russia as well, far removed from home, we were the best of friends and comrades and because we understood and were able to help one another.

Later, I learn of the death of Leutnant Tomasius. During all the operations undertaken with our company he was a distinguished, upright and exemplary officer. Then in March I read in the paper that Leutnant von Riedesel, my company commander in the winter operations as part of Major Wolff's battalion, has also been killed. In his self-control, reliability, uprightness and comradeship, he, too, for me, was a model officer.

He is to me just the same as Goldmann, my comrade in the armored vehicle to whose mother I was the first one to write. For over five months this was the sole news she had from her son. Where military operations are at their hardest, where life is the most hopeless and demands of a person the very last in body and soul, there comradeship and friendship reveal and prove themselves at their best. I had this experience with my friend and comrade Joachim Goldmann. For that reason he shall never be forgotten by me.

Being back in the homeland once again, in Germany, far removed from the noise of war, operations, deprivations and cold, seems to me at first to be something of a novelty, so firmly accustomed to everything had body and soul become in the last 7 months. But now, everything that one sees and perceives is seen anew and is evaluated according to a new standard. The profound impressions arsing from my 8 months in Russia will remain unforgettable for me throughout my entire life.

The Duties of the German Soldier
1. The Wehrmacht bears arms on behalf of the German people. It protects the German state and Fatherland, the people united in National

Socialism and its living space. The roots of its strength inhere in its glorious past, German national traditions, German land and German labor. Serving in the Wehrmacht is honored service to the German people;

2. The soldier's honor resides in the unconditional involvement of one's self for the people and Fatherland, including if necessary the sacrifice of one's life;

3. Courage in battle is the highest soldierly virtue. It requires toughness and determination. Cowardice is degrading; hesitation is not soldierly;

4. Obedience is the foundation of the Wehrmacht. Trust is the foundation of obedience. Soldierly leadership is based on a willingness to assume responsibility, superior ability and tireless care;

5. Great achievements in war and in peace arise only in the spirit of unshakable group action of leader and troops;

6. Group action requires comradeship. It proves itself especially in an emergency and in danger;

7. Self-confident but nevertheless modest, upright and loyal, God-fearing and honest, discreet and incorruptible, the soldier should be an example of manly strength for the whole people. Achievement alone merits pride;

8. The soldier finds his greatest reward and satisfaction in the awareness of his willingly accomplished duty.

Conclusion

Gefreiter von Wiedebach-Nostitz's record of, and reflections on, the events in which he participated paralleled the process of physical convalescence after he was medically evacuated to Germany. As the diarist writes of his recovery: "Body and soul can be fully healed." The reflective element in the diary manifests itself in references to God, typically but not surprisingly as he grapples with the aftermath of great danger and personal loss, such as the shock of seeing the broken bodies of Leutnant Behr and Unteroffizier Wohlfeil lying in the back of a military ambulance. And even though von Wiedebach-Nostitz recognizes the harsh, tactical exigencies that require the burning of villages to deny shelter to the enemy, he is not oblivious to the plight of Russian villagers driven from their homes.

Von Wiedebach-Nostitz's belief that God is watching over him highlights just one of the many paradoxes of individual and group behavior in war. The invading German army marched according to a plan of conquest; it brought untold misery, suffering, and destruction to the Russian lands. There are perhaps no atheists in a foxhole, but I interpret the references, even appeals, to God as one man's attempt to look past the NS regime's strategic goals and make some sense of the war and his place in it. Important here is not whether God did in fact watch over von Wiedebach-Nostitz but that he *believed* God would. A German soldier who believes that God will watch over him—just like the soldiers in the Red Army who did not succumb to Soviet atheism but continued to do their duty—has secured some part of himself that cannot be invaded by the NS regime.

7 The German Invasion in Soviet-Russian War Literature

> The rear lives by another set of laws and it can never merge in a moral sense with the front. Its law is life, the struggle for life, and we do not how to live in a holy manner: we know only how to die in a holy manner. The front is the holiness of Russian death; the rear echelons are the sins of Russian life.
>
> *Vasilii Grossman*

The central role allocated to agitprop in the Soviet state and the Communist Party's determination to own, control, and impose its own narrative on all explanations of Soviet affairs—both internal and external—required huge efforts during and long after the Great Fatherland War to shape its depiction in Soviet-Russian historiography and literature. Such control mandated a unique and pervasive instrument of censorship. By 1941, this instrument was a well-established feature of the Soviet ideological surveillance apparatus. The party had to explain not only why the Wehrmacht achieved such devastating tactical surprise (which implied incompetence on the part of the Red Army High Command, the intelligence agencies, and even Stalin) but also why the Red Army had been unable to rout the German invader. This failure was incompatible with strident preinvasion propaganda that the Red Army was trained and equipped to cope with the demands of modern war and could deal with any invader in short order. The historiographic analysis and literary treatment of the early part of the Great Fatherland War include a vast body of work that merits a separate study in its own right, yet it is too important to be omitted entirely here. This chapter, therefore, examines a selection of literary works devoted to the period 1941–1942: Vasilii Grossman's *Narod bessmerten* (The People Are Immortal [1942]) and his war diaries, Alexander Bek's *Volokolamskoe shosse* (The Volokolamsk Highway [1943–1944]), and Konstantin Simonov's

Zhivye i mertvye (The Living and the Dead [1959]). One of the most important developments related to an evaluation of these three works, and indeed the bulk of Soviet-Russian war literature published before 1991, was the release of vast amounts of documentary material about the role of the special sections and the NKVD. This material reveals and confirms the NKVD's obsession with documentation, okruzhentsy (encirclement survivors), and filtration and provides a new context for interpreting Soviet-Russian war literature.

Introduction

In 1939, a couple of months before Molotov and von Ribbentrop signed the German-Soviet Non-Aggression Pact, an interesting book—at least in terms of its fantasy plot—was published in the Soviet Union. Written by Nikolai Shpanov, Pervyi udar: povest' o budushchei voine (The First Blow: The Story of the Future War) is military science fiction, the story of an ideological war of the worlds in which fascist forces in Germany are defeated by the peace-loving Soviet Union. Although Shpanov identifies the main enemy as fascist (not National Socialist) Germany, he also blames the imperialist states of Britain and France for the outbreak of hostilities. The coordinated use of airpower, long-range bombers, and airborne and ground forces—all expertly led—ensures that the forces of fascist reaction are defeated. In The First Blow the armed forces of the Soviet Union are depicted as the most advanced in the world in terms of both equipment and doctrine.

Just how much stories such as Shpanov's influenced domestic perceptions of Soviet military performance cannot be precisely measured; however, there is no doubt that, in keeping with Marxist-Leninist theories about socialist realism and agitprop, these stories, along with other elements of the Soviet mass media, were intended to nurture a belief that the borders of the Soviet Union were secure and inviolable and that any aggressor would come to grief. To take just one example from Pravda: alongside its traditional and obligatory celebration of international proletarian solidarity, its 1 May 1941 edition reinforced the propaganda of military expertise and training. It published an order from Timoshenko, the people's commissar for defense, in which he declared that the Red Army "has enriched itself with military experience and is ready to give a crushing rebuff to any encroachment by the capitalists on the interests of our socialist state, or on the Soviet people."[1] Timoshenko also warned of the dangers facing the Soviet Union. Citing Stalin, he noted, "'In these conditions, the Red Army must keep its powder dry and remain in a state of permanent mobilized preparedness' so that 'no "chance events" and . . . no tricks on the part of our external enemies are able to catch us unawares.'"[2]

Regarding the veracity and credibility of the Soviet mass media, one thing can be said with some degree of certainty: where all sources of information and all interpretations of information are controlled by the state, with harsh penalties for dissenters, a substantial element of the population will succumb to state-controlled ideological narratives on just about any topic. From the state's point of view, it is not essential that people actually believe what they are told, as long as they act like they believe it. However, this pretense can be maintained only as long as it is not threatened by something at least as powerful as the state itself. If the Soviet fantasy world collides with some brutal physical reality that cannot be rendered inert by arrests, executions, denials, lies, and evasions, the state will find itself tested to destruction.

The constant stream of antifascist, we-are-for-peace, and readiness-for-war propaganda emanating from Moscow's mass-media machine right up until 22 June 1941 meant that any Soviet writer analyzing the summer retreat was faced with a truly daunting task: how to explain the element of surprise in the German attack; how to explain the Red Army's failure to destroy the German invaders on the border; how to counter the rumors of collaboration; how best to exploit any Red Army successes; and how best to counter the perception, despite all the Soviet propaganda, of German military prowess and the sense of hopelessness it engendered. Behind these questions lurked others that were probably best avoided completely—above all, the failure of the Non-Aggression Pact and the meaning of the notorious TASS communiqué of 13 June 1941. One option for writers in such circumstances was to leave the big picture to the papers and communiqués and concentrate on the small units and individuals, the civilians and soldiers who joined together to resist the German Leviathan. This is the central device of Grossman's The People Are Immortal. In Bek's The Volokolamsk Highway, the defense of Moscow takes center stage, and in The Living and the Dead, published after Stalin's death, Simonov tries to unravel some of the less flattering elements of the first six months of the German invasion.

Vasilii Grossman, *The People Are Immortal* (1942)

The People Are Immortal is set in August 1941, beginning with the imminent fall of Gomel' to the Germans. Within the limits of Soviet censorship, Grossman broaches the themes of national solidarity, encirclement, collaboration, and desertion. Much of the plot is driven by professional differences between Red Army officers and military commissars about how to react to the German invasion.

On the one hand, the message of Grossman's title cannot be clearer: no matter what the Germans do, they cannot win because the people—though not literally immortal—will survive these latest troubles and prevail. On the other hand, Grossman's reference to the people is not confined to the very brief Soviet period. Although Grossman sometimes gets carried away with the idea of Soviet unity among Ukrainians, Russians, Jews, Georgians, Belorussians, and Tartars, his notion of the people is deeply and remotely rooted in the non-Soviet past: it stresses historical continuity, tradition, and evolution. This emphasis on the longevity of the people and their traditions suggests two things: first, it is not clear where the 1917 Revolution fits into Grossman's vision of the people, and second, resistance to the German invaders cannot possibly be confined to what is understood as Soviet, given the short existence of the Soviet state. In appealing to the people, Grossman is looking back to Russia's long, troubled, and sometimes glorious past.

The appeal to ancient traditions and culture as the source of Russian resistance is evident is one of the central characters: the ordinary soldier Ignat'ev. The influences, traditions, and interests that have molded him are conspicuously Russian, rather than Soviet. His love of the land and his knowledge of ancient songs (gleaned from a solitary and mysterious wise woman in his village) are distinctly non-Soviet. Above all, Ignat'ev derives his strength from the land and exemplifies to a striking degree what German philosopher Carl Schmitt had in mind when he wrote of the connection between the partisan and the defense of his native soil, his telluric ethos. Again, in defiance of anything Soviet, Ignat'ev exemplifies a spirit of pantheism and ancient paganism, the essence of some wood demon that cannot be overcome by the Germans' modern weapons: Russian soul (dusha) and spirit (dukh) will trump German metal, guns, and Blitzkrieg.

This certainly fits Grossman's view of the sources of resistance, and it is reinforced by Grossman's masterful depiction of the German air raid in which the ancient town of Gomel' is destroyed. His description of the death agonies of a horse is especially powerful. That Grossman is appealing to a much bigger historical context than the Soviet one is implied by the reference to Tacitus's The Annals of Imperial Rome, which is found next to one of the civilians killed in the air raid. The significance of The Annals—its documentation of tyranny, terror, and civil war—is not just to highlight the permanence of war in human affairs and ongoing imperial rivalries; Grossman intends, I suggest, to awaken certain parallels between Tiberius and Stalin. A line from a speech by Tiberius, cited by Tacitus, also seems to capture the sense of Grossman's title and might even have inspired it: "Rulers die; the country lives forever."[3]

In Grossman's eyes, the destruction of Gomel' constitutes a war crime. However, Grossman's view of enemy behavior generally has a historical context that he is reluctant to acknowledge:

> The enemy was trampling all over the life of the people: he knocked down the crosses on the graves where mothers and fathers were buried; he burned children's books; he marched through those orchards where their forefathers had planted apple and cherry trees; he stepped on the throats of grandmothers telling children the fairy tales about the golden cockerel; he hanged the cask makers, the blacksmiths and the querulous, old night-watchmen. Ukraine, Belorussia and Russia had known nothing like it. There had never been anything like this on Soviet territory.[4]

German troops undoubtedly did knock down crosses, but Grossman conspicuously ignores the fact that Communist Party atheists relentlessly persecuted believers in Russia long before the arrival of the German army. He also betrays an element of contempt for his readers: had they all forgotten who desecrated the churches and converted them into grain silos and workshops? Soviet atheist campaigns were not directed exclusively against the Orthodox Church. In Gomel', the setting of Grossman's story, rabbis who objected to the closing of religious schools were brought before courts. Large synagogues were turned into restaurants.[5] Grossman's reference to the forefathers planting apple and cherry trees alludes to a *tsarist* time, a *Russian* time, a time of private property long before the party seized the land and dispossessed the peasants. It is all well and good for Grossman to portray the Germans as crushing and censoring Russian folk tales as part of their war on Russian folkways (folkways, it should be noted, that long predated the arrival of the party), but who introduced a brutal system of censorship that suppressed the ancient folk cultures of Ukraine and Russia? For anyone who could remember the fate of Vladimir Maiakovskii, one of the early poster boys of Soviet proletarian poetry, Grossman's image of Germans stepping on grandmothers' throats is somewhat unfortunate, since it evokes lines from Maiakovskii's poem "Vo ves' golos" (At the Top of My Voice [1929–1930]), in which the poet describes himself as stepping on the throat of his own song, suppressing his creativity for the good of the collective (Maiakovskii later committed suicide). Furthermore, when Grossman tells us that the Germans hanged people and that "there had never been anything like this on Soviet territory," he deliberately ignores the civil war, the genocide in Ukraine, the untold misery caused by collectivization, and the purges. To be fair, Grossman can hardly refer to party-orchestrated genocide and other afflictions visited on Russians, Ukrainians, and Belorussians in what is intended to be a propaganda tract. It would have been personal and professional suicide. So, in the manner of the Germans stepping on the throats of Russian grandmothers, Grossman follows Maiakovskii's lead and steps on the throat of his own song—or, perhaps, breaks his own pen.

Grossman does not totally evade the misery of collectivization and its consequences, however. They emerge in the character of Kotenko. He is the symbol and substance of the Ukrainian or Russian who, dispossessed or destroyed by collectivization, hopes the Germans will restore his fortunes and the land taken from him. But Grossman misconstrues the wellspring of Kotenko's grievances: it is not envy (zavist') toward the beneficiaries of the Soviet new order. Envy is one of the social-psychological levers exploited by the party to dispossess the wealthier, harder-working peasants. There is, in fact, no fundamental difference between the Communist Party activists inciting a poisonous, envious hatred toward successful or ordinary peasants and the National Socialist Party's demonization of Jews in Germany. It is not envy of the new party caste that drives Kotenko—he shows no obvious desire to acquire the trappings of power. He is motivated by jealousy: he is jealous of his property that has been taken from him and seeks its return. Now, in the middle of a war, as the Germans are about to enter the village, Kotenko's longing for his property appears base, utterly selfish, and bereft of any sense of solidarity with his fellow villagers—and Grossman intends it to be seen this way. But however narrowly selfish Kotenko is, his behavior highlights the fact that the Soviet state undermined social cohesion and solidarity with its pursuit of class war; as a consequence, it did not enjoy total legitimacy among all strata of the constituent populations of the Soviet Union.

The theme of private property, which figures so prominently in Kotenko's calculations, is also evident in the last hours of Mariia Timofeevna Cherednichenko, the mother of a senior military commissar and a prime beneficiary of the new political caste. She muses whether this will be the last occasion when she bakes bread in her own oven, bread made with her own wheat. In the Soviet state, ovens and bread are not the property of individuals. The fact that she refers to the oven and wheat as her "own" is an indirect recognition that Kotenko may have a point: the party has declared war on human nature and institutions by trying to eradicate the boundary between "yours" and "mine." Moreover, baking bread for her *own* consumption is a selfish act that is not intended to benefit the other villagers. Whereas Grossman's view of Kotenko's desire to recover his property is hostile, Vasil' Bykov's treatment of those dispossessed by collectivization is far more sympathetic in *Znak bedy* (The Sign of Misfortune [1983]). In *Stuzha* (The Great Freeze [1993]), another outstanding Bykov account of partisan warfare, the author notes that party activists destroyed millstones to prevent individuals from grinding flour and baking bread. Bread production could then be centralized and used as a form of socioeconomic control.

Having given us Ignat'ev, an essentially Russian soldier, and his immediate entourage, representatives of the people, Grossman must now provide a vision of the people that unifies things Russian (and Ukrainian, Belorussian, Jewish, and Tartar) with things Soviet. This unity of people, party, and Soviet state is served by Bogarev, the military commissar. From the outset, this unity is awkward and artificial, and Bogarev is obviously a propaganda device on Grossman's part. He gives Bogarev, whose civilian occupation is professor of Marxism-Leninism, a platform variously to chide, to instruct, and to punish regular Red Army officers, among them a Hero of the Soviet Union, for their lack of professionalism. One can imagine that this sort of baiting did not go down too well with regular officers.[6] Grossman tells us that Bogarev is consumed by a hatred of fascism. Thus, one must ask whether he felt this way between 23 August 1939 and 21 June 1941, and if so, what ideological yoga did he use to justify it. Bogarev is least plausible when he is assessing the German army:

> Bogarev had carefully studied the orders of the German command. In them, he noted a pervasive ability for organization. The Germans bombed things, plundered and burned things in an organized and methodical manner; the Germans were able to organize the collection of empty tins in military encampments; knew how to work out the complex movement of a massive column with thousands of details and were able to carry out these details on time with mathematical precision. There was something vile, something inconsistent with the free mind of a human being in their ability mechanically to submit,

unthinkingly to march, in the complex and massive movement of a million-strong mass of soldiers forged together in discipline. This was not the culture of reason, but the civilization of instincts, something that was derived from the organization of ants and other herd animals.[7]

There are some obvious objections to this assessment of German military behavior. First, the organization, planning, and execution of an invasion on the scale of Barbarossa must be thorough and painstaking. Given that the Red Army is retreating in disarray and that Gomel', where Grossman's story begins, is about to fall, German planning and organization seem to have none of the alleged flaws and disadvantages Bogarev identifies. Second, Bogarev's description of the Germany army—a million-strong mass marching to war as a disciplined whole—is not that far removed from the image of the Red Army and the Communist Party standing together to confront the fascist hordes. This image is projected by the propaganda of Bogarev's immediate employer, the Red Army Political Directorate, and is indeed a staple component of 1 May celebrations. One senses that what really irritates Bogarev, and possibly his creator, is that he would like to be able to describe the Red Army as a disciplined whole. Third, Bogarev's likening of the German army to "the organization of ants and other herd animals" comes very close to mimicking the NS regime's racial-ideological views of Slavs: the Germans are not fully human; they are insects to be eradicated. In denigrating the Germans as insects, Bogarev reveals himself to be a true follower of Lenin, who urged the mob to rid Russia of all "harmful insects" and "bugs," the rich and the bourgeoisie. Moreover, this perception of the Germans as ants and herd animals is hardly consistent with what a German prisoner tells Bogarev about Hitler: "Hitler—he told Bogarev—is not the creator of national values, he's an aggressor. He has captured the diligent, industrial culture of the German people, like an ignorant bandit who has driven away the magnificent car built by a doctor of technical sciences."[8] How does a nation whose military is bereft of reason (despite its obvious successes) maintain its industry? Can this assessment of Hitler's impact on Germany be equated with what Lenin and Stalin have done on an even greater scale in the Soviet Union?

Despite pretensions to military omniscience and the status he enjoys as a military commissar, Bogarev's assessment of the German army is challenged. For example, the division's chief of staff expresses a totally different view of German arms: "He highly rated the ability of the German General Staff in mobile warfare, the mobility of the fascist infantry and the ability of its air forces to operate with the ground forces."[9] Likewise, the head of the operations section sees the success of the German advance in terms of speed, terrain, and the geometry of topography—factors that apply to both sides, regardless of ideological differences. This is an implicit rebuke aimed at Bogarev, since the objective factors governing war cannot be permitted to be negated by ideological diktats.

A more substantial challenge to Bogarev comes from Myshanskii, an infantry company commander. He praises the mobility of the German army, the high level of coordination between the air and ground forces, the quality of the German General Staff, and their military culture. Myshanksii concludes: "The whole of strategy and tactics has been turned upside down."[10] This is a cue for Bogarev to start another tirade about German failures:

> Well, we're not children—said Bogarev—we know, we're dealing with the strongest army in Europe, with equipment, well, I'll tell you straight, which is superior at this particular phase of the war. Indeed, what is there in general to be said? Everything has been said; we're dealing with the Germans. Well, here it is, comrade Myshanskii, I have been listening to you very carefully and I am obliged to give you a little lecture. There's a need for it. You must learn to despise fascism; you must understand that fascism is the basest, the most wretched, the most reactionary thing on earth. It is a vile mixture of substitutions and theft in the widest sense of these words. This vile ideology is absolutely without any creative element at all. One has to despise it to the very depths of one's soul. Do you understand? . . . Fascism's entire military doctrine has been totally and utterly copied from the old plans of the German General Staff, worked out by Schlieffen. All their flanking attacks, wedges and the rest have been slavishly copied. The tanks and airborne assaults used by the fascists to surprise the world have been stolen: the tanks from the British; the airborne assaults from us. I am constantly amazed by the horrendous, creative sterility of fascism: there is not a single new military method! Everything has been copied. Not a single major invention! Everything has been stolen. Not a single new type of weapon! Everything has been borrowed. In all areas, German creativity has been sterilized. The fascists are incapable of inventing anything, writing books and poems and producing music.

They are stagnation, a swamp. They have contributed one element
alone to history and politics: organized bestiality and banditry! . . .
As the unit's military commissar I forbid you to utter words which are
unworthy of a patriot and which do not correspond to the objective
truth. Do you understand that?[11]

Bogarev's ideological rant explains some of the reasons for the Red Army's
dire plight in the summer of 1941 and the baleful influence of the commissar caste on planning and operational decisions. Serving the purposes of
agitprop, Bogarev's ideas and the fact that he is permitted to deliver them
without any serious challenge highlight not just the unjustified status enjoyed by these party functionaries but also the damage done to the morale
of the officers. The essence of Bogarev's tirade is precisely the opposite of
his insistence on "objective truth." It marks the assertion of ideological
fanaticism over objective truth.

For example, if what Bogarev mistakenly calls fascism in the context of
National Socialist Germany is indeed such a vile entity, one conversation
stopper for Myshanskii—though probably not a very good career move—
would have been to ask why the German-Soviet Non-Aggression Pact was
ever concluded. Even if, as Bogarev asserts, Schlieffen's ideas were copied
by a new generation of German officers, the fact is, they worked. In any
case, the adoption of the Schlieffen *Sichelschnitt* to attack northern France in
1940 was merely a diversion, since the main attack came farther south. One
must ask: if the fascists, as Bogarev calls them, have merely copied flanking
moves and wedges, why is the Red Army not countering these moves with
maneuvers of its own? The alarming thing about German military doctrine
is that it pioneered a type warfare that the Red Army was unable to match.
It is irrelevant whether tanks were invented by the British or airborne forces
were developed by the Red Army. The fact that the Germans have taken the
operational deployment of tanks to a higher level does not deny the British
the continued use of tanks. Ideas cannot be stolen. What is decisive is the
manner in which such forces, whether armored or airborne, are used and led.
In this regard, the German army is well ahead of its rivals. Despite Bogarev's
ravings, Myshanskii is essentially correct: the Germans have indeed turned
strategy and tactics upside down, and the Red Army is struggling to cope.

This is emphasized by two incidents. The first involves the aftermath
of an attack mounted by the regimental commander, Mertsalov, who is,
incidentally, a veteran of the Russo-Finnish War and a Hero of the Soviet

Union. Once again setting the agenda, Bogarev insists that the attack must be considered a failure, since too many of the enemy escaped. But this failure is due to a lack of all-arms cooperation—a quality the Red Army needs but, in the Germans, is somehow seen as bad. Bogarev criticizes Mertsalov for failing to command properly. One might ask how he can command properly when he must answer to his immediate army superiors and tolerate Bogarev's unsolicited advice. Bogarev's meddling, a consequence of dual command, raises an obvious question: if the Red Army is underperforming, who or what is to blame? An important element in Bogarev's evaluation of the attack is that it all comes down to *vnezapnost'* (suddenness), hinting that this more or less explains the Germans' success after 22 June 1941. This serves a clear propagandistic purpose but avoids the question of why and how the Germans managed to achieve *vnezapnost'*. Though undoubtedly a major factor in the immediate success of the German invasion, suddenness alone cannot explain continuing German military success. On the contrary, it points to serious shortcomings in the Red Army, which are now being addressed as the war progresses.

The second incident arises when a Soviet company encounters the Germans. Grossman describes the enemy advance as "the classic movement of German motorized columns, tried and tested," which he acknowledges was responsible for overrunning Poland, France, the Balkans, and Greece.[12] This does not correspond with Bogarev's ravings about the robotic nature of German operations. The use of "classic" to characterize these thrusts—a motif that occurs more than once in this story—suggests that the Germans have indeed taken tactics and all-arms cooperation to a new level. The question here is whether Grossman is deliberately (and maybe not so subtly) undermining Bogarev, thus paying lip service to the role of military commissars. Possibly, but then Myshanskii's views are undermined by his lack of aggression toward the Germans (the name Myshanskii suggests "mouse" in Russian). Perhaps he is too much in awe of the Germans and psychologically neutralized, which prevents him from responding with sufficient aggression. Thus, Myshanskii takes his company through a forest instead of crossing the open field, as ordered. The company becomes separated, and when it eventually rejoins the main force, the men are in disarray, and some have deserted. One of the deserters is apprehended, and Mertsalov orders that he be shot in front of the unit (*pered stroem*). Indicated here is the impact of Stalin's Order № 270. In addition, when Myshanskii is reunited with the main force, he is not wearing his badges of rank—a crime, according to Stalin's order. Myshanskii's justifies his actions as follows: "The sole correct thing seemed to me to disperse the men and break through the front in isolation."[13] Although this decision is based more on stealth than on aggression, it is by no means tactically illiterate. Moreover, Myshanskii is almost certainly correct when he maintains that they have fallen into a "classic encirclement,"[14] which only inflames Bogarev, since it hints, once again, at German tactical superiority. For his sins, Myshanskii is demoted to the ranks, another punishment provided for by Order № 270.

Earlier in the story, when Myshanksii points out to Mertsalov that they are encircled, he is reprimanded. Later, Mertsalov must acknowledge that they are indeed encircled. The mere thought of being encircled inspires dread, one suspects, because of the stigma inspired by Stalin's Order № 270 rather than for any military reason. Mertsalov's—and Bogarev's—reaction to Myshanskii's observation is to shoot the messenger (figuratively, not literally). Bogarev's reaction to Myshanskii's observation about falling into a "classic encirclement" is not only at odds with his earlier plea to Myshanskii to be bound by the objective truth—that they are encircled is an empirical fact—but also inconsistent with his reaction to the observations of others. For example, when Nevtulov (a soldier and politruk who read extracts of his diary to Bogarev and earned the latter's approval) comments that the German aerial formation is "the classic formation before an attack,"[15] he gets no reprimand from Bogarev.

The final attack in which the Soviet forces manage to break the encirclement represents not just a local tactical triumph for the Red Army but a wider, symbolic triumph of Soviet arms. The opposing German commander is Oberst Bruchmüller, and the name is significant; a German artillery officer of the same name pioneered mass, precision artillery attacks in World War I. The techniques used by Mertsalov to overcome Bruchmüller are the same ones used by the Germans—techniques that Bogarev earlier derided as evidence of ant-like slavishness. Grossman concludes his story with Ignat'ev and Bogarev supporting each other as they limp away wounded after the attack: Communist Party, Red Army, and people are one—at least on paper.

The Bogarev-Myshanskii opposition in The People Are Immortal can be read as a device used by Grossman to put forward various interpretations of the war, although, from a propagandistic point of view, Bogarev's are supposed to carry more weight. However, an entry in his wartime diaries indicates that in creating this binary opposition, Grossman may have been relying on, and reflecting, what he saw as a feature of Russian psychology:

In this war I have observed only two feelings in relation to what is taking place: either extraordinary optimism or total, unrelieved gloom. The transitions from optimism to gloom are rapid, sudden and happen easily. There is no middle ground. Nobody lives by the idea that this is a long war; that in this war hard, unremitting work alone, month after month, will lead to victory, and even those who talk about it in such a way do not believe it either. There are merely these two feelings: the enemy has been defeated, the first one; or it is impossible to defeat the enemy, the second one.[16]

If the two extremes identified by Grossman can be applied to Bogarev and Myshanskii—Bogarev representing the view that the Germans will be beaten, Myshanskii representing the view that they cannot—this suggests a lack of realistic ideas about how to counter the Germans. Clearly, the Germans are not invincible, nor are they the unimaginative military robots Bogarev seems to think they are. Both positions are extreme. The message here is that Russians, Ukrainians, and others must endure the unendurable. For the time being, that is the best there is.

Vasilii Grossman's War Diaries
(August 1941—Winter 1941–1942)

Grossman served as a war correspondent from August 1941 until the end of the war, when he entered Berlin with the Red Army. During the war Grossman kept a series of notebooks that were finally published in 1989. These notebooks, which sometimes resemble a diary, contain more than the author's observations about the course of the war. They depict a vast gallery of astonishingly diverse individuals who are often larger than life and amusing, like characters from a Gogol novel. They also contain some desperately moving moments, revealing the real hardships and struggles in the daily lives of Russians and others. The first four notebooks cover the period from August 1941 to the winter of 1941–1942, and the entries show that Grossman relies on them for many of the characters and incidents in *The People Are Immortal*.[17] Indeed, the notebooks play the same role in his two major postwar Stalingrad novels: *For a Just Cause* (1952) and *Life and Fate* (1988).

When one reads the notebooks alongside *The People Are Immortal*, it is possible to identify the various soldiers, officers, commissars, and civilians encountered by Grossman who also appear in thinly disguised form in the story. However, Grossman's view of the war as recorded in his notebooks is altogether more somber and objective than The People Are Immortal. These discrepancies reveal considerable tension between Grossman the astute, objective observer and chronicler, and Grossman the war correspondent who must operate within the ideological constraints of Soviet mass media. For example, Grossman is highly critical of the way some Soviet papers are reporting the war: "In a leading article I came across the following phrase: 'The severely battered enemy continued to attack in a cowardly manner.'"[18] He singles out another correspondent for a lack of realism and satirizes the hyperbolic content: "Ivan Pupkin killed 5 Germans with a spoon."[19] Some entries in the notebooks are used verbatim in The People Are Immortal; sometimes they appear with significant changes, highlighting the differences between what Grossman records and what is eventually published.

All the main themes of The People Are Immortal—collaboration, patriotism, desertion, execution, the role of military commissars, Red Army professionalism, and okruzhenie—are dealt with in the notebooks. Of note is that Grossman's view of commissars and other ideological functionaries diverges from the official view that they are exemplars of ideological commitment who enjoy the same level of military competence as Red Army commanders. Grossman's first encounter (after a two-hour wait) with N. Nosov, an editor who is also a regimental commissar, leaves him unimpressed: "I pondered the fact that this comrade was, to put it mildly, not that clever and that it was not even worth waiting two minutes to talk to him."[20] At a meeting presided over by brigade commissar Kozlov, Grossman observes that not all the commissars who are being sent to the front are full of martial ardor, and some of them are trying to shirk their assignments. One of the more impressive commissars Grossman meets is Nikolai Alekseevich Shliapin, whose account of operating behind German lines, followed by a fighting return to the Soviet side, appears to be the basis for the same story in The People Are Immortal. It is entirely possible that the fictional Bogarev is based partly on Shliapin. I say partly because Shliapin is more concerned with practical considerations such as good order, discipline, and morale; he does not engage in the ideological diatribes that Bogarev indulges in. Shliapin's account of one of the more successful breakouts from German encirclement started on 7 July 1941, when a group of soldiers led by General Boldin joined Shliapin's unit and Boldin assumed overall command. The success of Boldin's group and the eventual breakout are, in fact, cited by Stalin in Order № 270 as an example of how Soviet troops should behave when encircled.[21] Many of Grossman's notebook entries report instances of encirclement (okruzhenie), and they describe the chaos, uncertainty, and breakdown of command and control that paralyzed the Red Army in the summer of 1941. One striking omission from these entries is any comment about Soviet soldiers who managed to return to their own lines and were suspected of behaving badly. Thus, Grossman records the case of Captain Glushko, who escaped encirclement, but makes no mention whether the officer was subjected to filtration by the special sections. Another Soviet soldier was captured by the Germans, shot, and left for dead. He survived and managed to get back to Soviet lines, but there is no hint from Grossman that this soldier was regarded with suspicion. An almost identical incident was featured in the Russian television series *Shtrafbat* (The Penal Battalion [2004]): a junior Soviet officer is shot and buried by the Germans, but he manages to return to Soviet lines, whereupon he is arrested on suspicion of being an enemy agent, interrogated, and sent to command a penal battalion as punishment. The mistrust generated by any association with *okruzhenie* inspired paranoia and panic, undermined morale, and led to criminal activity. To quote Grossman:

> Here is a story from a brigade commissar. A technician-quartermaster of the 2nd rank who had recently escaped from encirclement and who, for unknown reasons, suddenly suspected the commissar and commander of a rifle regiment who called in at his hut of espionage, shot them dead in the yard. He took their possessions and money and buried the bodies in a shed. This technician-quartermaster was shot before the assembled command staff of the division. He was shot dead by the oldest colonel.[22]

Another glaring omission in Grossman's notebooks is the absence of any thoughts on encirclement or any mention of Order № 270. The order was read out to all troops down to the company level, and it seems inconceivable that Grossman could be unaware of the order and what it meant. It is possible that Grossman's omission is simply a matter of prudence. Entries that were critical of Stalin and the NKVD certainly could have led to his arrest if the notebooks fell into the wrong hands. Yet there is no reference to, or analysis of, Stalin's two orders (№s 270 and 227) in Grossman's two major postwar novels either: *For a Just Cause* and *Life and Fate*. This is even more unusual because Grossman records in his notebooks that German soldiers have been ordered by Hitler to stand fast—the words he uses are *ni shagu nazad* (not a step backward)—yet at no point does Grossman make any explicit reference to Order № 270 or, later in the summer of 1942, Order № 227.

Grossman's notebooks contain multiple examples of collaboration, desertion, and disaffection with Soviet power, suggesting that not all Soviet citizens viewed the arrival of the Germans as an unmitigated disaster. The behavior of Kotenko in The People Are Immortal was most likely inspired by the following entry: "An old man was waiting for the Germans. He laid a table with a tablecloth and set out food. The Germans came and plundered everything. The old man hanged himself."[23] The reactions of another civilian indicate deep resentment of the Soviet regime: "The old man, the watchman, observes in silence as we pick the apples. He talks about the prerevolutionary owners, recalls all the details, their names, their first names and patronymics. At the moment this is common."[24] This last observation is a concession that dissatisfaction with the Soviet regime is widespread. Grossman cites other examples: schoolteachers who are quite happy to live under German occupation; a husband and wife, both doctors, whose loyalties are split—he joins the partisans, and she serves the Germans.

Numerous examples of poor morale and a breakdown in military discipline are also found in Grossman's notebooks. In an entry dated 13 October 1941, Grossman records that one section deserted to the Germans with the slogan "Down with Soviet Power."[25] In another entry dated 24 October 1941, a commander is reported as saying, "Hitler will drive us to Siberia."[26] Later, in an incident that bears some resemblance to the disciplinary chaos that affected the tsarist army in the latter stages of World War I, the rank and file express outright hostility toward commanders. To quote Grossman: "Red Army soldier Kazakov said to the platoon commander: 'I've been pointing my loaded rifle at you for a long time.'"[27] On occasion, a breakdown in discipline results in summary justice:

> Red Army soldier Evstreev refused to go to his post, justifying his refusal by saying he was wet. On 20 October he deserted his post, having left the machine gun crew. He went to the 7th Company where among the soldiers he said: "The commanders are making fun of us; they're drinking the last drop of our blood and filling their faces." During the conversation with the politruk he got into an argument, declaring that "there'll soon be a time when we'll raise you up on the point of a bayonet as well." The politruk shot him dead with his pistol.[28]

Grossman's wide-ranging observations on the nature of war show him to be a restless investigator trying to understand the complexity of human behavior. Frequently, this leads Grossman to coin aphorisms or make generalizations in the hope of defining some facet of war or formulating some essential truth, much as a scientist (Grossman was a chemist before he turned to writing) would try to describe the behavior of matter in an experiment. Grossman's aphorisms—some are his, and some are collected from others—are analogous to the laws of chemistry and physics: they are epistemological, Tacitean shorthand. Their function is to impose order on the terrifying chaos of war, to permit the author to apprehend what he encounters.

Grossman's aphorisms show that he understands that war is not merely a military phenomenon but one with social and psychological manifestations. Thus, he notes, "Green eyes cut the heart without a knife."[29] Envy, which the party exploited in the collectivization campaign and is using again now, with the arrival of the Germans, is proving to be explosively divisive. Nor could any thinker on the nature of war object to the following: "The spirit (dukh) of an army is a great and elusive force but it is a reality."[30] From commissar Shliapin, Grossman cites the following: "Understanding departs and confusion remains."[31] The original Russian relies on the use of tolk (understanding), as opposed to confusion (bestoloch'): tolk vyidet, a bestoloch' ostanetsia. Shliapin maintains that a commander must see though the chaos and confusion and understand the core, the underlying trends, so that he can formulate a response in the form of orders to troops. Judging by the eminently sensible measures taken by Shliapin to ensure order and discipline, what he means by tolk—and this is what catches Grossman's attention—is that an assessment of any military situation, certainly at the tactical level, must be based on military, not ideological, norms. If military tolk is forced out, ideological bestoloch' will occupy the space, with disastrous results. Later, Grossman clarifies what he means by grasping the moment and the role it plays in the conduct of war: "War is an art. In it coexist elements of calculation, cold knowledge and intellectual experience along with inspiration, chance and something quite irrational (the battle for Zaliman near Pesochin). These elements, they coexist, and sometimes they are hostile to one another. This is like musical improvisation which is inconceivable without brilliant equipment."[32] The notion of war being an art resists any ideological reductionism. It places the commander center stage, and he must exercise his judgment based on training and experience. It provides no obvious function for dual command, the curse of the Red Army.

Two military aphorisms cited in the notebooks are used in The People Are Immortal. Grossman notes: "The dialectic of war consists in the ability to conceal oneself, the ability to save one's life and in the ability to fight and to give one's life."[33] This observation (or something very close to it) forms the basis of the tension between Myshanskii and Bogarev, and even allowing for the contrived ascendancy of the latter over the former, the tension is never decisively resolved in favor of either protagonist. Another insight into the nature of war is taken from an unknown Soviet soldier: "Animals and plants fight for survival but people fight for domination."[34] In The People Are Immortal, Grossman uses this quotation with an important change. Instead of "people," which recognizes a universal propensity to wage war for survival and domination, we find "Germans,"[35] implying that the struggle for domination through war is a uniquely German trait. This might suit the propaganda purposes of Grossman, his editors, and the censor, but the implication that the Germans are somehow biologically unique—even superior—plays into the hands of the NS Herrenvolk propagandists.

Grossman's notebooks are imbued with a deep, unconditional love for Russia and its people. Despite the dreadful calamity that has befallen Russia, there is hope, as suggested by the title The People Are Immortal. Among the women, especially those who seem untouched or unmoved by Soviet power, Grossman detects a wisdom and strength nourished by the folkways of ancient Russia, and especially by its religion. In fact, Grossman the scientist seems fascinated by the enduring strength and tenacity of religious faith. He records that a handwritten leaflet was found in the town of Iampol on which was written: "In the city of Jerusalem the Savior's voice was heard during the morning service: he who prays—just one—shall be saved."[36] Grossman is clearly moved and impressed by the resilience and faith of an old woman he meets in Tula. She dreams of her son, most likely killed at the front, and tells Grossman and his colleagues: "Last night the devil appeared before me and buried his nails into the palm of my hand. I started to pray: 'May God arise and may his enemies be scattered,' but the devil paid no attention. So then I began to curse him in foul language and he went away immediately. And the day before yesterday my son, Vania, came in the night. He sat on the table and looked through the window. I shouted 'Vania, Vania' but he kept quiet the whole time, looking through the window."[37] This grieving mother's reaction to the loss of her son is related to old Russia (Rus') rather than the Soviet period with its aggressive state-sponsored atheism. Her complete and simple faith in God, her generosity when she herself has so little, identifies her with the ethos of the Holy Fool, the iurodivaia, which is most likely the inspiration for the mysterious Bogachikha in The People Are Immortal. At the time, Grossman was agonizing over the fate of his own mother, last heard of in Berdichev, and he writes as if he and his colleagues have encountered the very soul of Mother Russia:

> If we are victorious in this terrible, cruel war then it will be because among us there are magnificent hearts in the depths of the people, such righteous people possessing such a magnificent soul which desires nothing, like these old women, the mothers of those sons who in great simplicity lay down their heads "for their brothers," so easily, so generously like this old woman from Tula, this impoverished old woman who gave of her food, her light, her firewood and her salt. These hearts, like the righteous ones in the Bible illuminate with their strange light our entire people, their cupped hands: but they shall be victorious.[38]

The words used by the woman to chastise the devil—*Da voskresnet Bog i ras-tochatsia vragi Ego* (Let God arise, let his enemies be scattered)—are taken from the book of Psalms. The full English version reads: "Let God arise, let his enemies be scattered: let them also that hate him flee before him" (Psalms 68:1). This citation from the Bible is somewhat out of place in a society where atheism has become the official cult, supposedly displacing Russian Orthodoxy.[39] Moreover, when the woman prays that those who hate God will flee, this cannot apply solely to the German invaders. When Grossman acknowledges the role of these righteous ones in the struggle, he is recognizing the limitations of Soviet ideology (Marxism-Leninism) to move hearts and bodies in the fight for survival—something implied in the view that the "the people are immortal."

Alexander Bek, *The Volokolamsk Highway* (1943–1944)

Set in the autumn of 1941, *The Volokolamsk Highway* is an account of the Red Army's desperate and ultimately successful attempts to stem the German advance on Moscow.[40] In Soviet terms, the themes covered by Bek are highly controversial: encirclement, cowardice, desertion, Soviet military competence, the trustworthiness of the Soviet media, and the multiethnic solidarity of the Soviet Union. The narrative device adopted by Bek is to embed (to use contemporary jargon) a journalist with a Soviet infantry regiment and have him try to persuade the Kazakh regimental commander, Baurdzhan Momysh-Uly, to recount his experiences as a senior lieutenant and battalion commander in the battle for Moscow two years previously. This is a useful device, as the overall effect is that of a documentary based on a series of extended interviews with the Soviet commander. The interviewee now enjoys the elite status of a Guards colonel, and he initially refuses to be interviewed because, as he tells the journalist, "Lying is hateful to me and you will not write the truth."[41] He eventually relents, which enhances the reliability and veracity of the story.

Whether prompted by death, German military prowess, encirclement, or isolation, fear is the dominant theme in The Volokolamsk Highway, and Momysh-Uly spends much of his time trying to counter its effects so his men will not succumb. To begin with, the commander criticizes the journalist for writing stories that portray Soviet soldiers as "supernatural beings." This criticism is somewhat cynical, since the bulk of Soviet writing does indeed portray soldiers as supermen and as people who are bereft of normal feelings. Momysh-Uly's view, which is very much in line with Soviet pedagogy and education, is that heroism can be taught or inculcated; it is not innate. The purpose here is to challenge the idea that the Germans are innately superior—a view held by a lot of Soviet soldiers—and thus prepare them to stand fast when ordered to do so. Implicitly conceded here is that much of German behavior and doctrine is superior to its Soviet counterpart. Apart from references to "suddenness" (vnezapnost'), this story makes no attempt to explain why the Red Army was caught so woefully unprepared on 22 June 1941.

Momysh-Uly's approach to dealing with fear is that it can be overcome by appeals to duty, loyalty, comradeship, Rodina (motherland), and, when necessary, ruthless measures against desertion and cowardice. These methods adopted by Momysh-Uly have been used by armies throughout history; the missing consideration is the competence of Soviet commanders and whether they inspire confidence in their men. Desertion, apathy, and a general state of apprehension cannot be attributed solely to faint hearts and cowardice. Soldiers have a right, at the very minimum, to be led by competent officers. When that competence is lacking—and is clearly understood to be lacking—soldiers will not be willing to take risks, and who can blame them? Competent commanders inspire a sense of loyalty to themselves and to the greater cause. Thus, when Momysh-Uly and his colleagues look to overcome fear among their men—especially the fear of German military prowess, which they see as the fundamental problem—they are obliged to consider their own roles as commanders.

Momysh-Uly's encounter with the psychological effects of encirclement (*okruzhenie*) occurs very early in *The Volokolamsk Highway*. As his battalion digs in, anticipating the German advance, small groups of Red Army soldiers from scattered units that have escaped the German net try to pass through the battalion lines. Momysh-Uly interrogates these soldiers, trying to ascertain what they mean by encirclement, since he admits, "On that morning I heard this word for the first time."[42] Of course, Momysh-Uly's claim is totally disingenuous: the problem of encirclement and retreat started the moment the war began, and encirclement was a major theme in Stalin's Order № 270, which was read to all the troops. It is simply not plausible that Momysh-Uly, a Red Army battalion commander preparing to defend the approaches to Moscow in the late autumn of 1941, had not already encountered the dreaded Russian O-word (*okruzhenie*) or that he was not familiar with the contents of Order № 270. In any case, the NKVD would have jolted his memory. There are two other consequences of Momysh-Uly's professed ignorance of *okruzhenie*: First, it undermines his credibility as a reliable witness and someone who cannot stand lying. Whether he approves of Stalin's thoughts on *okruzhenie* or not, Momysh-Uly is duty bound by Order № 270. That he is not undercuts his standing as a competent commander. Second, it points to the fact that Momysh-Uly has not been trained to deal with the tactical situation of encirclement, and when confronted with the facts on the ground, he is unable to adapt to the unfolding situation.

The point that emerges is that the soldiers are retreating because that is all they have ever done: flight and retreat are all they know. This is the precise state of mind that helps the Germans and that must be countered. Momysh-Uly's ire is aroused when one soldier, who is not wearing his badges of rank, tells him that he is a lieutenant, a platoon commander: "I don't know whether something changed in my face but something inside of me felt as if it had been hit: how could a platoon commander, a lieutenant, an officer of the Red Army flee, flee, in the guise of an ordinary soldier, from the front along with Red Army soldiers?"[43] Removing one's badges of rank constitutes a violation of military discipline, since it undermines the distance between commander and commanded. This becomes even more important for morale and discipline when troops are being subjected to the stresses of battle. However, removing one's badges of rank might be a reasonable precaution, especially for officers, in view of Hitler's Commissar Order. German soldiers might not be too assiduous when it comes to ascertaining whether a captured Red Army infantry officer is a military commissar or not. The other obvious point is, if this is the first time Momysh-Uly has encountered *okruzhenie*, why does he make no attempt to understand what has happened. The fact that he orders these soldiers to be arrested as deserters indicates that the default position of Soviet military discipline is a presumption of wrongdoing.

The same almost irrational, even fearful attitude toward encirclement and *okruzhentsy* appears near the end of the story when Momysh-Uly's own battalion—which is now encircled—is preparing to break through to the Soviet lines and encounters a group of stragglers. Momysh-Uly's instinctive response is to regard them as deserters and outcasts or, to use his word, *postoronnie*—an unusual term for one's Red Army comrades, regardless of the circumstances: "Once again my mood was gloomy: 'out of encirclement.' This word once again, which seemed to indicate some kind of an agreement, these wanderers in army greatcoats repeated it as they tramped across our lines from the Viaz'ma region. This word which forced itself on one's ears had become hateful."[44] What makes Momysh-Uly's attitude toward these stragglers disingenuous is that in Soviet terms, and certainly as far as the NKVD is concerned, both the stragglers and the men of Momysh-Uly's battalion, even if it retains the order and cohesion of a military unit, are soldiers who have been encircled and thus must be subjected to filtration.

Another incident reveals the brittle state of the Red Army. Momysh-Uly test-fires a machine gun in a forward position. The alarm is raised, and the Soviet soldiers start to abandon the position. Eventually, they are halted. In the course of this embarrassing episode, the section commander shoots himself in the hand; he is guilty of self-inflicted wounding—he is a *samostrel*. Momysh-Uly orders that the soldier be shot *pered stroem*. He justifies his decision to execute the traitor (is he a traitor?): "I am a human being. Everything human in me screamed: 'don't do this, show mercy, forgive!' But I didn't forgive. I am the commander, the father. I killed a son but several hundreds of sons stood before me. I was obliged by blood to imprint upon their souls that there never is and never will be mercy for a traitor!"[45]

This execution raises a whole series of questions about the demand for loyalty in the Soviet context. Momysh-Uly sees himself as something of an unforgiving biblical patriarch who, to protect the majority of his sons from the moral contamination of treachery, is obliged to have the traitor son killed. This represents a Soviet view of father and son. Whenever Momysh-Uly talks of *Rodina* (uppercase), it is always a *Soviet* motherland, whereas the motherland of the Kazakhs, Belorussians, Russians, and Ukrainians is always *rodina* (lowercase). In this regard, it should be noted that the battalion comprises one-third Kazakhs; the rest are Russians and Ukrainians. From a propagandistic point of view, this implies an integrated, multiethnic battalion united by love of the Soviet *Rodina*. In practical terms, differences in language, culture, and national allegiances are likely to assert themselves in the stress of battle and cause divisions. Nor is there any doubt about the economic policies of the *Rodina*: it is a "socialist *Rodina*,"[46] which in the case of Kazakhstan, represents a direct threat to the self-sufficient way of life of the steppe nomads. Momysh-Uly's own father is one such nomad.

Thus, when giving the order to kill the soldier, Momysh-Uly refers to him as "a traitor to the Motherland (*Rodina*) and violator of his oath."[47] The traitor's behavior is contrasted with that of another soldier, also a Kazakh, who is doing his duty to the Soviet *Rodina*, a long way from his own *rodina*. In fact, Bek conflates the Stavka, Stalin, the Kremlin, and the *Rodina*, a conflation that is reaffirmed when a politruk tells the soldiers that German fascism "treacherously attacked our Motherland [*Rodina*]."[48] The wording and the assertion are a direct allusion to Stalin's speech of 3 July 1941. Neither Bek nor Momysh-Uly provides any obvious reason why Kazakhs should be fighting in Russia for the Soviet Union. The uncontested assumption is not only that Soviet nationalism is an effective supranationalism but also that it is superior to any sense of Kazakh, Russian, or Ukrainian national identity. If loyalty to the Soviet *Rodina* trumps all other manifestations of national loyalty, this can only mean that in any conflict between, say, Kazakhstan and the Soviet Union, Soviet interests must predominate. Kazakhs (or Ukrainians) who draw attention to the human catastrophe of collectivization are acting in a way that is hostile to the Soviet *Rodina*.

Momysh-Uly's musings on shame and its role in combat motivation are also related to the theme of *Rodina* versus *rodina*: "Shame . . . have you ever thought about what shame is? If a soldier's sense of shame is killed in war; if this inner, condemnatory voice falls silent, no instruction, no discipline will move an army."[49] His thoughts on shame, the inner voice that commands duty, are undoubtedly correct and applicable to all soldiers in all armies. The complicating factor in the Soviet context is that, before the war, the regime tried to destroy any sense of individual shame in order to destroy any loyalty to individuals and families. In any conflict between the state and one's family, loyalty to one's village and family was deemed ideologically dubious—the new meaning of shameful. Shame is now something controlled by the state. Once the instinct to feel shame is suppressed, the inner voice cannot easily be heard. The other problem is that the source of shame is deeply rooted in the teachings of religion, shared history, culture, and language. Shame is based not on religious teaching alone but on a sense of loyalty to the past—to something bigger and more enduring than the individual. It is not clear that the worldview of Marxism-Leninism or any other materialist doctrine can ever be an adequate substitute. This inadequacy is revealed in musings from Momysh-Uly when he imagines the voice of shame taking control of soldiers deserting the battlefield: "No, stop! Flight is baseness and shame! You'll be despised as a coward! Stop, fight, be a worthy son of the Motherland [Rodina]."[50] The Russian word for son (syn) has both an abstract and a biological meaning, and they are differentiated by declension. When Momysh-Uly talks of a son of the motherland, he uses son as something abstract, figurative, and above all ideological. There is, I suggest, a mismatch between how soldiers see themselves—sons of real mothers—and how their masters see them—sons of some ideological construct that is cruel, unforgiving, rapacious, and hostile to their respective rodinas.

In addition to shame, patriotism is used by commanders to inspire a sense of duty. Again, there is an inherent and irreconcilable contradiction between Soviet patriotism and, say, Kazakh or Russian patriotism, as explained by Alexander Solzhenitsyn: "Patriotism is a feeling of total and permanent love for one's Motherland, with a readiness to make sacrifices for her, to share her misfortunes, without any obsequiousness, without any support for unjust claims, and openness in the assessment of her flaws, sins, and repentance for them."[51] If Solzhenitsyn is correct, Soviet patriotism cannot be an effective replacement for the love of Russia or Ukraine, principally because it is an ideological construct. Solzhenitsyn's warts-and-all patriotism that acknowledges flaws and sins represents a complete rejection of ideological Soviet patriotism. Furthermore, the etymology of the word patriotism draws on the notion that the nation is the father, and this patriarch is represented by a king or, in Russia's case, a tsar. But because of the brutal murder of the Russian royal family—the death of the father, a direct assault on Russian patriotism—the very notion of Soviet patriotism is irrevocably damaged or even doomed. Soviet patriotism will command the general loyalty of those with a predilection for political abstractions, but soldiers facing death are not moved or motivated by political abstractions.

Among the details of desertion, execution, and the fear and loathing aroused by okruzhenie in The Volokolamsk Highway, there are no direct references to the NKVD special sections: the NKVD acronym is entirely absent.

This is unusual because the NKVD played a major role in countering desertion and carrying out executions. By creating a situation in which Momysh-Uly takes it upon himself to have the *samostrel* shot without recourse to a military court, Bek bypasses the NKVD altogether. However, the NKVD's presence is hinted at by Captain Shilov, introduced by Momysh-Uly as follows: "He was not wearing a felt, ear-flapped cap, like all the soldiers and commanders of Panfilov's division but was wearing a camouflaged forage cap with infantry crimson edging. He uttered not a single word but even this manner of keeping silent, until addressed by a senior officer, along with his uniform and bearing betrayed a professional soldier."[52] The distinctive headgear with the crimson edging strongly suggests that Shilov is an NKVD officer and that the unit he commands is a blocking detachment that will be deployed against Momysh-Uly's battalion should it retreat without orders to do so. The apparently casual reference to Shilov's rounding up stragglers, *otstavshie*, implies barrier service (*zagriaditel'naia sluzhba*), a task routinely carried out by the NKVD.

Although *The Volokolamsk Highway* offers a flawed view of Soviet patriotism and the meaning of duty and shame in this context, it nevertheless reads something like a military instruction manual. General Panfilov, the division commander, instructs Momysh-Uly (echoing Napoleon's advice to commanders) that he must not wait for the Germans to attack but must seek an engagement: "Don't wait for an opportunity, go look for one."[53] To this end, Momysh-Uly dispatches large fighting patrols to engage the enemy and, he hopes, break the spell cast by the Germans. Momysh-Uly is also a proponent of the tactical and strategic advantages of surprise (*vnezapnost'*), seeing it first and foremost as a psychological weapon: "A blow to the psyche! Clearly this has been known since ancient times. And since ancient times this has been achieved by surprise [*vnezapnost'*]. And does not the art of battle, the art of tactics reside in the use of surprise to shatter the enemy and to protect one's own troops from the same effect of surprise?"[54] This undoubtedly has relevance for 22 June 1941 and underpins much of the success of the Blitzkrieg doctrine, which Momysh-Uly now regards as a failure: "One of the tactical principles of Blitzkrieg used by the Germans, evident in Poland, Holland, Belgium and France, was, as is well known, as follows: the Germans, having penetrated the line of the front at various points, surged forward, leaving scattered, isolated and demoralized enemy units behind them. In the area around Moscow the Hitlerites failed to do that."[55] On its face, this assessment is hardly contentious, although Bek fails to point out what Germany, in collusion with its erstwhile ally the Soviet Union, did to Poland. What made Blitzkrieg so successful in western Europe—shorter distances, vastly superior infrastructure (roads and railways), and far less demanding logistical problems—did not apply in the European zones of western Russia. There, the German army encountered much harsher terrain (in both summer and winter), poor road and rail communications, and a huge landmass, all of which complicated the German task. By themselves, these factors in the east would not automatically doom the Blitzkrieg doctrine—so brilliantly successful in western Europe, the Balkans, and Crete—to failure in western Russia. Critical factors included timing and the ability to make maximum use of good weather before the onset of autumnal rains and winter proper. Bek is correct to point out that the Germans failed to take Moscow, although it is not clear that this amounts to a failure of Blitzkrieg. By the time the Germans commenced the operation to capture Moscow, the war on the Eastern Front was five months old. This was no longer Blitzkrieg, since the element of surprise had long since been lost. By the time the Germans reached Podmoskov'e, the Blitzkrieg phase had passed, and the inevitable laws of space, time, manpower, and industrial capacity were slowly and perceptibly turning in favor of the Soviet state as it mobilized for total war. Even if the German assault on Moscow ground to a halt, this failure to take Moscow was not a failure of the Blitzkrieg doctrine per se or, indeed, of the post-Blitzkrieg phase of operations. Blitzkrieg provided the operational platform for the Germans to launch their attack on Moscow. Moreover, the mere fact that the Germans were able to achieve tactical surprise (vnezapnost') and had achieved other military successes by the time of the Moscow assault suggests that Blitzkrieg did not fail at all. Had Barbarossa been initiated in early May 1941, Moscow might well have fallen. In another respect, Bek (or rather, his narrator) unwittingly confirms the success of Blitzkrieg. If the psychological impact of Blitzkrieg had been fully eradicated, the shock-and-awe legacy of 22 June 1941 would have been eradicated as well. But in October and November 1941, Bek's narrator and his mentor, Panfilov, are still obsessively pondering ways to overcome the awe inspired by the Germans. The prominence of the themes of desertion, okruzhenie, and overcoming fear demonstrates that the effects of vnezapnost' and its corollary Blitzkrieg have not been fully eradicated.

Konstantin Simonov, *The Living and the Dead* (1959)

Published after Stalin's death, during the literary thaw of the late 1950s and early 1960s, *The Living and the Dead* remains one of the best accounts of the early part of the war. It reveals in painful detail the complete chaos caused by the German attack and the inability of too many senior Soviet officers to prosecute modern war. Simonov, anticipating Baklanov's *Iiul' 41 goda* (July 1941 [1965]), addresses the question of how the Germans were able to achieve such devastating surprise along the front. Why was nothing done in time? Why were so many frontline units without commanders on the first day of the war? Very early in the narrative, Simonov provides some overt signs and hints that many Soviet units are fleeing the battle zone without offering any resistance to the Germans. The two main characters in the novel are Sintsov, a political instructor (politruk) who undergoes a series of trials that raise some contentious issues in the first months of the war, and Serpilin, a senior officer whose loyalty to Stalin and the Soviet state remains steadfast despite his arrest in 1937.

Soviet readiness, or the lack thereof, emerges somewhat innocently in the opening paragraph: "Like millions of other families the first day of the war caught the Sintsov family completely unaware. A war, it seemed, had long been expected but even so at the very last moment it came crashing down like snow on one's head. Obviously, it was quite impossible to prepare oneself in advance for such a massive misfortune."[56] On one level, this apparently matter-of-fact introduction conveys the state of mind of millions of Soviet citizens when they learned that the Germans had attacked the Soviet Union on Sunday, 22 June 1941. Yet this opening statement also hints at a far more serious question: were the state agencies charged with being alert to external threats and taking the necessary countermeasures up to the job? Individuals and families might be caught unawares, but that should not be true of the state and its agencies. Again, it might be impossible for an individual to prepare for such a shock, but surely it is the state's duty to prepare itself for this eventuality. Ultimately, this is Stalin's failing.

Despite a severely disrupted rail network, Sintsov heads toward the front on a train that is full of politruks and commanders of the Western Special Military District. He ponders why so many of these essential personnel were absent from their posts, given the expectation of war: "How could this happen when a perception of a looming war had been hanging in the air since April, neither Sintsov nor the other soldiers on leave could understand. . . . People who were guilty of nothing felt themselves to be guilty and became very nervous at every long stop."[57] The reference to April is another criticism of Stalin and the state agencies (a few pages later, Sintsov says there was a smell of war in the air six months ago). Moreover, the fact that the Soviet Union has finally been attacked by a real enemy and not by Trotskyite phantoms, the legacy of the purges (never very far away in this novel), is implied by the sense of nervousness. Those who are "guilty of nothing," like the commanders were in 1937–1938, fear that they will be arrested as scapegoats. In fact, Simonov's specific reference to the obvious unease of the officers of the Western Special Military District may be construed as a pointer toward the fate of General Pavlov, the real-life commander of that district.

The stunning success of the Luftwaffe in destroying so many Soviet planes on the ground naturally raises the question of why the Red Air Force was so comprehensively outplayed and crushed. Some of the answers emerge in the fate of Simonov's character Lieutenant General Kozyrev, who is shot down in one of the early air battles. It turns out that Kozyrev, a Hero of the Soviet Union, is a famous air ace who served in Spain and was lionized in the Soviet papers. With his spine and legs broken after bailing out of his aircraft, Kozyrev reflects on his career:

> And for the first time in his life he cursed the day and hour—of which before he had always been proud—when, after Khalkin-Gol, Stalin had summoned him and promoting him directly from the rank of colonel to lieutenant general, had appointed him to command the fighter arm of an entire district.
>
> Now, staring death in the face there was nobody to lie to: he was not up to the job of commanding anyone apart from himself and his squadron. In essence, he became a general but remained a senior lieutenant. This was confirmed from the very first day of the war in the most dreadful manner and by no means with him alone. These lightning promotions, such as his, were the result of his impeccable bravery and the awards paid for in blood. But he did not know that the general's stars given to others and to him conferred no ability to command thousands of people and hundreds of aircraft.[58]

On its face, this personal failure might be dismissed as just that, but it hints at the consequences of the purges that struck the Soviet armed forces in 1937–1938. The rapid promotions enjoyed by Kozyrev and his colleagues, based on their successes in Spain and the Far East, were made possible by the mass culling of senior officers in all three services and the need to replace them. The normal sequence of promotion, based on progression through the necessary staff courses and mastery of command and control, did not take place. The following observation goes to the heart of what went wrong, at least in the Soviet air force, in the period leading up to 22 June 1941:

> He [Kozyrev] recalled his lack of concern about the fact that a war would begin and how badly he commanded when it started; he recalled his aerodromes where half the aircraft were not combat ready, the aircraft burned on the ground, his pilots desperately trying to take off under bombardment and dying without managing to gain sufficient height; he recalled his own contradictory orders, which he, crushed and stunned, issued in the first days, hurtling about in his fighter and saving almost nothing at all.[59]

Kozyrev's unsuitability for high command is further demonstrated when a radio message from a colleague goads him into setting off alone to fight the Germans. It may suit Simonov's purposes to cast the brave Kozyrev as one of the scapegoats for the disaster, but the responsibility extends much higher. Kozyrev's admission that he largely ignored the possibility of war is a barely hidden pointer to Kozyrev's superiors and, above all, Stalin. Simonov is once again hinting at what befell General Pavlov, who (like Kozyrev) served in the Spanish Civil War, was awarded the Hero of the Soviet Union, and enjoyed rapid promotion. From a professional point of view, Pavlov was completely overwhelmed by the German assault. Arrested and shot, he was, quite apart from his own shortcomings, a convenient scapegoat for his master. This is implied by Kozyrev, who echoes the opening sentence of The Living and the Dead: "Indeed, the war caught them unawares; they had not managed to rearm; and indeed many others and he had commanded badly and lost their nerve from the very beginning."[60] This is a truly shattering indictment of the Soviet military under the control of Stalin.[61]

In contrast to Kozyrev, brigade commander Serpilin, who is eventually promoted to the rank of general, exemplifies the competent and loyal Soviet commanders who were arrested during the purges. Serpilin is a dedicated soldier of the revolution. While teaching at an academy, he is arrested and sent to Kolyma. Assuming that Germany is the Soviet Union's most likely enemy, Serpilin has been learning German and keeping abreast of the latest developments in tactics and doctrine. In other words, he is a thorough professional, whereas Kozyrev's bravery and revolutionary enthusiasm are not enough. However, in the context of 1937–1938, Serpilin's preparations for war clearly imply a criticism of the belief that Germany poses no threat, and they lead to his arrest. He is charged with possessing German field manuals, learning German, and stressing in his lectures the tactical doctrine being developed in the Wehrmacht. In the paranoia of the Great Terror, he is deemed guilty of disseminating "propaganda about the superiority of the fascist army."[62] Soon after the German invasion, Serpilin is released and reinstated. His attitude about what has befallen him is disconcerting and perplexing, since it provokes no reassessment of his attitude toward the Soviet state. He considers his arrest and incarceration "to be a monstrous misunderstanding, a mistake, a stupid error. And communism was and remained for him a sacred and unsullied cause."[63] Serpilin's loyalty is not exceptional either in Soviet-Russian war literature or among the biographies of real victims of the purges who were arrested and then released.

One flaw in Serpilin's reasoning is that it provides no clear explanation of why so many of his colleagues were also arrested, incarcerated, and shot. All these arrests and executions cannot plausibly be dismissed as a series of monstrous errors. On the contrary, they point toward something planned and systematic that Serpilin either chooses not to see or is prevented from seeing by his loyalty to the "sacred and unsullied cause." One unintended consequence of Simonov's attempt to reconcile Serpilin the reinstated victim of 1937–1938 with Serpilin the loyal soldier of the Soviet regime is that if Serpilin will not or cannot recognize that there is something fundamentally wrong with the Stalin regime, it provides some support for Stalin and his failure to see the panzer juggernaut hurtling toward him. It mitigates Stalin's failure to act in good time and in good order, but it also undermines Serpilin's implied criticism of Stalin's failure to act. In the same way that Serpilin is unable to see the real nature of the Stalin regime, Stalin is unable or unwilling to see the real nature of Hitler's intentions. Toward the end of the novel, after Serpilin has successfully led the remnants of his division out of *okruzhenie*, the issue of Soviet readiness for war emerges in a conversation between Serpilin and a colleague, Ivan Alekseevich, who works in the Soviet General Staff:

> Listen, said Serpilin, having leaned over the table and looking him
> directly in the eyes, you were occupying the very same place on the eve
> of the war. Tell me: how did it happen that we didn't know and if we

did know why did you not report it? And if he did not listen, why did
you not insist? Tell me: I just can't be satisfied with what I know. I've
been thinking about this since the first day at the front. I've not asked
anybody, but I'm asking you.[64]

Serpilin does not indict Stalin, yet he cannot fully reconcile Stalin's supposedly high regard for the army and the events of 1937–1938: "For whom was
this necessary? And how could Stalin allow this to happen?"[65]

Caught up in the Soviet retreat soon after the start of the war, Sintsov observes firsthand how the Soviet agencies grapple with the escalating problem
of tens of thousands of Red Army soldiers who have become separated from
their units in the chaos caused by the German advance. A troika is hastily
convened to try deserters and other suspicious types, and Sintsov is enlisted
to keep the records. German air attacks are expected, so the military judge
setting up the troika orders, "Now we'll dig the trenches and then we can
get to work."[66] Under the circumstances, this seems normal. The word he
uses, *shchel'*, is a slit trench required in the event of air attacks. However,
in the context of dispensing rough summary justice to deserters, the word
is ambiguous, and a *shchel'* can be construed as a grave for those who will
be shot. Digging graves before the accused have been tried indicates a due
process based on the presumption of guilt, not innocence. This, of course,
is the principle of revolutionary, party, fast-track justice under which the
prewar troikas operated during the Great Terror. This parallel with the
purges is also implied by the death of a Red Army soldier who, having lost his
mind, screams and shouts, urging people to run to avoid being surrounded.
After he has been shot, a captain says of the soldier's death: "A dog's death
for a dog."[67] This was the favored phrase of Vyshinskii, Stalin's tame judge,
during the purges. Hurriedly convened, the troika to which Sintsov has
been assigned also works with indecent haste. There is neither the time nor
the willingness to hear the detainees' full stories, so innocent men will be
punished. The Sintsov-Simonov view of these detained soldiers is markedly
different from that found in *The Volokolamsk Highway*:

And the main thing was that nearly all those detained were neither
saboteurs, nor spies nor deserters, they were simply moving from one
place to another, searching for some person or other or something and
did not find anything because everything had become displaced and
moved from its positions. Coming under shell fire and bombardments

and having heard all the horrors of the German airborne landings and tanks, several of them, fearing captivity, buried and in some cases tore up their documents.[68]

Given the circumstances of the retreat, this is an entirely reasonable assessment. Of great importance here is the vexed question of documentation, which plays a major role in Sintsov's fate.

Much of the plot in The Living and the Dead is driven by the military reality of okruzhenie and the way Soviet agencies—in particular, the special section of the NKVD—treated okruzhentsy. This affects both Sintsov and Serpilin: Serpilin leads his division back to the Soviet lines; Sintsov, having survived encirclement once, finds himself encircled again and is regarded with profound suspicion once he makes it back to the Soviet lines a second time—this time, without his documents and party card. Okruzhenie is exhausting both physically and psychologically; then, once the ordeal is over, the soldiers are presumed to be guilty of some offense—desertion, cowardice, or espionage—until the NKVD is satisfied that they are not. For most Western readers of Soviet-Russian war novels, the NKVD's obsession with okruzhentsy seems unjust and cruel, since the Western attitude toward Allied escapees is to admire their skill and determination, not to suspect that they have returned to do the bidding of the German or Japanese intelligence services or that, because they were encircled or captured, they are cowards.

No sooner have Serpilin and his men returned to the Soviet lines than the full weight of an NKVD investigation is brought to bear on them. Wounded, Serpilin is immediately transferred by plane to Moscow. This indicates that he is not entirely trusted and, in view of his past, will be interrogated to ascertain his loyalty.[69] The same fate is about to befall the remnants of the division when a three-member commission, including a representative of the NKVD, turns up. The soldiers are formally congratulated on their successful return, but there is obviously a presumption of guilt and wrongdoing. For example, until all the necessary formalities have been completed, the soldiers are to be regarded not as a military unit but "as a group temporarily formed in conditions of encirclement, which as such has already completed its tasks, and since that is the case now it no longer exists as a group and those who have been charged with taking an interest in this matter will henceforth consider the question of each person individually, taking into account their rank and appointment and how each one conducted himself in encirclement."[70]

Revealed here are some insights into the methodology of the NKVD and its special sections and just how damaging they are to military morale. The unit has been fighting for more than three months—since the start of the war—and the remnants have made their way back to Soviet lines. The very factors Serpilin used to raise morale and instill fighting spirit and, above all, divisional pride—the divisional banner (*znamia*) plays a special role—are now being systematically dismantled and undermined by this troika as a prelude to filtration. The very qualities that helped the men make it back are now deemed a threat. For this reason, the troika wants to remove them from the front line as soon as possible, thus physically and *psychologically* separating them from other soldiers at the front. This NKVD policy is clearly intended to destroy any group or unit identity, solidarity, and pride in arms so that each soldier can be interrogated individually and subjected to all the ploys and ruses of the divide-and-rule policy. This explains why they are regarded not as a unit but merely as a group of soldiers. The men's status as soldiers has been removed by this bureaucratic sleight of hand, and their transport in a vehicle convoy observing strict intervals suggests that they are being treated as prisoners under escort, not as soldiers who have done their duty. Similarly, the NKVD officer, Major Danilov, insists that the men hand over all weapons. Initially, one presumes that he means only enemy weapons captured along the way, but a challenge from Shmakov, Serpilin's commissar, makes it clear that Danilov's order refers to all weapons: "And why do we have to hand them over?—said Shmakov—captured or issued weapons, these are our weapons, we made our way back with them. What do we have to hand them over for?"[71] Given that this is a war zone, the demand for the weapons makes no sense, unless its real purpose is to disarm soldiers who are suspected of wrongdoing and might offer armed resistance. The prerogatives of the NKVD are confirmed by Danilov: "Military personnel being sent for sorting and formation are not permitted to bear arms and in any case not captured weapons. The weapons are to be handed over and not to be taken into the rear area. Here, there is nothing more to be said."[72] It should be noted that the standard NKVD jargon for the process of interrogating and vetting *okruzhentsy* is filtration (*fil'tratsiia*), not sorting (*sortirovka*), as used by Danilov.

The question of loyalty also surfaces because so many of Serpilin's men have exited *okruzhenie* armed with German weapons. They have discarded their Soviet-issued, bolt-operated Mosin 1891/1930 rifles in favor of the much-prized German MP 38 machine pistols. This is not only a rejection of Soviet small arms but also a criticism of the Red Army's failure to provide suitable numbers of handheld automatic weapons, which gave the German infantry a huge advantage in the close-quarter encounter.

When he is alone with Shmakov, Danilov tacitly refers to filtration: "While we have still not got to know your people, and you know them, how in your opinion—he emphasized the words 'in your opinion,' making it clear that that opinion was for him by no means the end of the matter—are you able to answer for each one of the people that came out of encirclement with you?"[73] Shmakov's reply is that by returning to Soviet lines, rather than staying with the Germans, they have answered the question. Danilov is concerned that some of the men might be spies. (It would have been interesting to see Danilov's reaction to the fact that Shmakov had picked up a German agitprop leaflet and given it to Serpilin.)[74] The plausibility of Shmakov's position is partially undermined when he tells Danilov that he served in the All-Russian Special Commission for Combating Counterrevolution, Speculation, and Sabotage, one of the organizational precursors of the NKVD. Again, in response to Danilov's warnings about "vigilance," Shmakov insists that one must have faith in one's men: "Without belief this is not vigilance but suspicion, panic!"[75] Shmakov is hinting at the mind-set of the Great Terror and the purges. This is all well and good, but did Shmakov believe that Trotskii, Tukhachevskii, and the others were guilty, or did he lack revolutionary vigilance?

Further differences are revealed between the institutional ethos of the NKVD and that of the Red Army. When a unit manages to return to Soviet lines, a formal parade is held to mark its return. Danilov insists that this parade be held in the rear—one suspects that this is a ploy, since once the men are transferred to the rear and separated, there will be no parade—but another officer secures the military commander's permission to hold the parade at the front. Evident here is a struggle for supremacy and authority between the NKVD and the professional military.

Danilov's insistence that all the captured weapons be handed over before their journey to the rear leaves some three-quarters of the men unarmed. This leads to disaster and slaughter when they come in contact with the fast-moving enemy. But before he is hoisted by his own petard, Danilov ponders the situation of the *okruzhentsy*: "It is one thing when soldiers come out of encirclement alone, in twos and threes, without uniform and documents and another matter when a whole military unit breaks through retaining its weapons, documents and badges of rank."[76] This distinction is not entirely plausible. There are cases of soldiers escaping in small groups, and in fact, this improves their chances of success.

Units of the SS destroy the largely unarmed column, leading to the very circumstances that Danilov finds so suspicious—soldiers escaping in twos and threes. Sintsov, accompanied by Zolotarev (a Red Army soldier who plays an important role in Sintsov's final rehabilitation) and a female medical orderly, escape the butchery and head east. Zolotarev retains his Soviet-issued rifle, the orderly has a revolver, and Sintsov is unarmed. This is not a military unit but a group of desperate survivors, and Danilov's ideas about the proper behavior in *okruzhenie* are rendered ridiculous. They leave the injured medical orderly with a woodcutter and his stepdaughter. To hide her real identity in the event the Germans turn up, she now wears civilian clothing and decides either to bury her documents or to give them to Sintsov. Under the circumstances, these are all sensible measures, yet they conflict with Danilov's idea of what is appropriate, never mind Stalin's. The same decision-making approach applies to the revolver. Sintsov gets rid of it and tells the orderly: if the Germans don't turn up, she won't need it, and if they do, having the gun would be fatal for her and her hosts. This is sound reasoning, yet in Danilov's scheme of things, it amounts to a dereliction of duty or something worse.

This is Sintsov's second time facing *okruzhenie* and its aftermath, and documents play a crucial role in his life. Indeed, one of the critical themes in the novel is the obsession with documents, as this is reflected in the title: the living have documents; the dead do not. Without documentation, a person exists in some bureaucratic no-man's-land, like one of the living dead. In part, this obsession with documents arises from the very real and justified fear of German saboteurs and spies. There is, however, a specifically Soviet and Stalinist dimension that predates the war and relates to the frequent re-registration of party members and purges of party ranks when "unreliable and hostile elements" were expelled. Retention of one's documents—especially the all-important party membership card—is a test of loyalty. Thus, party bureaucrats and the NKVD assume that any soldier, politruk, or military commissar who returns without the necessary documentation has committed some offense.

Sintsov's nightmarish ordeal begins when Zolotarev, believing that Sintsov has been killed in a German bombardment, removes his documents and his jacket, with its badges of rank. This saves Sintsov's life when he is captured by the Germans; because he is not identified as a political functionary, he escapes summary execution (another hint from Simonov that Danilov's approach is wrong). Zolotarev hands the documents over to a senior officer, where they languish until they eventually come to light to rescue Sintsov's honor and corroborate his story—which is also supported by the written statement submitted by Zolotarev upon his return to Soviet lines. In Soviet terms, this is a happy outcome. However, before this moment of vindication and ideological salvation, Sintsov undergoes a series of grueling adventures—he is captured by the Germans, escapes, and undertakes an exhausting trek before returning to Soviet lines, only to find Moscow under siege and on the verge of mass panic. Sintsov's path to salvation begins with his acceptance into a militia unit that is defending Moscow. He distinguishes himself in battle and is decorated. In the end, Zolotarev's statement and the recovery of his personal documents work their magic.

Zolotarev also plays a role in another episode involving documents. As Serpilin's unit moves east, it picks up two stragglers. One of them is Zolotarev, and the other is Colonel Baranov, a senior staff officer who has no documents and wears no badges of rank. Baranov explains his lack of documents by saying that he put on Zolotarev's spare shirt, and his party card and other documents were burned with their vehicle. None of this convinces Serpilin, who orders that Baranov be reduced to the rank of private. Baranov eventually commits suicide. In a twist, it turns out that it was almost certainly Baranov who denounced Serpilin in 1937, leading to his arrest and incarceration. In Serpilin's assessment of Baranov, we see not merely the exposure of an envious careerist but also one reason why the Red Army was so disastrously unprepared in 1941:

> Teaching in the academy, Baranov would be ready to support one doctrine on one day and another on the following day, to call black white and white black. Skillfully adapting to what seemed to him would please the "higher-ups," he was the sort of person who would support even clear errors based on no knowledge of the facts which he knew only too well. . . . Reports and statements about the armies of possible enemies were his hobbyhorse. Seeking out their actual and imaginary weaknesses, he obsequiously passed over in silence all the strong and dangerous sides of a future enemy.[77]

Truth is a pervasive theme in The Living and the Dead, as Sintsov strives to be believed or agonizes over what can be believed in the Soviet mass media, and Serpilin seeks answers to the lack of readiness on 22 June 1941. When Baranov's widow wants to know the circumstances of her husband's death, Serpilin tells her that her husband was killed; he withholds the truth that, having disgraced himself, Baranov took his own life. This is a noble lie to protect not just Baranova, who is serving as a military doctor, but also her sons, who are at the front. Serpilin's behavior toward Baranova is in complete contrast to the way people behaved *and were expected to behave* toward those who had been arrested in the 1930s. Then, the families of arrestees were shunned as criminals and outcasts. By treating Baranova so humanely, Serpilin implicitly criticizes this past behavior.

Sintsov's obsession with the truth arises from the fact that he starts the war as a party journalist, a cog in the party propaganda machinery. The essential problem for Sintsov is that he is aware of a contradiction between what he has seen on the ground firsthand (albeit only one small part of the front) and what is being reported:

> In the sitreps [situation reports] they have written about the major battles in the border regions, and a bare three days ago I was unable to get from Borisov to Minsk. What are you supposed to believe, the sitrep or what I saw with my own eyes? Or perhaps both are true, perhaps further on, by the border, there are severe but successful defensive battles under way and I merely happened to be in a zone where the Germans had broken through; that I have lost my mind through fear and I am unable to imagine what is happening in other places?[78]

Sintsov finally realizes the worthlessness of the prewar propaganda trumpeting the Red Army's invincibility: "And with utter fury he recalled the novel about a future war which he had read two years ago in which the whole of fascist Germany had been smashed to pieces from the first blow of our aircraft. That author ought to have been on the Bobruisk highway two weeks ago!"[79] Simonov's use of the phrases "future war" and "first blow" are almost certainly references to Nikolai Shpanov's *The First Blow: The Story of the Future War* (1939). The point here is that Soviet propaganda about victorious defensive battles is not plausible, whereas German leaflets claiming that the Soviet Union has lost the war are all too believable to Red Army soldiers in headlong retreat. When Serpilin dismisses the content of German leaflets as "a plausible lie and nothing more,"[80] he more or less concedes that German propaganda is effective and that the Soviet side has no means of countering the Germans. Moreover, despite Serpilin's willingness to dismiss the content of German leaflets as a plausible lie, he is not willing to consider whether what happened to him in 1937 can plausibly be dismissed as an error or whether it is reasonable to accept that "suddenness" alone can explain the Soviet failure to stem the German Blitzkrieg.

Conclusion

The People Are Immortal, *The Volokolamsk Highway*, and *The Living and the Dead* represent a very small sample of Soviet-Russian literature devoted to the first months of the German invasion. Nevertheless, they manage to convey something of the disaster that overwhelmed the Soviet Union. All three works also reveal the inability of state propaganda to triumph over inadequate military readiness and professionalism. For example, in *The People Are Immortal*, Commissar Bogarev's tirades about German military shortcomings, at the very moment the German army is sweeping away everything before it, do not even qualify as propaganda. Bogarev's ravings are embarrassing nonsense, as the future author of *Life and Fate* may have intended.

If one had to identify the key theme common to all three novels examined in this chapter, it would unquestionably be *okruzhenie* and the treatment of the *okruzhentsy*. Grossman, Bek, and Simonov try in various ways to address this theme without violating what is *politicheski pravil'no* (politically correct), but without much success. The major obstacle in *The People Are Immortal* is the ubiquitous and unconvincing Bogarev; in *The Volokolamsk Highway* it is Momysh-Uly's implausible claim that he is encountering the dreaded O-word (*okruzhenie*) for the first time; and in *The Living and the Dead* it is Serpilin, who, despite his sympathy for soldiers who have been encircled through no fault of their own, offers no valid reason why such soldiers should be regarded with suspicion.

Whatever the vast majority of authors of Soviet-Russian war novels think about the theme of *okruzhenie* and Stalin's role in the countdown to 22 June 1941, they all proceed from the assumption that the Soviet Union was the victim of an unprovoked attack by Germany. This seemingly indisputable fact of twentieth-century history is, however, challenged by Soviet defector Vladimir Rezun, who, writing under the pseudonym Viktor Suvorov, argues that the Soviet Union was planning to attack Germany and was thus the aggressor. Suvorov's startling claim, with potentially devastating consequences for Soviet-Russian war literature and the history of the twentieth century, is the subject of the penultimate chapter.

8 Viktor Suvorov, the Stalin Attack Thesis, and the Start of World War II

> On the other side, on 22 June, the formation of the Soviet forces did not indicate any *immediate* intentions to attack.
>
> *Generalfeldmarschall Erich von Manstein,*
> Verlorene Siege

The standard and accepted narrative of the start of World War II runs more or less as follows. On 1 September 1939 Germany attacked Poland. France and Britain delivered an ultimatum to Hitler that all German forces must be withdrawn immediately, which he ignored. Following the expiry of the deadline set by Britain and France, they both declared war on Germany just after 1100 hours on 3 September. Poland fell to the Nazis. Nine months later, western Europe was overwhelmed and the British were forced to retreat from the European continent. After conquering western Europe, Hitler turned on Yugoslavia and invaded Greece and Crete; Rommel was dispatched to North Africa to salvage Italian fortunes. The final move in Hitler's aggressive plan, and the one that led to the war becoming truly global, was the invasion of the Soviet Union. According to this narrative, Hitler is the clear and obvious aggressor, and his ambitions were the primary cause of World War II. This narrative of how and why the war started, and by whom, is convincing and well documented, and it is the subject of Viktor Suvorov's *Ledokol: Kto nachal vtoruiu mirovuiu voinu?* (Icebreaker: Who Started the Second World War? [1992]). In this chapter I examine what I call the Stalin attack thesis, evaluating it on the basis of Suvorov's assertions and in light of new declassified archive material published since 1991.

Introduction

War itself is Suvorov's starting point. He argues, convincingly, that Marx, Engels, Lenin, and certainly Stalin valued war for its ability to destroy states and their social and economic structures. If a war were long and exhausting enough, it could create the necessary chaos and vacuum of power that the small but well-organized and well-disciplined communist parties could exploit. Once they occupied this vacuum of power, they could impose the ideological program derived from Marxism-Leninism on an exhausted society or its disorganized remnants. Undermining the tsarist war effort in World War I and promoting instability in Russia were thus primary and urgent preconditions for the Leninist seizure of power in 1917 and the consolidation of Soviet power thereafter. It is from these basic premises and historical facts that Suvorov's Stalin attack thesis (SAT) emerges. Stalin learned from Lenin: by a combination of planning and opportunism, Stalin sought to create a long and exhausting war that would cause chaos and instability in Germany—the prime target of Stalinist foreign policy planning—which could then be exploited to justify a war of liberation. Stalin, according to Suvorov, did everything he could to expedite Hitler's rise in the hope and expectation that Hitler would embark on a series of wars that would exhaust Germany, preparing the way for liberation-invasion by the Red Army. In this scenario, Germany was to be the icebreaker, the tool of Stalinist policy preparing the way for revolution and conquest.

Essential to this Stalinist policy was that Germany be lured into a war on two fronts. According to Suvorov, this was the primary aim of the Non-Aggression Pact. The intention was to clear the way for Germany to attack Poland and therefore provoke the Anglo-French guarantees given to Poland. Therefore, the British and French declaration of war against Germany marks the moment when Germany faced, unknowingly, the dramatically enhanced threat of a war on two fronts. This paved the way for Stalin to proceed with plans to attack Germany, which was now at war with Britain and France.

Suvorov argues that because the Soviet Union did not immediately act to carve up Poland, as Germany did, it looks as if the Germans started World War II.[1] Also, because the Soviet side did not attack Poland from the east as Germany attacked from the west, the German army had to face the entire Polish army and suffered greater losses. If Poland had been forced to deal with both armies at the same time, it would have collapsed much sooner. An interesting question here is, if the Soviet Union and Germany had invaded Poland at the same time, would Britain and France have considered themselves duty bound to declare war on the Soviet Union as well as Germany. This would not have been a desirable outcome from Stalin's point of view. Worse still, based on Suvorov's assessment of Stalin's intentions, if Germany and the Soviet Union *had* carved up Poland together on 1 September 1939, Britain and France—realizing they could not declare war on Germany without declaring war on the Soviet Union as well—might have failed to do either. Perhaps mindful of this possible outcome, Stalin decided to test Anglo-French resolve with regard to German behavior before invading eastern Poland on 17 September 1939. In any case, the fact that Britain and France did not declare war on the Soviet Union, which together with Germany violated Polish sovereignty, adds hypocrisy and recklessness to the criticisms of Anglo-French defense guarantees to Poland.

Lenin's signing of the Brest-Litovsk Treaty with Germany was clearly against Russia's national interest, but it made tens of thousands of German troops available for deployment in the west, prolonging the war and, as events showed, weakening Germany internally. Suvorov is quite clear that the Brest-Litovsk Treaty anticipates the Molotov–von Ribbentrop Pact: "Lenin's calculation in 1918 and Stalin's calculation in 1939 are one and the same: let Germany fight in the west; let it exhaust itself and the Western Allies at the same time."[2] Any calculations that a war between Germany and the Anglo-French alliance would be a protracted affair were brutally shattered when the Wehrmacht overran the Anglo-French armies in a matter of weeks, not years, in the summer of 1940. Yet all was not lost for Stalin. Although France was conquered, Britain was not, and the defeat of the Luftwaffe effectively put an end to German plans for an invasion of Britain. If Germany, while still at war with Britain, attacked the Soviet Union or the *Soviet Union attacked* Germany, Germany would face a war on two fronts, with no chance of victory. This, in essence, is the SAT.

What makes the SAT especially troublesome, and potentially fatal for the existing account of the origins of World War II, is that Suvorov applies his training and experience as a Soviet intelligence officer, a Soviet insider, to the task, bringing an instinctive, intuitive feel for Soviet behavior. Moreover, much of the SAT is based on a close reading of published Soviet material, especially that published after Stalin's death. Based on these primary sources, Suvorov's arguments and analyses are often robust, insightful, and not easily dismissed. In short, Suvorov presents a serious challenge to the established narrative. Nor can his arguments be summarily dismissed merely because he is a former GRU officer, a Soviet defector, and an individual who, in the eyes of the Russian Federation even after the end of the Cold War, is considered a traitor. This was the standard manner in which revelations of Soviet behavior were played down or dismissed when brought to the attention of Western audiences by Western politicians and academics with Soviet sympathies. Still, by the standards of all the protagonists in the Cold War, and certainly the intelligence agencies, Suvorov *was* a traitor. What better way to antagonize his former masters, who have condemned him to death in absentia, than to attack the Great Fatherland War—specifically, the endlessly trumpeted claim that the Soviet Union was the noble and *innocent* victim of Nazi aggression?

Even if the SAT cannot survive scrutiny, anti-Soviet and anti-Russian forces that are uninterested in careful argument will use it to demonstrate that Russia, whether Soviet or otherwise, is a menace to European security. Thus the SAT has political utility that goes beyond 1939–1941 and beyond the end of the Cold War. Yet Suvorov's arguments must be assessed on their merits. If the SAT can withstand critical assessment and turns out to be accurate and internally consistent, the consequences for the history of the twentieth century would be sensational, since it would support one of the staples of NS propaganda: that Barbarossa was a crusade against Asiatic Bolshevism. Suvorov's method in *Icebreaker* is to identify a number of political, economic, intelligence, strategic, and military indicators that, taken together, demonstrate beyond reasonable doubt that Stalin was planning to invade Germany but that Hitler, sensing the danger or acting on sound intelligence, preempted Stalin by launching his own attack on 22 June 1941.

Military Indicators

Suvorov devotes considerable attention to pre-1939 developments in Soviet military equipment and doctrine, arguing that they are consistent with an offensive mind-set and that the most likely target was Germany. Thus, the scale of Soviet armament innovation and production attracts his attention. It was indeed huge. However, given the West's earlier intervention in the affairs of the fledgling Soviet state, the ever-present risk of civil war, the fear of invasion from west and east, and the sheer size of the Soviet state to be defended, a massive arms industry was required to equip large armed forces, and this in itself was not evidence of planned aggression. That said, the range of Soviet innovation is striking. Suvorov claims that Soviet tank production concentrated on the *bystrokhodnyi tank* (BT)—literally, the "fast-moving tank." Because the BT ran on wheels, Suvorov concludes that, owing to the lack of proper roads in Russia, it must have been intended for use outside of Russia—most likely in the states to the west, with their superior road infrastructure. This interpretation has some merit until one realizes that the Germans made a clear and effective distinction between wheeled armored vehicles and tanks and that German tanks were all tracked, not wheeled. A tank with wheels is confined to roads, so it loses the advantage of cross-country movement. A tank with tracks can move on both. Likewise, the Soviet Union's production of amphibious tanks, indicated by the prefix "P" (*plavaiushchii*), is not necessarily evidence that these tanks were intended to cross rivers beyond Soviet borders. They could have had internal security and defensive applications as well. Though almost certainly incapable of crossing the major rivers in western Russia such as the Desna, Dnieper, and Oka, amphibious tanks probably could have coped with small rivers and small tributaries.

Having highlighted the high quality of Soviet planes—the MiG-3, Yak-1, Pe-2, Il-2, and Il-16—Suvorov then has to account for the Soviet air force's evident failure to deal with the Luftwaffe on and after 22 June 1941:

> The answer is simple: by far the biggest part of Soviet pilots, including fighter pilots, WERE NOT TAUGHT THE SKILLS OF AIR-TO-AIR COMBAT. So what were they taught? They were taught to attack ground targets. Soviet bomber and fighter manuals trained Soviet pilots to conduct one massive, sudden, offensive operation in which the Soviet air force in one blow would catch the enemy air force on its aerodromes and seize air superiority.[3]

This is certainly consistent with propaganda tracts such as *The First Blow* and with the doctrines being developed by Soviet air strategist Aleksandr Nikolaevich Lapchinskii in books such as *Vozdushnye sily v boiu i operatsii* (Air Forces in Battle and in Operation [1932]) and *Vozdushnaia armiia* (Air Army [1939]). But any air force that is trained solely for the task of ground attack is woefully unprepared and lacks flexibility. The case for a well-trained and expertly led defensive fighter arm was clearly demonstrated by the Royal Air Force in the summer of 1940, when it defeated the Luftwaffe. The lessons for the Soviet Union were obvious, and one can assume that they were studied by the Soviet General Staff. Moreover, the strategic plans prepared in 1940–1941 all contained an air plan that envisioned taking on enemy air forces in the air. Everything Suvorov writes merely highlights one urgent question: why was there no preemptive attack against Luftwaffe bases in

Table 8.1. Glider Orders for Soviet Airborne Forces for 1941 and 1942, Submitted by General Zhukov, Chief of Staff of the Red Army, 16 June 1941

	Quantity (Troop Capacity)	
Type	1941	1942
5-seater gliders	500 (2,500)	1,000 (5,000)
11-seater gliders	1,000 (11,000)	3,000 (33,000)
11-seater hydroplane gliders	200 (2,200)	500 (5,500)
20-seater gliders	300 (6,000)	1,000 (20,000)
Total gliders	2,000	5,500
Total troop capacity*	21,700	63,500

Source: № 558, "Zapiska nachal'nika genshtaba Krasnoi Armii generala armii Zhukova narkomy aviatsionnoi promyshlennosti [SSSR], 16 iiunia 1941 g.," 1941 god, 2:366–367.
*Based on the total allocation of seats, the maximum glider lift capacity would amount to 21,700 men in 1941 and 63,500 men in 1942, a threefold increase.

the Generalgouvernement before 22 June 1941? According to Suvorov, the Il-2 was intended primarily for the ground-attack role: "Aerodromes were its most important target."[4]

Throughout the 1930s the record-breaking achievements of Soviet pilots, the so-called Stalinskie sokoly (Stalin falcons), were featured in the Soviet press. This adulation was accompanied by the cult of the parachutist, which was widely promoted among Soviet youth. Parachute training and the mastery of a wide range of infantry skills had obvious military applications. Suvorov claims that the huge training effort devoted to raising airborne units is irrefutable evidence that the Soviet Union was planning a war of aggression, since parachutists and glider-borne units are not needed in a defensive war. But this is not always the case. In a very large state like the Soviet Union, covering eleven time zones, large airborne formations make it possible to deploy troops very quickly on remote borders in response to invasion. It should be kept in mind that the Soviet Union was also worried about a war on two fronts—from Germany in the west and Japan in the east. Suvorov interprets the scale of Soviet glider production as another indication of aggression. Mass production of gliders in 1941, he argues, implies that they were intended for use in 1941, not 1942, since they could not be stored outside in winter weather.[5] However, increased glider production was planned for 1942, which would have been after the supposed start date of any Soviet offensive against Germany. The full scale of planned glider production for 1941 and 1942 is shown in table 8.1. Significantly, Zhukov's order for glider production is dated 16 June 1941.

Suvorov relies heavily on published Soviet sources in which airborne operations are discussed. However, one must bear in mind the propaganda function of the Soviet media. These reports may have been intended to let the Germans know that the Soviet military was alert to the threat posed by German airborne units. Suvorov states that in December 1940 senior Soviet officers discussed the nature of surprise attacks with Stalin at a secret meeting. These surprise attacks were referred to as "special operations of the initial period of the war,"[6] and the plan was to use airborne and glider units in conjunction with preemptive air strikes to destroy enemy aircraft on the ground and then capture the aerodromes.

According to Suvorov, two new armies—the 16th and 17th Armies—were created in June 1940, and every effort was made to keep them top secret. Suvorov interprets this as evidence of hostile Soviet intent: "The further to the west, to the north and to the south the German divisions went, the more Soviet armies were created. Let us imagine that Hitler had gone even further, having landed his troops in Great Britain, having captured Gibraltar, Africa and the Middle East, how many divisions would Stalin then have created on the unprotected German border? And for what purpose?"[7] However, this huge increase in Soviet divisions does not necessarily indicate hostile intent; it could mean that Stalin was being perspicacious and thinking ahead.

Had Hitler succeeded in occupying Great Britain, North Africa, and the Middle East, Germany's industrial and war-making capacity would have been dramatically increased. There would have been no need to maintain a huge army in the Mediterranean zone—now under Axis control—or in North Africa. The Middle East oil fields would have been at the disposal of Germany. All British bombing of German cities would have stopped. There would have been no need to maintain a huge U-boat fleet. There would be no Lend-Lease and no second front. America would have played no part in Europe. The entire capacity of the advanced industrial economies of Britain, France, and Holland would have been at the disposal of Germany. All this industrial, economic, and military might could be turned against the Soviet Union, and if the Germans could incite the Japanese to attack from the east, the Soviet situation would be dire indeed. Thus, one might argue that the frenetic creation of divisions by Stalin was based on the very real fear that German arms, having so comprehensively overwhelmed France, Norway, and Holland, and having forced the British to retreat from the European continent, might succeed in rolling up North Africa and the oil fields in short order as well. If Hitler controlled the oil reserves of the Middle East, Romania's oil—the focus of so much Soviet effort, according to Suvorov—would be irrelevant. Thus, Stalin was preparing for the possibility that Germany—now the sole, undisputed master of all of western Europe, the Mediterranean, North Africa, the Suez Canal, and the oil fields of the Middle East—would make good Hitler's boast about *Drang nach Osten* and initiate the final reckoning with the Soviet Union. In such a scenario, there was no doubt that the German occupation forces would make every effort to recruit British, French, Dutch, Danish, and Norwegians to participate in the pan-European, anti-Stalin crusade, just as Ukrainian nationalism was being exploited.

The influence of Marxist-Leninist ideology on Soviet military doctrine meant that it was not enough for the Red Army to invade and occupy a foreign state. The next phase was to sovietize the occupied territory. Sovietization meant the identification, deportation, arrest, and, when necessary, execution of elements known or deemed to be hostile to Soviet power. According to Tukhachevskii, and cited by Suvorov, the aim of war "is to secure the free use of violence."[8] The point here is that the end of war is not the end of violence; it is the phase when violence can be used freely. Quoting Tukhachevskii once more: "Every piece of territory occupied by us is, after its occupation, Soviet territory where the power of the workers and peasants shall be exercised."[9] Vladimir Triandafillov, considered by Suvorov to be the father of Soviet operational art, also believed that occupied territory should be quickly sovietized and that special personnel should be trained and used for this purpose. The parallels with the German occupation regime are obvious. After the Red Army was defeated, the *Einsatzgruppen* and SS units were deployed to eradicate all opposition to German rule. Since they were the masters of their occupation zones, they had achieved the situation envisaged by Tukhachevskii in which they could use violence freely. One of the NKVD's primary missions was to impose order and sovietize occupied territory, but these functions were standard long before 1941 and were not the product of any plan to invade Germany. These methods had been used to totalitarianize the Soviet state before 1939 and would be used against eastern Europe after 1945. Thus, the existence of specialized NKVD formations and execution squads is not a critical indicator in the sense in which Suvorov interprets it.

Dismantling Fortifications

Some of Suvorov's most effective arguments in support of the view that Stalin planned to attack Germany concern the destruction of the security zone in the border region and the dismantling of the Stalin Line. A defender (in this case, the Soviet defender) should create a security zone that stretches back from the border and is occupied by light but highly mobile forces. The aim is to deny the enemy (in this case, the German army) the opportunity to achieve a major success by surrounding and destroying substantial Soviet forces in a surprise attack. The light forces maintained in the security zone should engage the enemy in a series of attritional attacks that disrupt the enemy's momentum and wear him down. The advantage of surprise is lost. This is *malaia voina*, which was prosecuted with outstanding efficiency by the Finns in the Winter War against the Red Army. Doctrinally, this is sound, and on paper, the fact that Stalin abandoned this policy invites suspicion of his real motives. Suvorov correctly notes that one consequence of the Non-Aggression Pact was to make the existing defense zone even stronger, since it was further behind the border. Moreover, as Suvorov notes, the lessons of the Winter War underlined the importance of the defensive zone. In this regard, Meretskov's orders to dismantle the zone and move units up to the new border make no sense.[10] The weakness in Suvorov's interpretation is that it is based on the assumption that the Red Army was capable of waging *malaia voina* with the same level of efficiency as the Finns. The Red Army's own assessment of its performance in the Winter War rejects that option.[11]

Suvorov sees the preservation of so many bridges across the river Bug as further evidence of Stalin's plan to attack Germany.[12] The standard explanation, properly rejected by Suvorov, is that Soviet commanders were idiots. I suggest that the bridges were not destroyed because this would have alerted the Germans to the fact that the Soviet side suspected something. In the language favored by Stalin and Zhukov, the Germans would have interpreted the destruction of the bridges over the Bug as a provocation. Furthermore, a massive road- and rail-building program initiated in the border region after Zhukov's appointment as chief of the Soviet General Staff is not conclusive evidence of a Soviet attack. Improving road and rail communications and making access to the region easier served a defensive purpose as well. There is clearly a balance to be struck here: on the one hand, Soviet troops would benefit by having better road and rail communications on their side of the border; on the other hand, this improved infrastructure could assist an invader. Exactly the same considerations applied to the Germans on their side of the border.

The Stalin Line was the unofficial name given to a series of reinforced fortifications along the western borders of the Soviet Union. It consisted of fifteen *ukreplennye raiony* (reinforced regions), each with a front of about 100 to 150 kilometers (62 to 93 miles) and a depth of about 30 to 50 kilometers (18.6 to 31 miles), with the flanks secured by the Baltic and Black Seas.[13] Unlike the Maginot Line, the Stalin Line was built in secrecy. Situating the reinforced regions well behind the lines means that the enemy lost much of the advantage derived from a surprise attack. The puzzling aspect is why the Stalin Line was dismantled before its replacement, the so-called Molotov Line, was built, and why it was dismantled at all, assuming that two defensive lines are better than one. If, as Suvorov claims, the Molotov Line and the road and rail infrastructure being built at the behest of Meretskov, Beria, and Zhukov were intended to be new rear areas for the Red Army attack, this still does not explain why Stalin refused to acknowledge the German buildup and then act in a timely manner. Suvorov argues that before the Polish campaign, Guderian was ordered to strengthen the fortifications on the border to mislead the Poles: the Soviets would take the view that German intentions were defensive, not offensive.[14] Suvorov argues that since German fortification work on the border was done with offensive intentions, similar work being carried out on the Soviet side must have been done with the same offensive intentions in mind.[15] This is a non sequitur.

Suvorov's Interpretation of Stalin's 5 May 1941 Speech

On 5 May 1941 Stalin delivered a secret speech to the graduates of Soviet military academies in Moscow. The speech plays a major part in Suvorov's evaluation of Stalin's military intentions toward Germany. His analysis of Stalin's speech is based on what others said about it in published sources and memoirs before the full text was published, which occurred in 1998. Thus, Suvorov's analysis is necessarily and unavoidably fragmentary, but it identifies some of the speech's essentials. For example, according to Suvorov, and consistent with the published version, "Stalin called Germany an aggressor, an invader, the subjugator of other countries and peoples and forecast that such a policy will not end in success for Germany."[16] Suvorov also claims that "Stalin imagined a war against Germany but WITHOUT a German attack on the Soviet Union, and with a completely different scenario for the start of the war."[17]

Suvorov argues that the best-known part of the speech is Stalin's statement that "war with Germany will not begin before 1942."[18] There is no reference to 1942 in the text of the published speech and no such wording. However, the speech was not formally recorded by a stenographer, so the statement could have been included in the speech but omitted from the record, although this seems unlikely. G. M. Dimitrov, who attended the event, made a detailed record of the speech, and the final part of his transcript cites Stalin as follows: "*Our policy of peace and security is at the same time a policy of preparing for war. There is no defense without an offensive. It is necessary to educate the army in the spirit of the offensive. It is necessary to prepare for war.*"[19]

Suvorov maintains, citing Admiral Nikolai Kuznetsov's book *Nakanune* (On the Eve [1966]), that immediately after Stalin's 5 May speech, Zhukov (by now chief of the Soviet General Staff) issued a directive in which he names Germany as the most likely enemy in any war.[20] This directive is probably the one contained in the second volume of *1941 god* and dated 15 May 1941.[21] The editors of that volume note that although the maps were dated 15 May, the document itself was prepared earlier: "It was compiled, apparently, immediately after Stalin's speech to the graduates of the military academies on 5 May."[22] There is nothing to show whether Zhukov's plan was accepted or rejected. However, anecdotal evidence from Zhukov indicates "that Stalin categorically rejected the proposal."[23] Suvorov notes that although the directive had not been published at the time of his writing, V. A. Anfilov cites one part of it in his 1971 memoirs (*Bessmertnyi podvig. Issledovanie kanuna i pervogo etapa Velikoi Otechestvennoi voiny* [The Immortal Feat of Arms: An Investigation of the Eve and First Stage of the Great Fatherland War]): "Over fifty years only one phrase from this top-secret document has infiltrated into the press: 'be prepared on the order of the High Command to launch swift blows in order to rout the enemy and to switch military operations onto his territory and to seize important positions.'"[24] The wording cited by Suvorov is not in Zhukov's directive dated 15 May, but similar wording is contained in a series of directives sent to the Western, Kiev, and Odessa Special Military Districts and dated 20 May. For instance, Zhukov's directive to the Western Special Military District states: "Given favorable conditions all the defending troops and army reserves of the district are to be prepared, on the order of the High Command, to launch swift blows."[25] Zhukov's directive to the Kiev Special Military states the following: "Given favorable conditions all the defending troops and army reserves of the district are to be prepared, on the order of the High Command, to launch swift blows in order to rout the enemy formations and to switch military operations onto his territory and to seize favorable positions."[26] His directive to the Odessa Special Military District is the same as that sent to Kiev.[27] The wording in the two directives to Kiev and Odessa is nearly identical to Suvorov's quotation from Anfilov's memoirs.

Suvorov claims that all this reinforces what he sees as Soviet intentions: "Had there been one word in this directive about defense, the marshals and communist historians would not have failed to cite it. But the entire remaining text of 5 May [1941] in no way lends itself to being cited. Even fifty years after the end of the war the directive still remains top secret."[28] To begin with, the Zhukov directive dated circa 5–6 May, 1941 envisages the possibility of Germany initiating aggression against the Soviet Union, not the other way around. The plan is intended to be primarily defensive, with provisions for counterattacks. The mission of the Western Special Military District is as follows: "by means of stubborn defense on the front of the Druskeniki and Ostrolenka to provide secure cover for the Lida and Belostok sectors."[29] Potentially devastating for much of Suvorov's SAT is the following, which occurs in paragraph VI of the directive (Covering the Concentration and Its Deployment): "At the same time it is necessary to take the utmost measures to accelerate the construction and equipping of reinforced regions and, in 1942, to begin the construction of reinforced regions on the border with Hungary, and, additionally, to continue the construction of reinforced regions along the line of the old state border."[30] Applying Suvorov's reasoning, the building of reinforced regions on the border with Hungary in 1942 has to be seen as a purely defensive measure, which rules out any Soviet offensive against Germany in 1941.

The same emphasis on defense is found in the three directives to the Western, Kiev, and Odessa Special Military Districts. Thus, the primary mission of the Western Special Military District is follows: "With the aim of providing cover for the mobilization, concentration and deployment of the troops of the district, you [commander] are personally, with your chief of staff and head of your operational section, to work out a plan by 20 May 1941."[31] Zhukov specifies six main tasks for the defensive mission: (1) to deny the enemy's land and air forces access to the land and airspace of the district; (2) by means of stubborn defense of the reinforced regions along the border, to provide firm cover for the mobilization, concentration, and deployment of the district's troops; (3) by means of air defense and the air force, to provide for the normal functioning of the railways and the concentration of troops; (4) by all possible types of intelligence available to the district, to determine in good time the nature, concentration, and formation of enemy troops; (5) by active air force operations, to secure air superiority and, through powerful blows on the main railway junctions, bridges, crossings, and enemy troop formations, to interdict and delay the concentration and deployment of enemy troops; and (6) to deny the enemy the option of dropping and landing parachutists and sabotage groups in the territory of the district.[32] Kiev and Odessa were required to prepare similar plans by 25 May.

However, an effective rejection of the SAT, based on Zhukov's orders, is not entirely robust. For all their emphasis on defense, there is no good reason why they could not serve as the basis for a preemptive strike, especially if Zhukov assumed—and Stalin could finally be convinced—that the Germans were planning to do much the same. The assaulting units had to be prepared, and toward this end, the mobilization, concentration, and deployment of troops to be used either in defense or in offense had to be secured. This emphasis on defense and aggressive action might be seen as a warning from Zhukov—which was probably as far as he could go with Stalin—that the military districts had to step up their levels of readiness. If all the necessary defensive measures were implemented and the mobilization, concentration, and deployment of troops behind the line occurred without interruption, this would change the meaning of Zhukov's warning order and the directive to be prepared to act on an order of the Soviet High Command, given "favorable conditions." There is undoubtedly some ambiguity and room for maneuver here. On the one hand, the requirement to be prepared to move forward in "favorable conditions" might mean that the Red Army, having weathered the initial surprise German attack, should go over to the counterattack. On the other hand, should the Western, Kiev, and Odessa Special Military Districts manage to mobilize, concentrate, and deploy their forces without provoking a German attack, the interpretation of the directive "to be prepared, on the order of the High Command, to launch swift blows in order to rout the enemy formations and to switch military operations onto his territory and to seize favorable positions" would change quite dramatically. In such conditions, this could be construed as an order to launch a preemptive strike against the Germans across the border and, depending on its initial success, to exploit it.

In this regard, a directive from Zhukov to the commander of the Western Special Military District, dated 12 June 1941, is significant, indicating either the reinforcement of the district or offensive preparations. Zhukov informs Pavlov that from 17 June to 2 July 1941, the following units will be arriving in the Western Military District: 51st Rifle Corps (98th, 112th, and 153rd Rifle Divisions), 63rd Rifle Corps (546th Corps Artillery Regiment and 53rd and 148th Rifle Divisions), and 22nd Engineer Regiment. Significantly, the unloading of these units is to be organized by an order of the General Staff; the formations will not be part of the Western Military District and will not come under the command of the Military Council; and only the commander of the district, the representative of the Military Council, and the chief of staff are to be informed of their arrival. As a further precaution, Zhukov orders: "Open references by phone or by telegraph in connection with the arrival or unloading of these troops are categorically forbidden."[33]

The Published Version of Stalin's Speech and the Stalin Attack Thesis

The published version of Stalin's 5 May 1941 speech does not provide direct support for Suvorov's interpretation. There are, however, elements in the speech that do not lend themselves to a clear-cut interpretation and could be construed as indicating plans for a preemptive strike against Germany.

Regardless of statements made in the All-Union press and broadcast by TASS, Stalin has his gaze firmly fixed on the nature of the German war machine and what it means for the military doctrine and equipment of the Red Army. Stalin seems to grasp that for all the comforting and at times bellicose noises being made by the Soviet media, the danger represented by Germany and its allies is understood by the Soviet people and reassurances are required, especially for those who may soon be called on to defend the Soviet Union. For this reason, the speech is generally free of Marxist-Leninist incantations.

Stalin begins by stressing the work that has been undertaken over the last four years to modernize the Red Army: its mobility and firepower have increased, and the speed of its aircraft has dramatically improved. Interestingly, Stalin claims that the significance of the military outcomes at Lake Khasan and Khalkhin-Gol has been exaggerated by those who fail to appreciate that the Japanese army was not a modern army. This is an unusual claim to make about an army that has repeatedly demonstrated its ability to wage war at the peak of modernity and its total mastery of the surprise attack and Blitzkrieg. It might also be interpreted as a putdown of Zhukov, the victor at Khalkhin-Gol. According to Stalin, ideas for the reconstruction of the Red Army have been derived mainly from the experiences of the Russo-Finnish War and the war in the west, by which he means the German defeat of Anglo-French forces in the summer of 1940.

Suvorov has argued that the thinly armored, wheeled BT was clearly intended to be used on roads in Germany and that this indicated planning against Germany. However, Stalin's assessment of Soviet tanks implies that if such plans were ever considered for the BT, they have now been discarded. Here, for example, is how Stalin characterizes Soviet tanks: "Our tanks have changed the way they look. Earlier, all our tanks were thinly armored. These days that is not sufficient. These days armor 3–4 times thicker is required. We have tanks of the first line, which will tear up the front. There are second- and third-line tanks: these tanks accompany the infantry. The firepower of our tanks has increased."[34]

The changes outlined by Stalin that have taken place in the tank and artillery formations, the provision of mortars, and the aviation formations are in some ways a description of the German army. He notes, for example: "It is possible to have a good command stratum but if we do not possess modern military equipment it is possible to lose a war."[35] However, the problem is one of doctrine and command as much as equipment, and Stalin has very little to say about the organizational and doctrinal changes that any rational appraisal of the Red Army's woeful performance in the Winter War would merit. That doctrine and leadership matter was clearly demonstrated by the Germans' success against the Anglo-French alliance in the summer of 1940. As Heinz Guderian has pointed out, France had the biggest army in western Europe, and the total number of tanks at the disposal of the Anglo-French forces in May 1940 was about 4,800—more than double the 2,200 available to Germany.[36] Moreover, French tanks were better armored and were superior in terms of gun caliber. German tanks were faster and, critically, they were better led and deployed in accordance with a superior doctrine.

A large part of Stalin's speech is devoted to the question of how and why the Germans were able to defeat the Anglo-French forces. When Stalin argues that the German army is not invincible, he is clearly trying to respond to the long run of German successes (the airborne invasion of Crete was only two weeks away). Stalin accounts for German success by arguing that after its defeat in 1918, the German army applied itself anew to the study of war. To quote Stalin: "The Germans critically analyzed the reasons for their defeat and found ways to organize their army better, to train and to equip it. The military thinking of the German army progressed. The army was equipped with the very latest technology and taught the latest methods in waging war."[37] In contrast, the French became complacent and—to use one of Stalin's favorite expressions—dizzy with success.

Particularly notable is Stalin's emphasis on the reasons for the Germans' success in the Franco-Prussian War of 1870 and their defeat in 1918.

According to Stalin, the decisive factor was that the war in 1870 was on one front, whereas the war in 1914–1918 ended up being a two-front one. Therefore, Stalin's assumption—and not just his—is that, for Germany, a two-front war must always lead to defeat. But it also seemed to him that *Hitler accepted this strategic reasoning.*

Stalin argues that the French army did not merely stagnate; its status plummeted, and French soldiers were viewed with disdain. This analysis is essentially Marxist, since the reason for this decline in status was, according to Stalin, that the spirit of capitalism became more important than national defense. What this fails to take into account is the devastating effects of World War I on the French national psyche, arising mainly from the fact that the war was prosecuted entirely on French soil and, as a consequence, the destruction was dreadful. Thereafter, France was willing to go to almost any lengths to avoid war. Appeasement, as in Britain, was respectable. Concerning the fate of the French army, Stalin concludes: "The army must enjoy the exclusive concern and love of the people and government: in this is the source of the greatest moral strength of the army. The army must be cherished. When such moral support does not emerge in a country, there will not be a strong and combat-effective army. This is what happened in France."[38] This is undoubtedly true, but it sounds wholly insincere coming from a man who did so much to weaken his army during the Great Terror, who imposed the incubus of military commissars, and who, in six weeks time, would regard any Soviet soldier who was captured or encircled as an especially depraved species of traitor.

German military success was also due to the fact that Germany had preached liberation from the restrictions of the Treaty of Versailles, something Stalin does not condemn. But now, according to Stalin, slogans of liberation from Versailles have given way to slogans of aggression.[39] Was this intended to steel the hearts and minds of the graduates, or was it a warning to Germany, knowing that the contents of his speech would not remain secret for long?

An obvious inconsistency in Stalin's speech is the acknowledgment that the Red Army has been obliged to study the war in the west and the assertion that, "from a military point of view, there is nothing special in the German army, in its tanks, artillery and planes."[40] This might have impressed some of the graduates, but it must have made Zhukov and other competent officers, such as Georgii Isserson, wince. The question is obvious: If, as Stalin claims, the German army is nothing special, how did it manage to achieve such stunning military successes? How did this same army, dismissed by Stalin on 5 May 1941, manage to lay siege to Stalin's namesake city from late August 1942? Again, one wonders what prompted Stalin to claim that "the German army has lost the desire for the long-term improvement in its military technology."[41] The lessons of World War I showed that Germany, even though blockaded by the Royal Navy, achieved wonders of improvisation and invention. Exactly the same would happen in World War II, even as Germany waged a war on two fronts and was being squeezed by the Anglo-American-Soviet vise.

If any support for the SAT can be found in Stalin's speech, it would be in the final part. Here, in a rejoinder to an earlier speaker, an unnamed tank major-general, Stalin says that the defensive line, presumably the Stalin Line, had been built for use "until such time as we had reequipped our army and supplied it with modern means of war."[42] Stalin concludes:

> Now it is necessary to switch from the defense to the offensive. . . .
> Conducting the defense of our country, we are required to operate
> in an offensive manner: to move from defense to a military policy
> of offensive operations. We have to reconfigure our education, our
> propaganda, agitation and our press in the spirit of attack. The Red
> Army is a modern army and a modern army is an attacking army.[43]

Stalin's conclusion can be construed as a warning that sometime in 1942—based on rumors—there will be a reckoning with Germany. However, if this is a warning or an attempt to deceive Hitler, the Führer would have no incentive to act in accordance with Stalin's timetable and every incentive to act in accordance with his own. That Stalin is signaling a policy based on offense cannot be taken to mean that an attack against Germany is imminent.

Dismantling of the Soviet Partisan Network

Though victorious in the civil war, the Soviet state remained weak and vulnerable to Western aggression and intervention. One solution to the threat from a conventionally superior enemy was to train, equip, and maintain a number of partisan units. In his article "Edinaia voennaia doktrina i Krasnaia Armiia" ("A Unified Military Doctrine and the Red Army"), Red Army commander Mikhail Frunze made the case for *malaia voina* and the role to be played by partisan units. Frunze argued that partisan forces that acted boldly and with determination and that displayed high levels of initiative could largely negate a technologically superior enemy. To ensure success in these operations, the partisan detachments had to be trained and equipped well in advance, since doing so would be far more difficult once an enemy had invaded. In fact, Frunze repeatedly stressed the need for advance planning. Between 1924 and 1936 substantial progress was made: schools were set up, groups were formed and trained, and rations and arms dumps were established. From a doctrinal standpoint, the Red Army accepted that partisans would play a major role in any future war.

In 1937–1938 the partisan infrastructure and the partisan movement were more or less disbanded. Suvorov argues that Stalin was responsible for the destruction of the partisan movement as war approached and that this was an offensive strategy and yet another indicator of Stalin's plan to attack Germany. Aleksei Popov, the author of a study of the NKVD's role in the partisan movement, argues that the destruction of the prewar partisan infrastructure and some of its cadres was due to "a shift in military thinking which would not permit war to be waged on one's own territory. However the very concept itself emerged from the atmosphere of fear created by the terror in relation to one's own people."[44] The scale of the terror and strategic vandalism at this critical moment is clear. The partisan infrastructure was not merely destroyed; many of its instructors and planners were physically eliminated. To quote Popov:

> Practically all the partisan cadres were destroyed as a result of the repressions of 1937–1938. Many officials in the Soviet General Staff, the NKVD and district party secretaries were repressed who at the start of the 1930s trained the partisan movement and Red Army commanders who had special partisan warfare training. The network of partisan warfare schools commanded by competent leaders was broken up and the partisan groups and detachments were disbanded.[45]

The disbanding of the partisan networks and the repression of its commanders and trainers should be seen not as part of a plan to attack Germany but as a move that was consistent with Stalin's attack on the Red Army and the judicial murder of so many talented commanders during the Great Terror. If Stalin saw some Red Army commanders as a threat to his grip on power—the ever-present risk of Bonapartism—it would be quite logical to regard the partisan movement, inspired by Frunze's theories of *malaia voina*, as a threat as well. The Soviet partisan movement was well trained and well equipped; by the very nature of partisan warfare, it was prepared to operate under cover, independently, in secrecy, and in defiance of authority. From one perspective, the partisan movement was something of a private army, and given that it was trained and led by the Red Army, it could be used to bypass the NKVD's conventional internal security measures should the Red Army decide to move against Stalin. Moreover, the partisan movement had bases all over the western Soviet Union, and in the event of any coordinated action against the Communist Party and Stalin, it would make an effective instrument in a coup. I suggest that Stalin's decision to disband the partisan movement in 1937–1938 may well have owed something to Hitler's decision to decapitate Ernst Röhm's *Sturmabteilung* (SA) in 1934. The SA in Germany and the partisan movement in the Soviet Union both represented existential threats to their respective leaders.

Warnings from Winston Churchill and Richard Sorge

The fact that Churchill personally warned Stalin of Hitler's plan to attack the Soviet Union is one of those famous moments in the countdown to 22 June 1941. Stalin's failure to act is often cited as evidence of his incompetence. Suvorov defends Stalin: given Churchill's avowed hostility toward the Soviet Union, Stalin had no good reason to trust Churchill, who had a vested interested in seeing Germany embroiled in a war on two fronts. That much is true, but the defense becomes less convincing when one considers that Churchill's warning was backed up by many reports from the NKGB and NKVD: Churchill's warning fit an emerging pattern. Moreover, Suvorov argues that Stalin had every reason to believe that Churchill was actively trying to embroil the Soviet Union and Germany in a war, yet according to Suvorov, Stalin was already planning to attack Germany. Churchill's warning, assuming that Stalin was intending to attack Germany, would have alerted Stalin to the fact that he needed to act before Hitler. Furthermore, the warning letter from Churchill could have been published in *Pravda* and issued as a TASS communiqué on the day the Soviet Union attacked Germany, using it to justify the preemptive strike. How, then, would Churchill react to the Soviet attack? Would he pledge British support for Stalin, or would he let the two states fight it out?

Stalin also ignored Soviet agent Richard Sorge's warning of the German invasion. Sorge had been ordered to return home and refused, thus forfeiting all trust. With regard to Sorge's reports, Suvorov argues that "the reports from Sorge remain just that: reports. The GRU does not believe ANY reports and is acting correctly. Reports accompanied by evidence are required."[46] The immediate response to this claim is that the evidence was there, and from many unrelated sources. Furthermore, in the autumn of 1941, Stalin believed Sorge's report that the Japanese were going to move south, even though there was no good reason to do so. And even if Sorge provided "evidence" of Japanese intentions, why would the psychopathically suspicious Stalin take it at face value and not assume that it had been fabricated by an agent now declared to be a *nevozvrashchenets* (non-returner) and possibly working for the Germans? Suvorov's explanation of why Stalin decided to believe Sorge is not convincing, and his claim that neither Stalin nor Golikov trusted documents makes it even less credible. If Stalin did not trust documents, what was the nature of the "evidence" provided by Sorge? If it was not documentary evidence, what was it? Given the nature of intelligence work and spying and the fact that Sorge was in Japan, the evidence could only be documentary. I suggest that Stalin believed Sorge about Japanese deployment in the autumn of 1941 because Sorge had correctly reported the date of the German invasion of the Soviet Union.

Given his mistrust of documents, Golikov looked for other critical indicators of German intent. According to Suvorov, one key indicator Golikov found was sheep production.[47] Another allegedly key indicator was discarded oily rags used by German soldiers to clean their weapons. Suvorov summarizes the Golikov approach:

> Golikov reckoned (with complete justification) that very serious preparation would be required for a war with the Soviet Union. By far the most important element of Germany's preparations for war against the Soviet Union would be sheepskin jackets. A huge quantity would be required, not less than 6,000,000. Golikov knew that in Germany there was not a single division ready to fight in the Soviet Union. He painstakingly kept an eye on European sheep production. He knew quite precisely that as soon as Hitler had actually decided to attack the Soviet Union he would have to give the order to prepare the operations. The General Staff would immediately give the order to start production of millions of sheepskin jackets. This moment would inevitably be registered on the European markets. Regardless of the war, prices for mutton must stabilize and then fall because of the simultaneous slaughter of millions of animals. At the same moment prices for sheepskins would rise sharply.[48]

Is this really credible? The Soviet side also analyzed rifle and motor oil samples (the Germans were doing the same thing). They reasoned that if the Germans reckoned on knocking out the Soviet Union before the onset of winter weather, severe-frost-resistant oil and winter clothing (sheepskins) would not be required for a short—it was hoped—summer-autumn campaign.

Suvorov argues that since Golikov did everything possible to uncover German preparations for an invasion, Stalin had no grounds to punish Golikov. In addition, the reason Golikov failed to uncover any signs of a German offensive was that there was "no such preparation," insists Suvorov.[49] This claim is completely untenable, and it was untenable well before the release of new archival material after 1991. Given the mass of information from numerous sources that came across Golikov's desk before 22 June 1941, Suvorov's explanation is simply not credible. All too often, Golikov told his master what he wanted to hear. Also, Suvorov's explanation of Stalin's failure to punish Golikov is conveniently naïve in the context of his overall interpretation: since when did Stalin need an excuse to have people removed and shot or to invent scapegoats or enemies? The fate of General Pavlov and others murdered after 22 June 1941 speaks for itself.

The Soviet Defensive Plan

Suvorov's analysis of the all-important question whether Stalin had a defensive plan rests on the views of Anfilov, who argues: "Strategic defense is a compulsory form of military operations: it cannot be planned for in advance."[50] Is this really the case? Even if the precise details of an enemy attack are not known in advance and the enemy manages to achieve tactical surprise, contingency planning can be valuable. In the case of the western territories of the Soviet Union, topography imposed restraints on an attacking enemy that could be foreseen and planned for. The Stalin Line was built on just that premise, and partisan detachments were raised and equipped on the basis of similar assumptions, as was the bol'shaia zasechnaia cherta (the great abatis feature) on Russia's southern flank. These defensive plans and installations were intended not to stop an enemy attack but to blunt and retard an advance—in effect, to buy time.

Having conceded the unlikelihood of Zhukov and other Soviet staff officers not having a plan for all eventualities, Suvorov insists that they did not have such a plan because the Soviet Union intended to attack Germany, making a defensive plan unnecessary. This, according to Suvorov, explains why Zhukov and others (though not Pavlov) survived the disaster after 22 June 1941:

> Stalin did not have Zhukov and other war planners executed for one
> very simple reason: the task for preparing a plan in the event of a

defensive war was never assigned to them. Of what could they be accused? Zhukov, Vasil'evskii, Sokolovskii and the other outstanding strategists were given the task by Stalin to develop all kinds of other plans. These were very good plans but from the very first moment of a defensive war they were not needed in the same way that the autobahn tanks and the airborne corps were also not needed.[51]

The suggestion that Stalin—always ready to see enemies, plots, and wreckers—spared the lives of Zhukov and colleagues because Stalin had never instructed them to prepare a defensive plan is totally untenable. First, it ignores Stalin's willingness to execute people, with or without any pretext, especially when he needed scapegoats. Second, as chief of the Soviet General Staff, Zhukov was professionally obliged to plan for a defensive war, regardless whether Stalin had ordered him to. Failing to plan for an attack by Germany, Finland, Japan, or Romania—all potential enemies—would have been a dereliction of duty and, in the Soviet universe, would have merited *rasstrel* (execution by shooting). The point is brutally illustrated in Stadniuk's *Voina*: Stalin, seizing on Pavlov's lack of initiative, asks whether he has to tell his watch to tick or his heart to beat. In other words, Suvorov's explanation of why Zhukov failed to prepare a defensive plan is risible.

The other problem is that, even if an army is planning to attack, it should be prepared to revert to defense. In his memoir, Guderian characterizes the particular problems facing Germany as follows: "In view of the possibility of a war against several opponents at the same time, the strategy had to decide between defense on the adjacent fronts and attack against the most important enemies. It had to adapt itself to a change of the fronts to be attacked. . . . In its geographical position Germany was always compelled to wage a battle of the 'inner line' in which attack and defense alternated."[52] The army that had stormed across Europe saw the Blitzkrieg stall in the Moscow snow, yet, having withstood the Soviet counteroffensive, it was able to resume the offensive in the summer of 1942, when Hitler initiated *Fall Blau*, thus demonstrating its professional qualities. Surrounded at Stalingrad, 6th Army achieved wonders of improvised defense. Offense and defense are just different phases of war.

Nor was it the case, as Suvorov claimed, that the tanks designed to be used on German autobahns were rendered redundant. Why were they not used in 1944–1945, when the Red Army entered the German heartland? Also, it was not true that the Soviet airborne divisions and corps were no longer needed. One option would have been to deploy them en masse against the German rear as the German lines of communication became extended. Decisive, concentrated use of such forces based on Guderian's successful doctrine for German armor—*Klotzen nicht Kleckern*—might well have had severe consequences for the German offensive. That these corps could not be deployed because of German air superiority was another matter. They could have been used in a purely ground role, as the Germans would deploy their own airborne units later in the war.

Soviet Airpower and Planning

German success in the initial phase of Barbarossa owed much to the preemptive air strikes carried out by the Luftwaffe on Soviet aerodromes in the first hours and days of the invasion. Planning for these strikes relied on high-quality information derived from air reconnaissance. Soviet offensive planning would also require high-quality air reconnaissance operations conducted over a period of months, followed by the collation and analysis of data.

Suvorov refers to Soviet reconnaissance flights over German territory,[53] yet there are absolutely no references to any such flights in the two volumes of 1941 god, an omission that is unusual to say the least. Nor are there any reports of detailed Soviet air reconnaissance in those same volumes. Citing the 1977 memoir of Generalmajor of Aviation G. N. Zakharov (*Povest' ob istrebiteliakh* [A Story about Fighter Aircraft]), Suvorov says that air reconnaissance flights were carried out.[54] Unfortunately, this is not conclusive evidence of hostile intent, or at least not on the scale claimed by Suvorov. Any Soviet air plan that was intended to include a successful preemptive strike would require sustained and systematic air reconnaissance flights to obtain a substantial collection of analyses and photographs. Irregular flights by Soviet aircraft over German border territories do not constitute evidence of a planned Soviet offensive.

Suvorov's description of air planning and deployment of the Soviet air force in the period before 22 June 1941 leaves an impression of efficiency and well-implemented plans:

> Running concurrently with the redeployment of troops was an
> intensive transfer of aircraft. By night, with the pretext of training,
> aviation divisions and regiments in small groups were relocated to
> aerodromes several of which were located less than 10 kilometers from

the border: but more about this later. For the time being we merely recall that together with the combat aviation subunits, there was also a concentrated transfer of the very latest planes which had still not been incorporated into the aviations regiments and divisions.[55]

However, an altogether different view of Soviet preparation and the performance of Soviet airpower on the day the Germans invaded is contained in a report to Stalin dated 8 July 1941. The introduction to this report could not be more damning: "As a consequence of the fact that units of the air force in the Baltic Special Military District were not prepared for combat operations, and of the inefficiency and inertia on the part of several divisional and regimental aviation commanders bordering on criminal behavior, approximately 50% of the aircraft were destroyed by the enemy in the course of air strikes on aerodromes."[56] The author of the report goes on to note that aircraft were not relocated, there was an absence of antiaircraft guns, and where guns were available, there was no ammunition for them. Worse still, from the outset of the German attack, there was no communication with the aviation units. The 7th and 8th Aviation Divisions lost 300 aircraft, and losses for the 6th and 57th Aviation Divisions were comparable. The author explains that these losses were due to the district command's refusal to permit Soviet planes to take off and attack the enemy—perhaps more evidence of Stalin's warning to commanders not to succumb to provocation.

Control of surviving aircraft and aircrews was so poorly coordinated that aircraft were concentrated on a small number of airfields, offering exceptionally good targets to marauding German planes. One such concentration was discovered on the aerodrome at Pil'zino on 25 June 1941, and just one enemy fighter-bomber managed to destroy thirty aircraft. Enemy success was further facilitated by the lack of effective camouflage measures. The scale of the Luftwaffe's success was evident in the Baltic Special Military District (since 22 June 1941 the North-Western Front), where a total of fifty-three operational aircraft were all that remained of the 7th, 8th, and 57th Aviation Divisions.[57] The Luftwaffe had achieved almost complete air superiority.

Damaging for Suvorov's thesis were the state of logistics and supply and the availability of engines and spare parts. For example, there was a marked shortage of surfacing material for the MiGs, propellers for the VISh-22E and VISh-2, spark plugs for the 3 MGA, and ammunition and other parts for the BS. Such shortages, inefficiencies, and incompetence were not only symptomatic of negligence on the part of those responsible for maintaining defensive capabilities; they were also compelling evidence that no major Soviet offensive was on the verge of being launched against German territory.

The general impression of unpreparedness is also conveyed by Grossman. In the first of his wartime diaries, Grossman records what Lieutenant Colonel Nemtsevich has to say about the start of the war, much of which flatly contradicts Suvorov:

> Nemtsevich has remarkably interesting things to say about the first night of the war, about the terrible, headlong retreat. For a day and a night he rushed about in a lorry, picking up the commanders' wives and children. He called into a small house and saw that some of our commanders had been killed: apparently they had been killed by saboteurs while asleep. This had happened in the western districts. He says that in the night of the German invasion he had to make a phone call on some trivial matter and it turned out that the line was damaged. He wanted to phone in a roundabout way but that did not work either. He was angry about this but did not pay any great attention to this. At the start of the war many of the senior commanders and generals were at resorts in Sochi. Many of the tank units were busy with a change of engines; many of the artillery units had no shells; and aviation units had no fuel for the aircraft. When phone calls started to be received from the border at the higher-echelon headquarters about the fact that the war had started, several of the border regions received the answer: "Don't succumb to provocation." This was the element of surprise in the most brutal and terrible meaning of the word.[58]

The nature and source of this testimony are significant. The fact that senior commanders were absent, that tanks were being repaired, and that aviation regiments had insufficient fuel does not support Suvorov's claim that the Red Army was about to attack German positions across the border. Moreover, one would expect a senior aviation officer like Nemtsevich, stationed in the border region, to confirm a higher state of readiness.

Overall Assessment of Suvorov's Thesis

According to Suvorov, Stalin was planning to attack Germany in 1941, but Hitler attacked first, succumbing to the strategic error of waging war on two fronts. Suvorov's SAT rests on a number of indicators with varying degrees of weight. The task here is to assess the individual indicators cited by Suvorov and determine whether, in the aggregate, they support the conclusion that Stalin was planning to attack Germany in the summer of 1941. In fact, the process of evaluating the overall effectiveness of Suvorov's case is broadly analogous to that used to analyze Stalin's failure to heed warnings of a German attack.

In all, Suvorov provides about thirty indicators of what he considers evidence of a planned Soviet attack against Germany. Most of these have already been analyzed, but they are summarized here and accompanied by a synoptic analytical response.

1. Dismantling the defensive zone and moving Soviet troops to the new border. (Comment: Whatever the advantages of having light forces forward, a large display of force on the border could constitute a display of force and a deterrent.)

2. Formation of massive airborne forces and glider units. According to Suvorov, "Paratroopers are not needed in a defensive war."[59] (Comment: In a state the size of the Soviet Union, large airborne forces can be deployed very quickly to remote areas as a defensive response to aggression and as a counter to insurgencies. They can also be used in a ground role and to mount raids behind enemy lines.)

3. Mass production of gliders in 1941, indicating their use in that year, since they cannot be kept outside in the harsh Russian winter. (Comment: Plans show that glider production was scheduled to increase in 1942, after the Soviet invasion envisaged by Suvorov.)

4. Mass production of the bystrokhodnyi tank. (Comment: This vehicle would have been unsuitable for use in rough terrain, whereas a tracked tank could be used both on- and off-road. These vehicles were not used in 1945 when the Red Army entered Germany, and they played no part in the reorganization of tank units, as indicated by Stalin's 5 May 1941 speech.)

5. Stalin's 5 May 1941 speech. (Comment: This speech contains no specific clue about the date of a Soviet attack. Stalin's message concerning the German military is contradictory: it is clearly successful, yet it has stagnated. The emphasis on the Soviet offensive is a response to potential German aggression and therefore demonstrates growing alarm about a German attack.)

6. Intensive study of how to overcome the passes in the Carpathian Mountains and seize the Romanian oil fields. (Comment: This may have been simply planning. Any such operation could have been initiated after a German attack to the north.)

7. Formation of river flotillas. (Comment: These flotillas could have served defensive purposes on the large rivers of western Russia.)

8. Deportations from border zones. (Comment: This could have been intended to disrupt German agent networks across the border and make the task of interdicting German agents much easier. By itself, it is not an indication of offensive action on the part of the Soviet Union.)

9. Increased aircraft and tank production. (Comment: Both offensive and defensive operations require sufficient tanks. In this regard, note that the German army had about half the number of tanks available to the Anglo-French armies in the summer of 1940. Doctrine and leadership at all levels are decisive.)

10. An aviation doctrine based exclusively on a first strike against enemy aerodromes. (Comment: This is evidence of a poorly trained air arm. Even if the doctrine is based on a first strike, no modern air force can forgo training for defense and other air operations.)

11. Plans for the rapid sovietization of occupied territories in the aftermath of invasion. (Comment: Sovietization was standard practice, as evidenced by the ideological program inflicted on the constituent republics of the Soviet Union after the Bolshevik seizure of power. Had Germany been defeated, it certainly would have been sovietized, as the Soviet zone and eastern Europe would be in 1945 and after. However, the drive to sovietize is not evidence of an attack plan.)

12. Stalin's desire to destroy Poland (Molotov–von Ribbentrop Pact) and have a common border with Germany. (Comment: The Soviet occupation of Poland and then the Baltic states can be construed as territorial aggrandizement. It is conceivable that an independent Poland could have concluded a nonaggression pact with Germany aimed at the Soviet Union. That possibility is removed if Poland ceases to exist.)

13. Occupation of Bessarabia and northern Bukovina. (Comment: As in the case of Poland, these occupations can be construed as both defensive moves and territorial aggrandizement.)

14. The preservation of too many bridges over the Bug, which assisted the German advance. (Comment: The Red Army intended to use these bridges, so they were not destroyed. In addition, destruction of the

bridges would have alerted the Germans that the Soviet side was suspicious, and it could have been construed as provocation.)

15. Removal of barbed wire in the border zones by the NKVD. (Comment: This could have been a deluded exercise in trust, a signal from the Soviet side that as far as they were concerned, everything was in order.)

16. Destruction of the Stalin Line—the *ukreplennye raiony*—followed by work on the Molotov Line on the new German-Soviet border to the west. (Comment: A defensive line well inside the country—even if built on the tactically sound principle of weakening the impact of an enemy surprise attack—could be construed, in the atmosphere of the Great Terror, as counterrevolutionary, a Trotskyist conspiracy, wrecking, sabotage, and treachery because it was predicated on maintaining minimal forces on the border and encouraged enemy forces to attack the Soviet Union. Thus, those who advocated building this line of fortifications were traitors.)

17. Stalin's assumption of new posts in May 1941. (Comment: Stalin was cautious, devious, mendacious, and duplicitous. He judged the time was right for him to assume these posts, including head of the army. If, as Suvorov claims, this was an attempt to concentrate his power, then Stalin's silence on 22 June 1941 was a spectacular failure of leadership and a dereliction of duty bordering on cowardice; to borrow from the Soviet ideological dictionary, it was an act of wrecking, counterrevolution, and sabotage. At such a moment of supreme crisis, Stalin himself should have addressed the people of the Soviet Union, rather than delegating the job to Molotov. Stalin's initial cowardice was compounded by his failure to address the nation until 3 July 1941. That Stalin survived this loss of nerve and was not removed lends some weight to Suvorov's claim that "the resilience of the highest state, political and military leadership in critical and in supercritical situations is one of the most important elements of a state's readiness for war."[60] By "readiness for war," Suvorov means readiness for the offensive. The resilience of the Soviet state was tested not in offensive operations but in its astonishing capacity to endure losses of men and equipment, above all from 22 June 1941 to 3 February 1943. No other European state could have endured such losses and survived.)

18. Dismantling of the partisan bases in the western regions in preparation for a sabotage—offensive—role behind German lines. (Comment: The dismantling of the entire partisan warfare infrastructure—with

its schools, arms, and rations dumps—that had been built up at such great cost in the late 1920s and 1930s must be seen as part of the general attack on the higher echelons of the Red Army in 1937–1938. Created and maintained by the Red Army, the partisan warfare network was an army within an army. Stalin—sensible of the ancient warning *quis custodiet ipsos custodes* (who guards the guards themselves?)—saw it as threat, so it was destroyed in the general onslaught against the Red Army and its commanders.)

19. A high proportion of soldiers in the Soviet airborne divisions with German names. (Comment: It is not clear that the number of soldiers with German names was out of the ordinary. It can also be noted that German-speaking Soviet parachutists were deployed to test the loyalties of Volga Germans and other German-speaking Soviet minorities.[61] The presence of German-speaking soldiers and soldiers with German names in Soviet airborne units is not decisive in itself.)

20. The formation of the *Pinskaia voennaia flotiliia* (Pinsk Military Flotilla) and the construction of the Pinsk-Kobrin canal: "The sole significance of the canal was to enable ships into the Vistula basin and further to the west."[62] (Comment: The *Pinskaia voennaia flotiliia* could easily serve defensive purposes, as could the Pinsk-Kobrin canal.)

21. Deceiving one's own troops about the true nature of deployment—a sure sign of an offensive. (Comment: Deceiving one's own troops could also be a sign that Soviet officials recognized the danger posed by Germany and wanted to keep the troops in the dark. All armies operate on the need-to-know principle—that is, to prevent leaks, information is withheld from soldiers unless they need to know it to perform their operational duties. In addition, censorship, organized lying, and deception were routine in the Soviet Union; this type of deception enjoyed no special status.)

22. Creation of a second strategic echelon. "After Germany initiated a preventive war, the second strategic echelon (like the first) was used for defense. But that in no way means that it was created for that purpose."[63] (Comment: But that did not exclude the possibility that its primary purpose was defensive. Also, this measure could be designed to reinforce both the offensive and counteroffensive abilities of the Soviet state.)

23. Arming and deploying zeks (zeks are *zakliuchennye*, labor camp inmates) from the Urals, Siberia, and Trans-Baikal before 22 June 1941 and the presence of so-called Black divisions. (Comment: Zeks and the Black

divisions were expendable in the grand scheme of Soviet planning and must be seen as an urgent defensive measure.)

24. Releasing various senior officers from the gulag. (Comment: By the time these officers were released, the Great Terror had come to an end. Against the background of World War II, the release of these officers is evidence that even Stalin realized he could not afford to waste talent, although this failed to save Pavlov and others.)

25. Redeployment of air units close to the border. (Comment: Given that there were large numbers of Soviet troops on the border whose presence was intended to be defensive, the presence of supporting air units would be expected.)

26. The Red Army was not trained for defensive operations. (Comment: Citing Major-General Gretsov, Suvorov argues that there was no plan in the event the Soviet Union was attacked; there was only a plan for offensive operations.[64] Even if the Red Army was not trained for defensive operations—a profound weakness—Zhukov's plans emphasize the need to defend the borders. The directives he issued to the Western, Kiev, and Odessa Special Military Districts in May 1941 do not support Suvorov's view. Counterattacks can also serve defensive purposes. Suvorov contends that in both theory and practice, the German Blitzkrieg was "strikingly similar" to the Soviet theory of the deep operation (*glubokaia operatsiia*).[65] Blitzkrieg relied on the efficient cooperation of all arms: air, artillery, infantry, armor, airborne, and special forces. It required very high levels of training and command and control and devolved significant decision-making powers to junior leaders. No comparable doctrine existed in the Red Army, and the poor Soviet command and control (to mention just one failing) translated into chaos and predictable moves that played into the hands of German commanders. Whether the operations are primarily offensive or defensive, the qualities needed by commanders for the successful prosecution of the Blitzkrieg doctrine are the same, with an emphasis on flexibility. Even after the Red Army had recovered some of its composure in the summer of 1941, one finds very little evidence of these qualities.)

27. The fronts were formed before the war, indicating a hostile intent because fronts are formed only in wartime. (Comment: The formation of fronts before the war could indicate that some Soviet planners were anticipating a German attack and planning ahead. By itself, it is not an indication that the Soviet Union was planning to attack Germany. In

this regard, it can be noted that the North-Western Front was formed on the basis of the Baltic Special Military District on 22 June 1941.[66] Designating the special military districts on the border as fronts before an attack might have been picked up by German intelligence.)

28. Golikov found no evidence of serious German planning for an attack against the Soviet Union. (Comment: Given the amount of high-quality intelligence reports from many sources that had been accumulating since June 1940, this assertion carries no weight. Golikov's obsession with oily rags and sheep production is irrelevant when measured against the vast array of other intelligence data. Moreover, there is a glaring inconsistency between Suvorov's claim that Golikov found no evidence of serious German planning for an attack against the Soviet Union and his assertion that "a huge number of reports were coming in from the Soviet border about the fact that German officers were conducting intensive reconnaissance. This is a clear sign of the approach of war."[67] If German reconnaissance of the border was not taken seriously by Golikov, there is no good reason for Suvorov to see reconnaissance of the border by Soviet officers as evidence of a Soviet intention to attack Germany.)

The Stalin attack thesis also spectacularly unravels when examined alongside the devastating conclusions about the state of Soviet military forces in a report presented to Timoshenko by Voroshilov dated 7 December 1940.[68] The report focuses on the organizational structure of the Soviet armed forces, operational preparation, size and personnel of the Red Army, mobilization measures, status of the cadres, combat training of the troops, current status of various arms of service, intelligence work, antiaircraft defense, rear services, equipment and medical services, military innovation, and even the state of the Soviet military publishing houses. This document is a thorough, comprehensive, and often brutally frank review of the state of the Soviet armed forces at the end of 1940.

To begin with, Voroshilov points out that the 1934 statute regulating the Defense Commissariat is obsolete. The huge number of organizations and directorates—totaling thirty-four—and the dissemination of responsibilities complicate and delay the decision-making process. Another complicating factor is the existence of too many manuals, handbooks, and sets of regulations—at the time, about 1,080. Indirectly described here is the organizational chaos arising from the changes that tore apart the Soviet state in the 1930s—above all, the Great Terror. The climate of fear it created had a direct effect on the willingness of individual directorates and their staffs to show initiative and make decisions. In such circumstances, the safe position is to await orders and thus avoid accusations of wrecking (vreditel'stvo). This state of affairs is hardly optimal for overall military effectiveness at any time, let alone for the Soviet Union at the end of 1940.

Regarding operational preparation, the shortcomings are hardly amenable to rapid improvement. Most striking is the admission that the Soviet General Staff possesses no data concerning the condition of forces on the borders: "The decisions of the district military councils, the armies and fronts on this question are not known to the General Staff."[69] The report also notes: "Supervision of operational preparation in the districts [okrugi] is practically nonexistent."[70] Preparation for military operations in the likely theater of war is acknowledged to be weak in all respects. Some of the more glaring deficiencies are specified: no procedures have been established to regulate the work of the two main agencies critical for the smooth running of the rail network in wartime, the Narodnyi Komissariat Putei Soobshchenii SSSR (People's Commissariat of Communications of the USSR) and the Organy voennykh soobshchenii Krasnoi Armii (Organs of Military Communications of the Red Army); road construction is proceeding too slowly, mainly because too many agencies are involved and there is no general plan or clear direction; the aerodromes in western Belorussia, western Ukraine, the Odessa Military District, and the Transcaucasia Military District are "extremely weak";[71] there is no clear plan for engineering work, and arming of the reinforced regions on the western borders is a matter of the greatest urgency; and there are serious shortages in the provision of maps in the likely zones of military operations. Scarcely believable is the admission that the People's Commissariat of Defense has no precise figure for the overall manpower of the Red Army. Blame for this deficiency is placed firmly on the Main Directorate of the Red Army, whose calculation, in the words of the report, "is in an exceptionally neglected state."[72]

Mobilization plans—so critical for the SAT—are also in disarray. The report notes: "The Narkomat has no new mobilization plan."[73] The partial mobilization carried out in September 1939 (a reference to the Soviet invasion of Poland) revealed a series of failings that have still not been resolved. Among these are extreme negligence in the assessment of those subject to military service (the most recent calculation was performed in 1927), inefficient mobilization, a whole series of unrealistic calculations about cavalry and transport, and the absence of a policy strictly reserving manpower in time of war.

Severe criticism is also aimed at the training of military command cadres. Preparation is especially weak at the platoon and company levels. Teaching at the military academies is also deemed to be poor. The main criticisms are too much classroom work, lack of field exercises, and "saturating the teaching programs with general subjects to the detriment of military matters."[74] This last point may be taken as a hint that time allocated to lectures on Marxism-Leninism, dialectical materialism, the history of the Communist Party, and the wickedness of capitalism do nothing to prepare soldiers for modern war. Still more alarming, "in questions of the mastery of military knowledge there was no firmly regulated system and in a number of cases there was evidence of slackness followed by bouts of intense activity."[75]

Multiple and serious shortcomings are also noted in the combat training of Red Army soldiers: junior leaders are poorly trained (an area in which the German army is especially strong); tactical training in all areas is weak, especially small-unit reconnaissance; and tactical field training is very poor, with "an inability on the part of the troops to carry out what was required in conditions of a combat situation."[76] Another major shortcoming is instruction in all-arms cooperation: the infantry cannot maintain contact with a rolling artillery barrage, the artillery cannot support the tanks, and the air force is unable to cooperate with ground forces. For armed forces that are supposedly preparing to mount a surprise attack on the most formidable opponent in the world, these are exceptionally serious flaws. The report also notes an atmosphere of "false democracy" and "undermining of the commander's authority."[77] To what degree this lack of discipline can be attributed to the purges is not clear, but military discipline is unquestionably undermined by a climate of "vigilance" that encourages people to denounce so-called wreckers and enemies of the people rather than strive for military professionalism and excellence.

Turning to the various arms of service, Voroshilov concludes that in terms of military training, the infantry is by far the worst prepared: "Infantry armaments lag behind the modern requirements of battle, mortars and submachine guns have not been provided."[78] This would have predictable consequences when the Wehrmacht and Red Army eventually clashed. In addition, the *Voenno-Vozdushnye Sily* (VVS), the Soviet air force, is nowhere near ready to play a vital role in any first strike against the Wehrmacht. The introduction to the relevant paragraph could not be clearer: "In its development over the last three years the equipment of the VVS of the Red Army lags behind the speed, range, power of engines and aircraft armaments of the most advanced air forces of other countries."[79] The Air Force Directorate is criticized for failing to push for new designs (a thoroughly unjust criticism) and is blamed for the VVS's lack of dive-bombers.

The litany of failings and shortcomings just goes on: spare parts are inadequate, the network of aerodromes is insufficient, airfield maintenance cannot guarantee the operational use of aerodromes year-round, bombing accuracy is poor, aircrews cannot cope with bad weather, there is a lack of training in the use of mounted weapons, and pilot quality is poor. Because of poor pilot training, the incidence of major air accidents remains high. This matter came before Stalin. At a meeting of the Politburo on 9 April 1941, it was noted that "as a result of slackness, we lose, on average, on a daily basis, in air accidents and disasters 2–3 aircraft which amounts to about 600–900 aircraft a year."[80] No mention was made of aircrew losses, which, depending on the type of plane (bombers had bigger crews), could easily amount to 2,000 killed and injured annually. When called on to explain the high accident rate, Rychagov, the young commander of the air force, left Stalin in no doubt about the cause: "You force us to fly in coffins!"[81] One week later Rychagov was arrested. Other factors contributing to the high accident rates include lack of familiarity with the aircraft, poor discipline, lack of organization in training, and irresponsibility on the part of unit and brigade commanders.[82]

The SAT places special emphasis on the role of Soviet airborne forces. Here, too, the findings of the Voroshilov report are hardly propitious. Voroshilov notes, for example, that these units "have not received their due development" and "lag behind modern requirements."[83] A critical weakness is that combat training and the provision of aircraft is divided between two agencies, which weakens command, control, and training. The logical step, which has already been taken by the Germans, is to place parachute and glider troops under the control of the Luftwaffe and not divide training and transport between two arms (as eventually happened in Britain).

The role of armored units in any Soviet first strike is essential, but the signs are not good. There are delays in production and a lack of repair facilities; crucially, the tank units are not properly trained in all-arms cooperation. The lack of prime movers means that the heavy artillery lacks mobility. Things look somewhat better in terms of artillery, although there is a shortage of calibers over 203mm and a critical shortage of armor-piercing and incendiary ammunition. A deficit in binoculars is also noted; this may appear to be a minor problem, but it severely undermines terrain reconnaissance and the effective fire control of heavy machine guns, mortars, and artillery.

The scale of Soviet assault operations envisaged by Suvorov also requires highly trained and well-equipped engineers and signallers, but there are major deficiencies in both areas. Soviet military engineers lack modern road-building equipment, excavators, and deep-drilling platforms. There is also an exceptional shortage of barbed wire. Soviet military engineers are judged to be lacking sufficient training in surmounting reinforced zones and obstacles and in clearing minefields.[84] The main communications devices are telephones and telegraphs, which are admittedly obsolete. Radio communications are inadequate, and the provision of such equipment is progressing very slowly. There is also an acute shortage of equipment suitable for the transmission of high-speed and secure communications. In fact, these communications failures had been exposed earlier in the war against Finland and during the deployment in Poland, and they had obviously not been rectified. One advantage of the lack of modern all-arms communications was that it dramatically reduced the amount of intelligence data available to the Germans through radio intercepts, but this advantage was far outweighed by the Red Army's inability to exploit radio for command and control, with severe consequences for high-speed, mobile warfare. Insufficient quantities of modern radio equipment substantially contributed to the catastrophic command and control failures that rapidly became apparent after 22 June 1941. These logistical failings were used against Pavlov in July 1941.

Given the role played by intelligence in all phases of war, the report's admission in this regard is staggering: "The organization of intelligence is one of the weakest sectors in the work of the People's Commissariat of Defense. There is no provision for the organizational intelligence and the systematic receipt of data about foreign armies."[85] The explanation for this lamentable state of affairs is that the various organizations engaged in intelligence gathering do not communicate effectively with one another. Even in a matter as critical as the intentions of the Wehrmacht, there appears to be a tendency to withhold intelligence data. This failing is by no means confined to Soviet intelligence agencies. The currency of intelligence agencies is reliable, hard information, and when there is more than one state agency collecting and disseminating information, institutional prerogatives and rivalries can assert themselves, imperiling the state.

Once initiated, high-speed offensive operations require well-organized rear-echelon services, as the Germans would discover. The same would be true for any Soviet attack. But according to Voroshilov, the training of the command staff responsible for administering the rear echelons is poor. Over the last two years, there has been no special training in this all-important area, despite the clear order that all military exercises must include a training component for rear-echelon staff. Because of the security restrictions placed on the relevant manual, command staff are not familiar with the procedures to be followed. It apparently does not occur to Voroshilov that this may explain why the operations of the rear echelons have not been properly tested. Additional failings are noted: rear-echelon services have not been prepared in the territories annexed by the Soviet Union in 1939–1940 (the Baltic states and eastern Poland), and the 1940 equipment and armament plan for the military districts has not yet been released by the Main Directorate of the Red Army. The primary consequence of the latter is that "it is not possible to process the provision of troops in both peacetime *and wartime*."[86] A major failing of the military operations carried out in 1939–1940 was military supply administration, and at the end of 1940, "Military administration continues to remain in a neglected condition."[87] The provision of medical services is also judged to be unsatisfactory. The Medical Directorate is blamed for not providing well-trained medical personnel or ensuring the appropriate number of surgeons. However, the harshest criticism leveled at the Medical Directorate is that during the Soviet-Finnish war it played no part in burying the dead on the battlefield.[88]

The Voroshilov report offers no support whatsoever for Suvorov's thesis that Stalin was planning to mount a preemptive strike against the Wehrmacht in 1941. First, many of the failings of the Red Army that came to light in the Soviet-Finnish war and in the invasions of the Baltic states and eastern Poland—operations against far less formidable foes than the Wehrmacht—have still not been rectified. Second, given the breadth and depth of these failings, there are no plausible grounds for believing that they could have been eliminated in 1941. Third, although not admitted by Voroshilov, the institutional chaos in the Red Army must be seen as a direct consequence of Stalin's paranoia about plots and spies and his relentless purges and murders of Red Army officers. The result of these attacks on his own commanders is a lack of institutional continuity and confidence.

Conclusion

One of the greatest challenges posed by Suvorov's SAT is that some senior Soviet commanders have conceded that Stalin was indeed planning to attack Germany. Thus, commenting on Admiral Kuznetsov's book, *Nakanune*, Suvorov concludes:

> The admiral completely, openly and clearly is telling us that Stalin considered war inevitable and was making serious preparations for it. However Stalin did not intend to enter into war in response to German aggression but at a moment of his choosing. In other words, Stalin was making ready to strike first; that is to initiate aggression against Germany. But Hitler launched a preemptive strike and all Stalin's plans were ruined.[89]

Suvorov also cites General Ivanov, who, in his book *Nachal'nyi period voiny: po opytu kampanii i operatsii vtoroi mirovoi voiny* (The Initial Period of the War: Based on the Experience of the Campaigns and Operations of the Second World War [1974]), claims that Germany acted before Stalin could do so.[90] Given that there are senior Soviet officers ready to admit that Hitler merely beat Stalin to the start, one has to ask why Germany's attack is considered to be *verolomno* (treacherous) and why, in spite of their assessments, Stalin and the Soviet Union are viewed as victims rather than would-be aggressors. One possibility is that Soviet historians, former officers, and the party agitprop machine were playing a double game. Two completely different views of 22 June 1941—on the one hand, that the Germans were the aggressors, and on the other hand, that the Soviet Union was planning to attack Germany—might be seen as a face-saving formula: the military was well aware of the threat and was planning to do something about it, but Germany, acting treacherously, attacked the Soviet Union; Stalin, aware of Hitler's plans, lost his nerve and permitted nothing that would provoke the Germans. Thus, all the responsibility for the Germans' surprise attack falls on Stalin, not on the Red Army. Even if that were the case, it does not seem possible that if the Red Army were about to launch an attack it could not convert to defense when the Germans attacked first. Another factor that militates against the theory that Hitler attacked the Soviet Union because he suspected a Soviet preemptive strike is the absence of any evidence that German intelligence agencies were reporting a Soviet plan to attack Germany. Guderian's references on this subject, as noted in chapter 1, are too vague to carry any weight.

Regardless of their pretensions to peaceful coexistence and fraternity and their signing of treaties promising eternal friendship, all states engage in military contingency planning. In view of this brute fact of international politics, it is inconceivable that the Soviet General Staff did not consider the option of expanding Soviet power by force, with a view to sovietizing other states. Indeed, such aggressive expansionism was mandated by Marxist-Leninist doctrines of class war and global revolution. If Stalin's intention to attack Germany along the lines asserted by Suvorov in *Icebreaker* was serious, one would expect to find a detailed plan for such an undertaking. So far, no such plan has come to light. There are only two plausible explanations for this missing link: (1) no such plan ever existed because Stalin never intended to launch a preemptive attack against Germany, or (2) such a plan does indeed exist, but it has not been declassified. If such a plan ever came to light, it would be a stunning vindication of Suvorov's Stalin attack thesis—a brilliant historical-analytical *Meisterstück* (masterpiece). But it would also mean that the Western view of World War II, especially the relationship between National Socialist Germany and the Marxist-Leninist-Stalinist Soviet Union, would be changed forever. That being the case, would the Russian Federation ever sanction the full publication of Stalin's plan to invade Germany in July 1941, undermining the whole view of World War II and the heroic nature of the Red Army?

9 The Legacy of *Unternehmen* Barbarossa

> As far as high-speed mechanized troops are concerned and their location on the forward zone, one has, in general, to see the threat of their sudden concentration in the mere fact of their existence. These motorized troops, having carried out a march of up to 100 kilometers on the day before or even during the last night, turn up on the very border only at that moment when the decision has been taken to cross the border and to invade enemy territory.
>
> *Georgii Isserson*, New Forms of Combat

To this day, the coordinated diplomatic and military planning at the heart of *Unternehmen* Barbarossa remains a model of how to confuse a future enemy with assurances of nonaggression while simultaneously planning a surprise attack. For this reason, among others, Barbarossa warrants careful study, certainly by military planners. The stamp of Barbarossa can be found not only on the Japanese attack on Pearl Harbor and some of the closing campaigns of World War II—the Normandy landings in June 1944, for example—but also on the Israeli-Arab Six-Day War (1967), the Soviet invasion of Czechoslovakia (1968), Soviet plans to attack NATO across the inner-German border during the Cold War, and Operation Desert Storm (1991). Other questions arising from Barbarossa are these: Why was the Soviet regime caught unprepared (complicated in part by the sensational claims of Viktor Suvorov)? And how did Hitler influence the decision whether to make the capture of Moscow the highest priority?

Introduction

There is, of course, one major difference between Unternehmen Barbarossa and the D-Day landings in 1944: there was no nonaggression pact between Britain and Germany that might have led one side to miss the threat. The Germans knew that a landing would be attempted at some stage and were able to take various measures to prepare for it. For their part, the Anglo-American planners were aware that the enemy—an enemy that had repeatedly demonstrated astonishing powers of recovery on all fronts of the European theater of operations—awaited their arrival. Unlike the British army that had exited the European continent in the summer of 1940, the Wehrmacht in France was not psychologically weak in the summer of 1944; it was ready and resolved to fight. The critical problem facing the Allies was therefore how to deceive the enemy concerning the time and place of the landings. In terms of the intelligence battle, the Allies played a masterful hand, confusing and misleading the enemy intelligence services such that total surprise was achieved on 6 June 1944. Even after the Normandy landings, the Germans continued to believe that they were just a diversion. One outcome was that some German units were held in reserve; if they had been deployed on D-Day, they could have affected the success of the landings.

With regard to the period immediately before the outbreak of hostilities in the Six-Day War and the Soviet invasion of Czechoslovakia, there are some elements that bear a resemblance to the state of German-Soviet relations before the launch of Barbarossa. If the preemptive strikes against Egypt and Syria were to stand any chance of success, Israeli planners knew they had to maintain the fiction that Israel was unprepared for war and willing to negotiate, while simultaneously preparing to seize the initiative. To undermine the resistance of Czechoslovak leaders, Soviet negotiators talked publicly of socialist solidarity and fraternity while mobilizing the forces of the Warsaw Pact for intervention. Even allowing for this unequal confrontation, Soviet deception and intelligence measures, refined in the invasion of Hungary twelve years previously, were impressive. By the time Czechoslovak politicians recognized the truth, it was too late.

Soviet planning for an attack across the inner-German border to defeat NATO forces in a molnienosnaia voina owed much to Isserson. All forces, certainly the armored and mechanized infantry divisions, along with their support services, were located as far forward as possible. This concentration of forces had taken place over years, and once established, it was regarded as the norm. Then, all that was required was an escalation in diplomatic and political tension—ideally, outside the main zone of intended operations, possibly the Middle East—and the Soviet shock armies would be deployed, taking NATO forces in Germany by just enough surprise to ensure the necessary momentum to bring Warsaw Pact forces to the French coast.

With regard to Desert Storm, the situation was more akin to the D-Day landings. In this case, the occupier had considerably less military expertise than the Anglo-Americans' opponent in Normandy, but Iraq was expecting an attack and had to be taken by surprise. When the advantages of technology and training so overwhelmingly favor one side, as they did in Desert Storm, tactical surprise is not essential, but it is desirable. In the period leading up to the invasion of Iraq in March 2003, the role played by intelligence data was crucial, as it was in Barbarossa. Whereas Stalin chose to ignore reliable intelligence material pointing to a German invasion, senior Anglo-American politicians and military leaders were accused of tampering with intelligence material in order to justify military action against Iraq to a skeptical public. These charges have yet to be fully investigated. Mindful of what happened to those individuals who crossed Stalin, Soviet intelligence officers justified telling the boss what he wanted to hear. American and British intelligence officers had no such excuses. Highlighted in both cases—the Soviet Union in 1941 and the American-led invasion of Iraq in 2003—is that leaders who exert too much pressure on their intelligence agencies court national catastrophe (in the case of Stalin) or policy disaster (in the case of the US-led coalition).[1] Hitler's arrogance about what would happen after the start of Barbarossa anticipated the arrogance and unbridled optimism of the US-led coalition that invaded Iraq. Both invaders were taken aback by the insurgencies they unleashed, and both struggled to contain them.

Barbarossa and Stalin

As David Glantz states in his operational analysis of the German invasion of the Soviet Union, "The most vexing question associated with Operation Barbarossa is how the Wehrmacht was able to achieve such overwhelming political and military surprise."[2] There were, he argues, a number of plausible reasons for Stalin to reject the possibility of a German attack: warnings and hints from the British that Hitler was planning to attack were seen as an attempt of the British side to foment a war between Germany and the Soviet Union, and the Soviet side had succumbed to the Germans' deception plan. However, even allowing for the fact that "the purges had decimated

Soviet intelligence operations as well as the military command structure,"[3] Soviet intelligence assets were performing very well, judging by the material in the two volumes of 1941 *god*. There was plenty of evidence from a variety of sources that the huge buildup of German forces was not inconsequential. Confronted with these data, neither the intelligence services nor the leader to whom they reported could afford to assume that these large-scale deployments of men and equipment were benign, certainly not in the tense and uncertain atmosphere of Europe in 1941. The Soviet failure is even more unforgivable and inexplicable because of Stalin's role in destroying the Polish state. All the negotiations with von Ribbentrop over the Non-Aggression Pact and the secret protocols told him everything he needed to know about Hitler. Having seen the methods Hitler used against Poland, Stalin had no right to assume that the Soviet Union would never fall victim to those same methods. In this regard, Isserson's analysis of how the war between Germany and Poland started is masterful and prescient, which probably did nothing to raise his stock with his dear leader after 22 June 1941.[4]

Zhukov indirectly acknowledges the importance of Isserson's analysis in the published version of his memoirs (1969). He makes the unusually candid admission that senior Soviet figures (not just Stalin) failed to grasp the nature of the new type of war pioneered by the Germans:

> The sudden transition to the offensive on such scales, with all the immediately available and earlier deployed forces on the most important strategic lines of advance, that is the nature of the assault itself, in its entire capacity, was not envisaged by us. Neither the People's Commissar, nor I, nor my predecessors B. M. Shaposhnikov, K. A. Meretskov and the leadership stratum of the General Staff had reckoned with the fact that the enemy would concentrate such a mass of armored and motorized troops and deploy them on the very first day by means of powerful, concentrated formations on all the strategic lines of advance with the aim of inflicting shattering, tearing blows.[5]

In a supplement published after his death, Zhukov, having confirmed that the 13 June 1941 TASS communiqué contributed to a dangerous sense of complacency among the border troops, goes much further in his criticism of Soviet conceptual awareness and planning:

But by far the most major deficiency in our military-political strategy was the fact that we had not drawn the appropriate conclusions from the experience of the initial period of World War II; and the experience was available. As is known, the German armed forces suddenly invaded Austria, Czechoslovakoslovakia, Belgium, Holland, France and Poland and by means of a battering-ram strike consisting of huge armored forces overran the opposing troops and rapidly achieved their mission. Our General Staff and the People's Commissar had not studied the new methods for the conduct of the initial period of a war, and had not imparted the corresponding recommendations to the troops for their further operational-tactical training and for the reworking of obsolete operational-mobilization plans and other plans linked to the initial period of a war.[6]

From an outstanding field commander such as Zhukov, these criticisms, aimed at himself and others, are a fitting endorsement of Isserson.

Regarding whether Golikov, the head of the GRU, had accepted the explanation that deployments in the east were tied to German operations in the Balkans, attention should be drawn to an analysis carried out by Golikov on behalf of the Soviet General Staff. He notes that the buildup of German troops and equipment had not been halted by German operations in the Balkans. Over the last two months (March and April 1941), the number of German divisions in the border zone with the Soviet Union had risen from 70 to 107, and the number of tank divisions deployed had increased from 6 to 12.[7]

Finally, Glantz points to institutional failings as the main reason for the Soviet Union's failure to act in good time: "In retrospect, the most serious Soviet failure was neither strategic surprise nor tactical surprise, but institutional surprise. In June 1941 the Red Army and Air Force were in transition, changing their organization, leadership, equipment, training, troop dispositions and defensive plans."[8] On its face, this seems plausible. Unfortunately, it shifts attention from the role played by Stalin. Stalin attacked the security institutions—NKVD, Red Army, and GRU—on which he relied. The institutions that emerged after these terror attacks were gravely weakened. Their institutional failings can be directly attributed to Stalin: they were Stalin's institutions. Characterizing the outcome of Stalin's murderous paranoia—and in terms of the Red Army's ability to prosecute modern war, it was almost suicidal—as institutional failings understates Stalin's responsibility. Stalin's judicial terrorism also highlights the ideological failures of Marxism-Leninism and its internal obsession with class war, which were clearly inimical to the cool appraisal of military affairs and the need to prepare for modern war. Appeals to Russian nationalism, which were implied in Stalin's radio address of 3 July 1941 and made explicit during the battle for Stalingrad, are further evidence of ideological failure. The emphasis on class struggle by Soviet military theorists such as Tukhachevskii, Frunze, and Triandafillov was wrong, and it distorted military planning and the assessment of intelligence data.

Here it is essential to recapitulate the damage inflicted by Stalin's purges. There were four main effects on the Soviet armed forces, all of which were disastrous: experienced commanders were removed; the subsequent personnel replacement policy resulted in inexperienced commanders being promoted before they were ready; professional competence and morale were undermined; and, after 22 June 1941, political control was tightened even further as a consequence of the command and control failures brought on by the purges.

First, and most obviously, the purges led to the removal of large numbers of middle-ranking and senior commanders, men who had come through the civil war and gone on to study modern war and the impact of technological changes, especially in armored warfare, and to formulate a new doctrine suitable for the Red Army. Being arrested and executed did not, in itself, mean that a commander was of exceptional caliber, but even moderately competent officers at all levels who are experienced and have passed the necessary training courses—the backbone of any army—are not easily replaced, especially in wartime. It is impossible to know how a Red Army that had not been subjected to Stalin's purges would have performed in the summer of 1941. However, it certainly would have been much better prepared to take on the Germans. That said, even an unscathed Red Army would have had to contend with the grave handicap of Stalin's refusal to heed intelligence warnings and act on them. An interesting question here is whether senior Red Army commanders in an army that had been untouched by purges would have tolerated Stalin's vacillation in the face of obvious danger. Even after 22 June 1941—such was the climate of paranoia—a disbelief in high-quality intelligence data and the practice of telling the boss what he wanted to hear continued. For example, the volume of high-quality information being passed on by the British traitors Anthony Blunt, Kim Philby, Donald Maclean, John Cairncross, and Guy Burgess to their Soviet handlers aroused suspicions in Moscow that Blunt and the others were double agents.[9]

The removal of so many commanders at all levels and throughout the institutional structure of the Red Army meant that their replacements lacked the experience and training to command the posts they now occupied. Many of the newly promoted, called *vydvizhentsy*, surely knew that the bizarre accusations leveled against their former superiors were false, making them far more vulnerable to and more dependent on ideological considerations, rather than purely military ones. As a result, military professionalism suffered, and personal initiative was stifled.

The arrest, public vilification, and execution of so many commanders undermined discipline and weakened junior officers' confidence in their superiors. In fact, a climate was created in which junior commanders with personal grudges or those driven by ideological vendettas were encouraged to denounce their superiors for lacking vigilance (*bditel'nost'*), engaging in wrecking (*vreditel'stvo*), or succumbing to ideological deviation (*uklonizm*). Predictably, the result was a severe weakening of morale, an eradication of unit cohesion, and a collapse in professional solidarity. History provides plenty of examples of outnumbered armies defeating numerically larger and better-equipped foes, but no armed forces, ancient or modern, can function with poor morale and an absence of unit cohesion and where the heroes of yesterday are vilified as traitors.

The damage done by the purges to doctrine, equipment procurement schedules, training, deployment, morale, effective command and control, and leadership was evident immediately after 22 June 1941, but even when confronted with the catastrophic results of their purges of the Red Army, Stalin and his party apparatus were unable to see that the unfolding disaster was a consequence of their vendettas. On the contrary, they saw it as evidence of treachery on an unimaginable scale. In this grotesque scenario, the basic principle of the purges, they persuaded themselves, had been correct: it had just not gone *far enough*. What was now needed to restore the situation, they believed, was not less party control but more, and so they reinstated dual command, among other things. Dual command was not merely a very public display of the party's lack of faith in the Red Army, which was soon picked up by enemy propagandists. Being the very opposite of the German doctrine of *Auftragstaktik* (military tradition that stresses personal initiative), without which all-arms operations could not properly function, it complicated command and control (to put it mildly), playing straight into the hands of German commanders and enhancing their already demonstrably superior tactical leadership.

Barbarossa's failure to deliver the knockout blow and the subsequent failure to take Moscow suggest that December 1941 was the moment Germany lost the war. At best, it could expect a long war of attrition in a struggle against the combined might of the United States, the British Empire, and the Soviet Union, with predictable consequences. At the risk of being accused of Anglocentrism, I suggest that the failure to destroy or capture the defeated British Expeditionary Force at Dunkirk, and certainly the failure to invade England in the summer of 1940, marked the moment when Germany's chances of winning the war were, if not fatally damaged, at least severely undermined. Granted, as von Manstein has explained only too clearly, the risks of Operation Sea Lion were enormous, but if successful, the rewards would have been stunning. That Hitler was prepared to attack the Soviet Union before Britain had been eliminated is doubly puzzling. First, it suggests that Hitler did not consider the threat posed by Britain serious enough to warrant giving it immediate priority. Second, the risks of attacking the Soviet Union and failing were far greater than the risks of attacking England and being defeated. Here, the factor of time was critical for German ambitions: if the Soviet Union could be defeated in a short campaign, the full weight of German arms could then be turned against Britain. The longer the campaign on the Eastern Front lasted, the more resilient Britain would become and the greater its capacity to mobilize British military might. An alliance between Britain and the Soviet Union would then be a near certainty. That the British were a meddlesome force in the Balkans and a ubiquitous and aggressive presence in the Mediterranean in the months immediately before Barbarossa, though frequently thwarted by German intervention, was evidence enough of what lay in store for Germany if Britain was not checked.

Instead of invading England and, if succeeding, changing the strategic situation in Europe to his overwhelming advantage, Hitler turned east. The Blitzkrieg failed, and by the middle of December 1941, Germany found itself at war with the United States, Britain, and the Soviet Union. The advantages of surprise and the benefits of ruthless treachery that had served Hitler so well since 1933 had now been exhausted. The military, technological, and doctrinal advantages Germany had enjoyed from September 1939 to December 1941 were now being matched and surpassed by its opponents.

Reasons for the Failure of Barbarossa

The factors that contributed to the failure of Barbarossa can be summarized as follows: (1) time, space, and terrain; (2) inconsistent attitudes toward nationalism; (3) the brutal treatment of Soviet prisoners of war and commissars; (4) the role of the *Einsatzgruppen* (the mass murder of Jews); (5) plans for agricultural exploitation and the retention of Soviet collective farms; (6) the assumption that the Soviet Union would collapse very quickly; (7) Hitler's failure to make a radio address to the Soviet people; and (8) failure to pursue military objectives—the capture of Moscow—to the exclusion of everything else, as recommended by Guderian and other generals.

Time, space, and terrain, along with weather, are factors in the planning and execution of all military operations. The Blitzkrieg doctrine was best suited to the distances and terrain found in western Europe. Even though there were natural and artificial terrain obstacles in the western theater of operations, these could be overcome, as the Germans demonstrated, without losing momentum because the operational area was so much smaller. Moreover, the advanced infrastructure of western Europe—highways, roads, railways, and bridges—facilitated and accelerated the Blitzkrieg, since the invader could exploit them for the rapid deployment of men and equipment and for purposes of resupply. Another advantage arising from the smaller operational area in western Europe was that the invader could seize assets—arms factories, power stations, dams, ports, ships, and food production plants—in a coup de main before they could be destroyed. In western Europe a scorched-earth policy was neither realistic nor psychologically acceptable to the inhabitants. On the Eastern Front, however, there was often time to evacuate major assets, especially plants and factories further east; where evacuation was not possible, industrial assets such as dams could be prepared for demolition. In the east the invader had to reckon with poor-quality roads and rail lines that were often rendered unusable by rain and snow.

The German invasion of the Soviet Union was also characterized by inconsistent and duplicitous policies toward nationalist movements. In the planning phase of Barbarossa, nationalist movements in Ukraine were exploited by the Abwehr, and the threat posed by these movements was taken very seriously by the NKVD. In contrast, the highest levels of the RSHA (the main terror and police agency of the NS regime) regarded nationalist movements with suspicion, and German planning documents make it clear that there was never any serious intention to abolish the Soviet collective farm system; this would be retained to maximize agricultural production for Germany.

However, there is evidence that some German administrators were willing to grant a degree of local autonomy in the occupied areas. One of the more interesting experiments took place in the Orlov district. The 2nd Panzer Army permitted the creation of the autonomous Lokot region, based on the village of Lokot. By the end of the summer of 1942, the Lokot self-governing region had expanded to include eight regions of the Orlov and Kursk districts, with a total population of about 581,000. All German troops were withdrawn, and the region was given self-governing status. To quote the recent work of a Russian historian:

> German troops, headquarters and command structures were withdrawn beyond the borders of the district, in which the whole spectrum of power was conferred on an Oberbürgermeister, based on a ramified administrative apparatus and numerous armed formations made up of local inhabitants and prisoners. The only demands made of the self-government were that supplies of foodstuffs were delivered to the German army and that it prevented the growth of a partisan movement.[10]

It turns out that the Lokot self-government even had its own political party, *Narodnaia Sotsialisticheskaia Partiia Rossii* (The People's Socialist Party of Russia), and its main aim was the destruction of the communist system and the collective farms. The leaders of this experiment saw a self-governing Lokot as the basis for the rebirth of Russia. One can only imagine the frenzy of hatred this experiment aroused in Stalin and Beria when they eventually got wind of it.

The question arises: to what extent did the existence of this self-governing region assist the Germans and impede the Red Army before and during the battle of Kursk in 1943? Once the battle of Kursk was over, there is no question that the whole area would have been scoured by SMERSH for any official who had worked in the administration. The fate of the 581,000 inhabitants after the Germans withdrew is not clear. It would have taken SMERSH many months, maybe years, to filter all those it considered unreliable, and this must have generated a massive amount of documentation, which is apparently still classified. German initiatives such those in Orlov would have been far more effective had they been launched from the outset.[11]

Harsh treatment of Red Army prisoners, often stemming from callous indifference, was a disastrous mistake. Such treatment was predicated in part on the assumption that the campaign would be over quickly and that any mistreatment of prisoners would have a negligible impact on German operations. The Germans' attitude toward prisoners and commissars soon became known on the Soviet side of the front, and the longer the campaign dragged on, the more such policies hardened Soviet resistance. Combined with the mass shootings of Jews by the *Einsatzgruppen*, the treatment of Soviet prisoners of war helped the Soviet regime. These killings supported a sense of *Soviet* solidarity that could possibly overcome the ethnic heterogeneity and fissiparous nature of the Soviet Union. To this end, Hitler's failure to make a radio address to the Soviet people immediately after the invasion must be seen as a lost opportunity. A direct radio appeal (reinforced by a massive airdrop of leaflets) in which he promised self-rule, abolition of the collective farms, restoration of the church, and an end to communism and in which he urged the people to turn against their oppressors—the NKVD, the commissars, and the party—would have caused utter panic among Stalin's entourage. But this did not happen, and the peasants were exploited just as ruthlessly by the German occupiers, which undeniably helped the Soviet regime.

A year later, on the eve of the Stalingrad counteroffensive, the consequences of this German error would be fully grasped by the utterly cynical Commissar Getmanov in Grossman's *Life and Fate*: "It is our good fortune that the Germans in the course of just one year did more to make themselves hated by the peasants than anything the communists did over the last 25 years."[12] Getmanov rather conveniently ignores the civil war and the genocide in Ukraine, but there is much truth in what he says. With victory secured, there would be time enough for the German occupiers to renege on these tactical, time-buying promises. The time for implementing the ideological program would have been after the Soviet state had been knocked out. Nonmilitary objectives that were launched before the Soviet Union had been defeated complicated and compromised the essential task of accelerating the collapse of the Soviet state. Again, the full force of the German propaganda machine should have been used to send the message that the German army had come to liberate Russia from communism. The failure to do so was probably based on the belief that such assurances would not be necessary, since the campaign would be a short one. Such considerations bring us to the question of what the primary military objective should have been in 1941.

One question that continues to engage historians of the Barbarossa campaign is whether Hitler's decision to head south in August 1941 predetermined the outcome of the eventual resumption of the drive on Moscow. For example, Glantz argues that Germany's best chance to take Moscow was in October 1941.[13] In contrast, Guderian and others maintain that the

August 1941 decision to go to Ukraine was the main cause of the failure to take Moscow. Citing various factors that he believes would have thwarted German plans to take Moscow in September, Glantz nevertheless concedes that the Germans might have captured the city then. However, that would have been just the start of the Germans' problems: surviving the winter in a devastated city, protecting their exposed and extended flanks, and withstanding an attack from a Red Army now numbering 5 million men.[14]

The obvious riposte here is Guderian's insistence on the pressing need to go all out for Moscow. Given the requirements of modern war, the defense of Moscow in 1941 relied on the Soviet rail network. In fact, the critical importance of the rail network for offensive and defensive purposes was well appreciated by Triandafillov, who identified fast and effective *rokirovka* (lateral troop movements) as crucial for deployment. The loss of Moscow would have meant the loss of all rail and river links to other parts of the Soviet Union, thus effectively preventing the necessary *rokirovka* and interfering with the movement of reinforcements from the Soviet Far East. Moreover, any Soviet threat to the German flanks and rear was predicated on a supply chain for the Red Army and the Soviet High Command's ability to move men and equipment by road and rail. If the German attack had succeeded in September, no buildup of offensive forces would have been possible, and the threat posed by millions of Red Army soldiers would have been reduced, since they would have been cut off from their supply bases.

The other factor to consider is the political impact on the Soviet Union if the Germans had taken Moscow. Guderian made a case for an all-out attack on Moscow in a meeting with Hitler:

> I explained that from a military standpoint it came down to the total destruction of the enemy forces that had suffered so badly in the recent battles. I depicted for him the geographical significance of the Russian capital that was, I said, completely different from Paris, for example, the traffic and communications center, the political center and an important industrial region, the fall of which, apart from its having an obviously shattering effect on the morale of the Russian people, must also have an impact on the rest of the world. I drew attention to the mood of the troops who expected nothing else than the march on Moscow and who, so inspired, had already, I said, made all the necessary preparations to this end. I tried to explain that after achieving military victory in this decisive thrust and over the main

forces of the enemy the industrial regions of Ukraine must fall to us much sooner when the conquest of the Moscow communications network would make any possible deployment of forces from north to south extremely difficult for the Russians.[15]

Guderian also pointed out that the German supply problem would be easier to deal with if everything were concentrated on Moscow. In addition, it is was essential to move before the onset of the *rasputitsa*.

Guderian's views find some support from von Manstein, who maintains—with the benefit of postwar hindsight—that Hitler underestimated the strength of the Soviet system and its ability to withstand the stresses of war. The only way to destroy the system, he argues, was to bring about its political collapse from within: "However, the policies that Hitler permitted to be pursued in the occupied territories by his Reich Commissars and the SD—in complete contrast to the efforts of the military circles—could only have the opposite effect."[16] This is an obvious point to make, but how do von Manstein's objections to German policies in the occupied territories fit with his own order issued on 20 November 1941? This lapse in memory notwithstanding, von Manstein's assessment of the policies being pursued by Hitler underlines the inner contradictions: "So while Hitler wanted to move strategically so as to destroy Soviet power, politically, he acted in complete opposition to this strategy. In other wars differences between the political and military leadership have often occurred. In this situation both elements were controlled by Hitler with the result that the Eastern policy conducted by him ran strictly counter to the requirements of his strategy and perhaps denied it the chance of a quick victory."[17] Von Manstein believed that the defeat of the Red Army would achieve Germany's economic and political goals. However, capturing Moscow was the key component: "After its [Moscow's] loss the Soviet defense would be practically divided into two parts and the Soviet leadership would no longer be able to conduct a uniform and combined operation."[18]

Conclusion

The period from 1 September 1939 to 22 June 1941 lends some support to Colin Gray's view that, although it is an intellectual convenience to accept a strict demarcation between war and peace (the title of Tolstoy's classic novel *War and Peace* is an indicator of how deeply this binary division is embedded), there can be a situation in which there is neither peace nor war or, rather, there is peace in war and war in peace.[19] In this situation, the conditions for a future war are being created amid circumstances that, to most people not immediately involved with problems of war, appear to be peace. This view suggests that peace is not permanent; it is merely a transitional phase during which old conflicts can be reignited or new conflicts can emerge, often unforeseen, because they are driven by political and technological change.

Diplomacy plays a crucial role in this transitional phase. It is in the diplomatic arena that new conditions and new threats arising from these new conditions are perceived or, rather, are open to being perceived. In these conditions, diplomacy can function as either an instrument to *avoid* war or one to *prepare* for war, a policy pursued by Hitler and clearly identified by Churchill and Isserson. Thus, Gray's thesis of war in peace and peace in war implies some modification of the Clausewitzian idea that war is a continuation of policy by other means. War is not merely a continuation of diplomatic policy by other means: war and diplomacy are not discrete entities; they constitute a single entity used by all states to further their interests, assert their honor, and deal with their fears. This entity is power. Thus, in the conditions we traditionally call peace, a state uses diplomacy to advance its interests (moderately or aggressively), and in the conditions we traditionally call war, the state uses force to advance its interests. Both policies, war and diplomacy, are parts of the same entity we call power. The origins of the relationship between diplomacy and war and the nature of power were first enunciated by Thucydides, and they have certainly been modified and reformulated by Machiavelli, Bismarck, and, more recently, Kissinger. However, in the twentieth century, Hitler's recognition that diplomacy and war are a single entity, and the degree to which this entity became an instrument of his will, remains one of the most important legacies of the NS regime and the planning for Barbarossa.

Finally, and most importantly, there was the human cost. What made Barbarossa and the war on the Eastern Front so appalling was not, to quote Omer Bartov, that "Nazi Germany exercised barbarism on an unprecedented scale" or that "its declared intention was extermination and enslavement."[20] What made it so appalling was that both Germany and the Soviet Union demonstrated a shocking capacity for barbarism, extermination, and enslavement. Clearly, this was an ideological war, but the first moves were not made on 22 June 1941. The first moves toward this *Weltanschauungskrieg* were made by Lenin's Soviet state. By effectively declaring the Soviet state free of all international norms, free of all moral and ethical obligations in its pursuit of global domination and class war, Lenin promulgated an intoxicating, nihilistic idea that was fully apprehended and applauded by the author of *Mein Kampf* and informed his own cult of German exceptionalism based on *das Herrenvolk*.

Appendix A   Translation of Lavrentii Beria's
Memorandum to Stalin, 5 March 1940

USSR   Top Secret
The People's Commissariat of Internal Affairs   5 March 1940
March 1940
№ 794/B

TsK VKP (b)
To Comrade Stalin:

At the present time large numbers of former officers of the Polish army, former police officers, members of the intelligence agencies, members of Polish nationalist, counterrevolutionary parties, participants of uncovered insurgent organizations, deserters and others are being held in the prisoner of war camps of the NKVD USSR in the western districts of Ukraine and Belorussia. All of them are sworn enemies of Soviet power and consumed by hatred of the Soviet system.

The prisoners of war, the officers and policemen, situated in the camps, are making every effort to continue their counterrevolutionary work and to conduct anti-Soviet agitation. Each one of them only waits to be freed so as to be able to take an active part in the struggle against Soviet power.

A number of counterrevolutionary organizations in the western districts of Ukraine and Belorussia have been uncovered by the agencies of the NKVD. In all these counterrevolutionary organizations an active leadership role is being played by former officers of the former Polish army and former policemen and gendarmes.

Among the deserters who have been detained there are those who have illegally crossed the state borders and additionally a considerable number of persons have been uncovered who are members of counterrevolutionary espionage and insurgent organizations.

In all, not counting soldiers and NCOs, a total of 14,736 former officers, officials, estate owners, policemen, gendarmes, prison warders, settlers and intelligence agents are being held in the prison of war camps. More than 97% of them are Poles by nationality.

Among those being held there are:

Generals, colonels and lieutenant-colonels: 295
Majors and captains: 2,080
Lieutenants, junior lieutenants and cornets: 6,049
Officers, junior police commanders, members of the border guard and gendarmerie: 1,030
Rank-and-file policemen, gendarmes, prison guards and intelligence agents: 5,138
Officials, estate owners, priests and settlers: 144

In the prisons of the western districts of Ukraine and Belorussia a total of 18,632 are being detained of whom 10,685 are Poles. This includes:

Former officers: 1,207
Former police intelligence agents and gendarmes: 5,141
Spies and saboteurs: 347
Former estate owners, factory owners and officials: 465
Members of various counterrevolutionary and insurgent organizations and various counterrevolutionary elements: 5,345
Deserters: 6,127

Proceeding from the assumption that they are all inveterate, incorrigible enemies of Soviet power the NKVD of the USSR considers the following to be necessary:

I. That the NKVD of the USSR recommends that:

(1) the cases of the 14,700 persons, the former Polish officers, officials, estate owners, police officers, intelligence agents, gendarmes, settlers and prison guards;

(2) and additionally that the cases of those arrested and located in the prisons of the western districts of Ukraine and Belorussia and that the number of 11,000 persons, the members of various counterrevolutionary espionage and sabotage organizations, former estate owners, factory owners, former Polish officers, officials and deserters be examined on the

basis of a special procedure with the application of the highest measure of punishment, shooting.

II. The examination of the cases shall be conducted without summoning the arrestees, without the presentation of any charge and the resolution concerning the termination of the investigation and concluding verdict shall be completed in accordance with the following procedure:

(a) with regard to persons being held in prisoner of war camps in accordance with material provided by the Directorate for the Affairs of Prisoners of the NKVD of the USSR;

(b) with regard to persons arrested in accordance with material from files presented by the NKVD of the Ukrainian SSR and the NKVD of BSSR.

III. The examination of the cases and the issuing of the verdict shall be the responsibility of a three-man panel comprising comrades Merkulov, Kabulov and Bashtakov (Head of the First Special Section of the NKVD, USSR).

People's Commissar of Internal Affairs
Union of SSR
L. Beria

Source: "SSSR Narodnyi Komissariat Vnutrennikh Del, ot 5 marta 40 g., № 794/B, Tovarishchu STALINU," in *KATYN: Documents of Genocide. Documents and Materials from the Soviet Archives Turned over to Poland on October 14, 1992*, ed. Wojciech Materski (Warsaw: Polish Academy of Sciences, 1993), 18–21. The document is also reproduced in A. N. IAkovlev et al., eds., *Katyn': Plenniki neob"iavlennoi voiny*, in the series "Demokratiia," *Rossiia. XX VEK, Dokumenty* (Moscow: Mezhdunarodnyi fond, 1997), 384–390.

Appendix B Translation of Stalin's Speech in the Kremlin to Graduates of the Academies of the RKKA, 5 May 1941

Comrades, permit me on behalf of the Soviet government and Communist Party to congratulate you on the completion of your studies and to wish you success in your future work.

Comrades, you left the army three–four years ago. Now you will be returning to its ranks and you will not recognize the army. The Red Army is not the same army it was a few years ago.

(a) What represented the Red Army 3–4 years ago?

The basic arm of service was the infantry. It was armed with a rifle that had to be reloaded after each shot, with handheld and mounted machine guns, with howitzers and with a gun possessing a muzzle velocity of up to 900 meters a second. The aircraft had a speed of up to 400–500 kilometers an hour. The tanks had thin armor able to withstand a 37mm gun. Our division numbered up to 18,000 soldiers, but that was still not an indicator of its strength.

(b) What has become of the Red Army at the present time?

We have reconstructed our army and we have armed it with modern military equipment. But first of all one has to say that many comrades exaggerate the significance of the events at Lake Khasan and Khalkhin-Gol from the point of view of military experience. There we were not dealing with a modern army but with an obsolete one. I do not want to say to you that all this means that you are being deceived. Of course, Khasan and Khalkhin-Gol played their positive role. Their positive role consisted in the fact in the first and second instance we defeated the Japanese. However, we drew the real experience in the reconstruction of our army from the Russo-Finnish War and from the contemporary war in the west.

I said that we have a modern army armed with the latest equipment. What is the state of our army today?

Before, there were 120 divisions in the Red Army. Today, there are 300 divisions in the army. The divisions themselves have become somewhat smaller but more mobile. Before, there were about 18,000–20,000 men in a division: now there are about 15,000.

Of the total number of divisions about a third are mechanized. There is no talk of this, but you must know this. Of 100 divisions, two-thirds are tank divisions and one-third mechanized. In the current year the army will have 50,000 tractors and trucks.

Our tanks have changed the way they look. Earlier, all our tanks were thinly armored. These days that is not sufficient. These days armor 3–4 times thicker is required. We have tanks of the first line, which will tear up the front. There are second- and third-line tanks: these tanks accompany the infantry. The firepower of our tanks has increased.

As for artillery, earlier there were a great number of howitzers. Modern war has brought about a correction and heightened the role of guns. Dealing with enemy fortifications and tanks requires shooting over open sights and with a shell possessing a great muzzle velocity, up to 1,000 meters and more a second. In our army a large role is now allocated to heavy gun artillery.

Aircraft: earlier, the ideal speed of aircraft was considered to be in the range of 400–500 kilometers an hour. These days that is lagging behind. We have sufficient quantity of aircraft and are producing massive quantities of aircraft reaching a speed of 600–650 kilometers an hour. These are first-line aircraft. In the event of a war these aircraft will be used first. They will clear the way for our relatively obsolete aircraft such as the I-15, I-16 and I-153 (Chaika) and SB. If we deployed these first they would be shot down.

It is possible to have a good command stratum but if we do not possess modern military equipment it is possible to lose a war. Earlier, insufficient attention was devoted to such cheap artillery, but valuable types of weapons like mortars, they were neglected. These days we have modern mortars of various calibers in service.

Before, there were no motorcyclist units. Now we have created them, this motorized cavalry, and we have them in sufficient quantity.

In order to control all this new technology new army command cadres are required who have mastered the art of modern war.

These are the changes that have taken place in the organization of the Red Army. When you arrive in the units of the Red Army, you will see the changes which have taken place.

I would not have mentioned this but our military schools and academies are lagging behind the modern army. Here Comrade Smirnov delivered a report and spoke about graduates, about their instruction on the basis of new military experience. I disagree with him. Our military schools still lag behind the army. Students are still being taught on the old equipment. So, I was told that in one artillery academy the men are being instructed on a 3-inch gun. Is that so comrade gunners? [Stalin turns to the gunners.] The military school lags behind the army. The air force academy is still teaching students to fly on old planes—I-14, I-16, I-153 and the SB. One must not teach people on old equipment: teaching them on old equipment means turning out poorly qualified people.

This backwardness is additionally encouraged by the programs. In order, you see, to instruct the new and to do it in a new way, the program has to be changed and a lot of work is required for that. It is far easier to teach according to the old programs: there is a lot less fuss and bother. Our military schools must and are able to rebuild their instruction programs for the command cadres on the new technology and to make use of the experience of modern war. Our military schools are lagging behind; this lagging behind is natural. It is necessary to get rid of it.

You will arrive in the army and there you will see the latest developments. In order to give you some idea, I have talked about the reorganization of our army.

Why did France suffer defeat but Germany was victorious? Is, in actual fact, the German army invincible?

You will arrive in your units from the capital. The Red Army soldiers and commanders will ask you questions about what is happening now. You studied in the academies, you were there at the heart of the leadership, tell us what is happening around us. Why was France defeated? Why did Britain suffer a defeat and why was Germany victorious? Is the German army really invincible? Our commanders not only have to command and to give orders—that's a small part—they also have to be able to talk to the soldiers: to explain to them the events taking place; to talk to them man to man. Our great military leaders were always closely linked with the soldiers. One must operate like Suvorov.

You will be asked: where are the reasons that explain why Europe has been turned upside down? Why was France defeated, and why was German victorious? Why did Germany turn out to have a better army? This is a fact that Germany turned out to have a better army both in terms of equipment and organization. How is this to be explained?

Lenin said that beaten armies learn well. Lenin's idea also relates to nations. Defeated nations learn well. Having been defeated in 1918, the German army learned well.

The Germans critically analyzed the reasons for their defeat and found ways to organize their army better, to train and to equip it. The military thinking of the German army progressed. The army was equipped with the very latest technology and taught the latest methods in waging war.

In general there are two sides to this question. It is not enough to have good equipment and to be well organized; one needs lots of allies. Germany studied the lessons of the past, precisely because defeated armies learn well.

In 1870, the Germans defeated the French. Why? Because they fought on one front.

Were the Germans defeated in 1916–1917? Why? Because they fought on two fronts.

Why did the French not learn anything from the previous war of 1914–1918? Lenin teaches us: the party and state will perish if they refuse to see the shortcomings, get carried away with their successes, rest on their laurels and get dizzy with success.

Victory caused French heads to spin; it made them complacent. The French let slip, and lost, their allies: the Germans took them away; the French rested on their successes; French military thought did not progress; it remained at the level it was in 1918. No concern was given to the army and it was offered no moral support. A new moral code emerged, one which corrupted the army. Soldiers were treated with disdain. One started to view army commanders as failures, as people of another era who, not possessing plants, factories, banks and shops, were forced to join the army. It was so bad that the girls would not even marry a soldier. It was only such a negligent attitude toward the army that could account for the fact that the military apparatus was in the hands of the Gamelins and Ironsides, who had little understanding of the art of war. Such was the attitude toward the military in Britain as well.

The army must enjoy the exclusive concern and love of the people and government: in this is the source of the greatest moral strength of the army. The army must be cherished. When such moral support does [not] emerge in a country, there will not be a strong and combat-effective army. This is what happened in France.

In order to prepare well for war, it is necessary not only to have a modern army but also to prepare the army politically.

What does it mean politically to prepare an army? Politically to prepare an army means having a sufficient number of reliable allies from neutral countries. Germany, in starting the war, coped with this task, but Britain and France failed to do so.

So these are the political and military reasons for the defeat of France and the victory of Germany.

Is the German army in actual fact invincible? No: there are not and never have been any invincible armies in the world. There are the best armies, there are good ones and there are weak ones. Germany started the war and in the first period moved in accordance with the slogan of liberation from the yoke of the Versailles Treaty. This slogan was popular and encountered the support and the sympathy of all those aggrieved by Versailles. But now the situation has changed. Now the German army acts on the basis of other slogans. It has displaced slogans of liberation from Versailles by slogans of aggression.

Using slogans of aggression and conquest the German army will not enjoy success. These slogans are dangerous.

While Napoleon I waged a war under the slogan of liberation from serfdom, he met with support, had allies and enjoyed success.

When Napoleon I started to engage in wars of conquest, he found many enemies and met defeat.

Insofar as the German army wages war under the slogan of crushing other countries and the subordination of other peoples to Germany, the adoption of this slogan will not lead to victory.

From a military point of view, there is nothing special in the German army, in its tanks, artillery and planes.

A significant part of the German army is losing the ardor which existed at the start of the war. Furthermore, boasting, complacency and conceit have appeared in the German army. German military thought is not progressing; its military equipment is lagging not only behind ours, but as regards aircraft America is starting to overtake Germany.

How could it happen that Germany has prevailed?

1. Germany succeeded here because its defeated army learned, rebuilt itself, reconsidered old ideas.

2. This happened because Britain and France, while successful in the last war, did not seek out new avenues, did not study. The French army was the dominant army on the continent.

That is why up to a certain moment Germany's fortunes started to improve.

But Germany is already waging war under the flag of domination of other nations. Insofar as the old slogan aimed at Versailles united those dissatisfied with Versailles, Germany's new slogan is divisive.

In the sense of long-term military development the German army has lost the desire for the long-term improvement in its military technology. The Germans consider their army to be the most perfect, the best, the most invincible. That's true enough.

From day to day it is necessary to perfect an army.

Any politician, any statesman who permits a feeling of complacency, may find himself facing the unexpected, as happened to France before the catastrophe.

Once again, I congratulate you and wish you success.

The First Response of I. V. Stalin at the Reception

Permit me to propose a toast to the leadership cadres of our academies, to the heads, the teachers, to the eradication of lagging or falling behind in the matter of studying modern military equipment.

Why has this lagging behind occurred? Firstly, it is easier for the teachers to teach the old equipment which is already familiar to them. In order to teach students on the new equipment, the teachers themselves have to know it and study it. They have to relearn. In the academies teaching is being done on the basis of the old programs. That's the first reason. The second reason is that our army supply agencies are not passing on the new equipment to the schools and academies. It is necessary to pass on this new equipment for the students to master so that the lagging behind of our schools and academies can be eradicated.

The Second Response of I. V. Stalin at the Reception

To the health of the gunners! Artillery is the most important arm of service: the artillery is the god of modern war. Artillery is to be found in all arms: in the infantry; in the armored formations and on planes.

To the health of the tank soldiers! Tanks are mobile artillery protected by armor. On tanks one can carry guns up to 130mm.

To the health of the airmen! There are two types of aviation. Long-range aviation, this aviation for attacking the rear, for conducting operations in support of partisans, but this does not have huge significance. Short-range aviation has by the most decisive significance, which has been underestimated and which has been kept down. Here it is a question of aviation directly operating with artillery, tanks and infantry. Here it is a question of fighter, ground-attack aircraft.

To the health of the cavalry! We have reduced them somewhat but now the role to be played by the cavalry is exceptionally great and we don't have a lot.

The role of cavalry in modern war is exceptionally great. It will pursue the retreating enemy units, penetrating the lines. In particular, it is required while pursuing the retreating artillery units not to allow them to take up new fire positions and settle on them.

To the health of our signallers and our glorious infantrymen! Here I would not call them infantry. Modern infantry are people dressed in armor, motorcyclists, tank soldiers.

Concerning the significance of the self-loading rifle: one soldier armed with a self-loading rifle is the equivalent of 3 soldiers armed with an ordinary rifle.

The Third Response of I. V. Stalin at the Reception

A General-major from the tank troops speaks. He proposes a toast to the Stalinist foreign policy of peace.

Comrade Stalin: Permit me to make a correction. A policy of peace has secured peace for our country. A policy of peace is a good thing. Up to the moment, the time we built a line of defense until such time as we had re-equipped our army and supplied it with modern means of war.

And now after we have rebuilt our army, after we have generously supplied it with the equipment for the conduct of modern war, when we have become strong, now it is necessary to switch from the defense to the offensive.

Conducting the defense of our country, we are required to operate in an offensive manner: to move from defense to a military policy of offensive operations. We have to reconfigure our education, our propaganda, agitation and our press in the spirit of attack. The Red Army is a modern army and a modern army is an attacking army.

Source: Rossiiskii tsentr khraneniia i izucheniia dokumentov noveishei istorii, fond 558, Opis' 1, delo 3808, listy 1–12.

Appendix C Translation of TASS Communiqué, 13 June 1941

Even before the arrival in London of Mr. Cripps, the British ambassador to the USSR, but especially after his arrival, all kinds of rumors concerning "the imminence of war between the USSR and Germany" started frothing up in the British and in the foreign press generally. According to these rumors: (1) Germany had allegedly made territorial and economic demands of the USSR and that negotiations between Germany and the USSR were now under way between them about concluding a new, much more tightly binding agreement; (2) that the USSR had allegedly rejected these demands and in connection with which Germany had started to concentrate its troops on the borders of the USSR with the aim of attacking the USSR; (3) that, for its part, the Soviet Union had allegedly started to intensify its preparations for a war with Germany and was concentrating its troops on the borders of the latter.

Regardless of the obvious senselessness of these rumors, national circles in Moscow nevertheless consider it necessary, in view of the persistent inflation of these rumors, to authorize TASS to state that these rumors are the clumsily concocted propaganda of forces which are hostile to the USSR and Germany and interested in the further expansion and unleashing of war.

TASS can state that: (1) Germany has made no demands at all of the USSR and is not advocating any new, more closely binding treaty at all in view of which there can be no negotiations taking place on this matter; (2) according to information available to the USSR, Germany is also unswervingly observing the conditions of the German-Soviet Non-Aggression Pact, as is the Soviet Union, in view of which, in the opinion of Soviet circles, rumors concerning Germany's intention to flout the pact and to mount an attack against the USSR are baseless and that the redeployment of German troops relieved from operations in the Balkans to the eastern and to the northeastern regions of Germany, which is taking place, is connected, one assumes, with other reasons which have no bearing on Soviet-German relations; (3) the USSR, as part of its peaceful policy, has observed and intends to observe, the terms of the Soviet-German Non-Aggression Pact on the basis of which rumors concerning the fact that the USSR is preparing for war with Germany are false and provocative; (4) the summer call-up of Red Army reserves and the forthcoming exercises which are now being conducted have as their aim nothing other than the instruction of reserves and the testing of the function of the railway network, exercises which are carried out, as is known, every year. Consequently to depict these Red Army measures as being hostile to Germany is, at the very least, ridiculous.

Published in *Izvestiia* 14 June 1941

Source: A. N. IAkovlev et al., eds., *1941 god, v 2-knigakh*, in the series "*Demokratiia*," *Rossiia. XX VEK, Dokumenty* (Moscow: Mezhdunarodnyi fond, 1998), 2:361.

Appendix D   Translation of the Formal Interrogation Record of General Dmitrii Grigor'evich Pavlov, 7 July 1941

Question: Have the reasons for your arrest been stated to you?

Answer: I was arrested in the afternoon of 4 July [other sources state 6 July FE] this year in Dovsk where I was informed that I had been arrested on the order of the Central Committee. Later, I spoke with Mekhlis, the deputy representative of Sovnarkom, and he stated that I had been arrested as a traitor.

Question: In that case, get on with the testimony of your treacherous activity.

Answer: I am not a traitor. The defeat of the troops which I commanded occurred for reasons that did not depend on me.

Question: The investigation has information pointing to the fact that your behavior in the course of a number of years was treasonous, and that this was especially evident in deeds, which came to light during your command of the Western front.

Answer: I am not a traitor. There were no malicious motives in my actions as front commander. Also, I am not guilty of the fact that the enemy has managed to push so deeply into our territory.

Question: How, in that case, has this occurred?

Answer: To begin with, I shall have to outline how the situation in the military operations of German troops against the Red Army started.

At one o'clock in the morning of 22 June of this year I was summoned to front headquarters on the order of the People's Commissar. Corps commissar Fominykh, a member of the Military Council and the front chief of staff, General-Major Klimovskikh, also went there with me.

The first question the People's Commissar asked me over the phone was: "Well, how's everything with you, quiet?" I replied that a very large movement of German troops was being observed on the right flank, and that according to a report from Kuznetsov, the commander of the 3rd Army, there had been a nonstop flow of German motorized and mechanized columns into the Suval'skii salient over the last 36 hours. According to his report as well, in many places in the Avgustov-Sapotskin sector on the German side, the barbed-wire obstacles had been removed. On other sectors of the front I reported that I was especially alarmed by the Bialopodliaska formation.

In answer to my report the People's Commissar replied: "You, just be a bit calmer and don't panic. In any case get your headquarters together this morning. It's possible something untoward will happen but look here: don't act on any provocation. If there are individual provocations, then call." That was the end of the conversation.

In accordance with the instruction of the People's Commissar I immediately summoned all the army commanders to the high-frequency radio net and ordered them to report to army headquarters along with their chief of staff and operational sections. I also proposed to the army commanders that they bring their troops up to a state of combat readiness and that they occupy their battle fortifications including even the unfinished reinforced concrete ones.

In response to this instruction Kuznetsov replied that in accordance with the earlier orders issued by me he had allocated ammunition to the troops and at the present time he was occupying the defensive fortifications.

Golubev, the commander of the 10th Army, reported that after the war games had ended his corps headquarters had been left for the command of the troops in that place specified by the plan. I warned Golubev to maintain his troops in full combat readiness and to expect my further orders.

Korobkov, the commander of the 4th Army, reported that his men were ready for battle. He promised to check the state of combat readiness of the Brest garrison. To this end I pointed out to Korobkov that the garrison must be in that place, as specified by the plan and I suggested that he act immediately to carry out my order.

The commander of the district air forces, Kopets, and his deputy, Taiurskii, who had reported to my headquarters, informed me that the planes had been brought to a state of complete combat readiness and had been distributed on the aerodromes in accordance with the order of the People's Commissar for Defense.

This conversation with the army commanders went on for about two hours of the night.

At 0330 hours the People's Commissar for Defense summoned me to the phone once again and asked me whether there was anything new.

I replied to him that at the moment there was nothing new to report; that communications with all the armies were functioning and that the respective orders to the commanders had been issued.

At the same time I reported to the People's Commissar for Defense that in spite of the proscription issued by Zhigarev, the chief of the air force to refuel the planes from the reserve fuel and to replace the engines with the reserves, I gave the order to Kopets and Taiurskii. The People's Commissar approved my order. I promised to report the latest situation in my sector after further discussions with the army commanders.

In the course of the next 15 minutes I received the following information from the army commanders.

From the commander of the 10th Army "all is quiet"; from the 4th Army "everywhere is quiet and the troops are carrying out the task set by you." In answer to my question whether the 22nd Tank Division had moved off from Brest, I received the answer: "Yes, it is moving out along with all the other units." The commander of the 3rd Army replied to me that nothing new had occurred. Ivanov's troops—Ivanov is the head of the reinforced zone—are in the reinforced positions. The 56th Rifle Division had been deployed to the place assigned to it in the plan; the 27th Rifle Division was also in its allocated position. About one month before the start of military operations, it had been transferred by me from Sapotskin–Grodno to Avgustov, and then to Graevo, Sukhovy. These positions had been confirmed by the General Staff.

I set off to report the new situation to the People's Commissar for Defense but before I was able to contact Moscow, I was phoned by Kuznetsov who reported: "Along the entire front there is artillery and rifle and small-arms fire. Over Grodno up to 50–60 aircraft are bombing the headquarters. I was forced to go into the cellar." Over the phone I told him to put "Grodno 41" into operation (the established password for the cover plan) and to go all out and occupy, with his headquarters, the assigned position. After that I urgently called Belostok. Belostok replied: "At the moment it is quiet on the front."

At approximately 0410–0415 hours I spoke with Korobkov, who also gave me the same answer: "Everything is quiet with us."

After about 8 minutes Korobkov passed on the following: "Aircraft are swooping down on Kobrin, on the front there is horrendous artillery fire." I instructed Korobkov to activate "Kobrin 41" and ordered him to take control of his men and start to act with complete responsibility.

I reported immediately and precisely everything which had been reported to me by the army commanders to the People's Commissar for Defense. The latter replied: "Operate in accordance with the situation."

Question: After how many minutes did you report to the People's Commissar for Defense the message from Kuznetsov concerning the fact that the enemy in the region of his army's dispositions had opened fire with artillery and small arms?

Answer: I reported Kuznetsov's message to the People's Commissar for Defense after about 10–12 minutes.

Question: Continue with your exposition of the situation developing at the front.

Answer: After I had reported to the People's Commissar for Defense the order was given by me to headquarters to establish contact as specified by our plan and particularly via radio communication. A check of the high-frequency means showed that communications with these armies had been cut. At approximately 0500 hours Kuznetsov reported the situation to me via the intercity phone line in a roundabout manner. He informed me that enemy troops were being held by him but that all of Sapotskin was ablaze since it was the target of especially heavy artillery bombardment and that in that sector the enemy was attacking but that so far the attack was being beaten back.

At about 0700 hours Golobev sent a radio telegram message that there was an exchange of small-arms fire along the entire front and that all attempts by the enemy to penetrate into our territory had been beaten back by him.

General Semenov—the deputy front chief of staff—reported to me that Lomzha had been captured by the enemy, but had been ejected from Lomzha by a counterattack of the 6th Cavalry Division. At that time the radio link with the headquarters of the 10th Army started to function intermittently. In response to my demand precisely to indicate the situation of our units, the headquarters of 10th Army reported in code where what divisions were located and the situation, from which it was apparent that units at the front were successfully repulsing the enemy attacks and inflicting huge casualties on him. Enemy infantry with comparatively small amounts of tanks were operating against the units of 10th Army such that by a rapid blow in the region of Semiatichi the communications battalion of the 113th Division was caught and surrounded by the enemy. Into this sector the enemy had brought major mechanized units and our troops were engaged in a stubborn battle with them. In several places under pressure from enemy tanks our infantry was withdrawing in the general direction of Briansk. In this situation report, it was stated that the commander of the 10th Army was throwing the tank units of the 13th Mechanized Corps into the attack (there were about 200 tanks in all) and committing the entire corps to participation in the overall battle and that he indicated that he would also use the 6th Mechanized Corps, which was subordinated to him for the operation.

Question: How did you assess this report from the commander of the 10th Army?

Answer: I took it to mean that the enemy was attempting to contain the operations of the 10th Army by use of its infantry and with minor tank forces from the front and was striving to deliver a more powerful blow from the direction of Drogochin, Nagainovka or to the north of the gap between the Belovezhskaia forest and the Suprenevskie woods.

Question: With regard to this, what instructions did you give to the commander of the 10th Army?

Answer: The commander of the 10th Army was given the order immediately to deploy the antitank brigade to his position and to deploy it in the region to the west of Mikhalovo, to the line to the south of Belostok.

I also instructed Golubev that the deployment of the 6th Mechanized Corps into the battle must be carried out in order to achieve the strongest possible blow, having advised him to familiarize himself thoroughly with the situation and act accordingly. In this message I pointed out that Boldin, my deputy, would be coming to him.

Question: Did you report this new situation to the People's Commissar for Defense?

Answer: Situation reports to the People's Commissar for Defense, in accordance with the instructions of the General Staff, were sent in good order.

Question: Did any instructions reach you from the People's Commissar for Defense?

Answer: I received instructions of the General Headquarters in connection with the situation.

Question: How did events develop further?

Answer: Having received very fragmentary information from the headquarters of the 4th Army about the fact that this army intended to launch a counterattack against the enemy in the region of Zhabenko, I was somewhat confused by this message, not understanding how in such a short space of time the 4th Army could withdraw 30 kilometers from Brest. I contacted Korobkov and received the answer from him that he lost contact with the 49th and 75th Rifle Divisions. He knew the location of the 75th Rifle Division and maintained contact with it via liaison officers. Korobkov reported that he was throwing Oborin's corps into a counterattack against large enemy mechanized forces and that he would inform me of the attack's outcome.

From subsequent information it was evident that on that day Zhabinka had changed hands 7 times and that everywhere our infantry pushed out the enemy infantry but that Korobkov under pressure from the enemy's mechanized units had nevertheless withdrawn to Kobrin. I gave instructions that Korobkov was to be informed via radio-telegram that he not take arbitrary decisions and should not abandon positions so easily and that he should fight on each sector until he had received authority from front headquarters to withdraw.

Delegated officers were sent by me to Korobkov under direct and categorical orders to demand from the headquarters and command staff of 4th Army, having ordered that both the army commander and the chief of staff report with countersigned documents, where what units were and in what state. Simultaneously with this order I moved the entire 113th Rifle Division on ahead, in the direction Kartuz–Bereza, to help Korobkov, and place it at his disposal. In order to accelerate its redeployment the entire motor-transport regiment, located at Starykh–Dorogakh, was designated. Furthermore, Korobkov was instructed that the line in the region Kartuz–Bereza must be prepared for defense and for covering the transfer of the 55th Division. All these measures were then reported in good time to the People's Commissar for Defense.

In the second half of the day Kuznetsov reported that of the three radio transmitters at his disposal, two had been smashed and that the one remaining was damaged. He requested that another radio be delivered to him. Over this period information from him arrived that Sapotskin had been abandoned by our troops, and Kuznetsov, with a trembling voice, stated that, in his opinion, the 56th Rifle Division only remained as a number. I replied to him that it was far too early to panic and that he should gather his men together. I asked Kuznetsov what he was doing with the 85th Rifle Division. He answered that the 85th Rifle Division, having been deployed on a line to the west of Grodno and under pressure from heavy enemy tanks, had started to withdraw to the south and southeast, but that he, Kuznetsov, was throwing Steklov's tank division into a counterattack and was endeavoring by means of this to recover the position of the 85th Rifle Division. In response to my question about what was the situation on his right flank, Kuznetsov answered that there, in his opinion, the situation was catastrophic, since the uncoordinated and scattered units in the region of Koze (to the north of Grodno) were holding the enemy pressure with difficulty and that the rifle regiment located between Koze and Druskeniki was crushed from the rear by a strike of major mechanized units, but that he was gathering everything together that he had and thrusting to Koze. Finally, Kuznetsov asked: "I feel that we must abandon Grodno, in which case how do we proceed with the supplies and the families of the command staff, many of whom are already in enemy hands?" I answered that when leaving any positions, stores and all goods which cannot be removed are to be destroyed completely. Kuznetsov passed the phone over to Biriukov, a member of the Military Council, who again asked what to do about the families. I replied: "Once the battle has started, the task of commanders is not to concern themselves with families but to concern themselves with the conduct of the battle."

In a subsequent message the headquarters of 3rd Army reported that the enemy was approaching Grodno and that our troops were leaving the city. On Kuznetsov's order the dumps were blown and the army replenished itself with shells.

On the same day Golubev, sensing the strongly developing enemy pressure from Semiatichi in the direction of Briansk–Bel'sk, without having assessed the situation, reported that the enemy was on the approaches to Bel'sk, whereas in fact the enemy was still fighting in the Briansk area. Golubev decided to throw in his mechanized corps.

Assessing the entire situation, I judged that the headquarters of the 3rd Army had left Grodno and transferred to Luno but the enemy was not applying any special pressure in pursuit of 3rd Army. On the left flank of 10th Army the enemy with great effort was exploiting his success and squeezing our units. On the remaining sectors of the 10th Army all attempts by the enemy to mount an offensive had been repulsed. In the 4th Army there was a sense of complete confusion on the part of the command, control of the troops had been lost and the enemy was rapidly exploiting his success, with his axis of advance along the Bobruisk–Brest highway.

In connection with the situation the 6th Motor-Mechanized Regiment was ordered by me to attack the enemy from a start line in the direction of Briansk with the mission of destroying the enemy's mechanized units in the region of Briansk and, on completion of that task, to concentrate everything in the region of Volkovysk at my disposal. This order was sent in duplicate: liaison officers by plane and by radio.

In the sector of the 3rd Army we had lost the Avgustovskii region. In the sector of the 10th Army, the units remained in the same region where they were due to be in accordance with the plan, apart from the left flank, where the enemy had occupied Tsekhonovets and was moving toward Briansk.

Units of the 4th Army were fighting for Zhabenko, but I found out that during the move out of Brest units of the 42nd and 6th Divisions and the 22nd Tank Division came under very heavy enemy artillery fire which in the first instance was concentrated against the buildings housing the command staff and then in the second phase along the streets and roads and on the vehicle parks. I learned that by use of this fire the enemy had inflicted considerable losses on the equipment of the artillery leaving Brest. I became aware of this from the corps commander and tank division.

Question: What conclusions, as the front commander, did you draw about the outcome of the first day of the battle?

Answer: I came to the following conclusions from the results of the first day's fighting: that against the center of 10th Army the main enemy was infantry and that our infantry was successfully beating back all enemy attacks. Against Kuznetsov, on the right flank, in the direction of Sapotskin heavy enemy tanks had been deployed which could not be penetrated by our 45mm artillery and that the enemy, having broken our defense, brought up infantry behind the tanks. On Kuznetsov's right flank an entire regiment of a major enemy mechanized formation was routed, which had come from the north, from Lithuania, comprising 2–3 mechanized divisions and 2–3 motorized divisions. This caused me great concern for the possibility of turning this blow around by means of a mechanized unit in the direction of Lida.

Question: What measures were taken by you, as front commander, to forestall the front's being broken?

Answer: On the right flank I instructed the 3rd Army—exploiting the attack of the 11th Mechanized Corps in the direction of Sapotskin—and the units of the 85th Division of the same division, to occupy a second defensive line to the west of Grodno and on to Sukhovolo, with the front facing north. I ordered Kuznetsov to round up the scattered units of the 56th Division and to place them on the right bank of the river Neman and defend Grodno and the direction to Lida.

Aware of the blow from Lithuania, I ordered the commander of the 21st Rifle Corps (headquarters in Lida) to occupy a defensive line to the west of Lida, the antitank brigade to the northwest, the 17th Rifle Division in order to hold the line so as to win time and to enable the 37th and 24th Rifle Divisions to concentrate in the region to the northwest of Lida and to secure the right flank from the strike out of Lithuania from the direction of Orana, establishing contact with the Lithuanian units, which was carried out by the commander of the 21st Rifle Corps but no units were found by him in the region of Orana.

Question: Did you convey your decision to the commander of the 21st Rifle Corps in the manner of an order?

Answer: Yes, this order was conveyed to the commander of the 3rd Army as well, who was instructed that from the moment he received the actual order the commander of the 21st Rifle Corps came into his order of battle.

Along the left flank I had already ordered the following: the 55th Rifle Division had moved out of Slutsk in the direction of Kartuz–Bereza. The division was being redeployed in motor transport with the task of forming part of the 4th Army and closing off the Slutsk line of advance. Moreover, the 143rd Division, which had arrived in a special train, had finished its concentration in the Obus–Lesno region, with the mission to strengthen units of the 4th Army in order to mount a counterstrike in the direction of Kartuz–Bereza or Milovitsa, according to the situation. Also, the 131st Division was located in the same region, having prepared a line on the river Shchar, and in expectation of launching a blow, according to the situation, against either Ruzhany or Pruzhany.

But the 10th Army, after I had instructed Boldin to mount a strike using the mechanized corps in the direction of Briansk, with the mission to rout the enemy's mechanized units in that region, was, on completion of that mission, to withdraw into my reserve in Volkovysk, then having received the Stavka directive, to mount an attack in the northern direction with the cavalry-mechanized group with the mission to restore the situation in the region of Grodno. Having set the new mission to the cavalry-mechanized group of the 10th Army, I designated General-Lieutenant Boldin as commander to carry it out and he arrived to the position in good time.

At the same time, and in order to control the operations of 3rd and 10th Armies and manage the attack of the cavalry-mechanized group, Marshal Kulik set off on 23 June 1941 and arrived at the headquarters of 10th Army.

Later on, we had a report about the 6th Mechanized Corps that it had not carried out the first task. For reasons which are not known to me, Golubev, the commander of the 10th Army, had not released it for the attack. The corps changed its area of concentration, standing to the east of Belostok in the region of Valila. The 29th Motorized Division occupied the front of Sokolka, and to the southwest.

Question: Did you consider these measures sufficiently comprehensive to restore the situation?

Answer: No, they were insufficient but I could do nothing more since I did not have the units.

Question: Was the enemy formation operating against you known to you?

Answer: No, not precisely. This information was clarified in the course of the battle and by air reconnaissance. On the first day of the battle the presence of major enemy mechanized formations became clear in the region of Brest, Semiatichi and Zhabenka and also that there were major mechanized formations in Lithuania in the region to the west of Orana. Up to 4–5 rifle divisions were advancing against the 10th Army, and in the direction of Sapotskin–Grodno 3 rifle divisions with heavy tanks were advancing.

Question: Did you take all measures to provide the armies with radio equipment?

Answer: Yes, regarding that matter all measures were taken by me. When, on the first day of the battle, Kuznetsov phoned me and requested that a radio be sent since his existing three had all been destroyed, I demanded them from Moscow via plane. At first, I got no answer from Moscow but after repeated demands from me they did answer and sent 18 radio sets but up to the day of my arrest these radio sets had still not been received.

Question: Why in spite of all this have the Germans succeeded in breaking through the front line and penetrating our territory?

Answer: Three mechanized corps fell on the Brest sector opposite the 6th and 42nd Divisions without warning. That created numerical superiority for the enemy and also superiority in terms of equipment. The commander of the 4th Army, Korobkov, having lost control and, by all accounts, having lost his head, was unable to close, with any sufficient degree, the main sector with his forces even if by bringing up for that purpose the

49th Division to the sector. A huge mass of bombers were deployed by the enemy against the 6th and 42nd Divisions in that sector. According to Korobkov's report the planes systematically attacked our infantry positions and the enemy dive-bombers knocked out one gun after another. Enemy air superiority was total, all the more so as a consequence of the fact that our fighters already on the first day, without even getting off the ground, had suffered considerable damage from a simultaneous enemy air strike on all our aerodromes at 0400 hours in the morning. On that day up to 300 aircraft of all types were destroyed, including trainers. All this happened because it was dark and the planes could not get airborne. I was personally unable physically to check how the planes were sited on the aerodrome, whereas at the same time the air force commander, Kopets, and Taiurskii, his deputy, Listrov, his deputy for political affairs, and the air force chief of staff, Taranenko, reported to me that the order from the People's Commissar for Defense concerning concentrated dispositions had been implemented by them.

Question: Did you have any reports that enemy aircraft had appeared on the border?

Answer: I received such a report at the same time as the bombing started. The central air observation and reporting post in Minsk received a report that the state border had been crossed by enemy aircraft after 4 minutes. The border aerodromes were notified considerably sooner but were unable to get the aircraft airborne since *the pilots were not trained for nighttime flying* [emphasis added].

Question: How did events at the front further develop?

Answer: On 23 June the front headquarters received a telegram from Boldin, which had been sent to 10th Army at the same time concerning the fact that the 6th Mechanized Corps has only one-quarter of its fuel remaining. Taking into account the necessity for fuel, the fuel supply section from the outset of the very first day of fighting had sent all the fuel available in the district to Baranovichi for the 3rd Mechanized Corps; that is 300 metric tonnes. Based on the General Staff plan the remaining fuel for the district was located in Maikop. Moving fuel any further forward than Baranovichi could not be done because of the damage done to the railway network and stations by constant enemy air attacks.

On the front of the 4th Army the following can be noted. On the second day, the enemy, relying exclusively on airpower and tank units with motorcycle units, approached Kobrin. Our units, poorly controlled by Korobkov, the 4th Army commander, were forced under the pressure of superior enemy forces to abandon Kobrin. The abandoning of Kobrin was assessed by me as causing the exposure of 10th Army's left flank and threatening the army with encirclement. I sent my assistant from the higher education institutions, Khabarov, to the army with my strict order to execute, if necessary, any number of people, but to stop the withdrawal of 4th Army and to ensure that the army headquarters took firm control of things. In order to assist 4th Army, the order was given at the same time to deploy the 121st Rifle Division in the direction toward Rozhany and to accelerate the tempo with which the 55th Division was being brought up to the line, Kartuz–Bereza. The 155th Division, occupying a firm defensive line in Slonim, was ordered to be ready to turn from the Volkovysk highway to Rozhany; that is also to assist 4th Army.

This order was delivered to divisional commanders and Korobkov by liaison officers via Baranovichi and on planes.

At the same time, with the aim of preserving the Baranovichi sector the 17th Mechanized Corps (without support units) was ordered to secure the Baranovichi road junctions from the side of Obus–Lesna; that was very conscientiously carried out by the 17th Corps, even in conditions of complete encirclement.

On the second day, and all day, enemy aircraft subjected the aerodromes to attacks. Where the 143rd Fighter Regiment of the 43rd Aviation Division was located, the enemy carried out 12 attacks on the aerodrome.

As a consequence of this the aerodrome at Losnitsa was bombed out and the administrative units, teaching and civilian, unable to fly, were all put out of action. The air force command relocated the regiment to the Slepianka aerodrome. At the same time, and on the second day, the enemy inflicted damage on the railway junctions at Orsha, Borisov, Bobruisk, Osipovichi, and totally destroyed the artillery dump at Gainovka.

On that day the enemy lost 27 aircraft.

On the second day, units of the 10th Army, apart from army headquarters, remained in their positions. Army headquarters changed its command post, moving away to the east of Belostok in the region of Valila. Units of the 4th Army, being constantly squeezed by enemy mechanized units and planes, continued its withdrawal to the line Pruzhany and Bereza–Kartuzka.

Over the course of the second day, the 3rd Army moved forward by about 13–17 kilometers in the direction of Grodno.

Concerning losses in men and equipment over the course of the first and second days I have no information at all, apart from a general report from Kuznetsov who informed me on the first day that the 56th Rifle Division had ceased to exist. In actual fact the division had lost about 25% of its men by the end of the first day and by the morning of the second, one unit appeared on the left riverbank of the Neman, and another unit on the Neman's right bank.

Although the 85th Division of the 3rd Army had suffered losses, it was still fully operational.

The 27th Division of the 3rd Army had become cut off but occupied a solid defensive position along the area Sukhovy–Genions and established contact with 2nd Division of the 10th Army.

My conclusions from the third day are as follows: the enemy had moved rapidly forward from the Brest sector by means of major mechanized forces with huge air support, which had targeted our infantry and artillery.

Question: What measures were taken by you in order to implement a turn-around?

Answer: In order to deal with the rapid enemy advance, the first thing undertaken by me on 23 June was to deploy all available bombers for the exclusive purpose of bombing the advancing enemy in the region of Kobrin. The moving out of the 55th Division from Slutsk to the region of Bereza–Kartuzka was accelerated so that it was possible to close this sector by a whole, organized formation. The 121st and 143rd Divisions were placed at the disposal of the commander of the 4th Army. The 143rd Division was continuing its unloading and concentrating in the region of Obus–Lesna.

Question: What was the outcome of these measures taken by you?

Answer: The results were that for one 24-hour period we were able to stop the enemy in the region of Bereza–Kartuzka.

Subsequent events unfolded in the following manner such that after our report to the Stavka about the severe situation in the Brest sector and after the report about the fact that enemy mechanized units were mounting a strong blow in the direction of Bel'sk to Gorodok, apparently, with the mission to cut off units of the 10th Army, the order was received: all units are to be withdrawn to the line of the river Shchar. This order was passed on to 10th Army, sent twice by radio, was acknowledged, and was duplicated to all armies by plane and parachute. In order to oversee the implementation of the order special delegates were sent to each army. This group of delegates was ordered to seek out Marshal of the Soviet Union Kulik, in the area of 10th Army. The units received the order and began its implementation.

At the same time, in order to secure a planned withdrawal of units to the line of the river Shchar, positions had already been prepared by me and at full capacity by the units of the 155th 121st and 143rd Divisions, and they occupied that line.

The 55th Division, operating in the Brest sector and proceeding to its line, was subjected to attack by no less than three tank divisions, accompanied by a large quantity of bombers, and was cut off and thrown into the forest on both sides of the highway. In such a way and simultaneously with the occupation of the Shchar, a breach in the left flank occurred once again. The enemy surged toward Slutsk. Orders were personally delivered by me to the chief of staff, Sandalov, to occupy and to prepare the Slutsk reinforced region for defense, personally to go out to the 55th Rifle Division with the army commander, to impose a harsh disciplinary regime and to compel the division to defend on the former state border, and with units of the 143rd Division to launch a counter-strike in a southern direction with the mission to cut the highway in the Kartuz–Bereza area.

I did not manage to ascertain how this order was carried out. I merely found out that units of the 55th Division were attacked on that day on the right flank; that is from the side of Baranovichi by not less than 60 tanks. The enemy's attack was repulsed by both artillery and by the infantry but even these operations demonstrated to me that the enemy in some unit or other had broken through to Baranovichi and in that way had emerged in the rear of the second formation; that is the 121st, 155th and 143rd Divisions. Nevertheless the measures taken by the commander of 17th Mechanized Corps, General Petrov, led to the destruction of up to 45–50 enemy tanks, which had broken through to Baranovichi.The remaining tanks set off in a southern direction.

I found out that on 24 June units of the 3rd Army had started to with-draw to the line of the river Shchar designated by the Stavka. The only thing of which I was not aware was where the 6th Mechanized Corps had been sent by the headquarters of 10th Army. According to my order it was due to arrive by means of a forced march ahead of the infantry and stand in the Slonim area in order to be ready to cut off any possible enemy counterattack with the aim of encircling the 10th Army from the south. This order was sent by me to the Stavka and approved.

On 25 June in the Vil'no sector, according to information from those who had fled Lithuania, the enemy had routed the 5th Mechanized Division, the national Lithuanian division had scattered and enemy mechanized units turned up on the right flank of the 21st Rifle Corps which forced us even more strongly to accelerate the move of the 50th Division to Vileika and the 24th Division to join up with the 21st Rifle Corps.

To the north of Lida, the 24th Division was attacked by not less than one enemy tank division and inflicted severe losses on the enemy, and then stopped on its occupied line with its front to the northwest.

The 37th Division, which had beaten off a tank and motorized infantry attack, with great losses for the enemy, had leveled its front and occupied one line with the 24th and 17th Rifle Divisions.

The enemy headed for Molodechno, bypassing the units of 21st Rifle Corps, without meeting any resistance, since there were no troops on that sector and none to be taken from anywhere. Having en route brushed up against the 50th Division in the Vileika region, the enemy occupied Molodechno and in so doing, severed the link between the formations of the 50th Division and the 21st Rifle Corps.

The commander of the 50th Division took the entirely correct and rational decision to withdraw and to occupy the Pleshchanitsa region in order to form a solid defense for the Minsk–Borisov sector.

After the enemy had captured Slutsk and Molodechno the troops in the reinforced regions of Minsk and Slutsk were brought up to full battle readiness. In order to strengthen the reinforced regions the 64th, 108th and 100th Divisions were moved up. The 100th Division was instructed to defend the northern salient face of Minsk. The 161st Division was left in reserve to the south of Minsk. Apart from the 100th Division, these divisions had only just completed their deployment.

The headquarters of the 13th Army which had been withdrawn was ordered to establish the Minsk front roughly along the line Pleshchanitsa–Minsk and Slutsk reinforced regions. The following units formed the army's order of battle: the 2nd and 44th Rifle Corps and the 20th Mechanized Corps without the administrative units. In such a way, a front was created covering Minsk and forces were amassed for a possible counterstrike in the event that it was required to withdraw the Minsk–Novogrudskii and Baranovichi formations.

On 25 June front headquarters received a telegram from the headquarters of 10th Army: "Units have arrived at the Zel'vianka River. All crossing points occupied by the enemy. Request support from the direction of Baranovichi."

I ordered the 10th Army to seize the crossings or to seek a route bypassing them across the river Neman or to the south through the forested expanses, depending on the situation. The troops were ordered to give more precise details of their location and to indicate the method of operation. At the same time, in order to ensure the correct operations of the troops situated on the line of the river Shchar, my assistant from the higher educational institutions, Khabarov, with an analogous group of delegates was sent to Petrov's headquarters by me. The delegates were required to take charge of the assistance of this formation for the withdrawal of units of the 10th Army, and they were then instructed where to go with these formations and in what direction.

By this time, as a result of successful battles in the Slonim area advanced tank units of the enemy had been destroyed and a map was taken from a dead officer, on which was indicated the entire attacking enemy formation, beginning with the river Bug and up to and including Baranovichi. From this map it was clear that the enemy was conducting an offensive with the strength of three mechanized corps and that along this line of advance this entire group had fallen upon a front which at the beginning consisted of two rifle divisions and then one rifle division.

Judging by the course of events it was possible to determine that in the Slonim area and in the Volkovysk region the enemy had apparently thrown in a mechanized division of the left-flank corps.

In the battles of the Minsk reinforced region the headquarters of a German corps was completely destroyed and all its documents were captured. From the documents it was established that 2 mechanized corps, reinforced by 3 motorized divisions were operating in this sector.

Throughout the 13th Army the army commander gave out the order on the basis of the personal instructions of the People's Commissar for Defense, conveyed via Marshal Shaposhnikov: "You shall fight for Minsk with utter determination and you shall fight right up to the moment of encirclement." This order was conveyed to all troops and by this order can be explained the stubbornness with which the troops fought against the many mechanized units, and having expended their armor-piercing shells, the units used ordinary bottles and water bottles full of petrol and set the German tanks ablaze. In such a way, the 100th Division alone managed to destroy not less than 100 tanks. The troops were advised by me of this method as early as the winter of this year based on the experience of battles at Khalkin-Gol. Nevertheless enemy mechanized units bypassed the reinforced Minsk region and, having dropped paratroopers in the region of Smelovichi, linked up with this assault and severed the Minsk–Borisov highway.

The supply route for the units remained along the Minsk and the Osipovichesk and Mogilev highways.

On the left flank by the time of my arrival at the front the enemy was approaching Starye Dorogi without encountering any organized resistance to his front at all, and on the basis of a report of the head of a supply dump at Urech'e was approaching Urech'e on that day with forces not less than a regiment of tanks which caused the head of the supply dump to set it alight, to blow it and then leave. There were no troops left to cover this sector.

On this position I ordered that platoons, companies and battalions were to be formed from the people of various divisions coming from the rear and to place them on the line of Starye Dorogi. At the same time the Bobruisk tractor academy was stood to and occupied in the Bobruisk area. All bridges across the river Berezina were mined and prepared for blowing. The remains of the 42nd Division—to be true very weak—and the 21st Locomotive Regiment took up defensive positions on the left bank of the river Berezina.

The task of blowing the bridges I allocated to Lazarenko, the commander of the 42nd Division. In the event that enemy tanks appeared and any threat that the crossings might be seized all bridges were to be blown; that was done by General Lazarenko when our units withdrew.

At about 0300 hours in the night of 27 or 28 June the chief of staff of the 13th Aviation Division received an order from me to leave the aerodrome with the onset of dawn so as not to subject the aircraft to complete destruction. This was done in very good time by the aircraft and at first light the aerodrome was occupied by enemy tank units. The whole time the enemy continued to seek and to find the crossings over the Berezina in the region of Ptatkovo–Domanovo.

In order to secure the river crossings the enemy employed the mass attacks of dive-bombers and a huge quantity of mortars. Over two days our aircraft had one essential mission: to bomb the enemy formation in Bobruisk.

In order to conduct discussions with the air force commander I came up with the following code: the northern group designated the region Smelovichi, northern 2 designated the region Pleshchanitsa and southern designated Bobruisk.

This code was established so that it would be possible to concentrate all the aircraft regardless of the situation on any one of these sectors by means of a simple order.

From 25 to 28 June there was no radio contact with either the 3rd or the 10th Armies. An attempt to get liaison officers there by plane ended with the planes being shot down. A large number of liaison officers were sent in vehicles by circuitous routes.

I do not know whether any of these liaison officers managed to get through to the headquarters of the 10th or 3rd Armies or not. People who turned up from the 3rd and 10th Armies came with information about the location of the headquarters of these armies or units usually about two days out of date. The 1st Antitank Brigade had lost contact with the 10th Army and had emerged from across the river Zel'vianka. The brigade returned without a single shell. It was stopped on the Berezina and immediately replenished with shells in order to defend the Berezina crossing.

Further on the fundamental task was set as follows: by all means and at any cost to seek out where our units were. Parachutists were dropped in the region of where our units were deemed to be with the task of handing over a coded telegram or to pass on the direction of withdrawal by word of mouth.

Marshal of the Soviet Union Kulik, whose fate at the present time is not known to me, was located with the 10th Army right up to the moment of my departure.

On the eve of my arrest, I found out when I was at front headquarters that a cavalry corps and allegedly the 113th Division had emerged from encirclement. As a result of the measures taken to restrain the enemy in the Minsk sector an exit gap on the Slutsk side had been maintained for units to the south of Minsk to Shatsk inclusively, to where all the units of the 155th, 121st, 143rd , 55th Divisions and the 21st Rifle Corps headed, apart from the 50th Division, which was ordered to take up a defensive position on the left bank of the Berezina river to the north of Borisov.

Taking the units to the river Berezina, I organized, in good time, covering detachments made up of various assembled units and military schools to cover the crossings in the region of Borisov, Berezino and the river Svisloch'. The mission of these detachments was to let through all our units across the other side of the river Berezina. The withdrawing units which were occupying the left bank of the river Berezina were ordered to hold the left bank, not allowing the enemy to cross the river.

The 47th Rifle Corps and the 20th Mechanized Corps were sent off to be used for a counterstrike in the general direction of Mogilev–Bobruisk so as completely to cut off the enemy tanks which had broken through to Rogachev.

I was unable to implement these measures since a new front commander arrived.

On the day of departure I was unable to report the status of units of the 3rd and 10th Armies, but I know from the condition of the troops that they will resist for a long time and stubbornly and will take all measures to get out of encirclement.

Over this whole period of the battles front headquarters worked flat out and had to acquire information by all possible means since the wire communications had totally failed to function. In the western regions it had been cut by local, anti-Soviet elements and saboteurs and individuals dropped by parachute.

The level of exhaustion of the chief of staff, General Klimovskikh, was so severe that I personally had to record the orders being dispatched in my notebook or personally had to check that they were being carried out or had to send special people selected from the political cadres in order to check.

I consider the enemy's massive superiority in tanks, his new equipment and his massive air superiority to be the main cause of these disasters.

Question: Can you specify the losses in manpower and equipment borne by the Western front during your leadership?

Answer: Up to the day of my arrest I had no information concerning either losses of men or loss of equipment. A unit of the 3rd Army and a unit of the 10th Army remained in encirclement. Their fate is unknown to me. As a consequences of the measures taken the remaining units were led out of encirclement and remained under command.

Question: Who bears the guilt for the penetration of the Western front?

Answer: As I have already indicated, the fundamental reason for the rapid penetration of German troops into our territory was the manifest superiority in airpower and tanks enjoyed by the enemy. Furthermore, on the left flank, Lithuanian units had been placed by Kuznetsov (Baltic Military District), which did not want to fight. After the first sign of pressure on the left wing of the Balts the Lithuanian units opened fire on their commanders and ran away. This enabled the German tank units to strike me from Vilnius. Alongside this the loss of control at the headquarters of the 4th Army by Korobkov and Sandalov of their units facilitated the rapid forward deployment of the enemy in the Bobruisk sector, and the failure of the 10th Army commander, General Golubev, to implement my order and to launch a blow on Briansk with the 6th Mechanized Corps with the aim of routing the enemy's mechanized formation, and after that to be at my disposal in the region of Volkovysk, deprived me of the opportunity of having any suitable strike force.

Question: Were there any treacherous actions on the part of your subordinates?

Answer: No, none. Several people were somewhat confused in the rapidly changing situation.

Question: And what guilt do you personally bear for the penetration of the front?

Answer: I took all measures in order to avert the penetration of German troops. I consider that I am not guilty of the situation which was created at the front.

Question: For how long have you commanded the Western Special Military District?

Answer: One year.

Question: Were the units of the district prepared for military operations?

Answer: The units of the district were prepared for military operations with the exception of the newly formed 17th, 20th, 13th and 11th Mechanized Corps. Moreover, in the 13th and 11th Corps, each one had a prepared division, the rest, having received recruits, only had basic training levels of equipment and then not in every case. The 14th Mechanized Corps had only one poorly trained motorized division and rifle regiments of tank divisions.

Question: If the main units of the district were prepared and you received the order to act in good time, this means that the deep penetration of German troops into Soviet territory can only be ascribed to your criminal actions as front commander.

Answer: I categorically reject that accusation. I have committed no treason or treachery.

Question: Along the entire length of the state border only on that sector commanded by you did German troops penetrate so deeply into Soviet territory. I repeat that this was the result of treacherous acts on your part.

Answer: The penetration occurred on my front because I did not have the latest equipment, as much as I wanted, as for example, the Kiev Military District.

Question: In vain you attempt to ascribe the defeat to causes having nothing to do with you. The investigation has established that you participated in a conspiracy as early as 1935 and that even at that time intended to betray the Motherland in any future war. Your present situation at the front confirms the information available to the investigation.

Answer: I have never been in any conspiracies and I have never moved in any conspiratorial circles. For me this accusation is exceptionally painful and false from start to finish. If there are any statements about me to that effect at all, they are demonstrably and totally the lies of people wanting by any means to blacken the name of honest men and so do harm to the state.

The interrogation finished at 1610 hours.

This is a correct transcription of my words and has been read by me. D. Pavlov.

The interrogation was conducted by:

Temporary executive officer, chief of the investigative unit, Third Directorate NKO USSR, Senior Battalion Commissar Pavlovskii

Investigator of the Third Directorate NKO USSR, Junior Lieutenant of State Security Komarov

Source: Tsentral'nyi Arkhiv, Federal'naia Sluzhba Bezopasnosti, Arkhivnoe-sledstvennoe delo № P-24000, listy 23–53.

Appendix E Translation of *Polozhenie o voennykh komissarakh Raboche-Krest'ianskoi Krasnoi Armii* (Statute Concerning Military Commissars of the Worker-Peasant Red Army), 16 July 1941

Confirmed by the Presdium of the Supreme Soviet of the USSR, 16 July 1941

1. The institution of military commissars shall be introduced in all regiments, divisions, headquarters, military-teaching establishments and institutions of the Red Army both at the front and in the rear.

2. The military commissar is the representative of the Party and Government in the Red Army and alongside the commander bears responsibility for the execution of the combat mission by the military unit, for the unit's steadfastness in battle and the unshakable readiness to fight to the last drop of blood against the enemies of our Motherland and honorably to fight for every piece of Soviet territory.

3. The military commissar is the moral instructor of his unit (formation) and the first defender of its material and psychological interests. "If the regimental commander is the head of the regiment, then the regimental commissar must be the father and soul of the regiment" (Stalin).

4. The military commissar is obliged to do his utmost to assist the commander, who is honestly and selflessly carrying out his combat tasks, in all his work, to strengthen the commander's authority and strictly to supervise the implementation of all orders issued by the High Command.

5. The military commissar is required to provide the Supreme Command and the government with timely information about commanders and political workers who are unworthy of the rank of commander and political worker and who by their behavior sully the honor of the Worker-Peasant Red Army.

6. The military commissar must inspire the troops for the struggle against the enemy of the Motherland. During the most serious moments of battle the military commissar is obliged by a personal display of courage and bravery

to raise the morale of his military unit and to achieve the unconditional fulfillment of the military order.

7. The military commissar is required to encourage and to popularize the best soldiers and commanders, to inculcate bravery, courage, cold-bloodedness, initiative and skill among the rank and file of the unit, to instill contempt for death and a readiness to fight to the very last against the enemies of our Motherland.

8. Relying on the vast masses of Red Army soldiers and commanders, the military commissar is obliged to wage a merciless struggle against cowards, panic-mongers and deserters, applying revolutionary order and military discipline with a firm hand. Coordinating his activities with the organs of the 3rd Directorate of the People's Commissariat for Defense, the military commissar is obliged to eradicate any manifestation of treason.

9. The military commissar shall lead the political organs and additionally the party and Komsomol organizations of the military units.

10. In his work the politruk is accountable to the regimental commissar, the regimental commissar to the divisional commissar, the divisional commissar to the Military Council of the army and to the Main Political Directorate of the Red Army.

11. All orders for the regiment, division, directorate and institution shall be signed by the commander and military commissar.

Source: KPSS o vooruzhennykh silakh Sovetskogo Soiuza: Dokumenty 1917–1968 (Moscow: Voennoe izdatel'stvo Ministerstva oborony SSSR, 1969), 307–308.

Appendix F Translation of *Erlaß über die Ausübung der Kriegsgerichtsbarkeit im Gebiet „Barbarossa" und über besondere Maßnahmen der Truppe* (Decree Concerning the Implementation of Military Jurisdiction in the Barbarossa Zone and Concerning Special Measures for the Troops), 13 May 1941

The Führer and Supreme Commander of the Armed Forces, Führer Headquarters, 13 May 1941

The primary function of military law is the maintenance of discipline among the troops.

The wide expanse of the operational areas in the East, the form of the combat leadership required as a consequence and the special nature of the enemy impose tasks on the military courts which during the course of military operations and until the first phase of pacification of the conquered territories, they will only be able to solve with their small establishment of personnel if military jurisdiction is, in the first instance, confined to its primary task.

This is only possible when the troops themselves respond to any threat from the enemy civilian population with the merciless use of arms.

Accordingly, the following orders are to apply to the Barbarossa zone, the operational zone, the rear area of the army and the zone of political administration:

I. The Handling of Criminal Offenses Committed by Enemy Civilian Persons

1. Criminal offenses committed by enemy civilian persons are until further notice withdrawn from the competence of the courts-martial and field courts.

2. Guerrillas encountered by the troops whether in battle or in attempting to escape are to be mercilessly put to death.

3. Additionally, all other attacks carried out by enemy civilian persons against the German armed forces, its members and other employees are to be put down by the troops on the spot by the severest means including the destruction of the attacker.

4. Where measures of this kind were absent or not in the first instance possible, elements suspected of an offense are to be brought before an officer. The officer shall decide whether the suspects are to be shot.

If the circumstances do not permit a rapid identification of individual perpetrators, collective punitive measures are, on the order of an officer with the minimum rank of a battalion commander, immediately to be implemented against villages from which the German armed forces are attacked from ambush or otherwise maliciously attacked.

5. It shall be emphatically forbidden to keep suspicious persons in custody in order to hand them over after the reintroduction of jurisdiction over the inhabitants.

6. The Supreme Commander of the army groups can, in agreement with the responsible commanders of the Luftwaffe and the Navy, reintroduce military jurisdiction over civilian persons in those places which have been sufficiently pacified.

With regard to the area of political administration this order shall be issued by the Head of the Supreme Command of the Armed Forces (OKW).

II. Dealing with Criminal Acts Committed by Members of the Armed Forces and Its Employees against Local Inhabitants

1. There shall be no compulsion to pursue acts committed by members of the armed forces or employees against enemy civilians even if the act is both a military crime and misdemeanor.

2. When making a judgment of such deeds any procedural measures are to take into account that the collapse in 1918 and the later time of suffering of the German people and the struggle against National Socialism, with its countless sacrifices made in blood, could be decisively traced back to Bolshevik influence and that no German has forgotten this.

3. Consequently the court shall examine whether in such cases a disciplinary punishment should be made or whether a court hearing is necessary. The court shall only order the prosecution of deeds against local inhabitants on the basis of military jurisdiction when it requires the maintenance of military discipline or the security of the troops. That applies, for example, to serious acts that stem from a lack of sexual restraint, that derive from

criminal behavior or provide evidence that the troops are threatening to run wild. As a rule criminal acts in which accommodation as well as supplies or other captured material are senselessly destroyed to the detriment of our troops are to be punished no less severely.

In every single case the ordering of preliminary proceedings shall require the signature of the court.

When assessing the credibility of statements made by enemy civilians extreme caution is required.

III. Responsibility of the Troop Commanders

Within the framework of their authority the troop commanders are personally responsible for ensuring that:

1. All officers in units attached to them are instructed in good time and in the most energetic form of the principles set out in paragraph I;

2. The legal advisers are informed in good time of the instructions and of the information communicated orally in which the political intentions of the political leadership have been explained to the army group commanders;

3. Only such judgments be confirmed that are consistent with the political intentions of the leadership.

IV. Maintaining Secrecy

Once promulgated this decree still enjoys the status of a protected secret as a secret command matter.

On Behalf

The Chief of the Supreme Command of the Armed Forces

[signed] Keitel

Source: Document 050-C, Exhibit USA-554, in *Trial of the Major War Criminals before the International Military Tribunal Nuremberg, 14 November 1945–1 October 1946*, Blue Series, 42 vols. (Nuremberg: n.p., 1949), XXXIV:252–255.

Appendix G Translation of *Richtlinien für die Behandlung politischer Kommissare* (Guidelines for the Treatment of Political Commissars), 6 June 1941

Attachment to OKW/WFSt/Abt.L/IV Qu

Nr. 44882/41 g. K. Chefs

In the struggle against Bolshevism one *cannot* reckon with the fact that the enemy will behave in accordance with humanitarian principles or those of international law. In particular, one must expect a hate-filled, cruel and inhuman treatment of our prisoners from *political commissars* of all types, as the actual bearers of resistance.

The troops must be aware of the following:

1. In this struggle mercy and any consideration of international law with regard to these elements are wrong. They pose a danger for our own security and the rapid pacification of the conquered territories.

2. The commissars are the originators of barbaric, Asiatic methods of waging war. Therefore it is necessary to move against them *immediately* and without delay, with all severity.

Consequently, if they are apprehended in battle or offering resistance they are in principle to be shot immediately.

Moreover, additional considerations are applicable:

I. The Operational Area

1. Political commissars who *oppose our troops* are to be treated according to the Decree Concerning the Implementation of Jurisdiction in the Barbarossa Zone. This shall apply to political commissars of all types and situations even if they are only suspected of resistance, sabotage or incitement thereto.

Attention is drawn to "The Guidelines for the Conduct of the Troops in Russia."

2. As agencies of the enemy's troops political commissars can be identified by the special badge—a red star interwoven with a gold hammer and sickle worn on the sleeves (for details see *The Armed Forces of the USSR*

OKH/Gen St d H O Qu IV Abt. Foreign Armies East (II) Nr. 100/41 g. dated 15 January 1941 under attachment 9 d). They are to be separated from the prisoners of war *immediately*; that is while still on the battlefield. This is required in order to deny them an opportunity of exerting any influence on captured soldiers. Provisions of international law guaranteeing protection to prisoners of war shall not apply to them. After they have been separated they are to be shot.

3. *Political commissars who are not guilty of any hostile behavior or are not suspected of same* are, in the first instance, to remain unharmed. Only some time later with a further penetration of the country will it be possible to decide whether remaining functionaries can be left in situ or whether they are to be handed over to the special units. Every effort is to be made to ensure that these units themselves undertake an examination.

When making a decision concerning the question whether "guilty or not guilty" the personal impression made by the commissar's attitude and manner shall in principle count for more than any act which it may not be possible to prove.

4. In cases (1) and (2) a brief report (report card) concerning the event is to be sent:

a) to the divisional intelligence officer from troops under command of a division,

b) to Corps and, so on, intelligence officers from troops which are directly subordinated to a Corps, Army, Army Group or Panzer Group.

5. All the above-mentioned measures must not stop the conduct of operations. Systematic search and cleaning up operations by combat troops are consequently to cease.

II. In the Army Rear
Commissars that are apprehended in the army rear on the basis of their suspicious behavior are to be handed over to the Task Force or Task Command of the Security Police.

III. Restriction of Courts-Martial and Field Courts
The courts-martial and the field courts of the regiments and commanders and so on may not be entrusted with the execution of the measures stipulated in paragraphs I and II.

Note: This translation is based on the text of the original document issued on 6 June 1941. All emphasis corresponds to the original document. The full German text of the Commissar Order, *Richtlinien für die Behandlung politischer Kommissare*, is widely available on the Internet and has been reproduced in many German works on the subject. See, for example, Gerd R. Ueberschär und Wolfram Wette, hrsg., *„Unternehmen Barbarossa": Der deutsche Überfall auf die Sowjetunion 1941, Berichte, Analysen, Dokumente* (Paderborn: Ferdinand Schöningh, 1984), 313–314 (the German archival reference is BA-MA, RH 2/v.2082).

NOTES

Abbreviations

IMT, Blue Series: *Trial of the Major War Criminals before the International Military Tribunal Nuremberg, 14 November 1945–1 October 1946, Blue Series, 42 vols.* (Nuremberg: n.p., 1949)

IMT, Green Series: *Trials of War Criminals before the Nuerenberg Military Tribunals, October 1946–April 1949, Green Series, 15 vols.* (Washington, D.C.: Government Printing Office, 1949)

OGB: *Organy gosudarstvennoi bezopasnosti SSSR v Velikoi Otechestvennoi Voine, tom vtoroi, kniga 1, 22 iiunia–31 avgusta 1941 goda* (Moscow: izdatel'stvo "Rus'," 2000); *Organy gosudarstvennoi bezopasnosti SSSR v Velikoi Otechestvennoi Voine: Sbornik dokumentov, tom vtoroi, kniga 2, Nachalo 1 sentiabria–31 dekabria 1941 goda* (Moscow: izdatel'stvo "Rus'," 2000); cited as OGB followed by the year, 1 or 2 to indicate the first or second half of the year (e.g., 1941/1), report number (№, if applicable), and page number

Preface

1. Gerhard L. Weinberg, *Germany and the Soviet Union, 1939–1941* (Leiden: E. J. Brill, 1954), 1.

2. See Roger Moorhouse, *The Devils' Alliance: Hitler's Pact with Stalin, 1939–41* (London: Bodley Head, 2014).

3. Weinberg, *Germany and the Soviet Union,* 2.

4. Robert Conquest, *The Great Terror: A Reassessment* (London: Hutchinson, 1990), 449.

5. Gerd R. Ueberschär und Wolfram Wette, hrsg., „*Unternehmen Barbarossa*": *Der deutsche Überfall auf die Sowjetunion 1941, Berichte, Analysen, Dokumente* (Paderborn: Ferdinand Schöningh, 1984).

6. Waitman Wade Beorn, *Marching into Darkness: The Wehrmacht and the Holocaust in Belarus* (Cambridge, Mass.: Harvard University Press, 2014), 236.

7. See *Operativnyi Prikaz Narodnogo Komissara Vnutrennikh Del Soiuza SSR № 00447, ob operatsii po repressirovaniiu byvshikh kulakov, ugolovnikov i drugikh antisovetskikh elementov, 30 iiulia 1937* (Operational Order of the People's Commissariat for Internal Affairs of the Soviet Union № 00447 Concerning the Operation for the Repression of Former Kulaks, Criminals, and Other Anti-Soviet Elements, 30 July 1937). This order provided two categories of punishment: arrestees falling into the first category were to be arrested and shot (*rasstrel*), and those in the second category were to be sentenced to eight to ten years in a labor camp. Decisions regarding arrest and execution were based entirely on notions of class, class warfare, and what those targeted for extermination *might do*, not what they had done. The executions envisaged by Order № 00447 totaled 75,950, which included 8,000 in Ukraine, 2,500 in the Kazakh republic, and 10,000 already in NKVD camps. The number of category-two arrests totaled 193,000, which included 20,800 in Ukraine and 5,000 in the Kazakh republic. Thus, the total number of repressions (executions plus incarcerations) equaled 268,950.

8. This was also acknowledged in a major Russian study published in 1997: "The mass deportations of Poles, the slave labor and the extermination of peaceful civilians, all of these things were constituent parts of the genocide against the Polish people. The aim was to erase the very concept of 'Poland' for all time." A. N. IAkovlev et al., eds., *Katyn': Plenniki neob"iavlennoi voiny*, in the series "*Demokratiia*," *Rossiia. XX VEK, Dokumenty* (Moscow: Mezhdunarodnyi fond, 1997), 42.

9. Moorhouse, *Devils' Alliance*, 300.

10. Omer Bartov, *The Eastern Front 1941–45: German Troops and the Barbarisation of Warfare*, 2nd ed. (Basingstoke, U.K.: Palgrave, 2001), 89. The brutal, mind-numbing indoctrination that was characteristic of the Red Army has also been identified by Roman Kolkowicz: "A large portion of the daily activities of the Soviet officer and soldier is taken up by repetition of the little understood Marxist-Leninist litany, and the military press does everything possible to add to political indoctrination. Periodicals and dailies repeat sterile formulas *ad infinitum*, and countless handbooks and textbooks add to this verbiage. Though the military consumer of this constant diet of political rhetoric may be numbed into a state of stupor, the Party leadership believes in the method as a way of realizing Makarenko's ideas on communist education, a belief that is reinforced by its reliance on Pavlov's theory of human behavior." Roman Kolkowicz, *The Soviet Military and the Communist Party* (Princeton, N.J.: Princeton University Press, 1967), 93.

11. Boris Pasternak, *Doktor Zhivago* (Milan: Feltrilleni, 1957), 519.

12. That these soldierly virtues existed before the rise of Hitler and independent of NS ideology is evident from the generous appraisal of German troops delivered by T. E. Lawrence as the British campaign in the Middle East neared its victorious conclusion in September 1918. Whereas the Turks and their Arab allies retreated in disarray, "exceptions were the German detachments; and here, for the first time, I grew proud of the enemy who had killed my brothers. They were two thousand miles from home, without hope and without guides, in conditions made enough to break the bravest nerves. Yet their sections held together, in firm rank, sheering through the wrack of Turk and Arab like armoured ship, high-faced and silent. When attacked they halted, took position, fired to order. There was no haste, no crying, no hesitation. They were glorious." T. E. Lawrence, *Seven Pillars of Wisdom: A Triumph* [1935] (Harmondsworth, U.K.: Penguin, 1988), 655. Although writing from the perspective of a Stalingrad survivor and former member of the Wehrmacht, Hauptmann Rudolf Krell (94th Infantry Division) leaves no doubt that German military steadfastness long predates the rise of Hitler and NS propaganda. As the end draws near in Stalingrad, Krell rebukes Generalmajor Lattmann for his use of the word "futile" to characterize further German resistance: "Finally, the German soldier has been taught throughout the centuries to stand fast where it is 'hopeless.' In the thousand year history of all peoples this attitude has always been demanded of soldiers as a self-explanatory duty and celebrated as such. The 'futile' concept stems in any case from the terminology of the enemy's conduct of psychological warfare

and it was stunning to hear General Lattmann in this place and at this time, among others, to keep availing himself of this word 'futile.'" Quoted in Frank Ellis, The Stalingrad Cauldron: Inside the Encirclement and Destruction of the 6th Army (Lawrence: University Press of Kansas, 2013), 148. Given that the German collapse at Stalingrad occurred a mere ten years after Hitler became chancellor of Germany, it does not strike me as plausible that these martial virtues could have been the exclusive outcome of NS propaganda.

13. V. I. Lenin, "Doklad na II Vserossiiskom s'ezde politprosvetov 17 oktiabria 1921 g.," in Sochineniia, vol. 33 (Moscow: Gosudarstvennoe izadatel'stvo politicheskoi literatury, 1951), 46.

14. Bartov, Eastern Front, 152.

15. The death toll from this prolonged orgy of sadistic violence, which included mass rape, mass machine-gunning of prisoners, bayoneting competitions, and beheadings, is estimated at 260,000 to 350,000 victims. Iris Chang, The Rape of Nanking: The Forgotten Holocaust of World War II (New York: Basic Books, 1997), 4.

16. Bartov, Eastern Front, 153.

17. Ibid., 156.

18. Convincing arguments for this assertion have also been marshaled by Bernhard Chiari in his essay "Zwischen Hoffnung und Hunger. Die sowjetische Zivilbevölkerung unter deutscher Besatzung," in Verbrechen der Wehrmacht: Bilanz einer Debatte, ed. Christian Hartmann, Johannes Hürter, and Ulrike Jureit (Munich: Verlag C. H. Beck, 2005), 145–154. To quote Chiari: "What at the turn of the century had served as the basis for training soldiers now reached the whole of 'Soviet society.' Masculinity

and a feeling of political community formed, with the propagation of violence as a legitimate way of solving problems, an inseparable combination. The right and the ability to exercise violence externally and internally was something that the Soviet Union used to an exorbitant degree. . . . Indeed, in the course of many years a permanent state of war with the non-communist milieu dominated the behaviour of the Party leadership" (152–153).

19. V. I. Lenin, "Kak organizovat' sorevnovanie?" [1929], in Sochineniia, vol. 26 (Moscow: Gosudarstvennoe izadatel'stvo politicheskoi literatury, 1949), 371.

20. Ibid., 375, emphasis in original.

21. Ibid.

22. Max Hastings, Armageddon: The Battle for Germany 1944–45 (London: Macmillan, 2004), 480.

23. Christian Hartmann, Wehrmacht im Ostkrieg: Front und militärisches Hinterland (Munich: R. Oldenbourg Verlag, 2010); Christian Hartmann, Operation Barbarossa: Nazi Germany's War in the East, 1941–1945 (Oxford: Oxford University Press, 2013). The latter is an English translation of Unternehmen Barbarossa: Der Deutsche Krieg im Osten, 1941–1945 (Munich: Verlag C. H. Beck, 2011). The English version is a short but highly effective study of the main questions associated with the war on the Eastern Front.

24. All the main contributions to the Historikerstreit were eventually published in a single volume: Historikerstreit: Die Dokumentation der Kontroverse um die Einzigartigkeit der nationalsozialistischen Judenvernichtung (Munich: R. Piper, 1987). Two immediate observations can be made about the articles in this

collection. First, only one contributor refers—briefly—to Vasilii Grossman's novel *Life and Fate*, which had appeared in German translation in 1984 and was reviewed by Heinrich Böll, "Die Fähigkeit zu trauern," *Die Zeit* 49 (30 November 1984): 11–12. Grossman subjects both totalitarian regimes to a forensic analysis and concludes that very little separated them, making its virtual omission from the *Historikerstreit* odd, to put it mildly. Second, no contributor made the connection with the Maoist genocide (1959–1962), which was implemented for much the same reasons as the Holodomor but led to millions more victims.

25. Hartmann, *Wehrmacht im Ostkrieg*, 484, 485, 514.

26. Alexander Watson, *Ring of Steel: Germany and Austria-Hungary at War, 1914–1918* (London: Allen Lane, 2014), 268.

27. Ibid., 132.

28. Geoffrey P. Megargee, *War of Annihilation: Combat and Genocide on the Eastern Front, 1941* [2006] (Plymouth, U.K.: Rowman & Littlefield, 2007), xiii.

Chapter 1. *Unternehmen Barbarossa*

1. Christian Hartmann, *Wehrmacht im Ostkrieg: Front und militärisches Hinterland* (Munich: R. Oldenbourg Verlag, 2010), 445.

2. Erich von Manstein, *Verlorene Siege* [1955], 19 Auflage (Bonn: Bernard & Graefe in der Mönch Verlagsgesellschaft mbH, 2011), 154.

3. Ibid., 161–162.

4. Ibid., 165, emphasis in original.

5. Heinz Guderian, *Achtung-Panzer! Die Entwicklung der Panzerwaffe, ihre Kampftaktik und ihre operativen Möglichkeiten* (Stuttgart: Union Deutsche Verlagsgesellschaft, 1937), 164.

6. Ibid.

7. Heinz Guderian, *Erinnerungen eines Soldaten* [1950], 9 Auflage (Neckergemünd: Kurt Vowinkel Verlag, 1976), 38–39.

8. Guderian, *Achtung-Panzer!* 165.

9. Ibid., 177.

10. Ibid., 202.

11. Ibid., 205.

12. Ibid., 206.

13. Ibid., 189.

14. Ibid., 161.

15. Ibid., 201.

16. Studying the Italian campaign in Abyssinia, Guderian came to a number of conclusions: (1) the peacetime network of roads influences the course of operations; (2) the network is not fixed and must be expanded in wartime; (3) improvised roads can be created that are suitable for tracked and cross-country vehicles; (4) the speedy establishment of these improvised roads favors the surprise deployment of mobile forces; and (5) mobile armies require road-building units and the necessary equipment. Guderian, *Achtung-Panzer!* 210–212. All these considerations are relevant for Barbarossa. When Guderian examined the use of tanks in Abyssinia and the Spanish Civil War, he concluded (correctly, as it turned out) that neither campaign offered a realistic trial of the tanks' value because the deployments were too small. In the Soviet Union, by contrast, Marshal Grigorii Kulik and General Dmitrii Pavlov advocated that large tank formations be broken up (based on the use of tanks in the Spanish Civil War).

17. Guderian, *Erinnerungen eines Soldaten*, 46.

18. Ibid., 48. For all his political prescience and interest in weapons, it is not clear that Churchill grasped the full significance of the changes being pioneered by Guderian. In contrast, Hitler immediately saw the potential of panzers. When Hitler visited Guderian during the Polish campaign, even he was astounded to learn that a concentration of Polish antitank guns had been destroyed by panzers and not by Stukas. Guderian himself attributed the low German losses in the Polish campaign largely to the panzers: "The tanks are a weapon that saves blood. The trust of the men in the superiority of their weapons had been markedly strengthened by the success in the corridor. The enemy had suffered the complete loss of 2–3 infantry divisions and a cavalry brigade. Thousands of prisoners and hundreds of guns had been captured." Ibid., 65.

19. Ibid., 51.

20. The advantages of deploying armor throughout the Ardennes, the basis of von Manstein's attack plan, had also occurred to Churchill. In a meeting in France on 14 August 1939, General Edward Spears, Churchill's personal representative with the French government, recorded that Churchill warned against the assumption that the Ardennes was impassable to armor: "'Remember,' he [Churchill] said, 'that we are faced with a new weapon, armour in great strength, on which the Germans are no doubt concentrating, and that forests will be particularly tempting to such forces since they will offer concealment from the air.'" Martin Gilbert, *Prophet of Truth: Winston S. Churchill*, vol. 5 (London: Minerva, 1990), 1101.

21. Guderian, *Erinnerungen eines Soldaten*, 80.

22. Ibid., 85–86.

23. *Manifest der Kommunistischen Partei*, 1848, para. I.

24. V. I. Lenin, "Printsipy sotsializma i voina 1914–1915," in *Sochineniia*, vol. 21, (Moscow: OGIZ, 1948), 272–273.

25. David M. Glantz, *Soviet Military Operational Art in Pursuit of Deep Battle* (Abingdon, U.K.: Frank Cass, 1991), 2.

26. Mikhail V. Frunze, "Edinaia voennaia doktrina i Krasnaia Armiia," in *Izbrannye proizvedeniia*, tom II (Moscow: Voennoe izdatel'stvo Ministerstva oborony Soiuza SSR, 1957), 5.

27. Ibid., 7.

28. Ibid., 8.

29. Ibid., 8–9.

30. Ibid., 10.

31. Ibid., 13, emphasis in original.

32. Ibid., emphasis in original.

33. Ibid., 17.

34. Ibid.

35. Ibid.

36. Vladimir K. Triandafillov, *Kharakter operatsii sovremennykh armii*, 1st ed. (Moscow: Gosudarstvennoe izdatel'stvo, otdel voennoi literatury, 1929), 5, emphasis in original.

37. Vladimir K. Triandafillov, *Kharakter operatsii sovremennykh armii*, 3rd ed. (Moscow: Gosvoenizdat, 1936). The introduction was downloaded from a Russian website that specializes in military matters (http://militera.lib.ru /science/triandafillov1/index.html). I am indebted to the compilers of this website, which is a valuable research tool.

38. Triandafillov, *Kharakter operatsii sovremennykh armii*, 1st ed., 27.

39. Ibid., 29, emphasis in original.

40. Ibid., 49, emphasis in original.

41. Ibid., 96, emphasis in original.

42. Ibid., 132.

43. Ibid., 161.

44. Ibid.

45. Ibid., 162.

46. Ibid.

47. Ibid., 163, emphasis added.

48. Ibid., 172.

49. Ibid., 177.

50. Georgii S. Isserson, *Novye formy bor'by (Opyt issledovaniia sovremennykh voin)* (Moscow: Voennoe izdatel'stvo Narodnogo Komissariata oborony Soiuza SSR, 1940), 3.

51. Ibid., 23.

52. Ibid., 24.

53. Ibid., 28.

54. Ibid., 30.

55. Ibid., 32.

56. Ibid., 37.

57. Ibid., 52.

58. Ibid., 54.

59. Guderian, *Erinnerungen eines Soldaten*, 136.

60. The full text of *Weisung Nr. 21* is cited in Guderian, *Erinnerungen eines Soldaten*, 455–457. It can also be found in many standard histories. See, for example, Gerd R. Ueberschär und Wolfram Wette, hrsg., „Unternehmen Barbarossa": *Der deutsche Überfall auf die Sowjetunion 1941, Berichte, Analysen, Dokumente* (Paderborn: Ferdinand Schöningh, 1984), 298–300.

61. Guderian, *Erinnerungen eines Soldaten*, 132.

62. The planning and trials for an invasion of Britain may have benefited the later Russian campaign. Thus, Guderian records that wading methods developed for Sea Lion were used to cross the Bug. Water up to a depth of four meters could be waded. Ibid., 139.

63. Ibid., 151–152.

64. Ibid., 153.

65. *Effects of Climate on Combat in European Russia*, CMH Pub. 104-6 (Washington, D.C.: Center of Military History, US Army, 1952), 51.

66. Document 872-PS, in IMT, Blue Series, XXVI:393.

67. Alfred Philippi, *Das Pripjetproblem. Eine Studie über die operative Bedeutung des Pripjetgebietes für den Feldzug des Jahres 1941* (Darmstadt: Verlag E. S. Mittler & Sohn, 1956), 22. Sources consulted by the author provide different figures for the total surface area of the Pripet forest-marsh (*Poles'e*). Thus, the online *Encyclopedia Britannica* gives a total surface area of 104,000 square miles (270,000 square kilometers), whereas the relevant entry in the *Malaia Sovetskaia Entsiklopediia*, 3rd ed., vol. 7 (1959), 310, gives the much lower figure of 38,000 square miles. The English-language Wikipedia entry uses the same figure as that cited by (EB). A total surface area of 90,000 square kilometers is cited in the German-language Wikipedia entry. The figure of 13.2 million hectares (132,000 square kilometers or 50,965 square miles) was derived from a study carried out by the National Academy of Sciences of Belarus and was provided by the Belarusian and Ukrainian affiliates of the Ramsar Trust. I am grateful to Tatiana Trafimovich (Belarus) and Aleksandr Kozulin (Ukraine) for their assistance.

68. During their trial, Pavlov and his chief of staff Klimovskikh stated that work on the new reinforced regions, which had started at the end of 1939, had not been completed by the time of the German invasion. Of the 600 new fire positions, only 189 had been equipped, but not completely. See № 437, "Protokol sudebnogo zasedaniia Voennoi kollegii Verkhovnogo suda SSSR po delu Pavlova D. G., Klimovskikh V. E., Grigor'eva A. T.

in Korobkova A. A., 22 iiulia 1941 g.,"
OGB, 1941/1, 387.

69. Viktor Suvorov, *Ledokol: Kto nachal vtoruiu mirovuiu voinu?* (1992), s Vladimir Bukovskii, "Monument chelovecheskoi slepote," (Moscow: Izdatel'skii dom, Novoe vremia, 1993), 74.

70. Guderian, *Erinnerungen eines Soldaten*, 156. Guderian's assessment of dust damage was confirmed by other commanders. Few tanks had dust filters, and "quartz dust was sucked into engines, which became so ground out that many tanks were rendered unserviceable. In other tanks the abrasive action of dust reduced engine efficiency and increased fuel consumption; thus weakened, they entered the autumn muddy season which dealt them the death blow." *Effects of Climate*, 48.

71. Guderian, *Erinnerungen eines Soldaten*, 192.

72. Ibid., 196.

73. Vasilii Grossman, *Gody voiny* (Moscow: Izadatel'stvo Pravda, 1989), 284.

74. Guderian, *Erinnerungen eines Soldaten*, 197–198.

75. Ibid., 137.

76. Grossman, *Gody voiny* (1989), 304.

77. Guderian, *Erinnerungen eines Soldaten*, 224. When citing temperatures, Guderian does not indicate Celsius or Fahrenheit. I have assumed he is using Celsius.

78. Ibid., 234.

79. *Effects of Climate*, 4.

80. Guderian, *Erinnerungen eines Soldaten*, 231. Guderian writes that the matter of winter clothing was not taken seriously by Oberkommando des Heeres (OKH) until 30 August 1941 and that Hitler bore no responsibility for the army's lack of winter clothing, since the

Luftwaffe and SS were well equipped. The general assumption in the army was that the Soviet Union would be defeated in eight to ten weeks (ibid., 137). However, even if the Soviet Union could be knocked out before the onset of winter, German occupation forces would still require winter clothing and equipment.

81. Carl von Clausewitz, *On War* [1832], ed. and trans. Michael Howard and Peter Paret (Princeton, N.J.: Princeton University Press, 1989), 143.

82. Between 1 January and 31 March 1942, German 4th Army, for example, suffered 96,535 casualties, 14,236 of which were directly due to frostbite. *Effects of Climate*, 6. Clausewitz's observation on weather is even harder to fathom, given his knowledge of the ordeals suffered by Napoleon's army in Russia.

83. Document 1157-PS, in IMT, Blue Series, XXVII:32–38.

84. Document 126-EC, in IMT, Blue Series, XXXVI:135–157.

85. Ibid., 137.

86. Ibid., 138.

87. Ibid.

88. Ibid., emphasis in original.

89. Ibid., 140.

90. Ibid., 141.

91. Ibid., 145, emphasis in original.

92. Ibid., 148–149.

93. № 235, "Soglashenie o vzaimnykh tovarnykh postavkakh na vtoroi dogovornoi period po khoiaistvennomu soglasheniiu ot 11 fevralia 1940 g. mezhdu soiuzom sovetskikh sotsialisticheskikh respublik i Germaniei, 10 ianvaria 1941 g.," in *1941 god, v 2-knigakh*, ed. A. N. IAkovlev et al., in the series "Demokratiia," *Rossiia. XX VEK, Dokumenty* (Moscow: Mezhdunarodnyi fond, Kniga pervaia, 1998), 529–530. All subsequent references use a shortened format based on

the report number (№), short title (1941 god), volume number, and page numbers.

94. Ibid., 530.

95. German officers interrogated after the war confirmed the importance of controlling agricultural production and thus maintaining the Soviet system of collective farms: "Local procurement improved in direct ratio to the ability of the German civil government detachments to regulate cultivation and harvests. Local potato supplies were sufficient until the autumn of 1941, and thereafter they ran short. Vegetable cultivation was generally limited to small garden plots which barely covered the needs of the civilian population. Fruit was available only in the south, and then in limited quantities. Forage is plentiful in summer; sufficient pasture land is available in almost all parts of the country." *Effects of Climate*, 58.

96. Document 126-EC, 146, emphasis in original.

97. Food control was an important and successful part of British counterinsurgency policy during the Malayan emergency (1948–1960). The aim was to restrict the amount of food reaching the insurgents.

98. Document 1526-PS, in IMT, Blue Series, XXVII:298–324.

99. Ibid., 299.

100. Ibid.

101. Document 1017-PS, in IMT, Blue Series, XXVI:548, 547–554.

102. Ibid., 553.

103. "Die neue Agrarordnung, Erlaß des Reichsministers für die besetzten Gebiete Vom 16. Februar 1942 (MitBIRKO, s.27)," in *Das Recht der besetzten Gebiete. Estland, Lettland, Litauen, Weissruthenien und Ukraine. Sammlung der Verordnungen, Erlasse und sonstigen Vorschriften über Verwaltung, Rechtspflege, Wirtschaft, Finanzwesen und Verkehr mit Erläuterungen der Referenten*, herausgegeben von Alfred Meyer u.a. (Munich: Verlag Beck, 1943), 57, 56–64.

104. Ibid., 59.

105. Document 126-EC, 155.

106. Document 089-USSR, in IMT, Blue Series, XXXIX:368.

107. Judicial Notice, in IMT, Blue Series, XXXIX:588–594.

108. "Erlaß des Reichsministers für die besetzten Gebiete," 56.

109. Ibid.

110. Ibid., 57.

111. These cuts are also consistent with observations made by Werner Maser, who argues that evidence was withheld from the defense at Nürnberg: "There are numerous indications that already in 1945 documents were seized, removed from the defense, or even stolen." Werner Maser, *Nürnberg: Tribunal der Sieger* (Düsseldorf: Econ Verlag, 1977), 173. He later notes that "German and foreign archives were at the disposal of the prosecution but not of the defense" (ibid., 404). See ibid., 547, for similar concerns about access to documents.

112. Document 050-C, *Erlaß über die Ausübung der Kriegsgerichtsbarkeit im Gebiet „Barbarossa" und über besondere Maßnahmen der Truppe*, 13 May 1941, in IMT, Blue Series, XXXIV:249–256. This includes the follow-up order from Keitel, dated 27 May 1941, that all copies were to be destroyed (ibid., 257).

113. Much the same function was served by the "Richtlinien für das Verhalten der Truppe in Rußland" (Guidelines for the Conduct of the Troops in Russia), which was issued on 19 May 1941. It identifies Bolshevism as a deadly

enemy of National Socialist Germany and its people, and it highlights the artificial nature of the Soviet state and the fact that it is held together by the naked violence of the Bolsheviks. German soldiers are warned that Asiatic soldiers in the Red Army are "inscrutable, unpredictable, underhanded and unfeeling" and that close contact with the population is a threat to their health. See Ueberschär und Wette, *Unternehmen Barbarossa*, 312.

114. Document 050-C, 253.

115. Ibid., 254.

116. Ibid., 255.

117. Ibid., 257.

118. Document 221-L, in IMT, Blue Series, XXXVIII:86–94.

119. Ibid., 87.

120. Ibid., 88.

121. Ibid., 92.

122. IMT, Blue Series, IV:9.

123. Document 052-C, in IMT, Blue Series, XXXIV:259.

124. Document 148-C, in IMT, Blue Series, XXXIV:502.

125. Ibid., 503.

126. Document 411-D, in IMT, Blue Series, XXXV:85.

127. Ibid.

128. Ibid., 85–86.

129. Document 4064-PS, in IMT, Blue Series, XXXIV:130.

130. Richard J. Evans, *The Third Reich at War 1939–1945: How the Nazis Led Germany from Conquest to Disaster* (London: Allen Lane, 2008), 49.

131. Demographic data are derived from sources cited by Hartmann, *Wehrmacht im Ostkrieg*, 651.

132. For Rosenberg on the Jews, see Document 2665-PS, in IMT, Blue Series, XXXI:67. In the original German, the final sentence reads: "Für Europa ist die

Judenfrage erst dann gelöst, wenn der letzte Jude den europäischen Kontinent verlassen hat."

133. Il'ia Erenburg and Vasilii Grossman, eds., *Chernaia kniga*, vol. 1 (Zaporozh'e: Interbuk, 1991), 28.

134. Document 2273-PS, in IMT, Blue Series, XXX:79.

135. Hartmann, *Wehrmacht im Ostkrieg*, 657–658.

136. Ibid., 658.

137. See, for example, "Hunting Jews in Szczuczyn," chapter 8 of Waitman Wade Beorn, *Marching into Darkness: The Wehrmacht and the Holocaust in Belarus* (Cambridge, Mass.: Harvard University Press, 2014), 184–205.

138. Hartmann, *Wehrmacht im Ostkrieg*, 568. Between 22 June 1941 and February 1945, some 5,734,528 Soviet soldiers were captured by the Germans. On 1 January 1945 there were 930,287 in captivity. It is believed that about a million Soviet prisoners worked as either *Hilfswillige* (auxiliaries) or *Freiwillige* (volunteers) for the German armies in the east. According to Fremde Heere Ost, about half a million prisoners escaped or were liberated by the Red Army. The remaining 3.3 million, or about 57 percent, perished in the camps or were shot. About 2 million of them had died before the start of 1942. Christian Streit, "Die Behandlung der sowjetischen Kriegsgefangenen und völkerrechtliche Probleme des Krieges gegen die Sowjetunion," in Ueberschär und Wette, *Unternehmen Barbarossa*, 198.

139. Hartmann, *Wehrmacht im Ostkrieg*, 568.

140. See Simon Sebag Montefiore, *Stalin: The Court of the Red Tsar* [2003] (London: Phoenix, 2004), 369–390.

141. № 330,"Iz zapisei, sdelannykh

dezhurnymi sekretariami, o posetite-
liakh I. V. Stalina za period s 21 po 28
iiunia 1941 g.," OGB, 1941/1, 98–105.

142. Ibid., 105, notes.

143. The decree declaring the reintroduction of commissars in the Red Army
made specific reference to the civil war:
"All these circumstances in the work of
political workers, which are connected
with the transition from peacetime
to wartime, demand that the role and
responsibility of political workers be
raised, similar to that which took place
during the civil war against foreign military intervention." See "O reorganizatsii
organov politicheskoi propagandy i vve-
denii instituta voennykh komissarov v
Raboche-Krest'ianskoi Krasnoi Armii,"
in KPSS o vooruzhennykh silakh Sovetskogo
Soiuza: Dokumenty 1917–1968 (Moscow:
Voennoe izdatel'stvo Ministerstva oborony SSSR, 1969), 305.

144. In his autobiography, Zhukov
comments on the role of junior leaders
in modern armies: "My many years of
experience reveals to me that where no
trust reposes in junior commanders,
that where there exists a constant surveillance of them on the part of senior
officers there can never be a proper,
junior-leader stratum, and consequently
there will not be any good subunits."
G. K. Zhukov, Vospominaniia i razmyshleniia (Moscow: Izdatel'stvo agentstva
pechati novosti, 1969), 39. Although
these comments are made in the context
of Zhukov's experience as a senior
noncommissioned officer in the tsarist
army, they have a much greater relevance
for the intrusive and damaging ideological supervisory role exercised by commissars and politruks in the Red Army.

145. Grossman, Gody voiny (1989),
278.

146. Manstein, Verlorene Siege, 183.

147. "Predislovie," OGB, 1941/1, ix.

148. Guderian, Erinnerungen eines
Soldaten, 213.

149. To quote an American study:
"The most unusual characteristic of the
country is the climate, which affects
terrain and vegetation and determines
living conditions in general. The climate
leaves its mark upon the Russian and
his land, and he who steps for the first
time on Russian soil is immediately
conscious of the new, the strange, the
primitive." Effects of Climate, 1.

150. Ibid., 56.

Chapter 2. The Commissar Order

1. Heinrich Uhlig, "Der
verbrecherische Befehl. Eine Diskussion
und ihre historisch-dokumentarischen
Grundlagen," in Vollmacht des Gewissens,
band II (Frankfurt am Main: Alfred
Metzner Verlag, 1965), 295.

2. Hoth agreed with Hitler: "He [Hit-
ler] issued an order; it was quite impossible for me to assume that he intended
a crime in issuing this order. Even today
I think that that was not really Hitler's
intention; I know his intention really
was to protect the troops against the
commissars. I do not think that Hitler
had any criminal intent." IMT, Green
Series, X:1110–1111. Moreover, according
to Walter Warlimont, information from
Hitler's intelligence services supported
the contention that German prisoners
would be harshly treated, and Hitler
argued that the atrocities committed by
the commissars in the Baltic states and
Finland justified harsh measures.

3. IMT, Green Series, X:27.

4. Ibid., 1083.

5. Ibid., 1090–1091.

6. Ibid., 1103.

7. One participant in the group assembled by Heinrich Uhlig to ponder the Commissar Order, Oberstaatsanwalt (public prosecutor) Wilhelm Hölper, argued that, given the traditions of the German officer corps, it was "inconceivable" that such an order could be issued. Uhlig, Vollmacht des Gewissens, 328. The German officer corps' collusion with Hitler over the Röhm problem provides one clue to how the inconceivable occurred.

8. IMT, Blue Series, XX:609.

9. IMT, Green Series, X:1078.

10. Erich von Manstein, Verlorene Siege [1955] (Bonn: Bernard & Graefe in der Mönch Verlagsgesellschaft mbH, 2011), 176.

11. Ibid.

12. Convention Relative to the Treatment of Prisoners, with Annex, Geneva, 27 July 1929, League of Nations Treaty Series, vol. 118, № 2734, 343–409.

13. Heinrich Uhlig is one of the few German historians to remind us about the functions of the military commissars in the Red Army in such uncompromising terms. Since the late 1970s, too many German historians have shown a marked reluctance to discuss the ideological-punitive role of the military commissars, resulting in a certain imbalance in the analysis of the Commissar Order.

14. In the files examined by Römer, there was only one example of a German general who refused to abide by the Commissar Order: General Otto Stapf, commander of the 111th Infantry Division. See Felix Römer, Der Kommissarbefehl: Wehrmacht und NS-Verbrechen an der Ostfront 1941/42 (Paderborn: Ferdinand Schöningh, 2008), 467.

15. Ibid., 12.

16. V. I. Lenin, "Kriticheskie zametki po natsional'nomu voprosu [1913]," in Sochineniia, vol. 20 (Moscow: OGIZ, 1948), 10, 18, emphasis in original.

17. Römer, Der Kommissarbefehl, 512.

18. № 282, "Vystuplenie Po radio zamestitelia Predsedatelia Soveta Narodnykh Komissarov SSSR, narkoma inostrannykh del SSSR V. M. Molotova v sviazi s napadeniem fashistskoi Germanii na Sovetskii Soiuz 22 iiunia 1941 g.," OGB, 1941/1, 15.

19. For example, in a speech delivered in Edinburgh on 25 September 1924, Churchill attacked the Soviet treaty favored by the British Labour Party and described Russia as "one of the worst tyrannies that has ever existed in the world. It accords no political rights. It rules by terror. It punishes political opinions. It suppresses free speech. It tolerates no newspapers but its own. It persecutes Christianity with a zeal and a cunning never equalled since the times of the Roman Emperors." In the same speech, Churchill objected to giving the Soviet Union money, which made it possible for the "Soviet sect" to retain power and spread its "filthy propaganda." See Martin Gilbert, Prophet of Truth: Winston S. Churchill [1976], vol. 5 (London: Minerva, 1990), 48. Churchill returned to the question of Soviet tyranny in his election manifesto of October 1924. In Russia, he noted, "A tyranny of the vilest kind has been erected," and huge numbers of people "of both sexes and of every class have been executed or murdered in cold blood." Ibid., 54.

20. V. I. Lenin, "Pis'mo D. I. Kurskomu" [1922], in Sochineniia, vol. 33 (Moscow: Gosudarstvennoe izdatel'stvo

politicheskoi literatury, 1951), 321, emphasis in original.

21. Ibid.

22. Richard Pipes, *Russia under the Bolshevik Regime, 1919–1924* (London: Fontana Press, 1992), 401.

23. This unwillingness to consider that the crimes of the Soviet regime were on a par with those of Nazi Germany (or even worse) and that NS crimes cannot be divorced from the crimes of Lenin and Stalin is by no means confined to German scholarship. Obvious English-language examples are Ian Kershaw, *The Nazi Dictatorship: Problems and Perspectives of Interpretation*, 2nd ed. (London: Hodder & Stoughton, 1989), and Ian Kershaw and Moshe Lewin, eds., *Stalinism and Nazism: Dictatorships in Comparison* (Cambridge: Cambridge University Press, 1997). The essential counter to Kershaw is Stéphane Courtois et al., *The Black Book of Communism: Crimes, Terror, Repression*, trans. Jonathan Murphy and Mark Kramer (London: Harvard University Press, 1999), whose contributors document the crimes of the Soviet state and other communist regimes, crimes that include genocide.

24. Uhlig raises a similar question when he asks: "Was this order [Commissar Order] part of a total military-political conception or was it one of those catastrophic errors to which brutal politicians and army leaders of all nations occasionally succumb?" Uhlig, *Vollmacht des Gewissens*, 294. In both NS Germany and the Soviet Union, orders such as the Commissar Order and the Katyn order, respectively, were clearly not accidental and certainly not occasional. They reflected the very essence of the two totalitarian states.

25. Römer, *Der Kommissarbefehl*, 161.

26. Römer is correct when he asserts that the Wehrmacht was "one of the support structures of the NS regime" (*Der Kommissarbefehl*, 568). However, it must be borne in mind that the Red Army fulfilled exactly the same role for the Soviet regime. It was created by the one-party Soviet state and (unlike the Wehrmacht, which grew out of the Reichswehr) had no tradition of professional independence, which had not been entirely eradicated in the Wehrmacht.

27. V. I. Lenin, "Proletarskaia revoliutsiia i renegat Kautskii [1918]," in *Sochineniia*, vol. 28 (Moscow: OGIZ, 1950), 216, emphasis added. Cited with approval by Lenin, the wording is derived from Marx and criticized by Kautskii as evidence that the "dictatorship of the proletariat" would lead to a concentration of power in one individual or a small group of individuals, which would indeed be a dictatorship as normally understood. Lenin's attempts to defend Marx and to neutralize Kautskii failed, since the very dangers Kautskii warned of in his essay "The Dictatorship of the Proletariat" (1918) were evident in November 1918—two months after the start of the Red Terror—when Lenin was attacking Kautskii. In any case, total control of political and economic life amounts to a dictatorship and is the first step toward the creation of a totalitarian state. Also relevant here are observations made by Lenin in an article first published ten years earlier, in which he identified the two errors responsible for the collapse of the Paris Commune: first, the proletariat had failed "to expropriate the expropriators," and second, they had suffered from a surfeit of magnanimity toward their enemies. Lenin believed

that the proletariat "should have exterminated its enemies." See V. I. Lenin,
"Uroki kommuny" [1908], in *Sochineniia*,
vol. 13 (Moscow: Gosudarstvennoe
izdatel'stvo politicheskoi literatury,
1947), 438.

28. Römer, *Der Kommissarbefehl*, 162.

29. Ibid., 480.

30. Ibid.

31. Ibid.

32. Ibid., 482.

33. Whereas some historians have
concentrated too much on the role
of NS ideology in Wehrmacht behavior on the Eastern Front—showing a
distinct unwillingness, even a refusal,
to consider that the Soviet state was a
menace of the first magnitude and that
the dangers perceived by the German
planners were not imagined—Weinberg
heads in the opposite direction: "The
decision itself [to attack the Soviet
Union] is a purely military one and so is
the early planning. In spite of previous
speeches by Hitler and later propaganda
by Göbbels [sic] the decision to attack
the Soviet Union is here demonstrated
to have had *nothing to do with the system
installed in that country.*" He continues:
"The military plans were designed to
smash the Soviet Army; beyond this, the
German policy was simply to be one of
exploiting, expropriating, and exterminating as much as possible—brown
commissars were to replace the red
ones." Gerhard L. Weinberg, *Germany
and the Soviet Union, 1939–1941* (Leiden:
E. J. Brill, 1954), 171, emphasis added. It
is indisputable that brown commissars
were intended to replace the red ones,
but German policies of exploitation,
expropriation, and extermination
cannot be divorced from NS ideology
any more than similar Soviet policies

of exploitation, expropriation, and
extermination can be divorced from
Marxism-Leninism-Stalinism.

34. *KPSS o vooruzhennykh silakh
Sovetskogo Soiuza: Dokumenty 1917–1968*
(Moscow: Voennoe izdatel'stvo Ministerstva oborony SSSR, 1969), 308. The
reintroduction of the institution of
military commissars on 16 July 1941—
that is, some three weeks after the
German invasion—reveals that German
intelligence was either unaware that
the commissars had been withdrawn
after the Soviet-Finnish war; that the
commissars still wore their distinctive
badges of rank after their 1940 withdrawal; or that, in the first days after
the invasion, those who were shot as
commissars were not formally identified
as such but were shot because anyone
that "acts and looks like a commissar,
therefore must be a commissar." The
fact that military commissars were not
allocated—formally, at any rate—to
military units at various times certainly
does not mean that the RKKA was left
to its own devices. The main instruments of ideological supervision were
the special sections of the NKVD. See,
for example, № 138, "Prikaz narodnogo
komissara vnutrennikh del Soiuza SSR
№ 0032 "o rabote osobykh otdelov
NKVD Soiuza SSR, 14 ianvaria 1939 g.,"
in *Lubianka: organy VChk-OGPU-NKVD-
NKGB-MGB-KGB 1917–1991 spravochnik*,
ed. A. N. IAkovlev et al., in the series
"Demokratiia," *Rossiia. XX VEK, Dokumenty*
(Moscow: Mezhdunarodnyi fond, 2003),
601–602.

35. Christian Streit, "Die Behandlung
der sowjetischen Kriegsgefangenen
und völkerrechtliche Probleme des
Krieges gegen die Sowjetunion," in
Gerd R. Ueberschär und Wolfram

Wette, hrsg. „Unternehmen Barbarossa": Der deutsche Überfall auf die Sowjetunion 1941, Berichte, Analysen, Dokumente (Paderborn: Ferdinand Schöningh, 1984), 201n17.

36. Römer, Der Kommissarbefehl, 512.

37. Wette's comments on the Feinbild Bolschewismus (enemy image of Bolshevism) concocted by the Nazis are equally applicable to any image of fascism concocted by Soviet propagandists: "Characteristic for the new [NS propaganda] line was the use of the term Bolshevism increasingly to dispense with any differentiations and which was applied to all political trends and persons which, from an NS point of view, were deemed to be on the 'left.'" Wolfram Wette, "Die propagandistische Begleitmusik zum deutschen Überfall auf die Sowjetunion am 22. Juni 1941," in Ueberschär and Wette, Unternehmen Barbarossa, 121. Such targeting of political enemies had been used in the early 1930s by the Soviet regime—well before the Nazis adopted similar methods—which referred to any and all opponents of the Moscow line as "fascists." Any distinctions among fascism, corporatism, capitalism, imperialism, National Socialism, and free-market economics were deliberately abandoned. The German Communist Party even labeled moderate, left-of-center parties such as the Social Democrats as "social fascists." At any given time, and depending on the current line being imposed by Moscow center, any trend, person, or organization could be vilified as "fascist" or rehabilitated as "progressive" when ideologically expedient.

38. Römer, Der Kommissarbefehl, 339.

39. Courtois et al., Black Book of Communism, 75–76.

40. Römer, Der Kommissarbefehl, 280.

41. Ibid. Whereas Römer casts doubt on the reliability of the Wehrmacht's perception of commissars, Hartmann examines the German soldiers' perception: "Militarily and also politically, . . . the Soviet commissars were taken overwhelmingly by German soldiers to be exponents of the Stalinist apparatus of repression. Of course, in this case the brutally distorted images of National Socialism were not without effect. However, the mere constancy of this picture speaks for the fact that it would be decidedly too simple to dismiss the German experiences, as they are found in very large numbers in official and private reports exclusively as products of propaganda. 'Perception' is always a dialectical process which is not totally served by images of the inner world but far more from that which falls under the concept of 'external circumstances.'" Christian Hartmann, Wehrmacht im Ostkrieg: Front und militärisches Hinterland (Munich: R. Oldenbourg Verlag, 2010), 502, emphasis in original.

42. Römer, Der Kommissarbefehl, 39, emphasis added.

43. Ibid., 291.

44. Ibid., 291–292.

45. In this regard, note Hartmann's conclusion that Soviet documents support the German assessment of commissars based on the interrogation of Soviet prisoners: "While it is probably the case with the interrogations that they also served German prejudices, the captured [Soviet] documents arose completely independently of German expectations such that precisely this group of documents forms a very significant supplement to the German perspective." Hartmann, Wehrmacht im Ostkrieg, 503, emphasis in original.

46. Römer, *Der Kommissarbefehl*, 485.

47. As a war correspondent, Grossman had plenty of contact with commissars and recorded many of his encounters—not all of them positive—in his wartime diaries. By far the harshest portrayal of commissars is found in his postwar epic *Zhizn' i sud'ba* (Life and Fate [1988]). The older commissars Krymov and Mostovskoi, who took part in the civil war, are ideological fanatics who are unable to grasp the nature of the totalitarian state they have helped create and are finally devoured by it. The new generation of party commissars and apparatchiks—Getmanov, Neudobnov, and Osipov—are corrupt party careerists bereft of the revolutionary fervor characterizing Krymov and Mostovskoi. Harsh depictions of commissars and other party functionaries are also the norm in Viktor Astaf'ev's *Prokliaty i ubity* (The Damned and the Dead [1992–1994]), and they are far from being ideologically correct in Vasil' Bykov's *Mertvym ne bol'no* (The Dead Feel No Pain [1966]) and *Stuzha* (The Great Freeze [1993]). Declassified NKVD reports also create a totally different picture from the propaganda construct of the wise and respected military commissar. See the following in IA. F. Pogonii, i dr., *Stalingradskaia epopeia: Materialy NKVD SSSR i voennoi tsenzury iz Tsentral'nogo arkhiva FSB RF* (Moscow: Zvonnitsa-MG, 2000): № 49, "Dokladnaiazapiska OO NKVD STF v UOO NKVD SSSR o reagirovaniiakh voenno sluzhashchikh chastei Stalingradskogo fronta po voprosu uprazdneniia instituta komissarov v Krasnoi Armii, 14 oktibria 1942 g.," 227–229; № 51, "Dokladnaiazapiska OO NKVD STF v UOO NKVD SSSR o reagirovaniiakh voenno-sluzhashchikh chastei Stalingradskogo fronta po voprosu uprazdneniia instituta komissarov v Krasnoi Armii, 16 oktibria 1942 g.," 233–235; and № 53, "Dokladnaiazapiska OO NKVD DF v UOO NKVD SSSR o reagirovaniiakh lichno gosostava Donskogofrontana Ukaz Prezidiuma Verkhovnogo Soveta ob uprazdneni instituta komissarov i na prikaz NKO № 307, 17 oktiabria 1942 g.," 237–239.

48. Römer, *Der Kommissarbefehl*, 316.

49. Richard Pipes, *The Russian Revolution: 1899–1919* [1990] (London: Fontana Press, 1992), 823.

50. Mikhail Sholokhov, *Tikhii Don*, vol. 3, in *Sobranie sochinenii v vos'mi tomakh* (Moscow: Gosudarstvennoe izdatel'stvo khudozhestvennoi literatury, 1957), 226.

51. Ibid., 317.

52. Ibid., 318, 319.

53. In "Chetyre dnia" (Four Days), one of his short stories written in 1935, Grossman identifies the ideological fanaticism of the commissar-party caste, a theme that features prominently in his later work, especially *Life and Fate* and *Forever Flowing*. The setting of "Four Days" is the Polish-Soviet war of the 1920s. Some Soviet commissars are forced to hide in a town abandoned by the Reds and now occupied by the Polish army. While hiding from the Poles, the commissars stay with a local doctor, and their class hatred and envious rage erupt all too easily. One of the commissars, Faktarovich, who served in the Cheka, leaves little doubt about how he would resolve the class problem in the Soviet state: "Doctors, lawyers, accountants, engineers and all the professors are traitors. They are enemies of the revolution. I'd [shoot] them all!" Vasilii

Grossman, "Chetyre dnia," in *Staryi uchitel'. Povestii Rasskazy* (Moscow: Sovetskii-pisatel', 1962), 51. I am not suggesting that Grossman's work influenced German planners. However, there is no doubt that in the 1920s and 1930s, Soviet military commissars were portrayed and venerated as bearers of ideological orthodoxy and fanaticism. The German planners correctly identified the status enjoyed by these functionaries and the threat they posed.

54. G. Bezverkhnii, ed., SMERSH: *Istoricheskie ocherki i arkhivnye dokumenty* (Moscow: Izdatel'stvo Glavarkhiva Moskvy, 2003), 28. "All told, in the years 1941–1942, 157,593 people were condemned by the military tribunals of fronts and armies to execution by shooting for 'panicking, cowardice and arbitrary abandonment of the battle-field.'" O. S. Smyslov, *"Piatia kolonna" Gitlera: Ot Kutenova do Vlasova* (Moscow: Veche, 2004), 52. Smyslov provides no source, so the number cannot be verified. The number of executions cited by SMERSH for the period 22 June to 1 December 1941 (14,473) amounts to a monthly average, discounting the last week of June, of 2,894. Using this monthly average for the eighteen-month period from 1 July 1941 to 31 December 1942 results in a total of 52,092 executions; this is still high, but well below the total number cited by Smyslov. If the number of executions cited by Smyslov is accurate for 1941–1942—and assuming that the overwhelming majority of sentences were carried out—it is highly plausible that the number of executions carried out by the Soviet side during the Stalingrad battle, another moment of extreme crisis for the Soviet regime, was well into five figures.

55. IMT, Green Series, X:1093.

56. In this regard, note the views attributed to Oberstleutnant Henning von Tresckow: "If international law is going to be broken it ought to be first broken by the Russians and not by us." Cited in Uhlig, *Vollmacht des Gewissens*, 289.

57. Hartmann, *Wehrmacht im Ostkrieg*, 757. Not insignificant, as Hartmann notes, is that the lawless conduct of partisan war as a reprisal to the German invasion occurred *before* the full force of German behavior was clear (ibid., 710–711).

58. Despite Soviet propaganda regarding the role of partisans in the first Great Fatherland War, and thus the implication that Soviet partisans were kindred spirits, Soviet partisans—like Soviet military commissars—were subject to strict and total ideological control and were therefore not the same type of fighter encountered by Napoleon's forces in Spain and Russia. Ideological control meant that, from a Marxist-Leninist-Stalinist perspective, the Soviet partisan and, I suggest, the Soviet military commissar could not be bound by the Hague and Geneva Conventions. The ideological partisan's rejection of the customs and rules of war has real consequences, which are fully grasped by Carl Schmitt: "War in any case remains something that in principle is fundamentally circumscribed and the partisan stands outside of these limits. It becomes part of his being and existence that he even stands outside of any circumscription. The modern partisan expects neither justice nor mercy from the enemy. He has turned away from the notions of enmity based on the conventions of controlled and circumscribed war and moved into the zone of

another, a real enmity, which through terror and counterterror escalates to extermination." Carl Schmitt, *Theorie des Partisanen: Zwischenbemerkung zum Begriff des Politischen* (Berlin: Duncker & Humblot, circa 1963), 17, emphasis in original. This flouting of international law and killing of prisoners were the norm in the partisan war in Yugoslavia. Milovan Djilas, one of Tito's inner circle, told Stalin, "We did not take German prisoners because they killed all of our prisoners." See Milovan Djilas, *Conversations with Stalin* (New York: Harcourt Brace & World, 1962), 79.

59. Hartmann, *Wehrmacht im Ostkrieg*, 757.

60. Römer, *Der Kommissarbefehl*, 359.

61. Ibid.

62. Ibid.

63. Heinz Guderian, *Erinnerungen eines Soldaten* [1950], 9 Auflage (Neckergemünd: Kurt Vowinkel Verlag, 1976), 138. Römer provides a lot of evidence that flatly contradicts Guderian's claim that the Commissar Order was not carried out in his command. For example, he points out: "The middle sector of the Eastern Front was the main stage on which by far the greatest number of commissar shootings occurred. Of the total of 2,257 provable executions that can be attributed to combat formations, almost half—that is 1,083 shootings— can be attributed to the front-line troops of Army Group Center." Römer, *Der Kommissarbefehl*, 390. A total of 253 commissar killings can be verifiably attributed to Guderian's Panzergruppe 2. Ibid., 391.

64. Römer, *Der Kommissarbefehl*, 360.

65. Ibid., 361.

66. Ibid., 363.

67. Ibid., 367.

68. Hartmann, *Wehrmacht im Ostkrieg*, 487.

69. Waitman Wade Beorn, *Marching into Darkness: The Wehrmacht and the Holocaust in Belarus* (Cambridge, Mass.: Harvard University Press, 2014), 58.

70. Hartmann, *Wehrmacht im Ostkrieg*, 487.

71. IMT, Green Series, XI:515.

72. It is quite clear from the top-secret memorandum written by Sir Owen O'Malley, the British ambassador to the Polish government-in-exile, that the evidence against the Soviet regime was overwhelming. In responding to O'Malley's memorandum, Sir Alexander Cadogan, the permanent undersecretary of state, drew certain conclusions that are relevant to the Soviet role in the Nürnberg proceedings. As Cadogan acknowledged, Soviet responsibility for Katyn raised problems that were not new: "How many thousands of its own citizens has the Soviet regime butchered? And I don't know that the blood of a Pole cries louder to heaven that [sic] that of a Russian. But we have perforce welcomed the Russians as allies and have set ourselves to work with them in war and peace. . . . And one other disturbing thought is that we eventually, by agreement and in collaboration with the Russians, proceed to the trial and perhaps execution of Axis 'war criminals' while condoning this atrocity." See Allen Paul, *Katyń: Stalin's Massacre and the Triumph of Truth* [1991] (De Kalb: Northern Illinois University Press, 2010), 305–306. That the Soviet Union was one of the prosecuting states at Nürnberg, despite having committed the same kinds of crimes committed by NS Germany—mass murder, terror, genocide, deportation, and use of slave

labor—was one of the glaring inconsistencies in the principles governing the conduct of the International Military Tribunal. These flaws have been examined in detail by Werner Maser, *Nürnberg: Tribunal der Sieger* (Düsseldorf: Econ Verlag, 1977), 517–608.

73. Wojciech Materski, ed., *KATYN: Documents of Genocide. Documents and Materials from the Soviet Archives Turned over to Poland on October 14, 1992* (Warsaw: Polish Academy of Sciences, 1993), 18.

74. Ibid., 22.

75. IMT, Green Series, X:1058.

76. Timothy Snyder, *Bloodlands: Europe between Hitler and Stalin* (London: Bodley Head, 2010), 89.

77. In a memorandum dated 9 August 1940, the Border Troops Directorate of the NKVD referred to one of the lesser-known consequences of the Non-Aggression Pact: the NKVD and the Gestapo had exchanged prisoners. Apparently, the Gestapo interrogated the prisoners received from its NKVD colleagues to ascertain information about the situation in the Soviet Union and the location of Red Army units and weapons. See № 85, "Zapiska 2 otdela glavnogo upravleniia pogranvoisk NKVD SSSR nachal'niku 5 otdela GUGB NKVD SSSR Fitinu, 9 avgusta 1940 g.," in *1941 god, v 2-knigakh*, ed. A. N. IAkovlev et al., in the series "*Demokratiia*," *Rossiia. XX VEK, Dokumenty* (Moscow: Mezhdunarodnyi fond, 1998), 1:165. In addition, these interrogations may have provided rumors of the fate of the Polish prisoners at Katyn.

78. Snyder, *Bloodlands*, 151.

79. Ibid., 149.

80. The possibility that these operations were coordinated has not gone unnoticed by Russian scholars: "In all likelihood the close timing of the execution operations of the two totalitarian regimes was not coincidental. Evidence for this is the fact that the leadership of the NKVD USSR very soon gave orders for the compilation of lists of prisoners in the three special camps, requiring the domicile of their families, including those living in the German-occupied districts." A. N. IAkovlev et al., eds., *Katyn': Plenniki neob"iavlennoi voiny*, in the series "*Demokratiia*," *Rossiia. XX VEK, Dokumenty* (Moscow: Mezhdunarodnyi fond, 1997), 42. This NKVD procedure strengthens the case that the Germans either had foreknowledge of the Katyn killings or had strong suspicions that they were about to occur.

81. № P22, "Sekretnyi doponitel'nyi protokol," *1941 god*, 2:587.

82. Paul, *Katyń*, 68. Serov's meetings with Gestapo officials would have been documented in great detail, and his reports would have been sent to Beria and seen by Molotov and Stalin. If these reports are not among the eventually declassified documents, one must assume they contain material that would be embarrassing to the Russian Federation. In 1944 Serov was in charge of the repressive measures taken against anti-Soviet elements in Lithuania and, above all, against members of the Polish Home Army. Measures against the Polish Home Army were stepped up with the arrival of the Red Army.

83. Cited in ibid.

84. № 103, "1939 g., noiabria 10, Moskva.— Rasporiazhenie UPV NKVD SSSR A. G. Berezhkovu o Zhenevskoi konventsii i neobkhodimosti rukovodstvovat'sia v prakticheskoi rabote direktivami upravleniia," in IAkovlev et al., *Katyn'*, 89. The "Doctors' Geneva

Convention" most likely refers to the Convention for the Amelioration of the Condition of the Wounded and Sick in Armies in the Field (27 July 1929).

85. № 15, "1939 g. sentiabria 19, Moskva, Proekt 'polozheniia o voenno-plennykh,'" in IAkovlev et al., *Katyn'*, 78.

86. See № 347, "Spetsial'noe polozhenie o voennoplennykh', 1 iiulia 1941 g.," *OGB*, 1941/1, 141.

87. № 87, "1939 g., oktiabria 30, Starobel'sk, obrashchenie voennoplennykh-vrachei i farmatsevtov k K. E. Voroshilovu o protivopravnosti soderzaniia ikh v plenu," in IAkovlev et al., *Katyn'*, 173.

88. № 160, "1940 g., ianvaria 7, Starobelsk, Zaiavlenie gruppy voenno-plennykh-polkovnikov s trebovaniiami opredelit' ikh status i sledovat' pri-niatym mezhdunarodnym normam v obrashchenii s voennoplennymi," ibid., 297.

89. "Vvedenie," ibid., 25.

90. *OGB*, 1941/1, № 347, 141.

91. Two of the discussants in Uh-lig's group argued that, in the Nazis' view, "international law must be fully subordinated to the interest of the state." Uhlig, *Vollmacht des Gewissens*, 334. Friedrich August von der Heydte then set out this position in more detail: "National-socialist doctrine proceeded from the assumption that the state was only constricted by international legal norms insofar as it voluntarily bound itself by these norms and considered itself bound by them. In the final analysis, this doctrine of voluntary self-commitment means the denial of general international law which binds the state even against its own will and against its own interests. The doctrine of voluntary self-commitment includes in itself the eventual violation of

international law. The Commissar Order is merely the logical consequence of the Third Reich's theory of international law." Ibid. Wilhelm Hölper followed up this point: "In other words, in inter-statal relations the NS state knows only one norm: what is useful to the state is right." Ibid. Of course, these two assessments precisely articulate the Lenin-Stalin-Beria view of international law and underline the fact that the Katyn Memorandum was, to paraphrase von der Heydte, merely the logical consequence of the Soviet regime's theory of international law.

92. № 129, "1939 g., ne ranee dekabria 4, Starobel'sk-svodka na-chal'nika uchetno-raspredelitel'nogo otdeleniia starobel'skogo lageria V.P. Voronova o kolichestve voennoplennykh po chinam po sostoianiiuna 4 dekabria 1939 g.," in IAkovlev et al., *Katyn'*, 249.

93. See, for example, Materski, *KATYN: Documents of Genocide*, 27–99.

94. Römer, *Der Kommissarbefehl*, 12.

95. Robert Conquest, *The Great Terror: A Reassessment* (London: Hutchinson, 1990), 449.

96. *IMT*, Green Series, XI:341.

97. Römer, *Der Kommissarbefehl*, 13.

98. *IMT*, Blue Series, XVII:286.

99. Ibid., 293.

100. Document 054-USSR, in *IMT*, Blue Series, XXXIX:290–332.

101. Details of the handover of the latest batch of eleven files were reported on the website of the Instytut Pamięci Narodowej (IPN), Poland's Institute of National Remembrance, on 7 July 2011 (http://ipn.gov.pl). As of August 2014, the IPN website had not confirmed that the government of the Russian Federation had turned over any of the remaining thirty-five volumes to the Polish

government. Another possibility, as reported by the Polish paper *Wiadomosci*, is that the NKVD filmed some of the Katyn shootings or made a photographic record. See, for example, "NKWD filmowało rozstrzelania w Katyniu," 4 April 2008, http://wiadomosci.gazeta.pl /1,114873,5087514.html. Bibliographical data concerning these recent sources were derived from the Wikipedia article "Katyn Massacre" (accessed 23 July 2014). I am grateful to the compilers of the Wikipedia article for these leads.

Chapter 3. Dance of the Snakes

1. See Viktor Kravchenko, *I Chose Freedom: The Personal and Political Life of a Soviet Official* [1946], with a new introduction by Rett R. Ludwikowski (New Brunswick, N.J.: Transaction Publishers, 1989), 332.

2. Ibid. Roger Moorhouse's claim that "the Nazi-Soviet Pact plunged both the communist and fascist movements into an existential crisis" is not convincing. Roger Moorhouse, *The Devils' Alliance: Hitler's Pact with Stalin, 1939–41* (London: Bodley Head, 2014), 115. Had the Nazi and Soviet regimes not been totalitarian states, and had they permitted some form of opposition to state policies, the possibility of an "existential crisis" might be admitted. But by the very nature of the power exercised by Hitler and Stalin, both leaders could operate in ideology-free zones when it suited them. Even if Soviet citizens were perplexed by the pact, their views were of no consequence, and if they spoke out, they would be silenced in short order. Of the two leaders, Hitler probably had more difficulty presenting the pact, but the destruction of Poland was a suitable response to his critics.

3. № P13, "Dogovor o nenapadenii mezhdu Germaniei i Sovetskim soiuzom, 23 avgusta 1939 g.," in *1941 god, v 2-knigakh*, ed. A. N. IAkovlev et al., in the series *"Demokratiia," Rossiia. XX VEK, Dokumenty* (Moscow: Mezhdunarodnyi fond, Kniga pervaia, 1998), 2:576–577.

4. № P14, "Sekretnyi doponitel'nyi protokol," *1941 god*, 2:577.

5. № P15, "Raz'iasnenie k sekretnomu dopolnitel'nomu protokolu ot 23 avgusta 1939 r.," *1941 god*, 2:578.

6. Gerhard Weinberg makes three important observations on the pact and the secret protocol: First, and unusually, the pact came into force as soon as it was signed. Second, the pact would not be rendered "inoperative if one of the parties attacked a third country." These departures from the norm are easily explained by Weinberg: the first was presumably a consequence "of Germany's need for speed; the second since it was understood that Germany was about to attack Poland and that it was just to cover this contingency that the Pact was drawn up in the first place." A third point raised by Weinberg is that the clause of the secret protocol dealing with the Balkans was left deliberately vague, "since an attempt to define German and Russian interests in the Balkans precisely would have made any sort of agreement extremely difficult, perhaps impossible." Gerhard L. Weinberg, *Germany and the Soviet Union, 1939–1941* (Leiden: E. J. Brill, 1954), 48, 49.

7. For the full German-language text of the Gaus affidavit, see Document Hess-16, in IMT, Blue Series, XL:293–298.

8. Ibid., X:311.

9. Ibid., 312.

10. Ibid., 313–314, emphasis added.

11. Ibid., XIV:284.

12. Ibid., 286.

13. № P19, "Germano-sovetskii dogovor o druzhbe i granitse mezhdu USSR i Germaniei, 28 sentiabria 1939 g.," 1941 god, 2:585.

14. № P20, "Doveritel'nyi protokol, 28 sentiabria 1939 g.," 1941 god, 2:586.

15. № P21, "Sekretnyi doponitel'nyi protokol, 28 sentiabria 1939 g.," 1941 god, 2:586.

16. № P22, "Sekretnyi doponitel'nyi protokol, 28 sentiabria 1939 g.," 1941 god, 2:587. For the avoidance of doubt, this protocol differs from № P21.

17. 1941 god, 1:70.

18. № 11, "Zapis' besedy narkoma inostrannykh del SSSR V. M. Molotova s ministrom inostrannykh del Litvy IU.Urbshisom, 14 iiunia 1940 g.," 1941 god, 1:30.

19. Ibid., 32.

20. № 14, "Zapis' besedy narkoma inostrannykh del SSSR V. M. Molotova s poslannikom Latvii v SSSR F. Kotsin'shem, 16 iiunia 1940 g.," 1941 god, 1:33–35.

21. Ibid., 35.

22. № 15, "Zapis' besedy narkoma inostrannykh del SSSR V.M. Molotova s poslannikom Estonii v SSSR A. Reem, 16 iiunia 1940 g.," 1941 god, 1:35–37.

23. 1941 god, 1:70.

24. № 17, "TASS Soobshchenie, 16 iiunia 1940 g.," 1941 god, 1:39.

25. Ibid.

26. № 19, "Beseda narkoma inostrannykh del SSSR V. M. Molotova s poslom Germanii v SSSR F. Shulenburgom, 17 iiunia 1940 g.," 1941 god, 1:41.

27. № 25, "Soobshchenie TASS, 23 iiunia 1940 g.," 1941 god, 1:47.

28. № 11, 1941 god, 1:30.

29. № 14, 1941 god, 1:35.

30. № 15, 1941 god, 1:37.

31. № 26, "Beseda narkoma inostrannykh del SSSR V. M. Molotova s poslom Germanii v SSSR F. Shulenburgom, 23 iiunia 1940 g.," 1941 god, 1:48.

32. Ibid., 49.

33. № 28, "Beseda narkoma inostrannykh del V. M. Molotova s poslom Germanii v SSSR F. Shulenburgom, 25 iiunia 1940 g.," 1941 god, 1:53.

34. Ibid.

35. № 32, "Telegramma inostrannykh del SSSR V. M. Molotova polnomochnomu predstaviteliu SSSR v korolevstve Rumyniia A. I. Lavrent'evu, 27 iiunia 1940 g.," 1941 god, 1:61–62.

36. Ibid.

37. Ibid.

38. № 34, "Beseda narkoma inostrannykh del SSSR V. M. Molotova s poslannikom korolevstve Rumyniia v SSSR g. Davidesku, 27 iiunia 1940 g.," 1941 god, 1:63.

39. № P21, 1941 god, 2:586.

40. № 50, "Beseda narkoma inostrannykh del SSSR V. M Molotova s poslom Germanii v SSSR F. Shulenburgom, 13 iiulia 1940 g.," 1941 god, 1:112.

41. № 98, "Beseda narkoma inostrannykh del SSSR V. M. Molotova s poslom Germanii v SSSR F. Shulenburgom, 23 avgusta 1940 g.," 1941 god, 1:198.

42. № 87, "Nota NKID SSSR v posol'stvo Germanii v Moskve, 11 avgusta 1940 g.," 1941 god, 1:166–167.

43. № 62, "Telegramma zamestitelia narkoma inostrannykh del SSSR S. A. Lozovskogo polpredu SSSR v Velikobritanii I. M. Maiskomu, 23 iiulia 1940 g.," 1941 god, 1:125–126.

44. № 88, "Iz zapisi besedy narkoma inostrannykh del SSSR V.M. Molotova s poslom Germanii v SSSR F. Shulenburgom, 12 avgusta 1940 g.," 1941 god, 1:168.

45. Ibid.

46. Ibid.

47. № 234, "Beseda narkoma inostrannykh del SSSR V.M. Molotova s poslom Germanii v SSSR F. Shulenburgom i predstavitelem ekonomicheskoi delegatsii K. Shnurre, 9 inavaria 1941 g.," 1941 god, 1:526.

48. № 235, "Soglashenie o vzaimnykh tovarnykh postavkakh na vtoroi dogovornoi period po khoiaistvennomu soglasheniiu ot 11 fevralia 1940 g. mezhdu soiuzom sovetskikh sotsialisticheskikh respublik i Germaniei, 10 ianvaria 1941 g.," 1941 god, 1:527.

49. № 230, "Beseda narkoma inostrannykh del V. M. Molotova s poslom Germanii v SSSR F Shulenburgom, 6 ianvaria 1941 g.," 1941 god, 1:512.

50. № 111, "Beseda narkoma inostrannykh del V. M. Molotova s poslom Germanii v SSSR F Shulenburgom, 9 sentiabria 1940 g.," 1941 god, 1:219–220.

51. № 121, "Beseda narkoma inostrannykh del V. M. Molotova s poslom Germanii v SSSR F Shulenburgom, 27 sentiabria 1940 g.," 1941 god, 1:265–268.

52. Ibid., 266.

53. № 146, "Beseda narkoma inostrannykh del V. M. Molotova s poslom Germanii v SSSR F Shulenburgom, 17 oktiabria 1940 g.," 1941 god, 1:303.

54. Ibid., 304.

55. № 149, "Beseda narkoma inostrannykh del V. M. Molotova s poslom Germanii v SSSR F Shulenburgom, 19 oktiabria 1940 g.," 1941 god, 1:312.

56. № 147, "Pis'mo ministra inostrannykh del GermaniiI. von Ribbentropa k I. V. Stalinu, 13 oktiabria 1940 g.," 1941 god, 1:306.

57. Ibid., 309.

58. № 171, "Beseda predsedatelia sovnarkoma, narkoma inostrannykh del SSSR V. M. Molotova s minisitrom inostrannykh del Germanii I. Ribbentropom v Berline, 12 noiabria 1940 g.," 1941 god, 1:357.

59. Ibid.

60. Ibid., 357–358.

61. Ibid., 359.

62. Ibid., 361.

63. № 174, "Telegramma general'nogo sekretaria TsK VKP (b) I. V. Stalina narkomu inostrannykh del SSSR V. M. Molotovu v Berlin, 12 noiabria 1940 g.," 1941 god, 1:367.

64. № 172, "Beseda predsedatelia sovnarkoma, narkoma inostrannykh del SSSR V. M. Molotova s reikhskantslerom Germanii A. Gitlerom v Berline, 12 noiabria 1940 g.," 1941 god, 1:361.

65. Ibid., 362.

66. Ibid., 363.

67. Ibid., 364.

68. Ibid. The Soviet record of the minutes uses the word "Montre," which is the Russian transliteration of Montreux. I assume that what Hitler meant here was "Monroe," not "Montre."

69. That Göring, Hitler, and von Ribbentrop were trying to deceive the Soviet delegation about the effects of British air raids is clear from the record of Göring's comments to his planning staff: "From the activity of the British air force over the last days it can be seen that an effort is being made by means of intense attacks to have a decisive impact on oil-processing plants and tank storage depots. As a result everything must be done so far as possible to ameliorate the effects of these sorts of attacks." Document 1155-PS, in IMT, Blue Series, XXVII:31. This refers to British attacks in June 1940, five months before Molotov's visit to Berlin. A year later, with the German army fighting in the Soviet

Union and the exploitation of Russian lands now critical for the German war economy, Göring rejected any further reduction in domestic consumption to supply the troops on the Eastern Front. Civilian morale would suffer, and the homeland already had enough problems to contend with, British air raids being one of them. See Document 003-EC, ibid., XXXVI:106.

70. № 176, "Beseda predsedatelia sovnarkoma, narkoma inostrannykh del SSSR V. M. Molotova s komanduiush-chim VVC, ministrom aviatsii Germanii reikhsmarshalom Germanii G. Geringom v Berline, 13 noiabria 1940 g.," 1941 god, 1:371.

71. № 179, "Beseda predsedatelia sovnarkoma, narkoma inostrannykh del SSSR V. M. Molotova s reikhskantslerom Germanii A. Gitlerom v Berline, 13 noaibria 1940 g.," 1941 god, 1:376.

72. Ibid.

73. Ibid., 380.

74. Ibid., 381.

75. № 182, "Beseda predsedatelia sovnarkoma, narkoma inostrannykh del SSSR V. M. Molotova s ministrom inostrannykh del Germanii I. Ribbentropom v Berline, 13 noiabria 1940 g.," 1941 god, 1:386.

76. Ibid., 388.

77. Ibid., 390.

78. Ibid., 388.

79. № 192, "Beseda narkoma inostrannykh del V. M. Molotova s poslom Germanii v SSSR F Shulenburgom, 25 noiabria 1940 g.," 1941 god, 1:413.

80. № 193, "Beseda narkoma inostrannykh del V. M. Molotova s poslom Germanii v SSSR F Shulenburgom, 25 noiabria 1940 g.," 1941 god, 1:416.

81. № 243, "Beseda narkoma inostrannykh del V. M. Molotova s poslom Germanii v SSSR F Shulenburgom, 17 ianvaria 1941 g.," 1941 god, 1:543.

82. № 251, "Beseda narkoma inostrannykh del V. M. Molotova s poslom Germanii v SSSR F Shulenburgom, 23 ianvaria 1941 g.," 1941 god, 1:563.

83. № 312, "Beseda narkoma inostrannykh del V. M. Molotova s poslom Germanii v SSSR F Shulenburgom, 10 marta 1941 g.," 1941 god, 1:738.

84. № 296, "Beseda narkoma inostrannykh del SSSR V. M. Molotova s poslom germanii v SSSR F. Shulenburgom', 1 marta 1941 g.," 1941 god, 1:706.

85. № 334, "Beseda narkoma inostrannykh del V. M. Molotova s poslom Germanii v SSSR F Shulenburgom, 24 marta 1941 g.," 1941 god, 1:794.

86. № 303, "Beseda narkoma inostrannykh del V. M. Molotova s poslom Germanii v SSSR F Shulenburgom, 6 marta 1941 g.," 1941 god, 1:723.

87. № 334, 1941 god, 1:794.

88. № 312, 1941 god, 1:739.

89. № 334, 1941 god, 1:795.

90. № 314, "Iz soobshcheniia NKGB SSSR v TsK VKP (b) i SNK SSSR o dannykh, poluchennykh iz angliiskogo posol'stva v Moskve, 11 marta 1941 g.," 1941 god, 1:740, emphasis added. Cripps's view is supported by what A. A. Shkvartsev, a Soviet official in Berlin, reported to Moscow after attending a press conference given by the German Foreign Ministry. He noted that a specific question concerning the Axis Pact was raised: against whom or what was it directed? Shkvartsev also reported that "conversations among journalists about the deterioration of Soviet-German relations continue. As proof of this claim they cite the German-Finnish Treaty concerning the passage of German troops through Finland." № 127,

"Telegramma polpreda SSSR v Germanii A. A. Shkvartsev v NKID SSSR, 27 sentiabria 1940 g.," ibid., 274.

91. № 361, "Beseda narkoma inostrannykh del V. M. Molotova s poslom Germanii v SSSR F Shulenburgom, 4 aprelia 1941 g.," 1941 god, 2:22.

92. № 383, "Beseda general'nogo sekretaria TsK VKP(b) I.V. Stalina s ministrom inostrannykh del Iaponii I. Matsuoka, 12 aprelia 1941 g.," 1941 god, 2:72.

93. Ibid., 71.

94. № 439, "Beseda polnomochnogo predstavitelia SSSR v Germanii V. G. Dekanozova s poslom Germanii v SSSR F. Shulenburgom v Moskve, 5 maia 1941 g.," 1941 god, 2:168.

95. Ibid.

96. № 454, "Beseda zamestitelia narkoma inostrannykh del SSSR, posla v Germanii V. G. Dekanozova s poslom Germanii v SSSR F. Shulenburgom v Moskve, 9 maia 1941 g.," 1941 god, 2:182.

97. № 462, "Beseda zamestitelia narkoma inostrannykh del SSSR, posla v Germanii V. G. Dekanozova s poslom Germanii v SSSR F. Shulenburgom v Moskve, 12 maia 1941 g.," 1941 god, 2:194.

98. Ibid., 195.

99. № 494, "Zapiska starshego pomoshchnika narkoma inostrannykh del SSSR v TsK VKP (b) A. N. Poskrebyshevu s preprovozhdeniem pis'ma V. G. Dekanozova, 26 maia 1941 g.," 1941 god, 2:264.

100. Clark states that Stafford Cripps "presented to Stalin comprehensive evidence of the German plan (supplied by Hess)." Alan Clark, Barbarossa: The Russian-German Conflict 1941–1945 (Harmondsworth, U.K.: Penguin, 1966), 67.

101. Alan Bullock, Hitler: A Study in Tyranny [1952] (Harmondsworth, U.K.: Penguin, 1983), 646.

102. № 552, "Beseda pervogo zamestitelia narkoma inostrannykh del SSSR A. IA Vyshinskogo s poslom Germanii v SSSR F. Shulenburgom, 14 iiunia 1941 g.," 1941 god, 2:364.

103. № 597, "Beseda narkoma inostrannykh del V. M. Molotova s poslom Germanii v SSSR F Shulenburgom, 21 iiunia 1941 g.," 1941 god, 2:415.

104. № 608, "Beseda narkoma inostrannykh del V. M. Molotova s poslom Germanii v SSSR F Shulenburgom, 22 iiunia 1941 g.," 1941 god, 2:431.

105. OGB, 1941/1, № 282, 14.

Chapter 4. The Soviet Intelligence Assessment of German Military Intentions, 1939–1941

1. № 6, "Zapiska nachal'nika razvedupravleniia genshtaba Krasnoi Armii v TsK VKP(b)—I. V. Stalinu s preprovozhdeniem agenturnykh soobshchenii, № 251784ss, 4 iiunia 1941 g.," in 1941 god, v 2-knigakh, ed. A. N. IAkovlev et al., in the series "Demokratiia," Rossiia. XX VEK, Dokumenty (Moscow: Mezhdunarodnyi fond, 1998), 1:23.

2. Ibid., 24.

3. Ibid.

4. Ibid.

5. Ibid.

6. Ibid., 25.

7. "Ot sostavitelei," 1941 god, 1:10.

8. № 20, "Iz svodki 5 upravleniia RKKA o polozhenii v Germanii, Rumynii i Latvii', 19 iiunia 1940 g.," 1941 god, 1:42–43. Both sides were keeping an eye on each other. On 5 June 1940 contacts between a pilot working out of Leningrad and an Estonian captain, Karl Kavel'mar, revealed that the German police had asked the latter about the number

of Soviet troops, their bases, and their weapons in Estonia and about the Estonians' attitude toward the Red Army. On 22 June 1940 the navigator of a Lithuanian steamer stated that after France and Britain had been defeated, Germany would turn against the Soviet Union. The report noted: "He [the navigator] allegedly knows that in Germany at the present time tens of thousands of men from the ages of 16 to 20 years, who will be designated for airborne assaults in time of war against the Soviet Union, are being taught parachuting and Russian." Another source, the radio operator on board a Latvian steamer, had heard a number of Germans saying that "Germany's forthcoming military operations against the USSR will be essentially aimed at the seizure of Ukraine." № 35, "Soobshchenie glavnogo upravleniia pogranvoisk NKVD SSSR v GUGB NKVD SSSR o voennykh prigotovleniiakh Germanii', № 19/47112, 28 iiunia 1940 g.," ibid., 66.

9. № 22, "Iz svodki 5 upravleniia RKKA o polozhenii v Germanii', 21 iiunia 1940 g.," 1941 god, 1:44. However, in early July, undercover agents confirmed the scale of construction in the eastern border regions and reported major shipments of building material, cement, and iron from Hamburg, Lübeck, and Stettin to Memel, Tilsit, Königsberg, and Danzig. The aim of this fortification work, according to the report, was to construct a reinforced line that would "stretch along the Soviet-German border from Memel to Eastern Prussia via Poland to Slovakia." The report also notes: "The reinforced positions will be built using the latest word in technology and taking into account military experience and in their strength will

allegedly exceed the existing Siegfried Line." № 44, "Spetssoobshchenie GTU NKVD SSSR v NKVD SSSR o voennykh prigotovleniiakh Germanii, № 16/30141, 12 iiulia 1940 g.," ibid., 93. These claims were not exaggerations. German expertise and methods that had been devised to overwhelm the Belgian forts could now be used to build forts to counter those same methods. The state of German civilian morale also received some attention from the report's author, who notes that the "mood of the bulk of the German population is against a protracted war and the people hope for the conclusion of peace in the near future." In addition, "among the lower-paid category of workers there exists the opinion that the harsh procedures introduced in Germany will be maintained after the war and in peacetime." Ibid., 94.

10. № 23, "Sluzhebnaia zapiska komanduiushchego voiskami BOVO narkomu oborony [SSSR] Marshalu Sovetskogo Soiuza S. K. Timoshenko, b/h, 21 iiunia 1940 g.," 1941 god, 1:44–45.

11. № 41, "Zapiska nachal'nika 5 otdela GUGB NKVD SSSR v razvedupravlenie RKKA s pros'boi dat' otsenku materialam o podgotovke Germanii k voine protiv SSSR, № 5/8175, 9 iiulia 1941 g.," 1941 god, 1:90.

12. Ibid., 91.

13. Ibid.

14. Ibid. Fitin's July reports were generally well received and were regarded as valuable since they confirmed the reliability of other data. They did, however, prompt a list of specific requirements from Lieutenant-Colonel Kostomakha, head of the first subsection of the 5th Section of the Soviet General Staff's Intelligence Directorate. Specifically, Kostomakha wanted

to know the following: (1) why the Germans planned to include a German battalion in each Slovak regiment; (2) the strength, organization, and location of the Slovak army; (3) the precise location of the fortification work and the materials being used; (4) precise details about the main deployments by rail, with the dates; (5) unit locations, with an indication of their type and numerical designation; and (6) details of the major units located in Vienna, Krakow, Liublin, and Zamost'ia. № 83, "Zapiska razvedupravleniia genshtaba Krasnoi Armii nachal'niku 5 otdela GUGB NKVD SSSR Fitinu s preprovozhdeniem otsenki razvedyvatel'nykh materialov, № 252202ss, 7 avgusta 1941 g.," ibid., 161. Most of these clarifications involved basic intelligence tradecraft. Perhaps the most intriguing question from Kostomakha's point of view was how to interpret German plans to assign a German battalion to each Slovak regiment. I suggest that this was intended to be a force multiplier. German military expertise and leadership were being used to raise the general standard and make the Slovak regiment more effective. In this policy we see the start of another one that would be widely implemented on the Eastern Front after the invasion: the Germans would raise units from the disaffected republics of the Soviet state and use them, variously, as antipartisan, security, and police units in the rear areas.

15. Soviet intelligence officers paid close attention to rumors and any manifestation of organized anti-Soviet propaganda in the German-controlled or German-influenced zones and countries. In fact, these concerns featured prominently in many assessments. For example, on 23 June 1940 the NKVD border troops based in Lvov reported "a forthcoming breach of the friendship treaty between Germany and the USSR and German intentions at the end of July 1940 to initiate, jointly with Italy, France, Hungary, Romania, Turkey and Japan, military operations against the Soviet Union.." The report's author speculates that Ukrainian nationalist organizations were the most likely source of these rumors. Poles living in the border region believed the Soviet government was training a Polish Legion to be used against Hungary. "After the occupation of Hungary," the report's author states, "this legion will allegedly take part in joint operations with the Red Army against Germany." № 67, "Iz razvedsvodki upravleniia pogranvoisk NKVD Ukraine SSR o voennykh meropriiatiiakh Germanii i kontsentratsii germanskikh voisk v pogranpolose SSSR, № 55, 26 iiulia 1940," 1941 god, 1:131–132.

16. № 45, "Iz dokladnoi zapiski upravleniia pogranvoisk NKVD Ukraine SSR v NKVD Ukraine SSR o meropriiatiiakh rumynskikh vlastei posle prisoedineniia k SSSR Bessarabii i severnoi Bukoviny, № AB-0033974', 12 iiulia 1940 g.," 1941 god, 1:95.

17. Ibid.

18. Ibid., 96.

19. Ibid. That Romanian officers treated Jews very badly is supported by a diary entry (20 May 1941) from Oberleutnant Bente, an officer serving in the German 76th Infantry Division, which was stationed in Romania before the start of Barbarossa: "Harlau and Botosani (divisional headquarters is located there) are full of Jews, some two-thirds. These speak German. The Romanian officers treat the Jews

like shit but accept their hospitality."
Nachträge zu Bittere Pflicht, band 3, O11b,
76a-3.

20. № 53, "Zapiska zamestitelia
nachal'nika pogranvoisk NKVD SSSR
nachal'niku 5 otdela GUGB NKVD SSSR
Fitinu o perebroskakh i kontsentratsii
germanskikh voisk', № 19/47415, 13
iiulia 1940 g.," *1941 god*, 1:115. The
general thrust of Petrov's report to Fitin
was confirmed by General-Lieutenant
Maslennikov's report dated 14 July 1940.
The numbers cited by Maslennikov
were almost identical to those included
in Petrov's report, which may suggest
collusion between the two officers or
their reliance on the same source. №
55, "Iz dokladnoi zapiski zamestitelia
narkoma vnutrennikh del BSSR v NKVD
SSSR o sosredotochenii nemetskikh
voisk vblizi sovetskoi Granitsy, 14 iiulia
1940 g.," ibid., 116–117. The same figures
cited by Maslennikov and earlier by Fitin
were also contained in a report bearing
Beria's signature that was sent to Stalin,
Molotov, Voroshilov, and Timoshenko.
See № 58, "Zapiska NKVD SSSR v TsK
VKP (b)—I. V. Stalinu, SNK SSSR—V.
M. Molotovu i K. E. Voroshilovu, NKO
SSSR—S. K. Timoshenko o voennykh
prigotovleniiakh Germanii', № 2848/b,
15 iiulia 1940 g.," ibid., 119–120. General-
Lieutenant Golikov, in a report dated 15
July 1940, concludes: "The transfer of
German troops to the territory of the
former Poland and Eastern Prussia, and
in particular to the immediate zones
bordering the USSR continues. Up to
13 July 1940 the situation is that there
are up to 11 divisions concentrated in
Eastern Prussia and up to 26 divisions
on the territory of the former Poland."
№ 57, "Iz svodki 5 upravleniia RKKA o
sosredotochenii germanskikh voisk na

granitse s Litvoi, 15 iiulia 1940 g.," ibid.,
118–119.

21. № 60, "Svodka piatogo upravleniia RKKA po sobytiiam na zapade,
adresovannaia narkomu oborony SSSR
Marshalu Sovetskogo Soiuza Timoshenko, № 86/252104ss, 20 iiulia 1940
g.," *1941 god*, 1:121.

22. Ibid.

23. Ibid., 123.

24. Ibid., 124.

25. № 75, "Zapiska NKVD SSSR I.
V. Stalinu i V. M. Molotovu o voennykh
prigotovleniiakh Germanii', b/n, iiul'
1940 g.," *1941 god*, 1:143–144, emphasis
added.

26. № 77, "Iz razvedsvodki upravleniia pogranvoisk NKVD Ukrainskoi
SSR o voennykh meropriiatiiakh
Germanii v pogranpolose s SSSR po
sostoianiiu na 3 avgusta 1940 g.," 1941
god, 1:153.

27. № 89, "Iz zapiski NKVD SSSR
v TsK VKP(b)—I. V. Stalinu, SNK
SSSR—V. M. Molotovu, KO pri SNK
SSSR—K. E. Voroshilovu i NKO
SSSR—S. K. Timoshenko s preprovozhdeniem doneseniia rezidenta NKVD
SSSR, № 3214/b, 13 avgusta 1940 g.,"
1941 god, 1:169.

28. Ibid.

29. № 90, "Zapiska 5 otdela UGB
NKVD USSR nachal'niku 5 otdela GUGB
NKVD SSSR Fitinu s preprovozhdeniem
obzora o peredvizhenii nemetskikh
voisk, № 176969, 15 avgusta 1940 g.,"
1941 god, 1:170.

30. Ibid., 171.

31. Ibid., 172.

32. Ibid.

33. Ibid.

34. Ibid.

35. № 91, "Spetssoobshchenie GTU
NKVD SSSR—informatsionno-

razvedyvatel'naia svodka po Germanii, № 16/35498, 16 avgusta 1941 g.," 1941 god, 1:174.

36. Ibid., 175.

37. Ibid.

38. Ibid.

39. № 92, "Spetssoobshchenie GTU NKVD SSSR—informatsionno-razvedyvatel'naia svodka po Germanii, № 16/35500, 16 avgusta 1941 g.," 1941 god, 1:175–176.

40. Ibid., 176.

41. № 99, "Spetssoobshchenie GTU NKVD SSSR—informatsionno-razvedyvatel'naia svodka po Germanii, № 16/36974, 23 avgusta 1941 g.," 1941 god, 1:199.

42. Ibid.

43. № 95, "Zapiska narkoma oborony SSSR i nachal'nika genshtaba Krasnoi Armii v TsK VKP(b) I. V. Stalinu i V. M. Molotovu ob osnovakh strategicheskogo razvertyvaniia vooruzhennykh sil SSSR na zapade i na vostoke na 1940 i 1941 gody, b/n [ne pozzhe 19 avgusta 1941 g.]," 1941 god, 1:181.

44. Ibid. The threat posed by Finland was reiterated a month later in another critical intelligence assessment dated 18 September 1940. There was a growing awareness that Finland was preparing for war with the Soviet Union. Meretskov, the author, notes that the demobilization order issued after the Winter War has been rescinded, and reservists are being called up. The most striking aspect of this assessment is the complete absence of any mention of the Red Army's clumsiness in the Winter War; it fails to note whether any attempt has been made to address the weaknesses at all levels of command and control in anticipation of another war with a demonstrably effective and resilient enemy. See № 118, "Zapiska narkoma oborony SSSR i nachal'nika genshtaba Krasnoi armii v TsK VKP(b)—I. V. Stalinu i V. M. Molotovu o soobrazheniiakh po razvertyvaniiu vooruzhennykh sil Krasnoi armii na sluchai voiny s Finliandiei, 18 sentiabria 1940 g.," ibid., 253–260.

45. № 95, 1941 god, 1:181.

46. Ibid., 182.

47. Ibid.

48. Ibid., 183, emphasis in original.

49. Ibid., 184.

50. Ibid., 185, emphasis in original.

51. Ibid., 186.

52. Ibid., 187.

53. Ibid., 190.

54. Surprise attacks, especially if carried out at night, can help offset the disadvantages of inferior aircraft. This was clearly demonstrated by the British surprise air attack on the Italian fleet in Taranto in 1940. British biplanes, which took off from an aircraft carrier in the Mediterranean, inflicted major damage on the enemy and changed the balance of naval power decisively in favor of the Royal Navy. Likewise, in the stunning US victory at Midway, which resulted in the destruction of four Japanese carriers, the US aircraft were technically inferior to the latest Japanese planes. What secured the US victory at Midway was superb intelligence analysis, which gave the US attackers the element of surprise, and the skill and determination of the US Navy pilots, who were able to exploit the advantages.

55. № 95, 1941 god, 1:187.

56. № 117, "Zapiska narkoma oborony SSSR i nachal'nika genshtaba Krasnoi Armii v TsK VKP(b) I. V. Stalinu i V. M. Molotovu ob osnovakh strategicheskogo razvertyvaniia vooruzhennykh

sil SSSR na zapade i na vostoke na 1940 i 1941 gody, № 103202/ov, 18 sentiabria 1940 g.," 1941 god, 1:241.

57. Ibid.

58. Ibid., 245.

59. Ibid.

60. № 119, "Spetssoobshchenie nachal'nika razvedotdela ZAPOVO nachal'niku razvedupravleniia genshtaba Krasnoi Armii general-leitenantu Golikovu, № 44229, 19 sentiabria 1940 g.," 1941 god, 1:261.

61. Ibid., 262.

62. Ibid.

63. № 122, "Spetssoobshchenie GTU NKVD SSSR—informatsionno-razvedyvatel'naia svodka po Germanii, b/n, ne pozzhe 25 sentiabria 1940 g.," 1941 god, 1:268.

64. Ibid., 269.

65. Ibid.

66. № 134, "Zapiska narkoma SSSR i nachal'nika genshtaba Krasnoi Armii v TsK VKP (b)—I. V. Stalinu i V. M. Molotovu, № 103313/cc/ov [ne ranee 5 oktiabria 1940 goda]," 1941 god, 1:288–290.

67. № 138, "Zapiska nachal'nika razvedupravleniia Krasnoi Armii narkomu SSSR Marshalu Sovetskogo Soiuza S. K. Timoshenko s preprovozhdeniem agenturnogo doneseniia, № 252513ss, 10 oktiabria 1940 g.," 1941 god, 1:292.

68. Ibid., 293.

69. № 156, "Spetssoobshchenie GTU NKVD SSSR—informatsionnom-razvedyvatel'naia svodka po Germanii, № 16/48024, 25 oktiabria 1940 g.," 1941 god, 1:325.

70. Ibid.

71. № 158, "Soobshchenie NKVD SSSR narkomu oborony SSSR S.\K. Timoshenko, b/n [oktiabr' 1940 goda]," 1941 god, 1:328.

72. Ibid.

73. Ibid.

74. № 199, "Iz orientirovki osobogo otdela GUGB NKVD SSSR o meropriiatiiakh po presecheniiu deiatel'nosti germanskoi razvedki', № 4/66389, 30 noiabria 1940 g.," 1941 god, 1:428.

75. № 208, "Spravka 5 otdela GUGB NKVD SSSR s izlozheniem agenturnogo soobshcheniia 'Litseista,' do 14 dekabria 1940 g.," 1941 god, 1:449.

76. Ibid.

77. № 217, "Spetssoobshchenie GTU NKVD SSSR—informatsionno-razvedyvatel'naia svodka po Germanii, № 16/59101, 27 dekabria 1940 g.," 1941 god, 1:463.

78. Ibid., 464. A Soviet agent inside Germany reported that Germany would seize Ukraine and the Caucasus and that all Czechs would be resettled as administrators to run the economy. The Czech lands would then be colonized by the Germans. The source noted that the process of colonizing the Czech Republic and Moravia had already started: "Dozens of villages both in the Czech Republic and in Moravia are now being freed of Czechs and resettled by Germans." The source also reported that an attack on Britain would be initiated in the middle of March, and the Soviet Union would be attacked via Ukraine. № 240, "Soobshchenie istochnika 'Lauren' o planakh napadeniia Germanii na SSSR, 15 ianvaria 1941 g.," ibid., 538.

79. Two recent studies that cover the fate of Germans in eastern Europe at the end of the war and immediately after are Timothy Snyder, *Bloodlands: Europe between Hitler and Stalin* (London: Bodley Head, 2010), and Anne Applebaum, *Iron Curtain: The Crushing of Eastern Europe 1944–56* (London: Allen Lane, 2012). The mass deportations beggar

belief: oceans and continents of grief, starving children, homes lost forever, abandoned women, and men bereft of hope and faith. Germans, innocent and guilty, paid a dreadful price. In the words of Applebaum: "By the time it was finished, the resettling of the German populations of Eastern Europe was an extraordinary mass movement, probably unequalled in European history. By the end of 1947, some 7.6 million 'Germans'—including ethnic Germans, *Volksdeutsche* and recent settlers—had left Poland, through transfer or escape" (*Iron Curtain*, 132).

80. № 217, *1941 god*, 1:464.

81. № 224, "Zapiska nachal'nika shtaba KOVO po resheniiu voennogo soveta IUgo-zapadnogo fronta po planu razvertyvaniia na 1940 god, b/n [ne pozdnee dekabria 1940 g.]," *1941 god*, 1:484, emphasis in original.

82. Ibid., 493–494.

83. № 227, "Donesenie 'Meteora' iz Berlina o voennykh prigotovleniiakh Germanii ot 4 ianvaria 1941 g.," *1941 god*, 1:508.

84. № 242, "Iz razvedyvatel'noi svodki № 2 upravleniia pogranvoisk NKVD USSR o dislokatsii voisk i voennykh meropriiatiiakh Germanii v pogranpolose s SSSR po sostoianiiu na 14 ianvaria 1941 g.," *1941 god*, 1:541.

85. № 246, "Zapiska zamestitelia narkoma vnutrennikh del SSSR general-leitenanta Maslennikova zamestiteliu narkoma vnutrennikh del SSSR Merkulovu o dostavke v Germaniiu obraztsov ispol'zuemykh v SSSR nefteproduktov, № 18/8033, 18 ianvaria 1941 g.," *1941 god*, 1:549.

86. № 257, "Zapiska GUGB NKVD SSSR nachal'niku razvedupravleniia Krasnoi Armii general-leitenantu Golikovu, № 5/1674, 29 ianvaria 1941 g.," *1941 god*, 1:575.

87. № 268, "Soobshchenie NKGB SSSR Stalinu, Molotovu, Mikoianu, № 18/M, 8 fevralia 1941 g.," *1941 god*, 1:600.

88. № 277, "Spetssoobshchenie GTU NKVD SSSR—informatsionno-razvedyvatel'naia svodka № 9 po Germanii po sostoianiiu na 10 fevralia 1941 g.," *1941 god*, 1:656.

89. Ibid.

90. Ibid., 657.

91. № 288, "Spetssoobshchenie GTU NKVD SSSR—informatsionno-razvedyvatel'naia svodka № 11/4 po Germanii po sostoianiiu na 25 fevralia 1941 g.', № 16/9887-zh, 27 fevralia 1941 g.," *1941 god*, 1:682.

92. Ibid., 682–683.

93. № 281, "Agenturnoe soobshchenie "Dory" iz Tsiurikha ot 21 fevralia 1941 g.," *1941 god*, 1:676.

94. № 289, "Iz doneseniia rezidenta Berlinskoi nelegal'noi rezidentury razvedupravleniia genshtaba Krasnoi Armii 'Al'ty' ot 28 fevralia 1941 g.," *1941 god*, 1:683.

95. № 301, "Zapiska NKGB SSSR I. V. Stalinu, V. M. Molotovu, S. K. Timoshenko, L. P. Beria s preprovozhdeniem agenturnogo soobshcheniia, № 336/m, 6 marta 1941 g.," *1941 god*, 1:717.

96. № 308, "Zapiska NKGB SSSR I. V. Stalinu, V. M. Molotovu, S. K. Timoshenko, L. P. Beria s preprovozhdeniem agenturnogo soobshcheniia, № 339/m, 8 marta 1941 g.," *1941 god*, 1:734.

97. № 315, "Iz plana genshtaba Krasnoi Armii o strategicheskom razvertyvanii vooruzhennykh sil Sovetskogo Soiuza na zapade i vostoke, b/n, 11 marta 1941 g.," *1941 god*, 1:741, emphasis added.

98. № 321, "Soobshchenie NKGB

SSSR I. V. Stalinu, V. M. Molotovu, L. P. Beria s preprovozhdeniem agenturnogo soobshcheniia, № 488/m, 14 marta 1941 g.," 1941 god, 1:769.

99. A heightened security regime is also an indicator that a state wants to hide its intentions or mislead a potential enemy. In an earlier memorandum to Stalin, Molotov, and Voroshilov (17 August 1940), Beria had reported that all passengers (presumably those using the rail network) in eastern Prussia, regardless of whether they were civilian or military, were being subjected to strict control and monitoring. He also reported: "The populations of Berlin and other cities have been repeatedly warned of the necessity to prepare air-raid shelters and to ensure a complete blackout. A complete blackout regime has also been introduced in Eastern Prussia." № 93, "Zapiska L. P Beriia—I. V. Stalinu, V. M. Molotovu, K. E. Voroshilovu, S. K. Timoshenko o voennykh prigotovleniiakh nemtsev na territorii vostochnoi prussii, 17 avgusta 1940 g.," 1941 god, 1:176–177.

100. № 342, "Spetssoobshchenie NKGB SSSR narkomu gosbezopasnosti SSSR Merkulovu o prodvizhenii nemetskikh voisk k granitse SSSR i o voennykh prigotovleniiakh v prigranichnykh punktakh, № 1/2/42, 27 marta 1941 g.," 1941 god, 1:803.

101. № 316, "Spetssoobshchenie razvedupravleniia genshtaba Krasnoi Armii o napravlenii razvitiia vooruzhennykh sil Germanii i izmeneniiakh v ikh sostoianii, № 660279ss, 11 marta 1941 g.," 1941 god, 1:748.

102. Ibid., 758–759.

103. № 327, "Doklad nachal'nika razvedupravleniia genshtaba Krasnoi Armii general-leitenanta Golikova v

NKO SSSR, SNK SSSR i TsK VKP(b) vyskazyvaniia, [orgmeropriiatiia] i varianty boevykh deistvii germanskoi armii protiv SSSR, b/n, 22 marta 1941 g.," 1941 god, 1:776, emphasis in original.

104. Ibid., 778, emphasis in original.

105. Ibid., emphasis in original.

106. Ibid., 780.

107. "Spravka," 27 aprelia 1964 goda, 1941 god, 1:780.

108. № 351, "Svodka agenturnykh soobshchenii o moral'no-politicheskom sostoianii chastei germanskoi armii, b/n [mart 1941 g.]," 1941 god, 1:812.

109. Ibid.

110. Despite the high morale of the German army in the period leading up to the invasion, there were cases of German deserters being intercepted by the NKVD and, when interrogated, indicating signs of disaffection among the German troops. The authors of a report to Merkulov, dated 30 May 1941, argued that soldiers who supported Hitler did so because of "fascist propaganda," not realizing that Hitler's support was derived largely from the success of German arms. The use of "fascist" in this intelligence summary was unusual, since the preferred term was the more neutral germanskii. Also, instances of drunkenness, desertion, and other lapses in military discipline among German troops should be interpreted with caution. I suggest that the most likely cause of such behavior was the prolonged period of waiting and training and even boredom. Soldiers with too much time on their hands start to look for grievances, just as German sailors did in the 1918 naval mutinies. Boredom and inaction are corrosive; action is cohesive. See № 506, "Zapiska zamestitelia narkoma vnutrennikh del

SSSR narkomu gosbezopasnosti SSSR V. N. Merkulovu s preprovozhdeniem razvedannykh', № 18/8289, 30 maia 1941 g.," 1941 god, 2:279–282.

111. № 355, "Spravka 1 upravleniia NKGB SSSR po soobshcheniiu 'Zakhara,' № 106, 2 aprelia 1941 g.," 1941 god, 2:13.

112. Ibid.

113. Ibid.

114. Ibid., 15.

115. Ibid., 14.

116. № 362, "Soobshchenie 'Sofokla' iz Belgrada ot 4 aprelia 1941 g.," 1941 god, 2:24.

117. Ibid. A second report from the same agent noted: "The Germans intend to attack the Soviet Union in May. The starting point for this will be based on the demand that the Soviet Union join the Axis Pact and render economic assistance." According to this agent, the three main German army groupings to be deployed against the Soviet Union were the Königsberg group under the command of General Rundstein (this most likely refers to Generalfeldmarschall Gerd von Rundstedt), the Krakow formation under the command of Blaskowitz or List (Generaloberst Johannes List or Generalfeldmarschall Wilhelm List), and the Warsaw formation under the command of Generaloberst Ludwig Beck. '№ 363, "Soobshchenie 'Sofokla' iz Belgrada ot 4 aprelia 1941 g.," 1941 god, 2:25.

118. № 374, "Iz spetssoobshcheniia NKVD USSR v TsK VKP(b) Ukrainy o peredvizhenii nemetskikh voisk, № A-1250/SN, 9 aprelia 1941 g.," 1941 god, 2:52.

119. Ibid., 54.

120. № 376, "Soobshchenie vneshnei razvedki NKGB SSSR v razvedupravlenie genshtaba Krasnoi Armii o kontsentratsii nemetskikh voisk, № 2/7/2575, 10 aprelia 1941 g.," 1941 god, 2:56.

121. № 387, "Dokladnaia zapiska NKGB USSR sekretariu TsK KP(b) Ukrainy N. S. Khrushchevu [ne ranee 15 aprelia 1941 g.]," 1941 god, 2:79.

122. For more on this incident—the JU-86 crash-landed near Rovno (Ukraine)—see Christer Bergström, Barbarossa: The Air Battle: July–December 1941 (Hersham, U.K.: Chevron, 2007), 12. The unit of the Luftwaffe responsible for conducting air reconnaissance over the Soviet Union was Aufklärungsgruppe Oberbefehlshaber der Luftwaffe. Air reconnaissance flights over Soviet territory began in the mid-1930s, but systematic aerial reconnaissance of the Soviet Union started in October 1940 and continued right up to the start of Barbarossa. Until 15 June 1941, the main focus of German aerial reconnaissance was Soviet airfields. Immediately before the start of Barbarossa, these expert German aircrews were also used to air-drop Abwehr agents (Bergström, Air Battle, 12). Bergström's study reveals the German expertise in air reconnaissance operations. The fact that these reconnaissance flights were largely uncontested by the Soviet air force gave the German planners a huge advantage.

123. № 387, 1941 god, 2:80.

124. Ibid.

125. Another indication of the threat posed by Ukrainian nationalism was a Ukraine NKGB report to Merkulov dated 15 May 1941. According to Meshik, the author, the Germans had already formed a Ukrainian nationalist government headed by Colonel Mel'nik, and they had selected Kiev to be the seat of that government. № 469,

"Spetssoobshchenie NKGB Ukraine SSR narkomu gosbezopasnosti SSSR Merkulovu o peredvizhenii nemetskikh voisk, № A-1620/sn, 15 maia 1941 g.," *1941 god*, 2:211.

126. № 387, *1941 god*, 2:80.

127. № 392, "Spetssoobshchenie NKGB USSR narkomu gosbezopasnosti SSSR Merkulovu o peredvizhenii nemetskikh voisk, № A-1328/cn, 16 aprelia 1941 g.," *1941 god*, 2:87.

128. Ibid.

129. № 393, "Spetssoobshchenie razvedupravleniia genshtaba Krasnoi Armii o perebroskakh nemetskikh voisk v pogranpolose, № 660406ss, 16 aprelia 1941 g.," *1941 god*, 2:87.

130. Ibid., 88.

131. № 412, "Zapiska sovetskogo voennogo attashe v Germanii nachal'niku razvedupravleniia genshtaba Krasnoi Armii general-leitenantu Golikovu, 25/26 aprelia 1941 g.," *1941 god*, 2:113.

132. Ibid.,

133. Ibid., 116.

134. Ibid.

135. Ibid.

136. Ibid., 113.

137. Ibid., 117, emphasis added. Perhaps stung by Tupikov's frankness, Golikov reported to Stalin and his inner circle this storm-warning refrain: "The mass deployments of German troops from the deep rear of Germany and the occupied countries of Western Europe continue without interruption. The main streams of these deployments head in two directions: to our western borders; and toward the Balkans." № 413, "Spetssoobshchenie razvedupravleniia genshtaba Krasnoi Armii o raspredelenii vooruzhennykh sil Germanii po teatram i frontam

voennykh deistvii po sostoianiiu na 25.04.41 g'., № 660448ss, 26 aprelia 1941 g.," ibid., 119.

138. № 418, "Direktiva NKO SSSR voennomu sovetu moskovskogo voennogo okruga, № Org/2/522726, 29 aprelia 1941 g.," *1941 god*, 2:123.

139. Ibid., 124.

140. № 425, "Direktiva narkoma oborony SSSR i nachal'nika genshtaba Krasnoi Armii komanduiushchemu voiskami ZAPOVO general-polkovniku D. G. Pavlovu, b/n, [aprel' 1941 g.]," *1941 god*, 2:133–134.

141. № 424, "Zapiska NKGB SSSR I. V. Stalinu, V. M. Molotovu i S.K. Timoshenko [konets aprelia 1941 g.]," *1941 god*, 2:133.

142. № 435, "Zapiska NKGB SSSR I. V. Stalinu, V. M. Molotovu i L. P. Beria s preprovozhdeniem agenturnykh soobshchenii iz Varshavy, № 1452/m, 5 maia 1941 g.," *1941 god*, 2:154–155.

143. № 466, "Dokladnaia zapiska NKVD Ukraine SSR v TsK KP(b) Ukrainy o dislokatsii i stroitel'stve nemetskimi vlastiami aerodromov i posadochnykh ploshchadok v pogranichnoi s SSSR polose, 14 maia 1941 g.," *1941 god*, 2:199–200.

144. № 472, "Spetssoobshchenie razvedupravleniia genshtaba Krasnoi Armii o raspredelenii vooruzhennykh sil po teatram i frontam voennykh deistvii po sostoianiiu na 15.05.42 g., № 660506ss, 15 maia 1941 g.," *1941 god*, 2:213.

145. Ibid., 215.

146. № 473, "Zapiska narkoma oborony SSSR i nachal'nika genshtaba Krasnoi Armii predsedateliu SNK SSSR I. V. Stalinu s soobrazheniiami po planu strategicheskogo razvertyvaniia vooruzhennykh sil Sovetskogo Soiuza na sluchai voiny s Germaniei i ee

soyuzniki, b/n [ne ranee 15 maia 1941 g.]," 1941 god, 2:216.

147. Ibid.,

148. Ibid., 219, emphasis added.

149. Ibid.

150. The Timoshenko-Zhukov memorandum to Stalin was followed up by a detailed directive to the commanders of the Western Special Military District, Kiev Special Military District, Odessa Military District, and Baltic Special Military District, requiring them to come up with plans to cover the mobilization and defense of their respective districts. See № 481, "Direktiva narkoma oborony SSSR i nachal'nika genshtaba krasnoi armii komanduiushchemu voiskami ZAPOVO, ne pozdnee 20 maia 1940 g.," 1941 god, 2:227–232; № 507, "Direktiva narkoma oborony SSSR i nachal'nika genshtaba krasnoi armii komanduiushchemu voiskami pribaltiiskogo osobogo voennogo okruga, ne pozdnee 30 maia 1941 g.," ibid., 282–288.

151. № 513, "Agenturnoe donesenie "Ramzai" iz Tokio ot 1 iiunia 1941 g.," and № 514, "Agenturnoe donesenie "Ramzai" iz Tokio ot 1 iiunia 1941 g.," 1941 god, 2:303–304.

152. № 525, "Spetssoobshchenie razvedupravleniia genshtaba Krasnoi Armii o podgotovke Rumynii k voine, № 660586, 5 iiunia 1941 g.," 1941 god, 2:325.

153. № 528, "Spetssoobshchenie razvedupravleniia genshtaba Krasnoi Armii o voennykh prigotovleniiakh Rumynii, № 660606, 7 iiunia 1941 g.," 1941 god, 2:333.

154. Ibid., emphasis in original. A directive from the NKGB dated 9 June 1941 also reveals a profound sense of urgency with regard to German intentions: "Conditions in the contemporary situation confront all the intelligence agencies of the Soviet Union with what is by far the main task: the clarification of all questions connected with the preparation of war with the Soviet Union being carried out in the first place by Germany." № 531, "Direktiva NKGB SSSR narkomu gosbezopasnosti Ukraine SSR Meshiku po provedeniiu razveddeiatel'nosti v sviazi s voennymi prigotovleniiami Germanii, № 2177/m, 9 iiunia 1941 g.," ibid., 335.

155. № 544, "Iz soobshcheniia NKVD SSSR v TsK VKP(b) i SNK SSSR o narusheniiakh gosudarstvennoi granitsy SSSR s noiabria 1940 g. po 10 iiunia 1940 g., № 1996/b, 12 iiunia 1941 g.," 1941 god, 2:350. In one of the many meetings he had with Molotov on diplomatic matters, von Schulenburg requested permission for German aircraft to cross Soviet airspace en route to the Far East. The reason he gave was that the Germans wanted to deliver medical supplies and spare parts to a ship. Molotov reacted suspiciously, possibly because he assumed that the real purpose of these flights was to conduct air photographic reconnaissance. See № 207, "Beseda narkoma inostrannykh del SSSR V. M. Molotova s poslom Germanii V SSSR F. Shulenburgom', 12 dekabriia 1940 g.," ibid., 1:444–448. Von Schulenburg requested flight clearance again in February 1941 (№ 269, ibid., 1:603). At a meeting in April 1941, he sought permission for five German ships to return to the west via the northern maritime route (№ 361, ibid., 2:23). Again, the spying implications were obvious.

156. № 544, 1941 god, 2:350.

157. № 588, "Razvedyvatel'naia svodka NKGB SSSR o voennykh prigotovleniiakh Germanii, № 1510, 20 iiunia 1941 g.," 1941 god, 2:398.

158. № 556, "Soobshchenie, po-luchennoe vneshnei razvedkoi NKGB SSSR iz Shvetsii [ne pozdnee 15 iiunia 1941 g.]," 1941 god, 2:365.

159. № 561, "Telegramma posla SSSR v Velikobritanii I. M. Maiskogo v NKVD SSSR, 16 iiunia 1941 g.," 1941 god, 2:374.

160. № 570, "Soobshchenie NKGB SSSR I. V. Stalinu i V. M. Molotovu, № 2279/m, 17 iiunia 1941 g.," 1941 god, 2:382.

161. Ibid., 383, emphasis in original.

162. № 573, "Iz zapiski narkoma gosbezopasnosti SSSR I. V. Stalinu, V. M. Molotovu i L. P. Beria o massovom ot'ezde iz SSSR sotrudnikov german-skogo posol'stva i chlenov ikh semei, i ob unichtozhenii arkhivov posol'stva, № 2294/m, 18 iiunia 1941 g.," 1941 god, 2:384.

163. № 604, "Iz telefonogrammy UNKGB po L'vovskoi oblasti v NKGB Ukraine SSR, 22 iiunia 1941 g.," 1941 god, 2:422.

164. № 605, "Direktiva komanduiush-chego voiskami ZAPOVO komanduiush-chim voiskami 3-i, 4-i i 10-i armii, 22 iiunia 1941 g.," 1941 god, 2:423.

165. № 772, "Dokladnaia zapiska nachal'nika Lomzhinskogo operativ-nogo punkta razvedyvatel'nogo otdela shtaba Zapadnogo Osobogo voennogo okruga upolnomochennomu Osobogo otdela NKVD Zapadnogo fronta o rabote etogo punkta pered nachalom i vo vremia voiny, 4 ianvaria 1942 g.," OGB, 1942/1, 19.

166. Ibid., 20.

167. Ibid.

168. Ibid., 21.

169. Ibid.

170. The FSB view of this document is worth citing: "The present document is the latest in a series which graphically shows the lack of trust with which even officials in the intelligence agencies in the border districts, and, moreover, in Moscow related to reports about aggres-sion being planned by Hitler's troops. Among the very highest echelons of power the most valuable information about Germany's forthcoming armed aggression against the Soviet Union was considered to be false and provocative. It was precisely this approach to the assessment of exceptionally important information concerning the security of the state that was also one of the main reasons of Red Army failures in the first days of the war." OGB, 1942/1, 24, notes.

171. Document 1229-PS, in IMT, Blue Series, XXVII:72.

172. № 655, "Iz neopublikovannykh vospominanii marshala Sovetskogo soiuza G. K. Zhukova, ne pozdnee 1965 g.," 1941 god, 2:502.

Chapter 5. NKVD Operations during Barbarossa, 1941–1942

1. № 431, "Ukaz Presidium Verkhov-nogo Soveta SSSR obob"edinenii Narod-nogo komissariata vnutrennikh del i Narodnogo komissariata gosudarst-vennoi bezopasnosti v edinyi Narodnyi komissariat vnutrennykh del, 20 iiulia 1941 g.," OGB, 1941/1, 372–373.

2. № 284, "Direktiva NKGB SSSR № 127/5809 o meropriiatiiakh organov gos-bezopasnosti v sviazi s nachavshimisia voennymi deistviiami s Germaniei, 22 iiunia 1941 g.," OGB, 1941/1, 35.

3. № 309, "Direktiva NKGB SSSR № 136 o zadachakh organov gosbezopas-nosti v usloviiakh voennogo vremeni', 24 iiunia 1941 g.," OGB, 1941/1, 67–68.

4. Ibid., 67.

5. Ibid.

6. See Stéphane Courtois et al., The Black Book of Communism: Crimes, Terror,

Repression, trans. Jonathan Murphy and Mark Kramer (London: Harvard University Press, 1999), 106.

7. № 285, "Direktiva Narodnogo komissara vnutrennikh del SSSR i Prokurora SSSR № 221 o perevode lagerei, tiurem kolonii na voennoe polozhenie i provedenii drugikh meropriiatii v sviazi s nachalom voiny', 22 iiunia 1941," *OGB*, 1941/1, 36.

8. Ibid.

9. № 289, "Plan agenturno-operativnykh meropriiatii UNKGB i UNKVD po g. Moskvei Moskovskoi oblasti po obespecheniiu gosudarstvennoi bezopasnosti v g. Moskve i Moskovskoi oblasti v sviazi s nachavshimisia voennymi deistviiami mezhdu SSSR i Germaniei, 22 iiunia 1941 g.," *OGB*, 1941/1, 44–47.

10. № 316, "Prikaz № 1 nachal'nika garnizona g. Moskvy ob obespechenii obshchestvennogo poriadka i gosudarstvennoi bezopasnosti v g. Moskve, 25 iiunia 1941 g.," *OGB*, 1941/1, 79–80.

11. № 323, "Direktiva NKGB SSSR № 148 ob areste i predanii sudy voennogo tribunala rasprostranitelei panicheskikh slukhov, pytaiushchikhsia dezorganizovat' tyl, 26 iiunia 1941 g.," *OGB*, 1941/1, 86.

12. № 373, "Ukaz Prezidiuma Verkhovnogo Soveta Soiuza SSR ob otvestvennosti za rasprostranenie v voennoe vremia lozhnykh slukhov, vozbuzhdaiushchikh trevogu sredi naseleniia, 6 iiulia 1941 g.," *OGB*, 1941/1, 204.

13. № 328, "Iz dokladnoi zapiski nachal'nika UNKGB po Zhitomirskoi oblasti № Zh/491/1 v NKGB SSSR i NKGB Ukrainskaia SSR o provodimykh meropriiatiiakh v sviazi s nachalom voennykh deistvii, 27 iiunia 1941 g.," *OGB*, 1941/1, 93–95.

14. Ibid., 94.

15. Ibid.

16. № 313, "Postanovlenie Politbiuro TsK VKP (b) o sdache naseleniem radiopriemnykh i peredaiushchikh ustroistv, 25 iiunia 1941 g.," *OGB*, 1941/1, 75–76.

17. № 306, "Postanovlenie TsK VKP (b) i SNK SSSR o sozdanii i zadachakh Sovetskogo Informatsionnogo Biuro, 24 iiunia 1941 g.," *OGB*, 1941/1, 63.

18. № 332, "Prikaz NKGB SSSR, NKVD SSSR i Prokuratury SSSR № 00246/00833/PR/59ss o poriadke privlecheniia k otvetstvennosti izmennikov Rodiny i chlenov ikh semei, 28 iiunia 1941 g.," *OGB*, 1941/1, 114–115.

19. Ibid., 115, notes.

20. № 337, "Direktiva Sovnarkoma Soiuza SSR i TsK VKP (b) № P509 partiinym sovetskim organizatsiiam prifrontovykh oblastei, 29 iiunia 1941 g.," *OGB*, 1941/1, 121–123.

21. Ibid., 123, notes.

22. A. N. IAkovlev et al., eds., *1941 god, v 2-knigakh*, in the series "Demokratiia," *Rossiia. XX VEK, Dokumenty* (Moscow: Mezhdunarodnyi fond, 1998), 2:455.

23. Ibid., 459.

24. Ibid., 468.

25. № 378, "Postanovlenie 3-go Upravleniia NKO SSSR na arest Pavlova D. G., 6 iiulia 1941 g.," *OGB*, 1941/1, 210–213. Opposition to the general line of the party concerning collectivization was known as the right deviation (*pravyi uklon*) and was the ideological heresy attributed to Nikolai Bukharin, Aleksei Rykov, and Mikhail Tomsky. Any association with this heresy and its proponents was very dengerous.

26. Ibid., 211.

27. Ibid., 215, notes.

28. Ibid., 211.

29. Ibid.

30. Ibid., 212.

31. Heinz Guderian, *Erinnerungen eines Soldaten* [1950], 9 Auflage (Neckergemünd: Kurt Vowinkel Verlag, 1976), 74. There is a marked lack of biographical detail on Krivoshein from 1940 to 1953, when he retired or was forced to retire. This may indicate that he was implicated in some of Stalin's crimes, along with a number of other officials.

32. OGB, 1941/1, № 378, 212.

33. Ibid.

34. Ibid., 213.

35. Ibid.

36. Aleksandr IUr'evich Vatlin, *Terror raionnogo masshtaba: «Massovye operatsii» NKVD v Kuntsevskom paione Moskovskoi oblasti 1937–1938 gg.* (Moscow: Rossiiskaia politicheskaia entsiklopediia [ROSSPEN], 2004), 60.

37. № 408, "Postanovlenie Gosudarstvennogo Komiteta Oborony № GKO-169ss (№ 00381) ob areste i predanii sudu voennogo tribunala byvshego komanduiushchego Zapadnym frontom generala armii Pavlova D. G., nachal'nika shtaba Zapadnogo fronta general-maiora Klimovskikh V. E. idrugikh, 16 iiulia 1941 g.," OGB, 1941/1, 333.

38. Ibid.

39. № 435, "Postanovlenie sledchasti Upravleniia osobykh otedelov NKVD SSSR ob ob"edinenii sledstvennykh del po obvineniiu Pavlova D. G., Klimovskikh V. E., Grigor'eva A. T. i Korobkova A. A. v odno sledstvennoe delo, 21 iiulia 1941 g.," OGB, 1941/1, 377–378.

40. № 436, "Obvinitel'noe zakliuchenie po delu Pavlova D. G., Klimovskikh V. E., Grigor'eva A. T. i Korobkova A. A. 21 iiulia 1941 g.," OGB, 1941/1, 379.

41. Ibid., notes.

42. Ibid., 379.

43. № 437, "Protokol sudebnogo zasedaniia Voennoi kollegii Verkhovnogo suda SSSR po delu Pavlova D. G., Klimovskikh V. E., Grigor'eva A. T. i Korobkova A. A., 22 iiulia 1941 g.," OGB, 1941/1, 382.

44. Ibid.

45. Ibid.

46. Ibid.

47. Ibid.

48. Ibid., 383.

49. Ibid.

50. Ibid., 383–384.

51. Ibid., 384.

52. Ibid.

53. Ibid., 385.

54. Ibid.

55. Ibid., 386.

56. Ibid., 387.

57. Ibid.

58. Ibid., 388.

59. Ibid., 389.

60. Ibid., 390.

61. Ibid., 391.

62. Ibid., emphasis added.

63. № 438, "Prigovor Voennoi Kollegii Verkhovnogo suda SSSR po delu Pavlova D. G., Klimovskikh V. E., Grigor'eva A. T. i Korobkova A. A., 22 iiulia 1941 g.," OGB, 1941/1, 392–393.

64. Pavlov, Klimovskikh, Grigor'ev, and Korobkov were all shot. Kosobutskii was sentenced to ten years in a labor camp; Salikhov was sentenced to ten years in prison; Kurochkin received an eight-year sentence that was suspended until the end of the war, and he died in battle; Galaktionov was shot; Eliseev received a ten-year sentence that was suspended until the end of the war, was demoted and sent to the front. OGB, 1941/1, 334–335, notes. Pavlov and others

were posthumously rehabilitated on 31 July 1957. Ibid., 394, notes.

65. № 617, "Predpisanie narkoma vnutrennikh del SSSR № 2756/B sotrudniku osobykh poruchenii spetsgruppy NKVD SSSR o rasstrele 25 zakliuchennykh v g. Kuibysheve, 18 oktiabria 1941 g.," OGB, 1941/2, 215–220.

66. An exceptionally detailed account of the purges of military figures before and after the German invasion can be found in N. S. Cherushev, *Udar po svoim: Krasnaia armiia 1938–1941* (Moscow: Veche, 2003). Among other things, the author catalogs the destructive role played by Mekhlis in undermining the authority of commanders.

67. № 355, "Vystuplenie po radio Predsedatelia Gosudarstvennogo Komiteta Oborony I. V. Stalina, 3 iiulia 1941 g.," OGB, 1941/1, 164.

68. № 415, "Iz Postanovleniia TsK VKP (b) ob organizatsii bor'by v tylu germanskikh voisk, 18 iiulia 1941 g.," OGB, 1941/1, 343–345.

69. № 455, "Direktiva UNKGB i UNKVD po Kalininskoi oblasti № 807 nachal'nikam MPO NKGB, GO i PO NKVD o merakh po uluchsheniiu organizatsii partizanskikh otriadov i diversionnykh grupp, napravliaemykh v tyl protivnika, 29 iiulia 1941 g.," OGB, 1941/1, 417.

70. Ibid., 417–418.

71. № 368, "Iz dokladnoi zapiski NKGB BSSR v NKGB SSSR i NKVD SSSR ob organizatsii partizanskikh otriadov i grupp, 5 iiulia 1941 g.," OGB, 1941/1, 188.

72. Ibid., 192.

73. Ibid.

74. № 391, "Zapiska sekretaria TsK KP(b) Belorussii, chlena Voennogo soveta Zapadnogo fronta P. K. Ponoma-renko v TsK VKP(b) o razvitii partizanskogo dvizheniia na territorii respubliki, ne pozdnee 12 iiulia 1941 g.," OGB, 1941/1, 299.

75. Ibid., 300.

76. Ibid.

77. Ibid.

78. № 596, "Dokladnaia zapiska NKVD Ukrainskaia SSR № 40/378 v TsK KP (b) Ukrainy o deiatel'nosti istrebitel'nykh batal'onov i partizanskikh otriadov za iiul'–sentiabr' 1941 g., 6 oktiabria 1941 g.," OGB, 1941/2, 176.

79. Ibid., 177.

80. Ibid., 179.

81. The NKVD also made great efforts to ascertain the nature of the German regime in the occupied territories. After Soviet troops had abandoned Kiev, Poltava, Sumy, and Khar'kov, the NKVD planned to send lone agents or very small groups, consisting of no more than three persons, to these occupied cities. Their specific tasks were to ascertain (1) the state, national, and agricultural policies of the Germans in the occupied areas; (2) the state of the economy (industry, transport, agriculture); (3) German propaganda and its form (newspapers, leaflets, spoken) and the Germans' and the authorities attitudes toward religion; (4) attitudes of the local population—workers, collective farm workers, and intelligentsia—and the Germans toward deserters; (5) German material provisions for the winter campaign; (6) the political morale of German troops; (7) the effectiveness of Bolshevik propaganda and the political morale of the local population and their attitudes toward Soviet power; (8) the activities of partisan detachments in the enemy rear and what they required;

and (9) the disposition, movement, and strength of enemy troops. See № 673, "Plan meropriiatii operativnoi gruppy pri Voennom sovete IUgo-Zapadnogo fronta po sboru razvedyvatel'nykh dannykh o polozhenii v oblastiakh Ukrainy, vremenno zakhvachennykh nemetskimi voiskami, 12 noiabria 1941 g.," OGB, 1941/2, 302–303.

82. OGB, 1941/2, № 596, 180.

83. Ibid.

84. Ibid.

85. Ibid., 181.

86. Ibid.

87. Ibid., 182.

88. № 540, "Dokladnaia zapiska sekretaria Orlovskogo obkoma VKP(b) I. A. Khripunova 1-mu sekretariu Orlovskogo obkoma VKP(b), chlenu Voennogo soveta Brianskogo fronta V. I. Boitstovu o partizanskikh otriadakh, deistvuiushchikh v tylu protivnika, 8 sentiabria 1941 r.," OGB, 1941/2, 40.

89. Ibid., 42.

90. Ibid., 46.

91. OGB, 1941/2, 49, notes, citing T. A. Logunova, *Partiinoe podpol'e i partizanskoe dvizhenie v zapadnykh i tsentral'nykh oblastiakh RSFSR. Iiul' 1941–1943 gg.* (Moscow: Izdatel'stvo Moskovskogo universiteta, 1973).

92. № 307, "Postanovlenie Politbiuro TsK VKP(b) o meropriiatiiakh po bor'be s parashiutnymi desantami i diversantami protivnika v prifrontovoi polose, 24 iiunia 1941 g.," OGB, 1941/1, 64–65.

93. № 315, "Prikaz NKVD SSSR № 00804 o meropriiatiiakh po bor'be s parashiutnymi desantami i diversantami protivnika v prifrontovoi polose, 25 iiunia 1941 g.," OGB, 1941/1, 77–79.

94. № 376, "Direktiva NKGB SSSR № 190 organam NKGB prifrontovoi polosy o podgotovke kadrov signal'shchikov dlia ostavleniia na territorii, zakhvachennoi protivnikom 6 iiulia 1941 g.," OGB, 1941/1, 206.

95. № 473, "Ukazanie nachal'nika okhrany tyla Severnogo fronta nachal'nikam okhrany voiskovogo tyla 7, 8, 14 i 23-i armii ob usilenii bor'by s parashiutnymi desantami protivnika 6 avgusta 1941 g.," OGB, 1941/1, 456–457.

96. № 501, "Iz ukazaniia № 51 transportnogo otdela NKVD zheleznoi dorogi im. L. M. Kaganovicha otdeleniiam i operpunktam TO NKVD o preduprezhenii i presechenii vrazhdebnykh proiavlenii na transporte, 23 avgusta 1941 g.," OGB, 1941/1, 509.

97. Ibid., 511–512.

98. Before the war there were two categories of the Germans in the Soviet Union. The first category included communists who had fled Germany after Hitler came to power. They were regarded with profound suspicion and were often referred to as *chuzhie v nashei strane* (aliens in our country). Vatlin, *Terror raionnogo masshtaba*, 175. The second category included Soviet citizens who were ethnic Germans. They were not trusted either, as indicated by NKVD Order № 00439, which provided for the arrest of all German citizens working in defense factories. Ibid., 180. The mere existence of this order demonstrates that Germans and Germany were seen as a threat.

99. № 519, "Soobshchenie № 4 zamestitelia narkoma vnutrennikh del SSSR V. N. Merkulova narkomu vnutrennikh del SSSR L. P. Beria s kratkim izlozheniem plana meropriiatii po obiazatel'noi evakuatsii nemetskogo i finskogo naseleniia iz Leningradskoi

oblasti, 30 avgusta 1941 g.," *OGB*, 1941/1, 559.

100. Ibid., 560.

101. № 532, "Postanovlenie Gosudarstvennogo Komiteta Oborony № GKO-636ss o pereselenii nemtsev izg. Moskvy i Moskovskoi oblastii Rostovskoi oblasti, 6 sentiabria 1941 g.," *OGB*, 1941/2, 25.

102. № 569, "Dokladnaia zapiska zamestitelia narkoma vnutrennikh del SSSR B. Z. Kobulova v NKVD SSSR o reszul'tatakh operatsii po pereseleniiu nemtsev iz Moskvy i raionov Moskovskoi oblasti, 20 sentiabria 1941 g.," *OGB*, 1941/2, 123.

103. Although the numbers given total 479,891, two documents cite the figure 479,841. See № 504, "Pis'mo NKVD SSSR № 2514/B v TsK VKP (b) s predstavleniem proekta postanovleniia SNK SSSR iTsK VKP (b) o poriadke pereseleniia iz Respubliki Nemtsev Povol'zh'ia, Saratovskoi i Stalingradskoi oblastei, 25 avgusta 1941 g.," *OGB*, 1941/1, 521.

104. Ibid., 522.

105. № 507, "Ukaz Prezidiuma Verkhovnogo Soveta SSSR o pereselenii nemtsev, prozhivaiushchikh v raionakh Povolzh'ia, 28 avgusta 1941 g.," *OGB*, 1941/1, 539–540, emphasis added.

106. The NKVD applied the principle of collective guilt not just to deportees but also to German prisoners of war. Article 46 of the Convention Relative to the Treatment of Prisoners, with Annex (Geneva, 27 July 1929) is quite clear on this point: "Collective penalties for individual acts are also prohibited." See League of Nations Treaty Series, vol. 118, no. 2734, pp. 343–409. Article 11 also stipulates that "all collective disciplinary measures affecting food are prohibited." Of course, it could be argued that ethnic Germans who were Soviet citizens were not prisoners of war and therefore were not protected by the provisions of Article 46. However, that is not a satisfactory defense, since it is clear from NKVD documents that all Volga Germans were being punished because they were all suspected of being enemy agents and saboteurs. Thus, the principle being applied to Volga Germans by the NKVD was no different from that being applied to Soviet partisans and military commissars by the Germans. Volga Germans were deemed to be *potential* or actual spies and saboteurs and were punished collectively.

107. № 559, "Dokladnaia zapiska Stalingradskogo oblastnogo operativnogo shtaba v NKVD SSSR ob itogakh operatsii po pereselenii nemtsev za predely oblasti, 15 sentiabria 1941 g.," *OGB*, 1941/2, 107.

108. Ibid., 110–111.

109. Ibid., 111.

110. Courtois et al., *Black Book of Communism*, 88.

111. *OGB*, 1941/2, № 559, 110–111.

112. Ibid., 111.

113. № 570, "Dokladnaia zapiska NKVD SSSR № 2639/B v Gosudarstvennyi Komitet Oborony SSSR ob itogakh pereseleniia nemtsev iz byvshei Respubliki Nemtsev Povol'zh'ia, Saratovskoi i Stalingradskoi oblastei, 21 sentiabria 1941 g.," *OGB*, 1941/2, 124–125, emphasis added.

114. № 558, "Soobshchenie UNKVD Moskovskoi oblasti № 1/692 v NKVD SSSR ob okonchanii pereseleniia lits nemetskoi natsional'nosti iz raionov oblasti, 15 sentiabria 1941 g.," *OGB*, 1941/2, 106.

115. № 571, "Dokladnaia zapiska NKVD SSSR № 2640/B v Gosudarstvennyi Komitet Oborony s predstavleniem

proekta postanovleniia GKO ob areste i pereselenii v Kazakhstan nemtsev, prozhivaiushchikh v Krasnodarskom, Ordzhonikidzevskom kraiakh, Tul'skoi oblasti, Kabardino-Balkarskoi i Severo-Osetinskoi ASSR, 21 sentiabria 1941 g.," *OGB*, 1941/2, 125.

116. № 573, "Dokladnaia zapiska NKVD SSSR № 2642/B v Gosudarstvennyi Komitet Oborony s predstavleniem proekta postanovleniia GKO o pereselenii nemtsev iz Zaporozhskoi, Stalinskoii Voroshilovgradskoi oblastei, 22 sentiabria 1941 g.," *OGB*, 1941/2, 127.

117. № 609, "Prikaz NKVD SSSR № 001488 o meropriiatiiakh po pereseleniiu nemtsev iz Voronezhskoi oblasti, 11 oktiabria 1941 g.," *OGB*, 1941/2, 205.

118. № 612, "Prikaz NKVD SSSR № 001507 o meropriiatiiakh po pereseleniiu nemtsev iz Gor'kovskoi oblasti, 15 oktiabria 1941 g.," *OGB*, 1941/2, 208–209.

119. № 631, "Prikaz NKVD SSSR № 001529 o meropriiatiiakh po pereseleniiu nemtsev iz Dagestanskoi i Checheno-Ingushskoi ASSR, 24 oktiabria 1941 g.," *OGB*, 1941/2, 237–238.

120. № 657, "Prikaz NKVD SSSR № 001543 o meropriiatiiakh po pereseleniiu nemtsev iz Kalmytskoi ASSR, 3 noiabria 1941 g.," *OGB*, 1941/2, 269.

121. № 700, "Prikaz NKVD SSSR № 001790/k o meropriiatiiakh po pereseleniiu nemtsev iz Kuibyshevskoi oblasti, 26 noiabria 1941 g.," *OGB*, 1941/2, 355–356.

122. Christian Hartmann, *Wehrmacht im Ostkrieg: Front und militärisches Hinterland* (Munich: R. Oldenbourg Verlag, 2010), 768.

123. *OGB*, 1941/1, № 355, 163.

124. Hartmann, *Wehrmacht im Ostkrieg*, 772.

Chapter 6. 20th Panzer Division and the Diary of Gefreiter H. C. von Wiedebach-Nostitz

1. Rolf Hinze, *Hitze, Frost und Pulverdampf: Der Schicksalsweg der 20. Panzer-Division* [1981] (Meerbusch: Dr. Rolf Hinze, 1996), 21.

2. Ibid., 23.

3. Ibid., 32.

4. Ibid., 55.

5. Ibid., 74.

6. Ibid., 92.

7. Ibid., 91.

8. *Effects of Climate on Combat in European Russia*, CMH Pub. 104-6 (Washington, D.C.: Center of Military History, US Army, 1952), 16.

9. Hinze, *Hitze, Frost und Pulverdampf*, 102, emphasis in original. Von Thoma went on to serve in North Africa and was captured by the British at El Alamein in November 1942.

10. Ibid., 126.

11. Hitler's address ended with the following: "German soldiers! With all this in mind you are entering into a hard struggle and bear a heavy responsibility. . . . *The fate of Europe, the future of the German state, the existence of our people lies in your hands alone from now on. May the Lord help us all in this struggle!*" See "Aufruf an die Soldaten der Ostfront vom 22.06.1941," in *„Unternehmen Barbarossa": Der deutsche Überfall auf die Sowjetunion 1941, Berichte, Analysen, Dokumente.*, ed. Gerd R. Ueberschär and Wolfram Wette (Paderborn: Ferdinand Schöningh, 1984), 319–323, emphasis in original.

12. *Der Gasmann* (The Gasman, 1941) was a German comedy that had just been released.

13. *Der wilde Jäger* (The Wild Huntsman) was a popular German poem written by Gottfried Bürger.

14. The official Spanish designation for the Blue Division was División Española de Voluntarios. It was known as the Blue Division because of the blue shirts worn by the Falangists who made up the bulk of the recruits. It served with distinction on the Eastern Front, suffering heavy casualties and earning the respect and admiration of the Germans.

15. *Oberfunkmeister* is the chief radio instructor or chief radio officer.

16. *Frau Luna*, written by Carl Lincke, was first performed in 1899.

17. *Willi Forsts Operette*, written by Willi Forst, was first performed in 1940.

18. The diarist refers to these fighters as Gunicane. These may well have been British Hurricanes, which were delivered to the Soviet Union.

19. Hinze cites an incident in a village on the night of 23–24 December 1941 that bears some resemblance to that recorded by von Wiedebach-Nostitz: "To begin with, we drove along the village street and then we went crazy; that is we opened fire with all our weapons, like madmen, setting the houses ablaze and made Ivan really mad. That had, firstly, the purpose of illuminating the battle area, and, secondly, to force the Russians out into the cold and to break their morale. This was not without success, especially the sudden appearance of tanks which clearly paralyzed the enemy. He suffered losses. Meanwhile, the situation had become very uncomfortable for the enemy and compelled him to move out of the village and to withdraw. Later, in the light of the rising sun, the fleeing brown forms, which stood out very well against the snow, presented us with an impressive sight. Judging from the weight of fire returned, enemy strength was probably

about a battalion, though it may have been up to regiment strength. In long lines the Russians plodded through the knee-deep snow, often tripping on their long greatcoats. Eventually, our lack of ammunition and the cover offered to the fleeing Russians by valleys and folds in the land prevented the complete wiping out of the enemy. Many of them failed to reach the cover of the wood to where they were heading. They suffered very high losses." Hinze, *Hitze, Frost und Pulverdampf*, 103. Hinze makes no mention of any losses suffered by civilians, but it is highly likely that some civilians, caught between the two armies, were killed; others were rendered homeless, which in the winter conditions amounted to a death sentence.

Chapter 7. The German Invasion in Soviet-Russian War Literature

1. "Order of the People's Commissar of Defense of the USSR," *Pravda*, 1 May 1941, 1.

2. Ibid.

3. *Tacitus: The Annals of Imperial Rome*, trans. Michael Grant (Harmondsworth, U.K.: Penguin Books, 1989), 121. In the original Latin, the aphorism attributed to Tiberius is found in book 3, paragraph 6: *principes mortalis, rem publicam aeternum esse*. One Russian translation would be *praviteli smertny—gosudarstvo vechno* (rulers are mortal, the state is eternal). If Tacitus is the inspiration for the title, Grossman's use of "people" instead of "state" is making a nonideological point. Grossman's point is also made by Viktor Kravchenko with regard to the costs of Soviet industrialization: "whatever our secret political attitudes, we felt that Stalins come and go, but Russia remains forever, and it was the

industrial future of Russia that was at stake." Viktor Kravchenko, *I Chose Freedom: The Personal and Political Life of a Soviet Official* [1946] (New Brunswick, N.J.: Transaction Publishers, 1989), 195.

4. Vasilii Grossman, "Narod bessmerten," in *Gody voiny* (Moscow: OGIZ, 1946), 40–41.

5. Richard Pipes, *Russia under the Bolshevik Regime, 1919–1924* (London: Fontana Press, 1992), 364.

6. Bogarev anticipates Nikolai Krymov, who appears in both *For a Just Cause* and *Life and Fate*. Both men want to be military commissars, not merely functionaries in the Red Army's political directorate, and both are trapped in the ideological paradigm of Marxism-Leninism. In *The People Are Immortal* Bogarev's certainties are left intact; in *Life and Fate* Krymov's are shattered.

7. Grossman, *Gody voiny* (1946), 9.

8. Ibid.

9. Ibid., 15.

10. Ibid., 34.

11. Ibid., 34–35.

12. Ibid., 68.

13. Ibid., 103.

14. Ibid.

15. Ibid., 74.

16. Vasilii Grossman, *Gody voiny* (Moscow: Izadatel'stvo Pravda, 1989), 314.

17. The four diaries are (1) August–September 1941, Central Front: Gomel', Mena (Chernigovshchina), the road to Brianskii; (2) September 1941, Briansk Front; (3) September 1941; and (4) South-Western Front, winter 1941–1942.

18. Grossman, *Gody voiny* (1989), 247.

19. Ibid. Taking the lead from Stalin's speech of 3 July 1941, the Soviet mass media quickly made historical allusions to 1812. Grossman, in contrast, seems to argue that the German invasion of 1941–1942 may be sui generis: "There is this Kutuzov myth about 1812. The bloodied body of war is dressed in snow-white clothing of ideological, strategic and artistic conventions. There are those who have seen the retreat, and those who have dressed it up. There's the myth of the first and the second Great Fatherland Wars." Ibid., 314. This suggests to me that Grossman fully understands the difference between propaganda and an honest depiction of the war and might well imply some criticism of his own work—*Narod bessmerten*, for example.

20. Ibid., 248.

21. Stalin refers to Boldin as follows: "Deputy commander of the troops of the Western Front General-Lieutenant Boldin, finding himself surrounded by German-fascist soldiers in the area of the 10th Army near Belostok, organized detachments from those units of the Red Army which remained in the enemy's rear and which in the course of 45 days fought in the enemy's rear and broke through to the main forces of the Western Front. They destroyed the headquarters of two German regiments, 26 tanks, 1,049 light, transport and headquarters vehicles, 147 motorcycles, 5 artillery batteries, 4 mortars, 15 mounted machine guns, 3 submachine guns, 1 plane on an aerodrome and a dump of aviation bombs. More than 1,000 German soldiers and officers were killed. On 11 August General-Lieutenant Boldin attacked the Germans from the rear, broke through the German front line, and having joined up with our troops, extricated 1,654 armed Red Army soldiers and commanders, of whom 103 were wounded, from encirclement." "Prikaz Stavki verkhovnogo glavnogo

komandovaniia Krasnoi armii', № 270, 16 avgusta 1941 goda," *Voenno-istoricheskii zhurnal* 9 (1988): 26–28.

22. Grossman, *Gody voiny* (1989), 276–277.

23. Ibid., 311.

24. Ibid., 259.

25. Ibid., 297.

26. Ibid.

27. Ibid., 299.

28. Ibid. The incident involving Evstreev is used by Grossman in *Life and Fate*. See *Zhizn' i sud'ba* (Moscow: Sovetskii pisatel', 1990), 477. However, the following diary entry is inherently contradictory: "Political morale is good: Torokov, a deserter, has been shot in front of the assembled troops." Grossman, *Gody voiny* (1989), 299.

29. Grossman, *Gody voiny* (1989), 273.

30. Ibid., 296.

31. Ibid., 269.

32. Ibid., 313–314.

33. Ibid., 254.

34. Ibid.

35. Grossman, *Gody voiny* (1946), 39.

36. Grossman, *Gody voiny* (1989), 307.

37. Ibid., 285.

38. Ibid.

39. This is supported by the ideological lapse of a communist who seems to find more comfort in God than in Marx and Lenin: "The communist, Evseev, lost his notebook. Some Red Army soldiers found this notebook. A prayer which had been copied out was found inside it." Ibid., 307.

40. Two sequels were published after the war, *Neskol'ko dnei* (Several Days [1960]) and *Rezerv generala Panfilova* (General Panfilov's Reserve [1960]).

41. Aleksandr Bek, *Volokolamskoe shosse* (Moscow: Voennoe izdatel'stvo, 1959), 8.

42. Ibid., 17. Another historical inaccuracy occurs when Momysh-Uly records the appointment of a commissar: "Tolstunov had arrived in the battalion for an undefined period. To tell the truth, I am obliged to acknowledge the fact that I interpreted his presence as imposing something of a limitation on my authority. According to the rules Tolstunov enjoyed no rights in the battalion; he was not my commissar (at that time there were no commissars in the battalions)." Ibid., 155. Bearing in mind that this is October 1941, a year before the order removing dual command and abolishing the institution of commissars (9 October 1942), Momysh-Uly's claim about there being no commissars is wrong. With the Germans closing in on Moscow, and given the rate of desertion and low morale among Red Army troops, one would expect the regime to make full use of military commissars and to ensure that *revolutionary* order and discipline were imposed alongside *military* order and discipline. I suggest that Momysh-Uly's attitude toward the commissar—entirely correct, since he does represent a challenge to military authority—was formulated by Bek based on the later order, not the situation that obtained in October 1941.

43. Bek, *Volokolamskoe shosse*, 18.

44. Ibid., 197.

45. Ibid., 27–28.

46. Ibid., 91.

47. Ibid., 26.

48. Ibid., 31.

49. Ibid., 129.

50. Ibid.

51. Alexander Isaevich Solzhenitsyn, *Rossiia v obvale* [Russia in Ruins] (Moscow: Russkii put', 1998), 152.

52. Bek, *Volokolamskoe shosse*, 98.

53. Ibid., 77.

54. Ibid., 137.

55. Ibid., 223.

56. Konstantin Simonov, *Zhivye i mertvye* (Moscow: Gosudarstvennoe izdatel'stvo khudozhestvennoi literatury, 1961), 3.

57. Ibid., 13.

58. Ibid., 51.

59. Ibid.

60. Ibid., 52. The wording "caught unawares" (*zastat' vrasplokh*) is precisely what Timoshenko used in his *Pravda* article in which, he assures, the Soviet people will not happen with Stalin at the helm.

61. Amidst the chaos of the retreat, some Soviet officers are discussing the situation, and one of them makes the connection with August 1914: "The August 1914 catastrophe is studied in the academies and they make fun of Samsonov, but about themselves. . . ." Ibid., 31. The matter is not pursued, but Simonov manages to make the connection between tsarist and Soviet military incompetence, or at least to imply that one exists. In *August 1914* Solzhenitsyn makes any number of explicit parallels between Stalin's failure in 1941 and Samsonov's lack of military professionalism in 1914. Solzhenitsyn's assessment of the time-servers and careerists in the tsarist army and officers promoted beyond their ability clearly has great relevance for the rapid rise of Kozyrev, the behavior of Baranov, and the arrest of Serpilin in *The Living and the Dead*. Regardless of political systems, bureaucracies retain features in common.

62. Simonov, *Zhivye i mertvye*, 102.

63. Ibid.

64. Ibid., 398.

65. Ibid., 400.

66. Ibid., 19.

67. Ibid., 22.

68. Ibid., 20.

69. To begin with, in the encirclement phase there is some friction between Serpilin and the newly appointed regimental commissar Shmakov. Serpilin suspects that Shmakov's appointment may have something to do with his arrest and incarceration before the war. Given that remnants of the division have been encircled, there is suspicion that Serpilin might try to exact revenge and desert to the Germans (as Vlasov would do in the summer of 1942). Shmakov's appointment as regimental commissar occurs as a result of the Supreme Soviet decree issued on 16 July 1941, providing for the reintroduction of commissars in the Red Army. But despite any gloss from Simonov, the reinstitution of dual command does not suggest that all is well between the party and the army. On the contrary, it suggests that the party fears a collapse among the army and that senior officers might act to remove Stalin and the party apparatus. One month later, reinforcing this decree, Stalin issued Order № 270.

70. Simonov, *Zhivye i mertvye*, 174.

71. Ibid., 175.

72. Ibid.

73. Ibid., 178.

74. Shmakov hands the leaflet to Serpilin with the following comment: "But you read it, it's not contagious!" Ibid., 149. Any Soviet soldier found to be in possession of one of these leaflets was subject to arrest on suspicion of planning to desert. Simonov's treatment of this theme is obviously disingenuous.

75. Ibid., 179.

76. Ibid., 200.

77. Ibid., 143.

78. Ibid., 35.

79. Ibid., 70. Later, Simonov writes: "At first, it seemed to Sintsov that the truth about war was somewhere in the middle. But later he grasped that was not true; and that both the good and the bad were related by various people. But they merited or did not merit to be trusted not according *to what* they said but according *to how* they said something." Ibid., 65, emphasis in original. As a reliable criterion for establishing a speaker's veracity, this does not inspire confidence; politicians at all times and in all places exploit delivery in order to inspire, deny, prevaricate, and lie. Soon after Sintsov has drawn this conclusion, he listens to Stalin's 3 July speech and concludes that it marks "the end of illusions." Ibid., 67.

80. Ibid., 152.

Chapter 8. Viktor Suvorov, the Stalin Attack Thesis, and the Start of World War II

1. Viktor Suvorov, *Ledokol: Kto nachal vtoruiu mirovuiu voinu?* (Moscow: Izdatel'skii dom, Novoe vremia, 1993), 42.

2. Ibid., 18.

3. Ibid., 32, emphasis in original.

4. Ibid., 33.

5. Ibid., 123.

6. Ibid., 124.

7. Ibid., 142.

8. Ibid., 55.

9. Ibid., 55–56.

10. Ibid., 77.

11. See, for example, N. L. Volkovskii, ed., *Tainy i uroki zimnei voiny, 1939–1940, Po dokumentam rassekrechennykh arkhivov* (Sankt-Peterburg: Poligon, 2000).

12. Suvorov, *Ledokol*, 78.

13. Ibid., 88.

14. Ibid., 104.

15. Ibid.

16. Ibid., 173.

17. Ibid., 174, emphasis in original.

18. Ibid., 181.

19. A. N. IAkovlev et al., eds., *1941 god, v 2-knigakh,* in the series "Demokratiia," *Rossiia. XX VEK, Dokumenty* (Moscow: Mezhdunarodnyi fond, 1998), 2:295, notes, emphasis in original.

20. Suvorov, *Ledokol*, 182.

21. № 473, "Zapiska narkoma oborony SSSR i nachal'nika genshtaba Krasnoi Armii predsedateliu SNK SSSR I. V. Stalinu s soobrazheniiami po planu strategicheskogo razvertyvaniia vooruzhennykh sil Sovetskogo Soiuza na sluchai voiny s Germaniei i ee soiuznikami, b/n [ne ranee 15 maia 1941 g.]," *1941 god*, 2:215–220.

22. *1941 god*, 2:296, notes.

23. Ibid.

24. Suvorov, *Ledokol*, 182.

25. № 481, "Direktiva narkoma oborony SSSR i nachal'nika genshtaba krasnoi armii komanduiushchemu voiskami ZAPOVO, ne pozdnee 20 maia 1941 g.," *1941 god*, 2:228.

26. № 482, "Direktiva narkoma oborony SSSR i nachal'nika genshtaba krasnoi armii komanduiushchemu voiskami KOVO, ne pozdnee 20 maia 1941 g.," *1941 god*, 2:234.

27. № 483, "Direktiva narkoma oborony SSSR i nachal'nika genshtaba krasnoi armii komanduiushchemu voiskami odesskogo voennogo okruga, ne pozdnee 20 maia 1941 g.," *1941 god*, 2:240.

28. Suvorov, *Ledokol*, 182.

29. № 473, *1941 god*, 2:218.

30. Ibid., 219.

31. № 481, *1941 god*, 2:227.

32. Ibid.

33. № 547, "Direktiva narkoma

oborony SSSR i nachal'nika genshtaba Krasnoi Armii kommanduiushchemu voiskami ZAPOVO, № 504207ss, 12 iiunia 1941 g.," 1941 god, 2:356.

34. № 437, "Vystuplenie General'nogo sekretaria TsK VKP(b) I. V. Stalina pered vypusknikami voennykh akademii RKKA v Kremle', 5 maia 1941 g.," 1941 god, 2:158.

35. Ibid., 159.

36. Heinz Guderian, Erinnerungen eines Soldaten [1950], 9 Auflage (Neckargemünd: Kurt Vowinkel Verlag, 1976), 84.

37. № 437, 1941 god, 2:160.

38. Ibid.

39. Ibid.

40. Ibid., 161.

41. Ibid.

42. Ibid., 162.

43. Ibid.

44. Aleksei Popov, NKVD i partizanskoe dvizhenie (Moscow: OLMA-PRESS, 2003), 36–37.

45. Ibid., 37.

46. Suvorov, Ledokol, 309.

47. Ibid., 312.

48. Ibid., 313–314.

49. Ibid., 314.

50. Ibid., 325.

51. Ibid., 327.

52. Guderian, Erinnerungen eines Soldaten, 418.

53. Suvorov, Ledokol, 204.

54. Ibid., 206.

55. Ibid., 208.

56. № 382, "Donesenie zamestitelia nachal'nika 3-go Upravleniia NKO SSSR F. IA. Tutushkina I. V. Stalinu o poteriakh VVS Severo-Zapadnogo fronta v pervye dni voiny, 8 iiulia 1941," OGB, 1941/1, 220.

57. Ibid., 221. Detailed commentary attached to the report dated 8 July 1941 by the FSB archivists provides further insights into the devastating success of the Luftwaffe attacks. The basic statistics of the air assault are daunting. By the outset of hostilities, the Germans had concentrated 4,980 combat aircraft in the border regions. In the first hours of the air assault, twenty-six aerodromes in the Western Special Military District, twenty-three in the Kiev Special Military District, eleven in the Baltic Special Military District, and six in the Odessa Special Military District were attacked. Of the 1,200 aircraft lost by the Red Army on the first day of the invasion, the Western Special Military District lost 738 aircraft (62 percent). It has been argued that these devastating losses are attributable mainly to the fact that the Soviet military leadership had not managed to fully implement the Central Committee's resolution dated 25 February 1941, "O reorganizatsii aviatsionnykh sil Krasnoi Armii." It has also been acknowledged that there was an acute shortage of antitank and antiaircraft guns, which rendered the troops vulnerable to tank and air attacks. Such shortages of essential equipment do not support the view that Stalin was preparing to attack the German army. On the contrary, these failings suggest an armed forces in disarray. The late arrival of orders did not help. Another fatal contribution, as noted by the FSB archivists, was the presence of all kinds of conflicting rumors and views. For example, "A negative influence was the opinion which existed at that time that there would be no war; 'that Hitler is provoking us' and that 'we must not succumb to provocation.' Even after the war had started, several commanders considered that 'this is not a war but an

incident.'" *OGB*, 1941/1, № 382, 221–222. Again, such attitudes and indecision do not suggest an army imbued with offensive élan and about to attack the Germans.

58. Vasilii Grossman, *Gody voiny* (Moscow: Izadatel'stvo Pravda, 1989), 249.

59. Suvorov, *Ledokol*, 114.

60. Ibid., 304. Whereas Suvorov sees Stalin's assumption of the post of chairman of the Council of People's Commissars as a sign of hostility toward Germany, Weinberg argues that this act by Stalin "was regarded everywhere as a sign of a policy of further cooperation with Germany, designed to prevent war, and carried out by Stalin directly in person." Gerhard L. Weinberg, *Germany and the Soviet Union, 1939–1941* (Leiden: E. J. Brill, 1954), 162.

61. In his memoir of the 76th Infantry Division, Jochen Löser recalls that the troops entered a village populated by Germans—Swabians who had been brought to Russia by Catherine the Great. The villagers reported that the German-speaking parachutists who landed in the area were regarded as agents provocateurs. The assumption was that they had been sent by the NKVD to test the villagers' loyalty. See Jochen Löser, *Bittere Pflicht: Kampf und Untergang der 76. Berlin-Branderburgischen Infanterie Division* (Osnabrück: Biblio Verlag, 1986), 106.

62. Suvorov, *Ledokol*, 133.

63. Ibid., 248.

64. Ibid., 171–172.

65. Ibid., 142.

66. *OGB*, 1941/1, № 382, 220.

67. Suvorov, *Ledokol*, 280.

68. № Р31, "Iz akta o prieme narkomata oborony soiuza SSR S. K.

Timoshenko ot K. E. Voroshilova, 7 dekabria 1940 g.," *1941 god*, 2:622–631.

69. Ibid., 623.

70. Ibid.

71. Ibid.

72. Ibid., 624.

73. Ibid.

74. Ibid., 625.

75. Ibid.

76. Ibid.

77. Ibid., 626.

78. Ibid.

79. Ibid.

80. N. S. Cherushev, *Udar po svoim: Krasnaia armiia 1938–1941* (Moscow: Veche, 2003), 434.

81. Ibid., 435.

82. № Р31, *1941 god*, 2:627.

83. Ibid.

84. Ibid., 628.

85. Ibid., 629.

86. Ibid., 630, emphasis added.

87. Ibid.

88. Ibid.

89. Suvorov, *Ledokol*, 316.

90. Ibid., 317.

Chapter 9. The Legacy of *Unternehmen* Barbarossa

1. See Tyler Drumheller with Elaine Monaghan, *On the Brink: A Former CIA Chief Exposes How Intelligence Was Distorted in the Build-Up to the War in Iraq* (London: Politico's, 2007). The title of this book speaks for itself.

2. David M. Glantz, *Operation Barbarossa: Hitler's Invasion of Russia 1941* [2001] (Stroud, U.K.: History Press, 2012), 24.

3. Ibid., 26.

4. In 1939, at the start of the Winter War, Isserson had been appointed chief of staff of 7th Army. After the war he asked to be transferred back to his

prewar teaching post in the General Academy—a request that was approved. However, on 7 June 1941, one year after the publication of *New Forms of Combat*, he was arrested and charged with voting for a Trotskyite resolution in the 1920s and, more recently, participating in criminal operations in Finland during the Soviet-Finnish war. In essence, it was asserted that Isserson had failed to discharge his duties as chief of staff and that this caused the failure of Soviet operations against the Finns on the Karelian peninsula on 17 December 1939. At a subsequent tribunal, Isserson was sentenced to death. He appealed and was sentenced to ten years in a forced-labor camp and disenfranchised for an additional five years. Freed from exile in 1955, he died in Moscow in 1976. That Isserson was arrested two weeks before the Germans invaded—when the dangers he had warned of were well advanced, despite Stalin's inability and unwillingness to see them—suggests to me that Isserson's arrest was attributable more to his brilliant and, for Stalin, alarming analysis set out in *New Forms of Combat*, rather than any alleged professional misconduct while serving in Finland. In *New Forms of Combat* he had let it be known that his next project would be a study of the German campaign in France, a campaign that would once again demonstrate the inferiority of Soviet armored warfare doctrine and the importance of surprise. Had Isserson been permitted to return to teaching and scholarly pursuits in the summer of 1940, his study of the German campaign in France might well have provided another unwelcome and untimely warning for Stalin. For an account of Isserson's fate, see N. S. Cherushev, *Udar po svoim:*

Krasnaia armiia 1938–1941 (Moscow: Veche, 2003), 318–321.

5. G. K. Zhukov, *Vospominaniia i razmyshleniia* (Moscow: Izdatel'stvo agentstva pechati novosti, 1969), 272.

6. № 655, "Iz neopublikovannykh vospominanii marshala Sovetskogo Soiuza G. K. Zhukova, ne pozdnee 1965 g.," in *1941 god, v 2-knigakh*, ed. A. N. IAkovlev et al., in the series "Demokratiia," *Rossiia. XX VEK, Dokumenty* (Moscow: Mezhdunarodnyi fond, 1998), 2:505.

7. № 441, "Spetssoobshchenie razvedupravleniia genshtaba Krasnoi Armii o gruppirovke nemetskikh voisk na vostoke i ugo-vostoke na 5 maia 1941 g.," *1941 god*, 2:173.

8. Glantz, *Operation Barbarossa*, 27, emphasis in original.

9. Christopher Andrew and Vasilii Mitrokhin, *The Mitrokhin Archive: The KGB in Europe and the West* (London: Allen Lane, Penguin Press, 1999), 124.

10. S. I. Drobiazko, *Pod znamemani vraga: Antisovetskie formirovaniia v sostave germanskikh vooruzhennykh sil, 1941–1945 gg.* (Moscow: Eksmo, 2005), 62.

11. The Lokot experiment was set up by the commander of 2nd Panzer Army, Generaloberst Rudolf Schmidt, one of the Wehrmacht's more enlightened officers. This may explain why he was arrested by the NKVD in 1947 and sentenced to twenty-five years in a Soviet camp. High on the list of NKVD priorities would be the acquisition of the names of those Russians who worked and liaised with the Germans in setting up this autonomous zone.

12. Vasilii Grossman, *Zhizn' i sud'ba* [Life and Fate; 1988] (Moscow: Sovetskii pisatel', 1990), 165.

13. Glantz, *Operation Barbarossa*, 204.

14. Ibid., 205.

15. Heinz Guderian, *Erinnerungen eines Soldaten* [1950], 9 Auflage (Neckergemünd: Kurt Vowinkel Verlag, 1976), 181–182.

16. Erich von Manstein, *Verlorene Siege* [1955] (Bonn: Bernard & Graefe in der Mönch Verlagsgesellschaft mbH, 2011), 173.

17. Ibid.

18. Ibid., 174.

19. Colin S. Gray, *Another Bloody Century: Future Warfare* (London: Weidenfeld & Nicolson, 2005), 342–343.

20. Omer Bartov, The Eastern Front *1941–45: German Troops and the Barbarisation of Warfare*, 2nd ed. (Basingstoke, U.K.: Palgrave, 2001), 156.

SELECTED BIBLIOGRAPHY

Andrew, Christopher, and Vasilii Mitrokhin. *The Mitrokhin Archive: The KGB in Europe and the West.* London: Allen Lane, Penguin Press, 1999.

Applebaum, Anne. *Iron Curtain: The Crushing of Eastern Europe 1944–56.* London: Allen Lane, 2012.

Bartov, Omer. *The Eastern Front 1941–45: German Troops and the Barbarisation of Warfare.* 2nd ed. Basingstoke, U.K.: Palgrave, 2001.

Bek, Aleksandr. *Volokolamskoe shosse.* Moscow: Voennoe izdatel'stvo, 1959.

Beorn, Waitman Wade. *Marching into Darkness: The Wehrmacht and the Holocaust in Belarus.* Cambridge, Mass.: Harvard University Press, 2014.

Bergström, Christer. *Barbarossa: The Air Battle: July–December 1941.* Hersham, U.K.: Chevron Publishing, Ian Allan Publishing, 2007.

Bezverkhnii, G., ed. *SMERSH: Istoricheskie ocherki i arkhivnye dokumenty.* Moscow: Izdatel'stvo Glavarkhiva Moskvy, 2003.

Chang, Iris. *The Rape of Nanking: The Forgotten Holocaust of World War II.* New York: Basic Books, 1997.

Cherushev, N. S. *Udar po svoim: Krasnaia armiia 1938–1941.* Moscow: Veche, 2003.

Clark, Alan. *Barbarossa: The Russian-German Conflict 1941–1945.* Harmondsworth, U.K.: Penguin, 1966.

Clausewitz, Carl von. *On War* [1832], ed. and trans. Michael Howard and Peter Paret. Princeton, N.J.: Princeton University Press, 1989.

Conquest, Robert. *The Great Terror: A Reassessment.* London: Hutchinson, 1990.

Courtois, Stéphane, et al. *The Black Book of Communism: Crimes, Terror, Repression,* trans. Jonathan Murphy and Mark Kramer. London: Harvard University Press, 1999.

Djilas, Milovan. *Conversations with Stalin.* New York: Harcourt Brace & World, 1962.

Drobiazko, S. I. *Pod znamemani vraga: Antisovetskie formirovaniia v sostave germanskikh vooruzhennykh sil, 1941–1945 gg.* Moscow: Eksmo, 2005.

Effects of Climate on Combat in European Russia. CMH Pub. 104-6. Washington, D.C.: Center of Military History, US Army, 1952.

Erenburg, Il'ia, and Vasilii Grossman, eds. *Chernaia kniga,* vol. 1. Zaporozh'e: Interbuk, 1991.

Evans, Richard J. *The Third Reich at War 1939–1945: How the Nazis Led Germany from Conquest to Disaster.* London: Allen Lane, 2008.

Frunze, Mikhail V. *Izbrannye proizvedeniia, tom II.* Moscow: Voennoe izdatel'stvo Ministerstva oborony Soiuza SSR, 1957.

———. *Neizvestnoe i zabytoe. Publitsistika, memuary, dokumenty, pi'sma.* Moscow: Nauka, 1991.

Geneva Convention Relative to the Treatment of Prisoners, with Annex, 27 July 1929. League of Nations Treaty Series, vol. 118, no. 2734, pp. 343–409.

Gilbert, Martin. *Prophet of Truth: Winston S. Churchill* [1976], vol. 5. London: Minerva, 1990.

Glantz, David M. *Operation Barbarossa: Hitler's Invasion of Russia 1941* [2001]. Stroud, U.K.: History Press, 2012.

———. *Soviet Military Operational Art in Pursuit of Deep Battle*. Abingdon, U.K.: Frank Cass, 1991.

Gray, Colin S. *Another Bloody Century: Future Warfare*. London: Weidenfeld & Nicolson, 2005.

Grossman, Vasilii. *Gody voiny*. Moscow: OGIZ, 1946.

———. *Gody voiny*. Moscow: Izadatel'stvo Pravda, 1989.

———. *Staryi uchitel'. Povesti i Rasskazy*. Moscow: Sovetskii pisatel', 1962.

———. *Zhizn' i sud'ba*. Moscow: Sovetskii pisatel', 1990.

Guderian, Heinz. *Achtung-Panzer! Die Entwicklung der Panzerwaffe, ihre Kampftaktik und ihre operativen Möglichkeiten*. Stuttgart: Union Deutsche Verlagsgesellschaft, 1937.

———. *Die Panzerwaffe. Ihre Entwicklung und ihre operativen Möglichkeiten bis zum Beginn des grossdeutschen Freiheitskampfes*. Stuttgart: Union Deutsche Verlagsgesellschaft, 1943.

———. *Erinnerungen eines Soldaten* [1950], 9 Auflage. Neckergemünd: Kurt Vowinkel Verlag, 1976.

Hartmann, Christian. *Operation Barbarossa: Nazi Germany's War in the East, 1941–1945*. Oxford: Oxford University Press, 2013.

———. *Wehrmacht im Ostkrieg: Front und militärisches Hinterland*. Munich: R. Oldenbourg Verlag, 2010.

Hartmann, Christian, Johannes Hürter, and Ulrike Jureit, eds. *Verbrechen der Wehrmacht: Bilanz einer Debatte*. Munich: Verlag C. H. Beck, 2005.

Hastings, Max. *Armageddon: The Battle for Germany 1944–45*. London: Macmillan, 2004.

Hinze, Rolf. *Hitze, Frost und Pulverdampf: Der Schicksalsweg der 20. Panzer-Division* [1981]. Meerbusch: Dr. Rolf Hinze, 1996.

Historikerstreit: Die Dokumentation der Kontroverse um die Einzigartigkeit der national-sozialistischen Judenvernichtung. Munich: R. Piper, 1987.

Hoehne, Gustav. *In Snow and Mud: 31 Days of Attack under Seydlitz during Early Spring of 1942* [1948]. MS C-034. Washington, D.C.: Department of the Army, Office of the Chief of Military History, 1953.

IAkovlev, A. N., et al., eds. *Katyn': Plenniki neob"iavlennoi voiny*. In the series "Demokratiia," *Rossiia. XX VEK, Dokumenty*. Moscow: Mezhdunarodnyi fond, 1997.

———. *1941 god, v 2-knigakh*. In the series "Demokratiia," *Rossiia. XX VEK, Dokumenty*. Moscow: Mezhdunarodnyi fond, 1998.

Infanterie-Regiment 59 später Pz. Gren. Regiment 1934–1945. Gemeinschaft ehemaliger 59er 1948-heute, in Zusammenarbeit der Kameraden E. A. Beckmann, E. Jordan, W. Kirchner, und P. Weber. Hildesheim: Drücherei August Lax, [1983].

Isserson, Georgii Samoilovich. *Novye formy bor'by (Opyt issledovaniia sovremennykh voin)*. Moscow: Voennoe izdatel'stvo Narodnogo Komissariata oborony Soiuza SSR, 1940.

Jahn, Bruno H. *Die Weisheit des Soldaten: Versuch einer Deutung und Einordnung*. Berlin: Keil Verlag, 1937.

Keller, Bastian. *Der Ostfeldzug-Die Wehrmacht im Vernichtungskrieg, Planung, Kooperation, Verantwortung*. Norderstedt: GRIN Verlag GmbH, 2011.

Kolkowicz, Roman. *The Soviet Military and the Communist Party*. Princeton, N.J.: Princeton University Press, 1967.

KPSS o vooruzhennykh silakh Sovetskogo Soiuza: Dokumenty 1917–1968. Moscow: Voennoe izdatel'stvo Ministerstva oborony SSSR, 1969.

Lenin, V. I. "Doklad na II Vserossiiskom s''ezde politprosvetov 17 oktiabria 1921 g." In *Sochineniia*, vol. 33. Moscow: Gosudarstvennoe Izadatel'stvo politicheskoi literatury, 1951.

———. "Kriticheskie zametki po natsional'nomu voprosu" [1913]. In *Sochineniia*, vol. 20. Moscow: OGIZ, 1948.

———. "Printsipy sotsializma i voina 1914–1915" [1915]. In *Sochineniia*, vol. 21. Moscow: OGIZ, 1948.

———. "Proletarskaia revoliutsiia i renegat Kautskii" [1918]. In *Sochineniia*, vol. 28. Moscow: OGIZ, 1950.

———. "Zadachi proletariata v nashei revoliutsii" [1917]. In *Sochineniia*, vol. 24. Moscow: Gosudarstvennoe Izadatel'stvo politicheskoi literatury, 1949.

Manstein, Erich von. *Verlorene Siege* [1955]. Bonn: Bernard & Graefe in der Mönch Verlagsgesellschaft mbH, 2011.

Maser, Werner. *Nürnberg: Tribunal der Sieger*. Düsseldorf: Econ Verlag, 1977.

Megargee, Geoffrey P. *War of Annihilation: Combat and Genocide on the Eastern Front, 1941* [2006]. Plymouth, U.K.: Rowman & Littlefield, 2007.

Montefiore, Simon Sebag. *Stalin: The Court of the Red Tsar* [2003]. London: Phoenix, 2004.

Moorhouse, Roger. *The Devils' Alliance: Hitler's Pact with Stalin, 1939–41*. London: Bodley Head, 2014.

Murphy, David E. *What Stalin Knew: The Enigma of Barbarossa*. New Haven, Conn.: Yale University Press, 2005.

"Order of the People's Commissar of Defense of the USSR." *Pravda*, 1 May 1941.

Organy gosudarstvennoi bezopasnosti SSSR v Velikoi Otechestvennoi Voine: Sbornik dokumentov, tom vtoroi, kniga 1, Nachalo 22 iiunia–31 avgusta 1941 goda. Moscow: Izdatel'stvo "Rus'," 2000.

Organy gosudarstvennoi bezopasnosti SSSR v Velikoi Otechestvennoi Voine: Sbornik dokumentov, tom vtoroi, kniga 2, Nachalo 1 sentiabria–31 dekabria 1941 goda. Moscow: Izdatel'stvo "Rus'," 2000.

Organy gosudarstvennoi bezopasnosti SSSR v Velikoi Otechestvennoi Voine: Sbornik dokumentov, tom tretii, kniga 1, Krushenie "Blitzkriga" 1 ianvaria–30 iiunia 1942 goda. Moscow: Izdatel'stvo "Rus'," 2003.

Paul, Allen. *Katyń: Stalin's Massacre and the Triumph of Truth* [1991]. De Kalb: Northern Illinois University Press, 2010.

Philippi, Alfred. *Das Pripjetproblem. Eine Studie über die operative Bedeutung des Pripjetgebietes für den Feldzug des Jahres 1941*. Beiheft 2 der Wehrwissenschaftlichen Rundschau. Darmstadt: Verlag E. S. Mittler & Sohn, 1956.

Pogonii, IA. F., i dr. *Stalingradskaia epopeia: Materialy NKVD SSSR i voennoi tsenzury iz Tsentral'nogo arkhiva FSB RF*. Moscow: Zvonnitsa-MG, 2000.

Popov, Aleksei. *NKVD i partizanskoe dvizhenie.* Moscow: OLMA-PRESS, 2003.

Das Recht der besetzten Gebiete. Estland, Lettland, Litauen, Weissruthenien und Ukraine. Sammlung der Verordnungen, Erlasse und sonstigen Vorschriften über Verwaltung, Rechtspflege, Wirtschaft, Finanzwesen und Verkehr mit Erläuterungen der Referenten. Herausgegeben von Dr. Alfred Meyer, Gauleiter und ständigem Vertreter des Reichsministers für die besetzten Gebiete unter Mitarbeit von Dr. Walter Wilhelmi (Ministerialrat), Dr. Walter Labs (Oberregierungsrat) und Dr. Hans Schäfer (Landgerichtsrat) im Reichsministerium für die bestezten Ostgebiete. Munich: C. H. Beck'sche Verlagsbuchhandlung, 1943.

Römer, Felix. *Der Kommissarbefehl: Wehrmacht und NS-Verbrechen an der Ostfront 1941/42.* Paderborn: Ferdinand Schöningh, 2008.

Schmitt, Carl. *Theorie des Partisanen: Zwischenbemerkung zum Begriff des Politischen.* Berlin: Duncker & Humblot, [1963].

Sholokhov, Mikhail. *Sobranie sochinenii v vos'mi tomakh.* Moscow: Gosudarstvennoe izdatel'stvo khudozhestvennoi literatury, 1956–1958.

Simonov, Konstantin. *Zhivye i mertvye* [1959]. Moscow: Gosudarstvennoe izdatel'stvo khudozhestvennoi literatury, 1961.

Smyslov, O. S., *"Piatia kolonna" Gitlera: Ot Kutenova do Vlasova.* Moscow: Veche, 2004.

Snyder, Timothy. *Bloodlands: Europe between Hitler and Stalin.* London: Bodley Head, 2010.

Spitzy, Reinhard. *So haben wir das Reich verspielt: Bekenntnisse eines Illegalen* [1986]. Munich: Langen Müller, 2000.

Streit, Christian. *Keine Kameraden: Die Wehrmacht und die sowjetischen Kriegsgefangenen 1941–1945* [1978]. Bonn: Verlag J. H. W. Dietz Nachf. GmbH, 1991.

Suvorov, Viktor. *Ledokol: Kto nachal vtoruiu mirovuiu voinu?* Moscow: Izdatel'skii dom, Novoe vremia, 1993.

Trial of the Major War Criminals before the International Military Tribunal Nuremberg, 14 November 1945–1 October 1946. Blue Series, 42 vols. Nuremberg: n.p., 1949. Library of Congress, http://www.loc.gov.

Trials of War Criminals before the Nuerenberg Military Tribunals, October 1946–April 1949. Green Series, 15 vols. Washington, D.C.: Government Printing Office, 1949. Library of Congress, http://www.loc.gov.

Triandafillov, Vladimir. *Kharakter operatsii sovremennykh armii.* 1st ed. Moscow: Gosudarstvennoe izdatel'stvo, otdel voennoi literatury, 1929.

———. *The Nature of the Operations of Modern Armies,* trans. William A. Burhans, ed. Jacob W. Kipp. Cass Series on the Soviet Study of War. Ilford, U.K.: Frank Cass, 1994.

Ueberschär, Gerd R., und Wolfram Wette, hrsg. *„Unternehmen Barbarossa": Der deutsche Überfall auf die Sowjetunion 1941, Berichte, Analysen, Dokumente.* Paderborn: Ferdinand Schöningh, 1984.

Uhlig, Heinrich. "Der verbrecherische Befehl. Eine Diskussion und ihre historisch-dokumentarischen Grundlagen." In *Vollmacht des Gewissens,* band II, hrsg., von der europäischen Publikation e.V. Frankfurt am Main: Alfred Metzner Verlag, 1965.

Vatlin, Aleksandr IUr'evich. *Terror raionnogo masshtaba: «Massovye operatsii» NKVD v Kuntsevskom paione Moskovskoi oblasti 1937–1938 gg.* Moscow: Rossiiskaia politicheskaia entsiklopediia (ROSSPEN), 2004.

Watson, Alexander. *Ring of Steel: Germany and Austria-Hungary at War, 1914–1918.* London: Allen Lane, 2014.

Weinberg, Gerhard L. *The Foreign Policy of Hitler's Germany: Starting World War II 1937–1939* [1980]. Atlantic Highlands, N.J.: Humanities Press International, 1994.

———. *Germany and the Soviet Union, 1939–1941.* Leiden: E. J. Brill, 1954.

Wright Peter, with Paul Greengrass. *Spycatcher.* Richmond, Australia: William Heinemann, 1987.

Zawodny, J. K. *Death in the Forest: The Story of the Katyn Forest Massacre* [1962]. New York: Hippocrene Books, 1988.

Zhukov, G. K. *Vospominaniia i razmyshleniia.* Moscow: Izdatel'stvo agentstva pechati novosti, 1969.

INDEX